P9-DNS-424

25.44
MU
13 May 1992

G. STANLEY HALL

G Stanley Hall

DOROTHY ROSS

 *G. Stanley Hall*

THE PSYCHOLOGIST AS PROPHET

The University of Chicago Press
Chicago and London

The University of Chicago Press, Chicago 60637
The University of Chicago Press, Ltd., London
© 1972 by The University of Chicago
Quotations from letters of William James
© 1972 by Alexander R. James
All rights reserved. Published 1972
Printed in the United States of America
International Standard Book Number: 0–226–72821–8
Library of Congress Catalog Card Number:75-165180

To Stan

Just as a planet revolves around a central body as well as rotating on its own axis, so the human individual takes part in the course of development of mankind at the same time as he pursues his own path in life. But to our dull eyes the play of forces in the heavens seems fixed in a never-changing order; in the field of organic life we can still see how the forces contend with one another, and how the effects of the conflict are continually changing. So, also, the two urges, the one towards personal happiness and the other towards union with other human beings, must struggle with each other in every individual; and so, also, the two processes of individual and of cultural development must stand in hostile opposition to each other and mutually dispute the ground. But this struggle between the individual and society . . . does admit of an eventual accommodation in the individual, as, it may be hoped, it will also do in the future of civilization, however much that civilization may oppress the life of the individual today.

Sigmund Freud,
Civilization and Its Discontents

CONTENTS

x   CONTENTS

ILLUSTRATIONS

PREFACE

G. Stanley Hall is remembered best, perhaps, for bringing Sigmund Freud and Carl Gustav Jung to America in 1909 to lecture to an influential group of psychologists and scholars at Clark University in Worcester. Hall was sixty-five years old when he showed this early appreciation of psychoanalysis and gave Freud his first academic recognition anywhere in the world.

Hall already had behind him a series of other pioneer ventures in American science and culture. Only a few years before, in 1904, in his major book on *Adolescence,* Hall had formulated, for the first time, the modern concept of adolescence. Since the 1880s and 1890s he had led the child study movement, which briefly dominated American educational reform and created the matrix in which progressive education developed. Hall's child study efforts and those of his students, such as Arnold Gesell and Lewis M. Terman, helped create a host of special disciplines, from child development and educational psychology to mental testing.

During these same decades Hall became one of the first scientific psychologists and, together with William James, established the field in America as an academic discipline. In 1889 he became the founding president of Clark University, then a wholly graduate university devoted to scientific research and a model in establishing the scientific pattern of university reform in America.

Hall thus served as an early prophet of science, psychology, and youth, and he acted the part. An enthusiast, an impressive speaker, and a tireless worker, Hall wrote and spoke up and down the country to parents, teachers, physicians, clergymen, and professors; and at Clark he taught substantial numbers of educators and psychologists to spread his message. He told all who would listen that the science of psychology could transform and revive education and religion; that child-rearing and education were the most important tasks of the race; that adolescence, with its limitless potential for growth, was the golden age of life, to be prolonged as far as possible; that the understanding of childhood and sex and psychopathology should be at the center of scientific psychology. He thus delighted in taking on concerns scorned by his psychological colleagues, expecting fully to be vindicated in the future. In fact, he was for decades almost forgotten. Only recently have practitioners and historians in some of the many fields he influenced begun to pay him some heed and to sense, here and there, the importance he had in shaping modern American thought and culture.

The strengths which led Hall to his prophetic concerns and the weaknesses which led to his rapid disappearance from view were both connected to profound ambivalences in his thought. Hall belonged to the late-Victorian, post-Darwinian era whose very name expressed its transitional nature. His rhetoric and his work were permeated with both religion and science. His evolutionary theories were tied to dated concepts of biological race as well as more sophisticated ideas of nature and nurture. He wanted to be both the village preacher and the cosmopolitan man of science. He had a canny sense for the underside of every idea, the ambivalence that lurked behind every belief, and often managed to profess both sides at once.

Hall's psychological colleagues shared his devotion to science and his practical idealism, but most of them were a generation beyond him in age and outlook, and found the dualities of his nature offensive. They criticized his work for the weaknesses which resulted, and forgot the strengths that remained. His popular audiences, often moved by the same dual allegiances which claimed Hall, responded strongly to his message, only to move on in later years to more contemporary idioms. For the historian, Hall's double-dealing is a marvellous revelation of the complexities of his age; his thought picks up and exposes intellectual and cultural conflict.

Hall could reflect so well the problems of his era and the direction of future concern because he was a very unusual man. Those who knew him often thought of him as a peculiar genius. Hall understood the conflicting aspirations in his culture because his own personality was riven with conflict. His strength lay precisely in his determination to give intellectual expression to his conflicts and to continue seeking their intellectual solution until the end of his eighty-year span of life. On a personal level, Hall failed to achieve any satisfactory balance. His relationships with those who came close to him were difficult and characterized, like his ideas, by duplicity. The self-absorption which fed his intellectual achievement often led him to deal meanly with those around him. There remained always an enormous gulf between the private man and the public exponent of noble ideals. Hall poured the warmth and feeling and idealism he could not communicate in his personal life into a self-conscious search for experience and prophetic intellectual constructions.

From his birth in 1844 in Ashfield, Massachusetts, to his death in 1924 in Worcester, Stanley Hall came into contact with most of the intellectual and cultural currents of his time. The dynamics of his early break with religious orthodoxy and his advocacy of science and psychology are better understood and less remarkable, perhaps, than that of his later pioneer work in childhood, adolescence, and psychoanalysis. By following him closely along the whole path of his development, however, one gains a better sense of the intricate relations between the older culture in which Hall grew up and the newer one he forecast—without, I hope, losing sight of the novelty of his ultimate achievement.

I have tried to analyze Hall's life and work in terms suggestive for the larger problems of American intellectual and social history as well as for the histories of the many fields he influenced. Throughout, I have focused particularly on the point where Hall's ideas and behavior and the cultural forces which shaped them visibly intersect with his personal psychological development. At this level of ego psychology one can see the effects of deeper psychological forces within him and wider pressures from the society at large, without losing sight of his own particularity and integrity. At the same time, those readers who can, will be able to draw further psychoanalytic or sociocultural inferences from the material.

For all the detail of this volume, some readers may find their

special interests slighted. The experimental psychologist will find
no discussion of the methods and apparatus of Hall's early experimental work; the historian of religion will not find an analysis of the
institutional and doctrinal context of American Protestantism to
which Hall's mature psychology of religion was directed; the modern
psychologist or historian of the life cycle will find only a partial
sketch of the social themes Hall drew into his work and the lines of
influence his ideas and work sent into the future. I can only plead for
these and other omissions the inevitable limits of biography, an inevitably personal sense of priorities, and the fact that Hall's insatiable intellectual appetite eventually exhausted my own.

ACKNOWLEDGMENTS

I am grateful for the support provided for this study by a grant from the Fund for the Advancement of Education in 1961–62, a predoctoral fellowship from the Social Science Research Council during 1962–64, and a Public Health Service postdoctoral training grant in the history of the behavioral sciences from 1965 to 1968. I owe a particular debt to the Section on the History of the Behavioral Sciences of the Cornell University Medical College-Payne Whitney Clinic and to Dr. Eric T. Carlson, director of the section, who made the training resources of the clinic available to me and gave me great assistance and stimulus before, during, and since my appointment there from 1965 to 1967.

Beyond these, my chief debts of thanks are owed to my husband, Stanford G. Ross, for his encouragement and forbearance, to the late Professor Richard Hofstadter, who directed the dissertation on which this study is based; to Dr. David Shakow, formerly Chief of the Laboratory of Psychology, National Institute of Mental Health, who offered his interest and knowledge during the research and in reviewing the manuscript; and to my friends Dr. Donald Marcuse, who helped me to clarify my understanding of Hall's personality, and Dr. Barbara Finkelstein, who gave me the benefit of her keen interest and knowledge of education.

Very useful comments on the manuscript were given to me by Professor Walter Metzger, the late Barbara Cross, and Dr. Gardner Murphy. I want also to thank Dr. Murphy and Dr. Bernard Levy of

xviii   ACKNOWLEDGMENTS

the Department of Psychology of George Washington University for sponsoring my study during 1967–68.

One of the most agreeable aspects of my work has been the contacts it led to with other scholars working on related subjects. Professors Frank M. Albrecht, Joseph Brent, John C. Burnham, Max H. Fisch, Joseph Kett, Barbara Sicherman, Michael Sokal, and Richard Storr at various times shared their special knowledge with me and made my work more interesting and fruitful. In this regard, I owe special thanks to Professor Nathan Hale, Jr., whose frequent exchanges of facts and ideas have contributed substantially to the book.

The cooperation and assistance I received from members of Stanley Hall's family and Clark University were indispensable in carrying out this study. Dr. Robert Granville Hall lent me his collection of his father's papers and memorabilia, and, together with his wife, met my taxing demands for information and material with great courtesy. Members of the faculty and staff at Clark University gave me complete access to their materials on Hall and their knowledge of him, and made the task of research immeasurably easier and more pleasant. I want particularly to thank former president Howard B. Jefferson; Tilton M. Barron, the librarian, and his assistant, Miss Marion Henderson; Professors Seymour Wapner and Bernard Kaplan of the Department of Psychology; and to acknowledge the assistance of the late Professor Heinz Werner.

Many people who had known Hall or Clark University generously shared their personal knowledge with me. Interviews and materials were given to me by Hall's former students and colleagues, Professors Edwin G. Boring, Frank H. Hankins, Carroll C. Pratt, and Frederic L. Wells; and by a number of people associated with Clark University—Miss Florence Chandler, Dr. Burton Gates, Mrs. Gladys E. Diliberto, Professor Vernon Jones, Miss Marion Ross, Joseph Talamo, and Mrs. William M. Tanner. A number of others associated with Hall took the time to answer my questions in writing: Professors Harry Elmer Barnes, Raymond F. Bellamy, Samuel Flagg Bemis, George Allen Coe, Frederick Eby, Melvin M. Knight, Charles A. Kraus, S. D. Porteus, J. E. W. Wallin, and Miss Evelyn Douglass, Mrs. Robert H. Goddard, and Dr. Miriam Van Waters. I also very much appreciate the assistance given to me in obtaining Hall materials by Dr. Kurt R. Eissler, Ernst Freud, Dr. Hilda C. Abraham, and Miss Eunice Winters.

Many librarians aided me in the research. I am particularly grateful to William H. Bond, Curator of Manuscripts at the Houghton Library, Harvard University; Roland Baughman, Head of Special Collections, Columbia University Library; Kimball C. Elkins, Harvard University Archives; Wallace Nethery, Hoose Library of Philosophy, University of Southern California; Miss Margaret Proctor, Carnegie Institution of Washington; Martin Schmitt, University of Oregon Library; Murphy Smith, American Philosophical Society; Miss Frieda Thies, Johns Hopkins University Library; Miss Bessie Totten, Antioch College Library; and Wyllis E. Wright, Williams College Library.

I want also to thank Brenda McFarland Cayo for her expert and conscientious services in typing the manuscript.

Finally, acknowledgment is made to Sigmund Freud Copyrights, Ltd., The Institute of Psycho-Analysis, The Hogarth Press Ltd., and W. W. Norton and Co. for permission to quote from "Civilization and Its Discontents" in volume 21 of the *Standard Edition of the Complete Psychological Works of Sigmund Freud*, revised and edited by James Strachey.

Part One

BECOMING A PSYCHOLOGIST 1844–1880

1   BEGINNINGS IN ASHFIELD

Born in a small farming village in western Massachusetts in 1844, Granville Stanley Hall was raised in very modest circumstances and a conservative, puritan milieu. From his Congregational parents and community, Hall received both strong ties to his childhood culture and a fierce ambition to shine in the larger world. Struggling to satisfy both, it took Hall many years to gain the confidence to attempt an intellectual career, then to rid himself of the theological restrictions of his creed, and finally, to find a philosophical stance and vocation which would answer his divergent needs.

Hall traced his family lineage to the first groups of Protestant settlers in New England. His mother, Abigail Beals, was descended from John Alden, and his father, Granville Bascom Hall, from William Brewster. The first Hall of the family arrived only a few years after Alden and Brewster, perhaps in Governor Winthrop's fleet of 1630. Hall's nine generations of American ancestry were all of English descent, except for an occasional Scot or Irishman, and those he could trace came to Massachusetts before the Revolutionary War. Stanley's great-grandfather Hall had been an officer on one of the ships boarded in the Boston tea party; his great-grandfather Beals was noted for ecstatic piety and unwavering faith. Most of his progenitors, however, were ordinary farmers who had left the eastern coast in search of better farmland in the late eighteenth century. The Halls had settled in Ashfield, Massachusetts, and the Beals nine miles away in Plainfield, in the northwest corner of the state.

Pioneers in the first exodus westward across the ocean, his family only timidly participated in the later westward movement across the land.[1]

Abigail Beals Hall was born in Plainfield, the youngest daughter and middle child in a family of seven children. The religious fervor of her grandfather had passed to her. Her journal records the intensity of her religious life and her conscientious prayer "for more entire sanctification." Her children felt the gentle warmth of her pious nature and Congregational faith as they were informed of the presence of God in all the activities of the world and urged to attain moral and spiritual justification.[2]

Mrs. Hall's aspiration also extended to education. Almost the only member of her family to seek a higher education, she was able to spend only one year at the Albany Female Academy and then taught school a number of years until her marriage. She maintained her intellectual interests afterward through reading, and often read aloud to her family, not only from the Bible and *Pilgrim's Progress* but also, Hall remembered, from *Uncle Tom's Cabin,* Scott, Dickens, *The Spectator,* stories from Shakespeare, and numerous periodicals. Having meager outlets in her immediate life, Mrs. Hall's ambitions came to rest largely on her children's futures. That her eldest son Stanley[3] would enter the ministry was her fondest hope and the end toward which she encouraged his education.[4]

Stanley's father, Granville Bascom Hall, was less ardent in his religious life but not in his moral demands. A man of imposing stature and presence, he was a stern father.[5] He once gave his nine-

1. *LCP* (see List of Abbreviations), pp. 22–31, 52–53; "Julina Orpha Hall. Bowman's Ancestral Charts," HP; William A. Hallock, *The Mountain Miller* (New York: American Tract Society), no. 254.

2. *LCP,* pp. 27–47; Abigail Beals Hall to GSH, 13 Sept 1859, HP. Hall discovered the existence of his mother's religious journals late in life, and quoted from them at length in *LCP,* pp. 36–41. The quotation in the text is taken from a fuller copy of the journals in the possession of Dr. Robert G. Hall, entry for 6 Jan 1856.

3. Stanley Hall's birth certificate has never been located, so it is impossible to determine the name he was given at birth. From the time he entered college, he used the name "G. Stanley Hall" or "Granville Stanley Hall," but he was known familiarly as Stanley throughout his boyhood and mature life.

4. *LCP,* pp. 27–47, 79–83, 147; A. B. Hall to GSH, 13 Sept 1859, HP.

5. *LCP,* pp. 74–75, 80–85.

year-old son six rules of conduct which would help him "to be a good man if God lets you grow up."

> In the first place then, ask the advice of your parents. . . . 2nd, Hear all they have to say and remember it all. 3rd—Never reject their advice because *you cannot see* it to be wise. . . . 4th—Never allow yourself to lean to your own understanding when it conflicts with the experience of your elders. . . . 5th—Shun the person who would have you do anything that your parents disapprove. . . . 6th and last, Do not manifest a spirit of disobedience by making words before you obey.[6]

Hall's severity was not entirely unrelieved, and several letters which he wrote to his young son betrayed tenderness and affection, as well as demanding discipline.[7] It was his harshness, however, which most impressed itself upon Stanley. In character, if not in piety, Hall's father was a Calvinist of the old school.[8]

Like his wife, Granville Hall had shown ambition unusual in his family. The fourth of ten children of an Ashfield farmer, he was the only one to seek a career outside the immediate vicinity. He wanted to obtain a good education but managed only a few terms at a nearby academy. Later, after trying several occupations, he traveled west to Wisconsin to take up a half-section of land but soon gave up the attempt to settle there. Returning to Ashfield, he taught school for several years in nearby towns, where he met his wife. They were married on 25 March 1843. Soon after the marriage, he left his pregnant wife with his family in Ashfield and returned to Wisconsin for another year's residence to make good the title on his land for investment purposes.[9] He was still there some months after his son Stanley was born on 1 February 1844.[10]

6. "St. Nicholas" [Granville Bascom Hall] to GSH, 1 Jan 1853, HP.

7. G. B. Hall to GSH, 4 Aug 1850, HP; G. B. Hall to GSH, 3 Apr 1852; "St. Nic." [G. B. Hall] to GSH, 31 Dec 1853, GSH Memorial Volume, CUP.

8. Charles Eliot Norton, who was well acquainted with the Ashfield community, described Hall's father as "a strict Calvinist of the old school." C. E. Norton to Daniel Coit Gilman, 14 Feb 1881, GP.

9. *LCP*, pp. 59–73; *Vital Records of Ashfield, Massachusetts, to the Year 1850* (Boston: New England Historic Genealogical Society, 1942), p. 164.

10. Although no official record of Stanley Hall's birth exists, his marriage certificate as well as his earliest testimony supports this date. "Heiraths-Urkunde, Nr. 537," photostat, HP. His sister also confirmed this date to Louis N. Wilson. L. N. Wilson to Edward Bradford Titchener, 2 June 1925, TP. The question of his birth date arises because of discrepancies in Hall's own testimony. He changed the year

On his return, Granville Hall settled down to farming in the village of Worthington nearby. Although his wandering days were over, he did not retire to the ways of his fathers. He kept abreast of innovations in farming techniques and machinery, even inventing some of his own, and he lectured his son on what he called "putting brains into all our work." As president of the local agricultural club, he urged the application of science to agriculture, not through the dicta of theorists who have never tried to farm but through experimentation and observation. He took a prominent part in the activities of the community and spoke frequently on behalf of his favorite causes, temperance and antislavery. When the political upheaval of the fifties gave a brief voice to hundreds of such local leaders in Massachusetts, he was sent to the state legislature in 1855 on the Know-Nothing ticket. One of his techniques for agricultural improvement was drawn from the observation that "it was a sad day for the dairyman when foreign blood first flowed in the veins of his cow."[11]

Despite his efforts and intelligence, Granville Hall was able to wring only a modest living from the soil. Two other children were added to the family: a son, Robert, two years younger than Stanley, and a daughter Julina, three and one-half years Stanley's junior. When Stanley was about fourteen, the family was able to move to a somewhat larger farm in Ashfield; by dint of frugality and labor, the Halls were able to live in accord with the spare standards of the countryside and to contribute toward their children's education.[12]

Hall's position of leadership, as well as his stern respectability, made his family "among the most-respected" in the town,[13] but he was never entirely satisfied with his lot as a farmer. Having had

---

of his birth from 1844 to 1845 to 1846 as he grew older and the mature years remaining in his career grew fewer. Between 1901 and 1905, he also changed the day from 1 February to 6 May, probably in response to the fact that 1 February was the day on which Clark University celebrated Founder's Day to honor Jonas G. Clark, whose birthday was also on that day. Clark's will, published in 1901, bitterly criticized Hall and threatened for a time to remove him from the University. See GSH to E. B. Titchener, 7 Feb 1919, TP.

11. *LCP*, pp. 62–74.

12. *LCP*, pp. 62–63, 76–77. Robert Beals Hall was born 30 December 1845. *Vital Records of Ashfield*, 55. Julina Orpha Hall was born 16 August 1847. L. N. Wilson to E. B. Titchener, 2 June 1925, TP.

13. George W. Curtis to A[lphonso] Taft, 19 Aug 1875, HP.

larger ambitions in his youth and having sampled the more refined standards of the world beyond the New England countryside, he felt humiliated by some of the chores of farming. Forced to reconcile himself to being a farmer, Hall felt defensive and insecure.[14]

When Stanley, after his first year of college, wrote his father that he stood high in his class and would try for first rank, Hall replied characteristically:

Hard as it is to gain an honor, it is often harder to *support* it; so great is the *public tax* upon it. It has been my ambition to *more than answer public expectation*. To do this, we must not *raise* the anticipations of the public, or we must have inexhaustable resources from which to supply them. . . . I like your present standing, and only wish you power and means to sustain it.[15]

Though he was always ambitious for Stanley, he may have been too afraid of the possibility of failure to urge his son to a novel future.

Stanley felt that his father was more eager to have his assistance on the farm than to have him prepare for the ministry.[16] Although Stanley never mentioned this possibility in later life, his father may also have thought, as he told the farmers of his neighborhood, that to restore the dignity of the farmer and prevent the best young men from leaving the land, "we must educate our sons. We must educate them as farmers—practical, scientific, efficient, intelligent farmers."[17] Interest in scientific agricultural education was growing among the state's progressive farmers, and an agricultural college was founded in Massachusetts during the years Stanley was in college.[18]

Granville Hall's insecurities were embedded even more deeply in his family and in the locale. Seven of his brothers and sisters survived into old age, as did his father, and young Stanley often lived with these aunts and uncles in Ashfield for months at a time to attend nearby schools. Extremely conservative people, who thought their brother Granville's progressive attitude rather queer, they had

14. *LCP,* pp. 72–77.
15. G. B. Hall to GSH, 2 June 1864, HP.
16. *LCP,* p. 63; Louis N. Wilson, *G. Stanley Hall* (New York: G. E. Stechert, 1914), p. 24 (hereafter cited as *GSH*).
17. Address by G. B. Hall, ca. 1860, reprinted in *LCP,* pp. 65–72.
18. Albert B. Hart, ed., *Commonwealth History of Massachusetts* (New York: States History, 1927–30), 4:388–92.

adopted the deflationary attitude of that class of New England farmer who had for generations lived meagerly and uniformly amidst myths of plenty and progress. Stanley's successes were greeted with warnings of getting "too big for his britches," and his relatives would avoid a ceremony at which he was to appear lest they were thought to be proud of their nephew.[19]

The attitude of Stanley's kinfolk was shared by others in the small town whose jibes and teasings he remembered. Ashfield was, after all, a remarkably homogeneous world. An agricultural village, with only one tavern, several churches, three stores, and a post office at its center, it had been losing population since 1810. It contained about sixteen hundred people when Stanley Hall was born, about twelve hundred when he left it to go to college. There was reportedly only one Irish family among the Anglo-Saxon population.[20] Charles Eliot Norton, the Harvard litterateur who made Ashfield his summer residence, reported that the landscape reminded him of "the tamer parts of the English lake country," and he noted the neat and well-kept farms and the modest comfort of the people. "Whenever you see a habitation you see what looks like a good home."[21] It was on the relative scale of American dreams that the dwindling population of Ashfield had cause to feel defensive.

The local Congregational church served the Halls as the social focus of their religious life. Stanley went regularly to Sunday meeting and to Sunday school, and he participated in discussions on the quality of the local preaching and the moral and religious habits of the parishioners. Hall later called this web of gossip that wove round the village his introduction to psychology.[22] The school was an even more vital center for young Hall, the seat and source of that "mental improvement" toward which he was steered. Whenever there was a school term offered in the township, young Hall at-

19. *LCP*, pp. 48–57, 130; Wilson, *GSH*, p. 22.

20. Wilson, *GSH*, pp. 24–25; *LCP*, pp. 171–72; GSH, "Boy Life in a Massachusetts Country Town Thirty Years Ago," 1891, pp. 116–17; Frederick G. Howes, *History of the Town of Ashfield . . . 1742–1910* (Ashfield, 1912), pp. 102–5, 120–27, 135–36, 155–72.

21. Sara Norton and M. A. deW. Howe, eds., *Letters of Charles Eliot Norton* (Boston: Houghton Mifflin, 1913), 2:270–1.

22. A. B. Hall to GSH, [1866]; GSH to A. B. Hall, 15 May 1866; to his parents, 18 Feb 1867, HP; *LCP*, pp. 47, 105.

tended, and his work was constantly tested and watched by parents, kin, and neighbors. Oratory was the focus of much of the scholars' attention, and Stanley, from childhood on, wrote and spoke pieces before his assembled neighbors. He passed these tests with distinction, and came to be judged by the community as a boy whose abilities and ambition gave great promise for the future.[23]

The piety, ambition, and intellectual interest that were Stanley Hall's birthright might have been contained in one of the roles his parents and community tradition prepared for him. The tension between the desire for success and fear of failure that surrounded him might have pressed his ambition into common shapes. But Stanley responded to these pressures in a manner that led him into a less conventional future. Directed to make up for the disappointments of his parents' lives and achieve what they had failed, he implicitly accepted the charge but sought to fulfill it in terms more nearly his own. Absorbing the puritan imperatives of his parents and community, he tried to develop within their bounds a distinctive identity.

In a household ruled by a gentle mother and a stern father, Stanley gave his purest affection to his mother. The first born and eldest son, Stanley turned to her instinctively for sympathy; he confessed that "she alone was my confidante in nearly everything." Taunts from his boyhood friends, rather than any felt desire, made him begin to assert his independence.[24] When he grew older, he still longed for the trust and security he had felt in the relationship, and he invested his feeling for his mother in a beneficent view of the course of nature and in the Victorian image of the pure, ideal, maternal woman. His later complex feelings toward women suggest that his feelings toward his mother were neither so pure nor so unwavering when he had to go beyond the fundamental matrix of dependency and trust. Even at the end of his life, he liked to imagine his mother emotionally unfulfilled in her marriage, and he was astonished to discover through a cache of letters that she had shared a warm and intimate relationship with her husband.[25]

Toward his father, Stanley's feelings were always painfully

23. *LCP*, pp. 108–11, 117–18, 152.
24. *LCP*, pp. 36, 41–42, 85–86.
25. *LCP*, pp. 28–29, 84–85.

ambivalent. He felt real affection for him, he said, "although the very atmosphere of Puritanism chilled almost every manifestation of it." Stanley remembered him most vividly as a man of quick and violent temper who backed his demands for obedience with sudden slaps and cuffs and occasional beatings. The boy evidently gave him ample occasion to use such methods, quarreling with him and challenging his authority in small ways whenever he could. At the age of fourteen, he recalled, he finally induced his father to abandon physical force by putting up his fists and threatening to retaliate. His relations with his father, he said, "may have laid the foundations for a certain independence of authority and impatience of control."[26]

Stanley Hall never was, however, able to deal consciously with the hostility he felt toward his father. He admitted in his autobiography that "I distinctly felt a constraint removed whenever my father was absent," but he concluded that "I had for the most part only kindly feelings towards him." As a boy Hall might well have shrunk from admitting such hostile feelings, for they were severely proscribed by religious standards, by his mother's gentle nature, and by his own fear of his father's physical prowess. Hall had been often told of his father's superior strength and courage and his superior standing in the community. His father was even reputed to be something of a charming "ladies' man." Indeed, the elder Hall, with his ambitions and insecurity, his muted love and visible anger, his challenging strengths and debilitating distance, gave his son a peculiarly difficult inheritance.[27]

Hall recalled vividly an incident that occurred during the Civil War, just before he was to leave for college. His father secured him an army exemption and thus brought down on Stanley rebukes of shirking and cowardice from the town. Already planning to enter college and fearing battle, Stanley felt the complicity of his own desires in the event and recognized besides that his father, more courageous than he, would have loved to join the fight had he been able. Hall called this "the very sorest of all my memories."[28]

26. *LCP*, pp. 74-76, 85-86; "St. Nic." [G. B. Hall] to GSH, 31 Dec 1853, GSH Memorial Volume, CUP.
27. *LCP*, pp. 61, 75-85, 110.
28. *LCP*, pp. 147-50.

Caught in these ambivalent feelings, Stanley developed a character at once aggressive and constrained. He was "brutally prone" to "bully" his younger brother and sister, he confessed, and also those in the neighborhood he knew to be weaker than himself. His brother, who resembled his mother's family and was of a more demonstrative and pliant nature than Stanley, became the particular object of his attacks. Stanley felt his brother to be his mother's favorite.[29] Young Hall also turned much of his hostility inward. He was subject to feelings of intense self-consciousness and humiliation, and at early adolescence he was for a time very fearful of dying. He felt himself to be emotionally inhibited and was prevented even from demonstrating to his mother the affection he felt for her. The hostility he showed toward his brother and father was, he feared, the chief cause of unrest in the household and a deep cause of pain to his mother.[30]

Still another source of guilt was his emerging sexuality. Hall had been introduced to sex through the care of farm animals and through the precocious subterranean sex life at one of his early schools, and the attitudes of his parents had confirmed the lessons of these sources: his private parts were always called "the dirty place." Hall discussed candidly in his autobiography his feelings of guilt when he began to experience nocturnal emissions at puberty and the struggle he waged to prevent them and to keep from yielding to the temptation to masturbate. Hall felt his desires to be evidences of innate corruption and unworthiness which rendered him unfit for contact with young women. His guilt became the secret preoccupation of his youth, and it mingled with the shame he felt at escaping service in the army, so "there has been something like a penance motif in all my efforts ever since."[31]

Hall stated later that the adolescent struggle over masturbation led to alternating states of exhilaration and despair, "so that the cyclic psychoses of undue elevation and exaltation, succeeded by depression, are established."[32] Hall described the appearance of

29. *LCP,* pp. 43–44, 85, 377–78; Wilson, *GSH,* p. 25.
30. *LCP,* pp. 42–44, 76–77, 85, 377.
31. *LCP,* pp. 131–38, 149. An early manuscript essay by Hall, "History of a Pine Tree," may be indicative of his childhood problems with masturbation. GSH Memorial Volume, CUP.
32. GSH, *Adol,* 1:439.

manic-depressive cycles in connection with a number of critical experiences in his life, and he may well have felt them first in adolescence in connection with his sexual guilt.

Goaded by his own sense of inferiority and the imposing image of his father that still held him captive, Hall developed high ambitions. When he was fourteen years old, he took his gun with him, climbed a nearby hill and there spent a daylong vigil during which he vowed to leave the farm and "do and be something in the world."[33] The enormous emotional investment he put in his ideal future at the same time aggravated and assuaged his insecurity. His most intense adolescent fear was the fear of mediocrity. That he would fail in his goals and return to the family farm was both a dread prospect and a cushion of security which Hall held onto well into his maturity.[34]

The farm was too narrow a world for Hall's ambition and too closely dominated by his father for him to embrace it happily. But neither did the career his mother held out to him, the ministry, seem to capture his imagination. While accepting the tenets of his faith, he apparently showed no pious ardor nor any inclination to force himself to deeper commitment.[35] Hall's later work suggests that he possessed strong religious feelings, but his other traits could not so easily fit the model of religious piety.

Hall's own tastes ran toward literary and artistic activities, where he had greater outlet for his self-absorption and fantasy life. Hall was an active boy, not very fond of farm work and curious about his surroundings. Though he took advantage of the ordinary opportunities for amusement the community offered, he was also an exceptionally imaginative child. He seemingly had no close boyhood chums; instead, he spent much of his time alone, collecting species of whatnot, carrying out imaginary adventures, and conjuring upon the farmland the people and settings of the books and stories he knew. As Hall entered his teens, literature was his first love. He started an autobiography, kept a daily journal, and wrote poems, stories, and adventure tales by the dozen. Flushed by his local ora-

33. GSH, "Note on Early Memories," 1899, p. 507.
34. LCP, pp. 223–24, 377; Wilson, GSH, p. 23.
35. GSH to A. B. Hall [Feb 1864]; A. B. Hall and G. B. Hall to GSH, 4 Mar 1864, HP; LCP, pp. 29, 63.

torical success, he imagined himself speaking before huge and admiring audiences.[36]

At one stage, music, even more than writing, attracted him. Music was evidently the one form of emotional expression approved in Hall's puritan milieu. His father was profoundly moved by music and first taught his son how to play the violin. Stanley soon took a more serious interest in music than the elder Hall had bargained for and eventually prevailed upon his father to buy a piano, and took lessons for a year or two. The music touched his adolescent emotion—his one mastered work was Beethoven's *Sonata pathétique*—and it served briefly as a means of escape from the farm. Hall wrote in his journal before his sixteenth birthday,

> I want to get a musical education and certainly a common school education but F[ather] told me this evening that he should help me to get enough education to teach a common school after I must shift for myself[,] for as for helping me to a musical education he should not[.] [T]his makes me feel the worst of anything he ever said for any other parent worth 1500 dollars would not [*sic*] help their children some for I feel that if I am not a musition I shall be nothing more than a day laborer.[37]

Hall evidently lacked talent on the piano, however, and he abandoned his plan, though the fantasy of being a great concert pianist remained with him into his old age.[38]

A literary or musical career was a distant and impractical dream to Hall, one which he could hardly consider in the same serious terms that he knew from his puritan upbringing should apply to the hard business of life. The moral world created by Congregationalism and the rocky New England soil had formed his mind. The moral law which God had planted in human nature was the hard law of Duty. It was not literary grace or grandiose power which his parents and teachers praised but moral principle and the commonsense, traditional bounds in which it had been placed. As Hall

---

36. GSH, "Note on Early Memories," 1899, pp. 490–93, 500, 507–10; GSH, "Boy Life," 1891, pp. 108–12, 113–15; Wilson, *GSH*, pp. 22–23; *LCP*, pp. 89–104, 113–30, 374–75; "Autobiography of Stanley G. Hall," 1858 and 1859, HP; "The Lost Maden," 4 Nov 1857, HP; "Journal Commensing December 16, 1859," HP.

37. "Journal Commensing December 16, 1859," HP. I have retained Hall's original spellings throughout.

38. *LCP*, pp. 114–17; Wilson, *GSH*, p. 22.

had written at the Ashfield Academy in perfect obedience to his training,

Let us remember that life's greatest good consists not in the full gratification of our own individual propensities and instincts but in the memory of good deeds and kind actions done and a conscience void of offense toward God and man.[39]

Beneath this well-learned body of moral precept, as beneath the dominating sense of his parents hopes for him, Hall's own desires remained amorphous and submerged elements of his personality.[40]

Hall was nonetheless conscious of his promise and his power. For all his inner guilt and reliance on fantasy, he had acquitted himself well in his community. His first independent job at sixteen, as schoolmaster for a term in a neighboring hamlet, showed him to have a realistic sense of his authority and its limits, as well as real skill in handling the young people and their parents. Hall felt himself a success at the job, and the experience gave him confidence to subdue his inner uncertainties and test himself in a larger world.[41] In the absence of any other clear goal, he left Ashfield at eighteen to obtain the higher education that would prepare him for the ministry.[42]

39. MS composition book, "Life" [Oct 1861], HP.
40. *LCP*, pp. 147, 183–84.
41. *LCP*, pp. 138–43.
42. *LCP*, p. 151; Wilson, *GSH*, p. 30.

2 SELF-DEVELOPMENT AT WILLIAMS COLLEGE

Stanley Hall left Ashfield in 1862 for one year at Williston Academy in nearby Easthampton to finish his preparation for college. He found the separation from home and the transition to this more accomplished world very painful. The college preparatory course at Williston was designed for boys planning to enter Harvard and Yale, as well as the less stringent smaller colleges, and Hall worked as he never had before to finish in the middle of the class. He felt inferior to his more knowledgeable and mature classmates whose poised addresses made his own earlier oratorical successes seem paltry. Hall remembered the year as one of intense humiliation.[1]

The following year Hall entered Williams College, just thirty miles from Ashfield. Presided over by the famous Mark Hopkins and drawing to its student body boys from middle-class homes all over the Northeast, the college was still a favorite choice of the sons of the poorer Congregational farmers of western Massachusetts.[2] Hall again felt many of the students to be far more knowledgeable in the ways of the world than he and found the studies "fearfully hard" during the first terms, though he was able to rank sixth in a class of forty-three by midwinter.[3]

1. *LCP*, pp. 118, 151–55; GSH to A. B. Hall, 8 May 1863, HP.
2. Frederick Rudolph, *Mark Hopkins and the Log: Williams College, 1836–1872* (New Haven: Yale University Press, 1956), pp. 65–72; *LCP*, p. 159.
3. GSH to A. B. Hall, 20 Jan [1865]; GSH to A. B. Hall [Feb 1864], HP. Apparently Hall did well scholastically from that point forward. He was prob-

Halfway through this first year, Hall informed his parents that he had experienced religious conversion. The event came as a great surprise to them, and to Hall himself, for as they knew, he was "an infant in spiritual knowledge."[4] As Hall described the experience to his parents, the church offered him "rest and safety," and his keen desire for these ends enabled him to traverse the infinite distances of the spiritual universe in something over twenty-four hours:

The history of the change which I humbly pray has been wrought in me is brief. Yesterday [Sunday] morn I had not the slightest serious impression. I spent the morning, I am sorry to say, in the secular pursuit of study, attended church in the P.M. and involuntarily fell into a train of reflection which led me to conviction. My impressions were deepened by the sermon on the general subject "The Ark of Safety." I then and there resolved that God assisting me I would give myself no rest until I had found rest and safety therein. Then followed a season of fear, then doubt, and darkness, perplexity and painful anxiety. I sought the advice and counsel of Christians and their prayers, but no light. My conviction of sin and of the terrible doom which hung over me I fear were not strong enough and I thought that I could have no hope till they were more vivid. But the feeling paramount was all the while a desire, deep, strong and ardent to become a Christian. In accordance with the counsel of others I tried to give myself fully into the hands of Jesus, relying on his promises but got no light until this morning when I began to feel that a burden was very gradually lifted from my mind, as though the night of wrestling was far spent and the day was dawning. Gradually this feeling has increased during the day and I begin to feel such a delightful but indescribable change coming over me and now I can say without distrust, though it does once in a while creep in, that I think and hope I have found acceptance through the blood of the Lamb.[5]

Hall's conversion came as part of a religious revival which swept the college almost every year in early spring. The earnest comradeship of the movement seemed to contribute as much to his new enthusiasm and security as did the faith itself. Hall had joined one of the smaller fraternities and he found his society brothers deeply involved in the revival. As he wrote to his parents,

ably omitted from the listing of the top half of his class at the end of sophomore year because illness prevented him from completing his biennial examinations until early in his junior year. GSH to A. B. Hall, 20 Sept [1865], HP.

4. A. B. Hall and G. B. Hall to GSH, 4 Mar 1864, HP.

5. GSH to A. B. Hall [Feb 1864].

I feel great pleasure in attending prayer meeting. We have them in our rooms and in the public rooms. A society brother has just called on me in deep anxiety for his soul's salvation. I did what I could to dispell his doubts. . . . Two seniors in the society have just called. . . . We all prayed for this other member above mentioned. What a noble thing to have such men for society friends.[6]

By the end of another week, Hall had joined the vanguard of the apostles. "I never spent so happy or so profitable a week," he reported.

I can hardly realize this delightful change that has come over me. I look at everything from a new standpoint. I have found courage to take part in several meetings of our class and elsewhere.[7]

At the end of freshman year he was writing home confidently: "Coleridge says there is no feeling of more exquisite pleasure than consciousness of increasing knowledge and power." Hall felt himself "daily growing" in these respects.[8]

Hall's religious enthusiasm did not recur after his freshman year; his attitude toward revivals and religious commitment became perfunctory.[9] His separation from home and the challenge of his new environment had led him temporarily to seek refuge in piety, but even while confessing faith to his classmates, he had felt slightly ridiculous. He could not help observing that the particularly pious students were somewhat slow-witted.[10] With courage partly restored, he found the varied intellectual and social life at Williams more attractive than religious piety.

The formal course work at Williams was the least item of Hall's attention. For the first two years, the curriculum was an almost unrelieved series of exercises in Greek, Latin, and intermediate mathematics. The small faculty made few intellectual demands on its students and after the anxieties of freshman year abated, Hall was

6. Rudolph, *Mark Hopkins*, pp. 97–99; *Catalogue of the Officers and Students of Williams College . . . 1863–64* (Williamstown: Williams College, 1863), p. 29 (hereafter cited as *Williams Cat.*); GSH to A. B. Hall [Feb 1864], HP.

7. GSH to A. B. Hall, 5 Mar 1864, HP.

8. GSH to G. B. Hall, 13 May 1864, HP.

9. GSH to Julina Hall, 13 Jan 1866; GSH to A. B. Hall, 21, 28 Jan 1866, HP.

10. GSH to A. B. Hall [Feb 1864]; GSH to A. B. Hall, 5 Mar 1864; GSH to A. B. Hall, 20 Sept [1865], HP.

no longer challenged by his studies. When in junior year he was able to study subjects other than the classical fare, he found the experience exhilarating, but the coverage of history, natural science, and modern languages was erratic, and the work remained "very easy."[11]

Hall was left, as a result, with a great deal of free time, and like the other students at Williams, he was at no loss for using it. Extracurricular activities offered him the most congenial outlet he had had for his enthusiasm and artistic bent, and except for romantic adventures, which he was too fearful to attempt, he participated in nearly every activity available.[12]

Hall showed his first interest in natural science in his junior year when he joined the scientific club attached to the Lyceum of Natural History, the college's museum of geological and biological exhibits. Hall said later that his curiosity "somehow got an early tilt toward origins," that as a child he had been "unusually inquisitive about the origin of babies" and had been especially interested in seeds of plants and in animal embryos.[13] His first scientific interests, at any rate, followed in that line. The fossils collected by Edward Hitchcock at the Amherst museum stimulated his interest in paleontology. For a time, he considered participating in a field expedition to South America planned by the Lyceum club.[14] The catchwords of evolution already had some currency on the Williams campus. Hall was inspired by them to write an essay on the nebular hypothesis of the origin of the solar system and to consider some of the heresies suggested by Darwin's theory of the origin of species.[15]

11. *LCP*, pp. 156–58; Rudolph, *Mark Hopkins*, pp. 45, 221–22; *Williams Cat.*, 1863–64, p. 19; 1864–65, pp. 19–21; 1865–66. p. 20; 1866–67, p. 19; GSH to A. B. Hall, 20 Sept [1865]; GSH to his parents, 16 Sept 1866, HP.

12. Hall was a member of a fraternity, debating society, literary club, theological society, natural science club, amateur musical group, art association, chess club, and wicket club, and a participant in numerous student excursions. *LCP*, pp. 160–62, 165; Wilson, *GSH*, pp. 29–30; GSH to A. B. Hall, 20 Jan 1864; GSH to G. B. Hall, 13 May 1864; GSH to A. B. Hall, 3 Oct 1865; GSH to Julina Hall, 18 Nov 1866, HP.

13. *LCP*, p. 358.

14. Wilson, *GSH*, p. 29; *LCP*, p. 358; Julina Hall to GSH [Sept 1866], HP.

15. P. A. Chadbourne, "Darwin's Theory," *Williams Quarterly* 14 (Nov 1866, Apr 1867): 67–69, 153–57; *LCP*, p. 358. Hall claimed late in his life that at Williams he outspokenly advocated the theory that man was descended from the ape. *LCP*, p. 358. There is no contemporary evidence of this, however; throughout *LCP*, Hall generally exaggerated the extent of his earlier radicalism.

Hall gave most of his attention, however, not to natural science but to the open book of nature spread round the college. The natural surroundings were traditionally venerated at Williams; they were the reputed inspiration of her most famous alumnus, William Cullen Bryant, and the goal of innumerable student expeditions. At Williston, Hall still described the countryside prosaically: "The woods look quite green and on some trees the leaves have nearly got their full growth," he reported to his parents; at Williams, he turned to the flowery and ecstatic descriptions of nature admired by his peers. A day in the nearby mountains spent communing with nature he called "the richest day of my life."[16]

Hall's models of enthusiasm and taste came from the romantic literature that he began to read in great quantity in his sophomore year. Hall could draw on the substantial collection of modern literature amassed by the student literary societies and on the inspiration of two visits to the campus by Ralph Waldo Emerson himself. By midyear he numbered himself among "the literary characters of the college," a situation he justified to his parents by observing that they "are the most successful so far as I know in after life."[17] These "literary characters" combined the qualities of the "intellectual" and the "gentleman," two ideals which had emerged among the Williams student body alongside the older puritan ideal still officially upheld by the college. Hall was attracted to this literary ideal both for its serious intellectual content and its elegance of style and manner. He tried to match his wealthier classmates in elegant clothes and possessions, but these efforts at gentlemanly grace were doomed to failure by his meager financial resources.[18]

---

16. *LCP,* p. 164; Rudolph, *Mark Hopkins,* pp. 135–43; GSH to A. B. Hall, 8 May 1863; GSH to Robert Hall [June 1864]; GSH to Julina Hall [summer 1864]; GSH, "Excursion to Peters Hill," Aug 1865, HP; GSH to A. B. Hall, 21 Jan 1866, HP; GSH, "Bryant," 1866; GSH, "Editor's Table," 1867.

17. Rudolph, *Mark Hopkins,* p. 76; GSH to A. B. Hall, 9, 20 Jan 1865, HP; Wilson, *GSH,* p. 28. Emerson spoke in Williamstown on 31 July and during 7–14 Nov 1865. Hall claimed to have called on Emerson but, unlike his classmate, Charles Woodbury, left no record of their exchange. *LCP,* pp. 162–63; Charles J. Woodbury, *Talks with Ralph Waldo Emerson* (New York: Baker and Taylor, 1890), pp. 3–4; *Williams Quarterly* 12 (June 1865): 221; 13 (Nov 1865): 139–40, 146.

18. Rudolph, *Mark Hopkins,* pp. 76–77; GSH to A. B. Hall, 8 May 1863; 20 Jan 1864; 15 May 1866; GSH to G. B. Hall, 17 Mar 1865; GSH to Julina Hall, 18 Nov 1866; GSH to his parents [spring 1867], HP.

At the start of his junior year, Hall and his friends formed a club—the Junto—composed, as he wrote his parents,

of nine of the most talented and literary men (so called) in our class. . . . We meet three hours from six and a half to nine and a half every Saturday evening. . . . We converse as elegantly and politely as possible on literary questions, authors, politics, philosophy, and read Shakespeare and intend soon to institute parlor theatricals. I expect to gain very great good from the organization. Profanity, refreshments, smoking, drinking, impoliteness are contraband.[19]

According to Hall's recollection, the group

poured over and discussed Emerson, even his poems, Carlyle, Coleridge, Lamb, Wordsworth and the Lake Poets, Tennyson, E. P. Whipple, "Hamlet," "Macbeth," and other of the plays of Shakespeare, the Brownings and G. W. Curtis. We discussed Dante in translation, *Wilhelm Meister, Faust,* read some of the plays of Schiller and Lessing in English, and many others.[20]

Hall left evidence of his wide reading in quotations and allusions liberally sprinkled through his own literary efforts. He became an editor of the student literary quarterly and twice was elected Class Poet, an honor he considered "no especial compliment as there is no one else in the class that writes at all decently."[21]

When Hall went to a nearby town to teach school for the winter recess, he acted the part of a literary gentleman. Nursing side-whiskers and a mustache, he instituted literary exercises for the townspeople, gave his first public lecture—an hour-and-a-half discourse on "Society" with prepared "extempore" asides—and managed to speak to one group or another four or five times a week.[22] When Hall returned to Ashfield for his vacations, he attracted the attention of Charles Eliot Norton, the town's distinguished summer resident, and during his few visits with Norton, the scholar encouraged his interest in literature and art, urged him to read Ruskin, and made him feel a small part of the greater literary world.[23]

Hall's introduction to the larger world frightened as well as

19. GSH to A. B. Hall, 3 Oct 1865, HP. Hamilton Wright Mabie, later a popular essayist and journalist, was also a member of the Junto.

20. *LCP*, p. 161.

21. GSH to A. B. Hall, 20 Jan 1864; GSH to Julina Hall, 18 Nov 1866, HP.

22. GSH to Julina Hall, 13 Jan 1866; GSH to A. B. Hall, 21 and 28 Jan 1866, HP.

23. *LCP*, pp. 170–72.

stimulated him. Despite the Junto's effort to exclude such morally debilitating influences as profanity and refreshments, Hall could not avoid the disturbing effects of the literature itself. As he studied Emerson and the English and German romantics, he was forced to recognize how congenial their ideas were to some of his own ambitions and desires and how different their values were from those of his orthodox mentors. Although he relished the figure he cut as a "literary man," he could not forget the old strictures against selfish pride. By the end of his junior year, he was struggling painfully to reconcile the demands of his disparate masters.

Hall's reaction to the threat of his subversive impulses was recorded in "The Student's Sin," one of his first contributions to the *Williams Quarterly*, the student literary magazine. All the sins he berated were his own. He began with "conceit," and the sudden attempt to acquire the "etiquette of a gentleman," and went on to repudiate him "who slights the college course" in favor of the shifting sands of literary study. He warned against the dangers of speculation and fantasy and the failure "to eliminate little immoralities in thought or reading." Hall concluded that "there are no more fatal errors than those of ambition by which we reach too far, and attempt too much." Hall contrasted these overreaching sins of literature with the more humble attractions of the ministry, but the very terms of his praise betrayed his feelings. Because the minister is always close to God, Hall claimed, he "always lives on the summit of his glory. . . . The need of both the religious and literary world is a great life." Hall could try to reconcile himself to a religious vocation only by linking it to the romantic ambitions he was trying to disown.[24]

Hall elaborated on the consequences he feared from his ambitious speculation in a poem, "A Life without a Soul." It told the story of a young man who was banished in childhood from his father's home. Abandoned, he grew up as part of nature, communing with all her creatures but lacking that knowledge of God which only society, through religion, could teach. The poet, at the end, tells of his own fearful musing that perhaps matter could explain the world as well as spirit: "Of those worlds that at the

24. GSH, "The Student's Sin," 1866.

surface close, the one will always prove/Unsubstantial. . . ." Hall
was afraid that his intellectual daring would lead him to discover
that only half the world he knew and desired was substantial and
that in consequence, like the boy banished from home, he would
lose a deep part of himself.[25]

Hall used the conventional antagonism between head and heart
to express his conflicts. Literature, which had led him into heretical
speculation and stirred his ambition, he assigned to the "head."
Against these tendencies, he listed religion and morality, both allied with man's emotional nature, and experience and the concrete
world, anchors against the tides of fancy: all these Hall ascribed
to the "heart." "God has made head and heart fast together," he
concluded. "Let the scholar beware of the great sin of putting
asunder what God has joined."[26]

Hall's battle between head and heart paralleled suggestively the
differences between his parents and the conflicts involved in his
identifications with them. Hall's assertion of manly independence,
his intellectual adventurousness, seemed to arouse in him fears
associated with taking his father's place in the home—of breaking
asunder the marriage partnership, of banishment and loss—as well
as fears of losing the religious assurance and warm sympathy he
had known in his mother. Hall never entirely freed himself from
these childhood fears. They hindered his effort to support a masculine identity and motivated his need to temper intellectual ambition; they shaped the conflicts between reason and piety, idealism
and realism, that he later tried to resolve.[27]

As a senior Hall was allowed course work in philosophy and
literature, which may have helped him in his struggle between
head and heart. The principal course in philosophy was taught by
Mark Hopkins, president and patriarch of the college. Hopkins
surveyed the whole of existence from the lowest, inanimate forms
of organization to the highest forms of rational and religious experience in man. Though he emphatically disbelieved in natural-

25. GSH, "A Life without a Soul," 1866.
26. "The Student's Sin," 1866.
27. Cf. Ernest Jones's discussion of Freud's fear of his gift for imaginative
speculation, in *The Life and Work of Sigmund Freud* (New York: Basic Books,
1953), 1:295–97.

istic theories of evolution, his theistically oriented panorama of the graduated levels of existence opened up a cosmic view which Hall found impressive and which stimulated his interest in natural science and philosophies of nature.[28]

In his synthesis of mental, moral, and natural philosophy, Hopkins also gave some limited attention to psychology. He treated psychology in accord with the prevailing doctrine of mental faculties, though he also elaborated on it in a rather original way. A physician, as well as a philosopher, Hopkins may have been influenced by the popular phrenological tradition and introduced some anatomy and physiology into his course. Hall later, in a complimentary dedication, called him his "first teacher in physiology."[29] Hall did not, at the time, appear to be particularly stimulated by this initial exposure to the subject, but Hall's mature system of ideas, with its cosmic scope and its emphasis on the innate constitution of the psyche, bore striking resemblances to Hopkins's own system.

In his early years, however, Hall had good reason to turn away from Hopkins's ideas. Hall's most pressing concerns at the time were personal and ethical, and in Hopkins's system Hall must have heard only echoes of the traditional standards under which he chafed. In accord with the revised Calvinism of the New England theology, Hopkins believed in the congruity of self-interest and virtue, self-love and benevolence, culminating in the love of God. While this formulation could lend religious sanction to the worldly values of American society, it was the traditional concepts of moral virtue which controlled the equation and the traditionally accepted forms of self-interest which could gain their approval. They appeared, moreover, in a finished system, a final revelation which the young could not change. To a young man like Hall, who felt his own interests and desires to be painfully at odds with the injunctions of his orthodox heritage, Hopkins's traditional assurance of harmony could have little to say.[30]

28. *LCP*, pp. 166, 168.

29. Ibid., pp. 166–69, 183; GSH, *Aspects of German Culture*, 1881, dedication page.

30. *LCP*, pp. 166–69. The discussion of Nathaniel Taylor's revised Calvinism and Horace Bushnell's rejection of it in Barbara M. Cross, *Horace Bushnell:*

Hall turned therefore to John Bascom, the professor of rhetoric and later president of the University of Wisconsin, who stood on campus as an outspoken and somewhat heretical young challenger to the president.[31] He was the man, Hall later said, to whom "I owe most" at Williams.[32] From early in September of his senior year, when Hall started a course with Bascom,

he alone suggested to me reading, criticized personally and in detail my literary efforts, and encouraged me to break away from Sir William Hamilton, whose system was taught by the president, and to become interested in Mill, Mansel, Jouffroi and the Associationists.[33]

Hall chiefly remembered Bascom for his interest in John Stuart Mill and other of President Hopkins's philosophical antagonists, although Bascom's concessions to empiricist philosophy appeared to interest Hall less at the time than the romantic, rationalist, and individualistic strains in Bascom's thought.

Although Bascom too believed in the consonance of self-interest and virtue, he conveyed a far different sense of those terms than President Hopkins. Well-read in romantic literature, he stressed the central role of feelings in thought and conduct, and praised a romantic model of the creative artist and hero.[34] Influenced also by the idealism of the Reverend Laurens P. Hickok, he extolled the mind, which "lights us at every step of the ascent," and lyrically defended philosophy as a pursuit distinct from theology.[35] Most important, Bascom urged a young man not to let humility dampen self-cultivation; he should make of his life a thing of delight, "pos-

Minister to a Changing America (Chicago: University of Chicago Press, 1958), pp. 1–20, suggests many parallels with Hall's experience later in the century.

31. "The divergences of [Bascom's] standpoint from that of the president were marked and a source of great interest to us students in the later college years, as most of us took sides with one or the other." *LCP*, p. 157. Cf. Rudolph, *Mark Hopkins*, pp. 54, 225–27; Arthur Latham Perry, *Williamstown and Williams College* (New York: C. Scribner's Sons, 1899), pp. 651, 807–8.

32. *LCP*, p. 157.

33. Ibid.; *Williams Cat., 1866–67*, p. 19.

34. John Bascom, *The Principles of Psychology* (New York: G. P. Putnam's Sons, 1869), p. 275; *Ethics* (New York: G. P. Putnam's Sons, 1879), pp. 17–19, 35; *The Philosophy of English Literature* (New York: G. P. Putnam's Sons, 1874), pp. 238–64.

35. Bascom, *Science, Philosophy and Religion* (New York: G. P. Putnam's Sons, 1871), pp. 5–26; *DAB*. s. v. "Bascom, John"; Perry, *Williams College*, p. 812.

sessed of a light of its own."[36] Bascom was himself an example of
his ideals, according to a Williams student: he conveyed in the
classroom and in discussion his sense of the excitement and glory
of the philosophical enterprise and his confidence in its future
progress.[37] Judging from the new confidence and ease which Hall's
essays showed after several months of contact with Bascom, the
chief influence of Hall's teacher was to sanction some of his romantic impulses and intellectual goals and to strengthen his capacity
for independence.

In "The Inventive Mood," Hall's first essay in the new style, he
found a new unity in man's capacity for intellectual invention,

the union of the particular that comes from observation with the general
and intuitive that flows in unconscious abundance from the divine source.
Man becomes the marriage hall of the two worlds of understanding and
reason. This is the highest prerogative of our being, the harmony of harmonies implying hygiene, and an artist's knowledge of man on the one hand,
and on the other moral relations that culminated in sweetest piety.[38]

Speculative reason, which earlier had been assigned to the subversive "head," he now described soothingly as intuitive reason. Philosophical and poetical truth had its source in man's emotional nature
as well as his mind and descended ultimately from divine inspiration. Hall realized that "many, unconsciously and against their will,
erect barriers within themselves between their two erect expressions
of the universe, so that their two selves never catch a glimpse of
each other."[39] Now he could rely on the natural functioning of man
in the act of creative thought to unite head and heart.

Hall thus centered his hopes on philosophy rather than literature.
He may well have found this new goal a sounder and more realistic compromise between his need to conform to the standards his
parents had established and his desire to strike out on his own
course. Philosophy, because of its connection with theology, was
closer to the norms of the narrow cultural milieu in which Hall

36. Bascom, *Ethics*, pp. 132–33.
37. Edward A. Birge, "President Bascom and the University of Wisconsin,"
*Memorial Service in Honor of John Bascom at the University of Wisconsin, De-
cember 13, 1911*, pp. 35–38. Dean Birge was a student of Bascom's at Williams,
from 1869 to 1873.
38. "The Inventive Mood," 1866, p. 109.
39. Ibid., p. 110.

grew up than a literary career, as well as more suitable to his particular talents. Intellectual creativity, he had discovered, combined both "an artist's knowledge of man" and the "sweetest piety."

In order to achieve a philosophy that united his "two selves" and satisfied both his conscience and ambition, Hall ran roughshod over the boundaries of his mentors' thought.[40] He did not specify how two distinct modes of knowledge like transcendental reason and natural, discursive understanding could be joined together. Formulating the problem in different terms as his knowledge grew, and failing to meet fully the intellectual difficulties it presented, Hall remained determined throughout his life to effect a fusion between a limited understanding of natural phenomena and a farther-reaching knowledge of their meaning.

Hall was also unaware how much he would have to revise his traditional notions of morality if he were to follow his own creative inclinations. In describing how "the inventive mood" could be achieved, Hall urged reliance on the moral sense, which he still envisioned in the figure of "Christian . . . with his central moral self defined" in contrast to the immoral Faust, Manfred, Wallenstein. But in a vein unlike that of Christian, he also rested the inventive mood on the power of books to

carry us to the boundaries of others' thought, and set us to work with their tools on the verge of human knowledge. All the lustres of human thought should be spread as sails before the mind, to catch every breath of divine wisdom till man is harbored in his proper end.[41]

Hall gave up the image of Christian entirely by the end of the year. In his poem read at graduation, "Philanthropy," Hall named Prometheus as the greatest practitioner of this traditional virtue. The bringing down of knowledge from heaven to earth, "the love of truth, all for its own sweet sake," was the highest philanthropy.[42]

Hall found further encouragement to follow his own impulses

40. On the origin of the distinction between the reason and the understanding in the philosophies of Kant and Jacobi, and the theory of knowledge developed from it by Coleridge, Carlyle, Emerson, and the German romantic philosophers, see Arthur O. Lovejoy, *The Reason, the Understanding, and Time* (Baltimore: Johns Hopkins Press, 1961), pp. 1–99.

41. "Inventive Mood," 1866, p. 113.

42. "Philanthropy," 1867.

toward a life of creative intellectual work in John Stuart Mill. Toward the close of his last year, Hall read through quickly much of Mill's work.[43] Though this heavy dose of empiricism may have shaken Hall's orthodoxy, it did not stimulate him to an articulate examination of epistemology or psychology. Hall followed Bascom's interpretation and an essay by the English theologian James Martineau in terming Mill's philosophy adequate for sense experience but false in the realm of religious experience and intuitive truth.[44]

The portion of Mill's thought which roused Hall to the most sustained interest was his ethical theory. Hall thought he saw a way of reconciling the utilitarian theory of ethics with the intuitive theory of his mentors, thus making self-interest legitimate. Hall seized on Mill's reference to the possible existence of a "vague, instinctive impulse toward perfection," and concluded that "our whole nature [is] set toward the highest good," so that "motives and impulses all the way down to the very appetites, relay the higher nature in its march." We can redeem the word selfishness from its vicious associations, Hall concluded. "Duty to self includes and commands all other fields." Indeed, he found at the center of Mill's system, as of Mill's life itself, "a belief in, and a struggle toward an intense self-cultured individuality." By the time Hall left Williams, Mill had become his hero.[45]

Through his reading in romantic literature and his introduction to philosophy under John Bascom, Hall had invested his enthusiasm and ambition in the ideal of intellectual creativity. This ideal gave him both a psychological basis for his independent identity and an assurance of his own place in the intellectual world, a place outside the known and finished systems of his elders. In the next decades,

43. Hall claimed to have read everything of Mill's he could secure, except the *Political Economy*, which was too difficult for him. *LCP*, pp. 161–62. His essay on Mill suggests some contact with at least Mill's *Logic, Examination of Sir William Hamilton's Philosophy*, and *Utilitarianism*, and with his essays on poetry, Bentham, and Comte.

44. GSH, "John Stuart Mill," 1867, pp. 18–29; Bascom, *English Literature*, p. 313; Bascom, *Psychology*, pp. 398–401; James Martineau, "John Stuart Mill," in *Essays Philosophical and Theological* (Boston: William Spencer, 1866), pp. 83, 116–18.

45. GSH, "Mill," 1867, pp. 18–29; *LCP*, p. 162.

Hall's desire to live "on the verge of human knowledge" would be recast in the mold of natural science; but the basis for his life-long devotion to knowledge and the search for new knowledge was already formed. So too was his romantic tendency to see man's impulses, appetites, and feelings as the core of human nature. Man's nature is, he remarked in his essay on Mill, "only his emotional nature." Though eschewing this conception for a time, Hall would return to it under the aegis of evolutionary biology.

Hall moved away from his old moorings slowly and cautiously, however. He tried to make each novelty of thought bear traditional meaning; he put new substance into old terms and overlooked logical contradictions in favor of poetic and figurative agreements. It was no accident that he should have chosen as his model of self-development a philosopher who could never free himself from parental influences, John Stuart Mill. Nor was it accidental that he identified with the martyred Prometheus, a hero who was dreadfully punished and suffered over and over again for his defiance. There was both prudence and belief in Hall's effort of reconciliation. His desire to maintain a traditional veneer, even later when his thought became more radical, sometimes disguised his meaning from himself as well as from his audiences.

These early speculations also show how closely Hall's thought was linked to his passions. His philosophical goal, as he said of American philosophy generally, was "to intellectualize and thus harmonize all the diverse strands" in his character.[46] As he deepened his studies, he tried to formulate a view of the world and the organization of knowledge that would support and guarantee the unity and harmony he sought, and he continued to condemn in others the subversive impulses in himself which threatened to disrupt it.

In following the contours of his internal struggle, his thinking often fell into confusion; by the same token, his thought showed the seriousness and vitality of the effort to define himself through philosophy. His classmates said that "when Stan gets to thinking clearly, he will think greatly," and they considered him "the smart-

46. GSH, "Philosophy in the United States," 1879, p. 105.

est man" in their class.[47] Hall's persistent effort to give intellectual form to the full range of his emotional experience was the chief source of both the insight and confusion he would display in his intellectual career.

In 1867, at the age of twenty-three, Hall graduated from Williams College. A picture taken at that time shows him as an impressive and serious young man. About five feet ten inches tall and solidly built, with dark hair and side-whiskers framing his face, Hall's finest features were a high forehead and dark, deep-set eyes. When Stanley was still a boy, his father had pointed with mingled pride and despair at the promise of his "noble brow and towering forehead."[48] The lower half of his face showed features less finely formed, a thick mouth and sharp chin, which were soon to disappear behind the full beard Hall wore all his mature life.[49]

The young man of the picture, however, was still entirely exposed and entirely uncertain of his future. He briefly considered going into medicine, but that course must have seemed too great a departure from the literary and philosophical interests he had been nurturing.[50] Hall considered more seriously the possibility of studying abroad. He knew the German universities were the goal of aspiring American scholars, and he had been filled with enthusiasm at the sight of those just returned from Germany glowing with its virtues. By sophomore year he was already hoping to finish his education in Germany, but he soon despaired of ever being able to afford it: "that plan looks now like a fool's idea with no means of accomplishment." Neither Hall's parents nor family could finance study abroad.[51]

With graduate study in philosophy virtually nonexistent in the American colleges in 1867, the clerical profession was still the chief path open to a young man of philosophical interests and slen-

47. GSH to A. B. Hall, 3 Oct 1865, HP; Wilson, *GSH,* p. 35. Hamilton Wright Mabie wrote Hall some years later that he had been accounted "the chief asset of '67." H. W. Mabie to GSH, n.d., HP.

48. GSH to A. B. Hall, 23 [?] 1867, HP; "St. Nic." [G. B. Hall] to GSH, 31 Dec 1853, GSH Memorial Volume, CUP.

49. *LCP,* pictures facing p. 99.

50. Ibid., p. 183.

51. Ibid., pp. 154–55; GSH to A. B. Hall, 9 Jan 1865, HP.

der means. Hall wrote rhetorically to his parents as his college career came to a close: "I had fully resolved now to preach sometime but yet I cannot make it seem that that will be the ultimate. I do not think I have got the requirements for a pastor. What do you think?" Short of striking out on his own to earn money for study abroad, Hall had little choice but to follow the traditional path into the ministry, whatever he might ultimately hope for. He soon asked his parents to inquire about his entering Union Theological Seminary and, in the fall of 1867, enrolled there as a divinity student.[52]

52. GSH to his parents, 18 Feb 1867; [May or June 1867], HP.

3 ENTRY INTO A LARGER WORLD

For the sons of the Connecticut Valley colleges, raised in the new school theology of the Congregational and Presbyterian churches, Union Theological Seminary was the last and highest school for the education of their souls. The regimen prescribed for the aspirant clergymen must have seemed to Stanley Hall like an island of old New England in the midst of an alien metropolis. For the two years he initially spent at the seminary, Hall followed a course of study in scriptural exegesis, formal theology, and history of the Christian Church.[1] Compelled to supplement his income, he taught school, preached during the summer vacations in small towns not very different from Ashfield, and extended his forensic reputation to fifteen or twenty Sunday schools in the city, where "all my little fame is on one speech."[2]

Though most of the students lived within its walls or boarded nearby, the seminary had little control over their daily lives outside the classroom. Hall quickly took advantage of his access to the city to escape the confines of the clerical world. He recalled that it was during his first two years at Union that he was introduced to liberal

1. George Lewis Prentiss, *The Union Theological Seminary in the City of New York* (New York: Anson D. F. Randolph, 1889), pp. 36–37, 41–43; *Catalogue of the Union Theological Seminary, N. Y., 1867–68* (New York: New York Printing, 1868), p. 14; *1868–69*, p. 13; *1870–71*, p. 15 (hereafter cited as *Union Cat.*).

2. *LCP*, pp. 177, 180, 182; GSH to A. B. Hall, [fall 1867]; 26 May 1868; GSH to his parents, [summer 1868]; GSH to A. B. Hall, 10 Feb 1869, HP.

Protestant attitudes which distinguished between the orthodox doctrines of the churches and the essential spiritual and moral truths
they contained. He was "profoundly influenced" by Ernest Renan
and David Friedrich Strauss, whose critical lives of Jesus reduced
the orthodox, biblical view of Christ to a legend woven around an
entirely human and highly moral man or to a myth expressing human truths in imaginative form.[3] In addition, Hall was "particularly fascinated by the radical O. B. Frothingham," who preached
that God was wholly immanent in the natural universe and worked
"in and through human nature." Frothingham named as his authorities the new "method," the new "direction" of thought, the latest
speculative word, with an enthusiasm that must have impressed the
young Hall.[4]

Hall found further encouragement to escape from orthodoxy in
the exciting environment of New York City. The seminary itself
introduced its students to some of the more pernicious aspects of
the metropolis by sending them to mission work in the slums and
to preach to "fallen" women. Hall emerged from his labors with
the streetwalkers unscathed, he later gratefully recalled, and went
on to other unauthorized adventures. Although Hall formed a
friendship with at least one of his fellow students, his clandestine
excursions were conducted alone. He attended all kinds of church
services, from Catholic to Seventh-Day Adventist to Spiritist. He
tested the city's famous phrenologists and mediums, repeatedly
visited the police courts and the morgue, and dabbled in a few of
the reform movements of the day.[5] He "fairly revelled in the thea-
ter," from the high drama of Booth's Shakespeare to the fore-
runners of vaudeville burlesque at Niblo's Garden. Twice he went
to see "The Black Crook," a popular and scandalous ballet spec-

3. LCP, pp. 184–85. Hall also read Theodore Parker, Tom Paine, Charles
Kingsley, and Matthew Arnold.
4. LCP, p. 179; Stow Persons, Free Religion: An American Faith (New Haven:
Yale University Press, 1947), pp. 28–30, 42–56; O. B. Frothingham, The Religion of Humanity (New York: David G. Francis, 1873), pp. 7–17, 42–55, 84–
108.
5. LCP, pp. 178–81; GSH to his parents [Feb 1868]; GSH to A. B. Hall, 11
Apr 1868; 10 Feb 1869, HP. Hall attended the free-trade lectures of his former
teacher at Williams, Arthur Latham Perry, and other lectures on reform at Cooper
Union.

tacle which featured for the first time on the American stage one hundred female dancers very scantily attired. After the second visit, Hall wrote his parents that he "sat very near and this time was disgusted."[6]

Hall claimed that "it was because my life before had been so restricted that all the accumulated curiosity of years to see the world and what it really was and meant was irresistible,"[7] but this first taste of the variety of life hardly quenched his thirst. Secretly escaping from his respectable milieu, Hall would spend spare moments the rest of his life viewing boxing matches and cockfights, brothels and circuses, morgues and crematoria, just to get their "psychological flavor."[8]

Hall regaled his parents with tales of how he withstood the immorality around him, but even his assurances revealed how the city had undermined his received categories of thought:

My experience as a Christian has been deepened and enriched . . . a sense of the shallow character of preachers has grown on me. . . . I draw lines I never thought existed before. . . . I realize what corruption there is everywhere here in New York. . . . Everything is bought and sold, character, life, justice, gospel, and I have taken special pains all term to understand this city. I have *realized* a great deal that I knew before. . . . [9]

The city itself, like the work of Frothingham, Renan, and Strauss, instructed Hall in the difference between the essential qualities and the surface appearance of his Christian heritage.

At Union Seminary, Hall dared for the first time to think of becoming a professor of philosophy. Seminarians before him had gone on to study philosophy in Germany, and one of these, George S. Morris, became his idol. Later instructor in philosophy at Johns Hopkins University and professor at the University of Michigan, Morris was only a few years Hall's senior and had just returned from Europe when Hall met him. "I felt a great and, no doubt, extravagant, affection and admiration for him. . . . I looked up to him as fulfilling my very highest ideal—a man who had been

6. Arthur Hornblow, *A History of the Theatre in America* (Philadelphia: J. B. Lippincott, 1919), 2:96–101; GSH to A. B. Hall [fall 1867], HP.

7. *LCP,* p. 180.

8. *LCP,* pp. 578–80.

9. GSH to A. B. Hall, 11 Apr 1868; 10 Feb 1869, HP.

abroad and knew philosophy." Hall called on him several times
during his second year at Union, and the older man loaned him
books and encouraged his philosophical aspirations.[10]

Like Morris, Hall came under the influence of Henry B. Smith,
the professor of systematic theology at Union and the leading moderate theologian of the new school Presbyterians. Smith's own studies in Germany had led him to a keen appreciation of the philosophical thinking of his time and particularly of the great modern
innovator of the German evangelical church, Friedrich Schleiermacher.[11] He may have advised Hall—as he had Morris a few
years before—to study philosophy in Germany.[12]

The man whose influence proved decisive in Hall's future course
was Henry Ward Beecher, the famous orator-minister of the Plymouth Church of Brooklyn. Hall became one of a group of theological
students admitted occasionally to Beecher's study for discussion
and was much impressed by the way Beecher took issue with doctrines taught at the seminary. When Hall applied for membership
in Beecher's church, he recalled, he answered the minister's questions honestly: he told him that he believed less rather than more
of orthodox doctrine, and Beecher, commending him for his hon-
esty, admitted him to membership.[13]

Hall no doubt informed Beecher of his philosophical interest
and financial need, and Beecher gave him a note to Henry W. Sage,
the merchant who later was to become a major benefactor of Cornell University. Late in the spring of 1869, Hall's second year at
Union, he presented the note at Sage's office, and as Hall recalled
the incident, Sage grumbled to himself about the liberties his minister took with another's fortune, signed a check for $500 to the
amazed young man standing before him, and sent him from the
room. The check, to be repaid with interest in five years' time, gave

10. *LCP*, p. 184; GSH to Robert Mark Wenley, n.d., in Wenley, *The Life and
Work of George Sylvester Morris* (New York: Macmillan, 1917), pp. 152–53
(hereafter cited as *G. S. Morris*).

11. *LCP*, p. 178; Prentiss, *Union Theological Seminary*, pp. 260–70; H. B.
Smith, "The Relations of Faith and Philosophy" [1849], in *Faith and Philosophy,
Discourses and Essays* (New York: Scribner, Armstrong, 1877), pp. 1–48.

12. Wenley, *G. S. Morris*, pp. 88–89.

13. *LCP*, pp. 181–82; Wilson, *GSH*, p. 37; *DAB*, s.v. "Beecher, Henry
Ward."

Hall his first opportunity to realize his dream.[14] With $500, Hall could hope to study in Germany for about a year.[15] Leaving his theological studies in midcareer, he sailed in June 1869.[16]

The interest and excitement of the promised land was so great that Hall remembered feeling no loneliness on his arrival. Going first to Bonn, he spent a month there in a German home, improving his language ability and listening to theological lectures to train his ear. By August, Hall probably left Bonn to hike with a German companion through southern Germany and Switzerland, and in October he settled in Berlin for the year.[17]

From the start, Hall found the more liberal atmosphere of the German cities a delightful and instructive change from America. The free behavior he had observed in New York City he could easily have assigned to the degenerate poor or the corrupt rich, but in Germany he could not avoid the challenge of more liberal codes of behavior. Hall vividly remembered his first Sunday in Bonn, when he spied one of the university professors of theology at a pleasant beer garden, seated with his family around him and enjoying his beer. It did not take the young New Englander long to appreciate the continental spirit. "The hated Puritan Sunday which all my life before had been a dreaded day of gloom and depression now became one of joy and holiday recreation."[18] Hall's excursions and theatergoing were now pursued openly and he even began drinking beer in moderate quantities. Hall relished the beer for the feeling it gave him of being *ausgelassen*, "let out." He loved Germany, he later remarked,

because beyond the Rhine I found, so highly developed, qualities that I lacked but admired; namely, a capacity for sentiment, *Gemüt* or the power

14. *LCP*, pp. 182–83; Wilson, *GSH*, pp. 37–38.

15. On the cost of a year's study in Germany during the 1860s, see James Morgan Hart, *German Universities: A Narrative of Personal Experience* (New York: G. P. Putnam's Sons, 1874), p. 394.

16. Henry Ward Beecher, "To Whom It May Concern," 5 June 1869; GSH to his parents, 11–22 June [1869], HP. Hall claimed that he could not trust himself to face his parents' objections, and so left the country without returning home to say good-bye. *LCP*, pp. 183–85.

17. *LCP*, pp. 186–88, 195–96; Wilson, *GSH*, p. 39; GSH to his parents, 9 July 1869, HP.

18. *LCP*, pp. 187, 219; GSH to his parents, 9 July 1869, HP.

of abandonment to the moods, feelings, ideas, and companions of the present moment.

Germany, far more than Williams College or New York City, allowed Hall some expression of the emotional nature he held under constraint, and indeed, he may have had to physically leave his homeland and come to this reputedly heretical place to allow himself to relax those constraints.[19]

For the first time, Hall cultivated relations with women. Throughout his adolescence his interest in women had been "unusually dormant and repressed." If the nymphs of Niblo's Garden had roused his emotions, he at least felt obliged to report that he had felt disgust. In Berlin, the family with whom he boarded with three other students boasted four adolescent daughters and the group often entertained themselves together. He met still others, and with two of these "mädchen," Hall later wrote, "I lost my obsession of bashfulness" and felt real affection for them. "This experience had a profound effect upon my character. I realized that I was a man in the full normal sense of that word." Such an experience was most salutary, he believed, "especially if it is followed by years of chaste sublimation."[20]

On one occasion Hall ventured to tell his parents about his new style of life. One Sunday evening, he wrote, he had yielded to the persuasion of the company and practiced dancing in preparation for a ball. The elder Hall, still the stern father, rebuked his twenty-six-year-old son:

People have often spoken of the laxity of *German theology,* and hitherto, my fears have extended only to *that.* . . . But the circumstance forced upon my mind an almost forgotten Poem beginning thus: "Vice is a monster of so hideous mien. . . ."[21]

Hall's response to his father was more open than usual. He could

19. *LCP,* pp. 188, 220, 222.

20. Ibid., pp. 188, 220–21, 378. Hall had some social contact with young women when he taught school during his college vacations, but he was generally very critical of them and ill at ease in their company. GSH to Julina Hall, 13 Jan 1866; GSH to A. B. Hall, 21, 28 Jan 1866, HP.

21. Really "Vice is a monster of so frightful mein . . ." from Alexander Pope, *An Essay on Man,* Epistle II, line 217; GSH to Julina Hall and his parents, 15 Mar 1870; G. B. Hall to GSH, 7 Apr 1870.

not but hope that his father had "parodied his own real solicitude a little" and replied that dancing

is a mere form for me without the least fascination and by pleasing instead of offending the people I think I kept the law of love on which the sabbath rests more than I broke it itself. My moral character to say the least is essentially fixed on principle . . . instead of being hauled by any such line as "Vice is a monster of such hideous mien."[22]

Hall was not entirely honest, however, for dancing was one of his real enjoyments. He still felt it necessary to close accounts of his excursions with some such remark as "Yet I go seldom out . . . I find very little satisfaction in this eternal attempt to be amused[.] I am sure it weakens character."[23] Puritan moral imperatives were too deeply implanted in his character to allow him full enjoyment of his German emancipation.

Although Hall told his parents that his chief studies would be in theology, he enrolled in the philosophical faculty at the university in Berlin.[24] The only theological subject he studied was the one most closely related to philosophy: systematic theology under Isaac August Dorner, the mentor of Hall's advisor at Union Seminary, Henry B. Smith. Dorner's theology was an attempt to compromise between Lutheran orthodoxy and the rationalist and subjectivist interpretations of Christianity propounded by Hegel, Schleiermacher, and their followers. Hall made a serious effort to understand Dorner's position, but he was more permanently affected by the radical insights of Schleiermacher himself, whose *Christliche Glauben* he studied in Dorner's seminar.[25]

Schleiermacher believed that religious faith was "neither a Knowing nor a Doing, but a modification of Feeling, or of immediate self-consciousness," the essence of which was "the consciousness

22. GSH to his parents, [Apr 1870], HP.
23. *LCP*, p. 116; GSH to G. B. Hall, [summer 1870], HP.
24. GSH to G. B. Hall, ibid.; Archiv der Humboldt-Universitat zu Berlin to the author, 2 Mar 1962.
25. *LCP*, p. 190. When Hall returned from Germany he worked up a set of notes which he and a German friend had compiled of Dorner's theological system and published it in the *Presbyterian Quarterly and Princeton Review*, 1872, 1873. Dorner protested that Hall's summary did not give "on the whole, a correct view of his system, and that it is inaccurate in several particulars." Henry B. Smith, "Dr. Dorner's 'Outlines of Theology,' " ibid., 3 (Apr 1874): 359.

of being absolutely dependent.''[26] The tendency of Schleiermacher's thought was to shift the problem of religion away from a supernatural God and toward the natural phenomenon of religious belief, to root religious belief in man's emotional nature, and to define religious feeling as the elemental feeling of complete dependence. These tendencies coincided with Hall's own growing liberalism in religion, his subjective cast of mind, and his own experience of religious belief; from this time forward, Hall's thinking about religion bore the mark of Schleiermacher's influence.

Hall's main effort was as a member of the seminar of Friedrich Adolf Trendelenburg, professor of philosophy at Berlin and the man under whom George Morris had studied a few years earlier.[27] Trendelenburg was one of the leading spirits in the critical movement in German philosophy that developed in response to the fragmenting intellectual situation of the mid-nineteenth century. This fragmentation had in turn been created by the collapse of religious assurance, the success and multiplication of the natural sciences, and the decline of the synthetic philosophical systems of the prior decades. By returning to the criticism of the limits and character of knowledge inaugurated by Kant, by applying historical criticism to the long tradition of philosophical speculation, and by learning from the methods and results of empirical science, the critical philosophers hoped to revitalize philosophical studies and to find some secure basis for restoring order to the intellectual scene.

Trendelenburg believed strongly in the value of historical criticism in discovering those elements of permanent value to philosophy, and his seminar when Hall attended it was devoted to Aristotelian studies. Trendelenburg attempted to overcome the dualism bequeathed by Kant and to establish a position of Ideal-Realism, based on a metaphysical conception of movement in nature. In his theory of movement, as in other aspects of his philosophy, he was much influenced by natural science, and believed that philosophy must base itself so far as possible on the results of empirical investigation. His work on the problem of knowledge and his respect for empirical study led him to an interest in psychology,

26. *LCP,* p. 190; Friedrich Schleiermacher, *The Christian Faith,* ed. H. R. Mackintosh and J. S. Stewart, (Edinburgh: T. and T. Clark, 1928), pp. 5, 12.
27. *LCP,* pp. 190–91.

and at the time of his death, two years after Hall studied with him, he was planning to write a treatise on psychology.

With no previous philosophical training in, or inclination toward, rigorous thinking, Hall appeared to appreciate only those aspects of Trendelenburg's thought for which he had been prepared. The main body of Trendelenburg's ideas entered slowly into his mind over the next decade as other influences and his general intellectual progress enabled him to grasp their significance. Hall wrote in 1878 that Trendelenburg's seminar "did not impress me so much then as since."[28]

At the time, Trendelenburg's emphasis on process and development encouraged him to "accept all I could understand of the Hegelian logic."[29] Although Hegel's influence in the German universities had already waned, adherents still existed, and Hall came into contact with the Hegelian professor of philosophy at Berlin, Karl Ludwig Michelet.[30] Hegel's majestic synthetic vision uniting rationalism and religion, reason and reality, strongly appealed to Hall. He was particularly impressed by Hegel's emphasis on development, his view that all ideas and institutions, and the absolute itself, existed only through a developmental process and were entirely conditioned by their developmental context.

The immediate impact of Hegel and Trendelenburg was to strengthen and confirm Hall's belief in the fundamental importance of historical process. Hall had encountered the idea of historical relativism first in the context of religious criticism and now philosophical criticism extended his insight. George Morris, himself a disciple of Trendelenburg, had been working in the history of philosophy in New York when Hall had first met and admired him and may have let Hall see the proofs of his book. It was through

28. GSH to William Torrey Harris, 17 Feb 1878, Harris Papers, Hoose Library, University of Southern California, Los Angeles.

29. *LCP*, p. 358.

30. *LCP*, p. 193; GSH to D. C. Gilman, rec'd 7 Oct [1876], GP. In a letter introducing himself to William T. Harris, Hall claimed that he had thought of writing something on Hegel's philosophy "ever since my senior year in college." [7 Oct 1871], Harris Papers. There is no other evidence, however, of Hall's having become interested in Hegel before his study in Germany. Many facts in this letter are distorted to give the impression of a deeper knowledge of Hegel than Hall in fact had at the time.

the influence of Morris, Hall later reported, that he first conceived an enthusiasm for the history of philosophy.[31] In Germany, Hall studied history directly, hearing the lectures of Johann Droysen and translating his *Grundriss der Historik*.[32] Modern historicism was, along with positivistic philosophies of natural science, the chief instrument of Hall's enlightenment and the foundation of his later conception of scientific knowledge and of psychology.

As Hall was taking up Hegel, he also proceeded more deeply into the second major area of his future interest. Trendelenburg's respect for natural science probably encouraged Hall to extend his interest in the biological sciences. Hall befriended an American medical student and under his direction began dissecting a human body. With his friend he also attended the surgical demonstrations of the director of the university's surgical clinic, Professor Bernhard von Langenbeck, and he may have heard some of the lectures of Emil du Bois-Reymond in physiology and of Rudolf Virchow, the renowned pathologist, in anthropology.[33] In Germany, a knowledge of the human organism and of scientific techniques must have seemed to Hall relevant to his philosophical interests.

After two months in Berlin and half a year in Germany, it became clear to Hall that he wanted to become a philosopher. Though he was living on a frugal scale, he knew his money would barely last the year and he sent requests to Henry Sage and to an uncle who had reserves, to finance more time in Germany so that he could take his Ph.D. degree.[34] His mother's response to his plan reminded him sharply of the disparity between his new ideals and those in which he had been raised.

31. GSH, "A Reminiscence," 1917, p. 297; Wenley, *G. S. Morris*, pp. 120, 154.

32. *LCP*, p. 189. Hall hoped to publish his translation of the *Grundriss*, but the plan never carried through. GSH to D. C. Gilman, rec'd 7 Oct [1876], GP.

33. GSH to his parents, 16 Dec 1869; [Apr 1870], HP; *LCP,* p. 189. Hall dabbled in a great variety of other subjects: physics, chemistry, economics, theology, Egyptology; and he claimed to have "heard enough of [Heymann] Steinthal in the psychology of language to get an impression of his personality." Hall admitted that "I had too little experience in note-taking at first to get much benefit from most of them, and some, even those I had paid for, were sooner or later abandoned." *LCP*, p. 189–90.

34. GSH to his parents, 16 Dec 1869, HP.

Now Stanley wherein is the great benefit of being a Ph.D. I think a *preacher* should be D.D. Just *what is* a Doctor of Philosophy? and wherein would it give you *credit, influence,* or usefulness?[35]

When Mr. Sage refused his plea and his money continued to dwindle, Hall became desperate. How, he asked his parents pointedly, could he manage to stay on? There was a great deal of Bible learning still to absorb.

I don't deny ambition, ambition which I have never dared to express but it is certainly in a good cause for I constantly narrow my studies to the single point of becoming a gospel minister which is my only great aim in this life.[36]

But even such a plea, as Hall could have known, would avail him nothing, for what resources his parents had were already committed toward giving his younger brother, following him through Williams, the same opportunities he had had.[37]

The Franco-Prussian War finally ended his hopes. Hall was excited by the outbreak of hostilities and his sympathy, like that of other visiting American students, was fully with his gracious hosts. He eagerly seized an opportunity to spend some weeks at the front as a war correspondent until the professional journalists arrived, but he found the war had occasioned a sharp inflation of the currency. The $300 his uncle had sent him was only enough to clear his debts and pay for his passage home.[38] In the late fall of 1870, after some fifteen to seventeen months abroad, Hall returned to the United States. A few years later Hall began to refer to this German trip as the traditional "triennium," or three-year period of study. He had wanted desperately to stay longer in Germany, and mentioning the longer period improved his chances of securing an academic appointment. The "triennium" abroad was also a more dramatic and fitting idea, so it pleased Hall ever after to say, and probably believe, that it was true.[39]

35. A. B. Hall to GSH, 18 Jan 1870, HP.
36. GSH to G. B. Hall [summer 1870], HP.
37. GSH to his parents [Apr 1870]; G. B. Hall to GSH, 7 Apr 1870; G. B. Hall, A. B. Hall, and Robert Hall to GSH, 1 Jan 1870, HP.
38. GSH to his parents, 20 July 1870, HP; *LCP,* pp. 194–95; Wilson, *GSH,* p. 40.
39. In the last available letter from Germany, Hall stated that he would arrive

Still without any permanent means of support and lacking sufficient preparation for any one profession, Hall returned to finish
his last year at Union Seminary. Again in an environment that
stifled his liberal impulses, Hall felt acutely frustrated.

I fairly loathed and hated so much that I saw about me that I now realized
more clearly than ever how possible it would have been for me to have drifted
into some, perhaps almost any, camp of radicals and to have come into
such open rupture with the scheme of things as they were that I should
have been stigmatized as dangerous, at least for any academic career, where
the motto was Safety First.[40]

It may have been on his return from Germany that Hall preached
a trial sermon at Union which, he liked later to tell, caused his professor to kneel and pray for his soul.[41] Hall kept the motto firmly
in mind, however, and managed to profess sufficient orthodoxy to
receive his divinity degree at the end of the year.[42]

Hall had by now decided definitely not to preach but instead to
use his Union degree as a credential for teaching philosophy in college.[43] By a stroke of good fortune, he found a liberal haven while
he finished at Union and looked about for a philosophical position.
George Morris, who was tutor to the sons of Jesse Seligman, a New
York banker, had just received an appointment at the University of
Michigan when Hall returned, leaving his place free for his younger
friend. Hall spent two years in New York in the congenial atmosphere of this liberal German-Jewish household, continuing on his
long road of enlightenment.[44]

Hall's rebellious feelings soon found an outlet in evolutionary

home by 1 October 1870, at the latest. GSH to his parents, 20 July 1870, HP. In
Union Cat., 1870–71, published in December 1870, Hall was listed as registered
and his New York address was noted. Hall's financial circumstances make it
likely that he returned by 1 October 1870, as he had planned, although he perhaps
could have returned as late as 1 December 1870 to register at the seminary. Hall's
first mention of a "triennium" occurred in a letter to Gilman applying for a job
at Johns Hopkins. GSH to D. C. Gilman, 31 July 1876, GP. In *LCP*, pp. 186–96,
and Wilson, *GSH*, pp. 39–41, the dates and the sequence of events of his journey
have been altered to accommodate this assertion.

    40. *LCP*, pp. 196, 223.
    41. Ibid., pp. 178.
    42. Wilson, *GSH*, p. 41.
    43. Ibid.; *LCP*, p. 196.
    44. *LCP*, pp. 196–98, 223; Wilson, *GSH*, pp. 41–42; Wenley, *G. S. Morris*,
pp. 119, 122, 153; *DAB*, s.v. "Jesse Seligman."

and positive philosophies. While he had heard something of Darwin's theory of the origin of species at Williams College, it is doubtful that he knew very much of the subject until he now came under the influence of a small group of positivists led by David Goodman Croly, managing editor of the New York *World*, and was inducted into the world of "radical thinkers."[45]

Croly, a disciple of Comte, was also interested in Herbert Spencer and in the program of sexual freedom advocated by John Humphrey Noyes. Hall followed closely a journal called the *Modern Thinker* which Croly put out between 1870 and 1873, and which served as a forum for himself, Noyes, and several others of Comtian and Spencerian persuasion.[46] John Fiske, in those days a young radical, occasionally spoke to the group and wrote for the *Thinker*. Hall also met George Ripley, the leading spirit of the old Brook Farm, who in 1870 had just returned from meetings in England with Spencer, Huxley, and Carlyle.[47] Hall recalled that by the end of those two years, he had gone carefully through Harriet Martineau's edition of Comte; read G. H. Lewes, an English philosopher interested in physiology and psychology; been "absorbed" by Fiske's *Cosmic Philosophy* and *Myth Makers*; and been "profoundly influenced" by Darwin, Spencer, and the English physicist and natural philosopher John Tyndall.[48] Hall also continued the scientific work he had begun in Germany. He heard medical lectures, probably at the College of Physicians and Surgeons, where classes were open to Union Seminary students,[49] though he did not gather evidences of Christianity from his medical studies as the seminary expected.

The first result of this varied exposure in New York and Germany to religious, historical, and philosophical criticism, to natural

---

45. In *LCP*, p. 179, Hall claimed to have begun to attend this "little club of Positivists" during his first year at Union. GSH to Wm. T. Harris, 9, 21 May, 19 June 1872, Harris Papers, suggest that Hall's chief contact with the New York Comtists occurred after his return from Germany.

46. *DAB*, s.v. "David Goodman Croly."

47. *LCP*, p. 179; GSH to Wm. T. Harris, 19 June 1872, Harris Papers; *DAB*, s.v. "George Ripley"; Milton Berman, *John Fiske: The Evolution of a Popularizer* (Cambridge: Harvard University Press, 1961), p. 104.

48. *LCP*, pp. 184–85, 222.

49. Wilson, *GSH*, p. 42; *Union Cat.*, 1870–71, p. 15.

science and positive philosophy, was to force Hall to abandon the supernatural world and to base his thinking henceforth on the ground of naturalism. Hall concluded that "Comte and the Positivists had pretty much made out their case and that the theological, if not the metaphysical, stage of thought should be transcended."[50]

Hall came to this conclusion only after serious struggle. The conception of nature that emerged from mid-nineteenth-century science seemed profoundly alien to human sentiments. Ordered by mechanical principles and moved by mechanical forces, giving rise to a succession of animal species and to man himself by the interaction of chance occurrences and physical processes, nature seemed to provide no warrant to those human desires for rational order and moral purpose in the universe which religion had hitherto guaranteed. Yet the longing for meaning and security, as the subjectivist critics of religion said, was itself part of human nature and the valid root from which all religion grew.[51]

The difficulty of reconciling the natural desires of the heart with the contemporary conception of physical nature was the burden of a representative document of Victorian spiritual travail, Alfred Lord Tennyson's *In Memoriam*, which Hall read over and over again until the pages of his copy were faded and worn and the long poem nearly committed to memory. "The poets helped me to clarity," Hall remembered, "most of all Tennyson."[52]

Tennyson represented the eternal indifference and wanton destructiveness of nature in the death of his beloved friend, Arthur Hallam; that his friend's life and his own mourning had lasting significance was the token Tennyson ardently desired of moral order in the universe. Through long struggle, the poet was able to achieve moments of reconciliation with his loss and to accept both the hard facts of nature and the force of his feelings. He concluded that both the heart's desires and man's knowledge of nature came from God and did not lie. "Let knowledge grow," he sang, "That mind and

50. *LCP*, p. 222.
51. Walter E. Houghton, *The Victorian Frame of Mind* (New Haven: Yale University Press, 1957), pp. 22, 69; John Theodore Merz, *A History of European Thought in the Nineteenth Century* (Edinburgh: William Blackwood, 1896–1914), 3:52–90, 162–74.
52. *LCP*, p. 185.

soul, according well,/May make one music as before,/But vaster." And in the end he forecast the development of a "crowning race," in whose hand nature would be "an open book." Tennyson's drama of doubt and return was as much a statement of faith in the ultimate rationality and moral beneficence of nature as of God, less a confession of theism than of pantheism.[53]

The faith Hall had won at Williams in the essential agreement between the truths of reason and the understanding was strengthened by Tennyson into a faith in the ultimate agreement of progressive knowledge and religious intuition. Anxious to remove any sharp divisions in existence, Hall henceforth tried to find Divinity within nature itself. The reconciliation of religious aspiration with the mechanical world-view propounded by science that Tennyson achieved in poetry, Hall hoped to achieve through philosophy. Having eschewed theology with Comte and Spencer, he did not think the metaphysical stage of culture was similarly obsolete.

The philosophical standpoint Hall took in New York was an eclectic Hegelianism. He had returned from Berlin interested in Hegel and within a year had made "digests" of his principal works and had tried to trace "the history of his philosophy down to the present." In the fall of 1871 he wrote to William Torrey Harris, the leader of a group of amateur Hegelian philosophers in St. Louis, embellishing his *curriculum vitae* with enlargements of his Hegelian knowledge and fanciful excuses for his absence of anything to show for it.[54] Hall had been following Harris's *Journal of Speculative Philosophy,* which published translations and commentaries on German and ancient idealism and encouraged the efforts of native talent. Like Hall, Harris had been influenced in his youth by transcendental literature and had attempted to link philosophy to the grounds of religion and art.[55] Hall asked Harris's advice on publishing an introductory work on Hegel in English, suggesting among other possibilities, a translation of the commentary on Hegel by

---

53. H. M. McLuhan, ed., *Alfred Lord Tennyson: Selected Poetry* (New York: Holt, Rinehart, and Winston, 1956), pp. 119, 220, and 118–220 passim; George Roppen, *Evolution and Poetic Belief* (Oslo: Oslo University Press, 1956), pp. 79–83.

54. GSH to Harris, [7 Oct 1871], Harris Papers.

55. Harris, "To the Reader," "The Speculative," *JSP* 1 (1867): 1–6.

Karl Rosenkranz, professor of philosophy at Konigsburg and one of Hegel's leading pupils. Harris replied with an offer to publish Hall's translation of the Rosenkranz in the St. Louis journal, and Hall immediately set to work. Portions of the commentary appeared in the journal over the next two years.[56]

Hegelian philosophy held many attractions for Hall. It provided him, first of all, with a confirmation of his experience of adolescent awakening and devotion to self-development, a justification of his feelings of growing consciousness and freedom, and a promise that "the universe itself might be comprehended and solved by mastering a few thousand pages." More than that, Hegel provided a "sense of universal 'explanatory solvency' ":

All conventionalities, and ideal institutions of society, church, state, family, schools, duty, etc., cease to exist merely and alone as brute material facts, and become clothes which the mind has made for itself rather than integuments which cannot be put off without vital lesion.[57]

Hegel gave Hall an Olympian vantage point from which to view and escape the conventional American world; yet its radicalism was limited to the play of ideas in the intellectual sphere.

Hegelian philosophy was also able to absorb into a philosophic system some part of both religion and evolutionary science. Rosenkranz belonged to the "right wing" of Hegel's followers who identified the Weltgeist with the traditional Christian Deity,[58] and this harmonizing of reason and the divine spirit seemed to Hall "the consummation of philosophic endeavor." Hall loved to conceive the Divine as the system of "reason which underlay and shaped all things," and to interpret Hegel's concept of history as "God coming to consciousness in man."[59]

56. GSH to Harris [7 Oct 1871]; 13 Oct 1871, Harris Papers; Karl Rosenkranz, *Hegel als deutscher Nationalphilosoph* (Leipzig: Duncker und Humblot, 1870); GSH, trans., "Hegel As the National Philosopher of Germany," 1872, 1873, 1874.

57. GSH, "A Note on Hegel, His Followers and Critics," *Aspects*, 154–56. This essay contains several pages on the appeal of Hegelian philosophy in America which were not included in an earlier version: "Notes on Hegel and His Critics," *JSP* 11 (Jan 1878): 93–103.

58. Karl Rosenkranz, "Correspondence," *JSP* 6 (Apr 1872): 175–81; Merz, *European Thought*, 4:15; Harold Hoffding, *A History of Modern Philosophy*, trans. B. A. Meyer (London: Macmillan, 1900), 2:288.

59. *LCP*, p. 358.

At the same time, Hall believed that the current tendency of natural science was to press on to the real nature of the thing itself, to seek, like speculative philosophy, "the central principle of all being and development."[60] Hall saw Darwinian evolution as the scientific analogue of Hegelian development. He wrote Harris,

No one that I have seen is disposed to oppose Hegel to the development theory. It seems to me that the 1st affords the only philosophic foundation for the latter. . . . I believe in the development theory in the sphere of nature . . . and that the laws of matter are the laws of thought, because of the higher belief that the laws of thought are primarily those of matter.[61]

Darwinian evolution and natural science would confirm and be confirmed in the Hegelian developmental philosophy.[62]

Hall thus went on to study Friedrich von Schelling's "Identity-philosophy," which tended to identify nature and spirit and to regard consciousness as the developing product of the evolution of nature. Hall remembered that it

treated all organic and even inorganic nature as steps in the unfoldment of a mighty process. Matter was sleeping mind. Mind was matter awakened, and vegetable and animal life and mind showed the stages of this awakening.[63]

As Hall's own interest in naturalism grew, he would turn repeatedly to Schelling's vision for inspiration.

Hall also found in the conservative interpretation of the Hegelian historical spirit a position at once safe and progressive. He believed,

60. GSH, "Anti-Materialism," 1872.

61. GSH to Harris, 21 May [1872]; 19 June 1872, Harris Papers. Hall wrote Harris, "I cannot see anything in the conception that the force which makes a flower blossom, or a sentiment glow, or a crystal to form, is a faint and distant replication of the force of all forces, viz., the primal antithesis and thesis of the infinite consciousness far back of the dawn of matter—which is inconsistent with the conception that the above phenomena are all developed, the later from the earlier, on the way to the full reflection and reproduction not only of their distant source but all the intervening processes. I think morphology is already showing the dialectics of evolution" (19 June 1872). Cf. Arthur O. Lovejoy, *The Great Chain of Being* (New York: Harper & Bros., 1936), pp. 242–333.

62. A similar appeal drew Hall to the work of Stephen Pearl Andrews, an amateur philosopher connected with Croly's group, whose "universology" seemed to Hall to "unite the positivistic with the speculative domains." GSH to Harris, 21 May [1872], Harris Papers; *LCP,* p. 179; S. P. Andrews, *The Primary Synopsis of Universology and Alwato* (New York: Dion Thomas, 1871).

63. *LCP,* pp. 358–59.

he wrote Harris, "in positivistic social science," but also "in that conservative restorative spirit which accepts and seeks to develop the present just as it is."[64] Again, Hegel could preempt and soften evolutionary science.

Despite Hall's circumspection, his abandonment of religious orthodoxy made it difficult for him to secure a position teaching philosophy, a task reserved in the traditional colleges for an irreproachable cleric, usually the president himself. When he first returned from Germany, Hall claimed to have applied at several colleges, including the University of Minnesota, and to have been refused because of his unorthodoxy.[65] Hall was acutely aware, as he lamented to Harris, that "the odium theologicum closes the positions that I desire and that otherwise might be open to me here,"[66] but he declared himself "still willing to sacrifice, as I have already done in more ways than one," for Hegel.[67] Hall moved easily into the martyr role that his heretical opinions opened for him. Hall was surprised at his parents' willingness to tolerate his liberal views as they grew older, and despite his continued apprehension, they apparently accepted with good grace his decision to teach philosophy.[68]

When in the spring of 1872 he still had not found a teaching position, he began to talk of a more speculative venture, a journal which would represent his own views and, he hoped, the American philosophy of the future. On consulting various philosophers in Cambridge and New York about his scheme, Hall was disappointed to find that there was "no common ground with the ultra orthodox. These men lay down a lot of theological postulates" and argue "that it is 'no use to try' to make a good Christian of Hegel." Nor were the Comtists he contacted willing to reverse their hierarchical arrangement of knowledge to the specifications of Hegelian metaphysics. Hall spoke vaguely of having a group of associates and supporters willing to undertake the venture with him, and he even elicited an offer from Harris to make the new journal a kind of east-

64. GSH to Harris, 21 May [1872], Harris Papers.
65. LCP, p. 196.
66. GSH to Harris, 13 Oct 1871, Harris Papers.
67. GSH to Harris, [7 Oct 1871], Harris Papers.
68. LCP, pp. 45, 253–54; HP, 1873–76, passim.

ern branch of the St. Louis journal, but the entire plan soon collapsed.[69]

It was not until late in the summer that Hall found a promising
opportunity to start his philosophical career. James K. Hosmer, a
young literary scholar Hall had met in Berlin, looked him up in
passing through New York. Hosmer was planning to vacate his
professorship of rhetoric and English literature at Antioch College
in Yellow Springs, Ohio, where his father was president of the
college, and he recommended the post to Hall. He may have told
Hall that his father would soon retire and that there might in that
event be an opportunity for him to teach philosophy, but the prospect of a fixed academic position was itself undoubtedly sufficient
to warrant Hall's acceptance.[70] At the age of twenty-eight, Hall
embarked for the Middle West and his first professional position.

69. GSH to Harris, 30 Apr, 21 May [1872]; 19 June 1872, Harris Papers.
70. GSH to Harris, 13 Aug 1872, Harris Papers; *LCP,* pp. 198–99; James K.
Hosmer, "Autobiography," typescript, pp. 187–91, Hosmer Papers, Minnesota
Historical Society, St. Paul; GSH to Hosmer, 8 Feb 1888, Hosmer Papers.

4 SEARCH FOR A PHILOSOPHY

Hall's academic appointment put only a temporary and superficial end to his restless studentship. Neither at the beginning nor the end of his four years in western Ohio was he truly a philosopher. The large ambitions and personal needs he was trying to satisfy through philosophy made formidable demands on his intellect, and he was not wholly pleased with his philosophical progress. The village culture which the college shared, somewhat more liberal and open in opportunity than that he had known in New England, tempted him with an easier, more familiar success. At Antioch Hall was still experimenting with roles, avoiding any firm commitments, and groping toward a philosophy and a vocation that would define his mature identity.

When Hall arrived at Antioch in the fall of 1872, the college had entered a period of decline. Since its founding under the presidency of Horace Mann twenty years before, Antioch had often found it difficult to compete for support among the dozens of small struggling colleges in Ohio, and its position was even more precarious under the depressed economic conditions of the 1870s.[1] Hall was required to teach French, German, rhetoric, English literature, and Anglo-Saxon—whose language and literature he had

---

1. S. C. Derby, "Antioch College," in George W. Knight and John R. Commons, *The History of Higher Education in Ohio* (Washington: U.S. Government Printing Office, 1891), pp. 128–37; Robert L. Straker, *The Unseen Harvest* (Yellow Springs: Antioch College Press, 1955), pp. 11–37.

not previously known—and to serve as college librarian, forensic coach, and drillmaster. During the second year, after President George W. Hosmer resigned, he became Bellows Professor of Mental Philosophy and English Literature. Abandoning Anglo-Saxon, to his great relief, he taught the senior course in philosophy along with French, German, and English literature. His chair, Hall later remarked, was a "whole settee."[2]

Although the small college required him to be versatile, Hall voluntarily enlarged the role. He occasionally worried that he might be spreading too much sail for his ballast, but once when the school year opened slowly, he felt that he needed "some little more activity." He promptly thought of projects other than learning philosophy to take up the slack.[3] Hall took over the direction of the college choir, participated in educational association meetings throughout the state, and lectured at Wilberforce, the nearby Negro college. With the traditional minister-president absent, he accepted the duty of preaching every other Sunday in the college chapel, and sometimes more often.[4] In the Unitarian setting of the college, Hall could speak his views more freely and still carry most of the students with him. Some of the subjects of his sermons suggest his liberal views: "The Philosophy of the Christian Fathers," "Christianity without Myth or Miracle," "Comparative Religions."[5]

Hall's sphere of activity soon branched from the college into the town of Yellow Springs. A village similar in culture to those he knew in New England, it provided an easy stage for his talents as a literary gentleman. Again he initiated literary society meetings and produced plays of Shakespeare. He joined the town's Masons and even brought literary exercises into their meetings. Hall worked his way to the Seventh Degree, the highest the local chapter could confer, and frankly revelled in the mysterious ritual.[6]

2. *LCP*, pp. 199, 201; *Catalogue of the Officers and Students of Antioch College, 1872–73; 1873–74; 1874–75; 1875–76* (Yellow Springs: Antioch College, 1873–76), passim (hereafter cited as *Antioch Cat.*); GSH to A. B. Hall, [9 Feb 1873], HP.

3. GSH to A. B. Hall, [9 Feb 1873]; GSH to his parents [4 Oct 1874], HP.

4. Wilson, *GSH*, pp. 53–55; *LCP*, pp. 199, 202; Straker, "Apprenticeship of GSH," pp. 6–7; Edward Everett Hale to GSH, 23 Aug 1875, HP.

5. GSH to his parents, 18 Jan 1875, HP; Wilson, *GSH*, p. 54.

6. GSH to A. B. Hall, [9 Feb 1873]; GSH to Robert and Sara Hall, 12 Nov

For the first time, Hall's salary enabled him to indulge his tastes. During the first year's new prosperity, he reported to his parents buying "another extravagant dressing gown, 13 broad quilted silk [stripes?], blue and twill palm figured, silk cord and tassel." Before long, his quarters boasted a "piano, quite a library and seven nice pictures and quite a portfolio of smaller works."[7] Such an impressive young bachelor soon became the focus of effort for the town's matchmakers, and his letters home became dotted with impatient references to anxious young ladies he could not dream of marrying until he had had one more trip to Germany. One of this band, Miss Cornelia Fisher, the daughter of a retired Cincinnati merchant, he was later to marry in Germany.[8]

A colleague described Hall at Antioch as "kind, impulsive, energetic, very sensitive . . . unsparing with his time, and very ready to assist the faithful students." On the other hand, Hall was "unrelentless with the shirk,"[9] and this firmness showed itself in his willingness to risk popular hostility in the cause of right. Hall exposed a "literary bureau" which sold essays to Antioch students, demanded heavy work from his students throughout the school year, and successfully countered the intense opposition these demands aroused.[10] Fittingly, Hall now thanked his parents for their severity.

When I see children spoiled by want of control and indulgence grow up without any earnest ideas or purpose of life I feel glad and thankful for what I used to call severity sometimes which I shall believe in for my children when they arrive, I think it deepens and straightens the nature and teaches self control.[11]

At once kind, impulsive, sensitive, and severe, it is understandable

1874; GSH to his parents, 24 Nov 1874; 18 Jan 1875; GSH to A. B. Hall, 29 Mar 1875; 21 Feb 1876, HP.

7. GSH to his parents, [Feb 1873]; GSH to A. B. Hall, [9 Feb 1873].

8. GSH to A. B. Hall, 29 Mar 1875; 21 Feb 1876; GSH to his parents, 15 Apr 1876; 30 Dec [1876], HP; LCP, p. 203. In GSH to Wm. James, 26 Oct [1879], JP, Hall claimed that Miss Fisher was the sister of one of his Union Seminary classmates and that he first met her in New York. There was, however, no Fisher from Ohio registered at Union during Hall's tenure there.

9. Wilson, GSH, pp. 53–55.

10. GSH to his parents, 31 Mar 1873; 12 Nov 1875; 30 Mar 1873, HP; LCP, pp. 202–3.

11. GSH to his parents, 12 Nov 1875, HP.

that he was also, as his colleague admitted, "often misunderstood."[12]
The only friendship Hall particularly recalled from these years was
the warm relationship he established with a woman colleague much
older than he who was a mathematician educated in Germany.[13]

Hall's varied talents, enthusiasm, and capacity for work nonetheless commended him to some of the elders of the community.
Hall came to the attention of Antioch's chief eastern Unitarian trustee, the Reverend Edward Everett Hale of Boston, and through Hale
and former president Hosmer, Hall was invited to preach to some
of the larger Unitarian churches of the state, occasions which gave
him the opportunity to meet some of the state's more substantial
business, political, and educational leaders.[14] Hall even began to
try to help solve the problems of the struggling college. He
drew up a complete plan of reform for the college shortly before
leaving, and he probably thought of himself as the young man
"with great executive force" whom Antioch needed as its new
president.[15]

Hall obviously enjoyed his success in the village culture and in the
state's Unitarian circles and welcomed the role of popular preacher
and organizer after his years of obscure apprenticeship. He was well
enough settled in his way of life at Antioch to discourage opportunities to leave. During his third year, he wrote his parents that he
was content to stay at Antioch for the time being, for "on the whole
I am growing here and not overworked and teaching just what I
want to teach."[16] Hall's comments about Antioch soon after he left
revealed, however, that he had felt constrained even by the liberal,
Unitarian doctrines of the college authorities, irked by the routine
tasks of teaching, and frustrated by his isolation from the intellectual
centers of the East. Beneath his easy successes, he could not forget

12. Wilson, *GSH,* pp. 53–55.
13. *LCP,* pp. 202–3.
14. Ibid., p. 201; GSH to his parents [Feb 1873]; 30 May [1873]; George
W. Hosmer to Judge [Alphonso] Taft, 16 Aug 1875; Hale to GSH, 23 Aug
1875, HP.
15. Hale to GSH, 23 Aug 1875; 23 Mar 1876; GSH to Mr. [Artemas]
Carter, 6 Dec 1875, HP. In his fictionalized tale of his life at Antioch, Hall had
the trustees make his young hero "the virtual head of the college." GSH, "A
Leap-Year Romance," 1878, p. 219.
16. GSH to his parents, 18 Jan 1875, HP.

his philosophical ambitions or his experience of cultural standards more enlightened than those of western Ohio.[17]

As a good Victorian, Hall felt "we are as naturally impelled to hide our wretchedness as our defects of mental culture,"[18] but he admitted to his parents that he often had to fight down "the blues" and "ennui."[19] Hall began to give lectures on the subject of pessimism during this period,[20] and his analysis of the appeal of pessimistic philosophies, like all his cultural criticism, had the pointedness and idiosyncracy of a sensitive reading of his own psyche. Pessimism, he said, fed on the present tendency to "callow, unphilosophical skepticism."

Men often lose their intellectual tastes, and even the tranquility of honest consciences. . . . The charms of domestic life are unexperienced or forgotten . . . while unattainable ideals fill many souls with nameless longings that make peace and contentment almost impossible.[21]

Hall's diverse activities and reading tempted him to shallow confusion; the duplicity of his beliefs and vocational desires denied him the tranquility of an honest conscience; the "charms of domestic life" were blocked by his uncertain financial position and reserve with women; and his feelings were buffeted by "unattainable ideals" and "nameless longings." Amidst this intellectual and emotional uncertainty, Hall clung to the relative familiarity and security of his outpost at Antioch and cautiously ventured toward a more satisfactory vocational role.

Teaching philosophy to a handful of senior students was itself not a demanding task for Hall. He substituted for the traditional instruction in metaphysics, logic, and ethics given by President Hosmer a more modern format that reflected his own wide inter-

17. GSH to Wm. James, 15 Feb 1880, JP; GSH to Prof. [A.L.] Perry [fall 1876]; GSH to D. C. Gilman, rec'd 7 Oct [1876], GP; GSH, "A Leap-Year Romance," 1878, p. 215.

18. GSH, "Democritus and Heraclitus," in *Aspects of German Culture,* 1881, p. 206.

19. GSH to his parents [4 Oct 1874]; 24 Nov 1874, HP.

20. GSH to Robert and Sarah Hall, 12 Nov 1874; GSH to A. B. Hall, 29 Mar 1875, HP.

21. GSH, "Democritus and Heraclitus," in *Aspects,* p. 205.

ests and the recent development of philosophy in Germany.[22] Outlining his philosophy course, he announced that

the historico-critical method is adhered to throughout in this department. No attempt is made at indoctrination. It is believed that with a fair understanding of the principles of Plato, Kant, Hegel, Spencer, and others, the mind is sufficiently restrained from dangerous extremes and errors.[23]

The acting president of the college confirmed that Hall's instruction was "mainly from the historical side, pointing up the strong and weak points of each system."[24] The new historical method allowed Hall to challenge the older religious tradition in the teaching of philosophy and open his students' minds to the clash of ideas. It was, too, reflective of his insatiable desire for intellectualized experience, a product of his desire to "get into sympathetic rapport with the most diverse types of personality and opinion," to appreciate their position from their own standpoint.[25] At the same time, it allowed him to attribute philosophical positions and counterpositions to third parties and avoid making any dangerous judgments himself. By this method, he stated, he hoped to avoid "all the *odium theologicum* . . . from whatever quarter."[26] By it, he also established a lifelong pattern of exposition by presenting succinct summaries of other people's views on a subject one after the other, without passing judgment on them, thus giving himself the benefit of both expressing and disowning their contrary opinions.

The caliber of Hall's instruction impressed the Antioch community as being "far above what is usually done in undergraduate classes" and won him an excellent reputation as a teacher.[27] Hall's teaching was not based, however, on any great depth of scholarship.

22. The first part of the course was devoted to psychology; the second, to the history of philosophy; and the third, mainly to aesthetics, an interest he had maintained since his discussions of Ruskin with Charles Norton during his literary college days. *Antioch Cat., 1872–73,* p. 16; *1873–74,* p. 13.
23. *Antioch Cat., 1874–75,* p. 18.
24. S. C. Derby to D. C. Gilman, [fall 1876], GP.
25. *LCP,* p. 86.
26. GSH to D. C. Gilman, 31 July 1876, GP.
27. *Antiochian* 2, ser. 2 (July 1875): 2; G. W. Curtis to A[lphonso] Taft, 19 Aug 1875, HP; E. E. Hale to GSH, 21 June 1876, GSH Memorial Volume, CUP; GSH to President Morgan, 23 Dec 1921, quoted in Straker, "Apprenticeship of GSH," p. 9.

Looking back on his philosophical efforts at Antioch, Hall felt "it was all poor cheap work." When he visited the University of Michigan to renew his acquaintance with George Morris, he was awed by "the extent" of Morris's library "and his familiarity with it."[28]

For the first two years at Antioch, Hall remained within the Hegelian camp and his interest was deepened by contact with Hegelian philosophers in St. Louis. At least once during these years, Hall made a pilgrimage to St. Louis, where he reported having "a delightful time with Harris."[29] Hall had early been aware that if his philosophical views were to be considered safe, he must avoid idealism as well as materialism, the "seductive extremes of modern thought,"[30] but he was carried away by enthusiasm.

While Hall remained fascinated with Hegel all his life, his wholehearted allegiance proved to be short-lived. After a visit to St. Louis during his third year at Antioch, Hall concluded that Harris and his men "seem better at their distance than upon personal acquaintance."[31] Hall did not specify what it was about the St. Louis gentlemen that had suddenly dimmed his enthusiasm. He discouraged an attempt to get him a philosophical appointment in the city,[32] and by the time he left Antioch, his interest in Hegelian philosophy had waned considerably.

Hall's visit to St. Louis, where Hegelian philosophy had the character of a transplanted provincial creed, may have reminded him that in the German universities Hegelian philosophy was outmoded and partially discredited. "It was this historical status of Hegelism," Hall wrote a few years later, "that first weakened its hold upon the writer's mind."[33] Hall may also have been discouraged by the somewhat cliquish monopoly Harris and his friends seemed to have on Hegel. It would take a very thorough indoctri-

28. Wenley, *G. S. Morris,* p. 154.
29. *LCP,* p. 22, 358–59; GSH to his parents [Dec 1874]; 18 Jan 1875, HP.
30. GSH, "Anti-Materialism," 1872, pp. 216–18.
31. GSH to his parents, 18 Jan 1875, HP.
32. Hall's friend James K. Hosmer was teaching literature at Washington University and hoped some professional philosopher could be hired to restrain the amateur speculations of the St. Louis group. Hall entered his name, but he named a prohibitive price for his appointment. J. K. Hosmer, "Autobiography," pp. 200–201, 210, 223–25, 247–48, Hosmer Papers. Hall asked for $2,500 in salary and a full professorship.
33. GSH, "Note on Hegel," *Aspects,* p. 154.

nation for him to equal or surpass Harris's authority on the subject.[34]

Behind Hall's enthusiastic allegiance and rather sudden disillusion with Hegelian philosophy it is also possible to see a considerable dimension of personal conflict. Hall's first experience with Hegelian philosophy turned into a lifelong love-hate affair. Philosophical idealism became the arch antagonist of his intellectual life, a foe which he berated in and out of context, yet an enemy whose substance he constantly toyed with bringing into his science. There is good evidence in the rhetoric Hall used about Hegel and idealism to suggest the kind of personal problems involved. Particuarly at times of personal crisis, the idealism syndrome, with its accompanying rhetorical outbursts, would appear in Hall's work.

As Hall described it, the youth first drawn to philosophical idealism was lifted into a state of exhilaration and then thrown down into the despair of nihilism. At first he experienced

an elation and exaltation that nothing else, unless it be paranoia or certain drugs, can give. Mind is supreme, has come to its own kingdom, cannot respect itself too highly as the cosmothetic creator and bearer of the universe.[35]

But this universal power also brought with it a universal responsibility. The youth realized everything in the world depended on his own psychic states.

He is reduced back to a hypothetical mesh of weltering, amoeboid psychic rudiments from which he must evolute himself.[36]

He was cast down into "the great disenchantment" and left at the end only with the sense of "aridity of heart" and an "enfeebled" will.[37] Here again was the cyclic manic-depressive pattern Hall said was established in youth by guilt over masturbation. Indeed, during his most severe crisis some years later, he publicly declared that philosophical idealism was no better than masturbation and pro-

34. Cf. the account of Bronson Alcott's visit to the St. Louis group in Henry A. Pochmann, *New England Transcendentalism and St. Louis Hegelianism* (Philadelphia: Carl Schurz Memorial Foundation, 1948), 34–53.
35. *GSH, Adol,* 2: 46.
36. Ibid., p. 535–37.
37. Ibid., p. 48.

duced just that effect in young men he knew.[38] Clearly, emotional conflicts idiosyncratic to Hall were involved in his experience of idealism.

The precise dynamics of Hall's emotional difficulties remain buried with him, but he himself distinctly assigned the danger of idealism to unconscious sources.

The energy of the instinct of idealization must not be misdirected or overdone. . . . [T]here is a saturation point. . . . [T]hat nine-tenths of life which is so deeply stirred at this age . . . cannot and should not be fully brought into the narrow field of youthful consciousness.[39]

The omniscient and omnipotent role into which idealism thrust Hall, "the titanic heaven-storming rage of absolute idealism," was fraught with dangers for him. At one point he spoke of it bringing "a kind of delicious mysticism, anticipating the realities of life from afar." At another point he feared that idealism would "lead men off the proper basis of their own true nature," perhaps even "counter to it."[40] Whatever desires and fears he felt, he retreated in face of them, as he had retreated at college from literature to philosophy in face of the overreaching ambitions transcendental literature had wakened in him. Hall eventually discovered that his intellectual ambition could be satisfied if it was enclosed by, and disguised in, natural science.

Hall's turn away from Hegel was also part of his slow intellectual maturation. Hall's understanding could have been deepened by the debate over Trendelenburg's critique of Hegel in the St. Louis journal during the early 1870s, by Morris's lucid criticism of Hegelian idealism in his essay on Trendelenburg published late in 1874, and by his own continued study of the history of philosophy.[41] As a result, Hall began to pay increased attention to the positive philosophers of natural science. He read more of Herbert Spencer,

38. See below, p. 254.
39. GSH, "The New Psychology," pt. 2, 1885, p. 240.
40. Ibid., p. 243.
41. Trendelenburg, "The Logical Question in Hegel's System," trans. Thomas Davidson, *JSP* 5 (1871): 349–59; 6 (1872): 82–93, 163–75, 350–61; A. Vera, "Trendelenburg As Opponent of Hegel," ibid. 7 (Jan 1873): 26–32; G. S. Morris, "Vera on Trendelenburg," ibid. 8 (Jan 1874): 92–94; Wm. T. Harris, "Trendelenburg and Hegel," ibid. 9 (Jan 1875): 70–80; G. S. Morris, "Friedrich Adolf Trendelenburg," *The New Englander* 33 (Apr 1874), 287–336.

Charles Darwin, G. H. Lewes, and John Tyndall and was especially attracted to Spencer's attempt to bring all of nature, animate and inanimate, conscious and material, under the laws of evolution. The atmosphere at Antioch was free enough to allow him to indulge his enthusiasm and to introduce Spencer into his philosophical lectures. When he left the college, he claimed that his philosophical work for the past years had been "nearly from the Spencerian standpoint."[42]

It was probably through Spencer that Hall contracted an enthusiasm for the subject which would soon unite his diverse philosophical interests and become the preeminent intellectual commitment of his life. Both Trendelenburg and Hegel had introduced Hall to psychology as a field of modern philosophy, but in 1870 and 1872 a second edition of Spencer's *Principles of Psychology* attempted to explain the development of human consciousness as a natural product of evolution. Beginning in the fall of 1873, Hall included lectures on psychology in his philosophy course.[43] When the first volume of Wilhelm Wundt's *Grundzüge der physiologischen Psychologie* reached him sometime after 1873, he was greatly excited by it;[44] Wundt's volume was the first systematic attempt to form a science of psychology from its bases in philosophy, physiology, and biology. When Hall left Antioch, he was convinced that "the application of scientific methods in psychology" was among the "marvelous new developments" in philosophy.[45]

During Hall's fourth year at Antioch, he was finally forced to come to a decision about his future. The struggling college was making itself over into a normal school and now had "too few pupils who study in the higher grades of philosophy to offer a man like Hall enough to do." Hall's work at the college was highly praised by the faculty and trustees, but as Edward Everett Hale admitted, they knew they could not keep him indefinitely.[46] Hall tried for an appointment at the new University of Cincinnati, and Hale mentioned him to Daniel Coit Gilman, president of Johns Hopkins

42. *LCP,* pp. 199, 359; GSH to D. C. Gilman, rec'd 7 Oct [1876], GP.
43. *Antioch Cat., 1873–74,* p. 13.
44. *LCP,* p. 200.
45. GSH, "College Instruction in Philosophy," 1876.
46. Hale to D. C. Gilman, 21 July 1876, GP.

University, but neither effort bore fruit. Although he still had no prospect of a position as the year drew to a close, he determined to take a year's leave of absence in which to work out his plans elsewhere.[47]

The appeal of Germany had not lessened during four years in the American Middle West, but Hall hesitated to return there to study.[48] He must have recognized that to enter the field of psychology would require more special training, but the prospect of another apprenticeship appealed to him less than a permanent philosophical appointment. Like dozens of other young scholars, Hall could not resist the possibility of a position at the new pinnacle of the American educational system.

In July, with the recommendation of Hale, Hall himself wrote to Daniel Gilman about the possibility of teaching philosophy at Johns Hopkins University. Enthusiastic to Gilman about the "new directions" and "new methods" in philosophy, he did not make clear what these were beyond the safe, "strictly historical methods" he promised to follow. Later, sending the beseiged president copies of his translations and reviews, he explained the lack of any written material which justly expressed his own views by saying that

in my own department, unlike those which are more special and technical, only the most deliberate maturity of thought could produce anything of value.

Gilman could not have been impressed with the caliber of Hall's work and was besides delaying the organization of the philosophy department in the hope of finding an established philosopher to take the chair.[49] His response to Hall's application was not encouraging.

Recognizing Cambridge as the chief intellectual center of the country, Hall had visited it previously, perhaps renewing his acquaintance with Charles Norton, and meeting President Charles

47. G. W. Hosmer to Judge [Alphonso] Taft, 16 Aug 1875, GP; Hale to GSH, 21 June 1876, GSH Memorial Volume, CUP; GSH to his parents, 12 Nov 1875; 15 Apr 1876; GSH to Mr. [Artemas] Carter, 6 Dec 1875, HP.

48. GSH to his parents, 15 Apr 1876, HP.

49. GSH to Gilman, 31 July 1876; rec'd 7 Oct [1876], GP; Hugh Hawkins, *Pioneer: A History of the Johns Hopkins University, 1874–1889* (Ithaca: Cornell University Press, 1960), pp. 53–55, 187–89.

William Eliot of Harvard.[50] In the absence of a permanent appointment, he decided to settle in Cambridge in September 1876 to hear
lectures at Harvard and then decide about returning to Germany.[51]
His decision to undertake further graduate training at the age of
thirty-two finally set him on the road to a professional career in
psychology.

50. Hale to GSH, 23 Mar 1876, HP; C. E. Norton to Gilman, 14 Feb 1881, GP; *LCP,* pp. 203–4.

51. GSH to Gilman, 5 Sept 1876; GSH to Prof. [A. L.] Perry [fall, 1876], GP. Hall stated in *LCP,* pp. 200, 203, and Wilson, *GSH,* pp. 58, 62–63, that upon reading Wundt's *Grundzuge,* he immediately determined to go to Germany to study with him, but was waylaid in Cambridge by the offer from President Eliot of a position in the English department and the prospect of a philosophical appointment. This story is not supported by contemporary evidence. The hope of a philosophical appointment at Harvard was never far from Hall's mind, but it was not a realistic prospect at the time of his decision to study at Harvard. The story appears to reflect Hall's desire to minimize the importance of his debt to William James.

5   PSYCHOLOGY IS THE WAY

One of the chief distinctions of the philosophy department at Harvard University when Hall arrived early in the fall of 1876 was the work offered in the new scientific psychology by the assistant professor of physiology, William James. Just two years older than Hall, James had convinced the Harvard authorities to let him give the first course in physiological psychology the year before, and Harvard was the only university in the country where the subject was taught.[1] Besides offering special work for graduate students, James gave an undergraduate course in the subject and arranged for the use of the physiology laboratory of his friend Professor Henry P. Bowditch of the Medical School.[2] Harvard had begun to make provision for graduate students and to offer the Ph.D. degree only four years before, in 1872.[3] It was undoubtedly the opportunity to pursue the "marvellous new developments" in psychology that convinced Hall to stay at Harvard.

In early September, even before he had permanently settled there, he and James wrote in concert to the *Nation* urging that the teaching of philosophy in American colleges be freed from subordination

---

1. Ralph Barton Perry, *The Thought and Character of William James* (Boston: Little, Brown, 1935), 2: 10–13; Paul Buck, *The Social Sciences at Harvard, 1860–1920* (Cambridge: Harvard University Press, 1965), pp. 178–79, 184, 188–90.

2. *The Harvard University Catalog, 1876–77* (Cambridge: Harvard University, 1876), p. 142 (hereafter cited as *Harvard Cat.*).

3. Samuel Eliot Morison, ed., *The Development of Harvard University* (Cambridge: Harvard University Press, 1930), pp. 452–54.

to religious purposes. In a letter signed with his initials, Hall complained that

especially the history of the leading systems of philosophy, ancient and modern, and the marvellous new developments in England and Germany, are almost entirely ignored. . . . The application of scientific methods in psychology by Spencer, Lewes, Lotze, Wundt, and others; the admirable textbooks now accessible in the general history of philosophy; the application of philosophical systems to history, politics, law and education, which have contributed to make these subjects centres of such fresh and eager interest under some of the great living German teachers, indicate how entirely our methods of instruction need to be remodelled.[4]

The uniformly critical tone of Hall's indictment of American philosophy bore witness to the undercurrent of frustration he had experienced as a student and teacher in the provincial, religiously oriented colleges which constituted the bulk of the country's system of higher education.

James's comments appeared anonymously in the editorial columns of the same issue, supporting in more moderate tones "G.S.H.'s" call for a reform of philosophy and pointedly excepting Harvard from the charge of "universal" academic stagnation. Inherently skeptical of exorbitant claims often made for natural science and its latest findings, James urged a balanced and careful examination of recent scientific developments in psychology. Nonetheless, he affirmed their importance, if only because they signified "a change in the method and *personnel* of philosophical study," and urged that the philosopher interested in the new movements gain a thorough training in physiology. "Young men who aspire to professorships and who will bear this in mind will, we are sure, before many years find a number of vacant places calling for their peculiar capacity."[5] James's faith in the future development of physiological psychology must have been a powerful encouragement to Hall to invest his time and effort in the new field. He obtained an instructorship in English at Harvard to pay his way and enrolled in the philosophy department as a candidate for the Ph.D. degree.[6]

4. GSH, "College Instruction in Philosophy," 1876, p. 180.
5. [William James], "The Teaching of Philosophy in Our Colleges," *Nation* 23 (Sept 1876): 178–79.
6. GSH to "Doctor," [late Sept 1876], Antiochiana, Olive Kettering Library, Antioch College, Yellow Springs; *Annual Report of the President of Harvard*

Hall was a relative stranger to the Cambridge intellectual world, and personal circumstances kept him from fully entering into it during the whole of his two-year residence there. Hall's duties in sophomore English proved time consuming and unpleasant and were made still more arduous by absences he was forced to take because of illness. Hall also endured a family tragedy. His younger brother, now married and the pastor of a church in Cambridgeport, became seriously ill soon after Hall arrived at Harvard and died that winter at the age of thirty-one. Hall's relationship with his younger brother had often been strained during the previous years. He remained closely enough attached to him, however, to board with the couple in Cambridgeport when he first came to Harvard and he must have felt deeply involved in his brother's illness and death.[7] After this tragic event, he moved to an inexpensive room in Somerville and only in December of his second year, took quarters close to the college where he could widen his acquaintance with the Cambridge men.[8] His grudging work in English meanwhile proved so unsatisfactory that his appointment was not renewed the second year. With the savings he had accumulated at Antioch, however, he was able to maintain his residence and finally concentrate all his efforts on his philosophical work.[9]

Hall took most of his work with William James in psychology. Besides the courses offered, he used James's room of experimental equipment and often went into Boston with him where he studied nervous physiology with Bowditch.[10] Sometime during his second year, James probably brought him into the philosophical club in Cambridge which had succeeded the earlier and more famous Metaphysical Club.[11] In the informal atmosphere of graduate study in

College, 1876–77 (Cambridge: Harvard College, 1878), pp. 7, 44–45 (hereafter cited as Ann. Rep. Pres. Harv.); Harvard Cat., 1876–77, p. 138.

7. LCP, p. 204; GSH to G. W. Hosmer, 1 Jan 1879, Hosmer Papers; GSH to A. B. Hall, 29 Mar 1875; GSH to his parents, 15 Apr 1876; C. W. Eliot to GSH, 12 Jan 1877; A. B. Hall to GSH, 30 Jan [1877], HP.

8. GSH to A. B. Hall, 9 Oct 1877; GSH to his parents, Christmas [1877], HP.

9. GSH to G. W. Hosmer, 1 Jan 1879, Hosmer Papers; GSH to A. B. Hall, 9 Oct 1877, HP; Harvard Cat., 1877–78, p. 166.

10. LCP, pp. 218–19; GSH to Gilman, 27 Jan 1877, GP.

11. GSH to A. B. Hall, 9 Oct 1877, HP; Perry, William James, 1: 712; Max H. Fisch, "Philosophical Clubs in Cambridge and Boston from Peirce's Metaphysical Club to Harris's Hegel Club," pp. 2–3, typescript, lent by the author.

those early days their formal work extended into conversation and visits to the James home. "I was immensely impressed and fascinated by his personality," Hall recalled, "and looked up to him, who was several years my senior, somewhat as I had done before to George Morris."[12] The philosophical friendship the two young bachelors formed was to be an important factor in Hall's development and in the future course of psychology in America. As was also the case in his friendship with Morris, Hall's emulation would eventually prove to cover a good deal of competitive hostility.

As the gifted son of an independent philosopher of comfortable means, James had matured under circumstances very different from those of Hall. Hall at twenty-six had had to defend himself against his father's reproofs for dancing on Sabbath eve by professing elevated moral principles, wheareas James at half the age had danced happily on a Sunday evening in Berlin under the approving eye of his father. When Hall was at Williams reading Emerson and arguing over Mark Hopkins's philosophy with a group determined to eschew profanity and heresy, James was breaking his philosophical teeth on conversation with Chauncy Wright and Charles Peirce and, occasionally over a bottle of whiskey, with Oliver Wendell Holmes, Jr. During their formative years, a monistic metaphysic seemed to Hall a seductive modern heresy against the dualism of his Congregationalist tradition; to James, raised on his father's Swedenborgian creationism, it seemed the traditional position of the religious mentality, which the critical and moral intelligence must somehow overcome. The gulf in culture and temperament that separated the Hall family of western Massachusetts from the James family of Cambridge had lent a very different quality to their experience and endowment.[13]

In their intellectual development, too, Hall and James shared basic interests overlaid with subtle, but important, differences.[14]

12. *LCP*, pp. 218–19.

13. Perry, *William James,* 1: 169–77, 202–9, 533–34, and particularly, 155–64, 181, 228–30, 507.

14. On James's thinking during these years, see, besides Perry, *William James,* 1, James's "Wundt's *Grundzuge der physiologischen Psychologie,*" *North American Review* 121 (July 1875): 195–201; "Remarks on Spencer's Definition of Mind As Correspondence," *JSP* 12 (Jan 1878): 1–18; "Are We Automata?" *Mind* 4 (1879): 1–22; "The Sentiment of Rationality," ibid., pp. 317–46.

Both were concerned with developing a philosophy that would respect the claims of naturalism as well as religion. Both were absorbed in the problem of knowledge Kant had bequeathed to nineteenth-century philosophy, the attempt to overcome the dualism of a phenomenal world known through man's conscious experience and a noumenal world beyond his knowledge. Having rejected Hegel's resolution of the Kantian dualism, Hall was all the more anxious to find another basis for establishing the reality and rationality of man's knowledge of the world. Both James and Hall had been drawn to the new empirical psychology as a promising attempt to throw light on epistemological issues by means of the prestigious techniques of natural science.

James was, however, already more learned in physiology and in British empiricism than Hall. Repelled alike by monistic philosophies and by large philosophical claims made in the name of science, James was thoroughly skeptical of Hegel, without having much knowledge of him, and had already outgrown an early enthusiasm for Spencer. In contrast, Hall's thinking was still rooted in the Hegelian idealism he was rejecting. His interest in natural science was by way of positivist philosophies, like Spencer's evolutionary cosmology, which aspired to large philosophical aims and a monistic, developmental framework. Whereas James worked out from his roots in British empiricism, it was through a critique of Hegel that Hall made his way to the new psychology.

The new, scientific psychology—or physiological psychology, as it was also called during its early decades—was formed during the last half of the nineteenth century from the convergence of concepts, problems, and methods of investigation in philosophical psychology, physiology, and evolutionary biology.[15] At the same time that philosophy came to deal increasingly with psychological problems through its focus on the problem of knowledge, the rapid development of physiology led to the study of the functioning of the nervous and muscular systems, the localization of functions in the brain, and the mechanisms of sense perception. The results of this work, like the insight furnished by evolutionary biology into the

15. On the origins of the new psychology and the work of its founders, see the Bibliographical Notes at the end of the volume.

place of the human animal in the biological world, led to the conviction that the mind could be studied in the same scientific manner as other physical and biological natural processes. Psychic processes were seen to exist in close dependence on the functioning of the nervous system, to be continuous with muscular processes, and to be approachable through experimental methods.

The paths along which the new discipline took shape were many and varied. Wilhelm Wundt, physiologist and philosopher, first brought them to a clear focus. He formulated the concept of a physiological or experimental psychology in the 1860s, outlined the subject in his pioneer text of 1873–74, and opened a psychological laboratory in the late 1870s.

The psychology of Wundt and his colleagues was a psychology of consciousness. Drawing on philosophical empiricism, they assumed the ultimate units of consciousness to be sensations and sought to analyze how these sensational elements entered into perception, association, and cognition. Their atomistic understanding of consciousness had been both fortified and extended by the new physiological understanding of nervous function. Physiology had isolated the sensory and motor nerves and pictured mental process as based fundamentally on a sensorimotor process: the nervous impulse traveled through the sensory nerve to the central nervous system, which then guided it into motor nerves and muscular reaction. The simplest unit of this process was the reflex action, the sensorimotor process unmediated by cortical processes or conscious reflection: more complex mental processes were often pictured as layered elaborations of the reflex model in the absence of any firm understanding of central nervous system function.

By utilizing this model, the new psychologists hoped to gain experimental knowledge of conscious processes. Wundt's classic reaction-time experiment recorded the time involved in a subject's reacting to a sensory cue. By complicating the experiment, Wundt attempted to isolate times for the intermediary processes occurring in the central nervous system as well, such as association and judgment. Wundt used the objective data of the times recorded, and the introspective accounts of his subjects about their perceptions and feelings during the experiments, to analyze the nature of association, attention, imagery, and the like.

One major line of interest among the new psychologists was the controversy inherited from Kant over whether the forms of thought, particularly the notion of space, were native to the mind or generated in experience. Geneticists had offered especially striking theories which, though they did not vanquish the nativists, pushed back the native component of spatial perception much further than philosophers had hitherto thought possible. In discussing the question of origins, Wundt and his colleagues also occasionally resorted to evolutionary biology, taking the discussion from the level of the individual mind to that of the development of psychomotor function in the species. These Kantian and biological concerns were directed, however, to the empirical analysis of consciousness as the chief task of the new psychology.

Hall entered into his work at Harvard with immense enthusiasm as he began to see that psychology might accomplish what Hegel had tried but failed to achieve.[16] His first exposition of his psychological views was in a critique of Hegel which he published in Harris's *Journal of Speculative Philosophy*. Hall found Hegel unable to meet the chief demand of contemporary psychology and philosophy: the transition "from the subjective-intensive to the objective-extensive . . . the central question of all recent psychology." He failed to extricate philosophy from the "see-saw of reality and ideality . . . in which the theory of knowledge has entombed her, remote from the common life of men and dead to the issues and impulses of science." He failed to face adequately the questions which psychology was now trying to answer: "Are mind and matter mutually exclusive or contradictory? Must the world be all one or all the other, or is there much that is common to, yet more than, both, as yet known?" Hegel's means of overcoming the dualism of mind and matter seemed far less satisfactory to Hall than those promised by the new psychology.[17]

Hall criticized on several counts Hegel's fundamental proposition that pure thought was the logical "prius" of existence. Space, Hall argued, fit Hegel's logical requirements for the necessary ground

    16. GSH to A. B. Hall, 9 Oct 1877; GSH to his parents, Christmas [1877], HP.
    17. GSH, "Notes on Hegel," 1878, pp. 95, 101.

and condition of existence far better than did pure thought. "Everything that is real and necessary must submit to the categories of space." Nor was pure thought "the simplest psychic process." Even in its most elementary form, thought was never "pure," never void of experience, and hence never "divorced from extension." Drawing largely on Trendelenburg's logical critique of Hegel, Hall went on to argue that the dialectic process was in no real sense genetic. Following Trendelenburg, he urged that motion itself, as an empirical principle, be considered "the 'prius' and the medium of all experience" and "the only aspect common to both thought and matter."[18]

Hall believed that psychology was now framing the problem of the relation of knowledge to the external world in such a way as to confirm Trendelenburg's theory. The new studies in physiological psychology suggested that each psychic movement or change "has at some point of the nervous system, as a counterpart or background, some demonstrable form of molecular or electrical change." Recent studies in psychology also suggested that the perception of motion was itself the simplest and most immediate sensation, out of which "all the higher faculties of the soul are developed." If psychology is correct, "a primitive immediacy, or absolute identity of subject and object at some point back of all of individual experience, perhaps, is thus postulated."[19] Hall was clearly taking the new psychology beyond its empirical base to solve his epistemological dilemma. He extended the physiological psychologists' genetic analysis of consciousness backward to the speculative beginnings of psychic life, less in the style of Wundt than of Spencer, who spoke of sense experience evolving from "a single primordial element of consciousness" and assumed a simple correspondence between the elementary units of consciousness and the elementary physical units at their base.[20]

Although Hall realized that "the facts upon which these inferences rest are, it need hardly be said, far too few to warrant any

18. Ibid., pp. 93–100.
19. Ibid., pp. 100–101.
20. Herbert Spencer, *Principles of Psychology* (London: Williams and Norgate, 1870–72), vol. 1, pars. 60–63, 129–31; Hugh Elliot, *Herbert Spencer* (New York: Henry Holt, 1917), pp. 233–90.

positive conclusion of this sort,"[21] he soon drew very positive conclusions. He undertook a study of the muscular perception of space as his doctoral dissertation and expected soon to make his "name and fame in philosophy."[22]

In his thesis, Hall suggested that the key to the relation between mind and matter lay in the muscular sense.[23] The muscular sense was composed of two different sources of sensation: sensations of motion transmitted to consciousness from terminal nervous organs in the muscles, and "feelings of innervation," sensations of force arising from the outflow of nervous energy from the central nervous system into the motor nerves. In both aspects of the muscular sense, Hall argued, the forms of external excitation and of subjective sensation were identical: the muscle moved, the nerve cells and fibers underwent mechanical changes or movements, and the consciousness registered motion. More important, this most elementary and immediate kind of sensation was inherently spatial. Hall postulated

a nativism which grants not only that there is nothing spatial in the intellect which was not first in sensation, but also that sensations may themselves be indefinitely compounded of psychic minima, each, however, having the spatial quale.

21. GSH, "Notes on Hegel," 1878, p. 100.
22. GSH to his parents, Christmas [1877], HP. His thesis was "The Perception of Space," Harvard University Archives, published as "The Muscular Perception of Space," 1878, pp. 433–50. Although Hall tried to duplicate in Bowditch's laboratory some of the physiological findings on which he based his theory, the thesis was a theoretical rather than an experimental study. Hall noted that he intended to submit five additional sections: "A discussion of local signs; Touch superceding muscular sense as sight does touch; Confirmatory, original observations on Laura Bridgman; Light and the Berkeleian theory; Metaphysical—Kant and Hegel." A copy of his published "Notes on Hegel" was eventually appended to the thesis and the list of proposed additions crossed out. The thesis was signed by Professors Bowen, James, and Hedge; Professor Bowditch may not have signed it because of his position in the Medical School, rather than in the philosophical department of the college.
23. Recent studies by Sigmund Exner and Karl von Vierordt had suggested to Hall that "motion is not a perception but an immediate sensation not implying any inferential knowledge whatever of time and space" and that the muscular sense, as the fundamental organ of motion, was "the most immediate of all the senses." GSH, "Notes on Hegel," 1878, pp. 99–100; "Muscular Perception," 1878, pp. 442–43. On the experiments of Exner and Vierordt, see William James, *Psychology*, 2: 171–76, and "The Spatial Quale," *JSP* 13 (Jan 1879): 73–75.

The muscular perception of space could form the link between the subjective world of thought and the objective world of extended matter.[24]

Hall used current biological speculation about the origin of psychic life in contractile tissue to further buttress his argument. Only gradually, as organic life evolved, did psychic processes retire from muscle to nerve fibers, cells, and more specialized organs. In the progression of organic life, as in the life of the individual, the most elementary muscular perceptions of space directly registered spatial movement.[25]

In stressing the role of muscular sensations in space perception and the construction of spatial perceptions from more elementary sensational units, Hall's theory cleverly brought into a nativist theory of space perception some of the positions characteristic of the geneticists.[26] Hall concluded that Trendelenburg's theory was largely demonstrated: "Movement explains all things." He announced triumphantly:

24. GSH, "Muscular Perception," 1878, pp. 433–47. According to John Bascom, *An Historical Interpretation of Philosophy* (New York: G. P. Putnam's Sons, 1893), pp. 318–19, Mark Hopkins "did not accept the doctrine of a direct knowledge of the external world in perception, but thought that we gain, in one act, a recognition of two opposing forces, mental and physical, in connection with muscular activity—an inroad of force from without, and our resistance to it." Hopkins "thus accepted a direct knowledge of force as force. . . . The mind already drops, in muscular experience, plumb to the bottom of things." Unfortunately, it is not clear that Hopkins taught this doctrine at Williams while Hall was there. Hall himself makes no mention of it, which may indicate that he did not know it, or that he had forgotten it, the idea perhaps making an unconscious impression on him.

25. GSH, "Muscular Perception," 1878, pp. 447–48. Hall followed Spencer, *Psychology*, 1: 427, in this analysis.

26. Cf. Theodule Ribot, *German Psychology of Today* (New York: Charles Scribner's Sons, 1886), pp. 68–133, and Edwin G. Boring, *Sensation and Perception in the History of Experimental Psychology* (New York: Appleton-Century-Crofts, 1942), pp. 28–34, 233–38. At a meeting of the Cambridge philosophical club on 6 April 1878, Hall read a paper which evidently stressed the genetic aspect of his theory. According to Cabot, "Mr. H[all] read a short paper on Space, endeavouring to bridge the chasm between the intensive quality of the feeling, & extensive quantity of Space, by dint of repetition,—many visual impressions coinciding together, & perhaps also coinciding with other sensible impressions, giving the notion of Extension,—& an aggregation of atoms & their developed forces on the other hand somehow potentiating themselves into feelings." Fisch, "Philosophical Clubs," pp. 1–3.

If subject is not one with object at some point in primordial space-perception it must remain eternally divorced from it in all the derived unities of external perception or reason. . . . Psychology is no longer content to hold belief in an external world as a mere act of faith or opinion. She postulates an ultimate Monism, and hopes one day to prove a rightful title to the bold nomenclature of the Identity-philosophy.[27]

Hall still considered Hegel's large philosophical goals "the legitimate aspiration of the philosophical sentiment."[28]

The same philosophical assumptions governed another psychological study Hall undertook at Harvard. He formulated a mechanical theory of color vision and performed several simple experiments in Bowditch's laboratory to test it, with inconclusive results. "The great interest which the physiologist feels in these investigations," Hall said, is due to their bearing on the great question whether there is an identity between the objective stimulus and the sensation registered in the sense receptor.[29]

Hall found in psychology an assurance of wholeness between the inner and outer world and between the fragments of his divided nature. The very newness of psychology, the limitless vistas it opened of progress through scientific methods, appealed to Hall's romantic commitment to creative intellectual work and self-development. The "assurance of Hegel that the problem of things is essentially solved," like the "confessed nescience of Spencer or the new Kantean school" now seemed to Hall "as fatal as a finality." Psychology was for one who preferred "the pursuit to the possession of

27. GSH, "Muscular Perception," 1878, pp. 446–50.
28. GSH, "Notes on Hegel," 1878, p. 103. Hall wrote Harris, 29 Apr 1878, Harris Papers, that his thesis was written from the standpoint of "essentially *Herbart,* Schleiermacher, and Ueberweg." Like Herbart, Hall grounded his empirical psychology in metaphysics. Hall considered himself part of "the growing school of Ideal-realism," a neo-Kantian attempt to identify the forms of thought native to the mind with external realities. The school was associated with the names of Friedrich Schleiermacher, Hermann Ulrici, and Friedrich Ueberweg, whose historical text was one of the principal sources of Hall's philosophical education. See Ueberweg, *History of Philosophy, From Thales to the Present Time,* trans. G. S. Morris (New York: Charles Scribner's Sons, 1872–74), 2: 136, 165, 170, 224, 244–52, 299–304.
29. Hall suggested that the cones were really a series of discs, progressively varying in diameter, which vibrated sympathetically to light waves of a particular frequency. GSH, "Color Perception," 1878, pp. 402–13.

truth" and hence satisfied his intellectual ambitions without suc-
cumbing to the hubris of omniscience.[30]

Hall's philosophical use of the new psychology offers an interesting insight on how the subject won its way into and emerged from
philosophy. For Hall, as well as for the discipline at large, it proved
to be a way station toward a more rigorously scientific outlook. From
its very beginnings in philosophical speculation, however, Hall's
psychology bore marks characteristic of his own later work and of
the functional direction of American psychology in general.

Hall's theory of perception was nativistic, yet argued in the
genetic style, and ultimately, his psychology would be the same.
Like his mentor William James, and like American faculty psychology and popular phrenology before him, Hall would conceive
of the individual mind as carrying within itself the pattern of its
experience. Unlike James, however, his approach was genetic
throughout. He still agreed with Hegel "that we may be said to
know a thing, even the mind itself, most truly when our thought has
followed all its changes in time, or has traced all its processes
above."[31] Though Hall dealt mostly with the origins of complex
perceptions from their sensational elements, a process which occupied a very brief span of time, and only occasionally with the origins
of consciousness in the evolution of animal life, his approach in
both cases was relentlessly genetic. When approached from the side
of Hegel and Spencer, the Wundtian analysis of consciousness could
reinforce the developmental point of view.

But the most important and pervasive characteristic of Hall's
psychology was his emphasis on movement and activity. His nativism and geneticism were parts of a larger tendency to view the mind
as an active agent, changing and developing through time, and to
view psychology as the study not of consciousness but of psychomotor process. Partly, of course, his motor emphasis supported
Trendelenburg, but one can hear a number of deeper echos in Hall's
theory.

Hall already pictured the mind as an energy system in which
there was a "constant influx of nervous energy into the muscles,"

30. GSH, "Notes on Hegel," 1878, pp. 101–3.
31. GSH, "Notes on Hegel," 1878, p. 100.

which responded to "every variation of sensation." Hall's authority
for this was Alexander Bain, who made the first modern attempt
to formulate a motor psychology. Bain's views had an important
influence on the British and American psychology which followed,
including that of William James. Hall also explicitly accepted Bain's
consequent belief that the whole body, not merely the brain, was
the organ of mind.[32]

The functional and evolutionary direction of British physiology
reinforced this tendency in Hall's thinking. Following John Hughlings Jackson, Hall already thought of sensorimotor processes,
rather than sensations, as the fundamental units of mind.[33] A few
months later, he remarked almost offhandedly, that

attention, to the physiologist, is essentially the expression of an instinct.
The mind pushes on from one impression to another by a native spontaneous
impulse of growth and development. . . . the direction and movement of
attention is like the successive waking of the different elements of psychical
life.[34]

This view of attention suggests an already deep-rooted tendency to
assimilate physiological concepts to the dynamic and developmental
terms he had learned in romantic literature and Hegelian philosophy. The physiologist in question was very likely Henry Maudsley, who traced both voluntary and involuntary attention back to "an
interest in the subject, arising either from ancestral affinities in the
individual's nature, or from affinities developed in it in consequence
of education," the former carrying the greatest weight in Maudsley's
mind.[35]

32. See Alexander Bain, *The Senses and the Intellect* (London: John W.
Parker, 1855), particularly, vol. 1, pp. 2, 60–62, 189, 324–29; Ribot, *English
Psychology,* pp. 196–97, 218; Richard Müller-Freienfels, *The Evolution of Mod-
ern Psychology* (New Haven: Yale University Press, 1935), p. 229.

33. Hall cited John Hughlings-Jackson, *Clinical and Physiological Researches
in the Nervous System,* 1877.

34. GSH, *Aspects,* p. 272.

35. *The Physiology of Mind* (New York: D. Appleton, 1878), pp. 316–23.
After discussing the influence of education, Maudsley went on, "Behind the
effects of education, however, are those inherited dispositions which have so much
weight in determining the character or temperament of the individual; what his
forefathers have felt, thought and done, though he has never known them,
assuredly has some influence upon what he will be inclined to feel, think and
do; he has inherited nervous substrata in his convolutions which are ready to

William James, too, had been influenced by this dynamic character of British psychology and physiology, and he surely pointed
out its importance to Hall. James was himself beginning to look at
mind in the light of Darwin's theory of adaptation, to view it as a
functional organ active in the adjustment between organism and
environment. It was undoubtedly James who drew Hall's attention
to Peirce's first exposition of pragmatism in 1878.[36] Without
referring to the source of his ideas, Hall quoted Peirce in support
of the importance of "the active part of our nature" in psychic
life.

All possible *truth* is practical. To ask whether our conception of chair or
table corresponds to the real chair or table apart from the uses to which
they may be put, is as utterly meaningless and vain as to inquire whether a
musical tone is red or yellow. No other conceivable relation than this between ideas and things can exist. The *unknowable is what I cannot react
upon.* The active part of our nature is not only an essential part of cognition
itself, but it always has a voice in determining what shall be believed and
what rejected.[37]

Hall maintained for the rest of his life the functional and pragmatic approach he had learned from the Cambridge environment.

Even before this influence, the first terms in which Hall heard
psychology discussed, those of faculty psychology and perhaps of
popular phrenology, presented the mind as an active agent vis-à-vis
its environment.[38] Moreover, the mixture of commonsense philosophy and Calvinist striving urged on him by his teachers at Williams
had made free will and moral choice seem the central elements of

---

take on, at the appropriate stages of his experience in life, the same kind of
function which they displayed in his forefathers."

36. Charles Peirce, "How to Make Our Ideas Clear," *Popular Science Monthly*
12 (Jan 1878): 286–302.

37. GSH, "Muscular Perception," 1878, p. 446. To support this position,
Hall also referred to Helmholtz's *Optik,* a source of Peirce's pragmatism as well.
Max H. Fisch, "A Chronicle of Pragmatism, 1865–1879," *The Monist* 48 (July
1964): 452, 464.

38. David Bakan, "The Influence of Phrenology on American Psychology,"
JHBS 2 (July 1966): 200–20, has suggested that phrenology, often combined
with faculty psychology, significantly influenced American psychologists toward a
functional approach, though they generally repressed the source of this influence.
On phrenology in America, see John D. Davies, *Phrenology, Fad and Science*
(New Haven: Yale University Press, 1955).

mind.[39] No one raised on this view could approach the new psychology without searching in it for analogs of the active, willing, choosing function of mind. Because Wundt's hypothesis of a feeling of innervation explained feelings of force or effort, the central quality of the will, "the origin of which empiricism could never otherwise explain," Hall regarded it as "epoch-making." He considered the hypothesis "an ulterior explanation of most, if not all, of the facts of physiological psychology."[40]

Not only the spirit of the active moral will but also the spirit of the American desire to be "up and doing" pervaded Hall's critique of Hegelian idealism and his motor-oriented psychology. Hall's interest in active, motor processes reflected the wide admiration of constructive activity and distrust of inward-turning contemplation. He observed that in the environment in which he had been educated, "self-knowledge was highly spoken of; but there was a prejudice against every sort of self-study or introspection as unpractical and paralyzing, save in a purely religious or ethical sense."[41] Though he recognized that this attitude was "simply superstitious," he never admitted that much of his own psychological insight came from introspection, and he was always happy to note when his psychology dealt with objective activities and behavior.[42] From the beginning, therefore, Hall's psychology was functional, developmental, dynamic, and vaguely behavioristic, and after an interlude of vain searching in physiological psychology for an adequate framework for these attitudes, they would reemerge, more powerful than ever, in his mature biological psychology.

Though Hall had drawn heavily on James's functional and empirical approach, his stance was rather different from his teacher's. James was not attracted to developmental analysis and he strongly

39. The whole senior philosophy course, Hall remembered, built up to a discussion of moral choice, which coincided in time with the Spring revival. *LCP,* p. 169.

40. GSH, "Muscular Perception," 1878, pp. 435, 440. For a critical examination of the concept of innervation feelings, see William James, *The Principles of Psychology* (New York: Henry Holt, 1890), 2: 492–518.

41. GSH, *Aspects,* p. 297.

42. The closest Hall came to such an admission was his confession in *LCP,* p. 445, that he had finally realized that no amount of training could supply the subtle introspective insight which the true psychologist possessed.

opposed the atomistic sensationalism Hall and Spencer shared. While Hall could feel secure only in a monistic universe, in which thought was identical with its material base, James tried to extricate the mind from any monistic principle which would rob it of its freedom and effectiveness in the world. One of the principal positions against which James was developing his pluralistic view was the evolutionary monism of the mind-matter school, to which he assigned "Clifford and Taine, Spencer, Fechner, Zöllner, G. S. Hall, and more besides."[43]

Hall's early work at Harvard revealed something of the quality of his imagination. Anxious to reach synthetic conclusions, he grasped quickly at the implications of a wide variety of ideas and drew them together into large patterns which laid bare some of the hidden and partial assumptions of his age. As imaginative and well-informed speculative exercises, his studies received some attention when they appeared. His thesis on the muscular perception of space was published in the fall of 1878 by *Mind,* the leading English journal of philosophy and psychology. His theory of color vision was published by the American Academy of Arts and Sciences and was discussed in *Mind* by an English Spencerian, Grant Allen, as an "ingenious . . . though somewhat speculative" effort.[44] In the Cambridge circle, Hall was known as something of a "queer genius."[45] He was still unaware of the enormous complexity of natural phenomena and drew conclusions from his data far larger than they warranted.[46] From careful and critical beginnings he was soon carried away by the implications of his theories to enthusiasm and certainty.

Despite Hall's intellectual rashness, however, his two years at Harvard changed him from a philosophical amateur to a serious

43. William James, "The Sentiment of Rationality," p. 336. See Philip P. Wiener, *Evolution and the Founders of Pragmatism* (Cambridge: Harvard University Press, 1949), pp. 101–5.
44. Grant Allen, "Mr. G. S. Hall on the Perception of Colour," *Mind* 4 (Apr 1879): 267–68.
45. James J. Putnam to Frances Morse [29 Oct 1879], Putnam Papers, Countway Library of Medicine, Boston.
46. Due to the paucity of evidence on the subject, for example, William James left it an "open question" whether feelings of muscular contraction and innervation involve a cognition of motion and hence space. He made no reference to Hall's study or conclusions. "The Spatial Quale," pp. 64–87.

scholar. His grasp of philosophy and science were by no means complete, but he had acquired the tools with which he could fruitfully continue his studies. Hall showed his new competence most clearly in a study he carried out in Cambridge during the summer of 1878. Using the new techniques of psychology, Hall examined Laura Bridgeman, an educated blind, deaf, and mute woman living at the Perkins Institute for the Blind in South Boston who held somewhat the same interest for her generation as Helen Keller did for a later one. Cut off from almost all sensation except touch since the age of two, she provided a test case for some of the early theories of the new psychology on sensation, perception, and their role in higher mental processes. Hall's careful study showed a wide knowledge of the new psychology and an ability to reason closely from empirical data to circumscribed conclusions as well as to speculate more broadly.[47]

Hall gave further evidence of his new competence and confidence in an uncompromising attack on "Philosophy in the United States," published in January 1879 in *Mind,* shortly after he left Cambridge. Hall described philosophical instruction at the large majority of the three hundred non-Catholic colleges in the United States as "rudimentary and medieval," a prey to "insidious orthodoxies," and conducted by unschooled "professorlings of philosophy." Though Hall twice repeated that conditions improved as one moved from west to east and from the smaller to the larger colleges, he concluded that "there are less than half a dozen colleges or universities in the United States where metaphysical thought is entirely freed from reference to theological formulae." Hall described in detail only the philosophical work at Harvard and devoted more space to Charles Peirce than to any other philosopher in the country. Hall called Peirce's recent articles on the logic of science "one of the most important of American contributions to philosophy."

Hall's treatment of the more popular schools of philosophy

47. "Laura Bridgman," 1879, pp. 149–72, reprinted, 1881, in *Aspects,* pp. 237–76. From his many findings, Hall concluded, for example, that Miss Bridgman had "sub-consciously" retained the knowledge of space and form learned in her first two years; that the muscular sense and sense of touch were capable of remarkable versatility in performing the functions of her other damaged senses; and that her facial expressions largely supported a hereditary theory of their origin.

showed his disillusion with the shallowness of his previous work. Discussing the St. Louis Hegelians, he characterized their philosophy as "beats and clicks of the triadic engine." The group of Comtists in New York who had first excited his interest in evolution were now labeled a "rather insignificant coterie" and noted only for "incoherency and assumption." Hall admitted that "very often the adoption of the formulae of the development-theory is so premature as seriously to interfere with the patient mastery of scientific details."

Although Hall's account of American philosophy was somewhat capricious—he singled out Mark Hopkins and Laurens P. Hickok for complimentary mention, for example, but did not even note the existence of James McCosh at Princeton—his comments were substantially just and perspicacious. The article was reprinted in America and has since become the standard contemporary source for the state of American philosophy during the third quarter of the nineteenth century.[48]

In June 1878, after passing an oral examination from Professors James, Bowditch, Everett, Hedge, and Palmer, Hall was awarded a doctorate of philosophy in the subject of "Psychology," the first doctorate awarded by Harvard's philosophy department and the first in the field of psychology to be given in this country.[49]

The rudimentary state of graduate education in America gave Hall little choice of position in 1878, despite his advanced degree. James preempted physiological psychology at Harvard. The Johns Hopkins University, to which Hall had already vainly applied, was interested in the new field, but James himself was then negotiating with President Gilman about the possibility of an appointment.[50] Though Hall still had connections in some of the western colleges, he confessed, "That [fate] will not send me west again is the only thing I really pray for."[51] Hall had hoped for years to return to Germany, and his friends in Cambridge urged him to go

48. See Herbert W. Schneider, *A History of American Philosophy* (New York: Columbia University Press, 1946), pp. 442, 455, 464.

49. *LCP*, p. 219; *Harvard Cat., 1878–79,* p. 179; Robert S. Harper, "Tables of American Doctorates in Psychology," *AJP* 62 (Oct 1949): 579–87.

50. Jackson I. Cope, "William James's Correspondence with Daniel Coit Gilman, 1877–1881," *Journal of the History of Ideas* 12 (Oct 1951): 617–20.

51. GSH to C. E. Norton, 3 Feb 1879, NP.

there for further training, for scientific psychology was flourishing in the German universities as nowhere else in the world. Although savings and an unexpected gift made the trip financially feasible, in June Hall was still trying to decide what to do. He may have hoped that James would accept an appointment at Hopkins in time to allow him to take his place at Harvard. No position appearing, however, Hall sailed late in the summer for a second pilgrimage to the German universities.[52]

52. GSH to A. B. Hall, 9 Oct 1877; GSH to his parents, Christmas [1877]; [June 1878], HP. The gift was from his former employer, Jesse Seligman.

6

GERMANY AGAIN AND NATURAL SCIENCE

The methods of physical science that had offered Hall the key to philosophy were being pursued in the German universities more widely and expertly than anywhere else in the world when Hall arrived there in 1878. With the aim of perfecting his mastery of physiology and its applications to psychology, he planned to study at Berlin, where Hermann von Helmholtz was lecturing and where Emil du Bois-Reymond directed a new physiological institute, and at Leipzig, where he would find the country's most eminent physiologist, Carl Ludwig, and where Wilhelm Wundt, pioneer of the new psychology, had opened his experimental laboratory.

Hall's interest in motor processes led him first to Berlin, the scene of his earlier German enlightenment, and to du Bois-Reymond's laboratory, where the physiology of the muscular system was under study. Hall worked chiefly with du Bois-Reymond's assistant, Hugo Kronecker, a bachelor not much older than himself, who lived near him and was socially as well as intellectually congenial. To Kronecker, Hall wrote James, "I have stood in much the same terms of intimacy and recipiency as last year to you, and to [him] I am likely to own a scarcely smaller debt of gratitude."[1] Kronecker and Hall embarked together on an experiment measuring muscle reaction to succeeding electrical stimuli to the spinal cord,[2] a project Hall called

1. GSH to Wm. James, [Dec 1878], JP.
2. GSH and Hugo Kronecker, "Die willkürliche Muskelaction," 1879, pp. 11–47.

"my central enthusiasm." From Kronecker, Hall "almost heard" that "the whole philosophy of life" could be written in the different forms of muscle curves. Hall's experiments with electricity soon led him to study physics and mathematics, and he began attending lectures in mathematics and mathematical electricity. "Just this independent look at nature," Hall wrote, "has opened new impulses and enthusiasm for me such as nothing else has."[3]

Hall was drawn further into physical science by his admiration for Helmholtz. Hall first approached Helmholtz in order to discuss constructing an experiment to test the theory of color perception he had formed in Cambridge, a theory at variance with Helmholtz's own. Although the great man was able to spend very little time with him and the experiment never materialized,[4] Hall found himself "amazingly lifted and impelled" by Helmholtz.[5] He began to attend his lectures in theoretical physics, at which Helmholtz's keen mind and masterful synthetic abilities conveyed to him the excitement of the rapid progress then being made in physics and physiology. To Hall, all of Helmholtz's thoughts seemed to bring "something newly created into the world." Helmholtz insisted, Hall wrote Professor Norton,

that the greatest and most important advancement of modern science during the last quarter of a century is the analysis of vision-hearing-touch etc. into their ultimate elements by physicophysiological methods. . . . This of course pleases me who am working in that line, and have long ago given up metaphysics in order to study psychology as a *natural science*.[6]

Helmholtz's attempt to subject the processes of life to physical and chemical explanation had captured Hall's imagination.

Carrying his enthusiasm still further, Hall came increasingly to feel that all the branches of philosophy

rest upon psychology, and that psychology is essentially a branch of physiology. The latter is by general consent and practice here already far too wide

3. GSH to Wm. James [Dec 1878], JP; GSH to Henry P. Bowditch, 23 Dec [1878], Bowditch Papers, Harvard University Medical School Archives, Boston; GSH to Wm. James, 15 Feb [1880], in Perry, *William James,* 2:21.

4. *LCP,* p. 208; GSH to Bowditch, 23 Dec [1878], Bowditch Papers; Helmholtz to GSH, 7 Nov 1879, GSH Memorial Volume, CUP.

5. GSH to Wm. James, 26 Oct [1879], in Perry, *William James,* 2:17.

6. 3 Feb 1879, NP.

a branch for a single specialist to profess. So it seems to me that the philosopher must take the brain nerves and muscles as his peculiar province and adopt without reserve the scientific method.[7]

As "a branch of physiology," psychology could be brought into what Hall thought of as the impending physical-chemical explanation of the natural world.[8]

Another scientific aspect of psychology that Hall had not previously been able to study was now open to him in Berlin: psychopathology. At Harvard, Hall had probably become aware of James's interest in the field and the commonplace attitude of the period that abnormal and pathological conditions were "nature's experiments," which could teach a great deal about normal conditions.[9] When he tested Laura Bridgman at the Perkins Institute for the Blind the summer he left for Germany, he became interested in the school for defective children and the insane asylum nearby.[10] In Germany, where psychiatry included both neurology and clinical psychiatry, Hall had a double incentive to take up the field. The somatic bias of European psychiatry supported the physicalistic views Hall was adopting.[11] He was impressed by the thoroughness and value of the postmortem anatomical examinations at the Clinic for Mental and Nervous Diseases at the Charité in Berlin, and he struck up an acquaintance with Paul Flechsig, a neuropathologist and his next-door neighbor, who was preparing to take up his duties as professor of psychiatry at Leipzig.[12]

Hall was even more impressed, however, by his first clinical contact with mental illness. He began to attend the psychiatric clinic

7. GSH to Norton, 8 June 1879, NP.
8. Hall also heard lectures on the senses by Hermann Munk, an experimentalist in brain localization, and reported being "much impressed" with him. GSH to Wm. James, [Dec 1878], JP; GSH to Bowditch, 23 Dec [1878], Bowditch Papers. He also heard Friedrich Harms in psychology. Ibid. In addition, Hall at least began the year visiting the lectures of Eduard Zeller in philosophy, Adolf Lasson in logic, and Karl Reichert in anatomy. GSH to Norton, 28 Oct [1878], NP. He may also have heard something of Otto Pfleiderer in psychology or religion and Moritz Lazarus in comparative religion. GSH, *Founders of Modern Psychology*, 1912, pp. vi–vii.
9. Perry, *William James*, 2:5.
10. GSH to his parents, [June 1878], HP.
11. Erwin H. Ackerknecht, *A Short History of Psychiatry* (New York: Hafner, 1959), pp. 65–70.
12. GSH to Norton, 3 Feb 1879, NP.

of Dr. Karl Westphal, professor of psychiatry at the university and medical director of the Charité Clinic. Finding Westphal "extremely accessible," Hall spent a good deal of time with him visiting wards and discussing psychopathology. Hall reported that Westphal saw human nature

only through his psychiatric "specialis." Every trait and habit, that is at all pronounced as individual is a "beautiful and classic case" of something which may lead a man or woman to the mad-house.[13]

Hall himself began to find the classifications "so close that one comes to see mild traits of insanity in all one's friends."[14] Later in the year, when he traveled through Italy and Austria, he made a point of inspecting psychiatric facilities.[15] His subjective and scientific interest in mental illness, supported by his clinical experience in Europe, would later develop into one of the principal bases of his psychology.

When Hall moved on to Leipzig in the fall of 1879, the stimulating vistas of physical science continued to influence his work. He heard lectures on the kinetic theory of gases and reported that the chemical theories of Julius Mayer and Jacobus Van't Hoff, with their promise of bridging chemistry and physics on mechanical principles, "fascinate me."[16]

Hall attended the lectures of his former neighbor Flechsig on the microscopic anatomy of the brain and did "a bit of microscope work on nervous centres."[17] His principle work, however, was in physiology. He heard the lectures of Carl Ludwig and his asisstant, Johannes von Kries, and worked daily in Ludwig's laboratory.[18] With von Kries he experimented on reaction times when the place

13. GSH to Wm. James [Dec 1878], JP. On Westphal, see Gregory Zilboorg, *A History of Medical Psychology* (New York: W. W. Norton, 1941), p. 445.

14. GSH to Norton, 3 Feb 1879, NP.

15. Hall stopped in Vienna to hear several lectures of the psychiatrist Theodore Meynert, and to tour his hospital; Hall thought Meynert less advanced than his Berlin teacher, Westphal. In Italy, Hall was shocked at the terrible conditions in the asylums and the general backwardness of the Italians "in all psychophysiological matters." GSH to Wm. James, 31 Mar 1879, JP.

16. GSH to Wm. James, 15 Feb [1880], JP.

17. GSH to Wm. James, 26 Oct [1879], in Perry, *William James,* 2:17.

18. *LCP,* pp. 205–6; GSH to Wm. James, 26 Oct [1879]; 27 Dec [1879], in Perry, *William James,* 2:17, 19.

of the stimulus varied; their results threw into doubt previous experiments on the speed of the neural impulse in humans.[19] After
this study Hall worked alone under Ludwig himself on reflex action.
Hall hoped to disprove several points of Wundt's speculative theory of nervous innervation in reflex action, but though he learned
a great deal in the process, the work did not produce any positive
results.[20]

Believing that he needed more basic training in physiology
than in psychology, Hall spent a great deal more time in Ludwig's
laboratory than he did in the new laboratory of the pioneer of experimental psychology, Wilhelm Wundt. The first American to
join Wundt's laboratory, Hall carried on some work there but
never completed a publishable study. He heard Wundt's lectures
on psychology and also joined his seminar, which was entirely
devoted to the review of literature in psychology and physiology.[21]

The greater Hall's contact with Wundt's ideas during his study
in Berlin and Leipzig, however, the greater was his disillusion.
Echoing the criticism of the younger physiologists, Hall wrote
James that

Wundt is more and more exasperating. He seems to me a grand importer
of English ideas . . . and an exporter of the generalized commonplaces of
German physiology . . . inexact . . . and as a man who has done more
speculation and less valuable observing than any man I know who has had
his career. His experiments, which I attend I think utterly unreliable and
defective in method.[22]

Hall's judgment of Wundt was based partly on his growing competence as a laboratory scientist. The habit of work he had estab-

19. GSH and J. von Kries, "Ueber die Abhängigkeit der Reactionszeiten vom
Ort des Reizes," 1879, pp. 1–10. Cf. James, *Psychology*, 1:96.
20. Wilson, *GSH*, p. 47; GSH, *Founders*, p. 324.
21. *LCP*, pp. 206–7. At Leipzig, Hall claimed to have heard the introductory
courses of Hermann Kolbe in chemistry, Wilhelm His in anatomy, and Rudolf
Leuckart in zoology; to have taken a philosophy course from Max Heinze; and to
have occasionally heard the aging Herbartian pedagog and philosopher, Ludwig
Strumpell. He may also have heard something of Franz Delitzsch in biblical psychology and Moritz Drobisch in philosophy. *LCP*, p. 207; GSH, *Founders*, pp.
vi–vii.
22. GSH to Wm. James, [Dec 1878]; 15 Feb [1880], JP.

lished earlier stood him in good stead as he spent many hours a day in the laboratory, in addition to reading widely in the field.[23] Wundt himself commended Hall for a "rare knowledge of modern German scientific works" and for his "solid, independent judgment." Wundt described his work in the laboratory as being carried on "with great zeal and success." Ludwig too praised Hall for "the *Geist*" with which the experiments in his laboratory had been executed, and added that he had personally noted "the care and conscientiousness with which Dr. Hall works."[24]

Hall's newly critical attitude toward Wundt also reflected the turn he had taken toward physical science. Wundt's tendency to stray from an entirely genetic and mechanical theory of the will, as well as the speculative nature of some of his concepts, made his ideas appear to Hall a "trifle dreamy."[25] Hall planned to clarify his position in articles on Wundt and Helmholtz; and when James wrote him that he had contracted with Holt publishers to write a textbook of psychology, Hall replied that he too would write a text embodying his new psychological views.[26]

Since coming to Germany, Hall had written James repeatedly of his "gratitude" and "recipiency" toward him. The text he was writing, Hall assured James, would give him "a modest place— and not altogether unjustly—as your disciple and at best amplifier."[27] When, during the winter of Hall's second year in Germany, James wrote him that he hoped to come abroad the following summer and to talk with Hall there, Hall made haste to explain that James would find him *"aufgegangen* in empiricism." Listing the hours he spent in the laboratory and his new interest in physics, mathematics, and chemistry, Hall warned James of his new *"richtung."*[28] But Hall's fear of expressing disagreement with his former teacher was exaggerated. However much or little opposition he conveyed to James, their meeting was amiable and fruitful. They

23. Ibid., 15 Feb [1880].
24. Wilhelm Wundt and Carl Ludwig, letters of reference for GSH, n.d., copies, GP.
25. GSH to Wm. James, [Dec 1878], JP.
26. GSH to Wm. James, 26 Oct [1879], in Perry, *William James,* 2:17; GSH to Wm. James, 27 Dec [1879], JP.
27. GSH to Wm. James, [Dec 1878]; 31 Mar 1879; 27 Dec [1879], JP.
28. GSH to Wm. James, 15 Feb [1880], JP.

met in Heidelberg in July and, wandering around the hills outside the town, carried on, according to James,

the highest and most instructive conversation. . . . We talked twelve hours steadily on Friday, thirteen with a two-hour intermission at Kuhne's lecture on Saturday, and thirteen and a half without an instant's intermission yesterday.[29]

The exposure to German science had toughened Hall's mind. After three days of exchange on psychological matters, James pronounced his former pupil "singularly solidified" and declared generously that their student-master roles had been reversed.[30]

Hall's study of natural science in Germany led him to abandon metaphysics and to embrace psychology as a natural science. He now realized that historical and philosophical criticism had discredited traditional philosophy. No individual could hope to propound a single and final view of the universe. "The new criticism and historical methods have shown that personality is too limited in its essence for this to be possible." It was philosophy in the systematic sense that he called "at best the expression of personal opinion," never having "anything like authority over others," and damned as "metaphysics" or "mere speculation." The new generation, Hall asserted, had been "renouncing the speculative method, and by the creed, *ignoramus ignorabimus*, abandoning as hopeless all attempts at further progress in that direction."[31]

On the basis of the new psychology, Hall thought of forming a reconstructed, scientific philosophy which would be immune to the failings of the old metaphysics. Hall wrote to Professor Norton of

the question I have to meet so often from philosophical men of the older school. They say no results of psychology, derived even from the physio-

29. Wm. James to Bowditch, 19 July [1880], in Perry, *William James*, 1:382.
30. Wm. James to Gilman, 18 July 1880, in Cope, "James's Correspondence with Gilman," p. 624.
31. *Aspects*, pp. 98, 297, 299. The creed "We do not know. We will not know," to which Hall referred, was taken from the conclusion of Emil du Bois-Reymond's well-known address of 1872, "On the Boundaries of Natural Knowledge": "Against the riddles of the material world, the natural scientist has long been accustomed to express, with manly resignation, his *Ignoramus. . . .* However, against the riddle of what matter and force are, and how they may be able to think, he must once and for all time decide for the truth which is much more difficult to concede: *Ignorabimus.*" (Translated by the author.) In du Bois-Reymond, *Reden* (Leipzig: Veit, 1886), 1:105–40.

logical study of senses, nerves or muscles, can affect any of the principles of philosophy. These are mainly developed and established like the fine arts, etc. While to me it seems as if all philosophy must ultimately rest on psychology—or that at bottom perhaps, on physiology. A new psychol. to me implies a new set of fundamental standpoints in regarding all facts of mind.[32]

Hall now conceived of philosophy as an empirical study, whose questions would be answered by discovering through scientific methods how the mind actually worked. In the light of psychology, "new and vast questions arise, take definite discussable form, and become accessible to scientific methods."[33] Progress would follow the path Hall had already discerned when the physiological psychologists took the problem of the perception of space from epistemological debate to laboratory investigation.[34] This new psychology would join with the physical sciences to form a coherent view of all natural phenomena on mechanical principles.

Hall's study of muscular physiology and his attraction to the possibility of scientific synthesis led him to fasten on reflex action as the key to the new psychology. Characteristically, Hall quickly saw the possibility of constructing from the model of the simplest psychic process a whole psychology based on mechanical principles. Just what theory of reflex action Hall proposed to work out in his psychology text is impossible to say. He and James exchanged expectations of imminent publication and discouragement at the slowness of progress. Hall opened negotiations with Holt about publishing his text, and the question soon arose as to which book would be published first and in what form.[35] Hall's enthusiasm proved even more premature than James's, however, for James's text finally appeared twelve years later, whereas Hall's was never

32. GSH to Norton, 3 Sept 1879, NP.
33. GSH, *Aspects*, pp. 297–98.
34. Hall thought this process would lead to a basic reclassification of mental function. "Must we not have a radically new classification of mental faculties more fundamental than the almost mythic (as to its origins) one of feeling, intellect, will, and may it not be due to the falseness, or superficiality of our classification that so far it has not been possible to localize faculties in the brain?" GSH to Norton, 8 June 1879, NP.
35. GSH to Wm. James, 27 Dec [1879], JP; Wm. James to GSH, 16 Jan 1880, in Perry, *William James*, 2:20; Perry, ibid., p. 34; Henry Holt to Wm. James, 10 Oct, 12 Dec 1881, JP; GSH to Harris, 3 Nov 1880, Harris Papers.

written. Nor did Hall publish the articles on Wundt and Helmholtz that would have clarified his psychological position. The task of writing a comprehensive psychology in the terms of reflex action was extraordinarily difficult, and still taxes the psychologist today.

Hall's difficulty probably arose as well from the materialistic implications of his new line of reasoning. From the beginning of his speculation at Harvard on the identity of thought and matter, Hall had tried to avoid the consequences of an overt materialism. Since there was "a dialectical indifference . . . of organism and intellectual function," Hall claimed, one could conceive of psychophysical functioning in either material or psychic terms.[36] In Germany, Hall's problem became more acute, but he could now draw on the pragmatic critique of knowledge he had learned from Peirce. Hall announced that "mechanized knowledge" is simply "the most organized and *known* form of knowledge. Hypothetical mechanism is often merely the best and most serviceable sort of *memoris technica*, and is . . . in no sense a *Ding an sich*." Despite this distinction between a more sophisticated mechanism and the older substantial materialism which had been a chief target of American religious orthodoxy, Hall was reluctant to expose himself to the risk of an entirely mechanical theory. He hastened to add that "as science advances in the study of consciousness, its highest problem, it will perhaps find it no less serviceable to resolve all knowledge into the forms of self-knowledge, interpret force as will, etc."[37] Hall clearly had prudential doubts about committing himself to a thoroughgoing reflex theory of psychology.

While struggling unsuccessfully with a mechanical theory of psychology, Hall was also struggling, on another side, with an evolutionary doctrine that claimed to put his identity philosophy into scientific form. The theories of Ernst Haeckel, professor of morphology at the University of Jena, were at the center of academic debate in Germany during the period of Hall's residence there. Haeckel had expanded Darwin's theory of the origin of species and other partial developmental concepts into a cosmic

36. GSH, "Muscular Perception," 1878, p. 447.
37. GSH, "The Graphic Method," in *Aspects*, p. 72.

evolutionary philosophy. He theorized that the basic units of construction of the universe were plastidules or molecules of mind-matter, whose development into increasingly complex units proceeded by the laws of evolution. A comparative morphologist, Haeckel discussed the evolution of species according to the principle of recapitulation: the individual, in his development, repeats the course of evolution taken by the species. He considered his evolutionary biology to be a historical and philosophical science, one not subject to all the strictures of the exact sciences, but a science nonetheless, and one which could serve as a foundation for the others and for a unified world-view.[38]

Haeckel's theories were attacked during the 1870s by some of the most eminent scientists in Germany, who charged that he had confused the nature and limits of scientific explanation. His critics rallied around the ideas of du Bois-Reymond, whose address "On the Boundaries of Natural Knowledge" ended with the confession of philosophic ignorance Hall had quoted approvingly.[39]

Haeckel's theories also carried marked political connotations. Haeckel's thesis, interpreted as a brief for continual social change, attracted support among German socialists, and the conservative party blamed it for the rise of socialist agitation in the country. After the government prohibited the teaching of evolution in any form in the schools, Haeckel issued in 1878, the year Hall arrived in Germany, a manifesto for *Freedom in Science and Teaching*, which rallied the younger, more liberal academics to him.[40]

Though Hall never expressed himself publicly on the issue of teaching evolution in the German schools, it is likely that the critic of the closed philosophical mind of the American colleges felt strongly attracted to Haeckel's plea for free science and free teaching.[41] Hall also felt an attraction to socialism, though his aware-

38. Erik Nordenskiöld, *The History of Biology* (New York: Tudor, 1928), pp. 505–26.

39. Ibid., pp. 521–22; Merz, *European Thought*, 2:403 n.

40. Nordenskiöld, *History of Biology*, pp. 507–8, 520–22; Ernst Haeckel, *Freedom in Science and Teaching*, trans. T. H. Huxley (London: Kegan Paul, 1879).

41. Hall wrote Norton: "I cannot see how the currency of theories of evolution can be made responsible for social democracy as the aristocratic party urged." 3 Feb 1879, NP.

ness of the disrepute in which it was held in both American and German academic circles made him cloak his interest.[42]

The appeal of Haeckel's philosophical scientism was even stronger than that of his political position. Hall described the controversy as being between the younger generation of scientists who supported Haeckel and the generally "older men who applaud the *ignorabimus* creed of Reymond." Having thus prejudiced his case, Hall declared that Haeckel's theory did not make a "religion of science" and that science would not "be generally discredited by such harmless speculation." How much of Haeckel's theory was "ripe for scientific speculation" was only a problem of "method and policy." Virchow himself, Hall asserted, was no less evolutionary in his approach than Haeckel was in his. When the issue was "scientific" instead of "metaphysical" speculation, Hall was unable to see that many of the questions asked and formulations made in the name of science were subject to the same objections as those of traditional metaphysics.[43]

Hall's confusion on this issue was due partly to the same historical consideration which had led him away from metaphysics. People may doubt, Hall admitted, that the new scientific psychology will ultimately prove the identity of thought and matter.

> But does not psychology, as well as the history of philosophy, teach us that the outstanding questions of thought have always seemed settled in proportion as men's minds were shut, or as they confounded the limits of their own individual development or culture with the limits of possible knowledge?[44]

In the light of science's inevitable progress, problems and formulations even beyond its present scope appeared as programs for future research and prophetic visions of the land someday to be conquered. When Hall found himself listed in a new essay by James among the evolutionary monists who espoused a kind of atomistic identity of mind and matter, he promptly objected: "Would you mind omitting my name from the list of hylozoic atomists? No doubt you are perfectly justified from our letters and my 'Space,' but I *meant* only monism, as a postulate, or scientific hypothesis, and by no

---

42. *LCP*, p. 222; *Aspects*, pp. 58–65.
43. *Aspects*, pp. 150–52.
44. GSH, "Notes on Hegel," 1878, p. 102.

means as a proven truth."[45] Hall could overcome some of the scientific objections to Haeckel by calling on his expansive view of science.

Still, Hall did not commit himself in Germany to Haeckel's evolutionary doctrines. Their ambiguous scientific status still discouraged him. Hall himself repeated the strictures of the most rigorous scientists in Germany who said that those who accept evolution as a finality are those who need a "creed," and he reported that many post-Hegelians had found in evolutionism a "new messianic dispensation of Hegelism." To the physiologist, Hall said, evolution was simply "a morphological assumption."[46] Hall derided the popular philosophies that had been erected on the theory of evolution, and reported condescendingly that

the very phonetic elements of the word *Entwickelung* [evolution] were recently described by a humorous writer as fitting and filling the average vocal organs more completely than any other known combination of sounds.[47]

Many years later, long after Hall had formulated his own evolutionism, he reported in his autobiography that "as soon as I first heard it in my youth I think I must have been almost hypnotized by the word 'evolution', which was music to my ear and seemed to fit my mouth better than any other."[48] As with many of his ideas, the value he attributed to this anecdote was subject to reversal.

Evolutionary theories had played a complex role in Hall's intellectual development. For all its force in America and Germany, Darwin's theory entered into an intellectual world already thick with idealistic and normative conceptions of historical and evolutionary development. Darwinian naturalism joined with historical criticism to lead Hall to abandon a supernatural divinity, but from the first he had relied on the progress of knowledge to restore meaning and purpose to the natural world. When he considered Darwin more closely, he immediately absorbed his theory into Hegelian and then Spencerian philosophy.[49]

45. GSH to Wm. James, 26 Oct [1879], JP.
46. *Aspects*, pp. 110, 150, 158.
47. Ibid., p. 189.
48. *LCP*, p. 357.
49. Ernst Cassirer, *The Problem of Knowledge* (New Haven: Yale Univer-

In Germany, therefore, Haeckel appeared as an attractive scientific model of evolutionary thinking. Hall was still, moreover, interested in the romantic and dynamic philosophers, particularly those like Fichte, Schopenhauer, and Von Hartmann who conceived of consciousness as a form of volition. Hall was very critical of the pessimistic direction of the theories of Schopenhauer and Von Hartmann, but his early psychological predilections drew him to their dynamic viewpoint.[50] Though he eventually worked his way to an evolutionary biology separate from philosophy, his science always bore the marks of these earlier attachments. Evolution always implied normative conceptions for Hall and always centered on the historical process of development over time, rather than on the functional process of selection and adaptation which was the novelty and center of Darwin's theory. It also focused on those dynamic elements of the human psyche which linked man to his evolutionary past, the instincts.

Hall's acceptance of natural science in Germany satisfied his intellectual ambition yet left him somewhat troubled. One could overcome pessimism, Hall said, by "the perfect joy" which comes to one

who is perfectly enfranchised from authority,—at least, in some particular sphere which may be ever so narrow,—who becomes at last able to say, "Here no one can teach me anything more;" he who has invented or created something new in the world, and far more he who has passed beyond all selfish hope or mortal fear,—he alone knows the perfect liberty of the sons of God.

In its narrow, concentrated focus, its creativity, and its freedom from supernatural sanctions, science offered Hall a measure of both safety and independence. Yet Hall called his happiness with science "the perfect joy which lies in a full self-sacrifice."[51] To accept the narrow focus of science, Hall had to sacrifice his intellectual hubris and take on the martyr's role. To abide by the limits of science demanded by the more rigorous scientists, he would have to give up

---

sity Press, 1950), pp. 170–75, concludes that Darwinian evolutionary ideas spread as rapidly as they did in the nineteenth century because of the prior influence of Hegelian philosophy and its outcome in an historical approach to reality.

50. GSH, *Aspects*, pp. 175–85, 194–207.

51. Ibid., pp. 206–7.

the sentimental satisfactions of philosophy as well. Hall regarded a rigorous commitment to science as "thorough, honest, manly . . . without crudity, evasion, or a trace of sentiment or triviality," but he could not suppress his desire for a creed. Another cure of pessimism he offered was "faith in an evolution which is slowly but surely accomplishing before our eyes all worthy ideals."[52]

The extent to which science was for Hall a hard matter of self-control and discipline was evident in the anger he came to feel toward the German physiologist and philosopher, Hermann Lotze. Lotze's early work in physiology had been among the most influential in shaping an empirical viewpoint in psychology. A complex thinker, Lotze later outlined a philosophy which sharply separated value and meaning from the mechanistically ordered structure of nature. The early Lotze had been Hall's hero; the later Lotze now appeared to him as a threat to all he had come to accept. Hall maintained that

the line cannot be drawn too hard and fast between speculations like Lotze's and a truly scientific philosophy. The world of law is to him like the old dispensation, to be superseded, not entirely without a break in the development, by a new. He refuses to trust science to work out its own salvation. He is the noblest of modern sentimentalists. His demands upon the world for individual aesthetic enjoyment are exorbitant and almost unparalleled. It never occurs to his refined and subtle hedonism that man's right to happiness at all is as yet quite assumptive. I deem this position in its practical effects scarcely less than immoral and socialistic. We are in the world to work. It costs hard labor of muscle or brain to live, rear a family, be respectable, and provide for decent burial; and what right has this philosopher, idly perched upon his twig, to talk with such moving, maddening pathos about a world of "worths and goods to be purely and passively enjoyed," when his own department was never more hopeful and in such crying need of self-sacrificing toil as now?[53]

That Hall associated the "self-sacrificing toil" required by science with the "hard labor" demanded by the elemental conceptions of duty and respectability of his puritan nurture suggests that his pursuit of science drew support from the puritan moral imperatives on which his character had been formed. The "moving, maddening pathos" Hall felt in Lotze's call to passive enjoyment of the world's

52. Ibid., pp. 189, 206.
53. Ibid., p. 99.

beauties and goods threatened the discipline and self-control which upheld his pursuit of science. Lotze's unscientific "sentimentalism" was so dangerous to his equilibrium that he was driven to call it "immoral and socialistic"—from Hall's day to this, a characteristic American response to threats against respectable identity.

Hall did not resolve in Germany, nor for some years after, his conflicts over his identity as a scientist. Nonetheless, he was firmly committed to science. His earlier desire to live on the frontiers of knowledge took a permanent turn in Germany toward natural science. Hall was inspired by the practice of science in the German universities and by the different but large hopes claimed for scientific explanation by Helmholtz and Haeckel. He absorbed the ideal of scientific research which pervaded the German university and the idealized ends which the German scholar attached to *Wissenschaft*.[54] From this point forward, Hall tried to absorb his religious and philosophical interests into his scientific identity.

While Hall was struggling with his science, he was also engaged in a more personal struggle. Cornelia Fisher, the young woman two years his junior whom he had met in Yellow Springs, was studying art in Europe when Hall arrived in Germany in the fall of 1878, and he now renewed the acquaintance.[55] Hall disclosed virtually nothing, at the time or afterward, about his courtship or marriage, but upon leaving Antioch he had written a romantic short story that so literally transcribed real people and events at the college it caused a sensation there when published.[56] The hero of the story was, of course, Hall himself, and the heroine bore marked resemblances to Miss Fisher.

Hall's fantasy concerned the rocky courtship of a shy professor at a small provincial college and a strong-willed young woman of

54. Ibid., pp. 119–20. Hall's complex scientific motivations suggest how difficult it is to make any facile generalizations on the psychological sources of scientific endeavor. Not only can different and conflicting motivations feed an interest in science, but various conceptions of science can yield sharply different scientific ideals. On this point, see Robert K. Merton, "Science, Technology and Society in Seventeenth Century England," *Osiris* 4 (1938), and Lewis S. Feuer, *The Scientific Intellectual: The Psychological and Sociological Origins of Modern Science* (New York: Basic Books, 1963).

55. *LCP,* pp. 86, 210; GSH to Wm. James, 26 Oct [1879], JP.

56. GSH, "A Leap-Year Romance," 1878; GSH to Adelaide Hardy, 5 Dec 1913, "Antiochiana," Antioch College.

the town. Their relations were hampered by the fact the young man believed women were by nature, and ought to be, entirely submissive to men and dependent upon them. The feeling of absolute dependence was the core of religious emotion, as Schleiermacher had said. The feeling of dependence, the professor felt, was the highest and noblest emotion, and it was naturally and properly incarnated in Woman. His young woman friend, however, was insulted by such ideas, and the young man responded to her protests with stiff rejection. Only gradually, after alienating her suitor, did she come to see that his ideas were sound and that she was willing to give up all for love of him. In despair, she ran off to Europe to study art and was about to enter a nunnery when the young man, realizing that she had repented, rushed to her side to confess his love and claim her.

The motivation of the hero was not altogether clear in the story, and Hall alluded to disturbing emotional currents running under the surface. When the professor warmed to his lecture on the nature of woman, he spoke "more and more earnestly and disconnectedly, as he felt himself borne along on a new and more dangerous hobby of his." The heroine felt the intense hostility of his views. They seemed to her like the thrust of a "hard, cold fist in her face." But the heroine also noticed that her suitor appeared to suffer greatly, as though "distressed by some private grief or misfortune."[57] The professor's views of womanhood, were laced with a private theme of self-sacrifice. "The highest and most perfect form of emotion," Hall had his fictional preacher declare, "is a sense of complete dependence and unreserved self-surrender." Like Schleiermacher, Hall associated this passive position with receptivity to aesthetic impressions.

The religious sentiment—love for any and every worthy object, aesthetic susceptibilities which respond to beauty wherever found, and even conscience—all are but diverse forms of this supreme feeling, elements of what the poet described as the soul of eternal womanhood.[58]

57. "Leap-Year," 1878, pp. 215, 217.
58. Ibid., p. 319. For Schleiermacher, see John Herman Randall, Jr., *The Career of Philosophy*, 2: *From the German Enlightenment to the Age of Darwin* (New York: Columbia University Press, 1965), pp. 239–46.

These sentiments, according to Hall, carried one to the very brink of self-sacrifice.

> When the heart and the mind have once made the great surrender to those objects which are higher and larger and more glorious than they, there comes a sweetness, a strength, and a light, unknown before.

One-quarter of the human race, Hall declared approvingly, believed that "annihilation" was the supreme good and followed "this hidden secret sense, that urges them to 'some unknown good.' "[59] Quite understandably, Hall later remarked that the religious feeling of dependence "almost suggests Masochistic longings toward the transcendent."[60]

At the climax of the tale, the hero described a picture of the manger scene painted by the heroine. At the center was the Mother with Child, now "completely satisfied . . . in the supreme joy of motherhood," while a male figure knelt near her, with face averted. Further back stood a herdsman who resembled the young professor himself, his face dominated by "a tender sadness" which made the woodpile to the side "suggestive of a sacrificial altar."[61]

It is difficult not to see in the desire for dependence and self-sacrifice, the religious sentiments and "aesthetic susceptibilities" Hall ascribed to the female nature, feelings he himself powerfully felt. Victorian culture had assigned these characteristics preeminently to the woman's sphere.[62] On a personal level, Hall evidently

59. "Leap-Year," 1878, p. 218.
60. *Adol,* 2:127.
61. "Leap-Year," 1878, pp. 326–27.
62. On the image of masculinity and femininity in Victorian culture, see Houghton, *The Victorian Mind,* pp. 341–72; Peter T. Cominos, "Late Victorian Sexual Respectability and the Social System," *International Review of Social History* 8 (1963): 243–46; Patrick Geddes and J. Arthur Thomson, *The Evolution of Sex* (London: Walter Scott, 1889), pp. 3–30, 270–71. On one level, the sexes were both recognized to embody feelings—the man, more active and passionate feelings, the woman, more altruistic and sympathetic ones. The final formulation, however, tended toward the view "Man thinks more, woman feels more." Geddes and Thomson, p. 271. Apparently, in the concept of sex roles, as well as in the reality, feeling tended to disappear in the man under the constraints of reason and self-control and to emerge only in the woman, in idealized forms. For some evidence that these attitudes were strong in America as well as England, see Barbara Welter, "The Cult of True Womanhood: 1820–1860," *American Quarterly* 18

experienced severe conflicts over his identification with his father and a substantial desire to follow his mother. Hence, to secure his masculine identity, he had to try to repress or disown powerful feelings of dependence and a latent feminine identification. Hall's desire to reduce his female partner to complete submission reflected his need to keep these "feminine" desires within himself under control. Hall wrote this fantasy before he seriously took up natural science, so the "full self-sacrifice" demanded by science overlay much deeper conflicts. Hall's scientific identity reinforced his masculine identification by excluding these "feminine" concerns from its sphere but only at the price of denying Hall an intellectual outlet for his suppressed feelings and itself assuming a martyred stance.

Despite these difficulties in his responses to women, Hall carried on with the relationship. Whether Miss Fisher had been at the start of their friendship a very independent and strong-minded lady is not known. Hall described her only as a "sincere Presbyterian, very practical, etc." who very much resembled his own mother.[63] Surely Hall would have wanted a mate who had, beneath a modest exterior, the strength to satisfy his own need for dependence. In September 1879, when Hall was thirty-five years old, they were married in Berlin,[64] and James noted a new strength and confidence in his friend's letters.

Having married and begun to sense his competence, Hall looked forward to an end to the frustrations and insecurity of his long apprenticeship. Hall confessed to James that

what has had more influence [on my new mood] than anything else is the growing hope and prospect that I may earn my own bread, somehow, without filling a position which would limit my freedom in any way; the prospect of sometime having *my own* experience about some of the great interests of life at home, as they look *to me,* without considering how Eliot will

---

(1966): 151–74; David M. Kennedy, *Birth Control in America* (New Haven: Yale University Press, 1970), pp. 36–71, and William L. O'Neill, *Divorce in the Progressive Era* (New Haven: Yale University Press, 1967), pp. 62–65.

63. GSH to Wm. James, 15 Feb [1880], JP.

64. "Heiraths-Urkunde. Nr. 537," HP. Hall was very reticent in telling his American correspondents about his marriage, especially James, who had himself married in July the summer Hall left for Germany. James was somewhat chagrined to be told of Hall's marriage only through a postscript in a letter to Bowditch. Wm. James to GSH, 10 Oct [1879], HP.

like it, how it will affect my prospects, whether Hale or Bellows will fear that such a man in their philosophy chair will lead young men away from the Unitarian pulpit—(as at Antioch). I may have no influence at all, but I do believe I have some things in my head and note-books to say which are so true to *me* that it will be the supremest intellectual luxury to work and hunt around till I can get them said somehow.[65]

Hall was thirty-six years old when he wrote this to James, just a few months away from his final return to the United States and to more frustrations, prudential calculations, and, ultimately, self-expression.

65. GSH to Wm. James, 15 Feb [1880], JP.

Part Two

DOMESTICATING SCIENCE 1880–1892

7 AMERICAN OPPORTUNITIES

In the ten years from 1880 to 1890, Stanley Hall became one of the leading figures in American scientific and intellectual life. Poor and almost unknown when he returned from his postgraduate work in Germany, he was by the end of the decade the major psychologist in the country next only to William James, already well-known as an educational reformer and the spearhead of a brilliant and far-reaching experiment in American higher education. The current on which Hall rose to prominence was the rising tide of natural science in American culture. Hall's mastery of the scientific techniques then being applied to psychology, his conviction of the dominating importance of the scientific world view, and his ability to generate and organize latent enthusiasm for science enabled him to seize on a variety of possibilities for scientific advance and rapidly bring them to fruition.

The way hardly seemed clear to Hall, however, as he faced his return to the United States. He had been looking for a satisfactory position in America almost from the day he arrived in Germany. Already in his mid-thirties, he was finding it extremely difficult to establish a secure future. While the educational system in America was entering a period of transformation that could be expected to produce more opportunities in the future, he had chosen a field of specialization that was still novel, untried, and suspect to conservative educational leaders.

Johns Hopkins University, with a graduate department staffed by specialists, emphasizing the scientific disciplines, and dedicated to original research, was still the most likely and congenial answer to Hall's career problem. He ventured to hope publicly that Hopkins would soon establish "a chair of physiological psychology and another of the history of philosophy."[1] When James declined President Gilman's offer to lecture at Hopkins for two or three months in 1879, he suggested Hall for the job, this time more forcefully than he had before. With a channel to Hopkins again open, Hall solicited Gilman's consideration and again was refused.[2]

The following year Hall tried once more. "I am an enthusiast for my department," he pleaded, and physiological psychology should have a chance to grow on Baltimore's "richest virgin soil."[3] In July 1880, after James's and Hall's rambling conversation in Heidelberg, James added his weight decisively to Hall's case:

He is a more learned man than I can ever hope to become. . . . I feel his exceptional merits, moral as well as intellectual, so strongly that I cannot bear to think of his being any longer without a place commensurate with them. . . . He is much too good for any but a first rate University.[4]

Even with that recommendation, however, Hall was refused. Gilman reminded him that Hopkins already had three men—H. Newall Martin in biology and Charles S. Peirce and George S. Morris in philosophy—whose work touched more or less extensively on his field. "That which I had in mind is I think not covered by either of these gentlemen," Hall replied coldly, "and several lectureships are devoted to it in the German universities with which I am best acquainted."[5]

Besides being wary of establishing a field whose independent existence was still uncertain, Gilman was also pressed for funds. Uncertain return on the stock which formed the basis of the university's operating income acted as a pervasive check on expansion from 1877 to 1880.[6] Gilman might well have hesitated under those circumstances to take on the new psychology.

1. GSH, "Philosophy in the U.S.," 1879, p. 98.
2. Wm. James to Gilman, 18 Feb [1879] in Cope, "James's Correspondence with Gilman," p. 623; GSH to Gilman, 12 May 1879, GP.
3. GSH to Gilman, 19 June 1880, GP.
4. Wm. James to Gilman, 18 July 1880, in Cope, "James's Correspondence with Gilman," p. 624.
5. GSH to Gilman, 10 Sept 1880, GP.
6. Hawkins, *Pioneer*, p. 131.

Beyond Johns Hopkins, Hall had few possibilities.[7] He was continually hopeful of an appointment at Harvard if James should
leave for Hopkins or if one of the several elderly philosophers at
the college should resign, but neither possibility appeared imminent.[8] Moreover, according to James, Hall's critique of philosophy
in American universities had aroused considerable criticism at Harvard. Although Harvard had fared better than any other school,
Hall's summary methods, as well as the bad name given to all
American philosophy, would have antagonized the Harvard philosophers, particularly since the critique was published in one of the
leading philosophical journals in England. Hall replied that the
Harvardians' reaction was unjust and that he rather than they had
an accurate picture of what, on the whole, American philosophy
was like. He soon confessed, however, that he was sorry he had ever
written the piece and that it would surely prevent him from getting
a university position.[9]

As a temporary expedient, Hall asked James, Bowditch, and Norton for support in obtaining a course of public lectures at the Lowell
Institute in Boston. Hall wanted to speak on "Muscles and the
Will," a very different subject, he said, from James's Lowell Lectures only the year before on "The Brain and the Mind," but Hall
was not appointed.[10]

Fearing that "neither psychology nor philosophy would ever

7. Cornell had been forming a modern graduate school under the presidency
of Andrew D. White and Hall reported "a shadow of a chance which appeared at
Cornell only to vanish." There was also "a very vague and horrible contingency
that a new prof. of philos. may sometime be wanted in the new north of England
university and that my physiological bias *may* not hurt me," but this unappealing
possibility similarly disappeared. GSH to Wm. James, 31 Mar 1879, JP; GSH to
Norton, 8 June 1879, NP.

8. GSH to G. W. Hosmer, 1 Jan 1879, Hosmer Papers. When Andrew Pea-
body retired in 1881, Hall applied vainly for the Plummer Professorship of
Christian Morals. So far as knowledge of the subject, he wrote Eliot, "I could
make a pretty good claim. . . . I should be willing, though with less enthusiasm,
to undertake chapel work, if that is indissolubly connected with the chair. . . . If
any kind of pastoral work among the students at large is contemplated, . . . then
certainly I hold myself the least worthy of all for the place." GSH to Charles
Wm. Eliot, 18 Feb 1881, Eliot Papers, Harvard University Archives.

9. GSH to Wm. James, 31 Mar 1879, JP; GSH to Norton, 6 Nov [1878];
3 Feb, 8 June 1879, NP.

10. GSH to Norton, 3 Feb 1879, NP; GSH to Wm. James, 31 Mar 1879,
JP; GSH to Bowditch, 3 Sept [1879], Bowditch Papers; Perry, *William James,*
2:27.

make bread," Hall began to think seriously of studying medicine
and then decided that "the most promising line of work would be
to study the applications of psychology to education."[11] Hall was
certainly aware of the central interest that education had held for
psychologists from John Locke to Herbert Spencer, as he was aware
of the popular ferment in education in America. In his work at
Antioch and with the St. Louis Hegelians, he had become acquainted with the new generation of school administrators and
young women teachers who wanted to regard their work as a profession and discussed problems of educational reform with reference to basic differences of philosophy.[12]

In Germany, moreover, pedagogy, as the subject was called, was
beginning to attain some intellectual respectability. The reform of
the Prussian school system during the 1870s had drawn the academic community into discussions of the school curriculum and
methods of teaching, as well as academic freedom. The subject was
still a secondary and even incidental interest to those German philosophers and scientists who occasionally lectured on it at the universities, and reading most of the German pedagogical literature,
Hall admitted, was like "sifting a bushel of chaffy, philosophic
words for two grains of wheat." By the late 1870s, however, a few
German university scholars were beginning to devote their complete
attention to pedagogy; the history of education had aroused serious
interest; and the new psychology and evolutionary biology were
recognized to have important educational implications. The widespread German view that the educational system established after
the expulsion of Napoleon had been the chief instrument of national regeneration suggested to Hall the crucial role educational
reform might play in American society.[13] He came to think of
pedagogy as the chief field of practical application for psychology
and a key to moral progress.

Hall gathered pedagogical materials and, partly with this subject

11. *LCP*, p. 215.
12. *Ohio Educational Monthly* 21–24 (1872–75), passim; GSH, "Philosophy
in the U.S.," 1879, p. 99; GSH, *Aspects*, pp. 121–27.
13. GSH to Norton, 3 Feb 1879, NP; GSH, "Chairs of Pedagogy in Our
Higher Institutions of Learning," 1882, pp. 36, 39–41; GSH, "The Moral and
Religious Training of Children," 1882, pp. 26–27.

in view, made a rapid tour through Europe on his way back to America. His "superficial study" of schools in Germany, France, and England he considered "most fortunate and very determining in my later life."[14] Hall was correct in perceiving that on his return to the United States, and for many years thereafter, the demand for expertise in education would provide him with a popular and lucrative vocation.

Hall's trip was also designed to give him a rich sampling of Europe's scientific wealth. Spending only a few weeks in each country, he managed to hear or meet many of Europe's greatest neurologists, physiologists, and physicians.[15] Eventually, this exposure would serve him well. The broad range of his studies, his wide curiosity, and his ability to grasp quickly the drift of ideas enabled him to acquire an eclectic store of European ideas and insights that would distinguish him in a relatively provincial academic community that looked to Europe for light. Nevertheless, after seeing the giants of the continent, Hall had to return jobless to the United States, take a small flat in North Somerville, Massachusetts, and hope to find through his contacts in Cambridge some means of supporting his wife and their expected first child.

The first opportunity for Hall was an offer from Franklin Carter, the president of his alma mater, Williams College. Carter, a Latinist who held a German Ph.D., had replaced the old administration in 1876 in an attempt to bring instruction at Williams up to date. Although the aging Mark Hopkins continued to instruct the senior class in philosophy, Carter asked Hall to give a series of lectures during the fall term on the history of philosophy, which would be compulsory for the seniors and additional to Hopkins's course.[16]

Dealing largely with modern German philosophy, Hall found

14. *LCP*, p. 216.
15. The people Hall remembered seeing on this trip were: in Vienna, the physiologists Wilhelm Kuhne and Sigmund Exner, the psychiatrist Theodor Meynert, and the surgeon Theodor Bilroth; in Heidelberg, Kuno Fischer, the historian of philosophy and antagonist of Trendelenburg; in France, J. M. Charcot, A. A. Liebeault, and Hippolyte Bernheim, psychiatrists engaged in the study of hypnotism, and the psychologist Theodule Ribot; in England, the physiologists Michael Foster and J. S. Burdon-Sanderson. *LCP*, pp. 215–16.
16. *Williams Cat., 1881–82*, pp. 15, 31.

the class interested in the personal details of Kant's life but not in his philosophy, and their disinterest grew as the course proceeded. While the students continued to like Mark Hopkins's traditional course, before the end of the third year, they virtually "refused to hear [Hall] any longer."[17] Hall should have remembered that as a senior at Williams, he himself had joined a revolt against the uncustomarily long Latin assignments of the newly arrived young professor from Germany, Franklin Carter.[18] The college students of those years were jealous of their traditional right to do as little course work as possible. A general reform of the college curriculum and faculty standards probably would have been necessary for Hall's course to succeed.[19] Meanwhile, Hall supported Carter's efforts in this direction and as head of a committee appointed to investigate conditions at Williams helped to allay the fears of alumni that the college would deteriorate as a result of Carter's limited reforms.[20]

While the American college seemed still unready for Hall's advanced skills, he had somewhat greater success in addressing the small audience of liberal men interested in effecting a reconciliation between modern science and liberal religion. Hall arranged with Osgood publishers in Boston to bring out a collection of essays, including articles he had written from Germany for the *Nation*, some of the technical psychological studies he had published earlier, and some new material. Titled *Aspects of German Culture*, the heterogeneous work was held together by its defense of natural science in the American context. With its complimentary dedication to Mark Hopkins and its omission of his critique of American philosophy, the book seemed designed to render Hall and his subject acceptable in American academic circles.

Hall argued both in the name of science and Christianity. Young men influenced by science and accepting the results of German biblical criticism had a right to remain in the church, he asserted; they should not "withdraw from the Church because they are dis-

17. Perry, *Williams College*, pp. 738–40.

18. *LCP*, p. 164.

19. Hall may also have slighted his lectures during the second and third year as his prospects in psychology improved.

20. *Report of the Visiting Committee of the Alumni of Williams College* (Williamstown, 1884).

satisfied with its leaders" any more than they should turn away from politics "because it is now controlled by bad men." Through them, a new "re-habilitation" of Christianity could be effected.[21]

Hall attributed the evils and loss of faith that beset American Christianity to excessive rigidity and literalism, "positivism," and "materialism" in belief. The only cure was the deepening of the religious consciousness by the study of "precisely these German methods and results of investigation" so much feared. Christianity had to give up only "the old and baseless claim of absoluteness and universal validity." In place of a supernatural Divinity would be deeper moral and psychological truths, namely:

> a profound psychological meaning in the atonement, Trinity, etc.; a matchless didactic method . . . a moral and aesthetic cultus . . . an incomparable instrument of discipline and social order . . . the highest and most philosophical common sense, adapted to the practical needs of ordinary life.

The creed and ritual of the church was only a "useful and valuable symbol of truth" which was to be judged by its "moral and social effects."[22]

Hall's standard of practicality made him reluctant to oppose traditional religious practices. In return for the liberalization of religion, Hall tacitly offered a cessation of the "extreme and injudicious," the "gross and tasteless" criticism of religion that had been characteristic of her scientific opponents, and recognized the need to go slow, to refrain from opening the religious problem "prematurely," and to respect the need for "rigorous religious observances and beliefs" among a people "devoted like ours to trade and industry."[23]

Hall offered a similar pattern of reconciliation between science and traditional philosophy. Though he praised the attainments of science, with its narrow and penetrating focus, and denigrated individual, synthetic systems of philosophy, Hall was not entirely of one mind. Some "brief system" giving voice to the *Zeitgeist* could have only transient existence; still "it may be at the same time the most serviceable of all forms of intellectual work." Hall realized

---

21. *Aspects*, p. 316.
22. Ibid., pp. 16–17, 39, 309, 317.
23. Ibid., pp. 8, 14, 316.

that "the mind must have ideal objects" and that in the current state of intellectual and religious confusion, "a new comprehensive and *popular* answer to the ultimate questions of life and destiny may before long become imperative for the preservation of moral and social order." Even the scientific specialist needed some broader culture, some wider conception of the organization of knowledge, to avoid stunted growth or "fanaticism." The only alternative to such a comprehensive creed was the morbid pessimistic philosophy already popular in Germany.[24]

Though Hall's book found its way to only a very small audience, and he later complained of its "wretched" career,[25] it made a very favorable impression in liberal circles. Simply as a knowledgeable tour of the German scene, the book was valuable. *Mind* reported that

probably no other English-speaking student of psychology and philosophy has acquired half as much familiarity as Mr. Hall with every phase of the present intellectual movement in Germany, and his brightly-written sketches are full of instruction not easily to be had otherwise.[26]

Even more important was the mediating use Hall was able to get from the liberal German religious and philosophical ideas he had acquired.[27] Hall's intellectual contemporaries of the 1870s and 1880s were clearly favorable to the distinction he made between literal religious doctrine and its essential moral and psychological meaning, his belief that critical science would justify enlightened religion, and his emphasis on the practical necessity of belief to maintain moral and social order. Hall combined these views into a program which promised to save the essential qualities of all parties to the dispute. It was undoubtedly this ability to cut through old antagonisms that so impressed Charles Norton. He declared that "in fairness and clearness of statement and in keenness of analysis [Hall's book] is remarkable."[28]

The social stance Hall took on his return from Germany was

24. Ibid., pp. 50, 154, 299–302.

25. GSH to James R. Osgood, 29 Feb 1887, Benjamin Holt Ticknor Papers, Library of Congress, Washington, D.C.

26. *Mind* 6 (1881): 444.

27. Hall knew the work of Ludwig Feuerbach, Eduard Zeller, and Albrecht Ritschl, besides that of Schleiermacher. *LCP,* p. 184; *Aspects,* pp. 7–8, 15–16.

28. Norton to Gilman, 14 Feb 1881, GP. The *Christian Register,* a Boston

similarly moderate. Hall was in these essays highly critical of America's materialistic standards and business orientation, her provincial complacency and popular philistinism, and her shallow and decaying faiths. He spoke in the combined accents of the New England mugwump, of Charles Eliot Norton's cultural criticism, of the anti-materialistic critiques of America he had heard in Germany, and of the perennial American jeremiad against loss of faith.[29] Hall considered several responses to these pervasive ills. The most extreme, and the least acceptable, was the kind of thoroughgoing philosophical pessimism he had found in von Hartmann and Schopenhauer. Hall was continually fascinated by pessimistic views of the world, but he consistently denounced them as cowardly and morbid.[30]

Another extreme solution which briefly attracted his attention in Germany was socialism. Hall was acquainted with socialist activities in Leipzig, he was drawn to the colorful personality of Ferdinand Lassalle, and he claimed later to have read some of the work of Karl Marx and to have "half accepted" what he understood of it.[31] The tenor of Hall's cultural criticism suggests, however, that he could not have understood very much of socialism. He was undoubtedly attracted to its iconoclasm and radical rejection of conventional authority. Of necessity, however, he was repelled by these characteristics as well. Socialism was, too radical a doctrine to allow him to maintain the balance of his character or a successful career. Moreover, Hall spoke in derogatory terms of the "social democracy." Its aims were materialistic and selfish and its views were often primitive and superstitious; it could be defined "as the consensus of the incompetent upon properly professional questions."[32]

Between these two extremes of pessimistic resignation and revo-

---

Unitarian organ, found Hall's work "strong and satisfactory" and particularly praised his tendency to disavow metaphysical or reductionist materialism. Professor Frances Bowen, one of Harvard's philosophers, found it a very "instructive" survey of current German thought and was especially pleased by Hall's awareness of the need for philosophy to fill the vacuum left by decaying faiths and to counteract narrow specialization. Clipping from *Christian Register*, GP; Frances Bowen, "Aspects of German Culture," *Harvard Register* 3 (Mar 1881), pp. 160–61.
    29. *Aspects*, pp. 300–301, 306–9.
    30. Ibid, pp. 41–50, 175–85, 194–207.
    31. Ibid., pp. 58–65; *LCP*, p. 222.
    32. Ibid., pp. 21, 27, 31, 86.

lution, Hall chose the path of the moderate, constructive critic, declaring that "the most unfavorable aspects of our national life can be squarely faced, not only without lessening our patriotism nor cooling our optimistic ardor, but without a shadow of alarm or discouragement."[33] Hall based his optimism on the forces of progressive growth already present, on the commitment he had made earlier as a Hegelian to work out from the present, "just as it is." Even in his critique of American philosophy, he opted against overturning the American "materialisms of faith and business" but hoped instead that they were already changing for the better. One source of good, he said, was the invaluable philosophical discipline of the American Sunday. This institution gives "seriousness and poise to character, teaches self-control, self-knowledge, self-respect, as the highest results of every intellectual motive and aspiration."[34] It was only a few years since Hall had freed himself from "the hated Puritan Sunday," but the "philosophical" rather than the "hated" day became a recurrent motif in his attempts to draw the old, unscarred, into the new.

Despite his limited success as a cultural mediator, Hall soon found himself "in great need of something besides my unremunerative writing to keep up my spiritual regimen" and asked Professor Norton to mention to President Eliot the possibility of a University Lectureship at Harvard. Such lecture series offered subjects of popular interest not taught in the regular curriculum.[35] As Hall liked to remember the event, President Eliot rode out to his home one day in the fall of 1880, appearing suddenly as a knight on a charger, and offered him lectureships in pedagogy and the history of philosophy.[36]

Hall's lectures on the history of philosophy received some favor-

33. Ibid., p. 320.
34. GSH, "Philosophy in the U.S.," 1879, pp. 67–68.
35. GSH to Norton, 30 Sept [1880], Norton Papers, Houghton Library, Harvard University. According to Thomas Sergeant Perry, Hall was "penniless" in 1880–81 and "wandering about the Common actually hungry"; Adams S. Hill, professor of rhetoric at Harvard, took him in as an assistant that year but treated him shabbily. Virginia Harlow, *Thomas Sergeant Perry: A Biography* (Durham: Duke University Press, 1950), pp. 109–10.
36. *Ann. Rep. Pres. Harv.*, 1881–82, p. 49; *LCP*, pp. 216–17. Hall recalled that Eliot first offered him only lectures in pedagogy and that he requested specially to be given a series on contemporary German philosophy as well.

American Opportunities

able notice[37] but were overshadowed by the great success of his lectures on pedagogy, the first of their kind at Harvard. Unlike others in the series, they were held in Boston proper on Saturday mornings so that teachers of the city could conveniently attend, from February to April, 1881.[38] Francis Parker's innovations at the nearby Quincy schools had roused interest in educational reform, and the community looked forward to some definitive, scientific answers to the issues raised at Quincy.[39]

President Eliot himself was skeptical of the new subject. In introducing Hall's first lecture, it was reported, he was hardly able to pronounce the word pedagogy without evident distaste.[40] But Hall's own seriousness, the large and distinguished audience of local educators he held, and the enormous success of the lectures among the city's teachers soon dispelled the president's disbelief. Eliot wrote Hall, "Your pedagogy lectures are remarkably successful, and I think must result to your advantage."[41] The teachers heaped thanks on Hall and Eliot and hoped that the work would be continued. It was soon proposed that "among the new professorships established in Harvard College during the next five years, there should be a professorship of pedagogy."[42] For the two succeeding years Hall was asked to return as university lecturer in pedagogy. This was Hall's first success, and coming after so long a period of uncertainty, it was a triumph he remembered all his life.[43]

The educational system of Boston which Hall addressed in 1881, as in cities throughout the North and West, was the product of the movement for free public schools begun during the 1840s. Comprising elementary and high schools, the system was by 1880 over-

37. Clipping from *Christian Register*, GP.
38. *Ann. Rep. Pres. Harv., 1880–81*, p. 39.
39. "The University Lectures on Pedagogy," [10 Feb 1881], clipping, GP.
40. Ibid.
41. Eliot to GSH, 2 Mar 1881, GSH Memorial Volume, CUP. Hall remembered that Charles Francis Adams, the man who had brought Parker to Quincy, and John D. Philbrick, the Boston superintendent of Schools and Parker's current antagonist, were present. *LCP*, p. 217.
42. *Harvard Register*, 3:107, 301; Hart, *History of Massachusetts*, 4:190; *Ann. Rep. Pres. Harv., 1880–81*, p. 39.
43. *Ann. Rep. Pres. Harv., 1881–82*, p. 49; *1882–83*, p. 7; *LCP*, pp. 217–18; Lorraine Pruette, *G. Stanley Hall: Biography of a Mind* (New York: D. Appleton, 1926), pp. 114–16.

flowing with an influx of working class and immigrant children into primary grades and just beginning a period of rapid expansion of the high school. A class of professional administrators had already grown up to superintend the local systems, and in the interest of economy, cheaper corps of female teachers continued to replace men in the teaching force. Plagued by their low status in society, teachers, like their administrator leaders, were anxious to professionalize their occupation and supported the founding and improvement of normal schools and professional organizations.

When Stanley Hall appeared on the educational scene in 1881, the conservative cast of the educational system contained a small but growing reformist energy.[44] The conservative character of the educational system was set by the prevailing moralism of the teachers who staffed it and the leaders who organized and defined its purposes. Mid-nineteenth-century educators saw their task as the inculcation of a strong, inner moral guide, or character, a replacement for the external authority which no longer prevailed among the rapid changes of American society. Character was defined as the control of the lower passions by the higher faculties which God had implanted in man's nature and which religion and training would perfect. Much emphasis was placed on making right actions habitual so that character would be deeply and firmly ingrained.

Character building was presumed to be accomplished in part by direct moral training, but the heated sectarian conflicts over how much or little of religious doctrine that would include always put limitations on this part of the program. A chief means of moral training, as it turned out, was implicit in intellectual education: the substitution of higher, more civilized interests and sympathies for lower; the self-discipline learned from the sustained effort to master difficult and tedious materials; and the self-discipline learned from obedience to the school regime. In actual practice, teachers seldom separated their moral from their intellectual task. Behavior and learning were rewarded and punished in similar ways, both being

44. My interpretation of the conservative, moralistic character of the nineteenth-century educational system, with its contained romanticism, follows Michael B. Katz, *The Irony of Early School Reform: Educational Innovation in Mid-Nineteenth Century Massachusetts* (Cambridge: Harvard University Press, 1968), pp. 115–62. For further sources see the Bibliographical Notes.

considered the product of will. The mind, like the character, was expected to operate in an orderly, restrained and mechanical manner. Knowledge, like a fixed body of holy writ, was to be hammered into the student in much the same way as the traditional rules of conduct. The style of teaching these attitudes typically produced was that of the "drillmaster."[45] Intellectual functioning thus bore no resemblance to the life of the mind, but only to the pinched morality which encased it, a profound confusion of purpose and style which Hall and his generation of reformers would not entirely disentangle.

Within the moral conservatism of the schools, there was a dawning recognition of the uniqueness of childhood and the wisdom of adapting education to the child's nature at every stage of development. The desire for natural methods of education was part of the growing awareness that the child had available many virtuous and healthy impulses for development and that training was far more effective when it followed and used these impulses.

The influence of European romantic educators from Rousseau to Pestalozzi to Froebel had been essential in drawing the attention of American pedagogs to the peculiar nature of the child and the value of his native impulses. Under the spur of their influence, new methods of pedagogy were being imported from Europe and slowly being put into practice. The notion of there being disciplinary value in the very unpleasantness and dullness of instruction was giving way to the realization that the teacher must appeal to the natural interests and curiosity of the child. Grounded in Pestalozzi's theory that the child learned from the perception of natural objects rather than from ill-understood words, the "object method" was already widely hailed. The teaching of drawing, justified on the same grounds, was entering the curriculum. So, too, were physical education and a heightened interest in the pupil's health, both part of Pestalozzi's and Froebel's concern for the education of the whole child, a concern which found fertile soil in the unhealthful, overcrowded conditions in most urban American schools. Froebel's kindergarten was introduced during the 1870s and was quickly

45. See Barbara Finkelstein, "Governing the Young: Teacher Behavior in American Primary Classrooms, 1820–1880" (Ph.D. diss., Teachers College, Columbia University, 1970).

gaining adherents. A more humane school discipline, based on respect for the teacher, rather than on fear of punishment, was widely considered in urban schools the preferred approach, if not the one always possible to execute.

Naturalism often worked hand in hand with utilitarian and modernist impulses to reform the curriculum, as through the influential doctrines of Herbert Spencer and the elective system pioneered by Charles W. Eliot at Harvard. Colleges were giving greater weight to modern languages and natural science and these subjects were also making headway in the lower schools on the theory that they were more natural, more useful, and at least equally as moralizing as the older classical fare. Manual-training programs, too, were introduced during the 1870s.

By 1880 these methods according to nature had hardly begun to dissolve the rigid moralism and formalism of the traditional school. The chief obstacles to these methods lay in the very base of the educational system. Due to the economy forced on educators by public frugality, conditions prevailed in most urban schools which insured the survival of authoritarian and formalized methods: a teaching force of ill-educated and insecure young women and classrooms of upward of sixty children. In such circumstances, teachers were understandably concerned far more with discipline and order than with playing on the child's natural interests, and many of the innovations introduced were quickly reduced to sets of formal procedures, tediously repeated. Pestalozzi's concern that children learn from natural objects, for example, almost immediately became a standardized method of introducing subject matter which the young teacher learned by rote in normal school and routinely repeated with her students.[46]

Natural methods, moreover, were still held firmly in check by the prevailing moralism. The romantic American pedagogs found little difficulty in accepting the coexistence of their natural theories and their ultimate goal of character building. The child's deepest impulses, they believed, inclined him to tame his animal nature and seek spiritual ends. And they never doubted that the impulses nature

46. Will S. Monroe, *History of the Pestalozzian Movement in the United States* (Syracuse: C. W. Bardeen, 1907), pp. 36, 169–93.

provided were embryonic and imperfect so that they required training under a firm hand.

Romanticism had by the early 1880s, however, begun to attain
some momentum among educators.[47] Much of this romanticism
may have been merely rhetorical. Talk of the maternal woman who
could see with divine insight into the beautiful nature of the child
may have been a response to the feminization of the teaching force.
Such rhetoric would have pleased both the lady teachers themselves
and the male superintendents who sought a higher justification than
mere economy for their decision to replace male teachers by inex-
perienced young women. More profoundly, the experience of leaving the village of one's youth and of overcoming traditional orthodoxy for the more liberal, romantic, and scientific faiths of the new
era may explain in other educators, as well as in Hall, a deep longing
for the harmony of one's early years, rural and infantile. This
nostalgia was, however, a token of a new world entered into, a
distance achieved. By the 1880s, therefore, some educators both
sentimentally idealized the child and displayed a new ability to
understand and accept the child's natural pattern of development.

By 1880, the romantic prescription had also shown its essentially
radical potential to subvert the traditional moral framework in
which education had been locked. Francis Parker, a New Englander
who studied Pestalozzi and Froebel in Europe, became the first
American to accept the essence of the European romantic educators'
doctrines and hence to break through the formalized spirit and
traditional morality of the American system.[48]

Made superintendent of the small suburban school system of
Quincy, Massachusetts, in 1875, with a mandate for complete
reform, Parker was able to adopt many of the romantic prescriptions
on curriculum, methods, and discipline and achieve impressive results in terms of how much and how willingly the child learned.
His thoroughgoing romanticism allowed him not only to idolize

47. *PNEA* for the late 1870s and early 1880s shows the inroads of romantic
rhetoric among lesser educators as well as among the few more visible pioneer
reformers.

48. Michael B. Katz, "The 'New Departure' in Quincy, 1873–1881: The
Nature of Nineteenth Century Educational Reform," *New England Quarterly*
(Mar 1967), pp. 3–30.

"the little child" but to seriously trust the child's natural propensities. Allowing the child to be himself, Parker believed, would allow him to ascend through natural stages to full morality; and implicit in this belief, as in that of his romantic mentors, was the faith that the morality thus achieved would be a new and higher one than society currently enforced. Moreover, by the strong effect of his buoyant personality and personal training on a relatively small corps of teachers, he established in the teachers themselves a genuine desire for innovation and the energy and capacity to carry it through. The "Quincy system" became a local cause célèbre and an international attraction among educators, a focus for the American pedagogs who had been reared on tamer romantic ideas for two generations.

Parker's experiment at Quincy ended abruptly in 1880, however, after five years' trial, and Parker wandered about until he found a congenial home at the Cook County Normal School in Chicago in 1883. Essentially a lyricist, he did not turn his romantic ideas into a programmatic appeal. As a result, Parker's breakthrough merely added to the growing sectarianism and confusion among educators, each group advocating one or another reform, yet uncertain of the larger implications or unifying rationale of their efforts. In 1880 the National Education Association felt it necessary to create within itself an elite group, the National Council of Education, to pass on the conflicting doctrines besieging educators.[49]

The chief strength Hall brought to this educational scene, and the first new factor he contributed to it, was the authority of science. With science, Hall was able to elevate the romantic doctrine from a submerged and sectarian strain in educational thinking and practice to a dominant ideology of pedagogical reform. Hall's 1881 lectures to Boston schoolteachers rang with the power of modern science: they were composed almost entirely of vivid reports of the latest German educational methods, enlarged by references to psychological principles and educational history. His subjects of reading, arithmetic, physical culture, and the like took on more intellectual substance than his teacher audience had doubtless ever heard before. Although Hall received some nativist criticism for his reliance on

49. *PNEA*, 1882, pp. 77–87.

German example, his audiences were overwhelmingly enthusiastic, for his scientific authority gave them the hope of becoming truly professional.[50]

Their hope for some definitive answers to the questions raised by Parker at the nearby Quincy schools was also fulfilled by Hall. Eschewing any general discussion of educational theories, Hall nonetheless supported most of the "natural" methods of the romantic educators. On the crucial subject of school discipline, however, he favored physical punishment, if necessary, and bowed to the necessity of making the child conform to the school "machine."[51] His call to a scientific profession of education, at this point, therefore, was clearer than his romantic message.

After his successful lectures, Hall immediately began to delve more deeply into the implications of his ideas and the responses of his audience. In two articles for the conservative *Princeton Review,* published in 1882, he bearded the lion in its den with the subjects of moral and religious training.[52] Much of what Hall told his readers came from the mixed bag of moralism and progressivism American educators had been carrying for at least a generation, though he stated his position more forcefully than most and sanctioned it with the authority of German science.

Hall steadfastly took on his moral duties, claiming to follow the "German educators [who] call their department pedagogy . . . despite the unpleasant associations which the word calls up, because the term includes moral discipline in addition to mere didactics."[53] On the issue of religious training, he followed a tradition already well established of criticism of religious "precocity" in children.[54] Like the romantic theorists, he wanted to

50. Hall's lectures were reported in the Boston *Evening Transcript* for 5, 12, 19, 26, 28 Feb; 5, 12, 19, 26 Mar; and 2, 4, 9, 18, 25 Apr 1881. See also GSH, "American and German Methods of Teaching," 1881, pp. 319–21, and GSH, *EP,* 2:242.

51. Boston *Evening Transcript,* 18 Apr 1881.

52. GSH, "The Moral and Religious Training of Children," 1882, pp. 26–48, and "The Education of the Will," 1882, pp. 306–25.

53. "Moral and Religious Training," 1882, pp. 28–29.

54. As early as 1846, Horace Bushnell in his influential work on child nurture had criticized religious "precocity" on natural grounds. Religion should not impose by force at an early age, he said, doctrines and duties which properly belonged to adult life. Horace Bushnell, *Views of Christian Nurture* (Hartford:

inculcate religion as in a sense a growth or development, and in such a way that this natural predisposition be neither neglected, repressed, nor distorted. The pupil should, and in fact naturally does, repeat the course of the development of the race, and education is simply the expediting and shortening of this course.[55]

Similarly, in dealing with the training of the will, Hall upheld physical punishment and the need for absolute obedience in the young child, while building his disciplinary program on natural principles and the ideas of Herbart, who was not yet well known in America. Hall wanted to build discipline largely on the natural tendency to obey an authority figure who is loved and use all the child's own higher impulses, along with a strict but wise exercise of authority, to cultivate an unvarying habit of obeying the right. The end product of such a discipline is that the child

will choose in its slow-widening margin of freedom the state and act you have pre-formed, and will be all the less liable to undue subservience to priest or boss or fashion or tradition later.

A will so formed would have the power of "totalizing," bringing all its parts and powers to bear on each task one set oneself, thus both increasing one's effectiveness in the world and securing one against disappointment by defining expectations.[56]

Yet Hall did not see his inner-directed man entirely in the light his traditional readers did.[57] His reading of the child's nature sug-

---

Edwin Hunt, 1847). See also Henry Ward Beecher, "The Training of Children," in *Plymouth Pulpit*, fifth series, 1870–71 (New York: J. B. Ford, 1871), pp. 167–86. The criticism of "precocity" in American children uttered by British observers also may have been aimed at the early seriousness and moralism, and absence of "fresh ingenuousness and playfulness" among children of middle-class, pious homes; historians have generally taken the criticism to be focused entirely on the freedom and insubordination of the children. See Richard L. Rapson, "The American Child as Seen by British Travellers, 1845–1935," *American Quarterly* 17 (1965): 520–34.

55. "Moral and Religious Training," 1882, p. 32. Hall drew heavily on Froebel for the early years and the metaphor of growth, and on Rousseau for the years of childhood and adolescence.

56. "Will," 1882, pp. 310–14, 320. On Herbart's theory of moral training, from which Hall borrowed heavily, see Johann Friedrich Herbart, *Outlines of Educational Doctrine* (New York: Macmillan, 1901), pp. 140–218, and Gabriel Compayré, *Herbart and Education by Instruction* (New York: Thomas Y. Crowell, 1907). Hall also drew from Rousseau's emphasis on mental unity.

57. The historicity of the inner-directed man is much disputed. See Carl

gested that the child be given no doctrinal instruction in a particular religious creed until adolescence, the natural time of conversion. Although the acceptance of formal religion in adolescence was the final stage he explicitly discussed, he implied that it was not the final stage of development.[58] Hall also spoke more frankly about sex than previous educationists: on the authority of a leading German physiologist, he claimed that for a few years, nine-tenths of the average male adolescent's thoughts and feelings concerned sex. His conclusion from this was traditional: "Therefore . . . education should serve the purpose of preoccupation"; but his ascription of such importance to the problem was a novelty.[59] Hall's brief sketch of adolescence in this article was his first description of this stage of life, and it already contained in capsule his view of this period as one of plastic growth, centered on new sexual energies and religious concern, and requiring greater freedom from parental authority.

Finally, Hall drew some unorthodox conclusions from his picture of traditional will training, for at the end he felt that for all its usefulness, there was "something deeper, without which all our good conduct is more or less hollow." Sensing how seldom such a trained will actually does encompass all one's feelings and volitions, Hall declared:

Thrice happy he who is so wisely trained that he comes to believe he believes what his soul deeply does believe, to say what he feels and feel what he really does feel, and chiefly whose express volitions square with the profounder drift of his will.

In the end, however, Hall cautioned that acting on one's felt convictions and impulses was "an impractical if not dangerous ideal."

For most of us the best education is that which makes us the best and most obedient servants. This is the way of peace and the way of nature, for even if we seriously try to keep up a private conscience at all, apart from feeling, faction, party or class spirit, or even habit, which are our habitual guides, the difficulties are so great that most hasten, more or less consciously and voluntarily, to put themselves under authority again, reserving only the

---

Degler, "The Sociologist As Historian: Riesman's Lonely Crowd," *American Quarterly* 15 (1963): 483–97. He may only have been an ideal construction of conservative critics of American society.

58. "Moral and Religious Training," pp. 38, 47.

59. Ibid., p. 45.

smallest margin of independence in material interest, choice of masters, etc., and yielding to the pleasing and easy illusion that inflates the minimum to seem the maximum of freedom.[60]

The readers of the *Princeton Review,* who were accustomed to thinking that doing one's moral duty was the definition of true freedom, could not have been any happier than Hall with this crippling surrender to convention. In these early essays, Hall was clearly struggling with the implications of taking romantic educational doctrines seriously, for he saw that doing so often required the postponement of adult standards of behavior until well into adolescence and presented the prospect that natural impulses would suggest unconventional—possibly dangerous—goals for human development.

The first area in which Hall seemed able to accept these possibilities was that of religious training, the stage on which his own struggle to maturity had been principally fought. Here he spoke from personal conviction when he declared for the child's right to hold immature religious beliefs undisturbed and to outgrow naturally an early belief for a more mature one. Hall's assurance that there was a natural impulse toward religious belief probably allowed him to trust nature in this area more easily than in others. To some extent, the recapitulation theory resolved the conflict which might arise between the ideal of self-realization for the child and the claims of society, for in realizing its own nature, the child followed the route taken by all mankind.[61] For the believer in a progressively evolving nature and society, however, this was not a final solution. Hall believed that the mature form of religious belief nature had intended was the figurative, psychologized Christianity of his own persuasion, a belief just then forcing its heretical way to recognition; and he still hesitated to state that conclusion explicitly in these articles.

The moral implications of this romantic naturalism also appeared to trouble Hall. Its unwillingness to coerce the child sometimes

60. "Will," pp. 322–24.

61. See Charles E. Strickland, "The Child and the Race: The Doctrines of Recapitulation and Culture Epochs in the Rise of the Child-Centered Ideal in American Educational Thought, 1875–1900," (Ph.D. diss., University of Wisconsin, 1963), pp. v and passim.

rubbed against his grain, as he recalled the hard struggle and discipline of his own childhood and youth.[62] When he saw that all one's natural impulses could not be harmoniously enchained in the traditional morality, he concluded that one must suppress them and obey traditional morality. Implicitly, however, he was exploring the possibility of trusting these native impulses to construct a new morality.

The ideas of postponing adulthood and of building from the child's natural impulses to a new and higher adult morality were clear desires of the European romantic educators which Parker, as well as Hall, could understand. For Hall, however, they took on new power and troubling implications, by a fact which he was the first of the American educators to take serious account of: nature was no longer the idealistic force of the romantics, it was biological, and the pattern of development it imprinted in living creatures was the product of biological evolution.

Hall first feared that evolutionary theories might require a thoroughly laissez faire theory of education, for some young American neurologists around 1880 were suggesting that predetermined, hereditary characteristics were so fixed that individual responsibility was destroyed.[63] Hall quickly realized, however, that a reliance on the evolutionary gifts of nature did not require such a position; indeed, that they assumed an alert environment to husband and shape them. The long period of dependency and teachableness in human development, Hall, like Spencer, saw as a sign of nature's intentions.[64] Such a conclusion was particularly necessary because of the enormous power biological evolution attributed to the sexual and aggressive impulses. Like the more orthodox American educators before him, Hall always took it for granted that impulses potentially dangerous to civilization should be directed, fenced, and shaped to presentable forms.

The prescription to follow nature, however, also implied a will-

62. As Hall put it some years later, "All that a child is called upon to do that he abhors is hurtful, except so far as it trains the will." GSH, "Health of School Children As Affected by School Buildings," 1892, p. 170.

63. See Charles Rosenberg, *The Trial of the Assassin Guiteau* (Chicago: University of Chicago Press, 1968), pp. 100–101.

64. *Aspects*, pp. 126–27. On Spencer's view, see his *Education: Intellectual, Moral and Physical* (London: G. Manwaring, 1861), pp. 101–68.

ingness to let these natural impulses assume some direction in de-creeing their ultimate disposition, and the ardent embrace of progress which evolutionary theories produced only made more explicit the desire to form on their basis new, more advanced modes of life and a more progressive morality. In the realm of educational practice, this meant not merely appealing to the child's nature while imposing on him the traditional curriculum and moral demands, but allowing the child's nature to help dictate the curriculum, its order of presentation, and the methods of teaching and discipline. This change in the source of educational practice inevitably involved a change in authority and eventually wrought, as Lawrence Cremin has remarked, a "Copernican" revolution in the classroom.[65] Al-though Hall avoided drawing these conclusions in the *Princeton Review,* he soon made them the center of his educational program, trusting that biological evolution would prove an adequate guide to the task.

In the flush of approval from the *Princeton Review* for his rather timid romanticism, and fervid approbation from teachers for his call to science and naturalism, Hall conceived of an original ap-proach to educational reform which would combine educational romanticism with biological evolution and scientific methods. The idea—to base education on a scientific study of child development— was an inevitable extension of the romantic decree to follow the child's nature in an age of evolutionary science, but Hall was prob-ably the first person, scientist or educator, to make the extension in any sustanied way.

The study of child development by scientists was just beginning when Hall urged his program of "child study." A number of Ger-mans had made systematic observations on child development in the early nineteenth century, and after Darwin's *Origin of Species,* the pace of investigation somewhat quickened until a careful study by a biologist in 1881, Wilhelm Preyer's *Mind of the Child,* caught the attention of the scientific community and stimulated wide inter-est in the possibilities of a scientific understanding of mental de-velopment in the child. All of this work consisted of observations

65. Lawrence Cremin, *The Transformation of the School* (New York: Alfred A. Knopf, 1961), p. 104.

of the first few years of life and was not directly tied to educational application.

Within the pedagogical tradition, another line of work was leading in the same direction. Herbart had called not only for a scientific psychology but a scientific pedagogy as well. In the hands of a number of disciples, particularly at the University of Jena, Herbartian educational ideas were rising to prominence at the time Hall was finishing his studies in Germany. The psychological science Herbart espoused was actually different from the chief ideas of his disciples who, like Hall, tended to read back evolutionary meanings into some of Herbart's ideas and give them a prominence absent in the master. Such, for example, was Hall's biological interpretation of Herbart's abstract catalog of the natural interests of the child, on which all education should be based, and the "culture-epoch" theory of his followers Rein and Ziller, who called for a sequence of study in each subject which followed the cultural evolution of the race or nation.[66]

A number of scattered attempts at child study had already been made by the early 1880s. As early as 1869 and 1874 German school officials had conducted questionnaire studies of their pupils' knowledge, and these studies would serve as models for Hall's own first questionnaire.[67] James Sully, the English psychologist who would become a major figure in the movement, published his first brief studies of imagination and language in the child in 1880 and 1884.[68] In 1880, Charles Francis Adams, who had supported Parker's efforts at Quincy, foreshadowed Hall by two years in urging the superintendents of the National Education Association to revise their pedagogy in accord with the natural laws of assimilation and development of the child's mind and to make education a science,

66. Compayré, *Herbart*, particularly, pp. 113–25; Charles E. Strickland, "The Child and the Race," pp. 33–59, 148–200; Harold B. Dunkel, *Herbart and Herbartianism: An Educational Ghost Story* (Chicago: University of Chicago Press, 1970), chaps. 12, 13, 14.
67. F. Bartholomai, "The Contents of Children's Minds on Entering School at the Age of Six Years," *Städtisches Jahrbuch, Berlin und seine Entwicklung* 4 (1870); K. Lange, "Der Vorstellungskreis unserer sechsjährigen Kleinen," *Allgemeine Schulzeitung,* 18 Oct 1879.
68. Eduard Claparède, *Experimental Pedagogy and the Psychology of the Child* (New York: Longmans Green, 1911), p. 16.

worthy of university study, by basing it on the study of the development of the mind.[69] In 1881, apparently without contact with Hall, the Boston secretary of the education section of the American Social Science Association published a circular on the observation of infants. Speaking for "some educators" who were roused by recent scientific studies of animal psychology to wonder why the mind of the child did not deserve equal attention, she asked mothers or other interested observers to record such facts as the infant's first attention to stimuli, crawling, walking, and speech.[70] Although the association discussed child psychology at its next meeting, nothing further came of the effort.[71] The ideas behind child study, therefore, were in the air. It required only a charismatic leader to find it a popular base of support and give it programmatic appeal.

Hall's first call for child study came in a speech to the superintendents of the NEA in the spring of 1882, where he proposed it as the core of a new profession of pedagogy. "It is the fundamental law of mental development, as well of action and assimilation, that must be made the basis of methods of teaching, topics chosen and their order."[72] Soon Hall urged that training in child study for normal school students would provide them with that larger enthusiasm and finer sympathy for their young charges which would perennially revitalize teaching practice.[73] Hall thought he had in child study a means for regularly achieving what theretofore only the exceptional personalities of the educational pioneers had been able to inspire—enthusiasm and sensitivity in their teachers.

The first fruit of Hall's joint venture in psychological science and educational reform was his pioneering empirical study of the child's mind, "The Contents of Children's Minds," begun in the fall of 1882 and published in the spring of 1883. His study was in large part, as he himself called it, a study of children's ignorance. "The

69. James Dale Hendricks, "The Child-Study Movement in American Education, 1880–1910: A Quest for Educational Reform through a Systematic Study of the Child," (Ph.D. diss., Indiana University, 1968), pp. 40–45.

70. Boston *Evening Transcript,* 19 Mar 1881, p. 10.

71. *Journal of Social Science* 13 (1881): 189–92; 15 (1882): 1–55.

72. GSH, "Chairs of Pedagogy in Our Higher Institutions of Learning," 1882, pp. 35–44.

73. GSH, "Educational Needs," 1883, p. 287; "New Departures in Education," 1885, p. 149.

problem first had in mind was strictly practical; viz., what may city children be assumed to know and have seen by their teachers when they enter school." On this question, Hall's approach was sharp and his results stunning. Except for a few questions, the general knowledge Hall asked of the children was of the kind far more accessible to children raised in the country rather than the city, and he thus turned up very high rates of ignorance. That knowledge of country life constituted "general" knowledge and that it formed a superior mental training to knowledge of city life were explicit premises Hall never doubted in the pervasive rural nostalgia of his day. Parents should take their children for visits to the countryside, Hall said, to improve their "intelligence."[74]

Hall's analysis of his data in terms of the kinds of responses given, the age, sex, ethnic background, and prior kindergarten training of his children also supported the latest innovations being sought by the educational disciples of Pestalozzi, Herbart, and Froebel: the need of object teaching; the tendency of the child to learn first the concepts most common in his immediate environment; the need of relating new knowledge to that already firmly acquired according to Herbart's "law of apperception"; and the effectiveness of kindergarten instruction.[75] Hall's study, therefore, was an affirmation, in the name of science, of the reform efforts of his day which hoped to adjust education to the child's nature. His format and conclusions, moreover, were directly geared to school instruction, so that his suggestions could be weighed and applied by the enterprising teacher. The study was thus an immediate success in reforming educational circles and was reprinted several times in the decades following.[76]

The pedagogical aspect of his study was not its only feature, for as Hall got into the work he found "other purposes more psychological" taking shape. Hall added some questions about the child's beliefs, imagery, understanding of right and wrong, and asked for drawings and stories, as well. His analysis of the responses yielded suggestive insights on the working of the child mind. Hall noted,

74. "Contents," 1883, pp. 250, 253–57.
75. Ibid., pp. 269–71.
76. In pamphlet form by E. L. Kellogg, New York, 1893; and by Hall in *PS* 1 (1891): 139–73, and *Aspects of Child Life and Education*, 1907, pp. 1–52.

for example, how children used words for their "rhyme, rhythm, alliteration, cadence" quite independently of their meaning; and that "the lower strata of conscience are dislike of dirt and fear."[77] Hall interpreted the child's fanciful religious ideas as

resultants in form and shading of the manifold deepest impression which what is within and what is without have together made upon the child's soul. . . . [They] represent many strata of intelligence up through which the mind is passing very rapidly and with quite radical transformations. Each stratum was once with but a little elaboration, or is now somewhere, the highest culture, relegated to and arrested in an earlier and earlier stage as civilization and educational methods advance.[78]

The content of the child's mind, therefore, was the product not simply of what he observed around him but also of the inherited impulses which developed in him in the same sequence as they had developed in the history of the race. The metaphor of Comte and the romantics linking the pattern of development of the individual to that of humanity had become, in the days of post-Darwinian biology, the law by which ontogeny recapitulates phylogeny, making the child mind and primitive cultures into caches of vestigial and arrested forms of life. Although it was later to dominate his conception of psychological science, Hall did not yet attempt to apply the theory much beyond the sphere of religious beliefs, and his psychological findings remained fragments of the larger pedagogical study.

Hall seemed to recognize that the value of child study to psychology would depend in large part on his developing reliable methods, for he exercised great care in obtaining his information. He drew up the questionnaire only after preliminary questioning of children, used four trained kindergarten teachers, and carefully supervised their administration of the test to obtain accurate and uniform data. He was also concerned that his two hundred returns were not sufficient to yield a true average and attempted to select the sample so as to exclude the extreme ranges of response. Though "deeply sensible of many sources of inaccuracy which may limit their value," Hall was encouraged by his results to advocate further scientific use of the method, particularly in subjecting "single con-

77. "Contents," 1883, pp. 250, 257–58, 266.
78. Ibid., p. 264.

cept groups" to more detailed study with larger numbers of subjects. Hall hoped to get results that were to some degree probable,
despite their being remote from "mathematic certainty" and to find
the essential, "characteristic and typical" points to test for. In his
later use of the questionnaire, Hall did not always hold himself to
these standards, but this first use of it, one of the first in scientific
psychology, was a worthy forerunner of the improved questionnaire
methods developed since.[79]

Hall's study of 1883 opened up possibilities for him in both
education and scientific psychology, but the scientific value of child
study was still unproved and its educational uses readily at hand.
The inquiries from teachers following the "Contents" study were
so numerous that Hall issued a pamphlet in 1883 to enlist them in
securing information on child nature. Hall asked teachers to record
the "exact language" or behavior of the child, together with whatever other specific information about the child they could gather on
one of a number of topics, such as play, friendship and affection, the
"instinct of justice" and truthfulness, pronunciation and use of
words. Requesting that the information come from direct observation, but if that was impossible, from questioning children, their
mothers, or nurses, Hall's scientific concern was clearly diluted by
the effort to secure a large number of data.[80]

Hall also launched a polemical effort to establish child study as a
movement of educational reform. His first pedagogical lectures in
Boston had placed him immediately on the elite National Council
of Education, and he had been named to the influential Committee
on Pedagogics chaired by William Torrey Harris, superintendent of
schools in St. Louis from 1868 to 1880, U. S. Commissioner of Education from 1889 to 1906, and Hall's old mentor in Hegelian phi-

79. "Contents," 1883, pp. 250–52, 270–72. The kindergarteners were loaned to
him by Mrs. Pauline Shaw, benefactress of the Boston kindergartens. For a positive evaluation by a phychologist of Hall's methods in this study, see Robert I.
Watson, *Psychology of the Child* (New York: John Wiley, 1959), p. 11. Hall's
method has recently been compared to the "methode clinique" of Jean Piaget by
a psychologist who replicated Hall's study and got quite similar results. John C.
McCullers, "The Contents of Children's Minds: A Partial Replication," MS.

80. GSH, *The Study of Children*, 1883, pp. 1–13. Miss Sara E. Wiltse, one
of Hall's kindergarteners, was again loaned by Mrs. Shaw to act as chief depository
and tabulator for the results submitted.

losophy.[81] Harris's sympathy for some of the romantic pedagogical innovations was balanced by his basic concern for the civilizing function of intellectual education. He was, on the whole, an intellectualist defender of the traditional system over which he presided.[82]

The interest Hall's work was creating led to a full committee report on "Pedagogy as a Science" at the 1884 meeting of the NEA, but Harris obviously hoped to contain the new movement within the traditional framework. He and his allies took umbrage at the implication of Hall's program that their whole careers had been spent on a chimera, for they had thought themselves following a "science of pedagogy" all along. Harris sought to ignore Hall's whole argument and merely reiterated the "correct" principles on which pedagogy should be based.[83] Discussion from the floor, however, was very critical of Harris's intellectualist emphasis, and at the NEA meeting the following year, Hall triumphantly heard Harris urge that educators join with the "distinguished specialists" who were conducting scientific pedagogical inquiry.[84]

That same year, 1885, Hall issued a popular manifesto on "New Departures in Education." Hall lyrically extolled "the soul and the body of the healthy young child . . . filled . . . with reverberations from a past more vast than science can explore." He placed the whole progress of education on the use of objective methods in studying child development. Such study would discover

the lines of strongest interest and curiosity in children during each of the main periods of immaturity, and in what order, directions and rapidity their capacities unfold and may be safely set to work, and how much.

Hall named as the goal of natural education, not the traditional

81. *PNEA*, 1884, pp. 59, 62.
82. Whether Hall's professional opposition to Harris held underneath an intense ambivalent attachment, as was the case in his relations with William James and George Morris (discussed below, chaps. 8, 10, and 13), is not clear from the evidence. After their acquaintance in St. Louis, the meager correspondence I have found suggests a more formal manner and greater distance between them than existed with the others. Harris was nine years older than Hall and that may have made the difference. Harris to GSH, 28 Feb 1902, CUP, also suggests that Harris treated Hall with careful respect and deference.
83. *PNEA*, 1884, pp. 42–55.
84. Ibid., pp. 56–57; *PNEA*, 1885, pp. 91–96, 492–505.

moral character but the development of man, man raised to a new level of evolutionary progress.[85]

After this initial flurry, however, Hall did not follow up his opening. In the next several years he did not appear at NEA meetings, many of which were distant from the East Coast, and the subject was dropped from the agenda. In popular articles after 1885, Hall mentioned the promise of child study, but did not try to make it the spearhead of a movement of educational reform.[86]

His most popular exposition of the meaning of natural education during these years was curiously inconsistent with his child study premises. Hall narrated clearly and vividly how two brothers, over a period of about nine years, made a pile of sand at their summer cottage into a model city, and in the course of their work, developed an appropriate social morality. This is, Hall declared, "education according to nature. . . . All the power of motive arising from a large surface of interest is here turned on to the smallest part. . . . The unity . . . is, as it always is, ideal." But the ideals that had stimulated the boys, Hall recognized, were "their conceptions of adult life," not the uniquely childish ideals from a font of nature far deeper than present culture which his theory called for.[87] Hall was apparently not yet ready to systematically center his educational thinking on his child study doctrine.

Moreover, he was having real difficulty putting his scientific program into practice. He eventually published only two brief articles from the child study data that amassed from his call to teachers in 1883—the first, on the "collecting instinct," appearing only as a note to the *Nation*.[88] Neither study made a pretense of the careful method he had attempted in "Contents"; in the second, on children's lies, he found the accuracy of the returns so uneven, he could not even tabulate the results numerically. The most striking char-

85. GSH, "New Departures," 1885, pp. 145, 147–48, 150.

86. GSH, "Overpressure in Schools," 1885, pp. 338–39; Introduction to Paul Radestock, *Habit and Its Importance in Education,* trans. F. A. Caspari (Boston: D. C. Heath, 1886). Hall also arranged for a condensed edition of Preyer's *Mind of the Child* and wrote an introduction to the first volume, *The Senses and the Will,* trans. H. W. Brown (New York: D. Appleton, 1888).

87. "The Story of a Sand Pile," 1888, pp. 690–96.

88. GSH, "A Study of Children's Collections," 1885, p. 190; "Children's Lies," 1890, pp. 59–70.

acteristic of both studies was their subjects, for in both cases, it is difficult to find any except personal reasons for Hall's having chosen these topics from among the wide range of information he received.

Hall's interest in the "collecting instinct" reflected his own omniverous collecting as a child and his difficulties with collecting data for child study. On this instinct, Hall stated, "the induction and specialization of natural science rests; . . . even the gathering of the above data about this instinct rest upon it." Yet collecting values and scientific values may be directly opposed, Hall counseled, for data cannot just be collected mechanically but must be thought through and meaningfully organized.

It is such hard work to think, and there are so many proxies and simulacra of thought that deceive even well-trained men—it is so much easier to get ready to think, as the miser hoards in order to get ready to live—that the way of true science is indeed straight and narrow.[89]

Hall was apparently stymied by the chaos of material he had collected. As he told a teachers' meeting, child study thus far had produced more "new problems for further research" than "answers agreed upon"; the work was one "not of years, but of decades."[90]

Hall's efforts to launch the child study movement in the early 1880s also came to rest after 1885 on his pursuit of an academic career in science. Hall had been offered several chances to make pedagogy his principal occupation. After his second series of pedagogy lectures at Harvard, President Eliot asked Hall to submit a plan for a university department of pedagogy designed specifically for teachers. Hall drew up a program of lectures, practice teaching under observation, library facilities for pedagogical literature, and eventually, an experimental school, a summer course, and a museum. Hall was reluctant, however, to enter into such work as his principal occupation, and he strongly discouraged Eliot's obvious desire to have him participate, without flatly refusing.[91] Though far from insensitive to the popular success he could achieve in the field, Hall

89. GSH, "Collections," 1885.
90. GSH, "Pedagogical Inquiry," 1885, pp. 507, 510.
91. GSH to Eliot, 10 Apr 1882, Eliot Papers. By the fall of 1882 Hall also had in hand an offer to become a supervisor of schools in Boston, a position he regarded as "not unattractive as a field of practical psychology." GSH to D. C. Gilman, 18 [Mar] 1882, GP.

much preferred a career in scientific psychology. As he wrote Norton, "Just as soon as I fully see my way clearly to a livelihood in [psychology] the educational line of study will be speedily subordinated to it, as it is only one facet of *applied psychology*."[92] By 1883, when he sent out his child study circular, Hall already had one foot through the gate of mecca—the Johns Hopkins University. By 1885, when he abandoned the movement, he held a permanent and prestigious appointment there in psychology. While Hall turned to other pursuits, the idea of child study continued to take hold. When he returned to the movement in the 1890s, it and he were ready to attempt a full-scale reorientation of education toward the natural pattern of development of the child.

92. GSH to Norton, 2 June 1883, Autograph Collection, History Section, Payne Whitney Psychiatric Clinic, New York City.

BALTIMORE'S "RICHEST VIRGIN SOIL"

Before Hall had finished his first series of pedagogy lectures in Boston, at the beginning of March 1881, President Gilman offered him a chance to give a series of lectures at Johns Hopkins under a program similar to the Harvard series.[1] News of the success of Hall's lectures, the easing of financial pressures at the university, and a laudatory letter to Gilman from Charles Norton in February 1881 finally tipped the scale in Hall's favor.[2] Hall proposed to lecture on either contemporary German philosophy or psychology, and Gilman himself preferred psychology to pedagogy. The ten lectures on the new psychology were given in January 1882.[3]

Gilman was unable to attend because of illness, but Ira Remsen, the professor of chemistry, wrote him that the lectures were very successful and that he was "much pleased with them." Of Hall personally, he wrote, "There is a good deal in that man, it seems to me. I have seen him in private frequently, and have been much impressed by his clear-headedness."[4] Hall was described by Norton

1. GSH to Gilman, 5 Mar [1881], GP; GSH, *EP*, 2:242.
2. Norton to Gilman, 14 Feb 1881, GP.
3. GSH to Gilman, 5 Mar [1881], 24 Mar 1881, GP. According to an advance announcement of the lectures, Hall planned to discuss "the general characteristics of sensations, memory, genesis of the knowledge of time and space, concepts, classifications of psychic activities, nature and degrees of certainty, morbid psychology, development of intelligence in children, with general psychophysical conclusions." *Johns Hopkins Circulars* 1:160.
4. Ira Remsen to Gilman, 19 Jan 1882, GP.

at this period as a man of "singularly modest and reserved nature,"[5] an impression Gilman certainly would not have received from Hall's persistent letters of application. Hall's ambition, however, lay at some distance beneath a reserved but agreeable exterior. Only in public speaking and occasionally in personal intercourse did the warmth and forcefulness of his nature show through, impressing and inspiring his listeners. In March 1882, Hall was offered a three-year appointment to the philosophy department as lecturer in psychology and pedagogics, under the arrangement that he would teach half the year, during the spring term.[6]

The philosophy department at Johns Hopkins to which Hall was appointed consisted of two other part-time lecturers: Hall's old friend and idol, George S. Morris, and Charles S. Peirce, the philosopher and physicist friend of James, whose work Hall had already come to admire. No full professor in philosophy had yet been appointed, for Gilman and the trustees had failed to find a man of both eminence and safe religious views.[7]

Hall's position at Hopkins was thus quite insecure. All three of the young philosophers were anxious for a permanent appointment.[8] In the summer of 1883, after Hall's first half-year of teaching, Gilman was evidently still uncommitted to any one of his younger men and still looking for a prominent philosopher. Before he went abroad that summer he asked Hall to recommend the names of promising European philosophers and psychologists he might see. Hall obliged and, recognizing the instability of his position, implied that he in turn was trying to establish some connection with Cornell.[9]

In late January 1884, without prior notice, Gilman and the executive committee decided to drop Peirce at the end of the term. Gilman appears to have recognized Peirce's intellectual power and the importance of his philosophical work, but his decision was ap-

5. Norton to Gilman, 14 Feb 1881, GP.
6. GSH to Gilman, 18 Mar 1882, GP.
7. Hawkins, *Pioneer,* pp. 187–206. The professorship was offered to William James, preeminent among the younger American philosophers, but after wavering to and fro for almost two years, James declined the offer in favor of Cambridge. Cope, "James's Correspondence with Gilman," pp. 613–22.
8. Hawkins, *Pioneer,* p. 192; G. S. Morris to Gilman, 24 May 1883, GP.
9. GSH to Gilman, 29 May 1883, GP.

parently based on Peirce's personal characteristics.[10] Gilman then proceeded to choose between Hall and Morris according to the policy he had followed in other departments of appointing only one full professor. At the end of February, Hall wrote Gilman that he was dissatisfied with the part-time arrangement, that he had certain unspecified offers to teach elsewhere, and that he wished to know whether he could leave before the end of his contract if the contingency arose.[11] Such a propitiously timed letter undoubtedly confirmed the necessity of an immediate decision on the professorship. In April 1884, Gilman announced Hall's appointment as full professor of psychology and pedagogy.[12]

Hall thus achieved, at the age of forty, his first secure professional position. In Baltimore, he visibly expanded to his new eminence. The father now of two small children, Hall bought a substantial house with the ample salary of $4,000 the Hopkins professorship carried. Highly conscious of the social climate of this southern town, he attempted to enter into the life of the local gentry and even rode to hounds in full regalia.[13] When Hall appeared at the NEA the summer of his appointment, he swelled with pride at his now distinguished status.[14] Hall's appointment marked for him, as well as his subject of scientific psychology, a coming of age.

10. Hawkins, *Pioneer*. pp. 195–96; Jackson I. Cope and Max H. Fisch, "Peirce at The Johns Hopkins University," in Philip P. Wiener and Frederic H. Young, eds., *Studies in the Philosophy of Charles Sanders Peirce* (Cambridge: Harvard University Press, 1952), pp. 306–9. Cope and Fisch have suggested that Simon Newcomb, head of the Naval Observatory in Washington and part-time member of the Hopkins faculty, brought to Gilman's attention the derogatory personal information about Peirce which resulted in his sudden dismissal. Newcomb apparently acted on information from another person who subsequently saw Gilman directly. Simon Newcomb to Gilman, 22 Dec 1883, GP: "I have . . . taken occasion to inquire diligently of my informant, and am by him assured that every thing I had said was fully justified. Furthermore, he deemed it part of the obligation of friendship to make known to you the exact state of the case, and would avail himself of the first opportunity to do so." Who this second responsible party was has not been determined.
11. GSH to Gilman, 29 Feb 1884, Alumni Records Office, Johns Hopkins University.
12. *Johns Hopkins Circulars* 3:95.
13. *LCP*, pp. 244–46, 259; Dr. Robert G. Hall, interview, 17–20 May 1961. Robert Granville Hall was born 7 February 1881; Julia Fisher Hall was born 30 May 1882. Wilson, *GSH*, pp. 80, 108.
14. *PNEA*, 1885, pp. 492–503.

Hall's appointment at Hopkins clearly owed itself to the scientific character of his subject and the accommodating character of his advocacy. Hall's psychology, unlike Morris's speculative idealism, was in accord with the scientific emphasis of the university. Gilman was himself a geographer and thought of natural science as the prototype of all advanced university work.[15] Hall also offered the possibility of forming connections between the university and the pending medical school. James had originally recommended Hall as fitted to form "a connecting link" between the two institutions, and psychopathology had become one of Hall's chief interests.[16] The quality of Hall's critical intelligence, his wide knowledge of European science, and rich store of eclectic ideas must have made him appear as a man of great promise in an emerging science.[17] Morris, on the other hand, was not interested in science or the philosophy of science. Although he was a man of high intelligence and demonstrated intellectual accomplishment, neither Gilman nor his colleagues were equipped to appreciate the character of his work.[18]

Added to the scientific factor in Hall's favor was the less tangible one of personality. Hall was an ambitious man who was also ambitious for his subject. Morris, on the other hand, was a man of genuinely quiet and modest temper. Gilman wrote in 1882 that he liked Morris "personally very much . . . but he is not quite forcible enough to hold his own in face of Sylvester, Peirce [*sic*], Gildersleeve and other men among us who are strong and pronounced.

15. *LCP*, p. 226; Hawkins, *Pioneer*, pp. 65, 150–51; A. L. Hammond, "Brief History of the Department of Philosophy, 1876–1938," p. 8, Lanier Room, Johns Hopkins University Library; Frank M. Albrecht, "The New Psychology in America, 1880–1895," (Ph.D. diss., Johns Hopkins University, 1960), pp. 102–19. Hall's ability to include the history of philosophy under the mantle of scientific psychology also recommended him. In a letter to Gilman about Hall's proposed plans for psychology written sometime before 31 Mar 1884, GP, a member of the board of trustees, J. C. Thomas wrote: "I believe the University can do a wise work in thus emphasizing both branches of psychological work [experimental and historical] and making the course fit in with our existent faculties."

16. Wm. James to Gilman, 18 July 1880, in Cope, "James's Correspondence with Gilman," p. 624.

17. Hall's study "The Contents of Children's Minds," 1883, was the only significant psychological work he had yet produced, and it is doubtful that Gilman or other psychologists immediately recognized the importance of it.

18. Wenley, *G. S. Morris*, pp. 147–52; Hammond, "Brief History, Dept. of Philosophy," pp. 5–8; Hawkins, *Pioneer*, pp. 198–99.

He retires into his shell."[19] When Morris visited him one day, Gilman noticed that he was in "fine spirits as to the progress of his work this year," chiefly it would seem, due to Hall. He was full of his and Hall's plans for the department, his and Hall's similar backgrounds, his and Hall's cordial relations.[20] Compared to Morris, Hall must have appeared to Gilman the more dominating and original force in the department.

Most important, Hall was able to apply his force where Gilman felt the university needed it most—in establishing good feeling with the community at large. Hall's work in education was a major asset. It was at Gilman's urging, rather than his own desire, Hall later said, that pedagogy was included in his appointment.[21] In announcing Hall's appointment, Gilman emphasized the popularity and importance of his pedagogical work.[22] Hall was, moreover, willing to allay religious fears. Unlike Morris, Hall could offer a mutually supporting reconciliation between science and religion. Peirce himself testified to the importance of this consideration when he tried to win his job back by offering to effect a "modus vivendi" between science, philosophy, and religion.[23]

From the time Hall first wrote President Gilman and promised to follow "strictly historical methods" in his work, Hall had been conscious of the need to defend himself against any imputation of materialism or irreligion.[24] Before he was appointed to lecture on psychology at Johns Hopkins, he told Gilman how amiable his views were toward religion:

I am as far as *possible* from materialism in every form. My physiological studies of the nervous system bring me incessantly before the question of the identity of thought and matter and I can only say that my deepest private feeling . . . is that materialism is simply want of education. As to my religious sentiments, I am a graduate in divinity, and without agreeing entirely with all I hear, am in the habit of church-going, and indeed am still a nominal church member I believe. I do not think it is possible for any one to become deeply interested in philosophy without a devout respect

19. Hawkins, *Pioneer*, p. 199.
20. Gilman Diary, "1882–1887 to California & Alaska," 31 Jan 1883, GP.
21. *LCP*, p. 226.
22. *Johns Hopkins Circulars* 3:95.
23. Hawkins, *Pioneer*, p. 196.
24. GSH to Gilman, 31 July 1876, GP.

for religion growing more profound at every step. In fact this seems to me the taproot of all deep interest in philosophy whatever direction it may take. . . .[25]

Hall's defense rested on his denial of outright materialism, his practical willingness to abide by the formal requirements of organized religion, and the religious sentiments grounding his interest in philosophy.

The terms of the reconciliation Hall finally proposed were made known in his lecture on "The New Psychology," his inaugural lecture as professor of psychology delivered in October 1884. The importance of the religious consideration in his appointment can be gauged by the fact that Hall made this one of the principal themes of his lecture and then published it in the *Andover Review,* a journal of the liberal movement in New England theology.[26]

Outlining his conception of the field, Hall was careful to deny that scientific psychology was necessarily materialistic. Although the theory of reflex action provided a tentative, simple model of how the brain and mind work, this did not justify philosophical materialism. Hall had come to see "the logical impossibility of every purely materialistic theory of knowledge." Moreover, even if mechanical explanation were carried to its furthest limits,

the sense of utter incommensurability between these objective relations and the closer, more intimate consciousness of such acts and states would be sufficient as a corrective of materialism and as a positive justification of an idealistic view of the world.

Mechanism, presumably, was not the only view of the world which experience legitimately yielded.[27]

Hall's principal means of adding a spiritual dimension to the conceptions of scientific psychology was his fusion of natural science and religious sentiments. The phenomenon of instinct, Hall commented, ought not to be described teleologically, implying a con-

25. GSH to Gilman, 5 Jan [1881], GP. Hall was apparently stating his views in answer to a specific inquiry from Gilman. It may have been some years since Hall was "in the habit of church-going." [A. B. Hall to GSH, Christmas 1877], fragment, HP.

26. GSH, "The New Psychology," 1885, pp. 120–35, 239–48; Daniel Day Williams, *The Andover Liberals* (New York: King's Crown Press, 1941), pp. 28–31.

27. "New Psychology," 1885, pp. 124–26.

scious purpose or agent. On the other hand, just such a teleological description gives religious satisfaction and answers the deep need for design and purpose. Thus, he concluded, instinct shows us the wisdom on which we can rest and bestow our trust.[28]

In such a manner, the new psychology would rescue the "mythopoeic faculties" from their present bondage to crass theories, be they crass materialisms or crass religious dogmas, and open the way for deeper expressions of the religious sentiments. "Deeper psychologic insights," Hall insisted, "are to effect a complete atonement between modern culture and religious sentiments and verities." Hall ended his lecture lyrically:

The new psychology, which brings simply a new method and a new standpoint to philosophy, is I believe Christian to its root and centre; and its final mission in the world is not merely to trace petty harmonies and small adjustments between science and religion, but to flood and transfuse the new and vaster conceptions of the universe and of man's place in it . . . with the old Scriptural sense of unity, rationality, and love beneath and above all, with all its wide consequences.

The discoveries of psychology would justify man's religious sense of the "unity, rationality and love" undergirding existence. Hall restored the perspective and conclusions of idealism as a kind of poetic extension of the scientific world-view.[29]

Since liberal religious views would arise naturally from the scientific view of the world, Hall argued that there was no need to rudely unsettle religious opinion. In teaching philosophy in college, the professor must remember that the secret of education was adaptation. Truth must be given in a form which naturally expands with the growth of the mind, opening new meanings as the mind develops. Under the influence of science, the older, orthodox concepts would presumably change imperceptibly into the newer naturalistic faiths. The long struggle with doubt he himself had gone through only increased the danger of losing one's bearing and one's faith. Hall was outspoken about the practical considerations that sup-

28. Ibid., pp. 121–23.
29. Ibid., pp. 134, 247–48. Josiah Royce, in *Lectures on Modern Idealism* (New Haven: Yale University Press, 1919), pp. 236–37, pointed out that Hall took the idealist position when he said that the real world conformed to the image which practical and aesthetic values dictated.

ported such a program. "The average adolescent of to-day needs a basis for his morality in belief," he contended. The stability of character depends on the stability of religious convictions.[30]

The same standard of judgment guided Hall's strenuous objection to the teaching of idealistic philosophies, particularly the theory of knowledge, to college students. Hall's own experience of disillusion with this philosophic tradition was evident in the elaborate argument he offered. He sent questionnaires to between three and four hundred college seniors on their experience in college philosophy. Since more than four-fifths of those who replied appeared to have gone through some kind of adolescent crisis of belief, Hall concluded that the theory of knowledge would only "aggravate instead of . . . moderate the natural fever of eclaircissement." Teachers must realize, Hall said, that "there are problems it is simply immoral for individual minds to open." By eschewing these studies, Hall hoped to prevent the "surrender to the ideal" by which he himself had been threatened.[31]

Hall was critical of idealism not only on grounds of practicality. Like all other philosophical systems of the past, it did not offer living truth, but only a datum of cultures now dead. Philosophy was "but a more elaborate organization" of the customs and myths that constituted the psychological expression of a people and was to be studied, like these more primitive forms, as part of a natural history of mind. Although Hall claimed that this constituted merely one legitimate standpoint from which to regard the history of philosophy, and that psychology was not all of philosophy, he was in effect reducing philosophy, like religion, to the level of poetic truth.[32]

Hall combined imperfectly two different approaches in his reconciliation of science with religion and philosophy. On the one hand, he argued that religious and philosophical concepts constituted a kind of mythical truth which reflected psychological and moral needs and which should not be confused with the more austere concepts of science. On the other hand, he believed that scientific concepts generated, through a kind of poetic extension, these same religious truths. Why "mythopoeic" insights should be tied to the

30. "New Psychology," 1885, p. 247.
31. Ibid., pp. 240–43.
32. Ibid., pp. 129–30.

mechanical concepts of natural science was a question Hall never asked. Hall's first position, in its attempt to distinguish and separate the grounds of religious belief and scientific knowledge, was typical of the more sophisticated efforts of his academic contemporaries to deal with the problem. His second position was characteristic of the popular mechanical philosophies that would ease the way for the general acceptance of naturalistic doctrines of evolution. Hall characteristically combined them into one synthetic viewpoint.

Hall's grand design for infusing modern science with religious sentiments made a strong impression on President Gilman. Several months later in his annual commemoration day speech, an event celebrating the university's relationship with the town, Gilman described how each department contributed to the general welfare. When he came to psychology, he stressed its innocent relations with religion and quoted the finale of Hall's inaugural lecture. These views, Gilman asserted, confirmed his own belief that philosophy will stand firm on God, Soul, and Immortality and confirm the Gospel.[33] Neither Hall nor Gilman nor their audiences could have agreed on the meaning of those four words; it was apparently sufficient that they agree to use them.

Certainly, a large element of calculation entered into Hall's religious position. Hall had recognized since his days at Antioch that to teach philosophy in the conservative American environment, a young man must "bring his mind into some sort of platonising conformity with the milder forms of orthodoxy."[34] His calculation was probably exerted in the interest of his science as well as his own career. The conscious opportunism in Hall's position overlay, however, a store of genuine belief. Hall's passion for a unified view of human experience made him genuinely concerned to find scientific confirmation of his feeling for the "unity, rationality and love beneath and above all." This had been the aim of his philosophizing since the days when he had pored over Tennyson and it was to be so until his death. For the remainder of his life, Hall argued that science offered a truly religious world-view, of greater weight than

33. *Johns Hopkins Circulars* 4:43–49. Hall claimed, however, that the conservative President James McCosh of Princeton University severely criticized his appointment and his religious views. GSH, "Reminiscence," 1917, p. 299.

34. GSH, "Philosophy in the U. S.," 1879, p. 91.

philosophic and religious myths tied to merely personal or historic speculation. He consistently valued the practical strengths of traditional religion and treated the religious beliefs of others with circumspection. Hall thus maintained his reconciliationist stand long after it won him his Hopkins appointment and into the more secular years of the twentieth century when it became unfashionable. Hall did want to keep science separate from religion and philosophy for the purposes of science; for religious and philosophic purposes, however, he wanted to make them mutually reinforcing.[35]

Hall's professorship was the first chair in the new psychology in the country, and it gave the subject important recognition. It had, however, unfortunate consequences for philosophy at Johns Hopkins, for Hall protected his lone eminence in the department with great avidity. In this first institutional position in which he was not cast as a student and subordinate, he showed the disturbing personal qualities which were often to mar his career thereafter. The element of disguise and the undercurrent of passion which marked Hall's synthetic intellectual constructions were also noticeable in his personal relations, particularly in situations involving conflict and competition.

The year after Hall's appointment, with Morris planning to assume a full-time professorship at Michigan and Hall evidently entirely occupied with psychology, Gilman began looking for a man to fill a subordinate or coordinate chair in ethics.[36] Hall proved little help to him in his search. A transitional appointment was made to assure instruction in ethics for the undergraduates, but a philosophical professor was never found during Hall's tenure. Hall

35. Hawkins, *Pioneer*, pp. 187–206, writing from the point of view of the development of Johns Hopkins University, and Cope and Fisch, "Peirce at Johns Hopkins," pp. 284–308, writing from the standpoint of Peirce's career, have both portrayed Hall as a "promoter" whose religious views were a disguise for opportunism. Albrecht, "The New Psychology in America," pp. 102–19, on the other hand, writing from the viewpoint of the development of experimental psychology, has pictured Hall's motives as justifiable opportunism in the interest of science, joined by "a tendency to get carried away by his own rhetoric." In the light of a fuller account of Hall's life and thought, both these accounts appear to oversimplify his motives and ideas.

36. *Annual Report of the President of Johns Hopkins University, 1883–84* (Baltimore, 1884), p. 9 (hereafter cited as *Ann. Rep. Pres. Hopk.*); Hawkins, *Pioneer*, p. 201.

appeared to object to everyone Gilman suggested except those whom there was little likelihood of securing.[37]

Although Morris had already assumed his chair at Michigan, Gilman considered him for the post in August 1885. Hall's response to this prospect was entirely negative:

I sincerely hope there is something better than a light that is so *dry* and am very sure there is. . . . My own current and very deep conviction about Prof. Morris is that philosophically he represents just what ought not to be and never can be established and that he never can touch our best students.[38]

Morris, of course, was steeped in the philosophical idealism and theory of knowledge that Hall found so dangerous.

One would think, however, Hall might manage more consideration for someone who had been his friend since his days at Union Seminary, who had been his first hero in philosophy, and who had helped him at a critical stage of his own career. Indeed, Morris's enthusiasm over their joint efforts at Hopkins suggested that their acquaintanceship had ripened into warm friendship. For the brief period in which their terms in Baltimore overlapped, Hall and Morris frequented the same boardinghouse, where they had many conversations together and where Hall admired Morris's musical ability.[39] Hall wrote when he objected to Morris's appointment that he had been "outwardly" in very "friendly relations" with him.[40]

Outwardly, in fact, Hall had even assented to Morris's philosophical position. Hall told Morris that he completely agreed with his lecture "Philosophy and Christianity," an expression of Morris's theistic idealism. After hearing one of Hall's psychology lectures a few days later, Gilman noted in obvious amazement, "He told G. S. M. he was in complete accord with his last lecture."[41] Hall's "complete" agreement, of course, had been figurative. In his autobiography, Hall remarked that like his mother, he shrunk all his

37. GSH to Gilman, 9 July, 3 Aug 1884, Alumni Records Office, Johns Hopkins University; GSH to Gilman, 13 Aug 1885; 28 Aug [1885]; 6 Jan 1887, GP.

38. GSH to Gilman, 28 Aug [1885], GP.

39. John C. French, *A History of the University Founded by Johns Hopkins* (Baltimore: Johns Hopkins Press, 1946), pp. 77–78; Wenley, *G. S. Morris,* p. 153.

40. GSH to Gilman, 28 Aug [1885], GP.

41. Gilman Diary, "1882–1887 to California & Alaska," 31 Jan, 3 Feb 1883, GP.

life from open quarrels, or even disagreements, with people.[42] In a later discussion of feelings of pity and sympathy in adolescents, Hall revealingly described how that feeling can become "an extreme reluctance to dissent from the opinions or purposes of others, especially adults." Hall told vividly how such an adolescent could make

> long statements of religious views, purposes and intentions . . . which are held and perhaps actively assented to and helped along in a way which sometimes causes entire misapprehension by the adult; or they are mistaken as promises where none were intended. [In doing this, he] effaces himself to a degree that he finds an object of astonishment afterward.

Sometimes, Hall went on, this behavior is based on a feeling

> that makes any shade of disagreement seem a form of hardihood that is too much of a strain upon the callow character. . . . With Rousseau, there seems to have been a spice of conscious flattery in this sensitiveness. . . . Some carry their self-abnegation so far that divining by a rapport that seems almost mystic, the lines of tastes and likes they develop almost a passion for saying only what ministers to these.[43]

Hall could hardly have described better the kind of passionate acquiescence, with its underlayer of fear and propitiatory retreat, which he displayed toward Morris at Johns Hopkins and which also emerged in his relations with James and his colleagues at Clark. What he did not describe was the pervasive hostility he must have sensed in those around him to occasion such fear and appeasement and the level of hostility within himself that this verbal surrender disguised. Behind his deceptive relationship with Morris, Hall engineered his final defeat at Johns Hopkins.

Hall also helped to drive away from Hopkins two of the department's strongest students, James McKeen Cattell and John Dewey. Both young men had been at Hopkins when Hall began the first term of his lectureship in January 1883. Cattell that year held the department's single fellowship and was beginning, substantially on his own, the series of experiments on the measurement of simple mental processes which would reorient American psychology and set a new standard of experimental competence. When, at the end of the year, his fellowship was not renewed but was given instead to

42. *LCP,* p. 86.
43. GSH, *Adol,* 2:374–75.

Dewey, he left Hopkins to continue his work under Wundt at Leip-zig.[44] Dewey may have told Hall of his plan to write a psychology text and during his fellowship year, worked with Morris and Hall.[45] At the end of the year, he apparently wished to stay in the depart-ment, but because of Hall's opposition, his fellowship, too, was not renewed. As Cattell wrote his parents,

> Dr. Hall has not acted honorably towards me. When I was at Baltimore he praised me highly, said there was no one he would so gladly see holding the fellowship, but unfortunately, he had nothing to say in the matter, and Dewey was a great favorite of Prof. Morris's and Pres. Gilman's. He added he hoped the university authorities would grant him an assistant, and if so he knew no one so well fitted for the post as me. Pres. Gilman showed me Dr. Hall's recommendation for the fellowship. Dewey stood first and I fourth. Yet Dr. Hall always spoke to me rather slightingly of Dewey, and told me this year he was compelled to drop him. Dewey had handed in his applica-tion for renewal of the fellowship, but at Pres. Gilman's advice withdrew it.[46]

A few years later when Gilman suggested to Hall that Dewey or James Mark Baldwin return to the department to handle under-graduate instruction in philosophy, Hall declared them not compe-tent for the job.[47]

The best that can be said for Hall in this affair is that still insecure in his position and driven to appease all around him, he praised Cattell when with Cattell and agreed to Dewey's superiority when with Morris and Gilman, even though he secretly had come to doubt Dewey's merit because of his Hegelian philosophical stance. The worst that can be said is that at a time when he himself had not yet produced very much in his field, he felt safer without strong in-tellectual challengers around him and set about to eliminate them. As a result, when Hall left Johns Hopkins a few years later for even richer virgin soil, he left behind a very weak philosophy department and no psychology department at all.[48] American psychology and

44. Forthcoming DAB Supp., s.v. "James McKeen Cattell."
45. Hall wrote James, 8 May [1883], JP, that "my best man came to me with a plan to write an undergraduate text-book and I rather encouraged him to do so. . . . I think he could do it."
46. J. M. Cattell to his parents, 27 Oct [1884], CP.
47. GSH to Gilman, 6 Jan 1887, GP.
48. Hawkins, *Pioneer,* pp. 203–7.

philosophy as a whole did not suffer, however, for in the fast-growing institutional network of academia, Cattell, Morris, and Dewey had other opportunities available, and Hall transplanted the Hopkins psychology department elsewhere. This first revelation of Hall's interpersonal failings was privy to the people concerned, and Hall remained, in public, for a time longer, the emblem of psychology's rising scientific star.

9   HALL'S NEW PSYCHOLOGY

While Hall was testing the need of the educational market for his scientific services and establishing himself at Johns Hopkins University, he was also engaged in a serious attempt to work out viable theoretical bases for the new psychology. Hall's first problem was the very nature of the subject itself, for his adoption of natural science in Germany had not entirely dispelled the philosophical purposes and epistemological theories he had brought to psychology. In his book of essays published in 1881, he reprinted unchanged his essays on Hegel and on the muscular perception of space.[1] When William T. Harris, newly arrived in Cambridge, conducted a seminar on Hegel during Hall's first year back from Germany, Hall participated to the very end, unlike James and the other Cambridge members.[2] He was still thinking in terms of a simple mechanical model of psychophysiological processes that would allow him to find the elementary unity of consciousness bridging mind and the material world. When he undertook a study in the laboratory of Henry Bowditch of one class of optical illusions of motion, he thought he may have come "very near attaining the *quale* of a real, pure sensation."[3]

1. *Aspects,* pp. 153–74, 208–36.
2. Perry, *William James,* 1: 738; Max H. Fisch, "Philosophical Clubs in Cambridge and Boston," *Coranto* 2 (Fall 1964): 13–15.
3. GSH and H. P. Bowditch, "Optical Illusions of Motion," 1882, p. 301.

Hall was first led to a more sophisticated view of mental function by his investigation of hypnosis. He had been introduced to the subject in Germany by popular demonstrators claiming spiritualist powers. When Professor Rudolf Heidenhain of Breslau gave a scientific demonstration of hypnosis to counteract the influence of the popular mesmerizers, Hall went there to observe his experiments and published a report of his trip in *Mind*.[4]

Hall decided that the cause of the hypnotic state was a focusing of consciousness or imagination. He came to that conclusion reluctantly, however, for it seemed to place hypnosis outside the sphere of reflex processes which Hall thought of as the basis of scientific explanation in psychology. "If the cause of these states and phenomena is essentially psychic," Hall said, "the prospect of obtaining exact scientific explanations of these phenomena seems indefinitely postponed." Still, he was convinced that physiological psychology could throw much light on the subject and that "the secrets of the soul are somehow bound up in those of the nervous system."[5] On his tour of Europe en route home, he made a point of attending the demonstrations of hypnosis by J. M. Charcot in Paris and Hippolyte Bernheim in Nancy, although he probably stopped only for a very brief period of time at each place.[6]

A year after he returned to the United States, in the fall of 1881, he began further studies of hypnotism. He used Bowditch's laboratory to test a frequently hypnotized subject who was then appearing in Boston, and a year and a half later, evidently after much further reflection, published the results in *Mind* under the title "Reaction-Time and Attention in the Hypnotic State." Hall conceived his experiment as a test of the theory that hypnosis was a product of the "concentration of Attention."[7] In taking this position, and in stressing the similarity of hypnotic "concentration of Attention" with other normal and abnormal "concentrative" psychic phenomena, Hall was aligning himself with investigators from Braid to Bern-

4. GSH, "Recent Researches in Hypnotism," 1881, pp. 98–104, reprinted in *Aspects*, pp. 134–44.
5. *Aspects*, pp. 141–42, 144.
6. *LCP*, p. 216.
7. GSH, "Reaction-Time," 1883, pp. 4, 10–11.

heim who urged the psychological and normal character of hypnotic trance.[8]

Hall reasoned ingeniously that if the hypnotic state is one of intensified attention, and if the focusing of attention reduces reaction times—as the new psychologists believed—then a subject under hypnosis should register reaction times distinctly faster than those for the normal state. Hall obtained positive results which he took as tentative support of his thesis.[9]

The theory that hypnosis was best described as a "tonic cramp of the attention" seemed to account for many psychological phenomena of hypnosis, Hall thought, as well as for the meager physiological data available. On the molecular aspects of hypnotic cerebral changes, he admitted, "very little is known."

In the dread of admitting the study of psychoses [i.e., psychic processes] into physiology, we may speak of the "lability" of passion and irrepressible volition, or of the erethism of temper and that too with real and increasing advantage; but in the study of our central question, viz., what were all the causes which enabled our subject to reduce his reaction-time from 18 to 10 hundredths of a second, it simply shows lack of intelligence to ignore the psychological or subjective side of the problem.

This kind of psychic explanation in no way undermined the foundation of psychology in physiology, Hall declared.[10] Complex psychological phenomena could be understood in terms such as "lability" or "irrepressibility," terms borrowed from the physiological description of energy processes, but they could also be understood as functional psychological concepts. At a time when so little was known about nervous action, it was simply "unintelligent" to limit or distort psychological knowledge to primitive neurological specifications.[11]

---

8. J. C. Flugel, *A Hundred Years of Psychology* (London: Gerald Duckworth, 1951), pp. 100–107, 216.

9. "Reaction-Time," 1883, pp. 171–73. William James performed a similar investigation a few years later and got results which did not agree with Hall's. He warned against "making rash generalization from few cases about the hypnotic state." *Proceedings of the American Society for Psychical Research* 1 (Dec 1887): 246–48. Cf. Franklin Fearing, *Reflex Action* (Baltimore: Williams and Wilkins, 1930), pp. 206–7, 215–16.

10. "Reaction-Time," 1883, pp. 177–79.

11. Hall may have been influenced in the development of this view by George Beard, a New York neurologist who first described "neurasthenia" and who Hall

At the close of this study, Hall pointed to the danger of "mono-ideism" for modern specialists and asserted that "the psychologist who confesses to any one predominant rubric or system is an idolater." Hall undoubtedly meant by this assertion that he himself had abandoned allegiance to such a "predominant rubric." Hall's work from this point forward suggests that he had given up the attempt to make "reflex action" into the sole, fundamental concept of his psychology.[12]

The recognition that psychological processes might require complex psychological explanations rather than simple physiological ones undermined Hall's belief in the identity of thought and matter. The close contact Hopkins afforded Hall with so many excellent scientific minds, and his long hours of conversation with Charles Peirce, probably further encouraged Hall to abandon his physical and epistemological baggage.[13]

By 1887, Hall formally assented to the more sophisticated view of the English neurologist, John Hughlings Jackson, that "the use of all such terms as ideo-motor, physiology of mind and even psycho-physics is a logical cross division." The theory that mental and nervous processes were concomitant series "is far better, even as a working hypothesis, than the theory of identity."[14] Moreover, "science is not ontology, but phenomenology." The vexed questions of epistemology could be ignored by the scientist. On a dualistic hypothesis, the histologist could nonetheless use conscious activities as a guide to study brain structure, and that structure could in turn

saw much of both in Baltimore and New York." *LCP,* p. 235. Beard described hypnotic trance as "a functional disease of the nervous system," one which related "only to circulation and innervation, and not causing structural changes." His physiological theory of trance, which Hall quoted, likened the mind to a chandelier of gas-burners operating on a fixed quantity of "cerebral force." Beard, "A New Theory of Trance," *Journal of Nervous and Mental Disease* 4 (Jan 1877): 5, 13, 17. On Beard's theory of nervous and mental disease, see Charles E. Rosenberg, "The Place of George M. Beard in Nineteenth-Century Psychiatry," *Bulletin of the History of Medicine* 36 (May-June 1962): 245–59.

12. Taking his own advice to heart, Hall gave a number of shrewd objections to his own attention theory and warned against making it into a total psychological explanation. "Reaction-Time," 1883, p. 182.

13. *LCP,* p. 226. Hall said he was greatly indebted to Peirce for "facts, ideas and stimulus." Cope and Fisch, "Peirce at Johns Hopkins," p. 311. Cf. Müller-Freienfels, *Evolution of Modern Psychology,* pp. 154–63, 182–84.

14. GSH, "Psychological Literature," 1887, p. 163.

be used to illuminate mental function. On an idealist hypothesis of the modern type, "conceptions of mind and matter, of self-consciousness and motion, cannot possibly be disparate and incommensurable, because both are concepts, and equally ideal." Thus Hall concluded that "it does not make one hair white or black, whether we work by this [idealistic] hypothesis or by that of realism." Such an issue was extraneous to the scientific study of psychology.[15]

Hall's recognition that scientific psychology did not offer a solution to the problem of knowledge was a serious blow to him. Many years later he remarked on

the ancient grudge I bear the big four [Kant, Fichte, Schelling, Hegel] for absorbing so much of the energy of my own best years, which might have been better spent and for the waste of which I am myself an awful warning against this peculiarly inebriating speculative debauchery.[16]

Despite the bitter criticism of Hegel and philosophical idealism he had begun to issue over ten years before, Hall had continued to struggle with epistemological concepts and problems and to find ways to transfer the attractions of idealism to scientific naturalism. Another ten years hence, it would be clear that he still was not free of these philosophers' emotional hold on his thinking nor of his grudge.

Hall could, however, proceed to concentrate his efforts on a strictly empirical psychology. Hall had been exposed to two very different traditions of empirical thinking in psychology. The naturalistic tradition of Spencer and Haeckel had been based on biological principles of continuity and naturalistic observation of behavior of the entire evolutionary-devolutionary series. The physiological tradition of Wundt and the German experimental psychologists had focused on laboratory cross sections of the adult or ideal conscious mind and based its concepts on sensorimotor units overlaid with such traditional categories as intellect, will, and imagination.[17]

15. Ibid., pp. 163–64. Hall referred to Ernst Mach on modern idealism, probably his *Analyse der Empfindungen*, 1886.
16. GSH, "Why Kant Is Passing," 1912, p. 420.
17. Robert M. Young, "The Functions of the Brain; Gall to Ferrier, 1808–1886," *Isis* 59 (1968): 521–68, distinguishes these two traditions in British psychology and traces them both back to Gall. Gardner Murphy, *An Historical Introduction to Modern Psychology* (London: Kegan Paul, Trench, Trubner, 1929), pp. 351–52, has distinguished the physicalistic and evolutionary approaches to psychological science.

Hall's psychology at Hopkins attempted to include both these traditions. The new psychology he described in his inaugural lecture of 1884 had three principal divisions: the study of instinct, experimental psychology, and historical psychology. Of the three, experimental psychology was the field he considered the "more central, and reduced to far more exact methods,"[18] and it was the field to which Hall devoted most of his teaching and investigation during the Hopkins years.[19]

While he was occupied with this physiological tradition, however, his interest in the naturalistic approach deepened. Hall's interest in development had always been rooted in his introspective awareness of his own process of self-development and in his philosophical attraction to broad theories of evolution. At Hopkins, the interest in biological evolution pervaded the entire faculty and especially the brilliant department of biology.[20] Hall was probably influenced most strongly by his contact with William Keith Brooks, the professor of zoology, whom Hall had first met when they were both students at Williams. A thoughtful man, Brooks was engrossed in the problems of Darwin's theory of evolution, particularly in the problem of heredity. Though shy and rather difficult in formal contact, he treated his students and intimates to warm and stimulating conservation on his biological concerns. Hall said that "I saw more of and owe more to him than to any member of the faculty there."[21]

Hall's concern with development expressed itself in the experimental topics he chose. He worked on the genetically "primitive" sensations of the cutaneous surface and on those processes which he felt to enter most basically and generically into self-development, such as the sense of time and the coordination of asymmetrical bilateral functions. And he constantly looked beyond his laboratory

18. GSH, "New Psychology," pt. 1, 1885, p. 123.
19. Hall spent the major portion of his regular psychology lecture course on sensation, perception, psycho-physic law, reaction time, and brain localization. *Johns Hopkins Circulars* 2: 233; 3: 118; 4: 107; 5: 135; 6: 114.
20. Hawkins, *Pioneer,* pp. 300–303. Hall opened his psychology course for, among others, "those who desire to carry on the study of biology by experimental methods into the study of the psychic functions of animals and man." *Johns Hopkins Circulars* 4: 117.
21. *LCP,* p. 238; *William Keith Brooks: A Sketch of His Life by Some of His Former Pupils and Associates* (Baltimore: Williams & Wilkins, 1910); E. A. Andrews, "William Keith Brooks," *Science,* n.s. 28 (Dec 1908): 777–86.

results for the biological and developmental implications of his subject.

Hall evidently lectured in a small dwelling adjacent to the center of the main buildings which were used by the university, and it was probably in this building that he set up a small psychological laboratory in the spring of 1883.[22] He found four students at Hopkins interested in the new study who in the spring of 1883 became the first to engage in psychological "observation and experiment" as part of his lecture course: James McKeen Cattell, Joseph Jastrow, E. M. Hartwell, and John Dewey. In addition, Henry H. Donaldson, an advanced student of nervous physiology under the Hopkins biologist, H. Newall Martin, was interested in working with Hall.[23]

In January 1884, Hall was given a room in the new biology building specifically for psychophysiological research.[24] About a half-dozen students thereafter continued to experiment under Hall each year. Cattell left for further studies in Germany under Wundt, and Dewey soon dropped laboratory work, but Jastrow and Donaldson continued and were joined by newer Hall students, like Edmund C. Sanford, who later joined Hall at Clark University, and Jujiro Motora, one of the founders of modern Japanese psychology. During the year 1886–87, when the new physics building was opened, Hall was given four rooms.[25] The studies which emerged from this progressively larger series of laboratories were published in *Mind* under a special section for "Research," and later in Hall's *American Journal of Psychology*. In the fall of 1885, he began the Monday

22. Wilson, *GSH*, p. 66; J. M. Cattell, "The Founding of the Association and of the Hopkins and Clark Laboratories," *PR* 50 (Jan 1943): 63. Cattell remembered that he, Jastrow, and Donaldson helped Hall to set up the laboratory.

23. *Johns Hopkins Circulars* 2: 93. While Dewey, whose chief interest was philosophy, had no previous scientific training, Hartwell, a biology student, held a medical degree; Jastrow had already carried on psychological research under Charles Peirce, and Cattell had previously studied in Germany under Lotze and Wundt. See Morton G. White, *The Origins of Dewey's Instrumentalism* (New York: Columbia University Press, 1943), pp. 34–48; Joseph Jastrow, "Charles Sanders Peirce As a Teacher," *Journal of Philosophy, Psychology and Scientific Methods* 13 (Dec 1916): 724–25.

24. *Johns Hopkins Circulars* 3: 49; *Ann. Rep. Pres. Hopk., 1883–84*, pp. 93–94.

25. *Johns Hopkins Circulars* 3: 69; 4: 107; 5: 26, 70; 6: 114; 7: 74. On the issue of whether Hall's Johns Hopkins laboratories deserve to be called the first of their kind in the United States, see below, chapter 13.

night seminar in psychology which he would conduct for the remainder of his career.

In four studies which Hall carried out jointly with his students
at Johns Hopkins he left his only record as an experimental psychologist.[26] The study of bilateral asymmetry of function with E. M.
Hartwell was the first and poorest of the group. Using three or four
subjects, Hall and Hartwell tested for asymmetry in arm movements, in judgment of distance of arm movements, and in reaction
times to aural stimuli. What interested Hall in the subject was
"what influence upon the psychic development of animals and man
is due to the power to bring two symmetrical parts of the body into
contact," and he suggested that there was probably great selective
advantage in "self-consciousness or double dealing with ourselves."
But he could only confidently expect that future experimentation
on the subject would elucidate this problem.[27]

The experiments which followed were considerably higher in
quality; how large a part of the improvement stemmed from Hall's
growing expertise and how much from the fact that his later co-
workers were themselves talented experimentalists is impossible to
determine. Hall's study with Donaldson of "Motor Sensations of
the Skin" was the result of extensive experiment over a period of
eighteen months from which Donaldson, working on his own, had
already discovered the warm and cold temperature spots on the
skin.[28] Instead of the simple sensation of motion Hall had earlier
assumed to exist, he now discovered that so many types of sensation
contributed to the perception of motion on the skin, that it was un-
clear whether or not there was "a simple motor sense in the skin at
the root." This experiment was probably the most useful to the
psychological work then in progress, and its results were used by
Ladd and James in their analysis of the role of motor sensations and
"local signs" in perception. Hall also called attention to

26. Of the three published experiments carried out by Hall's students at Hopkins, neither the Donaldson paper on the temperature sense nor Jastrow's study
of the perception of space by disparate senses acknowledged any direction from
Hall. Lewis T. Steven's experiment on the time sense did owe its subject and
direction to Hall. See *Mind* 10: 399–416; 11: 393–404, 539–54.

27. GSH and E. M. Hartwell, "Bilateral Asymmetry of Function," 1884, pp.
93–109, particularly p. 103.

28. *Johns Hopkins Circulars* 4: 76.

the effect of disturbed dermal functions in affecting psycho-sensory sanity; the fact of the genetic origin of senses and central nervous system from the external embryological layer; the function of specialized dermal sensations in presiding over the exercise of the sexual activities; and the relation of what the old psychology roughly called Touch in giving us the primary qualities of matter.

The promise of the study of dermal sensation for Hall lay largely in its relation to pathological, biological, and developmental problems.[29]

Hall's study of rhythm with Jastrow held somewhat closer to the experimental data. It was a preliminary study of a subject on which little experimental work had been done. They tested discrimination and counting of rapid sounds, just noticeable differences of duration, and judgment of full and vacant time intervals. Jastrow later continued studies of the rhythmic factor in perception at the University of Wisconsin. Hall found that his subjects could discriminate sounds more rapidly than they could count them, counting being a complex act of motor innervation. These results seemed to him to cast doubt on "any extreme form of [Wundt's] hypothesis of the identity of apperceptive and volitional processes," but this was a temporary demurrer on the way to an acceptance of Wundt's theory.[30] Hall's interest in Wundt's concept of apperception testified to his continuing interest in dynamic conceptions.

29. GSH and H. H. Donaldson, "Motor Sensations on the Skin," 1885, pp. 557–72, particularly pp. 567, 572. Hall and Donaldson concluded that "it would seem that 'local signs' are quite heterogeneous, and that, in the strong tendency we have to move the touching dermal surface over objects in contact with it, we are seeking not merely to multiply but to diversify our sensuous data for judging the nature of the impressions and to fill up the dermal 'blind spots' between which impressions are sifted in to us." Ibid., p. 572. Cf. James, *Psychology*, 2: 155–76; George T. Ladd, *Elements of Physiological Psychology* (New York: Charles Scribner's Sons, 1887), pp. 411–13.

30. GSH and Joseph Jastrow, "Studies of Rhythm," 1886, pp. 55–62, particularly p. 59. In his *Founders of Modern Psychology*, 1912, Hall stated that Wundt's work on apperception was "the most original and valuable of Wundt's experimental work in psychology" (p. 377). It showed that "apperceptive and volitional reactions are essentially the same process . . . only different forms of the excitation of the will" (p. 385). On Wundt's theory of apperception, see Wilhelm Wundt, *Lectures on Human and Animal Psychology,* trans. J. E. Creighton and E. B. Titchener (London: Swan Sonnenschein, 1894), pp. 252–65; Murphy, *Historical Introduction to Psychology,* pp. 164–66; Walter B. Pillsbury, *Attention* (London: Swan Sonnenschein, 1908), pp. 264–80.

Hall's final experimental study with Motora, "Dermal Sensitiveness to Gradual Pressure Changes," applied the concept of psychophysical relations developed by Fechner to the discrimination of
continuously and gradually changing sensory stimuli, rather than
to discontinuous stimuli, and concluded that

we have here a new standpoint for viewing psycho-physic relations, and few
if any safe inferences from one to the other between the work of Weber and
Fechner and their successors and ours can be trusted.

While thus narrowing the field in which the Weber-Fechner law
could be applied, Hall went on to note the need for more work on
the "tickle-sense . . . where we have not yet learned to distinguish
subjective from objective sensations, and with respect to which the
mind of the adult is still in a rudimentary infantile condition."[31]

Hall's four experimental studies at Johns Hopkins entered fruitfully into the psychological discussion of his time. Edward Bradford
Titchener of Cornell University, the leader of traditional Wundtian
psychology in America, believed Hall's work was "exceedingly important both in itself and also for the general spread of experimental
ideas."[32] His work displayed considerable introspective talent as
well as ingenuity in devising apparatus and in recognizing the complexity of factors entering into the experimental situation. Like
most of the early psychologists, he used relatively few subjects and
observations, relatively crude equipment, and no statistical measures
of significance in evaluating results, but within these limits, Hall's
experimental methods were probably better than average for his
day.[33] Hall's interests lay elsewhere, however—in individual and
comparative development, abnormal phenomena, and questions relating to the emotions and to biological studies. The physiologically
based analyses of sensation, perception, and attention could not
reach these broader questions.

The second part of the field of experimental psychology as Hall
described it in his inaugural lecture was psychopathology, and here
Hall was closer to his real concerns. Cattell recalled that "the work

31. GSH and Jujiro Motora, "Dermal Sensitiveness to Gradual Pressure
Changes," 1887, pp. 72–98, particularly pp. 90, 98.
32. Titchener to S. C. Fisher, 9 Dec 1924, TP.
33. For an examination of the experimental techniques of the early American
psychologists, see Albrecht, "The New Psychology in America," pp. 139–49.

done in Baltimore . . . was largely physiological and psychiatrical. Hall was much interested in insanity and other pathological aspects of psychology."[34]

Hall's description of the field in his inaugural lecture reflected the sources of his own interest. Hall spoke both of the great promise in relating some kinds of insanity to cortical abnormalities and the necessity for "detailed explorations of the mental states of individual lunatics with the history of each illusion from its inception," thus echoing the somatic and clinical character of psychiatry in Europe. Rhythmic patterns of abnormal psychological phenomena might also be correlated with such cosmic rhythms as the weather and planetary movements. Although somewhat bizarre, this hope was not altogether unique in an age of deep faith in a comprehensive natural order underlying the disparate and arbitrary surface of phenomena.[35]

Hall also continued to display the personal, subjective interest in mental illness he had shown in Germany. The warning he gave in his inaugural lecture was certainly a token of his own experience and a product of real understanding.

The successful student of these [pathological] states requires the rare combination of an insinuating, sympathetic temper, of a perhaps itself infinitesimally neurotic type, with power to trace all morbid psychic phenomena in others to and identify them with fainter experiences of his own, along with the most objective discriminating sagacity. The infection of these states is so subtle in imaginative minds and the *katharsis* so long and serious that they should be undertaken by the general student of psychology very rarely.[36]

Hall found a new stimulus for his interest in this subject in his position at Johns Hopkins. The connection between psychopathology and the hospital and medical department which was to be opened at Hopkins had been recognized and welcomed by all concerned from the beginning of Hall's dealings with the university. Hall emphasized in his inaugural lecture the great opportunity that this subject presented for the projected medical school. Voicing

34. Cattell, "Founding of the Association," p. 63.
35. GSH, "New Psychology," pt. 1, 1885, p. 127. Cf. Freud's acceptance of Fliess's theory in Ernest Jones, *The Life and Work of Sigmund Freud* (New York: Basic Books, 1953), 1: 289–91, 304.
36. GSH, "New Psychology," pt. 1, 1885, p. 127.

the kind of scientific pride which was to help draw the American medical profession into the study of mental illness, Hall urged that physicians deal with the "mind and heart and imagination" of their patients, if only to remove them from the influence of popular quacks.[37]

Although the medical school was not to be opened during Hall's tenure at Hopkins, one of the four classes of students for whom he designed his psychology course was students of "psychiatric medicine." He lectured on "disorders of speech, illusions, the psychological aspects of insanity, localization studies in spinal cord and brain." From Hall's first term at Hopkins, he took his students regularly to the Bay View Asylum, Baltimore's institution for the pauper insane.[38] During the summer of 1884, Hall engaged as one of his first fellows, William Noyes, Jr., a graduate of the Harvard Medical school then interning at the Danvers State Lunatic Asylum, whom Hall had often worked with in Bowditch's laboratory.[39]

Early in 1885, the trustees moved toward the organization of the medical department and Hall's interest in the subject quickened. Hall wrote Bowditch, "My tastes, interest, reading etc. draw me more and more to make psychiatry, scientifically and not practically worked, the focus of my psychology," and he wondered if Harvard might give him an honorary M.D. degree which he would use "only to procure entree to opportunities in that one line which seem to me the key of all psychological studies as well as educational ones." Bowditch evidently did not grant Hall's request, but even without a medical degree, Hall helped inaugurate psychiatric work at the university.[40]

During the year 1885–86, William Henry Welch started his tenure as chief of the projected medical school and head of the first of the medical departments, pathology. Early in 1886, arrangements were made to tie the Bay View Asylum to the university so that instruction in mental disorders could eventually be given there.

37. Ibid., p. 128.
38. *Johns Hopkins Circulars* 4: 117; 5: 107; 6: 114; Cattell, "Founding of the Association," p. 63.
39. GSH to Gilman, 26 July [1884], Alumni Records Office, Johns Hopkins University.
40. GSH to Bowditch, 19 Apr 1885, Bowditch Papers.

Three doctors were appointed as visiting physicians, and Stanley Hall was appointed to "cooperate" with them "as an expert in the management of insane asylums."[41] It is impossible to say whether Hall, before the appointment of this committee or after, actually served as *"locum tenens* Superintendent, perhaps the only layman in medicine to occupy such a position," as he claimed.[42] Certainly Hall shared the responsibility with the physicians appointed for effecting important changes in the hospital.

The asylum at Bay View was a part of the city's almshouse, one of the worst class of mental institutions in the country. As a home for the "chronic pauper insane," it was a receptacle to which other hospitals in the area sent their least curable, least manageable, non-paying, and often dying patients. Within a short time after the Hopkins men took over, sanitary conditions and medical care improved so greatly that the death rate was sharply reduced and the scourge of infectious diseases practically eliminated; a "better class" of nurses was secured, and the "imbecile children" were removed from the asylum, although there was no place to which to transfer them except the almshouse proper. In the care of patients physical restraint was virtually abolished, the patients were put to work improving the building and grounds, and a public subscription started to provide funds for their entertainment and diversion. To what extent the scientific quality of psychiatric treatment improved is not known. One of the tasks assigned to Hall was to assist in arranging for a proper system of clinical records.[43]

During Hall's last year, Dr. Edward Cowles, medical superintendent of the McLean Hospital near Boston, one of the most progressive mental institutions in the country, came to Hopkins to study with Hall. Some years older than Hall, Cowles displayed both intellectual and personal compatibility with him, and their acquaintance soon ripened into friendship, perhaps the most solid friendship

41. Alan M. Chesney, *The Johns Hopkins Hospital and the Johns Hopkins University School of Medicine: A Chronicle* (Baltimore: Johns Hopkins University Press, 1943), 1: 94; *Ann. Rep. Pres. Hopk., 1886–87,* pp. 44–45; *Johns Hopkins Circulars* 5: 16.

42. *LCP,* p. 232.

43. *Annual Report of the Trustees of the Poor of the City of Baltimore . . . for the fiscal years ending December 31, 1886* (Baltimore, 1887), pp. 5–8, 63–67; *Ann. Rep. Pres. Hopk., 1886–87,* pp. 45, 38.

of Hall's later life.[44] Cowles acknowledged a large debt to Hall's influence. He shared Hall's enthusiasm for a scientific psychology, free of metaphysics, oriented to physiology, and a partner of psychiatry in the study of mental abnormality. He publicized Hall's work and the importance of his ideal of scientific research to a profession still isolated from scientific influences, and when he returned to McLean, he established a research laboratory at the hospital.[45]

Cowles also believed that one of the most important avenues of progress for psychiatry lay in "the proper analysis of the expressions and products of the diseased mind," as Hall had already urged.[46] Cowles argued in a lecture at Hopkins on "Insistent and Fixed Ideas" that "mental disorders may originate in the feelings or the intellect."[47] Hall too, had suggested in his earlier study of reaction time in the hypnotic state, that "the attention-theory . . . may enable us to regard many abnormalities and neural disorders as only exaggerations of states familiar to every normal mind, and . . . it enhances our conception of the power of the mind over the body."[48]

Thus, Hall shared at a very early stage in the modern reform of American psychiatry toward more enlightened asylum care, toward scientific study and treatment, and toward the understanding of psychological pathology in mental illness. When he went to Clark, he continued to exercise some influence in these directions. Although the first generation of scientific psychologists generally took an interest in the subject, Hall's inclusion of it within the sphere of experimental psychology itself and his close attention to clinical study was unusual in this country.[49]

Hall expended a considerable amount of effort at Johns Hopkins

44. *Johns Hopkins Circulars,* 7: 6–7, 57; R. G. Hall, interview, 17–20 May 1961.

45. Cowles, "The *AJP,*" *American Journal of Insanity* 44 (Apr 1888): 544–46; *Proceedings at the First Annual Banquet of the New England Association of Alumni of Clark University* (1907), p. 7; GSH, "Laboratory of the McLean Hospital, Somerville, Mass.," 1895, pp. 358–64.

46. Cowles, "The *AJP,*" p. 546.

47. Cowles, "Insistent and Fixed Ideas," *AJP* 1 (Feb 1888): 222–70.

48. "Reaction-Time," 1883, p. 181.

49. See David Shakow, "One Hundred Years of American Psychiatry," *Psychological Bulletin* 62 (July 1945): 430; Ackerknecht, *History of Psychiatry,* pp. 72–81.

on a third subject he did not even mention in his inaugural lecture, for he believed it lay beyond the pale of legitimate science: psychical research. During Hall's study in Germany between 1878 and 1880, he had first come in contact with the growing vogue of spiritualism in academic circles as well as among the public. Demonstrators of such phenomena as hypnosis, mind reading, mediumship, and clairvoyance were claiming that their performances were evidence for the existence of an ideal world of spirits and personal immortality. Leipzig itself was the home of a flourishing spiritualist society and of a serious journal on the subject. Hall established contact with some of the spiritualists of the Leipzig academic community, including Theodore Fechner, the founder of psychophysics, who was then wholly engrossed in mystical studies. While late in life Hall could admit that he had felt some sympathy for Fechner's "dreameries about souls of molecules, plants and planets," at the time he was anxious to disown such views and to substitute science for superstition.[50]

During the 1880s, intellectual circles in England and then in America took up the subject. The Society for Psychical Research, formed in Britain in 1882, included men of science as well as philosophers and overt spiritualists. When reports of their investigations began to appear yielding apparently strong evidence for thought transference, their American colleagues were forced to take notice. William James himself had talked in England with the researchers during their first year of work; among the American scholars in the field, he was then the most devoted and remained so. In the fall of 1884, an American counterpart of the British society was formed, but it was determined from the start to assume an objective attitude and named officers who were established scientists and largely skeptical of the favorable British results. Simon Newcomb became president and Hall was made one of the five vice-presidents.[51]

50. *Aspects,* pp. 75, 128–33; GSH to Wm. James, 27 Dec [1879], in Perry, *William James,* 2: 18; *LCP,* pp. 207, 360.

51. Albrecht, "The New Psychology in America," pp. 157–85; Rosalind Heywood, *Beyond the Reach of Sense* (New York: E. P. Dutton, 1961), pp. 36–111; "Formation of the Society," *Proceedings of the American Society for Psychical Research* 1 (July 1885): 1–4; Perry, *William James,* 1: 416.

Hall already believed that insofar as these phenomena purported to convey thought without any physical means or to attest to conscious minds beyond living individual minds, they were fraudulent; all such phenomena could be explained entirely by natural principles.[52] Since he believed that many of the psychic phenomena were created by deception, he began to study magic and in the course of a lifelong devotion to it became quite an expert performer as well as follower of the magician's art.[53] One can easily imagine that Hall would be attracted to this field of mystery and dissembling. He himself bade investigators beware of "the unfathomable passion for deceit, both conscious and unconscious, that sometimes runs in veins through the natures of men of best reputation and most honest purpose."[54] Hall developed formidable critical powers in this line which he used particularly in investigating and unmasking mediums.[55]

What was not accomplished by deception, Hall thought were tricks of another kind, "tricks of our automatic nature, subtle and manifold far beyond all conception." The capacities of the automatic nature that Hall had particularly in mind were unconscious muscular movements which can accompany thought and can be "read," abnormal acuity in sight and hearing, and the unconscious assimiliation of subtle cues from the environment.[56] He and his students experimented in thought transference but found only the "subtlety of sensation in hysteric subjects."[57] He perfected a number of codes by which thought transference could be feigned, such as slight toe movements under a shoe of thin leather that could be deciphered some distance away. Hall claimed to have demonstrated mind reading by one of these devices at his home one evening to a group of distinguished Hopkins scientists and found a number of them ready to convert to spiritualism before he revealed the trick.[58]

Never believing that positive results would emerge from the

52. GSH, "Psychological Literature," 1887, p. 140; *AJP* 7 (1895): 138–39.
53. R. G. Hall, interview, 17–20 May 1961.
54. GSH, "Psychological Literature," 1887, p. 140.
55. *LCP*, p. 235; GSH, Introduction in Amy E. Tanner, *Studies in Spiritism* (New York: D. Appleton, 1910), pp. xv–xvii.
56. GSH, "Psychological Literature," 1887, pp. 135, 140.
57. GSH to Bowditch, 14 Feb 1885, Bowditch Papers.
58. *LCP*, pp. 241–42.

work, Hall became the first of the scientific leaders to resign from the society in 1886 or 1887.[59] Hall's attitude toward psychical research was the predominent one among the new psychologists. The aspiring scientists could hardly welcome the fact that in the public mind the "new psychology" was often identified with the study of psychical phenomena. Nor in the face of religious opposition to their science could they help but resent the popular approval of spiritualistic projects.[60] Hall recognized that some of these phenomena were "possibly" morbid, but he appeared too much opposed to the subject on principle to use it, as James sometimes did, to carry forward his interest in psychopathology.

The two other major divisions of psychology Hall described in his inaugural lecture were very largely absent from his actual work at the university. Like Wundt himself, Hall included in his systematic outline of psychology large areas of study outside the laboratory experimentation on which the new psychology actually focused. One of these subjects Hall called historical psychology, by which he meant a natural history of mind, an attempt to "go back of finished intellectual products and discover man's fresh primary thoughts and feelings."[61] Like Wundt's category of historical psychology, Hall's included the study of animals, children and adolescents, primitive peoples, and folk beliefs.[62] Hall added the psychological analysis of philosophy itself, together with science, religion, and other intellectual products rooted in history and personality.[63]

In his lectures on psychology, Hall dealt with "psychological anthropology" and during his last year added "the psychology of

59. As one researcher after another brought forward negative or ambiguous results the *ASPR* itself disbanded. In 1890, the remaining Boston chapter made itself into the American branch of the British Society. Albrecht, "The New Psychology in America," pp. 167–78.
60. Ibid.; E. B. Titchener, "Anthropometry and Experimental Psychology," *Philosophical Review* 2 (Mar 1893): 192; GSH to Wm. James, 21 Dec [1886], JP; Wm. James to Titchener, 6, 21, 31 May 1899, TP; Titchener to James, 28 May 1899, JP.
61. GSH, "New Psychology," pt. 1, 1885, pp. 128–30.
62. E. B. Titchener, "Wilhelm Wundt," *AJP* 32 (Apr 1921): 165–66; Wilhelm Wundt, *Outlines of Psychology*, trans. Charles H. Judd (London: Williams and Norgate, 1897), pp. 276–309.
63. GSH, "New Psychology," pt. 1, 1885, p. 130.

religion." Although he allowed the Metaphysical Club for students and faculty which Peirce had organized to go out of existence, he paid a great deal of attention to philosophy from the standpoint of psychology.[64] Even while Morris was in the department, Hall lectured on "psychological ethics" historically considered and later held lectures and seminars on the history of ancient and modern philosophy.[65] Despite his claim to subordinate philosophy to psychology, he would later admit that he taught philosophy for its own sake, as a record of what the race has thought and as a counterbalance to narrow specialization. Indeed, his love of the subject increased as the years passed, and he lectured on philosophy almost every year for the remainder of his career, going back particularly to Plato and the ancients.[66]

The most notable absence from Hall's psychology lectures was the study of child development. Although he originally intended to survey "the evolution of the psychic faculties in children," he apparently did not lecture specifically on the subject.[67] Though Hall recognized that there were psychological conclusions to be drawn from the studies of children he made during the 1880s, he was also aware how far short of science they fell. Moreover, prescriptions for child rearing and education could never have the respect of his scientific colleagues in the way that his laboratory experimentation could. At Gilman's urging, he taught a Saturday morning course on pedagogy, open to local teachers, and undertook other pedagogical chores, but to these he took as elevated an approach as possible.[68]

The final division of the new psychology Hall outlined was the study of instinct, perhaps, he said, the most perennial and basic idea in psychology. It was not known whether instinct was really "lapsed . . . intelligence" or "rudimentary mind," Hall said, but he considered the term to cover "what is *a priori* and innate in man." This was for Hall a very large category. It included chiefly "impulses,

64. *Johns Hopkins Circulars* 2: 94; 3: 46, 70, 96, 138; 4: 28, 40, 66, 82; 5: 26.
65. Ibid. 3: 136; 4: 107; 5: 136; 6: 114; 7: 114.
66. GSH, "Philosophy," in *Decennial Celebration, Clark University, 1889–1899*, pp. 45–59; DAB, s.v. "G. Stanley Hall."
67. *Johns Hopkins Circulars* 4: 117; 7: 114.
68. *LCP*, pp. 226–27, 251; *Johns Hopkins Circulars* 3: 136; 4: 117; 5: 135; 6: 114; 7: 114.

desires, appetites," and "in a sense," even "conscience, and the movement and rest of attention."[69] Instinct also included what Hall called, after the English physiologist Benjamin Carpenter, the "automatic nature generally" or the realm of the "unconscious." In this class of phenomena were not only the functions of the autonomic nervous system but also all those processes beyond the range of attention and will.[70] Hall felt this concept to be congruent with the genetic findings of German physiological psychology. The "threshold" of sensation formulated in psychophysics and the "unconscious inferences" in the visual perception of space posited by Helmholtz seemed to Hall to indicate the existence of a vast network of unconscious processes which had only a neurological dimension until they attained sufficient intensity to reach consciousness. Hall was tangentially exploring this network in his psychical research.

Hall felt the deepest levels of psychological meaning to be concentrated in the category of instinct. Through it he denoted the "depth and breadth and number and subtlety of psychical processes underlying and overreaching and encompassing our conscious psychic activities."[71] Here, rather than in reason, he said, lies "much that makes the human soul really great and good." These phenomena, Hall said, "show a wisdom beneath us we cannot escape if we would, and on which, when conscious purpose and endeavor droop, we can rest back, with trust, as on 'everlasting arms.' "[72] In the concept of instinct, Hall appeared to find a psychological anchor for the religious feelings excluded from his science. By incorporating virtually the whole of the conative, affective, and unconscious realms of psychic life into the concept of instinct, Hall prepared the way for linking the problem of individual development to phylogeny.

At the moment, Hall thought of the study of instinct as the study of animal psychology. In the lower species one could observe the

69. GSH, "New Psychology," pt. 1, 1885, p. 122.
70. GSH, "New Psychology," pt. 1, 1885, pp. 121–22; "Psychological Literature," 1887, pp. 131, 140; William B. Carpenter, *Principles of Mental Physiology* (New York: D. Appleton, 1884), pp. ix, 22–25, 376–86, 515–17.
71. "Psychological Literature," 1887, p. 133.
72. "New Psychology," pt. 1, 1885, pp. 122–23.

instinctive behavior which was now innate to man. Pointing to recent English and German studies of bees, insects, and animals in nature, Hall urged that animals be observed in their native habitat rather than in the laboratory. Alternatively, Hall proposed devising questionnaires for hunters, pet-keepers, and the like, from whom "kernels of valuable observation and insight" might be obtained. By whichever method, Hall was pleased to note "the great methodical advantage of being objective" rather than relying on introspection.[73]

Hall devoted a section of his psychology course to "instinct" and to those subjects he thought to be somewhat related: psychogenesis, attention and personality, feeling and will.[74] Considering the importance Hall attached to the field, however, his attention to it was small. His energy and interests were already committed in a great many other directions.

The image which Hall's psychology of the 1880s presented to his contemporaries, and the image Hall himself tried to project, was that of a rigorously scientific discipline, centered on the experimental laboratory. Here Hall spent the greatest part of his efforts and here the scientific character of his program was most plainly visible. Although only three of the seven Ph.D.s granted under Hall's professorship went to men who would become experimentalists,[75] the laboratory aspect of the Hopkins work was the most in-

73. Ibid., pp. 121–22. Hall's conception of comparative psychology may also have been influenced by his contact in Leipzig with G. H. Schneider, "who is an enthusiast for studying the habits of ants, dogs, fish, etc." GSH to Wm. James, 2 / Dec [1879], in Perry, *William James*, 2: 18. At Clark University, after 1895, important pioneer studies were done on the "sensory and perceptual aspects and relations of the behavior of birds, rodents, and primates." Robert M. Yerkes, "Early Days of Comparative Psychology," *PR* 50 (Jan 1943): 75. With the limited budget of the university, however, Hall could never fund the animal work adequately, and he never tried to advance and promote it the way he did child study. See GSH to George F. Hoar, 24 Sept 1902; James P. Porter to GSH, 2 Nov 1909, CUP.

74. *Johns Hopkins Circulars* 4: 107; 7: 113.

75. Joseph Jastrow, E. C. Sanford, and Jujiro Motora. William H. Burnham became a specialist in pedagogy and hygiene, G. T. W. Patrick and J. H. Hyslop became philosophers rather than psychologists. So too did John Dewey, who was chiefly Morris's student but received his degree in 1884 from Hall after Morris had left the department. Woodrow Wilson took Hall's course and for a time thought of majoring in psychology, according to *LCP*, p. 240.

fluential on the development of American psychology, as one university after another established a psychological laboratory in the effort to become fully modern.[76] Hall's scientific stance also plainly extended to his vigorous opposition to psychical research and his tendency to treat philosophy as data for psychological analysis. Hall was to take a position within the psychological profession very largely on the basis of these scientific characteristics.

Alongside of this position, however, stood Hall's interest in a naturalistic approach to psychology with its own very different, scientific canon. The study of animal instinct and of historical psychology, as Hall conceived them, were amenable not to laboratory methods but to observation and insight. The chief thread which held these nonexperimental fields together was Hall's biological evolutionary viewpoint. Hall had not yet fully articulated or coordinated the evolutionary assumptions underlying these topics, however, nor hardly tried to integrate them into the physiologically based experimental psychology he had learned in Germany. In 1886 and 1887 the pace of Hall's laboratory investigation began to slow somewhat,[77] and his interest in organizing and propagandizing for scientific psychology quickened. Even before other factors appeared to remove Hall from the laboratory, he may have begun to retreat before the task of uniting his two disparate views of psychology and turned instead to the journalistic, entrepreneurial, and preaching functions for which he had greater talent.

76. C. R. Garvey, "List of American Psychological Laboratories," *Psychological Bulletin* 26 (Nov 1929): 653–54.
77. Hall worked on only one experimental study during the two years, his study of gradual pressure changes on the skin.

10 ORGANIZATION OF THE SCIENCE

Hall had demonstrated a flair for organizational affairs in the village culture of his earlier years, but it was not until he was well settled at Johns Hopkins that he showed the ability to exercise leadership in the academic and scientific communities. Indeed, while Hall was still a student in Cambridge, James had described him to President Gilman as "perhaps deficient in the practical and organizing qualities which the Johns Hopkins University especially needs *now* in its professors."[1] James, of course, had not seen Hall operate at Antioch. The deficiency James sensed in his student may well have been connected with the loose and hasty quality of Hall's thinking, for Hall was grasping at a multitude of conclusions before he had thought them through and planning more projects than he could possibly complete. But this rash enthusiasm was an asset in laying the organizational foundations of a young and insecure science. Hall's institutional accomplishments were among the most enduring achievements of his career.

In 1886, Hall started plans for an American journal of psychology.[2] Because work in so many different fields converged on the subject, Hall believed, the psychologist was likely to miss much of it unless it could be focused in a single publication. One of the

1. Wm. James to Gilman, 18 Jan 1879, in Cope, "James's Correspondence with Gilman," p. 621.
2. Wm. James to GSH, 1 Aug [1886], HP.

principal tasks of the *Journal* was to review the large body of scattered literature here and abroad that was useful to psychology.[3]

In 1887, when Hall undertook the task of founding the *Journal*, Hopkins had the only department specifically devoted to psychology in the country. Within departments of philosophy, perhaps a dozen scholars, like William James at Harvard, offered some instruction in the new psychology. Among them only James had laboratory facilities. Scattered interest could be expected from some philosophers, physiologists, psychiatrists, biologists, and psychical researchers, but to what extent the problems and assumptions of these various fields belonged in psychology was entirely uncertain. The attempt to found a journal on the prospect of such meager and eclectic support was certainly a daring and visionary effort.

Hall's faith in the future growth of psychology had the additional support of the Hopkins environment. Five technical journals had already been founded by the Hopkins scientists to publish their own studies and to give dignity and focus to their subjects. Since academic disciplines in this country were still in their infancy and professional organizations virtually nonexistent, the journals were private ventures, owned and published by those who had the initiative to undertake the responsibility and the requisite financial resources.[4] Hall was given his opportunity when R. Pearsall Smith, a spiritualist member of the American Society for Psychical Research, offered him $500 to start a journal. Smith assumed that the *Journal* would be favorable to psychical research; to what extent Hall tacitly encouraged that assumption is unknown.[5] Hall added his own money, began collecting subscriptions from interested parties a year before the first issue was due—James chided him on running "the greatest confidence game in N[orth] America"[6]—and in October of 1887, somewhat later than announced, the first issue of the *American Journal of Psychology* appeared. Hall was so blinded by enthusiasm, he ordered a greatly excessive number of copies printed, probably fifteen hundred. According to Hall, it took the *Journal* five years to recover financially from this extravagance.

3. GSH, "Editorial Note," 1887, p. 3.
4. Hawkins, *Pioneer,* pp. 73–76, 107–10.
5. *AJP* 2 (1888): 677; GSH, "The *AJP,*" 1921, pp. 1–3; *LCP,* p. 227.
6. Wm. James to GSH, 1 Aug [1886], HP.

In more basic ways, Hall himself never recovered, for the need to make good his personal financial loss and to maintain strict economy became an overriding concern in his management of the *Journal* for the rest of his life.[7]

Hall designed the *Journal* not merely to provide a means of expression for his colleagues but to focus and define the field. As he explained in an introductory editorial, the *Journal* was to be reserved exclusively for "psychological work of a scientific, as distinct from a speculative character." Besides reviews and notes, only "original contributions of a scientific character" would be accepted. What Hall meant by this definition was very much what he had described in his inaugural lecture at Hopkins: "experimental investigations" of the type already common to the new psychology; "inductive studies" in animal instinct, psychogenesis in children, and morbid and anthropological psychology; and lastly, studies in nervous anatomy, physiology, and morphology. "Controversy," he concluded, "so far as possible will be excluded."[8]

Hall's definition of scientific psychology was itself controversial, however. He had limited the *Journal* entirely to empirical studies. Introspective, theoretical psychology of the kind practiced by many of his contemporaries was pointedly excluded. Except for articles of unusual importance, philosophy could presumably enter the *Journal* only as data for psychological studies. Hall also excluded psychical research. The spiritualist inclinations of the original donor had been reduced to "hypnotism" among the list of topics to be covered in abnormal psychology.

The tone of the new journal was made even clearer by the contents of its first issue. The major articles were entirely experimental and physiological. Most of the extensive reviews of literature were on experimental or physiological subjects, and much of the rest on

---

7. GSH, "The *AJP*," 1921, pp. 1–3. Wilson, *GSH*, p. 67, states that Hall printed 1,500 copies of the first issue; *LCP*, p. 277, claims 3,000 copies. The conservative report is more likely to be true. In "Reminiscence," 1917, p. 299, Hall made his largest claim of financial loss: he put $8,000 of his own money into the *Journal* in its first few years, he said, and the venture "only five years ago began to show a clear balance." According to Titchener, Hall was "perpetually talking dollars, and bemoaning that he had no more." Titchener to S. C. Fisher, 9 Dec 1924, TP.

8. GSH, "Editorial Note," 1887, pp. 3–4.

psychopathology. The *Journal* clearly bore the stamp of its editor. All but one of the contributors and reviewers were Hall's colleagues or students at Hopkins, and Hall himself, besides contributing an article, wrote more than two-thirds of the sixty-seven pages of reviews. In his reviews, Hall set out aggressively to distinguish scientific psychology from its philosophical forebears. He delimited the true field of psychology by showing how far short of scientific standards fell three psychological texts by three outstanding representatives of the American philosophical tradition.

Of the *Psychology* of James McCosh, president of Princeton and the leading advocate of Scotch realism in America, Hall stated, "Judged from a scientific standpoint . . . little that is good can be said." Despite McCosh's surprising and admirable open-mindedness to the new scientific influences, he everywhere betrayed his essential imperviousness to them and in statement of fact was "inexcusably careless." Even from a philosophical point of view, McCosh's position was not realism, as he claimed, "but eclecticism in every respect, which makes that word philosophically offensive."[9]

Next in the line of attack was the psychology of Borden P. Bowne, professor of philosophy at Boston University and a Christian philosopher influenced by Kant and contemporary German idealism. Bowne's opposition to materialism, Hall said, was less a reasoned philosophical position than "hylephobia, or morbid fear of materialism," an affliction "now often regarded as a sacred madness, as epilepsy used to be. It befalls only the good." Hall suspected that Bowne's "ignorance and audacious defiance of authorities is a part of the disease, and thus as sublime as the filth in which white-souled anchorites gloried." Hall's vivid similes could hardly have been appreciated by the Christian critics of the new psychology.[10]

To the third philosopher, Hall was more respectful. John Dewey, formerly his student at Johns Hopkins, had attempted a college-level text of psychology. He had thought through afresh the facts of psychology from the point of view of Hegelian philosophy, and Hall praised the "vigor, coherence, and originality" of the young

9. GSH, "Psychological Literature," 1887, pp. 146–49.
10. Ibid., pp. 149–54.

author's work. In reality, however, Dewey had done little more than spread a web of Hegelian definition over the field:

That the absolute idealism of Hegel could be so cleverly adapted to be "read into" such a range of facts, new and old, is indeed a surprise as great as when geology and zoology are ingeniously subjected to the rubrics of the six days of creation.

Such "naive" effort was "pathetic." From the point of view of scientific psychology, Dewey's Hegelian idealism represented "a stage of development which minds that come to full scientific maturity are certain to transcend."[11] These critiques of American philosophy must have left no doubt in the minds of traditional philosophers that the new psychology which sought entrance to their departments and universities was not a tame cousin easily to be brought into the old family.

Hall did not stop at philosophy but went on to the new psychology itself. George Trumbull Ladd, professor of philosophy at Yale, and like James, just two years Hall's senior, had taught himself physiology and mastered the psychophysiological literature of England and Germany, though not himself an experimenter. A devout minister as well as a philosopher, he believed the new psychology to be in harmony with his philosophical and religious principles and wished to encourage its development as a science in America. His *Elements of Physiological Psychology*, published in 1887, was the first American text in the new field. Ladd had recognized Hall as a fellow scientific pioneer in the field by asking him before the book appeared "as an expert in such matters, to help me improve the book by correcting mistakes and revising its judgments."[12]

Ladd's *Psychology*, Hall was quick to point out, was the only text in English which did not merely illustrate some theory or system, but whose "system consists in a plain grouping of the facts which are allowed to speak out for themselves." Its merit was thus incomparably greater than any other single volume in English. Hall fulfilled Ladd's wish for correction rather better than the author probably intended, however, for he devoted the body of his review

11. Ibid., pp. 154–59.
12. G. T. Ladd to GSH, 30 Mar 1887, CUP.

to a detailed discussion of "the significant defects of the book, which it is hoped may be remedied in another well-revised edition."[13]

Hall argued that despite Ladd's mastery of the physiological literature, he lacked the full understanding and perspective of science which can come only to a man who has worked long hours in the laboratory at close quarters with the raw materials of nature. Ladd viewed psychology with the eyes of Peter Bell, "which seeing, see not." Moreover, in the last section of the work, "The Mind as a Real Being," Ladd went off wholly into philosophy. To Ladd, this demonstration of the insufficiency of physiological psychology to explain the existential facts of mind was the pinnacle and real love of his work, but to Hall it was simply extraneous. Ladd's statements were "mild and commonplace Lotzeanisms" with which he would not quarrel.

It can be said in any field of science that there is a something quintessential not yet explored. Science is not ontology, but phenomenology, and there is nothing in physiological psychology to disprove the author's creed nor our own.

Psychologists must now abandon these old philosophical problems and "really work on whatever theory."[14]

There was one type of research and theory, however, at which Hall drew the line. Hall gave his longest review to the latest volume of proceedings of the English Society for Psychical Research and a new treatise on psychical phenomena by four of the more enthusiastic English researchers. Although they claimed to have conducted their studies with foolproof scientific precautions, Hall threw a blanket of doubt over their methods. By exposing the "tricks of our automatic nature," he argued for alternative hypotheses which these researchers had never considered.[15]

Hall objected to psychical research not merely on the ground of faulty method; the subject did not belong in a science of psychology at all:

When we reflect how few are the well established facts that are exact and certain, and on the labor by which they were demonstrated, or on how rare

13. GSH, "Psychological Literature," 1887, pp. 159–60.
14. Ibid., pp. 162–64.
15. Ibid., pp. 128–44.

are well ordered cohesions of thought . . . and remember that modern
science is already the greatest achievement of the human race, to bring one
solid contribution, to which individuals are more and more content to spend
a life of labor, we are reminded of Kant's well-known simile of an island
surrounded by an unknown and very tempting, but foggy, stormy sea. In
this sense telepathy is of the sea and not of the land. . . . Spiritualism, in its
more vulgar form, is the sewerage of all the superstitions of the past.

Hall knew from personal experience with what great effort and
sacrifice science had provided a tiny, solid island of fact and order
in the midst of the waters. He knew that the methods by which
academic psychology hoped to understand the relation between
mind and matter were "far harder and slower. But it is by these that
we prefer to labor." Hall summarized his position clearly: "We
desire, for our part, to see the psychological movement . . . kept in
the severest sense, experimental and scientific."[16]

Within the wide field of psychological endeavor the *Journal* was
intended to reach, its first issue was naturally received very favorably in circles predisposed to scientific attitudes. *Science* declared
the new journal "an ornament to American science" which proved
the importance and strength of the experimental movement in psychology. The technical character of the articles and the *Journal's*
willingness to "fearlessly combat views opposed to or neglecting
[technical, scientific] considerations" were to be applauded.[17] Edward Cowles, representing the progressive tendencies in psychiatry,
found the scientific spirit of Hall's journal wholly admirable and
was careful to point out besides that it was not "materialistic" in
any objectionable sense.[18] Croom Robertson, editor of *Mind*, viewing the journal from Britain and taking the rights of scientific psychology to its own standards for granted, was struck on reading the
journal by "what a stimulus to psychophysical research Prof. Stanley
Hall has been able, alike by example and precept, to communicate"
and especially pointed out to English readers Hall's "searching"
review of British psychical research.[19]

To those psychologists not committed to Hall's scientific program, however, his restricted journal was hardly welcome. The

16. Ibid., pp. 145–46.
17. "Book Reviews," *Science* 10 (Nov 1887): 248–49.
19. "Notes," *Mind* 13 (Jan 1888): 149.
18. Cowles, "The *AJP*," pp. 544–46.

reaction of the first of the new American psychologists was a crucial indication of the divisive role the journal would play in American psychology. While James wrote Hall that he "relished" the Mc-Cosh, Dewey, and Bowne reviews "amazingly" and thought the Ladd review "admirable in every respect, and fully agree with each word of it," he was disturbed by Hall's review of psychical research:

> To take sides as positively as you do now and on general philosophic grounds, seems to me a very dangerous and unscientific attitude. . . . I should express the difference between our two positions in the matter, by calling mine a baldly empirical one, and yours, one due to a general theoretic creed. . . . I don't think it exactly fair to make the issue what you make it—one between Science and Superstition.

It was as easy for James to see the "theoretic creed" behind Hall's position on psychical research as it was for Hall to see the religious and philosophical motives that guided James's. Neither man could win the argument in those terms.[20]

Hall's opposition to psychical research was no novelty for James, however, and they had argued their positions before. James's chief objection to the *Journal* went deeper, so deep in fact that he could not bring himself to express it publicly. Hall had asked that James review the first issue of the new journal for the *Nation*. When James said that he would be glad to do a "note" on it, Hall replied with a letter that fairly leapt from the page in thick, black, passionate script:

> Don't you think there has been too much hard, boring, solid work put into the Journal of psychology and that the newness and significance of the departure it represents is too great to be represented by a *note* such as you intend for the *Nation*. The journal is full of faults . . . but it is a *very* new departure and a very significant one. The *worst* thing that could be done for it would be a brief and generally complimentary note. I beg you not to do that. Criticize it as vigorously as you will in any way but *please* don't offer the Nation whose words will have such an effect on it . . . such a note as your words suggest to me.[21]

Obviously stunned by the intensity of Hall's response, James tried to escape as graciously as possible.

20. Wm. James to GSH, 5 and 10 Nov 1887, HP.
21. GSH to Wm. James, 3 Nov 1887, JP.

Your letter aboùt the *Nation* notice, I confess embarrasses me a little. . . .
You implore me so vehemently to pay it no general compliments that for
fear of displeasing you I am quite paralyzed, and think that possibly Jastrow
. . . might write something that would please you better.[22]

Hall evidently told James to go ahead with the review, but five days
later James gave up the effort.

I have been trying to write the notice of the Journal for an hour or more,
but find that all spontaneity has left me for the purpose, and that between
my conscience towards the Nation, towards you, and towards myself, I feel
so paralyzed that to copy the prospectus and a table of contents is all I'm
good for. It doesn't do to have a slight job made formidable. . . . Pray don't
think me "put out" in the least. I started to write with the heartiest good
will to the job, but found myself so subtly inhibited that it would not go.
Tameness incarnate became the only possible line—and that wd. please
you as little as it pleases me.[23]

What it was that inhibited James can be seen in his comment on
Hall to Croom Robertson written just the day before while he was
struggling with the review. James described Hall as

a wonderful creature. Never an articulate conception comes out of him, but
instead of it a sort of palpitating influence making all men believe that the
way to save their souls psychologically lies through the infinite assimilation
of jawbreaking German laboratory-articles. If you try to draw any expres-
sible theoretic conclusion from any of them, he won't hear of it; what you
ought to do is to pass on to a lot more of them, and so *in infinitum*.[24]

James's objection lay in the aggressively empirical and experimental
character of the *American Journal*.

James had been against making the journal "too empirical" when
he first heard of Hall's plan for a psychological periodical. He had
written Hall:

If I were you I should not insist on too narrow an interpretation of the
word psychological, not make it too empirical, but admit a good deal of
argumentative matter, if such be forthcoming. . . . I may be able to send
you a few little empirical scraps within the year, tho' I'm doing now no
experimental work.[25]

22. Wm. James to GSH, 5 Nov 1887, HP.
23. Wm. James to GSH, 10 Nov 1887, HP.
24. Wm. James to Robertson, 9 Nov 1887, in Perry, *William James,* 2: 85.
25. Wm. James to GSH, 30 Jan [1887], HP.

The development of experimental psychology had aroused some skepticism in James from the beginning. Though committed by vocation and choice to a scientific stance, James, like Hall, craved philosophic significance. In 1887, moreover, he was nearing a decade's labor on precisely the kind of synthetic, speculative psychological treatise Hall condemned. There was certainly resentment, as well as opposition, in James's denigrating reference to "a few little empirical scraps" and to the review of the *Journal* as a "slight job." Thus, while the *Journal* purported to bring the various contributors to the new psychology together, it in fact tried to impose a narrower definition of the field than existed at the time and to exclude those who did not fall within its scope. In framing the *Journal* as he had, Hall had ignored James's advice and challenged his psychological position. His journal was a bid for the leadership of the new profession.

In the light of this purpose, James's ambivalence seems all the more understandable, and Hall's desire for his opinion all the more characteristic. Hall clearly wanted to provoke James to a response, wanted almost to be punished for his revolt. Hall wrote the philosopher Thomas Davidson, whom he had known since his Cambridge days:

I am longing to have some one attack [the Journal of Psychology]. It is very open to criticism and I am sick of the pallid, mostly goody things I see about it in the papers. . . . I am now longing to be told where I am *wrong,* in the plan and details of the Journal and will love forever the man who will criticize frankly and honestly from a different standpoint.[26]

The journal would not achieve its personal function if it only evoked praise.

To some extent, Hall's position was typical of the scientism of the new academic disciplines in the 1880s, and also reflected the characteristic effort of newly professionalizing sciences in America to aggressively define themselves.[27] At a time when the profession was so small and dispersed, however, and when so little consensus ex-

    26. GSH to Davidson, 6 Dec 1887, Thomas Davidson Papers, Yale University Library, New Haven.
    27. Hawkins, *Pioneer,* pp. 295–97; George H. Daniels, "The Process of Professionalization in American Science: The Emergent Period, 1820–1860," *Isis* 58 (1967): 151–66.

isted on the standards to be exercised, a journal might well have taken a less aggressive and divisive stand at the outset. Hall felt more keenly than most, perhaps, the tensions that were a part of his membership in both a new science and the older culture of the puritan village. His strident condemnations of philosophical speculation and his martyred acceptance of the slow, difficult methods of natural science were aimed at his own philosophical impulses. It may appear paradoxical that the first champion of a strictly scientific psychology in America was a man who was determined to formulate a scientific philosophy compatible with religion, that the first psychologist to publicly berate America's Christian philosopher-psychologists in the name of science was a man who was anxious to effect a reconciliation between science and religion. The ambivalence which made Hall so desirous of religious approval, however, also contributed to his aggressive scientism.

In the spring of 1888, Hall left Johns Hopkins to assume the presidency of Clark University, an entirely graduate university to be established in Worcester, Massachusetts, and the emphasis Hall put on psychology at Clark was important to the early development of the profession. The status of psychology was one of the considerations which initially led Hall to abandon Hopkins. Though several other aspects of the new venture attracted him, he was on the whole reluctant to leave the pleasant and profitable Hopkins environment. By such outward standards as the number of students he attracted to his courses, Hall's work was proving successful. The success of the department could also be seen in the large number of inquiries about it that had been received from all over the country and the large number of Hopkins college graduates who wanted to do advanced work in psychology.[28]

The department was, however, still very new, and the laboratory had never been formally recognized and subsidized by the university on a par with the other science laboratories. Nor did Hall's journal receive a subsidy from the university as did a number of the other journals organized at Hopkins.[29] Hall evidently feared that he

---

28. *Ann. Rep. Pres. Hopk.*, *1886–87*, p. 5; *1887–88*, p. 5; E. C. Sanford et al., "Communication Regarding Professor Hall's Departure," June 1888, Alumni Records Office, Johns Hopkins University.

29. *Ann. Rep. Pres. Hopk.*, *1884–88*, passim; Hawkins, *Pioneer*, p. 109.

might not be able to hold his own in the competition for funds. In March 1888, he wrote Gilman:

The chief consideration in my mind up to the present time is to know whether my work has so commended itself to the honorable board you represent that it might henceforth enjoy opportunities in the matters of aid for the Journal, apparatus and [salaries?] equal to the older departments of the university for further unfoldment in case I should decide not to go to Worcester.[30]

Gilman was probably not able to assure Hall of such opportunities. Financial conditions had been worsening since 1886, and in 1888 the university faced a serious crisis for funds which, among other things, forced the postponement of the opening of the hospital and the formation of the medical school for some years.[31] With seemingly unlimited prospects for expansion beckoning at Worcester, Hall resigned the following month, April 1888.[32]

When Hall left Hopkins, he probably took with him most of the psychological laboratory equipment.[33] Moreover, he brought his best-trained students to Clark: Donaldson, as assistant professor of neurology to work in physiological psychology; Sanford, as instructor to direct the psychological laboratory; and Burnham, as docent to work on education as related to psychology. With so much of its native talent and facilities gone, and its financial future insecure, Hopkins did not reestablish a psychological laboratory and department until 1903.

30. GSH to Gilman, 13 Mar 1888, Alumni Records Office, Johns Hopkins University. The copy of this letter reprinted in N. Orwin Rush, ed., *Letters of G. Stanley Hall to Jonas Gilman Clark* (Worcester: Clark University Library, 1948), p. 1, is badly garbled.

31. Chesney, *The Johns Hopkins Hospital,* 1: 95–96.

32. GSH to Gilman, 16 Apr 1888, Alumni Records Office, Johns Hopkins University. Hall later claimed that after he had publicly accepted the Clark position, the university offered to increase his salary from $4,000 to $5,000 per year, but by that time he felt bound to go to Clark. Amy Tanner, "History of Clark University through the Interpretation of the Will of the Founder" (May 1908), p. 37, CUP.

33. Hall claimed, *LCP,* p. 259, that "the apparatus of my laboratory [was] distributed among other departments." However, William O. Krohn, "Facilities in Experimental Psychology in the Colleges of the United States," *Report of the United States Commissioner of Education, 1890–1891,* 2: 1141, stated that the Clark laboratory "comprises nearly all the original apparatus used in the first laboratory in this country, that of Johns Hopkins University."

The psychology department Hall founded at Clark was distinguished not only by the talented nucleus brought from Hopkins but by the strength of fields related to the new psychology. Franz Boas was named docent in anthropology, while the biology department at Clark promised to be one of the most advanced and distinguished in the country. At the time of its opening and during its first years of operation, Clark University was widely heralded as the pure embodiment of the most progressive tendencies in American higher education, and the firm establishment of scientific psychology there was a token of its prestige and a stimulus to its diffusion.[34]

Clark's preeminence in psychology directly encouraged the enlargement of the Harvard experimental program. James was particularly sensitive to the standing of his university,[35] and when Clark appeared as a rival to Harvard in his own field he was quite wary. During the spring of 1890, the first year of Clark's operation, Hall opened with James the subject of institutional cooperation by writing him that he had advised his best student in philosophy and historical-ethical psychology to apply at Harvard "because you can do so much better by him in his lines at Harvard than we can." Hall concluded with the hope "that in the philosophical field at large Harvard University and this may continue to supplement and not duplicate each other."[36] Hall's proposal was probably prompted by the knowledge that James was planning to add a research laboratory to the Harvard department.[37] Hall was obviously hoping that Harvard would not expand its laboratory offerings sufficiently to compete with Clark and that Clark in turn would be free not to build a full philosophical department.

Such interuniversity specialization and cooperation, however, was not to be the course of development that American universities fol-

34. See below, chap. 11, and Albrecht, "The New Psychology in America," pp. 136–38.

35. During one of James's visits to Hopkins, when Hall repeated to him a remark by one of the chemists that more chemical work was being done at Hopkins than at Harvard, James was sufficiently aroused to check the fact with the Harvard chemists, refute it, and urge Hall to correct the misimpression at Hopkins. Wm. James to GSH, 22 Apr [1886], HP.

36. GSH to Wm. James, 29 Mar 1890, JP.

37. *AJP* 3 (Apr 1890): 278.

lowed. This time it was evidently James who retorted emotionally, for Hall promptly wrote back:

How you pervert my meaning! I am not assuming to be able to carry men beyond you, but we are fitting up four rooms at much expense and have four men solely for empirical study of physico-psychology, next year our arrangements will probably be complete. This as you know, is far more in this particular line than is now anywhere attempted. What I mean by not duplicating would be therefore, when you have men with a strong tendency to the experimental, or we to the introspective, historical, or ethical, for us to regard the departments of both institutions as if they were in one University so far as advising students as to their course goes. Is not this plain and reasonable?[38]

James's reaction was evidently more favorable to Hall's plans after this explanation, though he stipulated, and Hall agreed, that Harvard should not be expected to "turn away all men who want Experimental Psychology."[39]

The plan was not finally adopted, however. The year after this exchange, James raised $4,300 to establish a laboratory, and though he doubted the fruitfulness of the experimental movement, he expended great energy and pains to start the laboratory and put it under expert management. As he wrote to Hugo Münsterberg, the Freiburg psychologist whom he hired to direct the new laboratory, "We are the best university in America, and we must lead in psychology."[40] This kind of competitive spirit among American universities undoubtedly accounted in part for the rapid adoption here of scientific psychology, particularly since it was accepted by the two leading symbols of progressive university reform in the 1880s, Johns Hopkins and Clark.[41]

The final contribution Hall was to make to the institutional base of the new psychology was his organization of the American Psychological Association. Hall sent out invitations to at least twenty-six people interested in the new psychology to attend a preliminary meeting at Clark on 8 July 1892; almost certainly the idea of an association originated with him. Hall's conception of the association was liberal and statesmanlike; he invited the full range of psy-

---

38. GSH to Wm. James, 1 Apr 1890, JP.
39. GSH to Wm. James, 7 Apr 1890, JP.
40. Perry, *William James,* 2: 15; Wm. James to Münsterberg, 21 Feb 1892, in Ibid., p. 139.
41. Albrecht, "The New Psychology in America," pp. 134–38.

chologists regardless of how he differed with them personally or intellectually, from William James and his colleague in philosophy at Harvard, Josiah Royce, to John Dewey, then teaching at the University of Michigan, and James Mark Baldwin of the University of Toronto.[42] Hall evidently recognized that to attempt to restrict membership from the outset to those wholly in sympathy with his views and his personal leadership would have created open division in the profession and aroused opposition from many who were not firmly in his camp but whose support he needed. Moreover, his judgment in this instance was not clouded by a heavy investment of his own funds and effort, as was the case with his journal.

James, and perhaps Ladd as well, were nevertheless somewhat wary of Hall's intentions. James, who was in Europe at the time, could not have attended the meeting had he wished to, but according to Cattell, "James . . . was not at the beginning particularly favorable to the organization."[43] Ladd, though presumably he could easily have done so, did not attend.[44] Both, however, accepted membership, and perhaps half of the twenty-six charter members met in Worcester and elected Hall their first president. The council they elected to plan the first formal meeting and "to report a plan of organization" was not limited to those of Hall's persuasion.[45]

The representative character of this preliminary meeting evi-

42. *Proceedings of the American Psychological Association . . . 1892, 1893* (New York: Macmillan, [1894]), pp. 1–2; Joseph Jastrow, "American Psychology in the '80's and '90's," *PR* 50 (Jan 1943): 65–67; S. W. Fernberger, "The American Psychological Association, 1892–1942," ibid., pp. 34–36; Wayne Dennis and Edwin G. Boring, "The Founding of the APA," *American Psychologist* 7 (1952): 95.

43. J. M. Cattell to S. W. Fernberger, 17 Dec 1940, in Fernberger, "The APA," p. 35.

44. Dennis and Boring, "Founding of the APA," pp. 96–97. One account of the founding of the association, by a former student of Hall's and hence probably from Hall's testimony, stated that Hall "planned, in conference with Professor Ladd and others, a society of psychologists, and invited more than a score to meet at Clark University on July 8, 1892." Edward F. Buchner, "A Quarter Century of Psychology in America: 1878–1903," *AJP* 14 (July-Oct 1903): 413. If Hall did consult with Ladd, the fact of Ladd's absence and of Hall's issuance of the invitation in his own name, suggests some initial difference of opinion. The "others" Hall may have consulted could have been Sanford and the Clark psychologists. The fact that this account probably came from Hall himself, however, is no guarantee of its accuracy.

45. Dennis and Boring, "Fouding of the APA," pp. 96–97; *Proceedings, APA, 1892, 1893*, p. 1.

dently allayed whatever fears of exclusiveness Hall's sponsorship had portended. At the first formal meeting, held in December 1892 at the University of Pennsylvania, Hall presided and all the major psychologists attended, except James who was still in Europe. No qualifications for membership were suggested; no statement of aims or constitution adopted. A number of philosophically inclined psychologists were nominated for membership, and Ladd was elected president for the following year.[46] The effectiveness of this inclusive organizational policy and the mutual contact it initiated probably accelerated the desire in the profession for an equally inclusive psychological journal.

While the psychological profession was still small in 1892 when Hall served as the first president of the association, its rapid growth since he had founded the *Journal* five years earlier had justified his optimistic faith. Laboratories already had been founded at Wisconsin, Pennsylvania, Toronto, Columbia, Harvard, Cornell, and Yale, as well as at almost a dozen other institutions. Hall himself had granted nine doctorates at Johns Hopkins and Clark, and soon the newer psychology departments would begin to graduate students.[47] By the end of 1892, 31 members had joined the association. Four years later there were 74 members and by 1900, 127. By 1897, there were more doctorates in psychology awarded in the United States than in any other science except chemistry.[48] Entering the university structure at a time when it was beginning a rapid expansion, particularly in the direction of modern, scientific studies, psychology established itself in America far more quickly than even Hall expected when he found his way to the field in the 1870s and struggled for a place in the early eighties.

The ability of psychology to allay traditional religious objections also contributed to this result. As a science of the mind, psychology could easily have been considered the most dangerous of all the modern subjects that desired entrance to the university. It was ex-

46. Ibid., pp. 12–14.

47. C. R. Garvey, "List of American Psychology Laboratories," pp. 653–54; Robert S. Harper, "Tables of American Doctorates in Psychology," pp. 580, 585.

48. J. M. Cattell, "The Advance of Psychology," in *James McKeen Cattell, 1860–1944: Man of Science,* ed. A. T. Poffenberger (Lancaster, Pa.: Science Press, 1947), 2: 108; "Psychology in America," ibid., p. 455.

tremely reassuring that the three founders of the science in America
—James, Hall, and Ladd—were all desirous of maintaining traditional Christian belief and outspokenly declared their subject to
support it. Particularly Hall's efforts in the 1880s, so visible from
his posts at Hopkins and then Clark, eased the way at the critical
early stage.

After once gaining a foothold, psychology continued to show
itself accommodating to traditional religion by ignoring it, as outside its sphere of competence. As Hall declared at the opening of
Clark University,

> The natural instinct of every ambitious youth is to excel . . . to be an author-
> ity, to surpass all others, if only in the most acuminated specialty. Learning
> thus what true mental freedom is he is more docile in all other directions.[49]

Hall had early sensed, as Haeckel had in Germany, the conservative
safety and the capitulation to authority in the narrowed focus of
scientific expertise. He believed that "it is this method of self-control
and subordination, that has commended the scientific method in
psychology to the confidence of conservative administrative boards,
and by which its recent remarkable academic extension in the universities and colleges of this country has been made."[50] Hall's estimate of the situation in the 1880s may well have been sound. He
could also have added that students probably flocked to the new
field because it gave them, as it had given Hall himself, a scientific
format for earlier religious and philosophical allegiances.

49. *Clark University, Worcester, Massachusetts: Opening Exercises, October
2, 1889,* (printed by the University), p. 24.
50. *AJP* 3 (1891): 590–91. Hall, like James and others of his generation, was
himself too firmly rooted in religious concerns entirely to ignore the subject; he
periodically discussed the psychology of religion during his later years.

11   A TRUE UNIVERSITY

In January 1887, when Stanley Hall was just organizing the *American Journal of Psychology* at Johns Hopkins University, Jonas Gilman Clark, a retired businessman, and eight other gentlemen of Worcester, Massachusetts, petitioned the state legislature to incorporate an institution in Worcester to be known as Clark University. Even in an age of generous gifts by men of wealth to cultural institutions, the announcement of Mr. Clark's gift of one million dollars to the proposed university was impressive, the largest single gift to an educational institution in New England up to that time.[1]

Jonas Clark had been born in a small farming village close to Worcester in 1815.[2] Without formal education, he had started as a peddler, moved to California during the gold rush, and became a prominent San Francisco merchant. Exhausted at the age of fifty, he had put his money into securities and New York and Boston real estate, and set out on the first of five extended trips to Europe. There Clark and his wife made the rounds of fashionable resorts

1. Amy Tanner, "History of Clark University through the Interpretation of the Will of the Founder," (May 1908) CUP, pp. 15–19; Merle Curti and Roderick Nash, *Philanthropy in the Shaping of American Higher Education* (New Brunswick: Rutgers University Press, 1965).
2. This sketch of Jonas Clark is drawn from Calvin Stebbins in "Founder's Day. Clark University," *CULP* 1 (1905): 138–61; Susan Wright Clark, ed., *In Memoriam: Jonas Gilman Clark* (New York: Atlantic, 1900); Tanner, "Clark University," pp. 3–12; E. B. Titchener to L. N. Wilson, 5 Aug 1926, CUP.

and cultural landmarks, collected a group of mediocre paintings and a good library of rare and finely bound books,[3] and gathered an external knowledge of some of the leading European universities. As his health deteriorated, the childless Clark came to feel a need for some more definite purpose and lasting achievement in his life. In 1880, when he was sixty-five, he tried to find these by returning to his native grounds and, for the first time in his life, conducting charitable works. Slowly, he matured in his mind the plan for an educational institution which would bear his name.

Clark had left the area an obscure young businessman of no special distinction; he returned to join the local gentry whom he did not know and still held somewhat in awe. Clark's chief purpose was to "found something *in* and *for Worcester.*"[4] He hoped to win the esteem of Worcester by becoming a benefactor of the young men of the city who sought a higher education and by binding the local aristocracy to him in this noble project. Clark had sensed in Europe the value of high culture. He always kept several of his rare books around him; now and again he would take one of them up and stroke its cover. Clark's understanding of higher education was only superficial, but he determined to buy at second hand a bit of the prestige and elevation he sensed in it.

The character of Clark's business experience combined with his native reserve to produce a personality hostile in many ways to the demands of enlightened philanthropy. During his years in business, Clark had kept direct control of his affairs, and when his business grew to the point where he no longer had the stamina to supervise it himself, he sold it and invested his assets in relatively conservative ways. Clark's mentality never really grew beyond the limits of the small-scale entrepreneur on the rise. Among the businessmen of his age, he was not an imaginative or resourceful figure. One of his few personal friends described how Clark

was very reluctant to let things pass out of his hands and lose control of them. Thus, for instance, if he gave a valuable watch to a friend, and here I am using a case that actually happened, he gave it in such a way that it

3. L. N. Wilson, ed., "List of Books and Pictures in the Clark Memorial Collection," *CULP* 2 (1906).
4. J. D. Washburn to Gilman, 22 Jan 1887, GP.

was difficult for his friend to tell whether it was loaned to him or given outright.[5]

Stiff and formal in manner, he was inclined to keep his own counsel and to watch carefully at some distance before committing himself fully to any venture.

Clark proceeded to choose eight men to act with him as a board of trustees.[6] His first choice was Stephen Salisbury, whom, "for very obvious reasons, he desired to commit at an early stage to sympathy in his purpose."[7] Salisbury was the head of perhaps the wealthiest and most respected family in Worcester, which supported a number of the city's cultural institutions. A bachelor then in his sixties, he devoted his time entirely to the management of his fortune and philanthropies. Clark also chose early John D. Washburn, a lawyer and former congressman who served on Harvard's Board of Overseers and was later to leave Worcester to become minister to Switzerland. Washburn, a neighbor of Clark's, was the only trustee with whom he talked privately about his plans.

Perhaps the most distinguished member of the board, and the one whom Clark himself held most in awe, was Senator George F. Hoar, widely respected for his scholarship as well as for his accomplishments at the Worcester bar and the United States Senate. Clark engaged two other members of the bar and two businessmen. The only person of scientific training was a respected local physician who died before the university actually opened. He was later replaced, at Stanley Hall's suggestion, by Dr. Edward Cowles, the director of the McLean Hospital who had studied with Hall at Hopkins.

Clark's choice of trustees was, on the whole, fortunate. Nearly all of the eight gentlemen were well known to Worcester and respected in the community; yet six of the eight had had experience of a larger sphere of affairs. Four members of the board—Salisbury, Hoar, Washburn, and when he was added, Cowles—had an informed concern with educational matters. The two members most inclined to take an active interest in shaping the university, Washburn and Senator Hoar, were of this group.

5. Stebbins, "Founder's Day," p. 146.
6. On the board members, see *LCP,* pp. 280–87; Wilson, *GSH,* pp. 73–74.
7. J. D. Washburn to Gilman, 22 Jan 1887, GP.

Precisely what Clark intended his university to be when he announced its establishment in January 1887 was a matter of some debate at the time, as well as since, for his public pronouncements were vague and general.[8] The view that Clark originally wanted to found an undergraduate college for poor country boys and that he had to be convinced by others, chiefly by Hall, to found a university has been firmly established by the word of later commentators.[9] Contemporary evidence suggests, however, that Clark's ideas changed during the course of the development of the university. At the start, Clark wanted a university in the popular sense of the word, an institution embracing both collegiate work and the higher graduate work he had observed in the European universities.

The act of incorporation Clark presented in January 1887 contemplated "an institution for the promotion of education and investigation in science, literature and art."[10] In March, when a hearing was held on Clark's petition, a Cambridge gentleman reported that when he questioned Clark about his plans, Clark replied

that he had the Johns Hopkins University at Baltimore in his eye as a model, that he expected something higher than Harvard and that there would be the utmost breadth and freedom both of teaching and of investigation.[11]

The words of the founder himself, addressing the board in May 1887 on receipt of their charter, corroborates this view. Concerning the plan of the university, Clark pointed to Cornell and Johns Hopkins, "to the general scope, purpose and methods of which I would invite your special attention."[12] Finally, Stanley Hall remembered that Clark was

8. Tanner, "Clark University," pp. 18–19; *Clark Clippings, 1875* and *1887,* passim, CUP. The series of clipping books at Clark are variously titled (hereafter all books cited as *Clippings*); the date identifying the volume rarely conforms to the dates of the clippings therein.
9. E.g., W. Carson Ryan, *Studies in Early Graduate Education: The Johns Hopkins, Clark University and the University of Chicago* (New York: Carnegie Foundation for the Advancement of Teaching, 1939), p. 49. The chief source of this view is L. N. Wilson, "Some Recollections of Our Founder," *CULP* 8 (1927): 6–8. Wilson's understanding of Clark's original intentions, to which he was not privy, evidently arose from the period 1889–92, when Clark grew disillusioned with the university and turned his hopes exclusively on an undergraduate college.
10. Wilson, *GSH,* p. 75.
11. Edward C. Towne, "Letter to Editor," Boston *Advertiser,* 9 Mar 1887, in *Clippings, 1875,* CUP.
12. Wilson, "Recollections," p. 16.

profoundly impressed with two ideas; first, the necessity of giving young men an education that would fit them for "good citizenship and their work in life" and, second, the establishment of a university which, like the Johns Hopkins, should add to the sum of human knowledge.[13]

He saw no difficulty, as indeed Ezra Cornell and Andrew D. White saw no difficulty at Cornell, in combining an undergraduate college and advanced university education.[14]

Clark did, however, believe that the college would be the core of the institution from which the university grew. He told the trustees on receipt of their charter that he would start at once with the college, but

during the four years which will be occupied for this first class in its undergraduate course, we shall need to prepare other buildings and provide other facilities, that we may be in readiness for the members of this class or such of them as may desire to avail themselves of the opportunity, to enter at once upon the post-graduate courses, professional or otherwise. . . . These post-graduate and professional courses, allow me to say . . . should be made to embrace as wide a range as possible of Theology, Philosophy, Science, Literature and Art.[15]

In a manner understandable for a self-made man of his era, Clark believed in the slow and inevitable growth of institutions from small, well-planted seeds.

Clark had then, the general notion of a "university" in mind, but did not know how to proceed further. His gift would provide the university with a productive endowment of about $600,000, a sum equal to that of Dartmouth College in 1885 and far below the three million dollars available to Johns Hopkins and almost five million dollars of Harvard University in that year.[16] From the time of the granting of the charter in the spring of 1887, however, Clark appeared preoccupied with the construction of the university buildings, which he began at once and supervised closely.[17]

13. *LCP*, p. 261.
14. Tanner, "Clark University," p. 15; Laurence Russ Veysey, *The Emergence of the American University* (Chicago: University of Chicago Press, 1965), pp. 81–86.
15. Wilson, "Recollections," p. 17.
16. T. W. Goodspeed to J. D. Rockefeller, 22 Nov 1888, in Frederick T. Gates, ed., *Correspondence of the Founder and His Associates,* vol. 1, University of Chicago Special Collections.
17. Tanner, "Clark University," pp. 24–30; J. D. Washburn to Gilman, 3 Oct 1887, GP.

Washburn was concerned, however, with what the buildings would contain. He recognized "how absurd it would be" to attempt to imitate Harvard "with one, two, or five millions, and in less than a century." He thus thought to "set up something in *one of the great Departments of learning* . . . label it 'Clark University,' and place it as high as anything in that department has gone."[18] President Gilman of Hopkins suggested the establishment of a graduate institute of science or technology, possibly in connection with the Worcester Institute.[19] Washburn brought Senator Hoar into his consultations with Gilman, but by the end of the year, no clear idea had emerged. Therefore, they began to concentrate their efforts on finding a president, who "would have a very potential if not conclusive voice, in determining the scope and character of the institution."[20]

A number of men were proposed for the position, though no one candidate appeared close to appointment before Hall came to their attention early in 1888.[21] On 22 January 1888, Hoar wrote Clark that Hall had been recommended to him from several sources.[22] In 1888, Hall appeared in the academic world as a promising scien-

18. Washburn to Gilman, 22 Jan 1887, GP.
19. Washburn to Gilman, 22 Jan 1887; 4, 12, 16 Feb 1887, GP; G. F. Hoar to Gilman, 18 Feb 1887, GP. Washburn was anxious to avoid any rivalry with his own school, Harvard. After consulting with President Eliot, he hoped to make the institution "a useful out-work and strong support of Harvard." He would even try to get Clark to give one or two hundred thousand dollars directly to Harvard. Washburn to Eliot, 12 Dec 1887; 24 Jan 1887, Eliot Papers, Harvard University Archives.
20. Washburn to Eliot, 12 Dec 1887, Eliot Papers.
21. Gilman was convinced that Clark would have to "discover among young men, not well known, one who gives high promise." He suggested John Trowbridge, professor of physics at Harvard. Gilman to Washburn, 14 Oct 1887, GSH Memorial Volume, CUP. Other names that had come to the attention of the trustees were George Herbert Palmer, the Harvard philosopher; Charles Franklin Emerson, professor of natural philosophy at Dartmouth College; Henry Barker Hill, professor of chemistry at Harvard; and Edwin P. Seaver, a native of Worcester and superintendent of schools in Boston, to whom Washburn most strongly inclined. Washburn to Eliot, 12 Dec 1887, Eliot Papers. Clark himself had tried to engage as president Nicholas Murray Butler, but after an interview, Butler declined, as he said, the presidency of the "Mr. and Mrs. Jonas G. Clark University."
22. Tanner, "Clark University," p. 37. A recommendation may have come from the Reverend Edward Everett Hale, a regular correspondent of Hoar's who had respected Hall since he met him at Antioch. Wilson suggested that Hall may also have been recommended by President William De Witt Hyde of Bowdoin College. Wilson, "Recollections," p. 7.

tist, a rising leader of the new psychological profession, and a man of still publicly unquestioned character. He was, moreover, a native of western Massachusetts. At some early point, Hoar must have talked about Hall with Gilman. The president could commend Hall's ability without reservation and feel that he was enlarging opportunities for one of his ambitious young professors. In addition, he could not have been unhappy to remove the pressure for funds Hall put on him and to end the obstructions to obtaining other kinds of philosophical instruction Hall had placed in his way.[23]

After an interview with Hall, Hoar "was very favorably impressed indeed by his modesty, earnestness and good sense." After further interviews with several trustees and with Clark himself in Baltimore and then in Worcester, Hall accepted their offer of the presidency of the new university on 5 April 1888.[24]

Hall's willingness to take on this task rested partly on his large ambitions for psychology, which Johns Hopkins could no longer promise to fulfill, and partly on his large personal ambitions. Hall's skills in public speaking and persuasion had gone unused in the psychological laboratory and been exercised only in his homely activities in pedagogy. By 1888, moreover, he was reaching an impasse in his experimental work. Hall had been attracted to positions of community leadership since his years at Antioch, but he had never had the opportunity to exercise such leadership in a position that commanded the full respect of his intellectual and scientific loyalties. If the scope of the university materialized as Clark indicated that it would, Hall would find himself at the pinnacle of American higher education.

Despite these attractions, Hall had "misgivings in taking this step."[25] He may well have been reluctant to abandon psychological work for an indefinite length of time, as his executive duties would demand. Most likely, however, his "misgivings" were due to the difficulties already apparent in directing Jonas Clark's university,

23. Hammond, "Brief History, Dept. of Philosophy," p. 8, concluded "that there was some relief [at Hopkins] when Hall went on to the presidency of Clark."
24. Tanner, "Clark University," p. 37.
25. GSH to Gilman, 16 Apr 1888, Alumni Records Office, Johns Hopkins University.

but Hall's doubts were assuaged by the enlightened and congenial attitude of the trustees, particularly Washburn and Hoar, whose thinking already tended toward a limited establishment of graduate education. The official letter of the trustees offering Hall the presidency was exceptionally forthright in its offer of freedom:

In the work to which you are thus called the Trustees promise you a hearty and unselfish co-operation. They desire to impose on you no trammels; they have no friends for whom they wish to provide at the expense of the interests of the Institution; no pet theories to press upon you in derogation of your judgment; no sectarian tests to apply; no guarantees to require save such as are implied by your acceptance of this trust. Their single desire is to fit men for the highest duties of life, and to that end, that this Institution, in whatever branches of sound learning it may find itself engaged, may be made a leader and a light.[26]

Privately, Washburn added that "the letter I wrote you officially may be considered the charter of your liberties."

I was very particular that Mr. Clark should assent to [the trustees'] declarations fully and understandingly, and he has done so. I believe he will press no views of his own against your judgment, or that of the trustees.[27]

On the matter of buildings, Washburn realized, Clark would have his own way: "On that subject, he is quietly sure he knows more than any of us."[28] On matters of educational policy, however, Clark was expected to bow to wiser voices than his own.

Hall had proof of this situation in his own preliminary dealings with Clark. The university, as Hall conceived it, had its central core in the graduate department; an undergraduate division, if it existed at all, was subordinate in importance. Hall could exert an almost hypnotic power over his listeners when he was inspired by his subject, and such power he evidently exerted over Clark.[29] Before Hall accepted the presidency, he persuaded Clark to reverse his scheme: to found the graduate university first and let the college grow downward from that.[30] Hall must have counted heavily on the continued

26. Washburn to GSH, 3 Apr 1888, in Wilson, "Recollections," p. 21.
27. Washburn to GSH, 26 Apr [1888], CUP.
28. Washburn to D. C. Gilman, 3 Oct 1887, GP.
29. W. C. Ryan, interview with H. H. Donaldson, 22 Nov 1937, notes, CUP.
30. When Hall accepted his call, he acknowledged to Clark a "general understanding" to the effect that "the development of the college is to proceed in time, but in plans and endowment the University is to be the more important ulterior

effectiveness of his persuasive powers and on the prospect of the university being so great a success that an undergraduate department could be easily added.

Hall must also have worried about the funds that would be available to him. In announcing his gift, Clark linked his further gifts to donations from the community, and the trustees recognized his desire "to stimulate co-operation in other quarters" and hoped "that your example may find many imitators."[31] Despite this stipulation, however, it was tacitly understood by the trustees, and openly asserted in the newspapers, that Clark's gift was only the beginning of his ultimate benefaction. His fortune was rumored to be between five and eight million dollars, and as speculation about the university continued, the figure often rose to ten or twenty millions.[32] Washburn himself, though trying to plan soberly for a one million dollar endowment, could not keep his mind from running to the possibility that "two, three, four or five millions may be at our disposal."[33] Stanley Hall, with his high ambitions and vivid imagination, could hardly help but do the same.

In the spring of 1888, Hall left Johns Hopkins and moved to Worcester to begin to organize the university. As a guest living in Clark's home, Hall appeared to maintain very amicable relations with his patron. While Clark supervised the construction of the main university building and paid for the expenses that arose by his personal check, Hall began gathering advice from educational leaders and scientists. From every side, he found approval of the plan to found a graduate institution.[34] The reasonable course, Hall decided with Clark, was to open the university in five related departments of natural science—psychology, biology, chemistry, physics, and mathematics—and allow the university to grow out from that core.[35]

Hall convinced Clark to postpone the opening of the university

end in view." GSH to Clark, 5 Apr 1888, in Rush, *Letters of GSH to Clark,* p. 2.

31. Wilson, "Recollections," pp. 18–20.

32. Washburn to Gilman, 22 Jan 1887, GP; Tanner, "Clark University," pp. 18–19; *Clippings, 1875; 1887,* passim, CUP.

33. Washburn to Eliot, 12 Dec 1887, Eliot Papers.

34. Tanner, "Clark University," pp. 65, 95–96.

35. *Records of Clark University,* vol. 1, 17 April 1889, Office of the President, Clark University.

one year and to finance an extensive tour of European universities so that he could gather the most advanced thinking on higher education at its source.[36] Leaving his wife and family behind, Hall traveled for seven months, from late September 1888 to late April 1889, and traversed the map of Europe from the low countries to Scandinavia, Russia, eastern Europe, Greece, Italy, Germany, France, and finally, with little time left, Great Britain. For Hall, the interest of his tour extended far beyond the necessary university quarters. He spent much time and effort gaining access to the elite military training schools of Russia, whose colorful drill and famed discipline fascinated him. The ancient sites in Greece, an institute of oriental religion in Paris, and his standard run of brothels, circuses, and curiosities everywhere claimed his attention.[37]

Hall conducted considerable business in Germany, and his views of men and subjects were sometimes enlarged elsewhere in western Europe. The chief product of the tour, however, was in the realm of exchanged ideals. Everywhere Hall went he painted such a glowing picture of the high ideals and large prospects of the new Clark University, that the European reputation of the institution would long out-distance the reality. Hall himself strengthened his ties with the international university community and its common devotion to the advancement of specialized knowledge. As a result of this trip, his standards and loyalty would be even more firmly based in the ideals of this community and further removed from the Worcester milieu on which the support of the university would depend.[38]

Even before he left for Europe, Hall began to gather a faculty that could create an advanced university. Hall turned immediately to the reservoir of talent at Johns Hopkins to name Henry H. Donaldson in physiology and psychology, Edmund C. Sanford in psychology, and Warren P. Lombard in physiology.[39]

In June 1888, Hall also approached Franklin P. Mall, an asso-

36. *LCP,* pp. 264–65.

37. Ibid., pp. 265–78; Rush, *Letters of GSH to Clark,* 16–35; W. C. Ryan, interview with Warren P. Lombard, 21 Aug 1938, notes, CUP.

38. *LCP,* pp. 278–79. On the foreign interest in Clark University during its early years see *Clippings, 1890–96;* W. O. Krohn to GSH, 29 Jan 1892, CUP.

39. GSH to Clark, 19 May, 3 June, 22 July, 11 Aug 1888, in Rush, *Letters of GSH to Clark,* pp. 6–12.

ciate in pathology at Hopkins, but they could not agree on terms.[40] The following spring Hall opened negotiations again, for in Europe, he wrote Mall, "I repeatedly heard very pleasant commendation of you and your work." Hall engaged him as adjunct professor of anatomy.[41] Hall may also have heard in Europe of a young chemist, John Ulric Nef, then at Purdue, whom he secured for organic chemistry.[42]

Early in September 1888, shortly before he was to leave for Europe, Hall evidently met Franz Boas on the train to Cleveland, where both were going to attend the meeting of the American Association for the Advancement of Science.[43] In October, Boas then on the staff of *Science* magazine, wrote Hall about his work in areas of interest to Hall, and Hall replied that indeed these views were very congenial to his own.[44]

Hall discussed anthropology with specialists on his European tour, but he wrote Boas from London that the more he talked to European authorities, the more he realized the difficulties of organizing such a department in an American university.[45] Hall probably had in mind the extensive time the anthropologist would require away from the university. Hall may also have hesitated to hire Boas because of his predominant interest in physical anthropology. Hall believed that "the physical part of anthropology is a little stagnant and that the myth customs and belief side is the next to grow."[46]

Hall nonetheless offered Boas a position at Clark in August 1889, the first appointment in anthropology at an American university. Hall reminded him again of his feelings that myths, customs, and beliefs were more important than "craniology, pre-historic re-

40. GSH to Mall, 30 June, 4, 22 July [1888]; Mall to GSH, 9 Aug 1888, FPM.

41. GSH to Mall, 17, 28 Apr, 23 May 1889, FPM.

42. GSH to Nef, 29 Apr, 3 May [1889]; 7 May, 28 June, 9 July 1889, John Ulric Nef Papers, University of Chicago Archives.

43. Melville J. Herskovits, *Franz Boas: The Science of Man in the Making* (New York: Charles Scribner's, 1953), pp. 12–13; GSH to Clark, 10 Sept 1888 in Rush, *Letters of GSH to Clark*, pp. 13–14.

44. Franz Boas to GSH, [Oct 1888]; GSH to Boas, 19 Oct 1888, Franz Boas Papers, American Philosophical Society.

45. Ibid.

46. GSH to Boas, 31 Mar [1889], Boas Papers.

mains, or even industries."[47] Boas's position was to be that of docent, a position Hall borrowed from the German university and intended for young scholars, often in new and untried subjects, who would be free of all formal teaching duties except one course of lectures.[48]

Hall also sought out somewhat older men of proven accomplishments. Before he left for Europe he offered the directorship of the chemistry department to an eminent American chemist, Arthur Michael of Tufts University.[49] Albert A. Michelson, already well known for his work in the measurement of light waves, was teaching at the Case School of Applied Science in Cleveland, Ohio, when Hall offered him a professorship of physics.[50] Both men accepted.

In biology, Hall wanted to secure another proven man, William K. Brooks, whom he knew well at Hopkins. Hall made Brooks "a tempting proposition," but he declined the Clark position.[51] Hall was able to bring to Clark, however, the director of the Marine Biological Laboratory at Woods Hole, C. O. Whitman, as professor of invertebrate morphology.

In mathematics, Hall found his entire faculty at Hopkins. William Story, who was associate professor in the department, came to Clark as full professor, and brought with him his Hopkins associates, Oskar Bolza and Henry Taber.[52]

As every commentator on the subject has noted, Hall managed to select a remarkably talented faculty. According to Donaldson, the selection was largely the product of a network of personal acquaintance: in the early Johns Hopkins period, faculty people were always on the lookout for top men.[53] Hall had the men of Hopkins directly before him, where he could judge their work at first hand, and

47. GSH to Boas, 8 Aug 1889, Boas Papers.

48. *Clark University: First Annual Report of the President, October 4, 1890,* (published by the University), p. 14 (hereafter cited as *Ann. Rep. Pres. Clark*).

49. GSH to Clark, 12 Dec 1888, in Rush, *Letters of GSH to Clark,* p. 27.

50. "Journal. May, 1887–June, 1891," CUP.

51. Brooks to Gilman, 21 June [1889]; telegram, Gilman to Brooks, 1 July 1889, Alumni Records Office, Johns Hopkins University.

52. *Clark University Register, May, 1889* (published by the university).

53. W. C. Ryan, interview with H. H. Donaldson, 22 Nov 1937, notes, CUP.

through other Hopkins faculty and through his own wide contacts in America and Europe, he was well placed to gauge the reputations of others. Hall himself, moreover, had some expertise in a wide range of scientific activity and was thus able to judge correctly the talent of such young men as Lombard and Boas.

Hall secured his faculty at the least cost possible to the university. He assigned himself an ample $6,000 yearly but bargained relentlessly with his men on salaries and positions, making a number of them take less than they were earning at their previous posts. Professorial salaries ranged from Michelson's high of $3,500, to Story's $3,000, down to Mall's adjunct professorship at $2,000.[54] Hall could follow this policy because he knew, better than other college presidents of the day, what would attract the most talented scientists to him: minimal teaching obligations, maximum time free for research, and all the research equipment they needed.[55] Though Boas was then earning $2,000, for example, he accepted Hall's offer of $1,000 yearly on the understanding that his summers would be free to spend in fieldwork in the Northwest.[56] Again and again Hall emphasized these advantages to his prospective faculty, often alluding in vague and glowing terms to large plans for expansion of their departments and absolute freedom for research.

Hall did not always choose with prophetic vision. Charles Peirce applied to Hall as the first academic year opened, before Hall was pressed for funds and when he could easily have planned for lectures in logic. While Peirce continued to apply for a regular position or a course of outside lectures for many years thereafter, Hall pleaded the paucity of funds at Clark or obstructions placed in his way by the trustees.[57]

54. "Journal. May, 1887–June, 1891," CUP. Cf. William R. Harper, "The Pay of American College Professors," *Forum* 16 (1893): 96–109.
55. GSH to Mall, 2 Aug [1888]; 25 Apr 1889, FPM; W. K. Brooks to Gilman, 21 June [1889], Alumni Records Office, Johns Hopkins.
56. Boas to GSH, Aug 1889, Boas Papers.
57. GSH to Peirce, 8 Oct 1889, CUP; GSH to Peirce, 12 July 1890; 20 Feb, 1 June, 1 Sept 1900, Brent transcriptions of Charles S. Peirce letters in the Widener Archives, Harvard University. Hall may have been dissuaded by the same personal and moral considerations which moved Gilman to fire Peirce. Peirce's subject moreover, shared in Hall's general distrust of philosophy. Though Hall always replied to Peirce with the highest praise of the quality of his mind and work, he did not think logic had the importance of science: "Logic never led to

Hall also passed by a number of promising German professors, though not voluntarily. The German government was reluctant to let scientists leave Germany, so Hall's moves in this area were blocked. He then approached Hermann von Holst, professor of history at Freiburg and an expert on American institutions. Married to an American woman and a friend of Senator Hoar, von Holst was willing and able to come to Clark.[58] Hall, however, had not prepared Jonas Clark for the appointment.

When Clark saw Hall straying from what he had already admitted was the most reasonable plan, that of concentration in the natural sciences, he told Hall not to invite von Holst or any other European professors for the time being.[59] Since Hall had gone quite far in his negotiations with von Holst, he felt this incident as his first humiliation at Clark's hands and the first real warning of the betrayal to come.[60] It was equally an indication of Hall's inability to assess realistically the limits Clark placed on the university.

With its faculty complete, Clark University opened in the fall of 1889. In his address at the opening exercises, Hall described his exalted view of higher education, and the exalted conception of science on which it rested. Science appeared to Hall as the latest and commanding product of progressive evolution which incorporated and replaced the older religious and philosophical modes of thought. Science discovered the natural order that governed existence and supported man's moral, aesthetic, and reverential sentiments. It represented a mode of thinking destined to illumine and govern all areas of human life.

The university was to Hall the agent and guardian of this distinctively modern route to salvation. Hall saw

modern science in its pure high form as not only the greatest achievement of the race thus far, but also as carrying in it the greatest, though not yet

---

the discovery of anything. . . . At best it follows the discoverer, often at a distance, and may at best afterwards tell how his work was done." GSH, "Affiliation of Psychology with Philosophy," 1906, p. 300. Hall may also have continued to think of Peirce in the competitive terms he had applied to all his Hopkins rivals.

58. *LCP*, pp. 272–74.

59. GSH to Clark, 14 Nov, 12 Dec 1888, in Rush, *Letters from GSH to Clark*, pp. 23, 28; Clark to GSH, 4 Dec 1888, 3 Jan 1889, in *Early Proceedings of the Board of Trustees* (Worcester: Clark University, 1901), pp. 19–20.

60. *LCP*, p. 274.

well developed, culture power of the world, not only for knowledge but also for feeling and conduct. It is of this power that universities are the peculiar organs; to them is now committed the highest interests of man; from them and from science now comes the light and advancement of the world.

Through close scientific examination of some small facet of existence, the university students would feel "the profound and religious conviction that the world is lawful to the core" and would thereby experience "what a truly liberal education, in the modern as distinct from the medieval sense, really is." Here would be fashioned the new world-view which science was to disclose, the new natural unity which was to enlarge the unity of the Christian vision.[61]

This power of the university, Hall urged, gave it a unique role in society and evolution.

The university . . . should represent the state of science *per se*. It should be strong in those fields where science is highly developed, and should pay less attention to other departments of knowledge which have not reached the scientific stage. . . . It should be a laboratory of the highest possible human development in those lines where educational values are the criterion of what is taught or not taught[,] and the increase of knowledge and its diffusion among the few fit should be its ideal.

The university would train the modern specialist, the expert who was increasingly coming to govern the modern world. It would develop the new modern man, educated in and according to the principles of nature.[62]

Hall's was an elitist conception of the university, as he was well aware. Scientific research required enormous expenditure of money and effort; it required a long period of training as well as innate talent. He heartily approved the sentiment "The more and better books, apparatus, collections and teachers, and the fewer but more promising students, the better the work." Those who sought a constantly higher and deeper education represented "the struggle of talent to the full maturity and leadership which is its right."[63]

The young men who devoted themselves to this high ideal were to be freed of all sectarian or dogmatic restraints. Serving as the

61. *Clark University . . . Opening Exercises*, pp. 19, 24.
62. Ibid., pp. 18, 24.
63. Ibid., pp. 18, 31.

cutting edge of the progressive march of civilization, this young priesthood was to be allowed free rein in their "holy fervor of investigation that in its passion for truth is fearless of consequences." Relying on the ultimate saving power of scientific knowledge, society was to consecrate a group of its most talented and dedicated young men to its highest purpose, the advancement of the human race. Significantly, Hall chose white as his university's color.[64]

Hall's ideal view of the university had its origins in many sources, from John Bascom to Tennyson, Comte, Spencer and the German universities. Hall made scientific knowledge itself into the agent of evolution within modern civilization, the source of all present and future progress. Though in practice Hall's devotion to science represented a moderate political course of tactical reform and strategic retreat, in theory it was a bold and radical call for unending change and absolute scientific power. Hall's vision satisfied his intellectual ambitions, on a grand scale. Other university presidents introduced graduate education and scientific research into American higher education. Other scholars of the period were imbued like Hall with an almost religious faith in science and research. None, however, held to this faith with as great intensity or enthusiasm as Hall, nor articulated so well the elitist assumptions and sweeping idealism which underlay it.[65]

Hall recognized that this conception of a university was alien to the tradition of American higher education and therefore tried to link it to native ideals. Devotion to pure science, Hall argued, would, in the natural and unforced course of events, produce valuable practical results. While he heartily respected applied science and technical and industrial education, "these are as much out of place in a truly academic university as money-changers were in the temple of the Most High." Once science has understood the basic principles, "their applications are relatively easy and quickly learned." The chemical industry in Germany, which benefited from the progress of chemistry in the German universities, was an ex-

---

64. Ibid., p. 20; Wilson, *GSH,* p. 88.

65. In describing the belief among some scholars of the period that scientific research was a "Sacred Quest," Veysey concluded that "no one better personified this profound degree of enthusiasm for research than did G. Stanley Hall." Veysey, *Emergence of the American University*, p. 150.

ample of the "high and normal technological value of pure science."[66]

Business and science also shared a fundamental style, which was characteristic of modern industrial society. They were

severe schools of integrity. The directness, simplicity, certainty and absorption in work so characteristic of both are setting new fashions in manners, and even in morals, and bringing man into closer contact with the world as it is . . . binding the universe together into new unities and imposing a discipline ever severer for body and mind.

When their work is finished, Hall concluded, "all the highest and most sacred of human ideals will not be lost or dimmed, but will become nearer and more real."[67] Hall's fervid optimism and idealism temporarily overcame his usual alertness to popular demands and blinded him to the obstacles which still impeded an amicable partnership between university science and the business culture.

The fact that Clark himself was liberal in his religious beliefs probably accounts for the fact that Hall gave briefer mention to the harmony between university work and religion. Clark himself was determined that the university should be entirely nonsectarian and that teaching and investigation should be entirely free from pressures to religious conformity.[68] On this issue, Hall felt no conflict. Indeed, on all counts, Hall was determined to deny any "shadow of doubt or of fear"[69] and follow his vision.

In fact, the first two or three years of Clark University were a Golden Age which came closer to Hall's ideal of a university than any other institution in the country ever did. The university opened with eighteen members of faculty grade and thirty-four students. Of this group of fifty-two scholars, fifteen had studied or taught at Johns Hopkins University, nineteen had done graduate work at European universities, and twelve scholars not on the faculty already held Ph.D. degrees. As a group, they were uniquely well trained for and dedicated to scientific research.[70]

66. *Clark University . . . Opening Exercises*, pp. 14, 18, 21.
67. Ibid., pp. 11–12.
68. Stebbins, "Founder's Day," p. 152; Tanner, "Clark University," p. 11; *Clark University . . . Opening Exercises*, p. 7.
69. Ibid., p. 11.
70. *Clark Register, May, 1889; May, 1890.*

The setting of the university itself was appropriate to its purpose. Jonas Clark erected his buildings on the outskirts of the city, where pigs and chickens still wandered through the neighboring plots. One horse-car line ran out to the campus from the center of town. When the young men fresh from the magnificence of Heidelberg or Berlin stepped off it, they were at first somewhat taken aback by what they saw. At the center of a large field overgrown with tall grass and surrounded by a picket fence, stood two ugly brick buildings, eminently substantial but of ungainly proportion and awkward decoration. When they stepped inside, however, they found rooms of very ample dimensions and interior finishing of the highest quality. By the standards of the day, the buildings appeared wonderfully functional.[71]

Arthur Gordon Webster, a young physicist trained in Berlin under Helmholtz who came to Clark to work under Michelson during the second year, expressed the view of his colleagues when he said that the spirit of Clark was far more important than buildings: "the spirit of work, and work is life."[72] Despite the difficulties of gathering equipment and books the first year, the group immediately settled down to work. Surrounded by a provincial city, they centered their lives during the day and far into the night on their research and study. No group of seventeenth-century Puritan businessmen ever showed a greater devotion to disciplined work than the Clark scientists. And "Dr. Hall, President, as we call him," said Franklin Mall, "works harder than any of us do."[73]

The intellectual excitement generated by these talented enthusiasts was palpable. Louis N. Wilson, who began at Clark as secretary to Jonas Clark and Hall and became the university librarian, recalled that there was a constant tension in the air which was never equaled in later years.[74] With Hall only forty-five years old, most of his faculty in their early thirties, and the students a little younger, there was much informal contact and intellectual exchange among

71. Arthur G. Webster, in "Twenty-Fifth Anniversary of Clark University, 1889–1914," *CULP* 3 (1914): 60.

72. Ibid., p. 61.

73. Mall to Wm. His, 17 Jan 1890, FPM; Mall to L. N. Wilson, 19 July 1890, CUP.

74. L. N. Wilson in "Twenty-Fifth Anniversary of Clark University," p. 68.

them. "The years at Worcester were splendid," Donaldson recalled. Like others of the faculty, he was impressed with the caliber
of his colleagues and found Hall "a man of unusual mental gifts
and the most suggestive and stimulating person with whom I ever
came in contact."[75]

Instruction in such an environment was totally different from
that at other universities. The teachers were required to lecture only
two hours a week and often lectured even less than that amount,
expending their principal efforts on directing their students in research. Many of the students, in turn, gave one lecture or a course
of lectures sometime during the year in their field of special knowledge. There were no formal rules either of instruction or administration to limit the intellectual interest of either teacher or student.[76]

The example of Clark University and Hall's public advocacy of
university reform on its model markedly advanced the ideal of
scientific research in America, despite the fact that the splendor of
those early days at Clark lasted such a short time.[77] By the third
year, Mall was reporting that certain interesting political affairs
were taking a good deal of time away from his work,[78] but even
before then, Hall and the trustees were aware that their noble creation was in imminent danger of collapse.

75. H. H. Donaldson, "Memories for My Boys," typescript autobiography,
Donaldson Papers, American Philosophical Society. See also, Florence Rena
Sabin, *Franklin Paine Mall* (Baltimore: Johns Hopkins, 1934), p. 90.

76. *Ann. Rep. Pres. Clark, 1890*, pp. 13–15; Edwin D. Starbuck to Wm.
James, 29 Jan 1896, JP.

77. Julius Steiglitz, noted chemist of the University of Chicago, declared in
Science 26 (Nov 1907), p. 700, that "the greatest recent impetus to all branches
of research, including chemistry, came in this country, in my opinion, from the
founding of Clark University with research as its chief and almost exclusive field
and from the founding, only two years later, of the University of Chicago with
its strong graduate school." Clark's contribution to Chicago is discussed in the
following chapter.

78. Mall to Wm. His, 8 Jan 1892, FPM.

 *Part Three*

COLLAPSE AND RECOVERY   1890–1896

Within a few years' time, in the early 1890s, Hall was toppled from the crest of the rising scientific tide. His aggressive enthusiasm and his idealistic visions did not, as it turned out, wear well over time. He was faced, in middle life and at midcareer, with a series of losses and wrecked ambitions that might well have silenced him.

The series of events which brought Hall low began in the spring of 1890 with a personal disaster. As Hall's first year at Clark University was drawing to a close, on 15 May 1890, while he was away in Ashfield recovering from a severe case of diptheria, his wife and eight-year-old daughter were accidentally asphyxiated. Hall was notified abruptly and he returned to the rambling house in Worcester, now empty except for his nine-year-old boy.[1] It would be difficult to overestimate the importance of this tragedy to Hall's life and behavior in the following years. Just a few years before his parents had passed away in Ashfield, filling him with sadness for his lost childhood home.[2] Now he was almost entirely alone. He mourned his wife through the summer, went off to California, and thought

---

1. *LCP*, p. 326. For a detailed report of the accident as it was told in Worcester, see Pruette, *GSH*, pp. 95–96. No reliable information exists on the character of Hall's relationship with his wife and children before the accident; Hall himself is entirely silent on the subject.

2. *LCP*, p. 253; GSH, "Boy Life in a Massachusetts Country Town Thirty Years Ago," 1891.

seriously of withdrawing from Clark altogether.[3] His depression was evidently deepened by a sense of personal guilt:

If misfortune, affliction, or sorrow arouse, as they always do (so animistic are we at bottom toward the universe), the question, "Was this deserved?" then remembered offenses long latent in memory often revive, the categorical imperative is heard from, and the gnawings of conscience may deepen to remorse.[4]

Hall was nonetheless able to return to Clark in the fall and he tried to deaden his pain in long hours of work.

Hall's chief solace was a renewed faith in God. "There are times," he remarked to his students,

when you must look a great calamity right in the face and live it down; sympathy of others will not help, but only makes it worse. Then it is that you must "glory in death," that you must "accept the inevitable with joy." And you can't do that if you have not faith.[5]

Soon after the tragedy Hall urged "acquiescence in some of the great consensuses concerning ultimate problems of life, its origin and end."[6] Praising Eduard Zeller, a liberal German philosopher and theologian, who believed that Christianity was a mythical formulation of essential truths about the world, Hall declared himself a Christian:

we cannot deny that [Christianity] has grown far too consubstantial with our social, moral, intellectual and aesthetic life and development to be eradicated by any violence, or even to be intellectually distinguished and traced through all the long and subtle association, by which it has become ingrained in our inmost psychic character.[7]

This marks the end of Hall's struggle with his religious feelings and the Christian tradition in which they had been trained. Hall's expressions of psychologized Christianity and mythologized science became more lyrical and frequent in the months and years following the accident.

The regimen of work and faith could not entirely fill the isolation

3. *LCP*, p. 326.
4. GSH, *Adol*, 2:312. This passage appears in Hall's description of "conversion."
5. "Reports of the Plato Club," *Atlantic Monthly*, Sept 1894, p. 477.
6. GSH, "Phi Beta Kappa Oration," 1891, p. 116.
7. GSH, "Contemporary Psychologists, I. Professor Eduard Zeller," 1891, p. 170. On Zeller, see also Hall's biographical essay in his *Founders*, pp. 3–64.

of Hall's life in Worcester. Though surrounded by students and colleagues, he did not allow any of them to penetrate his reserve sufficiently to become a friend. The tragedy also appeared to separate father and son, rather than draw them together, and Hall became a distant, austere, and authoritarian figure to his boy.[8] Hall published that year a study of the psychological development of his two infants which he had done almost eight years earlier, feeling perhaps that this portion of his life was now closed.[9] Alone with his sense of loss and guilt, Hall needed the success of his professional ambitions and the maintenance of his position of authority more than ever before.

Hall's fondest dream instead began to fade. To Hall's utter horror and disbelief, Jonas Clark became disillusioned with the university and began to withdraw his support. The fatal difficulty lay in the failure of Clark's project to raise a sympathetic response in Worcester. Clark had counted on bringing the wealthy citizens of Worcester, led by those of the board, into his project. Clark never made any direct appeal for funds to his trustees, however, and never took them into his confidence on his plans for the university. They naturally felt disinclined, therefore, to put their own money into the venture or to encourage others to do so.[10] Ironically, Clark's silence was rooted in his desire to see how the university would succeed before sinking more of his capital into it. The university was thus considered "Clark's show." As in Baltimore, earlier, with Johns Hopkins University,[11] the wealthy men of the area were reluctant to subordinate their own wealth to an institution bearing someone else's name. Clark's personal unfriendliness and pretensions to a higher culture than Worcester afforded were also resented.[12]

8. Interviews, R. G. Hall, 17–20 May 1961, and Burton Gates, 6 Mar 1962.
9. GSH, "Notes on the Study of Infants," 1891, pp. 127–38.
10. Tanner, "Clark University," pp. 48–51.
11. French, *History of Johns Hopkins*, p. 101.
12. G. F. Hoar to Clark, 18 Apr 1892; G. F. Hoar to GSH, 6 May 1902; R. M. Washburn to L. N. Wilson, 4 Feb 1927, CUP. According to the Hoar letter, 1902, members of the city's Board of Trade reported after Clark's death that "the businessmen of Worcester would now be behind the University, although they had felt heretofore unwilling to commit themselves to anything that bore the name of Jonas Clark." During the first three years of the university's existence, it received from benefactors other than Clark himself only two gifts: one of $5,000

Nor did the university inspire the confidence of the larger Worcester public. The high goals Hall had set, the exalted tone he used in talking about devotion to "pure" science, the many foreign connections of the university, and the tendency of the professors to keep almost entirely to themselves made Clark an easy target for the city's anti-intellectualism and nativism.[13] These sentiments were fanned by one of the city's three major newspapers, which openly ridiculed Clark's reticence and Hall's concept of the university. Early in 1891, they featured a lurid account of vivisection occurring in the university laboratories which roused a local storm,[14] and the following fall attacked the proposal of Franz Boas to take physical measurements of thousands of the city's school children. The paper directed its spleen against the "professor" of German birth and education whose face was marred by a cruel mensur scar, and declared falsely that the children would have to be undressed for some of the measurements.[15]

As unpleasant as this antagonism was, it would not have been crucial to the development of the university were it not for the importance Jonas Clark attached to it. Clark was, in Hall's words, "exquisitely sensitive" to public opinion.[16] By the second year of operation, it was clear to him that in terms of material support and public approval, his benefaction had failed of its principal aim. In vain, Hall and various members of the board told Clark of the high reputation of his university in academic circles all over the world. Senator Hoar lamented that Clark seemed to "give great weight to the cheap talk and to cheap and ignorant persons and to pay no respect to the judgment of the scholars and experts and leading educators at home or abroad."[17] Clark was addressing himself to the local audience, and far from ingratiating him with his neigh-

from an anonymous Worcester citizen and another of $500 from a Philadelphia woman who had read about the university in the newspapers. *Clark Register, May 1890*, p. 21; Worcester *Gazette*, 18 June 1889, in *Clippings, 1887*.

13. Boston *Advertiser*, 16 Feb 1894, in *Clippings, 1875*.

14. Examples of the *Telegram's* early hostility are in the issues of 23 Jan 1887; 15 Apr, 3 Oct 1889. The vivisection attack ran in the issues of 9, 12, 16, 23, 30 Mar, 13 Apr 1890; *LCP*, p. 292.

15. Tanner, "Clark University," p. 131; Worcester *Telegram*, 8, 22 Mar 1891; Herskovits, *Franz Boas*, p. 14.

16. GSH interview, 24 May 1900, in S. W. Clark, *In Memoriam: J. G. Clark*.

17. G. F. Hoar to GSH, 27 Jan 1894, CUP.

bors, the university had only furthered his isolation and subjected him to considerable public abuse.

Clark was, moreover, alarmed at the rate of expenditure at the university. Continuing to pay all the bills with his personal check, he audited every item and marked the absence of any source other than his own pocket for the continuing high costs.[18] In the face of this situation, Clark began to withdraw. He had made up the difference between the endowment income of $28,000 and the expenses the first year, an amount of some $65,000. In the spring of that year, he pledged $50,000 for the following, second year. By the spring of the second year, Clark's health had deteriorated, largely, his doctors told him, because of the anxiety created by his hard work and worry on behalf of the university. In April 1891, he therefore decided to leave Worcester to regain his health. Still maintaining formal relations with his board, he attended a meeting for the last time, turned over to them the deeds and stocks which constituted his original gift of one million dollars, pledged an additional $30,000 for the coming, third year, and left without any further word as to his ultimate intentions for the university. Clark spent his time in New York and Europe and discouraged correspondence about the university even with Hall.[19]

Meanwhile, Hall and the trustees were aware of the sources of Clark's disaffection. To gain public approval, Hall turned to the one means of gaining it easily at his disposal: in 1891 the board voted to start a summer school for the area's educators, and that same year, Hall started an educational journal, the *Pedagogical Seminary*.[20] Hall had not wanted to contaminate his university of pure science with the subject of pedagogy or with extension courses. He had discouraged applicants who were interested in the subject and emphasized that the little work done on it at Clark was on a very high plane. Even the summer course he planned was at first designed for principals and superintendents, rather than ordinary teachers, and Hall's first issue of the *Pedagogical Seminary* entirely

18. Wilson, "Recollections," p. 8; Wilson, "Note," in Tanner, "Clark University," p. 44a.
19. *Early Proceedings*, pp. 34–53; Tanner, "Clark University," pp. 44a–b, 46; Clark to GSH, 3 Sept 1891, CUP.
20. "Records of Clark University," vol. 1, 3 Dec 1891; 9 Apr 1892.

ignored child study, taking instead an elevated, intellectual approach to educational reform.[21]

The board also considered returning to the plan of founding an undergraduate college, which would be better understood and have closer ties to the community. With Hall's encouragement, how- ever, they decided in December 1891 to put themselves on record as desiring to maintain the university according to its same high stan- dards and to add departments in the order of their relation to those already existing.[22] The university could not be turned overnight into an undergraduate college. None of its present faculty would wish to stay under such conditions. The entire research idea would have to be abandoned, and a small poor copy of the dozens of other established colleges in the area put in its place.[23] If the college were to be added to the graduate university, a substantial increase in funds would be needed.[24]

As the fourth year approached, the trustees wrote Clark of the urgency of the situation and asked for a definite statement of his future intentions.[25] Clark replied as clearly as he was ever going to do:

I wish to call your attention to our first work. . . . [Our President] advised Post Graduate work which would give us time to secure quite a number of students from whom we could select the most promising for teachers from our own men that we had fitted for the work. . . . we concluded to com- mence as he desired expecting to be able to adopt the Collegiate department and reduce our expenses as we should be fully equipped at the close of the third year. . . . There have been some obstructions placed in our way which we had not anticipated, and I am not sure the Institution is wanted in Worcester, especially in its present form. . . . I want you to have a statement made so that you can see at a glance what each department has cost . . . then you can decide if the work has been a fair compensation for the cost and trouble it has given us. My impression is that you will dispense with all but [of?] the five departments.[26]

21. GSH to J. P. Gordy, 2 Nov 1889; GSH to J. R. Potter, 6 Nov 1889, CUP; Worcester *Gazette*, 12 July 1891, in *Clippings, 1887.*
22. Tanner, "Clark University," pp. 54–58; *Early Proceedings,* p. 54.
23. Tanner, "Clark University," pp. 135–38.
24. Ibid., pp. 135–42. At a slightly later date, at the trustees' request, Hall drew up a plan for a Clark College, which he estimated to require an additional million dollars in endowment.
25. Tanner, "Clark University," pp. 61–62.
26. Clark to the Trustees of Clark University, 19 Mar 1892, CUP.

According to the standards by which Clark could judge, his expenditures had not produced commensurate results in Worcester. The university ought to change its course and reform on lines that would be more directly profitable.

Clark refused to make any financial commitment for the future beyond the coming, fourth year, for which he pledged $18,000, the smallest amount he had yet given for operating expenses. Should the trustees and Hall decide to ignore his advice and maintain the university in its present form, it was clear that Clark would fail to give even that amount again. Such, in fact, was the case. After the fourth year, Clark made no further annual gifts to the university.[27]

On receipt of this letter, both Hall and the trustees felt they had no choice but to ignore Clark's disapproval and try to maintain the university in its present form. They temporarily abandoned the possibility of building a university of the stature Hall had intended, and tried to maintain friendly relations with Clark in the hope of securing the remainder of his fortune at the time of his death.

The conflict at Clark between Jonas Clark's limited conception of a university and Stanley Hall's enlightened vision was similar to other conflicts that arose from the late nineteenth-century alliance of wealthy capitalists with academic institutions. In the development of universities during this period, the individual chiefly responsible for overcoming the conflicting pressures of financial support and intellectual ideals was the university president.[28] Like William Rainey Harper at the University of Chicago, the president was sometimes able to generate public support and funds for his institution himself.[29] Like Andrew D. White at Cornell, he was often able to resolve tactfully the differences between his several constituencies, compromising where necessary.[30] Partly because of

27. Ibid.; Tanner, "Clark University," p. 44a.
28. On the development of universities during this period and the role of the university president, see Veysey, *Emergence of the American University*, and Richard Hofstadter and Walter Metzger, *The Development of Academic Freedom in the United States* (New York: Columbia University Press, 1955), pp. 320–467, particularly pp. 414–15, 457–58.
29. Veysey, *Emergence of the American University*, pp. 366–80; Thomas W. Goodspeed, *William Rainey Harper* (Chicago: University of Chicago Press, 1928).
30. Veysey, *Emergence of the American University*, pp. 81–86, 348.

the obduracy of the circumstances themselves, and partly because of his own disabilities, Hall was unable to perform the mediating institutional role in which he was placed.

One might have thought Hall would perform his public role more successfully than he did, but the gulf between the purity of his aspirations for the university and the kind of favor he would have to court was evidently too much for him. Hall constantly alluded in his public speeches to the need for more funds and the glories of university philanthropy,[31] but he was proud of the fact that he had never resorted to personal solicitation.[32] Even in his public discourse with Worcester, he found it difficult to moderate his exalted language and to meet objections on their own grounds. In the vivisection scandal, for example, Hall avoided taking action for a month before checking the outcry decisively. He looked down on the trouble from his place in the scientific community as a "ridiculous mess."[33]

Most important, Hall could not bridge the gulf between Jonas Clark and the university's demands. Hall had two courses of action open to him. He could at the outset have protested Clark's continued control of the finances and forced a definite agreement on threat of resigning. In fact, at the first meeting of the trustees on Hall's return from Europe, Judge Devens, one of the most eminent lawyers on the board, protested candidly to Clark about the situation. Clark, however, considered the judge's protest a slur on his good faith and told the board merely that they could rely on his resources until he was ready to make a specific commitment. Judge Devens was inclined to resign at that response and other members of the board were disquieted. Putting the issue in terms of loyalty to himself, Hall urged Devens to stay on. After talking to Clark in private, he told the trustees that he felt Clark's intentions were honorable and ample.[34] Clearly, Clark gave Hall no more than the same promise to take care of the expenses he had made from the start. Bent on maintaining the institution of his dreams, Hall continued to think Clark could be managed.

31. See, e.g., *Clark University . . . Opening Exercises*, p. 290.
32. GSH in "Twenty-Fifth Anniversary of Clark University," pp. 49–50.
33. GSH to H. P. Bowditch, 22 Apr 1891, Bowditch Papers.
34. *LCP*, pp. 280–81; Tanner, "Clark University," pp. 47–48.

Hall's only hope, therefore, was to try to educate Clark to larger views and moderate his own grandiose plans so as to bring the two along together in harmony. Both Hall and the trustees did try to impress on Clark the importance of academic opinion and the fleeting character of public opposition in Worcester, but their efforts here were to no avail. Where Hall was personally derelict in his relations with Clark was in regard to the vital matter of money. Hall never gave Clark an adequate idea of the financial needs of a university. Hall initially told him, as Clark's last letter to the trustees stated, that expenses would decrease once the initial expenditures for equipment in the first few years were passed. In his first president's report, published in 1890, Hall declared that

an undergraduate department, a medical school, a technical school and even still more specialization in the existing departments, or new ones of any kind, could be developed from this basis [of five graduate departments] with comparatively little labor, time, and all but the last with little expense.[35]

Such statements were completely false. Hall apparently let Clark live in unreality because he himself lived there. Despite Clark's manifest unwillingness to pay the bills of the university even in its present small size, Hall liked to continue talking with him about such grandiose enlargements. At the end of the second academic year, he stopped in Washington to discuss with Simon Newcomb the founding of a department of astronomy at Clark,[36] and no doubt continued to make similar approaches around the country.

Hall's temperamental inability to express opposition in face-to-face contact, moreover, must have turned him into the kind of agreeable acquiescence and clever conformity he had displayed with Morris. Clark, particularly, with his stiff New England manner and frugal, authoritarian standards, must have reminded Hall of his own father. Instead of forthright discussion, therefore, Hall resorted to childish tricks. He would try to sell Clark on each item of expense as it came up and then try to get the check to the bank before Clark could change his mind and stop payment.[37] Clark recorded that once Hall "purchased $3,000 worth of material without the knowl-

35. *Ann. Rep. Pres. Clark, 1890*, p. 11.
36. GSH to Newcomb, 7 May 1891, Simon Newcomb Papers, Library of Congress.
37. W. C. Ryan, interview with H. H. Donaldson, CUP.

edge or consent of anyone[.] Brought in the bills and said the sheriff would be in possession that day unless the bills were paid."[38] The exasperation which must have driven Hall to that expediency can well be appreciated, but it hardly represented an enlightened method of educating Clark to his responsibilities.

The brilliance of Clark University in its opening years could not survive the withdrawal of Jonas Clark's financial support. The talented and ambitious faculty had been lured to Clark with promises of ample and expanding material support and were fertile in the conception of interesting and fruitful ways to spend money. As the funds to support their activities disappeared, they would inevitably leave for more promising places in the rapidly expanding university structure. Hall might have salvaged more of the true university than he eventually did, however, if he had not also alienated his faculty.

Hall tried to hide the true financial condition of the university from the faculty, but his attitude toward appropriations decidedly stiffened after the first year, and the faculty men became aware that the university was "incompletely endowed" and under some pressure for funds.[39] It was not this general condition, however, but Hall's methods of effecting economies and general deviousness that antagonized the men. Since he was faced with large fixed costs in faculty salaries and basic equipment, Hall concentrated on the weak links in his chain of obligations. As the funnel through which all requisitions for supplies, equipment, and alterations in the buildings had to pass, from a fifteen-cent item to an expensive one, Hall arbitrarily cut corners wherever he could.[40]

In the disbursements to younger members of the university, below faculty grade, Hall also had some leeway. With the lower salary paid to the docent, Hall got full-grade faculty work from Boas, by making him direct students and laboratory work rather than

38. [J. G. Clark], Memo on back of seating chart for New York State Bankers' Association dinner, 9 Feb 1897, CUP.

39. Memo by the dissident members of the faculty, of events at Clark University from October 1891 to 16 February 1892, typescript, p. 1, CUP; Tanner, "Clark University," p. 68.

40. Faculty memo, pp. 30–31; GSH to Boas, [1891], Boas Papers; GSH to J. U. Nef, 28 July 1892, Nef Papers; F. P. Mall, "Jan. 21, 1892"; "Lies, Meddling, etc." MS notes, FPM; Tanner, "Clark University," pp. 81–82.

merely lecturing and doing his own research as the position officially called for.[41] Hall's most destructive economies were applied to the assistants and fellows. Hall drove a hard bargain with the assistants and withheld the stipends of fellows in disciplinary actions. The most lucrative living allowance allowed to a Clark fellow was $200 per year, paid in eight monthly installments of $25, and on several occasions Hall refused to pay a month's stipend for late arrival or absences from the campus.[42] Such perverse economies made Hall's public pronouncements on the high place and lavish care the university gave to young and worthy research scholars particularly galling. As Mall complained, "Although he preached fine principles to the public[,] in action and management he was an autocrat."[43]

The unrest caused by these moves was increased by Hall's general methods. Hall was not only a strong president, on the model of university administration he early approved,[44] but an arbitrary one. He acted without consulting the professors concerned, and when they complained, Hall refused to reconsider and often even to discuss the matter.[45] Hall constantly shifted positions. When one professor complained about his fellow's reduced stipend, Hall cited a "two-day" rule about absences from the campus, a rule that had not previously been heard of. When another complained in a similar case, he was cited a "ten-day rule."[46] He changed terms that had

41. GSH to Boas, 6 Apr 1891; Boas to GSH, 4 June 1891, Boas Papers. As an alternative to a promotion in rank and pay, Boas wanted to remain in the Northwest for fieldwork until December of the academic year. Clark's opposition to absences of the faculty from their work at Worcester would have made Hall extremely wary of granting that request.

42. Faculty memo, pp. 31–32; H. H. Donaldson, "Autumn of 1891–to Spring, 1892," FPM.

43. F. P. Mall, "Part of Resumé," MS notes, FPM. The character of these exactions on his struggling young scientists suggests an element of perversity in Hall's motivation. To a man of Hall's penuriousness, the handling of large sums of Jonas Clark's money, as well as the free expenditure of his funds on a long and exciting trip through Europe, must have aroused a great deal of guilt and anxiety. Perhaps Hall inflicted the punishment he felt he deserved on his hapless wards.

44. *Report of the Visiting Committee of the Alumni of Williams College*, p. 8.

45. Faculty memo, pp. 31–32; Tanner, "Clark University," p. 74.

46. Faculty memo, pp. 30, 34–35; Ryan, interview with Lombard, CUP.

already been agreed to and sometimes clearly broke his word.[47] He told to one person what had been told him in confidence by another.

Even more important to some of the men was Hall's interference in their work. A man of many suggestions and stimulating ideas, Hall evidently did not hesitate to express them, particularly to Boas in anthropology, Mall in anatomy, and Donaldson in physiology. Donaldson appeared generally appreciative of Hall's ideas;[48] to what extent Boas felt benefited by Hall's desire to draw him into the study of "myths, customs and beliefs" is unknown.[49] Mall felt abused by Hall's attempts to "change my work."[50] Mall and Donaldson both resented, moreover, the suggestions Hall made to their fellows and believed he disrupted the work of two of them.[51]

To the faculty, all these arbitrary and devious methods were attributable entirely to Hall. Hall claimed, however, that they were forced on him by the necessity of conforming to the arbitrary and ill-educated will of Jonas Clark. To protect Clark personally and to keep the true state of affairs from the faculty, he had to go back on his word, promise tentatively until checking with Clark on the exact terms permissible, and cut expenses at Clark's command.[52]

To some extent Hall's behavior was prompted by the direct intervention of Clark. The most notorious case of this kind occurred when Hall told Michael, his head professor of chemistry, that his wife, who was also a chemist, could not work in the laboratory, despite the fact that Michael had agreed to come on Hall's express word that his wife would have access to it. When Hall gave his

47. Mall, "Jan. 21, 1892," FPM; Ryan, interview with Lombard, CUP; Faculty memo, p. 37.

48. Donaldson, "Memories," pp. 91, 93–94.

49. Boas's work also took a turn toward the study of abnormal conditions which may have reflected Hall's interest in psychopathology. Boas held a seminar on shamanism, including the "abnormal states of mind" connected with it and its relation to hallucinations, hypnotism, etc. One of his students was set to measuring the heads of insane people and idiots in New England asylums. See *Clark Register, May, 1890; Ann. Rep. Pres. Clark, 1891.*

50. F. P. Mall, "Lies, Meddling, etc.," FPM.

51. H. H. Donaldson, "Diary," 11 Feb 1890, Donaldson Papers; F. P. Mall, "Notes on Faculty Meeting," 19 Jan 1892, FPM; Tanner, "Clark University," p. 91; Mall, "Jan. 21, 1892," FPM.

52. Tanner, "Clark University," pp. 67–68, 83; *LCP*, pp. 293–94, 298.

permission to Professor and Mrs. Michael, he had known of Clark's objection to admitting women to the university but had hoped to handle him. Clark accidentally found Mrs. Michael in the laboratory, however, and Hall was forced to tell Michael to go.[53] In some matters of appropriation, as well, particularly on matters that required an alteration in his buildings, Clark exercised a veto.[54] Hall may often have found himself trapped between his sanguine hopes of convincing Clark and Clark's obstinate refusal.

A great many of the complaints of the faculty, however, cannot be laid to Clark's door. In failing to consult with his faculty, refusing to allow his decisions to be questioned, justifying his decisions with evasive and contradictory deceptions, carrying tales, tactlessly encroaching on the work of other professors and their students, and most of all, in his sharp financial practices with the men below faculty grade, Hall was acting under the compulsions of his own character rather than Clark's. Jonas Clark was absent from Worcester for increasing periods of time during these three years, leaving Hall in charge, subject only to review of the books when Clark returned.[55] In his review of appropriations, hiring docents and assistants, and reducing the stipends of fellows, Hall exercised his own control in as arbitrary and thrifty a manner as Jonas Clark would have done.[56] Moreover, Hall seldom shielded Clark. His constant and shifting blame of Clark or the trustees or both for his decisions was, in fact, one of the reasons for the faculty's dissatisfaction.[57]

As a result of these methods, some unease existed among the faculty even during the first year, and more during the second, of

53. Tanner, "Clark University," p. 82.
54. Ibid., pp. 66–67.
55. Ibid., p. 68.
56. This conclusion is supported by the fact that many of the alterations in appropriations were skillfully made. The professors complained that without consultation, the changes caused delays in their work and inconvenience, rather than that they were substantively inappropriate. See Sabin, *Franklin Mall*, p. 102; faculty memo, p. 33. In regard to the fellows, it is unlikely that Clark would have questioned the regular appropriation for fellowships unless Hall brought the matter to his attention. At the time of the most important action Hall took in this area, the fall of 1891, Clark was in Europe and had given Hall instructions to take complete charge of all university decisions. Clark to GSH, 3 Sept 1891, CUP.
57. Faculty memo, pp. 30, 34–35; Ryan, interview with Lombard, CUP.

Clark's operation,[58] but the men seemed willing to overlook them in the light of the high ideals of the university and the genuine opportunities Hall offered for research. Some of the men "were but little interfered with,"[59] and many of the complaints were of a trivial kind and difficult to prove. Two circumstances, however, catalyzed the latent discontent at the opening of the third year: the University of Chicago appeared as an alternative to the uncertain financial support at Clark, and Hall committed a particularly flagrant offense against one of the fellows.

From the time it had begun to organize in 1889, the Chicago university had had difficulty recruiting professors. As late as February 1892, it had no certainty of being able to offer graduate work in science when it opened in the fall.[60] Many in the academic world apparently felt that the promise of Rockefeller millions and the grandiose scheme of organization announced by Harper comprised an untrustworthy foundation. The facilities such a university would offer were it to succeed, however, had been wistfully appreciated by some men at Clark, especially as Harper came closer to establishing his institution.[61] Whitman and Mall were thus interested when Harper approached them in the spring of 1891[62] and Hall could not guarantee the funds to support or extend their work at Clark.[63]

58. Mall, "Jan. 21, 1892," FPM. At least two faculty men claimed they had also been wary of Hall even before they arrived. Donaldson had concluded from his dealings with Hall at Johns Hopkins that he was "untrustworthy." Warren P. Lombard, who traveled with Hall briefly in Europe during the year before the university opened, admitted to being "prejudiced against him from the start." In Europe, Lombard found Hall "going in where he wasn't invited, and getting himself into all sorts of odd and presumably disreputable places." Donaldson, "Memories," pp. 87, 91; Ryan, interview with Lombard, CUP.

59. Faculty memo, p. 1.

60. Thomas W. Goodspeed, *A History of the University of Chicago* (Chicago: University of Chicago Press, 1916), pp. 205–11; "Report on the University of Chicago, February 1, 1892," in Gates, *Correspondence of the Founder*, vol. 1, University of Chicago Special Collections.

61. Robert Francis Harper to Mall, 13 Apr 1892, FPM; Carl Ludwig to Mall, 2 Feb 1891, in Sabin, *Franklin Mall*, pp. 325–26.

62. C. O. Whitman to W. R. Harper, 2 June [1891]; Mall to W. R. Harper, 27 Oct 1891, WRH.

63. GSH to Mall, 9 June 1891, FPM. Hall told Mall that despite the "highest appreciation" of him and the "remarkable success and promise of your scientific work," he could not guarantee "the permanence or extension of your department here."

Whitman entered into a discussion with Harper about the possibility of establishing a biological research center on the inland lakes. A marine biologist, Whitman could not resist the fact that "some features of the location are not equalled anywhere else in this country." Harper, moreover, talked of being able to erect a laboratory building for biology, support a large department of related biological studies, and offer Whitman the large salary of $7,000. Whitman was soon able to conceive of founding at Chicago perhaps the "leading center of instruction and research" and opening a "new era in the Biology of this country."[64]

While such possibilities were being presented to him, Hall's actions reminded him sharply of the disadvantages of the administration at Clark. In the fall of 1891, according to Donaldson's memory,

A. D. Mead . . . a Fellow in Zoology under Whitman . . . returned to the University late because it had been necessary for him to nurse his mother, who was ill. The family income was a small one. Because he was late Hall refused to pay him his Fellowship stipend for the month, which, I believe, was $25.00.

Whitman was greatly incensed at the injustice of this case and demanded that Hall revoke his decision. When Hall repeatedly refused to reconsider, Whitman threatened to resign. Other members of the faculty and student body were aroused, and other instances of mistreatment of fellows and assistants soon came to light.[65]

In the midst of this agitation, Mall and Whitman accelerated negotiations with Chicago.[66] Harper's offers in definite form were less ample than he had earlier implied, however. Besides the laboratory building, Whitman urged, "the number and character of my colleagues is the most essential thing." Whitman stipulated the names and salaries of seven Clark men whom he wanted Harper to

64. C. O. Whitman to W. R. Harper, 2 June [1891]; 9 June, 30 July, 20 Sept, 19 Dec 1891, WRH.

65. Donaldson, "Autumn of 1891—to Spring, 1892," FPM; Donaldson, "Memories," p. 95.

66. Mall to W. R. Harper, 27 Oct 1891; C. O. Whitman to W. R. Harper, 19 Dec 1891, WRH. Mall also solicited an offer from the University of Michigan. George A. Hench to Mall, 8 Nov 1891, FPM.

take, and who presumably were anxious to come with him, including
Mall, Donaldson, Lombard, and Boas.[67] When Harper balked at
Whitman's high terms, Mall, who was very anxious that the scheme
should succeed, wrote Harper of their position.

> You will pardon me if I tell you proudly what I think the reason is why
> men of Whitman's stature are so attached to this place. They make of science
> a religion and the highest duty of a scientist is to add to knowledge. This
> place is founded on such an idea. . . . On account of much freedom here, in
> spite of our trouble (confidential), we cling to our ideals.[68]

In the light of these ideals and Harper's reluctance to guarantee
their realization at Chicago, Whitman, Mall, and a number of their
colleagues decided to make a concerted effort to improve conditions
at Clark.[69]

On 13 and 14 January 1892, Whitman, Mall, Donaldson, Lombard, Michelson, Nef, and Boas met to discuss the Clark situation
and its remedy.[70] Story and Sanford, who continued to cherish a
personal loyalty to Hall, refused to join in the discussions, although
they were notified of them. As a result of these meetings and the
common airing of grievances, the small matters that each had been
able to overlook swelled into a formidable body of complaint. The
men began to see a clear pattern of duplicity in Hall's behavior. The
only remedy, they decided, was to embark on a policy of complete
frankness and try to establish the ground rules for a new method of
administration.

What followed was a bizarre series of encounters between a
desperately uncomprehending Hall and an irate faculty goaded to increasingly aggressive action. Hall persisted in believing throughout
that the "whole trouble" arose from uneasiness with regard to the
faculty's positions and that as soon as he was assured of more funds
from Clark for the following year and could sign contracts, the
entire difficulty would disappear. Meanwhile, he tried to stall for

67. C. O. Whitman to W. R. Harper, 15, 26 Jan 1892, WRH.
68. Mall to W. R. Harper, 27 Jan 1892, WRH.
69. The following account of the faculty's attempt to reach an agreement with
Hall is taken from the faculty memo, CUP, except where otherwise indicated. It
should be noted that the memo is entirely silent on the concurrent negotiations
with the University of Chicago.
70. Bolza and Baur, a docent in paleontology, soon after joined in the negotiations.

time and to keep all word of the trouble from the one authority in the university who trusted him completely, the board of trustees.

Michelson, Lombard, and Donaldson first approached Hall privately with the grievances of the men and urged him to call a faculty meeting. Hall obliged, but he claimed not to understand the trouble at all and asked whether they "wished to see the President of the University humiliated." At a following meeting, the faculty presented a set of propositions which they hoped would serve as a basis for future harmony:

1. The Faculty and other Academic appointees are governed by only such rules as have been publicly brought to their notice.
2. At the written request of two or more members of the Faculty, stating the object of the meeting, the President will call a Faculty Meeting.
3. Members of the Faculty may propose for discussion any subject concerning the University or its members.
4. In matters pertaining to their studies, as distinct from their business relations to the University, Assistants, Fellows, scholars and students shall be responsible to the instructors by whom their work is directed.
5. The Faculty may elect their officers and committees, President excepted.

Although Hall had privately before assented to the propositions, he now raised difficulties. The trustees would need to approve them. They could only be acted upon at a regular meeting, and this was "a meeting of the Faculty, and not a Faculty Meeting." As Hall could not say, an official faculty meeting would be recorded in minutes open to the scrutiny of the board of trustees and the founder. The faculty's attempt to establish a policy of complete openness could take no account of Hall's desire to save face.

When Hall saw that no one would meet him except as a faculty, he reluctantly called the men together again in a formal faculty meeting. He allowed the propositions to be taken up and the faculty voted to accept them and have them transmitted to the trustees for approval at the earliest opportunity. However, Hall referred to the propositions as being formulated by a "body of men," and "several warm discussions" were required to make him "barely admit that we did not represent a conspiracy." At the end Hall urged secrecy, particularly that the matter not reach the trustees, the faculty having just voted to send the propositions to the trustees for approval.

The faculty's disappointment over Hall's behavior at the two meetings was profound. Their only means to bring the matter to the attention of the trustees, they felt, was to resign. Led by Michelson, they drew up a declaration of resignation as of September 1892, "owing to lack of confidence in the President of Clark University."

The trustees gave Hall their complete support. They referred the resignations to Hall

in whose impartiality, good judgment, clear understanding of all interests involved, and devotion to the interests of the University, they have entire confidence, with full power to represent the Board, and to take such action with regard to any or all of the resignations tendered, as he may deem advisable.

At a faculty meeting the following day, Hall read this decision to the men. Evidently strengthened by this support, he followed with a statement of his own which indicated for the first time that he might be able to come to an agreement with them:

As a contribution to this end, I wish first to waive all I did and said in connection with the late painful meetings. Under the peculiar circumstances it did not represent my deliberate view, and I desire to reconsider it.

As for the detailed complaints against him, Hall was sure that "as you gradually know all the facts, you will be certain to view me in a very different light," and he added that a recent letter from Jonas Clark "makes some things possible not so before."[71] In conclusion, Hall proposed

(1) A mutual redetermination of powers, rules, and methods of the Faculty. This would be slow, but should begin at once. (2) To open negotiations for the future with individuals, and with all, if funds will permit. These painful days may begin a better state of things, and nothing I can do shall be wanting to bring good instead of injury out of the discussion.

Expressing great satisfaction with the statement, the faculty informed Hall that they were "fully prepared to meet the President in the spirit of his remarks" and withdrew their resignations. They then agreed to Hall's plan that they confer with him and the trustees by means of a committee to consist of Michelson, Whitman, and Donaldson.

The first meeting with Hall on 4 February was a great disappointment to the new committee, for the equilibrium Hall seemed to have

71. No communication from Clark easing the financial situation at the university is known to have been sent at this time.

established two days earlier was shown to be most fleeting. Hall declined to consider the administrative propositions, saying "they opened the whole matter of the duties of the Faculty." He appeared to have no intention of bringing the trustees into the discussion and discussed a more detailed set of proposals introduced by the faculty[72] "in such a way that it seemed plain that he wished to filibuster." When this procedure continued for several weeks, the committee went directly to the trustees, and a committee of trustees finally appeared on campus to discuss the matter, on 16 February.

The trustees basically supported the faculty on their detailed proposals and refused to discuss the first and more basic set of administrative demands in detail. These were matters between Hall and the faculty, the trustees said, and did not require their approval. Since Hall had from the start told the faculty that he could not assent to them without the trustees' approval, this left him finally and clearly with his back to the wall.

During the six weeks that followed, "Hall was filibustering" and could not be made to discuss the propositions. At the same time, he was trying to reengage Nef and Whitman for the coming year, "but both refused to consider anything until the propositions had been acted upon."[73] Hall believed that the difficulties would disappear once he signed contracts for the coming year with his professors. The faculty believed Hall was trying to use his power of appointment to break the movement for administrative reform.

Hall destroyed any lingering hope of improved relations when he announced his decision on the propositions on 11 April. While he granted completely the full publication of rules, he agreed to call faculty meetings upon request only if he deemed it "necessary." He

72. The second set of propositions read: "1. Heads of Departments or of Laboratories have full control of the appropriations assigned for their use, with the option of ordering through the [president's] office or not, at discretion. 2. Heads of Departments or Laboratories have authority to engage scientific and laboratory assistants, and to determine their salaries. 3. No action affecting any Assistant or Fellow shall be taken by the University without consultation with the Head of the Department, or the instructor by whom his work is directed. 4. The Library Committee is to be appointed by the Faculty, and the rules are to be submitted to the Faculty for ratification. The Committee shall have power to expend money appropriated for books and journals." This last referred to Hall's exclusive control of the library list.
73. Mall, "Feb. 16–May 8," MS notes, FPM.

"desired" rather than guaranteed liberty of discussion in the meetings and reserved the right, with the trustees, to appoint the secretary and all standing committees of the faculty. Finally, Hall left the direction of the fellows and assistants to their professors in all matters pertaining to their studies "and not affecting the rules or policy of the University."[74] The faculty received this decision as a "huge joke. . . . The general conclusion was that we no longer had anything to fight for and that we make arrangements to connect ourselves with other institutions as soon as possible."[75]

Actually, Mall had convinced Whitman to accept Harper's offer, despite Whitman's lingering doubts of Harper's ability to fulfill his promises, on 9 April 1892, two days before Hall handed down his final decision. Whitman and Mall had been continuing negotiations with Harper throughout the winter, and Mall was particularly anxious for the "biological scheme" to go through, even during the brief periods when the faculty was hopeful of a settlement with Hall.[76] Hall's tactics had long since alienated them, and the attraction of the Chicago plan had long since taken root. Whitman's final acceptance and Hall's final decision now freed the other dissident faculty men to explore openly the possibilities at Chicago. Mall notified Harper of the situation, and in eight days he appeared personally in Worcester.[77]

Within a few hours of his arrival, Harper formally engaged five men in biology—Whitman, Mall, and three others. After further consultations, he left the decisions about Donaldson, Nef, and Michelson open "as there were side difficulties." Hall then sent for Harper and threatened to expose to the public his dastardly raid, as

74. GSH, "The President of the University has decided as follows . . . ," 11 Apr 1892, Boas Papers.

75. Mall, "Feb. 16–May 8," FPM.

76. C. O. Whitman to W. R. Harper, 14, 19, 21, 30 Mar, 2, 7 Apr 1892; [April, 1892]; Mall to W. R. Harper, 8 Feb, 7, 9 Apr 1892, WRH.

77. According to Donaldson, "Autumn of 1891—to Spring, 1892," FPM, and Sabin, *Franklin Mall,* p. 103, Mall notified Harper through his younger brother, Robert F. Harper, an Assyriologist and friend of Mall's from student days in Leipzig. R. F. Harper was in Europe at this time, however, and it seems unnecessary that Mall would choose this roundabout method of notifying Harper when he was already in direct contact with him. R. F. Harper to Mall, 13 Apr 1892, FPM. Neither Donaldson's nor Mall's accounts of the quarrel with Hall mentions the fact that Mall and Whitman were negotiating with Harper throughout.

an example of the methods of a "Standard Oil institution," unless Harper allowed him to keep certain men. Harper evidently agreed to make an effort in this direction[78] and, according to Hall, offered Hall himself a place at Chicago as professor of psychology.[79] Hall wanted particularly to keep his chemist, Nef, and had just promoted him to associate professor, claiming that his acceptance of the honor was an implied contract for the following year. When Harper left his office, Hall called in Nef and told him that "he could not break his contract." If necessary, Hall would take the case to court. Nef, against the wishes of Harper, resigned immediately. Thus, "Harper left with Nef and Michelson committed to him."[80]

In the end, two-thirds of all those of faculty rank and 70 percent of the student body left Clark in the spring of 1892. Half of those leaving went directly to the University of Chicago. Out of the ruins of Clark, Chicago had the foundation of distinguished departments in physics, chemistry, biology, and mathematics. When the university opened that fall, five of its thirty-one full professors were Clark men. Clark was left with only one distinguished department, psychology.[81] The declining financial situation at Clark would probably have led many of the faculty to Chicago under any circumstances, just as many of them had a few years before come to Clark in the wake of hard times at Johns Hopkins. Had Hall been able to deal differently with his faculty, however, a few might have remained and the university's reputation would not have suffered so sharp a setback.

Hall's conflict with his faculty came at an early stage in the development of American universities, when procedures of administration and the mutual powers of president, trustees, and faculty were not matters of common and accepted practice. Any man would have had difficulty in dealing with the ambitious and restless group of young men Hall had assembled at Clark. In the circumstances, however, Hall appeared to be totally inadequate to the task. The challenge of the faculty to his authority, coming atop the pressures

78. Mall, "Feb. 16–May 8," FPM.
79. *LCP*, pp. 296–97.
80. Mall, "Feb. 16–May 8," FPM; Tanner, *Clark University*, pp. 89–90.
81. *Ann. Rep. Pres. Clark, April, 1893;* Goodspeed, *History of the University of Chicago*, pp. 486–87.

placed on him by Jonas Clark and within a year of the tragic death
of his wife and daughter, were clearly too much for Hall's precarious psychological balance.

Hall at one point admitted to Mall the reason he could not approve the demand for faculty meetings and other procedures of
accommodation. He could never "attend a meeting in which he did
not know what was to be sprung upon him," he said. More centrally,
"The propositions could not be decided on their own merits," he
told Mall. "They would have been granted if [the faculty] had
not asked them. They came to him as a command, etc." To Mall,
this excuse was the final absurd lie of Hall's long history of lies. It
was, however, a significant exposure of the rigidity with which Hall
felt compelled to hold on to the narrowing realm over which he had
control.[82]

Hall's response to the conflict made him seem to the faculty to be
a devious and untrustworthy eccentric, as Donaldson called him; a
plain and simple liar, as Mall pictured him; a "Jekyll and Hyde
personality," as Lombard thought him to be; or a "pseudomaniac"
and "bass hypnotizer," as Whitman called him.[83] The nature of
Hall's disturbed behavior must have seemed particularly offensive
to men of science, devoted to the truth, in an age which valued
character so highly. As Mall commented, the "principle involved
was a religion and no doubt the same influence which made Christians martyrs."[84]

In face of Hall's behavior, the action of Sanford appears all the
more remarkable. Sanford evidently recognized the truth in some
of the men's grievances, but he recognized as well the inevitable
diminishment of Hall which their protest entailed. A man of gentlemanly demeanor and character, he steered his own course by a sense
of Hall's underlying worth and by a feeling of personal loyalty to
him. He also disliked insubordination. Titchener claimed that "what
characterizes [Sanford] is an unswerving rectitude combined with
an habitually deferential attitude to any sort of powers that be."

82. Mall, "Jan. 21, 1892" and "Feb. 16–May 8," FPM.
83. Donaldson, "Memories," pp. 91–95, Donaldson Papers; Mall, "Feb. 16–
May 8," FPM; Ryan, interview with Lombard, CUP; C. O. Whitman to J. U.
Nef, 4 Aug 1892, Nef Pepers.
84. Mall, "Jan. 21, 1892," FPM.

Though his decision to stay with Hall would require on his part self-sacrifice and infinite tact, he followed this path through the next thirty years of their association. Through all this period, the two men were cordial and correct, though never quite intimate friends, and Sanford sometimes regretted his decision. Had Sanford instead chosen to leave, the stature of the psychology department would have been threatened, the viability of the university in doubt, and the possibility of Hall's surviving the rub of academic and administrative contacts greatly reduced.[85]

Like the dissident faculty, Jonas Clark, too, came to feel that Hall was untrustworthy. During the summer of 1892, on a brief return visit to Worcester, Clark happened to meet Lombard and heard from him a frank statement of the faculty's position, including the nature of the faculty's dissatisfaction with Hall and Hall's tendency to blame Clark for his arbitrary actions. Lombard then later sent Clark a copy of Hall's statement to the faculty meeting of 2 February 1892, in which he admitted the error of his earlier behavior and implied that Clark, rather than he, was to blame for the misunderstanding.[86]

In the fall of 1892, Clark stated that he felt Stanley Hall had "deceived" him. Clark's natural reticence prevented him from elaborating on that charge; so its meaning has remained something of a mystery in the fog that has surrounded the early history of the university.[87] Hall advertised the view that Clark referred in this charge to Hall's failure to found an undergraduate college. Clark, however, did not appear to look on this failure as a deception, for the central premise on which the original plan was based, that Worcester would meet it with an outpouring of funds, had not materialized. There was a much more natural and obvious basis for

85. On Sanford, see L. N. Wilson, ed., "In Memoriam. Edmund Clark Sanford," *CULP* 8 (1925), and Titchener to E. G. Boring, 9 Nov 1923, TP. Lewis M. Terman, in "Autobiography," *A History of Psychology in Autobiography*, ed. Carl Murchison (New York: Russell and Russell, 1961), 2:320, stated that Sanford "seemed to have a particularly inhibited personality and was subject to nervous fatigue and states of depression." He temporarily expressed bitterness over his relations with Hall in Sanford to Titchener, 25 April 1924, TP.

86. W. P. Lombard to J. U. Nef., 12, 19 Sept 1892; statement by J. U. Nef, 1892, Nef Papers; W. P. Lombard to Clark, 20 Sept 1892, CUP.

87. Tanner, "Clark University," p. 69.

his feeling that Hall had deceived him in the disclosures of Lombard. That Clark's disillusion with Hall was a significant factor in his withdrawal of interest and funds from the university seems doubtful, for the pattern and causes of Clark's declining interest were already clear beforehand. Clark's distrust, however, did probably influence his ultimate bequest to the university.

The reaction of the trustees to the exodus of the professors remained closely tied to the version of the conflict Hall gave them. They recognized that Hall had made administrative mistakes, but concluded that Hall could be a very competent man and still be unable to "keep a hotel."[88]

Even after so large a part of the faculty left, Hall and the trustees kept to their plan of a graduate university, for the considerations which had dissuaded them from founding a college still held true. Pending Clark's demise, when they hoped a large bequest would allow them to resume their earlier, more ambitious plans,[89] they tried to maintain a university on the meager annual budget of $28,000. Hall hoped to find one man of stature for each of the departments, but even that proved difficult after word of the faculty's dissatisfaction with Hall circulated. No biologist could be persuaded to come to Clark except one of the former young fellows, Clifton Hodge.[90] In physics, Arthur Webster, the talented assistant in the department, became assistant professor. Story remained in mathematics, while instruction in chemistry limped along until 1895 when it was discontinued for some years. In number of faculty and students, the department of psychology, and the subdepartment of pedagogy which was soon added to it, dominated the small university.[91] Thus, in the end, necessity forced Hall to compromise his ideals. The university was reduced to a restricted scale and its precariousness encouraged him to admit within its bounds substantial concessions to the popular culture.

88. Faculty memo, pp. 21, 28.
89. Tanner, "Clark University," pp. 62–64, 90–91.
90. Ibid., p. 91; Wm. K. Brooks to Wm. H. Welch, [Sept 1898], Alumni Records Office, Johns Hopkins University.
91. *Ann. Rep. Pres. Clark, April, 1893*, p. 15; *Clark Register, 1894*, p. 45.

PROFESSIONAL QUARRELS

At times during the first decade of the new psychology in America, it appeared that Stanley Hall would become the preeminent leader of his profession. Like the two other natural leaders of the new discipline, James and Ladd, Hall was nearing fifty, while the other psychologists—Dewey, Sanford, Cattell, Baldwin, Jastrow, and Münsterberg—were fifteen to twenty years their junior. From the mid-1880s until 1883, Hall commanded the major bases of power in the new discipline, and until 1895 he often spoke for its rising scientific spirit more fully than either of its other two elder statesmen. Hall could not maintain this position, however. The collapse of his large hopes for Clark University, after only three years of its existence, inevitably constricted the influence he had hitherto exerted on the profession by sheer numbers. Whereas Hall's Ph.D.s still outnumbered all others at the turn of the century, Clark could not hope to keep pace with the rapidly expanding departments of the larger, wealthier universities.[1]

Nor did Hall's *Journal* propel him, as he had hoped it would, into leadership of the scientific movement within psychology. In the early days of the discipline, when enthusiasm and assertion were useful, Hall's journal venture could succeed. When the profession began to grow, however, and leadership required the skills

1. In 1898, thirty of the fifty-four doctorates in psychology awarded in this country had been awarded by Hall. Harper, "Tables of American Doctorates," p. 580.

of cooperation and compromise, Hall was found wanting. However firmly he advanced the scientific aspirations of his colleagues, he could not hold their allegiance without exercising judgment and commanding personal respect and trust. Hall's incapacity in this regard soon reduced the relative influence of his *Journal* and exiled him from leadership in the new American Psychological Association.

Part of the difficulty lay in Hall's renewed attacks on James and Ladd, in the name of science, in the review columns of his *Journal*. James's long-awaited *Principles of Psychology* first drew Hall's fire. In his preface, James had thanked Hall, as well as several others, for the inspiration of his "intellectual companionship,"[2] and Hall wrote James in a friendly vein before his review of the *Principles* appeared: "My own view—as you aid me more than anyone else to define it—differs from your standpoint somewhat more widely than I thought before I understood you." Hall hoped that it would "give no offense even for an instant."[3] In his review, however, Hall's tone was more belligerent. Though he admonished his readers at the start not to forget that "gratitude and admiration are predominant," he subjected the volumes to probably the most detailed and severe criticism they were to receive. Even his closing praise had its characteristic Hallian turn: "The good [in the book] is so very largely preponderant that many if not most of the gravest errors and defects might be eliminated in a radically revised edition."[4]

While claiming to eschew metaphysics, Hall charged, James had nonetheless brought in philosophical issues at every step and organized many of his conceptions around them, rather than around the natural grouping of the facts. James's philosophical concern was most apparent in the "strangely timid" manner in which this generally outspoken writer played "bo-peep" with the question of soul. The only real cohesion one could find in the book, Hall shrewdly remarked, was its attempt to refurbish in scientific terms the older philosophic conception of soul. Such, Hall believed, was

2. James, *Principles*, 1:vii. James also cited Chauncey Wright, Charles Peirce, James J. Putnam, and Josiah Royce.
3. GSH to Wm. James, [Jan 1891], JP.
4. GSH, "Review of William James's *Principles of Psychology*," 1891, pp. 578, 591.

the root of James's many-sided effort to enrich the mind's native perceptual content, active impulsive nature, and causal power.[5]

James confused psychology not only with philosophy but also with neurophysiology. The *Principles* showed Hall that psychologists knew almost as little of the exact workings of the nervous system and the brain as of the epistemological or metaphysical status of mind. James had used brain processes as his *deus ex machina,* and his jumbled and contradictory nervous metaphors amounted to a confused "meta-neurology."[6]

James's whole effort had been animated, Hall feared, not by the patient attitude of the scientist but by the speculative urge of the philosopher to grasp the whole of things. There was still too much to be discovered before such a decided arrangement of the facts would prove useful. It is "worse than waste," Hall said, "it is philosophic and scientific precocity and lack of self-control." Hall himself preferred to put his faith in a "future monistic synthesis" and trust that experimental science, with its reverent and lawful attitude toward nature, would in its own time substantiate the essential truths of religion through its understanding of man.[7]

To these major criticisms, Hall added a liberal dose of his characteristically unflattering insight into the personality of the author. Though he praised James's brilliance and versatility, he implied that the book sounded as though it were written with a shotgun or water hose, rather than sharply and cleanly with a rifle. So much did James's personality intrude on his work, that it sometimes reminded one of Rousseau or a cheap popular diarist. Just those revelations and distinctive marks of James's personality "will be valuable material for the inductive methods of the future in psychology."[8]

Earlier Hall had written James in a more generous manner:

[I] must before all congratulate you on what your Lotze called the highest human felicity—successful delivery ... of a legitimate and whole experience of one's knowledge, opinions and whole personality, a joy only possible to the philosophers. Now we have you sure and even death cannot rob us of

5. Ibid., pp. 578–80, 588.
6. Ibid., pp. 586–87.
7. Ibid., p. 590.
8. Ibid., pp. 585, 589–91. Hall referred to *Marie Bashkirtseff: The Journal of a Young Artist* (New York: Cassell, 1889).

you and everyone that reads the book will rejoice that you have tried and put yourself down. . . .[9]

Hall, having renounced the joy possible to the philosophers and pressed by his own inability to communicate his feelings straightforwardly or synthesize his psychological views, could not but view James's achievement ambivalently. The year James's text appeared, Hall finally published in his journal a brief history of the concept of reflex action, all that survived of his own attempt, begun contemporaneously with James's, to construct a synthetic system of psychology.[10] Hall made no mention of the use to which he had originally intended this material, for its meager dimensions must have been a bitter reminder to him of his own frustrated desire for synthetic meaning.

Hall also attacked Ladd's new text in a *Journal* review. It was pervaded by "an inability, now, alas, we fear, grown hopeless, to take the clear, consistent, scientific standpoint." Unlike his own first critique of Ladd, Hall this time did not attribute Ladd's deficiency to a weakness of scientific understanding. Ladd did not see that the old conflict of materialism and religion had been made obsolete by dynamism.

Nature is not yet heartily loved and trusted. The reason for this halting attitude, we believe lies not in the author's lack of long familiarity with the practical details of laboratory and clinic so much as in a sluggishness of religious perception, a lack of prophetic insight and depth.[11]

To the religiously committed Ladd, this was probably the crueler blow.

Hall's position in itself was not unpopular to his colleagues. James and Ladd also criticized each other's work forcefully and on some of the same grounds as Hall did.[12] The younger experimentalists were in sympathy with Hall's desire to eliminate all

9. GSH to Wm. James, 14 Oct [1890], JP.
10. GSH, "Sketch of History of Reflex Action," 1890, pp. 71–86. Hall turned the remainder of his historical notes on reflex action over to the Clark biologist, Clifton F. Hodge, and told him that they were originally collected for a history of the subject which was made unnecessary by the publication of a German treatise in 1881. C. F. Hodge, "A Sketch of the History of Reflex Action," *AJP* 3 (1891): 149.
11. GSH, "Psychological Literature," *AJP* 6 (1894): 477–78.
12. George T. Ladd, "Psychology As So-called 'Natural Science,'" *Philosophical Review* 1 (Jan 1892): 24–53; "Is Psychology a Science?" *PR* 1 (July 1894):

philosophical questions from psychology and to take a consistently empirical approach to all problems.[13] Moreover, the definition of psychology Hall defended against James and Ladd could not help but be exclusive and belligerent in a profession in which the philosopher-psychologists still about equaled in number the new experimentalists. Ladd, taking the older and wider view of science as any kind of ordered explanation of facts, could present his position as the "courteous" and "generous" one.[14]

It appears, however, that Hall created a level of ill-feeling in excess of the odium his purge necessarily produced. There was a degree of personal ambition visible in Hall's efforts which made him suspect to his colleagues. One gathers that it was Hall whom Ladd had in mind when he remarked that "my observations lead me to admit that not a few who cry most loudly in the name of 'science' show quite too plainly that it is chiefly for their own sakes," and not for science's sake, that they work.[15]

There was also a disturbing level of insult in Hall's criticism of his philosophic colleagues. Hall clearly had a talent for cutting to the bone. He often attributed the contour of the author's thinking to the immaturity or the peculiar style of his personality, thus producing the same kind of irate reaction as did the charges of "resistance" that Freudians were later to make against their detractors.[16] Quite naturally, James began to complain about "the raw philistinism of the Stanley Hall school."[17]

The personal and intellectual antagonism Hall aroused came to

392–95; Wm. James, "Plea for Psychology as a 'Natural Science,' " *Philosophical Review* 1 (Apr 1892): 146–53; "Psychology: Descriptive and Explanatory," *PR* 1 (May 1894): 286–93.

13. See Wm. L. Bryan, "On the Development of Voluntary Motor Ability," *AJP* 5 (1892): 125–32; E. W. Scripture, "The Problem of Psychology," *Mind* 16 (July 1891): 305–26; J. M. Cattell, "Mental Measurement," *Philosophical Review* 2 (May 1893): 316–32.

14. G. T. Ladd, "President's Address before the New York Meeting of the APA," *PR* 1 (Jan 1894): 1–21.

15. Ibid., p. 19. James was disturbed by Hall's refusal to allow the publisher of his journal to act also as the American agent for *Mind*. Wm. James to GSH, 10 Nov 1887, HP.

16. John Dewey to Wm. James, 10 May 1891, JP; Wm. James to W. F. H. Meyers, 30 Jan 1891, in Henry James, ed., *The Letters of William James* (Boston: Atlantic Monthly Press, 1920), 1:307.

17. Wm. James to J. M. Baldwin, 11 Jan 1891, in J. M. Baldwin, *Between Two Wars, 1861–1921* (Boston: Stratford, 1926), 2:204.

focus on the *American Journal of Psychology*. Hall's limitation of the *Journal* to empirical studies excluded most of the work of James and Ladd, the younger philosopher-psychologists like Dewey and Baldwin, and even the theoretical articles of the experimentally oriented psychologists like Cattell and Scripture. Although Hall printed the studies of Harvard students when they began to appear, and an occasional review from Cattell at Columbia, even the experimentalists were poorly represented in the *Journal* compared to Hall and his colleagues at Clark. Cattell, wary of Hall since his experience at Johns Hopkins, preferred to publish his experimental studies in *Mind*.[18]

Caught short of material, Hall would fill an entire issue with a long dissertation from one of his Clark students, most of which was speculative work out of place in such a journal.[19] In the reviews, the selection of literature reflected Hall's somewhat capricious taste; the reviews themselves were often just one or two paragraphs of brief summary without comment and were largely written by Hall and the men at Clark. The reviews of the books of some of Hall's rivals which resulted were regarded as "scandalous."[20]

By 1892, it became apparent that the volume of experimental work as well as general psychological work would soon greatly increase, but Hall's exclusive and capricious use of his authority had already alienated his potential supporters. The younger psychologists began to talk of founding their own publications;[21] Scripture, now at Yale, announced that he would publish the Yale studies himself in a separate Yale series.[22] Meanwhile, the traditional philosophers, who had hitherto opened their publications to the new psychology, began to retreat. In 1892, Jacob Gould Schurman, head of the school of philosophy at Cornell, announced a *Philo-*

18. In addition to the difficulty over fellowships, Hall mishandled a report of Cattell's first experimental work at Hopkins in a way which suggested to Cattell that he was trying to appropriate it. Cattell to his parents, 27 Oct [1884], CP.

19. GSH, "Reminiscence," 1917, p. 299.

20. Wm. James to J. M. Baldwin, 11 Jan 1891, in Baldwin, *Between Two Wars*, 2:204.

21. Wm. James to Münsterberg, 29 July 1893, MP; Cattell to Wm. James, 16 Sept 1893, MP.

22. Wm. James to Josiah Royce, 18 Dec 1892, in Perry, *William James*, 1:807.

sophical Review for philosophy and psychology which would not publish experimental researches, and Cattell thought that the attitude of the new editor of *Mind* suggested that experimental studies of psychology might not be welcomed much longer in the English journal.[23]

James was unhappy at the thought that "these little separate college tin-trumpets" were multiplying,[24] but was unwilling to throw his influence decisively behind Hall's journal. Early in 1892, Hall cordially offered to give James a special section in his journal for the work of the new Harvard laboratory, but James left the question open for a year to consult with Hugo Münsterberg, the head of the laboratory, who had not yet arrived from Germany.[25] During most of 1892 and 1893, James was in Europe and the initiative to create some wide consensus on publication fell to the younger psychologists. James personally preferred a philosophic monthly which would embrace Schurman's *Philosophical Review* as well as Hall's *Journal* and Scripture's proposed experimental series, but he recognized that "others will not feel as I do in this matter."[26] Traditional philosophy and psychology had already drifted too far apart to be rejoined.

The first formal meeting of the association in December 1892 was probably the occasion for Baldwin and Cattell, the leading voices of dissatisfaction with the *Journal,* to discuss some solution to the problem with Jastrow and Scripture. Later they were joined by the two newly arrived laboratory chiefs, Münsterberg and Edward Bradford Titchener, an Englishman who had finished his training with Wundt and been appointed to head the psychology department and laboratory at Cornell University.[27]

Cattell and Baldwin drew up two offers, one involving "a journal under President Hall's ownership and editorship," the other involving "the Am. Jour. owned and edited as a communistic enterprise." The first proposal included the appointment of a board

23. *Mind*, n.s. 1:138; [Cattell], "Not for the Public," CP.
24. Wm. James to Royce, 18 Dec 1892, in Perry, *William James.*
25. GSH to Wm. James, 16 Feb 1892, JP.
26. Wm. James to Royce, 18 Dec 1892, in Perry, *William James.*
27. Münsterberg to Wm. James, 22 June 1893, JP; Wm. James to Münsterberg, 29 July 1893, MP.

of cooperating editors whose majority decision could approve papers for publication equally with Hall. Alternately, the cooperating editors proposed to buy the *Journal* from Hall for $3,000. Should these proposals fail, Baldwin and Cattell would found a new journal.[28]

According to Cattell, Hall "led us to understand beforehand that he would accept either" proposal.[29] He had written Cattell in April 1892, before definite discussions began, that he would like to sell the *Journal* or get "cooperation on *almost any terms*."[30] When the negotiations began in earnest, however, Hall began to retreat. Constantly shifting his ground, he argued in the end for one year's delay, saying that he was prevented by a contract with his printer from doing anything for another year. The negotiations broke down completely by mid-July.[31] To Münsterberg he complained that he had been presented with "a list of conditions which I had no hand in making." Instead of recognizing the crucial issue of joint representation on the *Journal*, he argued that "the faults of my *Journal* have been chiefly caused by the need of economy. The whole thing is this."[32] With but a few changes of words, Hall could have been speaking of his refusal to negotiate the faculty's complaints about his administration at Clark.

Coming immediately on the heels of the collapse of his plans at Clark and the revolt of the faculty, any scheme that took the sole power over the *Journal* out of his own hands could not possibly have succeeded. Hall thought of the *Journal* as virtually synonymous with his own person.[33] At that point, a threat to his full authority over it must have seemed to him much the same as a threat against his very life. Nor did it help that Baldwin handled so much of the negotiations. Baldwin was himself a difficult and ambitious man, and he and Hall were already acrimonious opponents. Hall wrote Münsterberg that "Baldwin . . . I think is determined to be an

28. Wm. James to Münsterberg, 29 July 1893, MP; J. M. Baldwin and J. M. Cattell, "Proposition to G. Stanley Hall," CP.
29. Cattell to Wm. James, 16 Sept 1893, MP.
30. Cattell to Wm. James and G. T. Ladd, [summer 1893], CP.
31. GSH to Münsterberg, 19 July, 27 Aug 1893, MP.
32. GSH to Münsterberg, 19 July 1893, MP.
33. See below, p. 243.

editor and . . . is exceedingly peremptory and unpleasant in manner to deal with," a judgment Titchener confirmed.[34]

When the negotiations reached a stalemate in the summer of 1893, Baldwin and Cattell decided to proceed with their plan of founding another journal, but the two newest laboratory men in the country were still favorably inclined to Hall. Titchener was impressed by the kindness that Hall showed him. Some years later he explained to Cattell: "I always feel, personally, that Stanley Hall is the man to whom my allegiance is due over here,—as he was so actively kind to me when I first came, and had so little to gain by his kindness."[35] To an ardent disciple of the Wundt laboratory, moreover, Hall's position in 1893 as the preeminent American leader of scientific psychology would have counted heavily. Titchener continued to resist Baldwin's blandishments.[36]

Münsterberg, too, was favorably disposed toward Hall. Hall had offered him a contributing or associate editorship in his journal and Münsterberg preferred "one bad editor to a dozen good ones."

Hall is an established man who has achieved something, while the trio Baldwin-Cattell-Jastrow is not an authority under whose decisive voice I would care to humble myself. . . .

Even after Baldwin and Cattell abandoned the attempt to reach an agreement with Hall, he continued to waver.[37]

James was besieged with letters from Cattell and Baldwin, as

34. GSH to Münsterberg, July 1893, MP. Baldwin's peremptory manner and ambitions were reflected in the later account he offered of the negotiations: "The unwillingness of President Stanley Hall . . . to accept the terms offered him to fuse his *Journal* with our *Review*, made it impossible to include all the important names of American psychologists on our board of Consulting Editors. 'Barkis was willing' only on condition that everyone else accepted subordinate positions under 'Barkis.' " Baldwin, *Between Two Wars,* 1:64. Titchener later wrote Cattell: "I know that Baldwin treated [Hall] badly . . . I know too that Baldwin, in his effort to detach me, said things of Hall that were not true. Doubtless only in the zeal of the moment; but still, there they were." Titchener to Cattell, 31 July 1903, CP.

35. Titchener to Cattell, 26 Oct 1898, CP.

36. In Leipzig during the middle 1890s Hall was "regarded as more or less in good standing as [a] Wundtian." Charles H. Judd, "Autobiography," in Murchison, *History of Psychology in Autobiography,* 2:215.

37. Münsterberg to Wm. James, 22 June, 14 July 1893, JP. (Translated by the author from the German.)

well as Münsterberg, during the summer of 1893 about the negotiations going on in America. His initial reaction to the news was
favorable to the inclusion of Hall in whatever arrangement was
made, though he had so little confidence in Hall's management that
he wished Hall could be substantially excluded.[38] James had originally shared some of Münsterberg's doubts of a Baldwin-Cattell-
Jastrow editorship. "Cattell is absurdly narrow, and Jastrow too
neuropapery." Baldwin, however, was "a strong and broad man"
and the three together might produce good results. By the time
Baldwin and Cattell asked James for his support, they had evidently
convinced him that their review would not keep to the narrow
empirical limits he disliked.[39]

Two weeks later, Münsterberg too wrote James that he had
changed his mind.

I must today confess that I over-estimated Hall; he has, after all, lied to me
also, and, while I will not break with him, I must confess that I now
see nothing more to hinder the founding of a second journal under Cattell
and Baldwin.[40]

Probably, Hall's offer of an editorship to Münsterberg did not
really mean an editorship. James had rather expected such a result:

I am not altogether surprised that you have all come to grief in your
negotiations with Hall, his personal psychology is a very queer and tor-
tuous one, containing, however, elements of sincere devotion to truth. He
hates clearness—clear formulas, clear statements[,] clear understandings;
and mystification of some kind seems never far distant from everything he
does. Yet I think he does not mean to deceive, nor is he a liar in any vulgar
meaning of the term. He shrinks with an instinctive terror from any
explanation that is definitive and irrevocable, and hence comes to say and
do things that leave an avenue open to retreat—at bottom it is all con-

38. Wm. James to Royce, 14 Aug 1893, JP; Wm. James to Münsterberg,
6, 29 July 1893, MP. In the second letter to Münsterberg James wrote: "The great
trouble, I suppose is with Hall. He is absolutely without judgment, can't tell
good from bad, and hasn't a definite or clear idea in his head. Yet his enthusiasm,
initiative, and vast and vague bibliographic knowledge, together with what he
has done, give him certain *rights* which can hardly be ignored. If he could only
be nominal chief-editor, whilst someone else exerted the real power, that might
be the solution."
39. Wm. James to Münsterberg, 29 July 1893, MP.
40. Münsterberg to Wm. James, 26 July 1893, JP. (Translated by the author
from the German.)

nected with timidity in him—as a *dreamer* he is bold, when it comes to acting, he wills-and-wills-not. But what I least like in his journal and other writings of his as president, is the religious cant he finds it necessary to throw in. Yet in a certain sense even that is not insincerely meant! He has too complicated a mind![41]

James's description of Hall stands as the most perceptive comment on him to survive to the present day. For most of his contemporaries Hall had "too complicated a mind."

Hall was deeply hurt by the journal quarrel, though he characteristically claimed to "accept the inevitable with *Joy!*" Feeling himself repudiated, he did not come to the second meeting of the association in December 1893, at which Cattell and Columbia University were hosts. A number of experimentalists allied to Hall also failed to appear. James, now returned from Europe, attended his first meeting and was elected president, and Cattell secretary, for the following year. The association changed its policy of the previous year and voted to publish its proceedings independently instead of in Hall's *Journal*. The shift which thus took place at the 1893 meeting of the association represented a transfer of power away from Hall.[42]

Hall remained a permanent casualty to the journal quarrel. He came to association meetings only occasionally during the remainder of his life. Sanford and the other psychologists attached to Hall, however, returned the following year to association meetings, and all of them except Titchener began contributing to both Hall's journal and the new *Psychological Review*.[43] While Hall himself lost his central position in the profession, and while various personal and institutional rivalries were heightened, the profession itself was not permanently split by the journal quarrel. While many psychologists shared Hall's desire to have their discipline

41. Wm. James to Münsterberg, 11 Aug 1893, MP.

42. GSH to Münsterberg, 27 Aug 1893, MP; *Proceedings, APA, 1892, 1893,* pp. 28–29. Sanford, Titchener, Jastrow, and two former Clark fellows, Herbert Nichols and William Lowe Bryan, did not attend, but, conceivably, circumstances other than the journal quarrel could have kept them away.

43. S. W. Fernberger, "The APA. A Historical Summary, 1892–1930," *Psychological Bulletin* 29 (1932): 66; J. E. W. Wallin, "History of the Struggles within the APA," *Journal of General Psychology* 63 (1960): 289; Herbert S. Langfeld, "Fifty Volumes of the Psychological Review," *PR* 50 (Jan 1943): 148.

develop independently of both philosophy and neurology, the personal and institutional rivalries within the profession did not coincide with the intellectual disagreements. Five of the nine American editors of the new *Review* were philosopher-psychologists, and the other four represented physiological and experimental approaches. The only factor which united nearly all of them was their opposition to Hall's exclusive hegemony.[44]

In part, Hall responded constructively to the challenge of the new bimonthly *Psychological Review*. When it appeared in 1894 under the editorship of Baldwin and Cattell, with the cooperation of a distinguished board of American and European psychologists, he recognized that the excellence and representative character of the *Review* threatened to turn the *Journal* into a parochial organ. He therefore accepted Sanford and Titchener as coeditors with himself and gathered his own cooperative board.[45] Since the board's American members included only his own and Titchener's friends and sympathizers, the threat to his authority was minimized. The breadth of his own interests and the cohesion that remained in the profession kept the *Journal* from insularity.

The editorial Hall wrote to open the first issue of the *Journal* under the new arrangement, however, showed how disturbed he really was by the course of events. More perhaps than any other single event of the decade, it alienated Hall from his professional colleagues. "When the American Journal of Psychology was founded in 1887," Hall began,

it was a pioneer in its field. It represented the department of psychology at the Johns Hopkins University, was for years the only one of its kind in the country, and the establishment of which, as its subsequent history shows, was one of the boldest and most sagacious as well as one of the most success-

44. The nine editors associated with the *PR* were James, Ladd, Baldwin, Dewey, Fullerton, Donaldson, Cattell, Münsterberg, and M. Allen Starr, a psychiatrist of the College of Physicians and Surgeons in New York.
45. The effort it cost Hall to share the *Journal* even with his friends was apparent on the cover of the October 1895 issue of the *Journal*, the first to appear under the joint editorship. Hall listed himself, in large type and with full title, as editor of the *Journal*, "assisted by" Sanford and Titchener, their names in smaller type and without title, though the agreement had been that the *Journal* was to be edited by all three equally together. Eventually, Sanford offered to take the blame for this "regrettable mistake" and the listing was corrected in subsequent issues. GSH, Letter to the Editor, *Science*, n.s. 2 (Nov 1895): 734–35.

ful and beneficent steps ever taken by this leader of the new academic movement.

Using the *"Journal"* as a synonym for himself, he went on to claim that his influence had been responsible, through men who had been associated with him either as students or colleagues at Hopkins and Clark, for the founding of departments of experimental psychology and laboratories at Harvard, Yale, Pennsylvania, Columbia, Toronto, Wisconsin, and many other universities.[46]

Hall followed this braggadocio with a description of the "sharply defined field" to which the *Journal* was henceforth to devote itself, the "philosophical *standpoint* and character" it was to have. The standpoint he outlined was similar to the one he had shown in the *Journal* from the start, but he interspersed his outline with statements that were so much associated with criticisms of other psychologists that the outline must have seemed to many readers simply an excuse for vituperation. Hall's chief barbs were directed at the philosopher-psychologists, and particularly at William James. What the *Journal* was especially against, Hall said, was "mystic infiltration," the mixing of

the most opposite tendencies in rococo confusion in the same journal and even text-books, . . . "arm-chair professors," who lack patience for the tedious details of laboratory research as well as the instinct for concentration and specialization that can focus their efforts upon anything less than the entire field of psychology. . . . the disposition . . . to press imperfectly established observation into the service of old discussions concerning problems not yet soluble by science . . .

and so on.[47] James had become the chief focus of the hostility released by Hall's declining status.

Since the dislike and mistrust of Hall in the profession had already come into the open during the journal quarrel and been crystallized by it, James and the other psychologists implicated in Hall's editorial felt free to challenge him. James wrote immediately to Hall asking for a retraction: "I am astonished . . . to find you asserting that the department of exp. p. and the lab. at Harvard was founded under the influence of a Clark man." The idea was

46. GSH, "Editorial," *AJP* 7 (Oct 1895): 3–4.
47. Ibid., pp. 4–6.

"simply ridiculous." Herbert Nichols, a Clark Ph.D., was the only man Hall could have meant, and he came to Harvard after the laboratory was founded. Though he recognized how "contemptible" the beginnings were, James could not but mention his own early efforts in experimental psychology, "arm-chair professor" that he was. One of the things he had done was

inducting you into experimental investigation, with very naive methods, it is true, but you may remember that there was no other place but Harvard where during those years you could get even that.

Were it not that the honor of Harvard was involved as well as his own, James closed, he would let the matter pass, but now he must ask for a public correction of the record.[48]

Hall replied to James that he had thought Nichols to be "the first Harvard Instructor who was chiefly a lab man and experimenter, or first to offer a purely experimental course, or all of these." He meant soon to write something that would alter "the growing tendency to look askance at others' work, which I deplore." He concluded

I am no judge of how much should be allowed a Journal or a University in the way of self complacent utterances when it turns anniversary corners and wants to keep its courage up. If I have overstepped the line of propriety here, I am sorry. If you wish me to make any statement in the Journal tell me just what will satisfy you. This I heartily and sincerely desire to do.[49]

To which James replied coldly:

You ask what will satisfy me in the way of correction. Anything you like that withdraws the false statement. My activity in Harvard cannot be a matter of which you are entirely ignorant. I trust that you have submitted my letter to Sanford and Titchener who are of course as fully responsible as you are now for what the Journal prints.[50]

The angry desire to bring Hall to account soon led to the appear-

48. Wm. James to GSH, 12 Oct [1895], HP.
49. GSH to Wm. James, 16 Oct 1895, JP. In "the tendency to look askance at others' work," Hall was probably referring to a survey of psychology by Baldwin which gave him little credit for the establishment of the new psychology in America, although it did acknowledge his laboratory at Johns Hopkins as the first in the country. J. M. Baldwin, "Psychology Past and Present," *PR* 1 (July 1894): 363–91.
50. Wm. James to GSH, 19 Oct [1895], HP.

ance of four letters in *Science*, one each from James, Ladd, Baldwin, and Cattell, refuting Hall's claims before the entire scientific community. James explained that

I, myself, "founded" the instruction in experimental psychology at Harvard in 1874–5 or 1876, I forget which. For a long series of years the laboratory was in two rooms of the Scientific School building, which at last became choked with apparatus, so that a change was necessary. I then, in 1890, resolved on an altogether new departure, raised several thousand dollars, fitted up Dane Hall, and introduced laboratory exercises as a regular part of the undergraduate psychology-course. Dr. Herbert Nichols, then at Clark, was appointed, in 1891, assistant in this part of the work. . . .

Likewise Ladd speaking for Yale and Baldwin for Toronto pointed out that their own influence, rather than Stanley Hall's, had been decisive in starting laboratories and experimental departments at their universities. Cattell followed suit, denying that he was, in any real sense, a student of Hall's, for he had studied several years with Lotze and Wundt both before and after Hall came to Hopkins.[51]

A few weeks later, Hall replied in *Science* to this "well concerted quartet of letters." He tried to extricate himself from a number of his claims by pleading that he had not at all meant what his readers thought he had meant. On the laboratory question he argued that "In the development of a new academic 'department' a crucial point is, as I deem it, when an instructor is appointed whose central work and interest is in that line." Hence Scripture at Yale, Cattell at Pennsylvania and Columbia, Jastrow at Wisconsin and Nichols at Harvard had "founded" the experimental departments at those institutions. How Toronto got on the list, he had no idea.

This, and this alone, was my theme. Had it been of the pioneer work, no less crucial, which made these appointments possible, which was done by Profs. James, Ladd, and earlier by President McCosh and others, I should not only have desired to say nearly all they have said, but more. To Prof. James, especially, I owe a debt I can never repay, unless by trying to influence him to correct the views in which we more and more widely differ, some of which he will bear me witness I have earnestly tried to do.[52]

51. Wm. James, G. T. Ladd, J. M. Baldwin, and J. M. Cattell, Letters to the Editor, *Science*, n.s. 2 (Nov 1895): 626–28.
52. GSH, Letter to the Editor, *Science*, n.s. 2:734–35.

The psychologists in question were hardly mollified by such a retraction.

The literal truth of these claims and counterclaims lies almost entirely with the complainants rather than with Hall. It was not Hall's influence, but the work of other independent pioneers in the new psychology which accounted for the experimental departments Hall said he was responsible for founding. Yet the importance Hall felt himself to have had in stimulating the development of scientific psychology in America was not entirely exaggerated and the literal counterclaims of his opponents did not take adequate account of it.

There is also some doubt that the rooms James had fitted with psychological and physiological equipment since the mid 1870s deserved to be called the first psychological laboratory in America, as his letter to *Science* implied. Before that letter was written, Hall had called his Hopkins laboratory the first in America without evoking any response from James or others,[53] and in 1893, Baldwin, who was hardly inclined to inflate Hall's reputation, had called the Hopkins laboratory the first in this country.[54]

It is difficult to draw lines through the gradual course during which an institutional form takes on definition and shape. James received an appropriation and opened laboratory space for experimental demonstrations to students from 1875 onward, and he had another small room where he himself conducted research from 1877. However, these laboratories did not actually function as an integral part of a program of teaching and research, as Hall's did at Hopkins. Students were not directed in research projects and did not produce any experimental studies. Even the Hopkins laboratory, however, lacked formal recognition and regular subsidization from the university; Jastrow's laboratory at the University of Wisconsin was the first to achieve this status.[55]

Where one places the award of "first" depends, therefore, on the particular criterion of institutional development chosen. In this

---

53. GSH, "On the History of American College Text-Books," 1893, p. 160. Hall's history of college textbooks may have paralleled his address at the 1892 APA meeting; so he may have made the same claim at that time.

54. Baldwin, "Psychology Past and Present," p. 384.

55. Robert S. Harper, "The Laboratory of William James," *Harvard Alumni Bulletin* 52 (Nov 1949): 169–73; Albrecht, "The New Psychology in America," pp. 128–32.

case, it appears fair to say that Hall's laboratory was the first in this country to function as a university psychological laboratory in the modern sense, and it was recognition of this fact that led Hall's contemporaries to credit him with the first American laboratory, at least until his braggadocio called all his claims of accomplishment into question.[56]

Hall's need to "keep his courage up" by these exaggerated claims was painfully clear. As James himself admitted, there is usually no need to deny assertions of this type, "for the by-standers generally see truly."[57] But James and his colleagues were unwilling to trust to the eventual triumph of truth. The kind of figurative statements which Hall was accustomed to make could hardly be tolerated when they dealt with matters so close to his colleagues' personal pride. It is hardly to be wondered that their reaction to Hall's belligerent assertion was itself ungenerous. Cattell, as always, within the profession, a moderating influence, closed the series of letters in *Science* with the only acknowledgment of the important role Hall had played:

It seems a pity that President Hall, who has accomplished so much for the advancement of psychology in America, should claim . . . that he has accomplished nearly everything. . . . Even those who have done the most are representatives of such a movement, not causes of it.[58]

The consequences of what Titchener called the "unfortunate editorial"[59] disturbed Hall's relations with his colleagues for many

56. Professor Boring stated that "if obtaining space for experiments and performing them there constitutes founding a laboratory, James was ahead of Hall." In evaluating Wundt's title to the first laboratory in the world, however, he argued that "the fact that both Leipzig and Harvard had space for experimentation in 1875 does not mean that there was a tie, for Leipzig went ahead rapidly, whereas Harvard lagged with James." This latter consideration also applies to the comparison between James's and Hall's laboratories, for Hall's alone was the center of a sustained program of experimental investigation for both teaching and research purposes. Edwin G. Boring, "On the Subjectivity of Important Historical Dates: Leipzig, 1879," *JHBS* 1 (Jan 1965): 5, 7. After this incident, Cattell returned to calling Hall's laboratory the first in America. Cattell, "Founding of the Association," p. 62. So too did Sanford and Titchener, *Commemorative Number of the AJP* 14 (July-Oct 1903), dedication page.

57. Wm. James to GSH, 12 Oct [1895], HP.

58. Cattell, Letter to the Editor, *Science,* n.s. 2:628.

59. Titchener to Cattell, 31 July 1903, CP.

years thereafter. One immediate result was a break with James. Their relationship had been under increasing strain since Hall had come to Hopkins and begun to exert himself and his views against his former teacher. Considering Hall's sensitivity, James was not an easy man for Hall to deal with, for James too was jealous of his authority. In dealing with Hall, James inclined to robust, sometimes insensitive, assertion and used a subtle pedagogical tone.[60] The personal bond between the two men was still able to withstand these tensions at the time of the deaths of Hall's wife and daughter. James responded feelingly and Hall permitted himself momentarily to lean on his old friendship.[61] The following year, however, James was deeply hurt by the personal tone of Hall's review of his *Principles*. Hall's attack on "arm-chair psychologists" and philosophers who lacked self-control hit James almost as deeply as himself, for James, too, was temperamentally divided in his allegiance to science and philosophy.[62]

Whether some final straw followed the editorial controversy is unknown, but in late January 1896, James apparently wrote Hall to the effect that he understood Hall was "breaking off" with him.[63] Hall replied, of course, that he had "never dreamed" of such a thing and that *"I cannot understand your feeling at all* but sincerely wish to do so."[64] Two days later, a student of them both told James that he resented James and Hall "each telling me the other was a 'crank'. . . . It ought to make both of you happy and more congenial to know the high and sincere compliments each pays the

60. When James refused to review Hall's new journal for example, he appended a lecture on how it might be improved—all excellent suggestions, but a provocation he might well have foregone under those circumstances. Wm. James to GSH, 10 Nov 1887, HP. In the competition engendered by the close proximity of Clark and Harvard, James perceived Hall's specialization as a claim to be able to "carry men beyond" himself, a condition he could not tolerate. Hall also felt that certain courtesies were not equally exchanged when the two visited each other at Hopkins and Harvard. *LCP*, p. 235.

61. Wm. James to GSH, 16 May [1890]; 20 June 1890; 21 June [1890], HP.

62. Perry, *William James*, 1:227–332, 343–44; David Shakow and David Rapaport, *The Influence of Freud on American Psychology*, Psychological Issues, vol. 7, no. 13 (New York: International Universities Press, 1964), p. 38.

63. Perhaps when Hall spoke to the Graduate Club at Harvard during 1895–96 on "The Present State and Prospects of Psychology," he delivered his characteristic critique of James. *Harvard Cat.*, 1896–97, p. 150.

64. GSH to Wm. James, 27 Jan 1896, JP.

other."[65] The compliments were to little avail. Though the two probably never broke off formally, their friendship never recovered.[66]

Hall continued to intersperse his work with open or veiled criticisms of James's characteristic views[67] and he was never able to understand what part he had played in the quarrel. The explanation Hall became accustomed to make for the tensions in their relationship was that James resented the fact that Johns Hopkins University had chosen Hall rather than himself for the professorship of philosophy.[68] Hopkins, of course, had originally chosen James, who declined the offer; the two had never really been in competition for the appointment. It is clear, however, that Hall had felt himself to be competing with James from the start of their relationship. In Hall's autobiography, his relations with James constitute the most obscure and distorted section of the entire book.[69]

Relations between the psychologists at Clark and those at Harvard deteriorated further as Münsterberg, too, began to clash with Hall,[70] and as the Harvard scholars noted Hall's continuing exag-

65. E. D. Starbuck to Wm. James, 29 Jan 1896, JP.

66. Both men did attempt to heal the breach at least superficially. When James came to Worcester in 1899 to see Adolf Meyer, Hall invited him to tea and urged Meyer to urge James to accept. That year James briefly attended the conference Hall called to celebrate Clark's decennial, and he complimented Hall graciously on the excellence of the event. The next year James responded favorably to Hall's anti-Imperialism. In 1909 he again came to Clark for one day for the twentieth-anniversary conference and may have stayed with Hall as his guest. When James died, Hall joined, but did not write, the complimentary obituary of James which appeared in the *AJP*. GSH to Wm. James, 11 May 1899; GSH to Adolf Meyer, 11 May 1899, Adolf Meyer Papers, William H. Welch Library, Johns Hopkins University Medical School; *Clark University, 1889–1899: Decennial Celebration*, p. 38; Wm. James to GSH, 14 May 1900, HP; Wm. James to GSH, 8 Sept 1909, HP; "William James," *AJP* 21 (Oct 1910): 605. According to Dr. David Shakow, who now owns the volumes, James did not cut the pages on the copy of *Adolescence* that Hall gave him. Shakow to the author, 12 Apr 1965.

67. See, e.g., GSH, *Adol*, 2: 44–45, 292–93; GSH, *Founders*, pp. 412, 414, 454–55. Not until the end of his life, in *LCP*, p. 445, did Hall praise James for having the subtle introspective insight of the true psychologist.

68. W. C. Ryan, interview with Frederick E. Bolton, notes, CUP; R. G. Hall, interview, 17–20 May 1961.

69. *LCP*, pp. 203–4, 218–19.

70. Münsterberg and Hall clashed partly over the place of child study in psychology; see Larkin Dunton et al., *The Old Psychology and the New: Addresses before the Massachusetts Schoolmasters' Club, April 27, 1895, by Larkin*

gerated claims of the accomplishments of Clark University.[71] A critical attitude so pervaded the Harvard department that Robert M. Yerkes, a student there from 1897 to 1902, felt constrained from making contact with Clark men even though he knew important work was being done at Clark in his own field of animal psychology. He recalled that he was "given to understand that it was either indiscreet or bad form for a Harvard psychologist to try to cultivate friendly professional relations with G. Stanley Hall and his Clark associates."[72] The professional quarrels of the 1890s put Hall and Clark University on the defensive, and Hall's new psychology of these years soon confirmed this beleaguered stance.

Dunton . . . Hugo Münsterberg . . . William T. Harris . . . G. Stanley Hall (Boston: New England, 1895), pp. 14–26, 36–38. See also, Hugo Münsterberg to Wm. James, 24 Jan 1896, JP.

71. GSH to Hugo Münsterberg, 4, 7, 10 May 1895, MP.

72. Robert M. Yerkes, "Early Days of Comparative Psychology," *PR* 50 (Jan 1943): 75.

At the same time that Hall's hopes for Clark University were receding to very modest dimensions, and he was being displaced in the institutional leadership of his profession, he also had to find a new foundation for his psychological views. When he had left Johns Hopkins in 1888 he left laboratory work behind. During the first three years of his administration at Clark, most of his attention was demanded by the institution, and he carried in addition only the editorial work connected with his journals. During these years, Hall came to realize that he was unable to make experimental psychology into a synthetic framework for his disparate psychological concerns.

James's *Principles*, appearing in 1890, made Hall's sense of deficiency in this regard acute. While Hall wrote James that "you aid me more than anyone else to define [my own view],"[1] the standpoint Hall was able to construct vis-à-vis James was only a negative one, a declaration of being against certain trends in psychology which James exemplified. The concepts in psychology which Hall held to as "pregnant" with future promise: concepts of unconscious inference, threshold, nascence or continuity between brain and mind states, material monadism; the framework he sought in observation, experimentation, and individual and ancestral experience—all this would, he told James, create some future monistic synthesis, but as

---

1. GSH to Wm. James [Jan 1891], JP.

yet it did not cohere in his mind.[2] Between 1891 and 1895, Hall produced not a single piece of substantive psychological work. Instead, he gave vent to bitter attacks on "text-book makers and teachers of second-hand knowledge"[3] and admitted withal that "this attempt to unify is also an impulse of sanity. . . . And so it is with the impulse to stand for something and be a positif."[4]

The inability to create a work of intellect and to formulate a coherent world-view became the center of Hall's difficulties, for that original aspiration and persisting dilemma of his choice of scientific psychology as a vocation could no longer be evaded. Without the commanding institutional roles he had assumed in psychology and at Clark University to sustain his self-respect, Hall had to return to the task he had initially set himself, to find in scientific psychology a unified world-view which would illumine the phenomena of mental life with scientific understanding and religious meaning. The "strictly scientific" role Hall had chosen to pursue had failed to sustain the exalted position he sought institutionally; by 1894, it was clear to him that it also would not provide the intellectual unity he sought.

In that year, Hall turned fifty years old. The component of maturity Erik Erikson has described as "generativity," the ability to create and nourish children, ideas, and things,[5] had collapsed for Hall when the professional role he had tried to create for himself, like the family he had sustained, was decimated. Old age and death threatened to take him before the fruits of maturity had been secured. Indeed, a picture of Hall in his autobiography shows him to have physically aged a decade in the space of the few troubled years following the deaths of his wife and daughter. Scattered through Hall's writings in 1894 are evidences of profound feelings of malaise. As he commented to his students that year, "When we

2. GSH, "Review of William James' *Principles of Psychology,*" 1891, pp. 579–80, 585, 590.
3. GSH, "The New Psychology As a Basis of Education," 1894, p. 719; "Research the Vital Spirit of Teaching," 1894, p. 570; "On the History of American College Text-Books," 1894, p. 160.
4. "Reports of the Plato Club," *Atlantic Monthly,* Sept 1894, p. 471.
5. Erikson, *Identity and the Life Cycle: Selected Papers,* Psychological Issues, vol. 1, no. 1 (New York: International Universities Press, 1959), pp. 97, 153–56, 166.

are weak we fall apart, and the black horse of the Phaedrus takes the bit in its mouth."[6]

Hall described in 1894 a great fatigue which presented "the early psychic symptoms of old age,"[7] and Hall thereafter dated the onset of senescence from the age of forty-five to fifty.[8] The condition Hall described was one of "doubt" and "reserve." It was the curse of the scholar and critic who cannot create:

This habit of carping, this trick of collecting notes, this inability to put a work through, this dawdling erudition. . . . They live in an atmosphere of criticism, they collect notes, they wait, they dream, their youth goes by, and the night comes when no man can work.[9]

In terms clearly descriptive of his own life, Hall told "how to turn the freshness and spontaneity of youth into the premature ripeness of age, eliminating the noon-day of consummate manhood." In intellectual work, Hall complained, the youth

does not find companionship either warm or large. . . . He brings his most cherished convictions and ideals to a mart where others just as sacred and cherished are diverse and even contradictory. Instead of one there are many equally tempting lines of excellence, and [he is] always tempted to "change saddles." All the complexity of the world of science is open to him. If he takes a course in the History of Philosophy, and finds views to which his soul goes out, the next system overturns them. . . . He had a creed, but now doubts if even the world is real. He held a brief in one or more of the many causes of reform, but finds his indictments against Diabolos *nolle-prossed*. At every point he is thrown back upon himself, and pessimism has touched him with the Great Fatigue. He is a forlorn unit. He wanted to square himself with the universe, but finds it too large for him to catch its drift. . . . he feels that all things are alike true and alike false, while his heart is growing cold and his head gray in vain.[10]

Hall must have been describing the crisis of his own career; and his need to articulate and guarantee his mental unity in a synthetic in-

---

6. "Reports of the Plato Club," 1894, p. 360. Hall also declared that year, "Our moral rhythm is ethical, and the moral of it is never to lose your self-control. The moment you do, you are hysterical, more or less." GSH, "Remarks on Rhythm in Education," 1894, p. 85.

7. GSH, "Scholarships, Fellowships, and the Training of Professors," 1894, pp. 450, 452.

8. GSH, "The Dangerous Age," 1921.

9. "Scholarships," 1894, p. 451. This was Lang's description of the critical scholar at Oxford University, which Hall quoted approvingly.

10. Ibid., pp. 451–52.

tellectual system echoes his earlier protracted search for a career, a philosophy, and an identity. The crisis of his mature years reopened the problems and questions of his youth. The account he gave of the "Great Fatigue" unconsciously melted the stages of adolescence and senescence into one, and he explicitly noted "the strange rapport between stages of evolution and those of devolution," especially between those two stages.[11] Significantly, Hall first announced in 1894 that he was preparing a treatise on the subject of adolescence.[12]

The central experience of his earlier development—the surge of exhilaration and the despair of nihilism which was evoked in him by his study of Hegel and modern idealism—apparently revived in this later stage, for Hall reopened his attack on idealism with exceptional force.[13] In an article published in *Forum,* Hall accused the professors who teach epistemology of acting from

a morbid neurosis of cynicism, indifference, and selfishness. . . . These so-called espistemological vagaries [are] in some forms, hardly less than the physiological equivalents of self-abuse. I am well aware that this is strong language, but I have definite clinical cases in mind where just this effect has been produced.[14]

Hall reportedly went so far as to announce to Josiah Royce at a professional meeting in 1894 that his theory of idealism was similar to, and no better than, masturbation. Hall, moreover, said he could not understand why Royce became furious in response.[15] That Hall felt this connection strongly enough to present it as a rational proposition, in public, and to idealistic philosophers themselves, suggests

11. Ibid., pp. 450–52.
12. "Universities and the Training of Professors," 1894, p. 301.
13. Hall may have tried again to work through modern idealism to some intellectual haven, only to be trapped once more in subjectivism. The surge of "excelsior ambition," the desire for total dependence, and the fear of these desires, all of which were associated with this doctrine, in any case must have risen anew under the blows of this period.
14. "New Psychology As a Basis of Education," 1894, p. 712.
15. Frank E. Spaulding, "Clark University and Dr. G. Stanley Hall," in "One Schoolman's Philosophy," MS autobiography, pp. 611–12, in possession of Miss Lydia P. Colbey, Worcester, Mass. Hall remembered the event as an APA meeting at which the teaching of philosophy was discussed, but it may have been the meeting of the American Antiquarian Society in Boston, 25 April 1894, at which Hall delivered a paper "On the History of American College Text-Books and Teaching in Logic, Ethics, Psychology and Allied Subjects."

how pressing his emotional difficulties became during this crisis of
his middle years.

It is impossible to say how important a role sexual disorders
played in Hall's difficulties. The important themes of Hall's intellectual life emerged from personal experience, and it was at the
time of this crisis that the subject of sexuality became one of Hall's
chief intellectual concerns. In particular, two themes concerning
sexuality appeared in Hall's work for the first time. One was the
importance to psychology of recent disclosures of sexual pathology:

Painstaking monographs on the morbidities of love show not only its dominance but its plasticity, and how every manifestation of it, divorced from its
natural object in the other sex, may be evoked in the most literal and
physical way toward almost any object or act.[16]

Hall's insight into the plasticity of sexual feeling later became one
of the foundations of his genetic psychology.

The second theme was the beauty and nobility of the love of
young men, which Hall later often associated with the model of the
Greeks, though Hall disclaimed the Greek practice of carrying the
relationship to physical love. This sentiment informed Hall's ideal
of the university teacher. As mother's love increases when the number of progeny decrease, Hall said, the "work and love" of such
teachers "was more intense because so few could understand and
love them in return."[17] He would be willing to "transfer his own
choicest germs of work and promise, and be himself but dung—to
minister to the advent of real greatness."[18]

To what extent these ideas bespeak personal problems with
homosexual desires, abnormal manifestations of sexuality, or a pervasive sexualization of experience is not known. If Hall incurred any
sexual disturbances, they could not but heighten his anxiety and
augment the feelings of guilt, worthlessness, and impotence aroused
by his losses and failures.

If sufficiently severe, such feelings cannot long be borne. In
1894, Hall recounted Goethe's experience upon reading Shake-

16. "New Psychology As a Basis of Education," 1894, p. 717.
17. Ibid., p. 720. On Hall's Greek ideal, see *Adol,* 1: 513–23; 2: 107–8, 249–
59.
18. "Scholarships," 1894, p. 450.

speare of feeling "a most vivid sense of the infinite expansion of his existence," an experience which might well have been Hall's own and may have marked the upturn in his crisis.

Goethe said of Shakespeare that, at the first touch of [Shakespeare's] genius, something inspiring hovered above him; that he became his for life; that he was like one born blind on whom a miraculous hand bestowed sight in a moment; and that he had a most vivid sense of the infinite expansion of his existence. This experience men are repeating to-day as they see their own nature expanded till every form of animal life is but a branch of their own family tree.[19]

Evolutionary biology provided Hall with the vision of one's psyche as a microcosm of the entire living world, as a composite inheritance of the past, as an "echo-chamber" reverberating with the whispers of ancestors.[20] The experience of it, he said, was like a "new birth." His later descriptions of adolescent religious conversion drew partly on this middle-aged experience of despair and regeneration.[21]

Even more fully than his earlier conception of scientific phychology, this biological vision offered Hall an outlet for his need for both dependence and omnipotence within a framework of renunciation of complete individuality. Through it, he could avoid the damaging sense of guilt which arose from his failures. All history bore the responsibility; mother nature made him what he was, constituted his very being at this moment, and could be trusted to work through him to the progress of all mankind. Hall gave up what he later described as that "overblown Titanic heaven-storming individuality" which demanded to be judged "solely on our own merits or demerits."[22]

Accompanying this resignation, was a renewed love of nature,

the great mother of us all, the reservoir of every kind of force, the force that makes the electric light, that makes my heart pulsate, my food digest, that makes my voice, that makes my thought, that makes anything, everything.[23]

19. "New Psychology As a Basis of Education," 1894, p. 718.
20. See *Adol*, 2:61.
21. "New Psychology As a Basis of Education," 1894, p. 718; *Adol*, 2:301–53.
22. Ibid., p. 309.
23. "Nature Study," 1896, p. 157. Hall was drawn to evolutionary theories, he declared in *LCP*, p. 359, in part because "I conceived all creative processes as still active, all about me, and above all felt that there was nothing really dead but

To love nature, the "all mother," Hall declared, was "if not itself the *summum bonum,* at least it must involve most of the virtue and blessings of life."[24]

In this love of nature, Hall gave freer conscious rein to his feelings of dependence and of love. As the years passed, he confessed to "being more and more passionately in love with woman as I conceive she came from the hand of God. I keenly envy my Catholic friends their Maryolatry."[25] But, more important, Hall freed his sense of trust in the workings of his own nature and his willingness to accept in himself those feelings and interests he associated with the female nature. Since early manhood, Hall had relegated these "feminine" qualities to the mythopoeic comforts of religion, the lower regions of popular culture, and the dependent nature of woman, and had kept these realms separate from his scientific identity. Now, aided by his renewed sense of unity and subordination in the maternal nature, this earlier segregation began to break down.

In two remarkable stories which he wrote later in his life, Hall revealed how deeply his soul was divided into masculine and feminine ideals and how desperately he longed to unite them. As in his earlier tale of love at Antioch, Hall's fictional efforts barely disguised his fantasies. In "Preestablished Harmony," published in 1902, Hall described an encounter between an older, woman-hating bachelor professor and a young beautiful lady who turned out to be precisely like him in every movement, thought, and feeling, a veritable double of himself.

Walking from opposite directions into Boston Common, they collided at the center and performed an elaborate dance of identical, mirror-image movements in an attempt to move out of each other's way. But they were blocked, and the situation suggested to the professor "an indefinite perspective of inner harmonies, which might be the other's fate, counterpart, or what you will, just as the hypothetical Brundusian ass if exactly between the two

---

that there was everywhere life abounding, filling all possibilities everywhere, which gave and still gives the deepest intellectual satisfaction that I have ever known."

24. "Address at the Bryant Centennial," 1894, p. 67.
25. *Adol,* 1:646.

bundles of hay would surely die of starvation." It was clear that "they must both with stoic resignation accept the inevitable with what joy they could." Indeed, it became apparent that "some mystic agency was cadencing their souls into complete unison." They married and lived happily ever after, and the change which was thus wrought in the professor was regarded by his friends as something of a "miracle or conversion."

In an obscure footnote, which referred to hints of an active sex life between the two, Hall commented on the extreme compression of his story in terms of the classical unities of time, place, and action. One can easily regard it as compressed even more, to the space of his own psyche. Hall had never been able to escape the feminine ideal he carried within him, and this was especially true after 1890 when the collapse of his more masculine efforts threw him back on himself. Although Hall wished for a magical and complete union, the most he was able to achieve was a kind of feminization of his own identity and sublimation of his desires into intellectual creation.

This character of Hall's "conversion" was made clearer in the second story, "How Johnnie's Vision Came True," an account of the experience of a fourteen-year-old boy who, taking his gun with him, climbed a nearby mountain and vowed to do and be something great in the world.[26] The account precisely echoed the facts of Hall's own life and similar adolescent experience, except that it also described the fantasies the boy had on the mountaintop, something Hall did not include in his autobiographical account of the experience. On reaching the top, the boy first ran toward the sun, exclaiming

Oh, sun, help me. . . . Shine into and through me. I want to know all the world as you do. You never saw a shadow. You could not. And all I know is shadow darkening down into black ignorance. Don't set, but rise in my soul.

But the sun did set, and as the moon rose he saw his mother in it, as the sun had been his father. The womanly figure bent close to him, saying "Peace, my son, be strong, be calm," and also "Arise and shine as I do." The boy fell asleep and dreamt then of a

woman, mature and of the mingled charm of mother, sister and bride. . . . he rose to his feet and cast himself into her embrace, where he was pressed

26. *Recreations of a Psychologist,* 1920, pp. 128–46.

close to her heart till soon his lips met hers in a moment of such ecstasy as
he had never dreamed of before. "You must never leave me," he whispered
at last, and her soft, sweet voice replied, "Never. You shall obtain all you
seek. I shall be always with you. . . ."

In this story, too, late in life a real woman appeared who was the
very likeness of the boy's adolescent vision, and he, now a successful
widower, married her. When they climbed together on their honeymoon to the top of the mountain, they found

the remains of the old gun, from which the stock had rotted entirely away.
It was a symbol of the first stage of sublimation which had culminated in
the unique union not only of this man and his wife but of senescence and
adolescence.

That is, of adolescent fantasy into senescent reality.

Whether Hall did actually have this fantasy during his adolescent
mountaintop experience, or whether it was the product of later
dreams, it was still clearly seen and felt in his later life when he
recorded it in this story, and it clearly reflected the dominance of
the feminine moon ideal in his own life after 1894. The image of
the powerful, omniscient sun-father which Hall had struggled with
in his commitment to philosophy and science had abandoned him.
It was the feminine embodiment of love, calming and restoring him,
urging him to "Arise and shine as I do," which furnished the energy
and creative form for Hall's labors after his fiftieth year.[27] This
shift in the foundation of his identity never fully healed the division
in Hall's psyche nor dispelled his unease with himself and others.
Within limits, however, it was a healing strategy, enabling him to
recover and enlarge that capacity to unite his two selves by creative
intellectual work which he had forged in his youth.

Hall thus came to feel in his biological vision a new power of
"productiveness and creation," the special need of his desolate
middle years, a new ability to comprehend all nature.

It is as if God had come to consciousness in the human brain—that most

27. Howard R. Wolf, "British Fathers and Sons, 1773–1913: From Filial
Submissiveness to Creativity," *Psychoanalysis and the Psychoanalytic Review* 52
(1965), pp. 197–214, has argued that sons in British fiction during the course
of the nineteenth century changed from submission to open revolt against their
fathers, a revolt which often led them to base their own identity on the feminine
ideal of creativity and the heroic role of the artist.

complex of all tissues in the universe—more than ever before, as if it were a mouthpiece of things that never could have been spoken before.[28]

In the same passage of 1894 in which he described the expansion of consciousness to all animal life, he also declared that

every stage of human development has been marked by its own special form of productiveness and creation . . . now, God's creative prophets go up to meet him above the region of eternal frost, and bring down his law from the wild elements and mysteries of nature.[29]

That God-like function which Hall had always feared in meta-physics and surreptitiously sought in science perhaps again seemed within his capacity.

The chief inspiration for and fruit of Hall's new sense of promise was his dramatic turn to child study, after so many years of relegating it to a secondary position in his career. Quickly exploiting the ground swell of interest in child study among teachers and educators, he began to see child study as a part of scientific psychology as well as a pedagogic enterprise, and to throw himself fully into it.[30]

Hall's new enthusiasm was clearly related to his personal situation. He recognized that "this new and great movement should be preeminently the woman's science,"[31] and his conception of childhood and adolescence was rooted in those aspects of human nature he associated with femininity. Most important, child study promised success. At a time when all else he touched was losing ground, the praise and publicity his child study work aroused in educational circles must have been enormously gratifying. Hall seemed to have clear title to the leadership of the new movement; if it grew in proportion to its rise in the early nineties, he could dream of finding himself in a position of prominence and authority in some ways comparable to those he had just lost:

I am well aware that this will seem to be enthusiasm, and . . . though I stand today a minority of one, ten years hence most of you will agree with me. For if promises that are now springing up . . . are realized, it [the child study movement] is to be not only an educational renaissance, but a scientific re-

28. "Pedagogical Methods in Sunday School Work," 1895, pp. 719–20.
29. "New Psychology As a Basis of Education," 1894, p. 717.
30. Ibid., pp. 716–17.
31. "Practical Child Study," 1894, pp. 391–92.

construction that aims at the top and is the salvation and ultimate development and end and aim of creation and of history.[32]

Even in an age when eschatological language couched in the metaphors of science was fairly common, Hall's claim for child study
as the "end and aim of creation and of history" must have seemed
extreme. Such a claim, of course, was extreme for Hall himself and
he never again made it directly. In 1894, however, the emotional
need for success still far outran its realization.

Probably the greatest hope Hall saw in child study was its po-
tentiality to effect a "scientific reconstruction." Although it took
two more years for Hall to enunciate it clearly, the possibility of
constructing a synthetic view of psychology along evolutionary lines
must have been dawning behind his vision of 1894 and his child
study work. The attempt to extend the understanding of the evolution of the race to the evolution of mental life in the individual,
already explicit in the theories of Spencer, Darwin and Haeckel, was
being given detailed and substantial encouragement by the work of
the English biologist George John Romanes.[33] In 1895, as Hall was
formulating his new views, James Mark Baldwin published his
Mental Development in the Child and the Race, an attempt to draw
these sources into a formal genetic psychology.[34] Hall was undoubtedly influenced by these thinkers to attempt a genetic basis for his
psychology.

Probably an important catalyst in bringing Hall's pressing intellectual and emotional concerns together, was a more popular
biological treatise, Henry Drummond's *Ascent of Man,* published
in 1894 from his Lowell Lectures of the previous year. Drummond
was evidently among the "great biologers" who were Hall's in-

32. "Child Study in Summer Schools," 1894, pp. 335–36.
33. George John Romanes, *Mental Evolution in Animals* (New York: D.
Appleton, 1884); *Mental Evolution in Man* (New York: D. Appleton, 1889).
34. Baldwin recalled that during the years 1893–1903, "the new interest in
genetic psychology and general biology had become absorbing, and the meagerness of the results of the psychological laboratories (apart from direct work on
sensation and movement) was becoming evident everywhere. I began to feel that
there was truth in what James was already proclaiming as to the barrenness of
the tables and curves coming from many laboratories." Murchison, *History of
Psychology in Autobiography,* 1:4.

spiration at this time.[35] Drummond presented evolution as "the final revelation of the unity of the world" which could "comprehend everything under one generalization" and "explain everything by one great end." To Darwin's principle of natural selection by means of the struggle for survival, he added another principle that he considered far more important—"the Struggle for the Life of Others," or "altruistic Love," which developed in the course of evolution from the necessities of maternity. The human mother he regarded as virtually the highest product of evolution.[36] These views could easily have excited Hall's imagination at this moment in his life. By making love, particularly maternal love, a major element of evolution and a legitimate scientific concern, Drummond may have opened for Hall the possibility of a wider scientific identity than his earlier mechanical model of psychology had imposed.

Drummond also traced the development of the human body and mind according to the law of recapitulation, that each individual in development recapitulates the forms through which the race has evolved. The human mind, too, was a product of evolution, and the first key to this process was the mind of the child. Drawing on the work of Romanes, he asserted that "emotions . . . appear in the Mind of the growing child *in the same order as they appear on the animal scale*" and that the same parallelism would hold for the entire "mental faculty."[37] The speculative character of these generalizations must have given Hall some pause, but the promise they held for making child study the center of an evolutionary psychology was evidently irresistible.

In 1895, in his "unfortunate editorial," he declared that child study equaled the laboratory movement in importance and would soon relegate "much of the present adult psychology" to history's ash heap.[38] The following year he announced that the study of "the

35. "New Psychology As a Basis of Education," 1894, p. 719; "Address at the Bryant Centennial," 1894, pp. 67–69.
36. Drummond, *The Lowell Lectures on the Ascent of Man* (New York: J. Pott, 1894), pp. 11–36, 268, 321. Hall also knew Patrick Geddes and J. Arthur Thomson's, *The Evolution of Sex* (London: Walter Scott, 1889), which likewise described love as the universal dynamic in nature and altruistic love as the real law of evolution.
37. Drummond, *Ascent of Man,* pp. 72–73, 82–83, 119–35.
38. GSH, "Editorial," 1895, p. 8.

dispositions and impulses of children" and of animal instinct marked "the entrance of evolution into the study of all the faculties of the adult human soul in a way that cross-sections all other lines of endeavor." This study, Hall said, will provide

something like a perspective, that will enable us to distinguish the deeper and older things of the soul from those that are of recent acquisition. I think the old adult psychology, that all of us teach even now, is to be, radically but gradually, transformed into a new genetic psychology.[39]

By linking the developmental sequence in the individual psyche to the evolutionary sequence of all living forms, Hall had a biological basis on which to reconstruct scientific psychology. The insight of the romantic educational theorists which for over a decade had infused his pedagogical thinking now fully entered into his psychology.

This biological, genetic emphasis returned to the center of Hall's thinking the romantic awareness of the importance of emotional and dynamic processes. Hall subsumed both affective and cognitive processes under the category of instinct. "Instinct-feelings, as they are coming to be called," he said in 1895, "these constitute the man and the woman." Or again, "What constitutes life is the intensity and the variety and scope of what we feel." The center of psychological study, he said, ought to be "the feelings, the intuitions, the more instinctive processes." Hall singled out love as a particularly important topic, and he said that he meant by this, love conceived frankly, in its physiological, as well as psychological, manifestations.[40] He also implicitly returned to the connection he had earlier drawn between instinct and attention. The movement of attention, the rise of particular interests at various stages of development, was

39. "Modern Methods in the Study of the Soul," 1896, pp. 131–33.
40. "Pedagogical Methods in Sunday School Work," 1895; "Modern Methods in the Study of the Soul," 1896, pp. 131–33. Hall later changed the term to "feeling-instincts." In this view of feeling, Hall was probably influenced by his earlier reading of Maudsley's *Physiology of Mind*. "It is feeling or the affective life that reveals the essential nature of the man; it lies deeper in his nature than intellect, as the organic lies beneath animal life; it expresses the fundamental tone of his nerve element, which again is the result of its actual constitution or composition, inherited and acquired" (p. 351). He could also have been influenced later by Theodule Ribot, *The Psychology of the Emotions* (London: Walter Scott, 1897).

the product of the "evolutionary nisus that was given at impregnation."[41] Hall thus broke through the traditional division of mental
life into intellect, emotion, and will, and tied all three to conative
drives.

Hall regarded this dynamic viewpoint as a means of overcoming
the dichotomies in reality and knowledge Kant had posited. In his
description of the despair and nihilism into which the theory of
knowledge leads its victims, Hall remarked that one possible way
out was "a pleasant pathway of ascent through Wundt's theory of
attention and Fichte's conception of will," but this solution was
very difficult, he warned, and unnecessarily "implicates what God
made plain."[42] On another occasion, Hall suggested that escape lay
through Fichte's ethical stance and Schopenhauer's interpretation of
energy as will. "This fadges very well," Hall said, "with the Wundt
theory of attention and apperception as rudimentary will."[43] Wundt
had kept alive for Hall the dynamic character of consciousness he
had learned earlier from Fichte, Schopenhauer, and Von Hartmann.
Hall came to consider Schopenhauer's *The World As Will and Idea*
as "the most brilliant and perhaps in many respects the most insightful piece of modern philosophical literature."[44] Hall also came
to believe, like Spencer, that the impulses native to the individual
were acquired by experience in the race, thus seemingly resolving on
a phylogenetic level Kant's dichotomy between knowledge acquired
by experience and the forms of knowledge innate to the mind.[45]

The synthetic possibilities of evolution thus extended even beyond
scientific psychology. What was emerging, Hall claimed on another
occasion, was a kind of "biological philosophy . . . a view of life
far higher, broader and more unified than Plato, Aristotle, Kant,
Hegel, or even Darwin, Huxley and Spencer ever dreamed of," a

41. Hall believed that the problem of the movement of attention was "simply
tunneling into the genetic process from the other side of the mountain, if we only
assume that every movement of attention due to inner stimulation is an end result
of the very same evolutionary nisus that was given at impregnation." GSH,
Founders, p. 413. Hall could have been fortified in this conception by Theodule
Ribot, *The Psychology of Attention* (Chicago: Open Court, 1890).
42. *Adol,* 2:537.
43. "College Philosophy," 1900, p. 417.
44. GSH to Mr. Arnett, 31 Oct 1902, CUP.
45. Spencer, *Principles of Psychology,* vol. 1, par. 208; *Adol,* 2:41.

confirmation within dynamic matter of the age-old truths of the spirit.[46] By "mythopoeic" extension, Hall's science could now be entirely congruent with his religious and philosophical intuitions.

The view Hall reached by 1896 of genetic psychology-biological philosophy was to be the source of his insight for the remainder of his life and a chief source of the contributions he was to make to American psychology and culture. In large part, it grew out of the interaction between Hall's persisting romanticism, evolutionary ideas, and Hall's personal psychological dynamics. Evolutionary concepts supported and extended at every point the insights of the romantic poets and philosophers, and Hall's own self-awareness of the distinctive needs of childhood, the emotional upheavals of the adolescent search for identity, the dependence of each individual on the psychic accruals of his past, and the basal importance of feelings and instinctive impulses in shaping one's psyche and one's life.

Despite Hall's claim at the end of his life that he had embraced evolution, with a whole soul, at the first sound of the word,[47] the contemporaneous record suggests rather that he fully accepted evolution as the framework for his thought only in the middle 1890s. At least since his studies in Germany, he had been reluctant to flout the decree of the more positivistic scientists that synthetic systems constructed on the theory of evolution were only pseudo-scientific substitutes for a religious creed and belonged to the realm of popular culture. He accepted more limited evolutionary concepts within the confines of his science and his educational theory, but until the middle 1890s they remained minor or disconnected motifs. It was only after his wife's and daughter's deaths had convinced him of his need for Christianity and when he faced great personal pressures toward the construction of a unifying intellectual system that he could overcome the strictures of positivistic science.

These limitations in Hall were maintained by forces even more

46. "Psychological Education," 1896, pp. 228–29. In *Adol,* 2:539–48, Hall outlined his "new kind of *theologia prima.*" Hall declared his belief in three-dimensional space, in "being or ether," in energy, in "reason, law and cause in the universe," in "life abounding" throughout the universe, and in evolution as the survival of the best, or at any rate not the worst, in life.

47. *LCP,* p. 357.

powerful than his scientific norms. The rigorous scientists reinforced, in effect, dichotomies and exclusions which had been created by Hall's intrapsychic defenses and the Victorian culture. Hall personally needed what Victorian culture decreed: that the feminine, the feelings, the dependent, and the childish be held separate and subordinate to the masculine identity, and that they be admitted to consciousness only in the form of denatured idealizations. Hall's commitment to science had been so involved with his achievement of an independent, masculine identity, that his science was bound by the narrow base of his masculinity. The personal crisis of the early 1890s drove Hall back to the suppressed elements of his personality and greatly augmented their strength. His willingness partially to admit them to consciousness opened the way for his fuller appreciation of biological evolutionary theories. And the theories, in turn, gave Hall sanction to exercise his scientific imagination and intelligence over a wider field. Although he was never able personally to integrate what had been earlier segregated, he was able to use these elements intellectually.

The return to elements of his personality earlier suppressed also brought with it a return to earlier cultural themes Hall had embraced in his youth. The attraction of these themes had never faded, even while being shunted aside, and Hall came to realize how his romantic allegiance to the "heart" led toward the newer emphasis on feelings and instincts; how his attraction to Hopkins's graduated synthetic view of man, nature, and spirit fed his search for an evolutionary, biological philosophy. Hall came to admit that the older American theorists had been on the right track with their faculty psychology and their cosmic view.[48] Even more strikingly, Hall echoed Hegel and Comte in their search for a single structure of laws to describe the parallel development of individual consciousness and the consciousness of the human race; and like Comte as well, Hall enthroned Woman in both processes as the guardian and embodiment of affection and morality.

Hall always loved to declare that new wine really could be put into old bottles. He was himself only partly aware of the radical changes involved when the "heart" was conceived as "biological

48. *Adol,* 2:54.

drives" and when the only guarantee of unity in the cosmos was the dynamic impulsion man shared with nature. The sentiment and idealism attached to the older notions spread like fine mist over the harsher biological ideas, befogging their revolutionary implications and allowing Hall to advance bravely into the unknown.

The genetic psychology and philosophy Hall outlined by 1896 finally provided the intellectual unity and the wide outlet for his feelings and interests that he had sought. Equally important, it allowed him to unite in the role of a "creative prophet" the functions of both preacher and scientist. As the seer of childhood and the herald of a new, genetic psychology, Hall could use his great talents as a moral didact and enlightened voice of the people within the realm of science. Just as in the case of sex role, so with the narrowed specialization of occupational roles, Hall managed to break through some of the rigidity and limitations society imposed and create for himself a synthetic identity more expressive of his root tendencies. This new, prophetic role, of course, matched the sense of martyrdom and isolation Hall had always felt, and now more keenly, as a result of his institutional defeats. "This view is my own," Hall would remark, "and I fear shared as yet by no one else, least of all by my fellow teachers of psychology."[49] By turning to a genetic approach among colleagues who were mechanistically oriented, and taking up subjects they neglected or despised, Hall gave up his claim for leadership of the profession in the present, only to seek its fulfillment in the ultimate judgment of the future.

Freed from the canons of rigorous science, Hall turned out after 1896 volumes of richly rhetorical studies in the new genetic mode which were utterly unlike the chaste products of his colleagues' laboratories. He kept huge, loose-leaf notebooks on all his favorite themes and added to them as he doggedly reviewed popular and scholarly books in several languages. He would dip into them in turn for his lectures at Clark, his talks and articles, and then pile them together into books, relying throughout on his inspiration and enthusiasm to weld them into significant pronouncements, perhaps great cultural movements of the future.[50]

49. "The Methods, Status, and Prospects of the Child Study of Today," 1896, p. 187.
50. GSH, "Confessions of a Psychologist," 1901, pp. 93–95.

Like his manner of working, Hall's style displayed certain peculiarities. From the time of his return from Germany in 1881, his sentences tended to be long and in the Germanic manner; each thought was endlessly elaborated and qualified before uttered. Occasionally he would insert neologisms based on Latin or Greek roots without bothering to define them, parhaps as the Germans constructed new complex words from their simpler roots. Religious lyrics were woven in at points of climax in his scientific or philosophical argument. After 1896, these elements were often fired by the heat of passion and moral earnestness into a lush torrent of words. Hall's rhetoric sometimes produced clear expositions and eloquent appeals. At other times, it covered over masses of data insufficiently analyzed and ambiguity and evasion in the treatment of scientific issues.

Hall parted company with his psychological colleagues not only in his genetic approach and his style but also in his essential disregard of methods. By 1896, the definitions of scientific psychology formulated by the younger members of the profession were beginning to take for granted the scientific criteria Hall had fought for against James and Ladd, and to stress instead the quantification of data and the accuracy of experimental design and evaluation of results.[51] Hall called attention to the young Scripture's "pet foibles of exactness and precision," and quoted Aristotle to the effect that "it is the mark of a man unread and immature to insist on treating a subject with more exactness than the nature of the subject requires."[52] Hall became willing to use any method, no matter how far short of the sharpness and certainty of the methods of laboratory science, that would let him deal with the full span of topics he thought to be significant. On this issue Hall diverged from what was becoming the mainstream of academic psychology in this country.

The moral and religious overtones Hall attached to his work also progressively differentiated him from the new generation. During the first decade of the new psychology, Hall's concern with the mutual harmony of science and religion was welcome in the liberal

51. See, e.g., Edward W. Scripture, "Accurate Work in Psychology," *AJP* 6 (1894): 427–30.
52. GSH, "Psychological Literature," *AJP* 7 (1895): 146.

intellectual centers of the country. Hall's ability to turn the language of science into "mythopoeic" terms enabled him to tell groups of ministers and educational societies that psychology studied "the soul," that the undevout neurologist was mad, and that he himself, because he used the concept of attention as well as the principles of association to explain mental action, was a "spiritualist" rather than a "materialist" in psychology.[53]

This rhetoric, however, also found its way into Hall's professional studies. When Hall in 1887 attacked Ladd for seeing with the eyes of Peter Bell and hence not with the eyes of a scientist, his scientific readers should have been warned. For Hall saw in nature not only the intricate universe of scientific analysis but the moral and aesthetic rhythms which Wordsworth too had seen there.

By 1893, even William James was disturbed by the "religious cant" with which Hall felt it necessary to embellish his psychology, and the younger generation felt even less happy with it. When Hall told his students at a seminar in 1894 that he both believed and disbelieved in the Christian stories and did not want to be forced to state explicitly which kernels in them were true and which false, several of his students adamantly disagreed. What the young person wanted and needed, they retorted, was precisely an open and clear statement that would free him of his religious anxieties and allow him to go on with his studies unimpeded.[54]

One of the most talented of Hall's early students, William L. Bryan, left a record of his uneasy encounter with Hall's mixed bag of science and spirit. Hall had closed his part of Bryan's doctoral examination with the question: what ideas did Bryan most deeply "believe in and wish to teach to everybody?" The creed which Hall sought in answer was for Bryan too great an embarrassment to articulate. Afterwards, he hastened to write Hall not to believe him empty of such principles but only that "these things cannot be said."[55] This encounter may have represented differences in temperament between the two men as well as the different temper of their ages, but it is symbolic of the distance already growing up

---

53. GSH, "The Relations of Physiology to Psychology," 1890, pp. 698–99; GSH, "Psychological Progress," 1894, pp. 29–33.
54. "Reports of the Plato Club," 1894, pp. 472–73.
55. Wm. L. Bryan to GSH, 7 Feb 1893, CUP.

between Hall and the main body of younger experimentalists. Having considered Hall the very model of the new science when he came to study with him in 1891, Bryan recognized a few years later that Hall's eminence in the profession would rest in large part on the broad philosophical knowledge and interests he brought to it.[56] James and Ladd could have found a certain satisfaction in this turn of the wheel.

Ironically, Hall's marginal position in the profession probably accounted for some of the stability of Hall's later years. Relieved of the need to conform to the canon of science, Hall could give vent to all his interests and follow them in whatever direction they led. His expression of hostility in his *Journal* editorial, moreover, was finally pronounced enough to bring down upon him the wrath of his colleagues and thereby to relieve his sense of guilt. There was now realistic ground for the position he so often sought of self-sacrifice and self-abnegation. A decade later Titchener admitted that there was still "a great deal of feeling against Hall in the country."[57] Hall remained an outsider, and in this position he was subject to far fewer demands, both inner and external, than he had been as a competitor within the mainstream of psychology.

Hall was not entirely without support, however. He had his alliance with the loyal Titchener to sustain him. The fact that Hall emerged from the conflicts of the mid-1890s in alliance with Titchener was itself somewhat ironic. Titchener and Sanford, the director of the laboratory at Clark, enjoyed both personal and scientific congeniality. Sanford worked partly in the Wundtian tradition which Titchener deliberately carried forward, and Cornell usually supplied the personnel for the Clark laboratory.[58] But by 1898, Titchener realized that Hall, like James and Ladd before him, had become "cranky"; he had left the traditional limits of introspective experimental psychology and gone "mad on child business and the questionnaire."[59]

Hall, moreover, kept his firm grip on the *Journal,* indulging in the same editorial capriciousness and jealously guarding it from any

56. Wm. L. Bryan to GSH, 31 Jan 1891; 24 Aug 1893, CUP.
57. Titchener to Cattell, 31 July 1903, CP.
58. E. G. Boring, interview, 5 Mar 1962.
59. Titchener to Cattell, 20 Nov 1898, CP.

plan or person who smelled mildly of "merger" or "joint control."
Repeatedly Hall thought someone was trying to get hold of the
Journal and sent Titchener off to the attack, only to have him find
that no such raid was planned and that Hall, in Titchener's word,
had been "romancing."[60] Each of the three editors, Hall, Sanford,
and Titchener, was responsible for filling and editing an equal
number of pages in each issue. Since it was almost impossible to
meet that quota precisely, constant adjustments of editorial and
financial responsibilities were required between the three, and the
difficulties often caused delay in publication. Various proposals for
improving the *Journal,* moreover, seemed always obstructed by
Hall.[61]

Hall smoothed over the strain he caused Titchener by dangling
before him the prospect that he would soon retire and turn the entire
journal over to him. Hall put his co-editors under three-year contracts governing the financial and editorial conditions under which
the *Journal* would operate. As the years passed, Titchener became
more uneasy about the contract renewals, and Hall had to resort to
shrewder blandishments to continue on the old basis.[62] Titchener
confessed to Cattell that "at times he has almost driven me insane.
But I have kept a great respect and liking for him, through it all.
He is a gentleman, despite various ill considered actions."[63] Titchener never attributed Hall's behavior during their many quarrels
and difficulties to base motivation and hence was able to maintain a
basic respect for him.

Among the profession at large, Hall's personal isolation also
eased as time went on. Cattell attempted to restore contact with
Hall, and as editor of the rival review and the principal leader of
the younger generation of psychologists, his efforts were crucial in

60. Titchener to Cattell, 26 Sept 1906, 2 Oct 1906, CP; Howard C. Warren to
Titchener, 23 July 1910, TP; GSH to Warren, 17 Mar 1911, 25 Oct 1911, 28
Nov 1911, CUP.
61. L. N. Wilson to Titchener, 28 May 1901; W. B. Pillsbury to Titchener, 7
Aug 1902; A[ugust] Kirschmann to Titchener, 19 Jan 1904; draft of contract enclosed in E. C. Sanford to Titchener, 12 Jan 1907, TP.
62. Titchener to Cattell, 17 June 1904, CP; Sanford to Titchener, 12 Jan 1907,
6 Apr 1907, TP; GSH to Titchener, 14 Mar 1910, 23 Mar 1910, 27 May 1913,
TP; Titchener to H. D. Sheldon, 12 May 1926, TP.
63. Titchener to Cattell, 31 July 1903, CP.

alleviating ill feelings. Hall was himself moved by Cattell's gestures of "personal good will."[64] A number of the younger psychologists were drawn into contact with him as their interests dictated, and were perhaps surprised to find him, as Howard C. Warren of Princeton University remarked, "affable and friendly."[65]

One token of the limited respect accorded Hall by the profession as he grew older was an invitation to give a course of guest lectures at Columbia University in 1912, the same course William James had given earlier in the century. Hall obliged with perceptive sketches of Wundt, Helmholtz, Fechner, Lotze, and Zeller, all of them major figures in his own life and four of them founders of scientific psychology. Not the least of the merits of Hall's historical lectures was a new consistency in his evaluation of his psychological heritage. Hall praised Wundt and Fechner for their broad, philosophical interests leading out from science and even admitted his belief in Fechner's mystical idea of the existence of soul-life in all matter. The hero of the piece, as of Hall's study in Germany, was Helmholtz, though now Hall praised him for what he regarded as his own strengths: he was not a "method pedant" and he followed his problems freely across disciplinary lines.[66]

As was the case in the psychological profession, the new conditions at Clark University, too, formed an environment much more conducive to Hall's personal stability than had the initial, more promising state of the university. Hall could see his institution fighting bravely for high ideals against heavy odds and the hostility of the surrounding world, a vision which conformed sufficiently to fact to cause him little difficulty. Within the university, Hall no longer had the pressures of Clark over him and a pugnacious faculty under him. With the continued support of the trustees, his authority was virtually complete.

The faculty who stayed on or returned after the juncture of 1892 by that fact proved their personal loyalty. Many of the practices the

64. GSH to Cattell, 7 Mar 1898, 19 July 1899, 21 June 1900, 6 June 1901, 6 Sept 1904, 8 Sept 1904, 9 Dec 1905, 18 Jan 1906, 17 Aug 1908, 7 July 1909, CP; Titchener to Cattell, 7 Aug 1903, 23 Nov 1903, CP. Hall's thanks are in GSH to Cattell, 20 Nov 1903, CP.
65. H. C. Warren, "Autobiography," in Murchison, *History of Psychology in Autobiography,* 1:459.
66. GSH, *Founders,* particularly pp. 143, 304–5, 439, 449.

first faculty found objectionable, the succeeding one was willing to tolerate as Hallian eccentricity or to oppose by methods Hall found acceptable. The tact of Sanford, and next to him of William Burnham, another of Hall's Hopkins students, proved invaluable buffers, although there were occasional incidents, particularly between Hall and new faculty members.[67]

Hall and his small faculty went back to their work with a strong feeling of dedication. Hall had always maintained that the essential components of a university were present in the quality of its men and their dedication to science, not in its size. The reduced scale of operation made it even easier for those left to concentrate on their work and for students and faculty to retain the close relation and mutual stimulation which is the core of the educational process. The one ideal to which Hall remained true in deed as well as in word was freedom of the faculty to teach what they wished. Hall's wide suggestiveness and occasional conflicts that arose over the direction of students did not strike the faculty that remained as incursions on this freedom.[68]

Occasionally, the genuine intellectual distinction Hall nourished at Clark received some recognition outside. Hall gained the friendly notice of his academic colleagues, and the Worcester townspeople as well, by the Decennial Celebration he arranged at the university in 1899.[69] He invited five distinguished foreign scientists to speak at the celebration and afterward awarded them honorary degrees, among them, Santiago Ramon y Cajal, of the University of Madrid, whose work in histology was one of the principal sources of the neurone theory; Antonio Mosso, of the University of Milan, a pioneer student of physiology and development; and August Forel, professor of psychiatry at Basel and director of the Burgholzï Asylum. With all present praising the international character of university ideals, this brief event helped to set in motion an active exchange between American and European universities before the war. Hall could not help spoiling his brief return to eminence,

67. *LCP*, p. 351.
68. Ibid., pp. 302–4. See H. D. Sheldon, "Clark University, 1897–1900," *Journal of Social Psychology* 24 (Nov 1946): 227–47.
69. Tanner, "Clark University," pp. 127–28; Worcester *Spy*, 24 May 1900; *Science*, n.s. 11 (Apr 1900): 620–22; *Clark University, Decennial Celebration.*

however; to the chagrin of his American colleagues, he painted so glowing a picture of Clark to his foreign guests that some of them returned with the idea that Clark University was the only place in the country doing genuine university work.[70]

In substance, Clark University remained in this mold until Hall retired from the presidency in 1920. Although the final bequest of Jonas Clark eased conditions somewhat, it was not nearly as large as Hall had hoped. When Clark died in 1900, he left half of his five million dollars to the university, of which sum only about one-quarter went to the graduate department. Half was set aside for the establishment of a college with which Stanley Hall was forbidden by Clark's will to have any connection.[71] Indeed, Clark at one point had added a codicil to his will forbidding any bequest to the university if Hall were its president. A few years later, however, Clark withdrew the condition, requiring only that Hall have nothing to do with the collegiate department.[72]

Thus, over the next few years the chemistry department was restored and fellowships and faculty salaries slightly increased. Gifts from the town increased somewhat, allowing for occasional special expenditures, though the university and the new three-year college were never fully adopted into the philanthropy or the social world of the local gentry. The college existed amicably with the university; and its resources, like that of the library, which Clark also endowed separately, sometimes indirectly augmented those of the graduate department. Though still pressed for funds, Hall was assured of the continuance of his university on its modest scale and according to its high purpose.[73]

For a time his personal life, too, seemed to repair. In 1899 he married Miss Florence Smith, a teacher from Newton Centre, Massachusetts, who had attended the Clark summer schools, and went off the following summer on a honeymoon trip to Europe. Hall said only that his second wife was very unlike his first, and reports suggest that she was a plump, good-natured woman, not very pretty,

70. Hugo Münsterberg to GSH, 30 May 1901, MP.
71. Tanner, "Clark University," pp. 144–56.
72. Ibid., pp. 69–72.
73. "Ann. Rep. Pres. Clark, 1902–03," ". . . 1903–4," ". . . 1906–7," unpublished, CUP; Dr. David Shakow, interview, 13 Oct 1970.

entirely without pretense, and naively indifferent to conventional manners. Many found her a charming asset to the president, but others became aware of her growing pattern of eccentric and bizarre behavior over the years. It gradually became evident that she suffered from mental illness, and after ten years of marriage Hall arranged a separation. Eventually he was forced to commit her to the care of an institution, where she was diagnosed to have progressive arteriosclerosis of the brain.[74]

Hall's public image hardly changed through all these years. Of medium height, physically lithe and quick, he gave the impression of controlled energy. He seldom in public abandoned his pleasant manner. In odd moments, sometimes with a student, or most often alone, he would still be "getting the feel of things," particularly all those things his respectable milieu and puritan conscience forbid. Most of his self-conscious search for feeling and experience, however, went into pioneer ventures in education and psychology.

74. Pruette, *GSH,* pp. 101–4; Carl Gustav Jung to Emma Jung, 6 Sept 1909, in Jung, *Memories, Dreams, Reflections* (New York: Pantheon, 1961), pp. 365–66; Burton J. Rowles, *The Lady at Box 99: The Story of Miriam van Waters* (Greenwich: Seabury Press, 1962), pp. 81, 96; *LCP,* p. 575.

Part Four

PROPHECY   1891–1924

15 THE CHILD STUDY MOVEMENT

Hall's new vision brought him first to the study of child nature and educational reform. During the 1890s he led the way for a flourishing popular movement of child study, one which made up in scope and fervor for what it lacked in depth and persistence. The movement was already in decline in 1904, when he published its most important work, his study of adolescence, and Hall himself soon moved on to broader genetic concerns and the work of Sigmund Freud. Hall's message during this last thirty years of his life—his championship of health and self-expression for childhood, his idealization of adolescent experience, and his praise of the psychoanalytic point of view—found acceptance after his time in large segments of American education, psychology, and culture. He spoke during these years as a cultural prophet, whose need to understand and preach his own sense of life reached deeply enough to touch the problems and desires of later generations.

Hall was first drawn back to education in 1891 by the need of popular support for his university, and was gratified when the circulation of his first issue of *Pedagogical Seminary* in 1891 was "unexpectedly large."[1] Child study was in growing demand among educators. During the years Hall was not present at NEA meetings, there were repeated calls from the floor for more scientific peda-

1. *Ann. Rep. Pres. Clark, 1891*, p. 8.

gogical studies.[2] In the flaring social tensions of these years, Hall recognized that "education is the one thing in which men of all sects, parties, rank, or races, now agree."[3]

The ground swell of support which attracted Hall back to the leadership of the child study movement came from a variety of reforming sects within the profession. Stirred by their own theories and by Hall's earlier advocacy of child study, they looked to scientific psychology for support and guidance. In the vanguard of reform stood the most recent arrival to educational agitation, the Herbartians. These young pedagogs, just returned from study under Herbart disciples in Germany, were propagandists for the Herbartian methods of teaching and curriculum organization, and were at first willing advocates of a scientific study of the child's interests and learning processes. Behind them stood the older American reformers. There were members of the normal school at Oswego, New York, chief advocates in America of Pestalozzi's ideas, particularly his "object method."[4] Although the kindergarten movement was largely occupied with following Froebel's doctrines, a number of individual kindergarteners, like those Hall had worked with in Boston, joined him. Some physicians and the new teachers of physical education who were committed to his gospel of health were willing participants.[5] So too were adventurous administrators like E. H. Russell, principal of the normal school at Worcester, who in 1885 had instituted a program of child study for his students,[6] and Earl Barnes, professor of pedagogy at Stanford University, who in 1891 began conducting investigations of the attitudes of school children, using teachers in the state to gather data.[7] The reigning

2. *PNEA,* 1885, p. 349; 1888, p. 24; 1889, pp. 42–43, 275–76.
3. GSH, "Phi Beta Kappa Oration," 1891, p. 110.
4. *PNEA,* 1891, pp. 832–35.
5. For example, Laliah B. Pingree, the superintendent of Boston kindergartens, Dr. C. J. Enebuske and Amy Morris Homans, of the Boston Normal School of Gymnastics, and the physician, Dr. Edward Mussey Hartwell, were early supporters. "An American Pedagogical Society," 1891, *CW,* vol. 4.
6. *PNEA,* 1889, pp. 275–85.
7. James Dale Hendricks, "The Child Study Movement in America," pp. 98–99; "Twenty-Fifth Anniversary of Clark University," p. 66. Barnes said in 1896 that he had collected over two hundred syllabi circulated on child study from various sources and "nearly all of these can be traced directly or indirectly" to Hall's brochure of 1883, "The Study of Children." Barnes, *Studies in Education,* 1:12.

father of educational reform, Frances Parker, now principal of Chicago's Cook County Normal School, heartily endorsed child study,[8] and Hall always claimed "to wind up my watch and get inspiration" from Parker.[9]

Representatives of all these reforming groups flocked to the banner of science Hall held aloft in 1891 at the NEA meeting in Toronto. Appearing there for the first time since 1885, Hall pinned a notice to a bulletin board and attracted 150 people to unofficial discussions of "The Study of Children."[10] The following year at the NEA, Hall again attracted crowds to unofficial meetings.[11]

In July of 1892, Hall held a two-week summer school at Clark University on the "higher pedagogy and psychology"—an event repeated almost annually thereafter until 1903. Sixty-eight attended this first session, including a half-dozen principals of normal schools, a like number of city school superintendents, generally from small towns in the East, a few university professors of pedagogy, and the rest generally normal school teachers. The entire Clark faculty led these eager students from 8 A.M. to 10 P.M. through cram courses in the new psychology and progressive educational ideas, and left them, according to report, enthusiastic supporters.[12]

Hall catalyzed interest in the new movement the following summer in 1893 at the World's Columbian Congresses held in connection with the Exposition at Chicago. From this event, child study spread among laymen and professionals throughout the country and across the Atlantic. A series of educational congresses had been planned for the Exposition, but Hall broke out of the unified organization and led the progressives into a congress on "Experimental Psychology and Education," leaving the conservative faction, led by William Torrey Harris and James McCosh, to meet under the

8. Frances W. Parker, "The School of the Future," *PNEA*, 1891, pp. 82–90; "An Account of the Work of the Cook County and Chicago Normal School from 1883 to 1899," in U. S. Commissioner of Education, *Annual Report . . . 1902*, 1:261–62; and *PNEA*, 1889, pp. 479–82; 1895, pp. 418–29.

9. "Child Study As a Basis for Psychology and Psychological Teaching," 1892–93, p. 369.

10. *PNEA*, 1891, pp. 830–35.

11. *PR* 2 (1895): 102.

12. "A Summer School of Higher Pedagogy and of Psychology," CUP; "Dr. G. Stanley Hall's Summer School," *The School Bulletin* (Sept 1892), p. 4. Extensive reports of the summer school activities and lists of those enrolled were printed each July in the Worcester *Gazette* and are excerpted in *Clippings*, CUP.

title of "Rational Psychology and Education." Hall turned the entire three-day session of his congress over to child study.[13]

The child study congress attracted more attention and attendance than any of the other educational congresses. Preliminary reports of investigations appeared promising. Normal school principals and teachers, led by Barnes and the Oswego reformers, were already urging that child study be made a basic part of the teacher's professional training.[14] In the face of such support, Harris and his conservative allies in the NEA in 1894 allowed the formation of a Child Study Department in the association, with Hall elected its first president.[15] The department met each summer, elected new officers, heard brief reports of investigations, and discussed the practical value of child study to the teacher. The NEA and state and local teachers associations would provide the backbone of interest in child study.

Although Hall and others tried several times to erect a national organization to give the movement a central focus, outside the NEA, none was ever formed. Hall had proposed a national society for pedagogical research at his first child study meeting at the NEA in 1891, and the idea was greeted with enthusiasm by all concerned.[16] When he sent out a call for support in the fall, however, he chose as official sponsors only Massachusetts educators close to himself; no Herbartians were listed and the society quietly disappeared.[17] Repeatedly through the years the erection of a national organization would founder on sectarian antagonisms within the movement.[18] Hall was particularly antagonistic to the Herbartians, because of the reluctance many of them showed to abandon exclusive attention to Herbart. Their large number and the similarity of their ideas to his own also made them the chief challenge to his hegemony. He publicly criticized their sectarian attachment to the ideas of one man and

13. "The General Programme of the World's Congresses of 1893," 1 Jan, 1 Apr 1893, and "Official Program of the International Congress of Education . . . July 25–28, 1893," p. 25, Chicago Historical Society; New York *Tribune*, 16 Jan 1893.
    14. *PNEA*, 1893, pp. 713–85; *ER* 6 (1893): 160–61.
    15. *PNEA*, 1894, p. 995.
    16. Ibid., 1891, p. 835.
    17. "An American Pedagogical Society," 1891, CW, vol. 4.
    18. *PNEA*, 1893, pp. 714–15; 1897, pp. 825–26, 869; Wm. L. Bryan to GSH, 1 Nov 1893, 5 Jan 1895, CUP.

did not scruple to charge them with un-American subserviency to foreign doctrine, as he himself had been charged earlier.[19]

Hall's inability to unite the diverse support for child study into one organization mirrored the substantive dispersal of the movement. Neither the Herbartians nor the kindergarteners were ever entirely drawn into the movement. In 1892 the Herbartians formed a Herbart Club and in 1895, evidently pressed by the popularity of the child study idea, renamed it the National Society for the Study of Children, but the society engaged in discussion of Herbartian concepts and curriculum reform, not empirical study of child development.[20] A few prominent Herbartians and kindergarteners studied with Hall, cooperated in his efforts, and published in his journals; others worked in child study projects with which Hall was not directly connected, and others remained altogether aloof.[21]

The only other national, organizational focus for child study existed in the Illinois Society for the Study of Children.[22] The society was organized by the Chicago Superintendent of Schools after the inspirational Columbian Congress in 1893 and worked closely with Parker's Cook County Normal School. It succeeded in gaining the active support of the state's leading Herbartians and kindergarteners, as well as leading physicians. Beginning in 1894 it held a Child Study Congress for four days each summer which brought together workers from all over the country, including Hall. In 1895 and 1896 the congress boasted an audience of up to three thousand people, mostly teachers, parents, physicians, and clergymen.[23] The Illinois plan of organization was copied in a number of other states though no other state organization was as large or

19. Introduction to Herman T. Lukens, *Connection between Thought and Memory* (Boston: D. C. Heath, 1895); *PS* 3 (1894): 5; *PS* 3 (1895): 186–88. Hallians also criticized the formalized teaching method developed by the Herbartians; Barnes, *Studies in Education,* 1:203–12.

20. On the ambivalent relationship between child study and Herbartianism, see Dunkel, *Herbart and Herbartianism,* chap. 14; Strickland, "The Child and the Race," pp. 148–200; and Charles De Garmo, "The Principles of the Herbartian School," *Journal of Education* 40 (1894): 392ff.

21. Among those sympathetic to Herbart who joined Hall's efforts were Herman T. Lukens and Will S. Monroe. Patty Smith Hill, later of Teachers College, Columbia University, was the most prominent kindergartener influenced by Hall.

22. See the society's *Transactions,* published annually from 1894 to 1902.

23. *PS* 3 (1895): 198–200.

developed as substantial a program. Altogether, at least twenty-three states had organized child study efforts during the decade.[24]

Contemporaneously with this domestic movement, child study spread across the Atlantic. James Sully and three young women teachers came from Britain to attend the Chicago congress and were inspired by Hall to form a society for child study among psychologists, physicians, and teachers when they returned. The British movement, therefore, had direct roots in the American, and other movements around the world formed partly under the influence of American contacts and publications.[25]

As the preeminent spokesman for science and romantic naturalism in American education and as the leader of the burgeoning child study movement, Hall became a major power in the educational profession in the 1890s. As early as 1891, an educational journal declared that "What Dr. W. T. Harris is to philosophy, Dr. Hall is to psychology." Harris as the conservative and established power, and Hall as the progressive challenger, dominated the educational scene of the decade. His word was said to control many of the most important appointments in the professional hierarchy. After 1900, as his movement and his reputation dissipated, he still controlled for another decade the large network of students and disciples he had placed across the country.[26]

24. *PS* 3 (1896): 360–61; 4 (1896): 115. The superintendents of thirty-seven out of ninety-two counties in Illinois who were circularized in 1897 reported a noticeable and salutory interest in child study among some of their teachers. Wilbur Harvey Dutton, "The Child-Study Movement in America from its Origin (1880) to the Organization of the Progressive Education Association (1920)," (Ph.D. diss., Stanford University, 1945), pp. 88-90. A partial review of child study activities in the states can be found in Dutton, pp. 138–51. Annual surveys of child study, published during the height of the movement, give a more concrete picture. See, particularly, *PS* 3 (1895): 189-212; 4 (1896): 111–25; *PNEA*, 1895, pp. 893–906.

25. On the British society, see *PS* 3 (1895): 355–56. On child study organizations in Europe, Asia and Latin America, see Dutton, "Child-Study Movement," pp. 152–56; *PS* 6 (1899): 254–55, 372–81; 8 (1901): 510–14; 14 (1907): 130–34; and Herman T. Lukens to GSH, 6 Aug, 3 Oct, 16 Dec 1897; 5 Feb 1898, CUP. Hall's work was well known in France and Germany. Theta H. Wolf, "Intuition and Experiment: Alfred Binet's First Efforts in Child Psychology," *JHBS*, 2 (July 1966): 234, 238, surmises that Binet was influenced by reading Hall around 1890 when he moved into child psychology.

26. *Journal of Education* 34 (Oct 1891): 217; Frederick Eby to the author, 4 Oct 1962; Henry D. Sheldon to GSH, 25 Jan 1910, CUP.

Hall spoke to educators as the ambassador of science and the university, bringing the critical eye and scientific intelligence they themselves lacked. In the first issue of *Pedagogical Seminary* in 1891, Hall declared that the new universities must provide the leadership for educational reform. "The one source of vitality in every true educational system is at the top, and not at the bottom." Hall concluded that if education were left to regulate itself, it would result in schools "marvellously adapted" to their own environments, schools which would

stand for the naive unconscious instincts of the Volksoul—conservative only and utterly unprogressive. The impulse we plead for has its exactly opposite source where consciousness and science are at their clearest and best.[27]

While Hall soon abandoned this explicitly intellectualist stance in addressing his child study audiences, and often pandered to their sentiments, the claim for scientific superiority was always implicit in his child study work, and it always implied a hierarchy of evolutionary values contrary to that of his child nature theory.

Among psychologists, however, Hall found at first little support for his program of child study outside of his own circle, centered at Clark University. One of the most competent and respected of Hall's students, William L. Bryan, urged other psychologists to put their scientific tools to work for child study:

We promise a science of conscious life. . . . But we shall be false to all our promise, and we shall turn the confidence and sympathy which has endowed chairs and built laboratories, into derision and rejection if we confine our science to a little round of testing in the laboratory.[28]

Despite Bryan's plea, the main body of American psychologists were not in the 1890s directly concerned with education or developmental psychology. Laboratory experimentation on the adult human remained the core of psychology for those who worked in the Wundtian tradition. Those like Cattell at Columbia, who were transforming the Wundtian model into a functional and differential study of human behavior, were favorably disposed toward the pursuit of

27. GSH, "The Educational State," 1890, p. 719; "Educational Reforms," 1891, p. 12.
28. *PNEA*, 1893, p. 778.

applied and developmental subjects but seldom engaged in the work themselves.[29]

Only one other center of psychological interest in the study of child nature existed outside of Clark. At the University of Chicago, James Mark Baldwin was working on a developmental study of mental function which described the socialization of the child through the process of imitation. A unique figure in American psychology, Baldwin's work both anticipated Piaget's genetic exploration of cognition and stimulated interest in social psychology. John Dewey, who arrived at Chicago in 1894, was another philosopher-psychologist whose concern with development and the adaptive function of reason led him into educational theory. From 1896 to 1904, Dewey directed a laboratory school at the university which experimented with progressive ideas by actually trying them in the school. Both Baldwin and Dewey endorsed the child study movement somewhat reluctantly. They, like others in the profession who might otherwise have been interested, had reason to personally distrust Hall and would not have wanted to get involved too closely with him. They approved his basic goal but were skeptical of the scientific means and the educational message of the program Hall set out.[30] There was some feeling in the profession that Hall had so tainted child study with popular pseudoscience that no "respectable" scientist wanted anything to do with it.[31]

Hall and his disciples at Clark thus provided most of the scientific personnel the movement had during the 1890s, and they were quickly absorbed into the professional structure of education. By 1895 Hall had half a dozen of his students in chairs of psychology at major normal schools or in joint chairs of psychology and pedagogy in the middle and western state universities, and more followed after them.[32] These psychologist-pedagogs were joined by

29. Cattell, "Address of the President before the APA, 1895," in Poffenberger, *James McKeen Cattell*, 2:55.

30. John Dewey, "Criticisms Wise and Otherwise on Modern Child Study," *PNEA*, 1897, pp. 867–68; Baldwin, *Mental Development in The Child and the Race*, pp. 36–38. See also Nicholas Murray Butler in *ER* 12 (1896): 411–13.

31. E. D. Starbuck to Wm. James, 23 Aug 1902, JP.

32. *Clark University, Decennial Celebration*, contains a directory of the whereabouts of Hall's students to date, as does L. N. Wilson, ed., "Clark University Directory of Alumni, Faculty and Students," *CULP* 4 (1915).

an even larger number of professors of pedagogy and adventurous teachers who had little if any formal training in psychology. Together they provided the bulk of professional workers in child study.

Surrounding the teachers and professionals in the movement was a wide circle of popular support, chiefly among upper middle-class women, often college educated, who had the leisure and intelligence to devote to the cause. Popular interest in the idea was visible very early. In New York City in 1889, Mr. and Mrs. Felix Adler formed among their friends a Society for the Study of Child Nature which discussed such topics as the proper kinds of toys and punishments.[33] The American Association of University Women, noticing the early infant study of Millicent Shinn, their member in California, formed a study group around her in 1892 and then took up support of the work nationally.[34] Women's clubs across the country and the new parent-teacher associations also enrolled in the ranks after 1893.[35] The National Congress of Mothers, which first convened in 1897 and featured Stanley Hall as a principal speaker, owed something of their positive self-consciousness as mothers to the child study influence and warmly endorsed the movement.[36]

The women's reading circles and clubs which took up child study only occasionally tried original research; usually they discussed the findings and prescriptions coming out of the movement and attempted to apply them to their own children and their neighborhood school. Most likely, the women involved in these efforts were typically less aggressive and more conservative than their counterparts who were working for women's suffrage or interesting themselves in the social and political problems of immigrants and the poor. They apparently enjoyed Hall's traditional characterization of their differences from men and their proper superiority within the woman's sphere. They wanted to bring an intelligent concern and enlightened knowledge to their roles as mothers and homemakers rather than change or enlarge these roles.[37]

33. *PS* 3 (1895): 200.
34. *PNEA*, 1894, pp. 996–99.
35. Ibid., 1897, pp. 859–65; 1905, pp. 721–27; *PS* 15 (1908): 563–79.
36. *The Work and Words of the National Congress of Mothers. First Annual Session, 1897* (New York: D. Appleton, 1897).
37. Ibid., and *PNEA*, 1905, pp. 721–27; *PS* 15 (1908): 563–79.

Hall's leadership of this diverse interest in child nature was exercised chiefly through his powers of rhetoric and research. He constantly spoke to teachers and the public about the child study program and purposes, summing up the scientific work to date, offering suggestions for reform based on these findings, urging more work in various directions, and heralding the benefits which would soon emerge from the movement. Hall repeated his message from Boston to the Middle or Far West almost annually. In 1893–94 Hall gave thirty-four major public lectures, and though a count is not available, his pace apparently increased as the decade proceeded.[38] He figured at the end of his life that he had given over twenty-five hundred such talks in the course of his career.[39] Hall's lecture style has been described by numerous sources as extremely impressive.[40] Speaking with great sincerity and naturalness of manner, gliding easily from simple exposition to lyrical hyperbole, Hall's style evidently mirrored his complex message. Whereas a modern reader of the recorded word is most often struck by its nineteenth-century ornateness, Hall's audiences were impressed and moved by the simplicity and directness of his manner. Most of these talks were then published, often several times, in Hall's own journals and in other popular and professional magazines.

Hall's rhetoric was an important element in stimulating such wide interest in child study. With his canny sense of what his audience craved to hear, Hall both excited their interest in, and soothed their fears of, a science of the child. In his opening address to the new Child Study Department of the NEA in 1894, Hall began with no less a pronouncement than "Unto you is born this day a new Department of Child Study."[41] Hall's messianism, drawn from the critical events in his own life in 1894, also promised the anxious teacher a new professional basis for education in science. It was to be a science

38. *PS* 3 (1894): 181. Hall's former students constantly drummed up demand for his lectures across the country. See Thaddeus L. Bolton to GSH, 7 Dec 1896, CUP.

39. *LCP*, p. 304. Hall said that between 1886 and 1911 he gave over seven hundred lectures outside of Clark on educational subjects; this number would have been only a part of the number devoted to child study. *EP* 1:xiii.

40. "Biographical Sketch of President Hall," *American Journal of Insanity* 53 (1896): 317–22; *PS* 5 (1897): 297.

41. "Child Study," 1894, pp. 173–79.

subordinated to the needs and capacities of teachers, however. In a remark that was to be repeated constantly in the following years by all the leaders of the movement,[42] Hall asserted that child study was intended to benefit first and foremost the teacher—to make her forever young, sympathetic, and professional: only secondarily and almost incidentally would it benefit science.

The other major appeal Hall offered was his special combination of moralism and romanticism. In a passage which brought applause from his audience, Hall declared,

> The little child now standing in our midst is, I believe, again to be the regeneration of education, to moralize it, to make it religious, to bring the child (because it brings the school) home to the hearts of the men and women, where children should always find a warm place.

Hall offered the teacher an exciting format for familiar and comforting ideas. Indeed, he declared that "the feature of child study is that, like the Gospel, it makes old things new."

In a brilliant display of Hallian ambiguity, he outlined the chief goals of child study in educational reform: health was the first goal and he described the euphoria of true health so as to suggest a new dimension to his program; then he gave as concrete examples such things as a good appetite and sound sleep. The second goal was to help the teacher to "get the child in a condition of responsive sensitiveness to every aspect of nature . . . to get as many sensations and as many different views of life as possible." But again Hall's example was only the variety of experiences he had had as a young boy on the farm. Lastly, Hall wanted for the child psychological unity, a lesson he had learned in studying adolescence: "We must get at the personalities of the child," he said. Yet here again, the fundamental unity Hall described was the moral one of a life devoted to altruistic purposes. "Life is for service; it is not for self, and this idea should be implanted deeply in the heart of every child." Hall offered the child a new dimension of experience only to circumscribe it in the next breath with the clichés of nineteenth-century conventional wisdom. The romanticism of freedom and growth could hold underneath the traditional counsels of sound habits, agrarian nostalgia, and moral duty. Hall did develop a genuinely

42. *PS* 3 (1895): 209–10; 5 (1897): 299.

progressive program, but the movement flourished because he was able to draw into it both the enlightened yearnings and the conservative sympathies of his educational constituency.

Hall focused his efforts on changing the attitudes of those within the educational profession, and secondarily, the larger public. In 1891, he briefly recognized that most educational reform had been the work of influential laymen outside the profession, people who could mobilize the political power to change the underlying conditions which shape school systems and the professional bureaucracy. On a number of occasions he attacked such conditions as the low pay of teachers, overcrowded classrooms, and the subtle collusion of textbook publishers and politicians.[43] Understandably, for a man inclined to intellectual pursuits, however, Hall's political criticism was not at the center of his message. He did not concern himself with the possibility that constraints created by the society at large could determine the fate of his rhetorical efforts.

Hall shaped the child study movement also through his own research and through directing or stimulating the research of others at Clark and elsewhere. Hall's research was focused on the nature of the child, rather than the learning situation, although some child study workers did begin to investigate aspects of what happened to the child in the classroom. Hall often hoped publicly that someone would endow a model or laboratory school for him at Clark, like the schools run by Columbia University Teachers College and the University of Chicago, but no one ever did.[44] His theories of child nature and school reform therefore always remained rather general and he never tested or refined them in a real school situation.

The central method of Hall's own research and the means by which he drew large numbers of teachers and mothers into his scientific project was the questionnaire method. Hall compiled fifteen questionnaires during the academic year 1894–95, each on a particular topic, such as doll playing, children's lies, or children's fears.[45] A typical syllabus, on fears, for example, listed a great num-

43. See GSH, "The Case of the Public Schools," 1896.
44. "The Ideal School As Based on Child Study," 1901, p. 38.
45. The syllabi have been collected in a separate volume of CW, *Topical Syllabi*. The titles of most of them are listed in *LCP*, pp. 382–89. Each questionnaire is generally printed, in some part, in the study reporting on its results. In

ber of possible fears and asked for each one information about the age at which it appeared, intensity, manifestations, causes, and its "educational good or bad effects."[46]

Hall then distributed copies of the syllabi to about eight hundred correspondents all over the country, generally teachers in normal schools, sometimes superintendents, principals, or ordinary teachers.[47] One of the most intelligent and productive of Hall's correspondents, Miss Lillie Williams, a teacher at the Trenton State Normal College, described how she used the syllabi to elicit memories from her students of their own childhood feelings and experiences. Her students would then answer the syllabi themselves as reminiscences. The more talented and interested of her students would go on to observe children and gather data on some or all of the points on the questionnaire.[48] Other teachers might assign part of the questionnaire to older students as themes or directly question their students for answers. In this way, Hall gathered twenty thousand returns to his questionnaires that year.[49]

Hall and his students then attempted to analyze the data and publish their findings. Whatever their ultimate conclusions, the questionnaire would have served in the interim as a device to make teachers and mothers more sensitive to childhood experience. In 1895–96 he drew up sixteen syllabi, again sent them to about eight hundred workers and received sixty thousand returns.[50] In all, between 1894 and 1915, Hall distributed 194 questionnaires on child study topics.[51]

The impersonality and conceptual vagueness of the method seem peculiarly suited to Hall's strengths and weaknesses. For all their fragmentary character, much of the data was extremely suggestive,

---

addition, *AJP* 14 (1903): 96–106, lists the syllabi and the studies based on them, 1894–1902.

46. *Topical Syllabi,* CW, no. 8, 1st ser., "Fears in Childhood and Youth," 1895.

47. *PS* 3 (1895): 192–3.

48. Lillie A. Williams, "How to Collect Data for Studies in Genetic Psychology," *PS* 3 (1896): 419–23. See also William H. Burnham, "The Observation of Children at the Worcester Normal School," *PS* 1 (1891): 219–24.

49. *PS* 3 (1895): 192–93.

50. Ibid. 3 (1896): 359.

51. *LCP,* p. 382.

though the absence of any means for tracing the development of individual respondents was a serious handicap even for the kind of use Hall wanted to make of the data. He supplemented these findings with his own introspection and with casual observation of children within his reach. Though he had on the whole very little contact with children in the ordinary course of his scholarly life, particularly after his first wife and daughter died, he evidently used what opportunities he had to advantage, for occasional passages throughout his work clearly bespeak a keen observer of actual children.[52]

Hall's own researches were based on the questionnaire, but his overall view of the field and much of the work of his students and others extended beyond its confines. While it thus never dominated the movement completely, it did provide the glue which held a great majority of the teacher participants to child study. The questionnaire became the representative emblem of the movement and the chief target of the child study critics. After its demise, much of the significant child study work done within the method, as well as the large amount of work done without it, was forgotten. Hall and his colleagues, however, initiated themselves or stimulated in others much of permanent value.

Hall's child study program had its sources and stimulus in three different areas of reference: actual conditions in the schools, the belief in biological naturalism as the basis of education, and the scientific tools available for inquiry. Neither Hall nor his colleagues ever succeeded in bringing their grasp of all three of these areas into harmony. Many of the most cherished doctrines of the child study enthusiasts had little or no basis in scientific fact, while several fruitful types of scientific investigation gathered a momentum of their own and soon passed beyond the scope of the movement. Some of the findings most practically useful in the school contributed little to the scientific understanding of child nature, while some of the most practically desired results were never obtainable by the scientific means at hand. The work of the child study movement was thus extremely diverse, and the amalgam of ideology, investigation, and practical reform Hall put together was not entirely representa-

52. See, e.g., GSH, "Education of the Heart," 1909, pp. 31–38.

tive of the whole movement. As the preeminent spokesman for child study in America his words and his work carried great weight, but he often advocated unpopular positions and stimulated child study workers to challenge and oppose his views.

A major part of Hall's child study program revolved around the subject of physical development and health as the proper foundation for mental development. "An ounce of health, growth and heredity," Hall often told his audiences, "is worth a ton of education."[53] A great many avenues led to this subject and gave it centrality in Hall's mind. The schools grossly neglected physical development and hygiene. The romantic pedagogical reformers, and now the Herbartians, were concerned with the "whole man," the symmetrical development of all the child's native powers. Hall's biological and medical background and his interest in motor psychology also called attention to these factors. Finally, precise scientific tools were available to measure physical processes. Much of the work in this area was thus done by psychological or medical experts and produced durable results.

Studies of the physical growth of school children were among the first Hall called for. Norms of physical growth, he thought, would provide educators with sure standards by which to gauge arrested development, and hence a wide variety of diseases.[54] Franz Boas, docent in anthropology at Clark, was probably influenced by Hall's stance when in 1891 and 1892 he undertook a study of the growth of Worcester school children, which served as the basis for his series of growth studies of the 1890s. In them, Boas discovered the phenomenon of accelerated and retarded growth and the enormous variation among individuals in the tempo of growth, findings which dampened Hall's large expectations for the diagnostic value of this data.[55]

The health of school children had been a subject of public debate

53. GSH, "Heredity, Instinct, Feelings," 1898, p. 46. In "The Ideal School," 1901, p. 24, the proportion was a "pound" to a "ton."

54. GSH, "Child Study: The Basis of Exact Education," 1893, pp. 430–32. Hall knew of Henry P. Bowditch's first American study in 1878 on the growth of Boston school children.

55. J. M. Tanner, "Boas' Contributions to Knowledge of Human Growth and Form," in *The Anthropology of Franz Boas, Memoir of the American Anthropological Association,* ed. Walter Goldschmidt (1959), pp. 76–87.

long before the child study movement, as physicians since the 1840s had roused parents to complain of the ill effects of "overpressure" in the schools. The complaint reached its peak in the 1880s, after which the child study movement apparently channeled it into effective action.[56] Hall directed a great deal of rhetoric and research to problems of health. European studies of physical defects and illness in schoolchildren had already suggested alarming rates of defect which increased with age. Although Hall was well aware that the school could hardly be blamed for these defects in the absence of a control group of children not attending school, he often used these findings to awaken public concern for the real negligence of health that existed in the schools.[57]

Hall himself suggested the first study in America of hearing defects, done by his aide, Miss Wiltse, in 1888 in a Boston school, with the aid of a physician.[58] Simple eye and hearing tests became one of the staples of the child study workers, and regular tests by physicians soon became a standard part of the school program. The remedy of moving such children to the front of the class or seeing to it that they obtained medical correction often had such startling effects on children otherwise considered dull or grossly defective that this aspect of child study easily caught the popular imagination and became a favorite image of the entire movement.[59] Under the prod of child study experts, the concern about disease and defect widened to broader problems of school hygiene, from the proper style of desk to needed intervals of exercise and rest. Thus the child study movement evidently brought to fruition the earlier, independent efforts of physicians to improve health conditions in the schools. By 1910 medical health officers had become a new class of school official, and some educators, like William H. Burnham,

56. John Duffy, "Mental Strain and 'Overpressure' in the Schools: A Nineteenth Century Viewpoint," *Journal of the History of Medicine* 23 (Jan 1968): 63–79, discusses this complaint but does not link its disappearance after the 1880s to its absorption into the child study movement.
57. GSH, "Child Study As a Basis for Psychology and Psychological Teaching," 1892–93, pp. 367–68; "Child Study: The Basis of Exact Education," 1893, pp. 434–36; "Health of School Children As Affected by School Buildings," 1892, pp. 163–72; "Some Practical Results of Child Study," 1897, p. 167.
58. *PS* 3 (1895): 193.
59. *PNEA*, 1894, p. 997; 1895, pp. 893–94; 1896, p. 841; *PS* 3 (1895): 204; *ER* 14 (1897): 150–59.

Hall's colleague at Clark, had opened a new speciality in school hygiene.[60]

Muscular function was emphasized by Hall more strongly than any other area of child activity. In line with his general concern for physical health as the basis of mental well-being, Hall argued that muscular training was the proper foundation of mental education. Hall based this connection on a great variety of scientific findings, but the chief connection he described was a figurative one, in which the pattern of muscular movements formed a kind of paradigm for the whole mental apparatus.[61] Hall thus wanted muscular exercise integrated into activities which were meaningful for the whole child. He advocated free forms of exercise for school children rather than formalized gymnastics.[62] He approved the introduction of organized sports but soon opposed them when the degree of competitiveness and physical combat made them "brutalizing."[63] He continually urged manual-training teachers to tie their muscular training to genuinely functional and mentally educational projects.[64] Hall also pointed to the fact that constant muscular activity was natural for the child, and, therefore, the immense effort of the drillmaster teachers to make children sit still was harmful and useless.[65]

Hall introduced one issue into the discussion of muscular education which eventually proved both false and fruitful. He claimed that the incomplete development at birth of portions of the muscular and nervous systems suggested the early exercise of "fundamental muscles"—those which controlled the trunk and limbs—but not of "accessory muscles," which controlled the fingers. From this Hall concluded that learning to read and write ought to be put off at

60. The inauguration of health services in the school and the broader concern with school hygiene have been taken to be almost entirely the work of the medical profession. See, e.g. Cubberly, *Public Education,* pp. 604–611, and K. E. Veselak, "Historical Steps in the Development of the Modern School Health Program," *Journal of School Health* 29 (1959): 262–69.

61. GSH, "Child Study As a Basis for Psychology and Psychological Teaching," 1892–93, p. 367; *Adol,* 1:129–32, 156–58, 160–69.

62. *Adol,* 1:189–90, 195–96, 202–3.

63. Ibid., p. 157.

64. Ibid., p. 174–87.

65. Ibid., p. 161; "Child Study As a Basis for Psychology and Psychological Teaching," 1892–93, p. 368.

least till the eighth year, if not the tenth, and that the fine finger-work required in the kindergarten was harmful. He punctuated these conclusions with dire predictions of muscular and nervous disease for those whose finer muscles were "overworked."[66] The fact that fundamental muscles should be exercised before accessory became in the 1890's, even for Dewey, one of the few "settled principles" of child study.[67]

The issue called forth a number of pioneer studies, by Hall's students and others, of the ability of children at various ages to perform certain muscular tasks.[68] Although the sharp distinction Hall had drawn between the development of fundamental and accessory muscles was eventually discredited, the studies tended to support the more modest concern that children be able to perform without too great strain the muscular tasks they were set.[69] Only the experimental progressive schools of the following decades post-poned reading and writing to the seventh or eighth year, but Hall's program strengthened efforts in the public schools to reduce excess drill in penmanship during the primary years and helped reform the kindergarten program.[70]

Hall was so concerned about health, growth, and physical de-velopment because of his desire to overcome his own malaise and insufficiency and because these terms contained his search for a new, biologically based ideal of human development. Just as virtue was the highest achievement of man within the Protestant culture of Hall's youth, health became for Hall the optimum condition of man in an evolutionary world. It was the foundation of the new morality

66. Ibid., pp. 368–69; GSH, "Child Study in Summer Schools," 1894, pp. 333–34; *PNEA*, 1896, p. 863; *Adol,* 1:156–57. Hall's concern may also have arisen from the fact that he was unusually clumsy in the movement of his own "finer muscles." *LCP,* p. 122.

67. John Dewey, *Transactions of the Illinois Society for Child Study* 1 (1895): 18, quoted in Katherine Camp Mayhew and Anna Camp Edwards, *The Dewey School; the Laboratory School of the University of Chicago, 1896–1903* (New York: Appleton-Century, 1936), p. 475.

68. John A. Hancock, "A Preliminary Study of Motor Ability," *PS* 3 (1895): 9–29; *PS* 5 (1897): 293–99.

69. William L. Bryan, "The Hygiene of Motor Development," *PNEA,* 1897, pp. 279–80; Frederic Burk, "From Fundamental to Accessory in the Develop-ment of the Nervous System and of Movements," *PS* 6 (1898): 62–64; Everett Shepardson, "A Preliminary Critique of the Doctrine of Fundamental and Ac-cessory Movements," *PS* 13 (1906): 101–16.

70. See, e.g., C. C. Van Lieuw in *ER* 9 (1895): 172–86.

Hall found in nature, the goal of the individualist—as harmony and cooperation were the goal of the socially minded—in the newly secularized culture of the turn of the century. Typically, Hall's conception of health retained the more conservative emphasis on health as the product of good habits, while it moved toward a more romantic definition of health as the possession of all one's powers and their active, joyful exercise. Hall linked health with "euphoria," the maximum state of happiness which derived from the maximum use of one's powers.[71] The importance of normal health determined the need to measure, diagnose, and prevent abnormality and pathology; so these conditions, too, were pervasive themes in the Hallian child study literature.

From physical conceptions of health and development, Hall's ideal extended into the realm of mental health. Hall and other experts described for teachers the danger signals of mental illness in children they might watch for.[72] More often, however, Hall discussed mental health in a general way, as the product of mental unity. His lyrical praise of health folded together both physical and mental dimensions and assumed that mental health arose on the foundation of physical well-being.[73]

In the transitional culture in which Hall lived, the new standards of health and disease bore some of the same burden as the old standards of virtue and vice. The pervasive danger of disease and deviation which Hall and his colleagues pictured hanging over the younger generation had something to it of the old fear of sin. Although the studies of abnormalities in children were themselves meliorist in intent and enlightened in approach, some of the public apparently saw them in a traditional, pejorative light. One expert remarked in 1902 that among people hostile to child study, the movement stood chiefly for the idea that "certain children are peculiar or abnormal."[74]

The other major category of Hall's child study program concerned

71. *Adol,* 1:205.
72. *PS* 4 (1896): 3–40; 5 (1897): 293–98; *PNEA,* 1903, pp. 811–13; 1908, pp. 936–42; 1910, pp. 874–81.
73. Hall's discussions of mental unity drew loosely on the currently popular ideas of Herbart and Janet. *Adol,* 1: 162–63, 240–42, 308–10. In linking mental to physical health, he was following the popular phrenological tradition. See Davies, *Phrenology,* pp. 90–92, 106–17.
74. Frederick E. Bolton, in *PNEA,* 1902, p. 705.

the psychological and behavioral aspects of child development and education, and was most often undertaken in support of greater freedom and self-expression in the school. The formalized methods and traditional moralism of the typical drillmaster teacher were a ready target for his efforts. Hall's desire to establish a genetic psychology also impelled him and others to investigate the basic mental and emotional characteristics of child behavior. In this case, however, practical and theoretical needs were greater than the investigative capacities of psychological science. Hall's questionnaire was the chief method of inquiry. The best of the work produced was useful or suggestive, but the bulk of it was scientifically shoddy and practically worthless. Much of it was done by pedagogs ill trained in scientific techniques, who attempted to follow the letter of Hall's doctrines and methods but lacked his spirit, and so produced more conventional studies.[75] Despite these difficulties, however, substantial areas of useful study were opened.

Some areas of child behavior studied by Hall and his colleagues were specifically relevant to the school and produced tangible results. The study of children's art was achieving considerable vogue in Europe when Hall called attention to the revealing character of children's drawings in his "Contents" study. The subject was taken up early by other child study pedagogs.[76] While drawing had already entered the school curriculum, its goal was to teach the child to accurately reproduce reality and it was conceived in the drillmaster style of practicing lines, geometric figures, and techniques of draftsmanship. Child study investigators concluded that drawing was a form of self-expression for the child and that it naturally began with his drawing of whole figures, particularly the human figure. Hall repeatedly called attention to these conclusions, and his advocacy helped to set in motion the reform of art work in schools

75. For examples of some of the characteristically bad products of child study modeled on Hall's work, but far more conventional in tone, see the work of Dr. Reuben Post Halleck, whom Hall himself criticized, particularly, *PNEA*, 1897, pp. 833–43, and 1898, pp. 354–62; J. R. Street, a Hall student, in *PS* 5 (1897): 5–40, and 6 (1899): 267–313; and Theodate L. Smith, Hall's research assistant, in *PS* 11 (1904): 178–203, and 12 (1905): 27–54.

76. *PNEA*, 1895, pp. 895–98; *PS* 4 (1896): 79–110; Stephen Kern, "Freud and the Emergence of Child Psychology, 1880–1910" (Ph.D. diss., Columbia University, 1970), pp. 242–49.

and the emphasis on artistic self-expression which flowered later in progressive education.[77]

Indeed, Hall studied most school subjects as forms of self-expression. Under his aegis, the child's language was studied empirically and reports made of children's actual production of sounds and vocabularies at various ages, thus laying a foundation for child linguistics.[78] Many studies of what children liked to read and how literature could be used to draw out their natural interests and sentiments appeared. These generally stressed imaginative works and the mythical, heroic, and adventurous subjects which Hall advocated, though often they idealized and sentimentalized children's imaginative interests beyond recognition.[79] Science, too, Hall urged, was to be seen not as a systematic study but as a field in which the child could enlarge his love of nature and express his imaginative awareness of natural forces. This position, too, was often sentimentalized, though the most influential nature study work to come from Clark was a practical and unpoetic manual directing children in a program of raising animals and plants.[80]

Play was an expressive function of childhood stressed by the romantic educational reformers which Hall did much to encourage, by discussing the subject and directing his students' research into children's plays and games. Hall countered the thesis of Karl Groos, the chief authority on play, that children's play was a form of anticipation and practice for their later life tasks. Hall claimed that this was true only in small part and that much of children's play was reversionary expression of earlier activities of the race; thus

77. *PNEA*, 1896, p. 863; 1897, pp. 284–85; *PS* 9 (1902): 296–323.

78. Frederick Tracy, "The Language of Childhood," *AJP* 6 (1893): 107–38; "Children's Interest in Words," *PS* 9 (1902): 274–95; 10 (1903): 359–400; and several studies of child vocabularies, *PS* 11 (1904): 264–91 and ff.; 15 (1908): 63–74; 16 (1909): 64–103.

79. GSH, "Children's Lies," 1890, p. 67; "Address at the Dedication of the Haston Free Public Library Building, North Brookfield, Massachusetts," 1894, pp. 11–21; "Practical Child Study," 1894, pp. 391–92; *PNEA*, 1899, pp. 1044, 1051; 1900, pp. 123–45.

80. GSH, "Nature Study," 1896, pp. 156–58; *Adol*, 2:144–231; Edward L. Thorndike, "Sentimentality in Science Teaching," *ER* 17 (1899): 57–64. Clifton F. Hodge, professor of biology at Clark, developed the manual. It was printed in serial form in *PS* and then as *Nature Study and Life* (Boston: Ginn, 1902), which reportedly sold a million copies. Dutton, "Child-Study Movement," p. 98.

the free expression of these impulses was necessary to the later emergence of more civilized activity.[81]

Hall's insight into the nature of children's play could not be entirely contained, however, in his recapitulatory theory. His questionnaire study of dolls in 1896, for example, remarked that observation of doll play was the royal road to the child's personality. Hall saw that the "small scale of the doll world" allowed the child to work its will unimpeded and thus to project its own feelings and ideals onto the doll, revealing its own individuality more clearly than in real life.[82] Unfortunately, neither Hall nor his students followed this lead in their own later studies.

Ironically, Hall's emphasis on *free* play stemmed partly from his Calvinist conception of work. Hall hoped that work could someday be infused with the interest and zest characteristic of play, but in the meantime he repeatedly described work as a form of punishment, drudgery, and hardship. He thus hoped to keep play a completely different condition. Deweyesque attempts to direct the child's play toward industries and work activities struck him as making play into a kind of work and hence unsuitable.[83]

One of the outgrowths of his view was the serious pedagogical attention directed toward play. One of Hall's students collected thousands of examples of children's play activities and games, graded them according to difficulty and educational by-products, and attempted to make teachers familiar with them and their uses.[84] Several of Hall's disciples founded the playground movement in the late 1890s, which generated wide public support for public playgrounds and supervised recreational programs during off-school hours.[85]

Closely related to the play behavior of children was their tendency to socialize, particularly to form cliques, groups, gangs, clubs, and organizations. These were all natural forms of the child's

81. *Adol*, 1:202–3.
82. GSH and A. Caswell Ellis, "A Study of Dolls," 1896, pp. 160–63.
83. *Adol*, 1:232–33; GSH, "The Natural Activities of Children As Determining the Industries in Early Education," 1904, pp. 443–47.
84. G. E. Johnson, "Education by Plays and Games," *PS* 3 (1894): 97–133. See also *PS* 7 (1900): 459–78.
85. Dr. Luther Gulick and Dr. Henry S. Curtis. See "Clark Alumni Banquet, 1907," p. 32.

social instinct, Hall urged, and a number of his students collected questionnaire data on the typical forms of these groups. As was the case with play, Hall thought this group impulse a heritage of earlier times and less civilized kinds of social ties, and was anxious to keep its expression vigorous and true to the purposes of children and youth. He defended the street gangs of the slums as wholesome if they could be diverted from their criminal activities and urged leaders of youth movements to desist from imposing exclusively religious programs on their members.[86]

Since 1881, when Hall had urged a more "natural" development of the religious sentiment, liberal religious views had also been drawn from child studies. Hall early directed his child study efforts to reform of the Sunday school, and child study conventions in the 1890s often included a Sunday school section. He called for gearing early religious education to Bible stories and the postponement of doctrinal training till adolescence.[87] Not all of his emphases in this area were classically liberal, however. Hall favored an emotional conversion in adolescence. His stress of the animistic and pantheistic religious views of children and youth could be interpreted as endorsement of "superstition," and indeed he sometimes suggested that the Catholic church, with its symbols and rituals, was closer to the heart of the child than any other.[88] Hall's studies of the religious impulse in children and youth urged greater outlets for emotionalism, at the same time that they asked for less doctrinaire and sectarian attitudes.

Hall also found psychological evidence to support the importance he attributed to the biological distinction between the sexes. As evolution advanced, Hall believed, the sexes had diverged more and more sharply. The special role of women as childbearers of the race thus colored his analysis of sex-related differences from child-

86. Henry D. Sheldon, "The Institutional Activities of American Children," *AJP* 9 (1898): 425–48; *PS* 7 (1900): 300–350; *Adol*, 2:397, 428.

87. Barnes, "The Theological Life of a California Child," *PNEA*, 1893, pp. 765–71; *PS* 3 (1896): 363–412; 5 (1897): 293–99; 8 (1901): 440; GSH, "Some New Principles of Sabbath School Work," 1900, pp. 10–12.

88. *Adol*, 2:281–362; *PS* 6 (1899): 267–313; GSH, "Pedagogical Methods in Sunday School Work," 1895, pp. 719–20. Hall's religious views were "disquieting" to Unitarians. *Congregationalist and Christian World* 83 (1901): 169–70; Boston *Evening Transcript*, 31 Oct 1900.

hood onward. Hall himself did several studies of the "budding girl," the young adolescent girl just becoming aware of her femininity, and true to his conventional image of woman, he drew her as a changeable creature, much concerned with her clothes and appearance, who was essentially bored by intellectual subjects and her school studies.[89] In evaluating all the child study investigations, he discovered innate differences so profound as to warrant the separate education of women from puberty onward for their ultimate maternal role.[90] The unpopularity of this position in a profession which had embraced the coeducational high school stimulated a number of studies specifically designed to test Hall's doctrine. They soon showed that what differences there were between the sexes in childhood were either not significant or of a kind that would suggest a joint education as readily as a separate one.[91] Hall nonetheless clung to his Victorian views.

Beyond these more special studies of aspects of child behavior, Hall and other child study workers tried to uncover the more basic structure of emotions and interests characteristic of the childhood years. Hall's own questionnaire studies of children's lies, fears, and anger were the most penetrating of this group. Hall's studies were general attempts to survey a topic, looking out for suggestive facts and possible applications along the way. His data was provided by the thousands of questionnaire returns he sorted, condensed, and quoted at some length, giving the reader a real, if disjointed, sense of the quality and variety of human reactions not often publicly acknowledged. They may have helped to deepen the sensibilities and loosen the traditional moralism of his child study audience.

Hall's study of lies, published in 1890, perhaps the first systematic examination of this subject, was the most attuned to a practical message.[92] Against the traditional, severe proscription of lying, and

89. GSH, "The Awkward Age," 1908, pp. 149–56; "The Budding Girl," 1909, pp. 47–54.
90. *Adol*, 2:561–647; GSH, "Co-education in the High School," *PNEA*, 1903, pp. 446–60. On the widespread scientific belief in great psychological differences between the sexes, see Kern, "Freud and the Emergence of Child Psychology," pp. 101–10.
91. *PS* 3 (1896): 469–82; *PNEA*, 1903, p. 791.
92. GSH, "Children's Lies," 1890, pp. 59–70. See also "Children's Lies:

the drillmaster teacher's mechanical conception of truth, Hall argued that lying was a complex phenomenon and that most instances of lying were of a type that required understanding rather than punishment. Hall insightfully described the child's desire to find "easement from a rather tedious sense of the obligation of undiscriminating, universal and rigorously literal veracity." Many lies, Hall said, are a product of the child's "mythopoeic faculty," his "idealizing temperament," and thus part of the play instinct. "Its control and not its elimination is what is to be sought." Hall suggested severe punishment, physical if necessary, only for lies committed from a desire to show off or attract attention; only when faced with the idea of "self-indulgence" did he revert to the need for "hard and even hated tasks." In his sympathetic insights, as well as his lingering severity, Hall obviously spoke in this study from very personal experience.

The studies on fear and anger had something of the same impact. Hall's study of fears in 1897, one of a number of early systematic treatments of the subject, opened to the view of American readers the great number and range of fears to which children were liable, such as, fears of loss of physical support and orientation, water, animals, darkness, and disease. He discussed their probable causes in the child's own experience and in phylogenetic sources. Withal, Hall concluded, "The dominant impression left by such a study . . . is that of the degrading and belittling effects of excessive fears. . . . The courageous child will not succumb to fears, and has a passion for overcoming them." Hall could not keep from passing the traditional moral judgment and beclouding the enlightened lesson to be learned from his demonstration of the naturalness of childhood fears.[93] Similarly, his discussion of the wide variety of incitements to, and manifestations of, anger tended to support his observation that "anger . . . has its place in normal development." He seemed reluctant, however, to advocate openly any amount of release of anger and opted in the end for control.[94]

Their Psychology and Pedagogy," in *EP*, 1:345–87. Kern, "Freud and the Emergence of Child Psychology," pp. 157–62.

93. GSH, "A Study of Fears," 1897, pp. 147–249; Kern, "Freud and the Emergence of Child Psychology," pp. 151–54.

94. GSH, "A Study of Anger," 1899, pp. 516–91.

Despite these minor notes, Hall's studies opened to the teacher's view whole areas of child experience and motivation she had never before had to consider. Hall himself was clearly impressed by the questionnaire data on fears and was led to stress how "inadequate and partial" the conscious ego is, "a feeble, flickering, taper in a vast factory full of machinery and operatives, each doing its work in unobserved silence."[95] Nonetheless, Hall expected study of the instinct-feelings to put them within reach of conscious direction. Though he admitted that it was an open question "just how far the pent-up energy of anger can be metamorphosed from malignant to benignant work," he drew the conclusion ever after that anger, like love, fear, and all other emotions, could be educated to more realistic and constructive responses and goals.[96]

Such studies of lies, fears, and anger were meant to be studies not only of the child's basic emotional patterns but also of what Hall called juvenile "faults and vices." Just as feelings of fear and tendencies to lie were seen as inherited adjustments to an earlier animistic and savage past, now somewhat dysfunctional in modern civilization, the more extended range of faults from truancy to swearing, fighting, and even stealing were given a similar interpretation. With many of the minor vices, Hall took an even more lenient attitude, believing that if they were not allowed some juvenile expression, the natural means of controlling them would not then be developed. Hall did not always make clear whether the child must give them direct expression or only "vicarious cathartic expression," but he did argue that boys, at least, had to be allowed mild exploratory lies, truancy, slang, swearing, fighting, and the like.[97]

The focus of this analysis on natural forms of behavior which were out of keeping with the moral standards of the culture in which they appeared opened the way for a number of Hall's students to argue for a social view of juvenile delinquency and crim-

95. "Fears," 1897, p. 246.
96. "Anger," 1899, pp. 55, 75; "The Education of the Heart," 1899, pp. 31–38. See also *PS* 3 (1894): 330.
97. *Adol,* 1:325–410, 2:452–53; GSH, "Feminization in School and Home," 1908; *PS* 10 (1903): 200–266. On the problem of "vicarious cathartic expression," see Robert E. Grinder, "The Concept of Adolescence in the Genetic Psychology of G. Stanley Hall," *Child Development* 40 (1969): 359.

inality in general. As one student concluded, "The child is not a criminal. He has tendencies which are antagonistic to modern social standards." Since all inherit these tendencies, it is the environment in which the child is raised that makes him delinquent. The rigid environment which condemned these atavistic impulses, or the ignorant, poverty-stricken, and criminal environment which encouraged their overdevelopment were responsible for crime, not the inherited impulses themselves.[98] The staunchest advocate of this line of reasoning declared that "it is doubtful whether in three-quarters of the cases criminal tendencies are anything else than a convenient name with which to cover our social failure in education.[99] Hall himself accepted this environmental analysis, and in the area of adolescent delinquency, developed a relatively sophisticated social theory of criminality, though he also retained remnants of the hereditary degeneracy theory of Lombroso.[100]

Hall's studies of the natural impulses of the child were intended to serve a basic theoretical purpose, as well as a practically liberating one. Hall hoped the child study movement would uncover the "nascent periods" of the various powers and interests of the mind, the schedule of times at which they grow most rapidly and hence are most impressionable. He had early formed an idea of the development of the religious impulse, and he expected that a similar genetic scheme could be discovered for all the child's mental appetites. From the beginning he told his child study supporters that his

98. *PNEA*, 1904, p. 798. For other studies by Hall students see *PS* 8 (1901): 65–91, 350, and *PNEA*, 1898, pp. 910–16. Judge Ben Lindsey of Denver, founder of the juvenile court, agreed with this reasoning. *PNEA*, 1909, p. 742. Hall claimed that Judge Lindsey told him that "our literature has been the lamp to his feet." *PNEA*, 1908, p. 950. Earlier, Hall's students had given currency to degeneracy theories of criminal anthropology. Arthur MacDonald, docent in criminology at Clark, 1889–91, and afterward assistant in the U.S. Bureau of Education, popularized degeneracy theory in *Criminology* (New York: Funk and Wagnall's, 1893). George E. Dawson in *PS* 4 (1896): 221–58, concluded that both bad environment and bad heredity were involved.

99. *PNEA*, 1898, p. 910.

100. *Adol*, 1:325–410, particularly, pp. 340–44, 406–10. See also GSH, "Psychological Education," 1896, p. 235: "Strong souls can have, dominate, and use what in less developed ones would be disquieting symptoms of defect and disease. [Lombroso's idea of] perfect sanity . . . would not only be uninteresting but ineffective."

science would provide them with this chart of natural development, and they eagerly awaited such a definitive guide for all basic decisions on curricula and methods of teaching.[101]

Hall's own questionnaire studies did not yield the desired blueprint. In only a few instances did Hall feel his data trustworthy enough to distinguish patterns of feeling or behavior according to age. Often he suggested that a child's impulse was a hereditary survival from a much earlier age and that it had features in common with certain characteristics of primitive cultures, but he was never able to show that the timetable of evolution indicated to what age of childhood the impulse belonged.

Other investigators tried different approaches to the problem. Earl Barnes in 1892 had teachers question their pupils to discover their personal ideal. He found that the younger child's ideal was a chum or close personal acquaintance, while as the child grew older, he looked to the social and political order for his ideal figures. Girls, he discovered, increasingly chose masculine ideals. This study was often replicated with substantially similar results; Barnes did it again in England, where his results varied from the American pattern, showing the importance of different cultural and educational influences on children in the two countries.[102]

More specific studies attempted to locate by age the child's interest in particular subjects and types of phenomena. Series of studies were done in which children were asked to name and give reasons for their favorite selection in the school reader, or their favorite books. These led into somewhat more objective investigations of what books children actually drew from libraries, which selection from the reader they remembered best, or on which kinds of subjects they wrote the best themes. All of these studies yielded some interesting criteria as to the kinds of stories which children found appealing, but they did not reveal any uniform age-related pattern of specific interests in children.[103]

101. GSH, "New Departures in Education," 1885, p. 150; "Phi Beta Kappa Oration," 1891, p. 112; "Practical Child Study," 1894, pp. 391–92.

102. Barnes, *Studies in Education*, vol. 2; *PS* 7 (1900): 3–12; 10 (1903): 101–40; *PNEA*, 1903, pp. 754–59.

103. *PNEA*, 1895, pp. 904–5; 1899, pp. 1044–51; *PS* 7 (1900): 357–96; Barnes, *Studies in Education*, 2:203–12.

Those in and out of the movement who studied the data carefully saw that many of the results reflected what the child thought the teacher wanted to hear. Large numbers of choices and reasons, for example, were highly moralistic.[104] Some investigators also began to see that the results showed how the environment had trained the child's interest, far more than they disclosed any innate pattern of sensitivities.[105]

Hall's failure to produce this blueprint for education loomed increasingly large amidst the often vague and contradictory findings of child study. Nonetheless, Hall continued to predict, as hope waned through the decade, that a schedule of nascent periods was "impending."[106] The age span that could have proved most fruitful for a study of specific "nascent periods," of course, was the first six years of life, the period excluded of necessity from both the teacher-oriented child study movement and the questionnaire method. One of Hall's students, Arnold Gesell, escaped these limitations and later fulfilled something of Hall's ambition.

Although this most sought-after result of the movement was not achieved, a general picture of the child did emerge from Hall's studies, a picture that was echoed in much of the child study literature. The dominant characteristic of this child was its imagination. Motivated by strong feelings and impulses, the child lived in a world apart from adult civilized society and filled his experience with imaginative reconstructions of his inner and outer worlds. Even at the times when the child hungered for facts and seemed to take the world at face value, his attitudes and interests stemmed from more exotic needs. His impulses and fancies often roused the suspicion and hostility of the adult world; yet they represented the authentic line of development the child must take and education ought to follow.

There was in this picture, surely, beyond the familiar romantic portrait of the child, an echo of Hall's own childhood as an imaginative boy, living out his fantasies among the primitive pursuits of the farm, terribly conscious of how out of place and misunderstood his feelings and dreams were in the adult world immediately around

104. *PNEA*, 1898, p. 901; 1899, p. 1044.
105. Ibid., 1898, p. 901; *PS* 5 (1898): 497–511; 11 (1904): 498–507.
106. GSH, "Resumé of Child Study," 1899, pp. 347–49.

him. Perhaps Hall hoped to recover in this image his own lost childhood and the line of healthful development he had somehow lost.
His conception of childhood represented, too, a refuge for the impulses that still swept him beyond the sober conduct approved by
his professional peers. Hall gloried that unlike his "parched and
bankrupt" guild, children, at least, could show regret, boast and
brag, vigorously attack their enemies, embroider and evade the
truth—all characteristics of his own unprofessional behavior, now
justified, perhaps, by the design of nature.[107]

As the child study movement proceeded into the twentieth century, Hall increasingly focused his attention on adolescence. He was
able to discern in all the child study data a broad expansion of
interests and feelings occurring roughly at early adolescence. What
differentiated this stage of growth from earlier childhood was the
adolescent's larger social reference, his turn from self-absorption to
concern for others, and particularly, the importance of love, rather
than the earlier, more savage feelings. But underneath this new
portrait, Hall extended to adolescence the imaginative character of
childhood and his idealization of it as "the paradise of the race."[108]

107. GSH and T. L. Smith, "Showing Off and Bashfulness As Phases of Self-
Consciousness," 1903, pp. 197–98.
108. GSH, "Note on Early Memories," 1899, p. 496.

16 FROM INFANCY TO ADOLESCENCE

It was not until a decade of child study investigation had passed, and the failures of the movement were as visible as its strengths, that Hall drew together his suggestions into a comprehensive scheme of education. It was, perhaps, the persistingly fragmentary character of the child study findings that forced him to present his followers with a coherent pedagogy. The main thrust of Hall's message, however, even when it was not tied directly to pedagogy, had pervaded his earlier work, and Hall declared that "something like this has from the first animated all my own feeble educational endeavors."[1]

In 1901, Hall presented to the NEA and then published in the *Forum* his conception of "The Ideal School As Based on Child Study." He followed this piece the next year at the NEA with a summation of his views on secondary education, called "The High School As the People's College." Both these articles were widely circulated and acclaimed. Two years later, in 1904, Hall published his long-awaited two-volume study, *Adolescence.* An expansion of many aspects of his ideal educational program, *Adolescence* went far beyond to a comprehensive description of adolescent development and Hall's version of genetic psychology.

Hall's opening message in his essay of 1901, "The Ideal School"

1. GSH, "The Ideal School As Based on Child Study," 1901. Unless otherwise noted, the material below which refers to Hall's ideal school is found in this article.

—and always his principal message—was the injunction to follow nature. "Childhood as it comes fresh from the hand of God, is not corrupt, but illustrates the survival of the most consummate thing in the world." It followed from this ideal view of child nature that "the guardians of the young should strive first of all to keep out of nature's way." They should seek the "prolongation of human infancy, and the no whit less important prolongation of adolescence." Every invasion of this natural and leisurely course of development "has a certain presumption against it, and must justify itself by conclusive reasons." By thus asserting the priority of nature, Hall set nature against three ideals he meant also to include in his educational theory: civilization, democracy, and intellect. Hall stated the claims of nature so fervently, it was sometimes difficult to see the ways in which he brought these countervailing ideals into his vision.

Most of Hall's audience knew, however, as he often did himself, that if child nature was not corrupt, it was not totally good and uniformly ideal either; and that if the presumption must lie with nature, civilization, too, had some claims. Hall acquiesced to the child's learning to read at eight because "even if it be prematurely, he must be subject to special disciplines and be apprenticed to the higher qualifications of adulthood, for he is not only a product of nature, but a candidate for a highly developed humanity."[2] In *Adolescence,* Hall stated explicitly that discovery of the natural pattern of development of the child was only the first step toward an educational prescription. After that, he said, "we must decide" which element to allow to atrophy and which to encourage, for child nature as a whole and for each individual child.[3]

Hall was really telling his audience that on the inevitable continuum of nature and civilization, the balance ought to be weighted toward nature, and that the educator's decision to curtail or distort nature ought to be made only after a careful study of child development revealed the true character and direction of the impulses involved. Among educational theorists of the time, Dewey said later, the prescription to follow nature always implicitly acknowledged

2. *Adol,* 1:xi–xii.
3. *Adol,* 2:152.

the claims of society, but these claims were usually unarticulated.[4] Perhaps, for all the rising doubt and unease, men like Hall could still take for granted the structure of social and moral values around them. Certainly, the average American teacher did not need to be reminded of her civilizing function.

Against nature, Hall also posed the democratic doctrine of equal education for all. In an era of social Darwinism, Hall considered inequality the decree of nature, and democracy, the difficult and precarious achievement of civilization. Nature endowed children with differing capacities, Hall argued, and hence required different kinds and levels of education for each. All children had a right to be educated to the limit of their capacities, but not beyond. The kind of intellectual education which led to college was a vanity sought by multitudes who could be only harmed by it. "I would bring discrimination down to the very basis of our educational pyramid," he declared.

Hall adapted this view to the popular democracy of his constituents through the concept of "individualization." Throughout this period, he spoke of it as the key concept of the new education. For Hall, it meant educational methods adjusted to all the child's individual variations of age, sex, ability, and vocational expectation. He could advocate by this standard, methods geared to the natural stages of development of the child and its individual rate of progress. He could also justify on the grounds of individual variation such conservative measures as separate education for young women and a pyramidal educational structure with primary education for all, varied vocational and technical schools available for many on the secondary level, and collegiate and university instruction available only to those few with the highest scholastic ability.[5]

Hall's elitism based on nature fit well with the essentially moral and long-range goals Hall set for the educational process as a whole.

4. Camp and Mayhew, *The Dewey School*, p. 465. Thorndike pointed out that Hall did not abide by his own dogma but instead sensibly and insightfully urged that nature be abridged and shaped to civilized ends. Thorndike, "The Newest Psychology," *ER* 28 (1904): 221.
5. See also GSH, "Phi Beta Kappa Oration," 1891; "New Movement in Education," 1891.

Hall and the conservative disciples who echoed him clearly opposed any leveling, "socialistic" legislation.[6] What Hall hoped from his ideal school was a kind of "reformation," a human regeneration effected by the slow processes of education, and from that, the elevation of the race to "the higher maturity of the superman that is to be." Hall's inegalitarianism and his view of human progress as a long-range process of moral rejuvenation rather than one of immediate social and political action made his educational message politically conservative.

Within the social realm over which parents and educators ruled, however, Hall's message was one of meliorism. If nature provided the substance of the developing personality, the environment could ennoble or distort it at will. In America, hereditarian theories often led to environmentalist prescriptions. Hall's message put enormous pressure on teachers and parents to provide, as he said in *Adolescence,* "the most favorable environment and eliminate every possible cause of arrest or reversion."[7] If genius was possible for only a few, physical and mental health and development to the limit of one's capacity were within the range of all, if only the nurturing environment was sufficiently alert and informed. In this sense, Hall's message was characteristically liberal and democratic, shaping into modern and scientific form the belief in the possibility of improvement espoused since the rise of evangelical Protestantism and popular democracy. Weighted with the hope of individual advancement and the whole biological progress of the race, the tasks of child-rearing and education became for Hall the central tasks of life. All doctrines and all institutions of society, he constantly urged, were to be judged chiefly by their effects on the rearing and education of the young.

Nature also meant to Hall a devaluation of the intellect and of learning in comparison to the virtue, health, and sentiment that were nature's gifts. If the presumption was in favor of nature, Hall said of his ideal school,

We must overcome the fetichism of the alphabet, of the multiplication table, of grammars, of scales, and of bibliolatry, and must reflect that but

6. "Reports of the Plato Club," 1894, pp. 13–14; *PNEA,* 1902, p. 725.
7. *Adol,* 1:89.

a few generations ago the ancestors of all of us were illiterate. . . . that
scholars have argued that Cornelia, Ophelia, Beatrice, and even the blessed
mother of our Lord knew nothing of letters.

Hall's romanticism constantly carried him into sentimental idealizations of ignorance. Hall did not even notice the irony of attributing
the illiteracy of his female heroines to the findings of scholarship.
Science always remained for Hall the very apex of civilization, the
highest product of evolution, and yet its claims could not quite
reach the springs of his nostalgic yearning. Although intellectual
training had, in a very real sense, set Hall free, he could not help
but distrust its tendency toward ruthless destruction of the past in
which his sentiments were still rooted. Like Dewey, and other
scholars of their generation, he could celebrate the wings of enlightenment only if the intellect was tied firmly to the ground of real
life, concrete experience, and human sentiment.

The chief thrust of Hall's argument, however, as of Dewey's, was
not against intellect per se but against the restricted form of it which
prevailed in the schools. They urged a wider, freer kind of intellectual endeavor—in Hall's case, one more akin to the imagination
and more attuned to the feelings; in Dewey's case, one more related
to the social, problem-solving experiences of real life. Yet neither
was willing to exalt these processes as intellectual functions. Hall
most often spoke of his program for freely educating the imagination as a training of the feelings rather than the intellect; and Dewey
constantly drowned the expanding, conceptualizing intellect in
praise of experience.

Despite this romantic devaluation of intellect, Hall was simultaneously attached to the ideal of science and the high intellectual
standards of the university, and he simultaneously urged their claims
in education. His romantic pleas to follow nature were joined to
the demand for better intellectual training for teachers. He always
believed that the child craved intellectual substance of a high order,
though of varying kinds at different stages of development, and he
saw intellectual pleasures as the natural outcome of a properly
natural education:

The native interests and fresh eager curiosities of children are the sacred
buds of mental growth and should not be blighted by the dismal, dry
method work, which gives form where substance is asked for, and slowly

but surely breeds apathy, indifference and distaste for the exquisite pleasures of intellectual activity.[8]

In Hall's scheme, the university remained the refuge of pure intellectual training, while the schools below were to adapt intellectual materials to the impulses of child nature. Hall's entire program can be read as an attempt to develop intellect within the confines and categories of a romantically conceived child nature. It was a characteristically Hallian attempt to synthetically join the two poles of his own inclination and of educational theory.

Hall's conception of education outlined in "The Ideal School" conveyed this complex sense of the natural education needed in the schools. The kindergarten stage, Hall believed, should last from age two or three through seven, for he sensed at about the age of six "amid the increased instabilities of health . . . the ripple-marks of an ancient pubic beach now lifted high above the tides of a receding shore-line as human infancy has been prolonged."[9] He thus wanted these difficult transition years included in infancy rather than childhood proper. Hall conceived the kindergarten in the manner of what has become the classical progressive nursery school. In place of premature learning to read and write, he argued, or of the orthodox Froebelian "magic mongering" with the symbolic meaning of cubes and spheres, he suggested a wide variety of free-play activities, much firsthand contact with plant and animal life, adequate periods of rest, and ample snacks to "save the disposition" and provide lessons in table manners. Moreover, "Children should hear far more English and better and in the later years the ear should be trained for French or German." In healthful exercise, free play, and oral instruction in nature study and language conducted exclusively through the medium of exploring the world immediately around him, the child was getting, Hall thought, the best kind of preparation for intellectual, emotional, and physical development.

The period from about eight to twelve years Hall named the "juvenile" stage, a period of slower physical growth and relative stability, reminiscent of "some remote age . . . when our early forebears were well adjusted to their environment . . . before a higher

8. GSH, "Editorial," *PS* 2 (1892): 4.
9. *Adol*, 1:x.

and much more modern story was added to human nature." This period Hall thought was uniquely suited to the "drill, habituation and mechanism" necessary to acquire the rudiments of civilized knowledge. This was the period for intensive instruction in reading, writing, and arithmetic, though less drill was required in these elements than the nineteenth-century school imposed. If the child appeared capable, one or two modern foreign languages should be begun, taught by the oral method, and again if capable, Latin could be begun at ten and Greek at twelve. In all these studies, teaching methods should try to "show," "demonstrate," and not "explain," Hall urged, for "reason is still very undeveloped. The child's mind is at a stage when there is little in it that has not been brought in by way of sense." Here, then, was the place for that discipline, will, and authoritarianism Hall never wanted entirely to relinquish.

At the same time, however, Hall urged leaving plenty of "space and time" for what was "spontaneous and voluntary." This was the period of "tribal, predatory, hunting, fishing, fighting, roving, idle, playing, proclivities," which should be "developed in their season so that we should be immune to them in maturer years."[10] Hall thus wanted much free time left for play and spontaneous organizations. Within the school, drawing should be "a real expression of the child's soul, and the child would copy what he, and not what the adult, sees." Music should initially be taught as pure singing rather than note reading, that is, to educate the sentiments.

Most important, language should be taught always as a means of expression and not as a formal discipline. The student should "live in a world of sonorous speech" and keep reading and writing "subordinate to hearing and speaking." The child should only be asked to speak and write on themes upon which he feels strongly. "Our end is the cultivation of expression," Hall claimed, even if that expression be the vivid slang which comes "fresh from the mint where all words were made." The teacher, moreover, must be an expert storyteller, so that "the tales of Ulysses, Orestes, Siegfried, Thor, King Arthur and his Knights . . . perhaps Dante . . . perhaps some legends from ancient India . . . something from Grimm" all become familiar to the schoolboy. "I believe in the ethical virtue of

10. Ibid.

these things almost as I believe in the Bible, for they sink deep and transform," Hall declared. "Such stories discipline the heart and the attention at the same time, and implant a taste for good reading and a distaste for bad."

Thus, Hall pictured the latency period as a time of intensive intellectual instruction, instruction which would both impose rudimentary drill and elicit spontaneous self-expression. He retained a substantial dose of the traditional, mechanical learning, but circumscribed in time and supplemented by broader appeal to the feelings and imagination. The unitary methodology of education sought by Dewey and most of the progressive educators Hall explicitly left sundered at this stage of education into two distinct types which theoretically could coexist without infringing one upon the other.

In the area of adolescence, Hall called for a total break with traditional education. Beginning with puberty at thirteen and fourteen, and extending on into the twenties until sexual and social maturity was reached, this stage had always been closest to Hall's personal concern. Comments on adolescents and questionnaire studies on their interests had from the start been part of Hall's child study work, but the primary focus of the child study movement and of nearly all its support among educators was in primary education and the normal education of primary teachers. Around 1901, however, Hall began to turn his attention more frequently to secondary education and adolescence.

Apparently, Hall shifted his focus at this time because of his growing disillusion with the results of his child study efforts. In 1899, he began to object publicly to what many of his followers were doing in his name. It was almost inevitable that Hall should find himself in disagreement with some of the results of child study. The complexity of his theories assured the fact that those who heard him would often misunderstand his meaning, or would extract from his whole theory those things which supported their own inclinations, ignoring the ways in which every strain of his thinking was hedged about with different, limiting considerations. Hall's program, moreover, had never entirely represented the whole child study effort.

Speaking to a major convocation of teachers at the Chicago Kindergarten College in 1899, Hall denounced the excess of sentimentality and lax discipline which was being urged in the name of child study.[11] Educators agreed that "invariably . . . the maximum of child study has resulted in the minimum of child punishment."[12] Yet despite this most popular belief of his adherents, Hall persistently opposed the abandonment of physical punishment, at home and in the schools. All adult authority implicitly rested on superior physical power, he believed, and when that authority was challenged seriously and deliberately, physical punishment was necessary to maintain it. There were more damaging punishments inflicted by enlightened parents and by nature herself, Hall remarked frequently, than a little dermal pain.[13]

Nor should the civilized virtues be carried to excess, Hall told the Chicago teachers. The child must be allowed to fight and to hit back rather than turn the other cheek. Hall also criticized the sentimental children's books which appeared in droves to meet his findings about the animistic character of children's thought. As one listener reported Hall's words:

All that rot they teach to children about the little raindrop fairies with their buckets washing down the window panes must go. We need less sentimentality and more spanking. We are going child study mad.[14]

Though Hall himself often pandered to the sentimentalism of his popular audiences, he did not like the "sissified" version of his romanticism that resulted. He began to urge that the feminization of the teaching force was responsible for this kind of outlook and was a great danger in the schools, especially for boys.[15]

Hall's remarks caused a furor in Chicago, as the press broadcast his views under "startling headlines." The board of education promptly refused to dismiss teachers to attend the remaining sessions "where such alleged barbarisms were upheld."[16] A leading educational journal labeled Hall's ideas "reactionary." The direction of

11. GSH, "Education of the Heart," etc., 1899; "Corporal Punishments," 1899.

12. *PNEA*, 1893, p. 772. See also, 1895, pp. 262–63; *PS* 3 (1894): 47.

13. See also *Adol*, 2:534; GSH, "Anger," 1899, p. 64.

14. *New York Education* 3 (Nov 1899): 165.

15. GSH, "Some Dangers in Our Educational System and How to Meet Them," 1907, pp. 667–68; "Feminization in School and Home," 1908.

16. *Kindergarten Magazine* 11 (1899): 599–600.

modern culture is toward increasing refinement, the journal declared, not toward Hall's exaltation of physical strength.[17] Theodore Roosevelt, however, then governor of New York, wrote Hall personally to commend him on the "sound common sense, decency and manliness" of his views.[18]

In 1900, Hall also began to express himself on other aspects of the liberal, democratic, and humanitarian direction in which education was moving. The "extremely wide" application of the principle of public education for all, Hall feared, had gone too far.[19] So, too, had the teacher's concern for the most dull and difficult of her students. Pity was misdirected at

the undervitalized poor . . . moribund sick, defectives and criminals, because by aiding them to survive it interferes with the process of wholesome natural selection by which all that is best has hitherto been developed. . . . Pity has its highest office then in removing the handicaps from those most able to help man to higher levels . . . in ushering in the kingdom of the superman. The mission of pity in the world today is to minister to the needs of elite youth at the stage of later adolescence . . . to add to human euphoria

17. *New York Education* 3 (Dec 1899): 226–27.
18. Theodore Roosevelt to GSH, 29 Nov 1899, GSH Memorial Volume, CUP. The letter reads in full: "My dear Dr. Hall—I must write you to thank you for your sound common sense, decency and manliness in what you advocate for the education of children. Over-sentimentality, over-softness, in fact, washiness and mushiness are the great dangers of this age and of this people. Unless we keep the *barbarian virtues*, gaining the civilized ones will be of little avail. I am particularly glad that you emphasize the probable selfishness of a milksop. My experience has been that weak and effeminate men are quite as apt to have undesirable qualities as strong and vigorous men. I thoroughly believe in cleanliness and decency, and I utterly disbelieve in brutality and cruelty, but I feel we cannot too strongly insist upon the need of the rough, manly virtues. A nation that cannot fight is not worth its salt, no matter how cultivated and refined it may be, and the very fact that it can fight often obviates the necessity of fighting. It is just so with a boy. Moreover when it comes to discipline, I cordially agree with you as to the need of physical punishment. It is not necessary often to have recourse to it, but it is absolutely necessary that the child should realize that at need it will be resorted to. With my own children (who I think I can say, are devoted to me, and who are close and intimate friends) I invariably have to punish them once physically so as to make them thoroughly understand that I will unhesitatingly resort to such punishment if they make it necessary. After that by treating them with justice, which implies firmness as well as mercy, I hardly ever have to proceed to extremities again.
Mrs. Roosevelt is as much pleased with what you say as I am."
19. Worcester *Gazette,* 8 Jan 1900.

so that the plateau of the best half of the race will be high, so that the summits of human possibility may be easier attained.[20]

Equal education for all and special attention to the needy were contrary to the elitist character of evolution.

It may well be that Hall's growing distaste around the turn of the century for what educators were doing to the elementary schools led him to turn his attention to secondary education in the following years. The high school was still not overrun with female teachers and democratic aspirations. Hall was, moreover, completing his major book on adolescence; if the elementary teachers had misconstrued his meaning, perhaps those in the high schools would be more amenable to persuasion.

As earlier with primary education, the situation in the secondary schools which Hall addressed was ripe for an articulate spokesman of change. Public high schools had begun to appear in some number after the Civil War, but between 1880 and 1900 the number of such schools increased 750 percent. At that date about 12 percent of the high-school-age population was in the schools. Amid this rapid expansion, a chaos of variety in curriculum and standards existed. In 1894, the same year that saw the establishment of the Child Study Department at the NEA, a Committee of Ten outlined to the NEA a program of reform for secondary education. Chaired by Charles W. Eliot of Harvard and staffed by academic experts rather than educational administrators, the committee sought both to raise the level of high school work to a standard acceptable for entrance to the better colleges and to broaden the traditional college's acceptance of high school work beyond the standard preparatory courses of Latin, Greek, and mathematics.[21]

The committee's recommendations had a profound effect in shaping high school education in three areas. To introduce uniform standards the committee counted hours per week per subject, and years per study, as a uniform coin for judging preparation. They recommended four "courses" or lines of study the student could

20. GSH and F. H. Saunders, "Pity," 1900, pp. 590–91.
21. On the character of secondary education and the work of the Committee of Ten, see Theodore R. Sizer, *Secondary Schools at the Turn of the Century* (New Haven: Yale University Press, 1964).

pursue, and set them up in such a way that a core—more or less common to all four courses—should occupy the first two years of study, with greater freedom for electives in the last two years. Finally, the committee set up all four courses as, in effect, college preparatory courses. Whether or not the student was planning to go on to college, the committee thought, he would benefit most from having the subject taught in a manner suitable for college preparation. All four courses had a heavy bias toward languages, though the range of subjects widened from Latin and mathematics to include English, modern foreign languages, the modern sciences—physics, chemistry, and biology—and history. It was in urging the disciplinary value of these more modern subjects, and their suitability for college entrance, that the committee showed its chief liberality.

Until around 1910, perhaps, the committee's ideal dominated secondary educational circles, and high school programs all over the country showed an increasing approximation to the suggested curriculum organized into alternative courses. Even before that time, however, the pressure of mounting numbers of students who did not plan to go on to college, began to erode the committee's ideal. The standardization of subject units, and the organization of them around a core from which elective alternatives led in several directions would remain, but the college-oriented, language-centered curriculum would be diluted and fragmented.[22]

From its first appearance, Stanley Hall attacked the major premises of the committee report,[23] but it was not until 1901 that he began to issue more systematic criticisms of the high school and its subservience to the committee's ideal. His central objection was the subordination of the high school to the goal of college entrance and the preconceptions of college educators. The high school, as part of the ideal school, ought to be adapted to the distinct needs of adolescence, Hall insisted, and these were entirely different from the "uniformity and inflexibility," the "artificial programme . . . fitting not for the world but for college" which the committee had inspired.

22. Dewey, *Educational Situation*, pp. 50–79; Lawrence Cremin, "The Revolution in American Secondary Education, 1893–1918," *Teachers College Record* 56 (Mar 1955): 295–308.
23. GSH, "Remarks on the Report of the Committee of Ten," 1894.

Though himself an elitist, Hall's criticisms of the "unnatural" program of the intellectualists rode the rising tide of democracy in the high schools. It was altogether characteristic of Hall, therefore, that he should choose to call the major presentation of his high school program to the NEA in Chicago in 1902, "The High School As the People's College." Hall could not resist shaping his message to popular demand. According to an astute observer, Hall "gained perceptibly" in his popularity at the NEA Chicago meeting "by the choice of his topic," for "the entire West is charged . . . with fervor when the people's rights are championed."[24] Hall not only permitted confusion by the complexity of his views, he invited it by exploiting those views opportunistically.

In the high school, Hall asserted, education must make a complete break with drill and mechanism. The appeal must be to "freedom and interest. Individuality must have a far longer tether." Beyond that, the youth should be exposed to large, substantial doses of information: "facts, ideas, laws, and principles should be in the very atmosphere, for they are now the ingenuous youth's native breath. . . . He is all insight and receptivity." By the same token, however, the school should "let up on examination" and not require skill and accuracy. The power to appreciate and apprehend was greater than the power to reproduce accurately. "The fundamentals of the soul, which are instinct and intuition, and not pure intellect, are now in season." Evidently insight and curiosity were functions more of the adolescent's feelings and drives than of his intellect.[25]

In *Adolescence,* however, Hall made it clear that feelings were to nourish, not supercede, serious thought. If the adolescent

has no resources in solitude, cannot think without the visual provocation, is losing subjective life, enthusiasm for public, social, ethical questions, is crippled for intellectual pursuits, cares only in a languid way for literary prose and poetry, responds only to sensuous stimuli and events at short range, and is indifferent to all wide relations and moral responsibility, cares only for commercial self-interest, the tactics of field sport, laboratory occupations . . . then the school is dwarfing, in dawning maturity, the higher powers that belong to this stage of development.[26]

24. *Journal of Education* 55 (Mar 1902): 167–68.
25. "The Ideal School," 1901.
26. *Adol*, 2:465.

His call was for a different kind of intellectual education in the high school, lax in the more traditional intellectual standards but containing greater intellectual substance.

Hall's ideal of an intellectual life grounded in the feelings was almost always coupled with a severe critique of the ordinary high school teacher and his normal school training. Repeatedly Hall declared that "inadequate knowledge on the teacher's part is the chief high-school evil which instinctively seeks shelter, dignity, and ease in formalism."[27] The adolescent soul, Hall believed, "naturally storms its way to the center of things with a rapid impetuosity, but the methodaster and macerator blunts the intuitions." Not only the formalized methods of the high school teacher, Hall claimed, but his constant attention to objects of sense and to concrete things near in time and space, killed the youth's higher intellectual powers.[28]

Hall's ideal was the German secondary school teacher, who held a doctorate in his subject and was "a living fountain, not a stagnant pool." Hall wanted to abolish the lesson setting and recitations tied to inferior textbooks which American drillmaster teachers employed, and to make the teacher a real source of information. The intellectual standards of the whole system ought to be upgraded, Hall declared. The college teacher with a Ph.D. ought to teach in high school, the better educated high school teacher in primary grades, and so on down the line.[29]

The high school curriculum Hall recommended in his outline of the ideal "People's College" in 1902 was as radical a departure from the schools then in existence as was his intellectual spirit.[30] Hall's first point of attack was the great emphasis on the study of Latin in three of the committee's four courses, and in the high schools themselves, where large numbers of students sought to acquire this universal emblem of intellectual culture. For those who could and would go deeply into the study of antiquity, Hall felt the training

27. GSH, "How Far Is the Present High School and Early College Training Adapted to the Nature and Needs of Adolescents?" 1901, p. 656.
28. *Adol*, 2:462–65, 496.
29. "The Ideal School," 1901.
30. The high school program described below is also taken from GSH, "How Far Is the Present High School," 1901; GSH, "The Secondary School Curriculum," 1903; and *Adol,* 2:449–527.

entirely worthwhile, but for most who took it, it was no more than
a "sanctified relic," devoid of intellectual substance.

> It is a cheap subject to teach and can be made respectable and impressive
> to the pupil by less knowledge on the teacher's part than almost any other
> subject. . . . It is admirably adapted to the worst side of the recitation method
> now in vogue.[31]

The core of the curriculum, Hall felt, should be moved radically
toward the modern subjects and should consist only of three basic
subjects: English, science, and motor training.

English here, as in the lower school, should eschew formal language study for large amounts of reading, medieval legend, drama,
and oratory. Science should postpone the logical development of the
structure of the basic sciences until later, and teach astronomy,
geology, and biology as descriptions of our universe, with much
factual information, outline of basic theories, and historical, biographical treatment of the heroes of the science. Motor training
should include time for free play and sport; and a more vital
manual-training program should center on making toys and simple
scientific instruments of use in the school. History, mathematics,
modern languages, and all else besides this basic core should be left
to the students' elective choice.

If all students were educated in this "genetic" core, Hall said,
then those going to college and those not going on would each get
an equally sound education. Presumably they would be differentiated
in the kinds of electives they chose for Hall believed the majority
should have a vocational education. The college, in turn, ought to
take in anyone who wanted to come but graduate only those who
could meet its high standards. Thus, the high school curriculum
could shape itself to adolescents' real needs and ignore any uniform
prescriptions as to types of subjects and time devoted to them.

Although Hall spoke less often about college education, he believed that the college years, as a period of middle or late adolescence, ought to be subject to a similar regime as the high school.
The growing specialization of the college, with its introduction of
the new scientific knowledge into the curriculum was contrary to the

31. GSH, "The Secondary School Curriculum," 1903, p. 7.

needs of youth, Hall felt, and hence he advocated an updated form of the older curriculum of the nineteenth-century college. Philosophy and science ought to be taught as "cosmology or the philosophy of nature," with a broad outline of each science placed in a larger, evolutionary framework. The goal was to excite interest over a wide surface rather than to train in the exacting techniques of specialized scholarship.[32] From a radical critique of the old college while a young, aspiring scientist, Hall thus came full circle to become an appreciative defender of its merits. In the affairs of his own Williams College, Hall now supported the conservative alumni who wanted to halt the modernization of the college.[33] It was not the new knowledge itself that Hall opposed but its technically scientific form. Only in graduate school could the claims of logic, systematic conceptualization, and scientific method be finally and wholly met, and even there, if Clark University is the model, Hall opted for broad stimulation as well as careful specialization.[34]

Hall's plan of reform, unlike Dewey's, thus encompassed secondary as well as primary education and perhaps departed more from the existing school in the later than in the earlier stages. His educational goals were exceedingly complex. Beginning in the kindergarten years, when the child-centered program included spoken French and German, on through the college and university, where specialization often gave way to broadly humane interests, Hall offered a varied mixture of sweeping romantic rhetoric and ambitious intellectualism, of individualistic concern for the needs of each child and elitist judgments of educational goals. Hall's program of wide interests, rooted in the feelings, unencumbered with logical exactions, and yet reaching a high intellectual order, strikingly resembled his own intellectual style. On a personal level, Hall's peculiar genius made the pattern a success. As a system of pedagogy it had irremediable failings, as his own teaching in this style at Clark University would show.

Hall's educational theory nonetheless drew attention to a central problem of education—the extent to which curiosity and genuine intellectual growth are dependent upon their ties to the child's feel-

32. *Adol*, 2:527–54.
33. Perry, *Williamstown and Williams College*, p. 837.
34. See *LCP*, pp. 363–66, 373, 429.

ings and imagination. Hall assumed that systematic intellectual training inevitably followed the lines of a "dry" and "dead" logic and was necessarily incongruent with the nurturing of innate curiosities and the development of the emotions. Feeling, Hall thought, provided the motive force and the pattern which the intellect must grasp and follow. Since Hall's day, the psychology of Jean Piaget and the educational experiments of Jerome Bruner suggest that Hall underestimated the extent to which systematic conceptual thinking can answer a real need of youth, generate curiosity, and bring with it emotional and aesthetic satisfactions. Nor did Hall perceive that abandoning the intellectual discipline as a systematic enterprise everywhere except in the graduate university might work against the high intellectual standards he called for. The disparity Hall sensed between intellectual training and the student's own feelings and imagination has many dimensions, however, and has hardly been overcome, either in theory or practice. Hall's early work reminds us of the existence of these two poles of educational endeavor and the difficulty of orienting education to both of them.

In 1904, Hall added to this statement of his educational theory a full statement of his theory of adolescence. His two-volume study of this stage of life was his crowning effort in child study, but it followed his far-ranging mind quite beyond the pedagogical purposes and mental limits of the movement. The book was begun in 1894 and was not published until ten years later, when he was sixty years old. It was, virtually, his first book—the long-delayed masterwork of a man who had spent most of his life searching for his true metier and had not found it until middle age.

Adolescence was an intensely personal book, as much a revelation of his own personality as he had praised and castigated William James for writing in 1890. It contained not only Hall's systematic aspirations but the adventurous spirit he could never systematize. The book's subtitle aptly conveyed the character of the work: *Adolescence: Its Psychology and Its Relations to Physiology, Anthropology, Sociology, Sex, Crime, Religion and Education.* Hall's giant volumes contained masses of half-digested data from the enumerated fields, and more. The ideas it contained were tied to biological speculations that were barely plausible, at best, and were constantly embellished with lyrical references to the psychological truth of Christian doctrine. Large parts of the book were filled with unctuous[35] comments about sexuality. And if that were not enough, Hall frequently resorted to neologisms, which he seldom defined, to express the peculiarity of his mind. Interlaced with this mass of data and rhetoric, however, was a vivid portrait of the adolescent stage of life.

The stages of childhood Hall outlined in his *Adolescence* were those he had already worked out in the child study literature. Some of his analyses of the adolescent period and its proper education were also extended treatments of arguments he had already made —for a different kind of intellectualism in the high schools, for more extensive and more natural motor training, and for considering youthful transgressions as products of natural impulses mismanaged by the society at large. Hall labeled his chapter on this last subject "Juvenile Faults, Immoralities and Crimes," evidently not noticing that he was here, as in other areas, merely carrying over into adolescence many of the feelings and attitudes he had attributed to the earlier juvenile stage.

Hall's analysis of adolescence, however, centered on the unique characteristics of that stage. At the foundation of adolescence, according to Hall, was a rapid spurt of growth in body, mind, and feelings and a new endowment of energy, beginning around the time of puberty.

The floodgates of heredity seem opened and we hear from our remoter forebears, and receive our life dower of energy. . . . Passions and desires spring into vigorous life. (1:308)

This "new birth" broke up the old harmonies of childhood personality and hence initiated a period of "storm and stress" (1:xiii). The new powers and drives born in adolescence seemed to Hall "ancestral prepotencies struggling with each other for predominance, checking and favoring each other in a way that suggests the Herbart-Taine concepts of collisions and impacts at all angles, with sums of arrest and reinforcements" (1:242). Although the environment could enlarge or mute this upheaval, its essential cause was the riot of inherited biological impulses.

35. The word is E. L. Thorndike's, and entirely appropriate, in his review of *Adolescence*, in *ER* 28 (1904): 217.

Hall's sense of struggle was heightened by his somewhat Hegelian formulation that "the emotions develop by contrast and reaction into the opposite." Feelings come in pairs of "antithetic impulses." With real sensitivity to adolescent experience, Hall described alternating periods of overactivity and inertness; of strong self-feeling and distrust of self, in which the youth's "bravado" is needed to hide his own sense of unworthiness. Selfishness and altruism also alternated, and here Hall remarked

> that often those most tender and considerate, most prone to take pains, to prefer other's enjoyment to their own, and to renounce . . . and conquer the strongest natural desires . . . were those most liable occasionally to fall lowest in gloating self-gratification at the expense of others.

Other antithetic patterns of feeling and behavior Hall noted were defective and excessive sociability; "exquisite sensitiveness" coupled with "imperturbability and even apathy, hard-heartedness and perhaps cruelty"; passive, receptive moods and then a passionate desire to enter reality and become "an active and perhaps creative cause"; radical desires to remake the world, alternating with conservative, even reactionary, instincts; and finally, "high intuitions that anticipate maturity and even the best mental products of old age" combined with folly, childishness, and silliness. Through this simple category of "opposite feelings," Hall was trying to describe what is now thought of as ambivalence of feelings, as a variety of defensive strategies against unwanted feelings, and as the experimental virtuosity of the adolescent in search of identity. Radical impulses were only a small component of the erratic and stressful behavior of youth which set the adolescent apart from the adult world. (2:75–90).

Hall advocated a direct attempt to prolong adolescence so that as much as possible of this human endowment could be developed.

> The endeavor should be to prevent [the youth] from prematurely finding a support, to prolong the period of variation to which this stage of life is sacred, and to prevent natural selection from confirming too soon, the slight advantage which any quality may temporarily have in this struggle for existence among many faculties and tendencies within us. . . . It is thus that the soul explores the maximum area possible of human experience. (2:88–89)

Hence parents and teachers should provide the adolescent with a combination of "freedom that leans a little toward license" and "shelter and protection," so that nature might take its course (2:71, 91).

As much as Hall wanted to draw out potentialities, however, he also wanted to establish supression, sublimation, and control, so that order was progressively established. One of the reasons "nearly every latency must be developed," Hall said, was that otherwise "some higher power, that later tempers and coordinates it, lacks normal stimulus to develop" (2:90). The chief instrument of order was the self-critical faculties which developed during adolescence, and eliminated "contradictions and inconsistencies" (1:323–24). On another level, Hall described the process of control in terms of "inhibition" and "irradiation," processes somewhat similar to the Freudian repression and sublimation (1:162, 322–24). All adolescent emotions were somewhat plastic, Hall felt, but sexual energies in particular could be irradiated to other and higher endeavors (1:162; 2:140–41).

Hall's treatment of sexuality was the key item in determining where the balance would finally be struck between freedom and control. Hall believed that normal sexuality appeared first at puberty. His chief liberality was again the product of his personal experience: he discussed masturbation with great frankness and urged frankness with young people so that the dreadful anxieties and guilt imposed by secrecy could be dispelled. Hall was still not able to look upon masturbation as a natural phenomenon, however. He opposed it as a dangerous vice, repeated many of the pious warnings that were popular fare on the subject, and claimed that only nighttime emissions were normal (1:411–71).[36]

As to heterosexuality, Hall extolled sexual intercourse as "the most unitary act of a highly complex life" (2:120). Indeed, the subject of physical consummation brought Hall to his highest rhetorical pitch:

36. The physical and psychological dangers of masturbation were widely publicized in nineteenth-century science. Hall's effort to discard some of the more extreme views, while retaining much of the old tone, was evidently typical of the newer treatment of the subject after 1900. See Nathan Hale, Jr., *Freud and the Americans: The Beginnings of Psychoanalysis in the United States, 1876–1917* (London: Oxford University Press, 1971), pt. 1; Kern, "Freud and the Emergence of Child Psychology," pp. 48–52, 96.

Every gemmule is mobilized and the sacred hour of heredity normally comes when adolescence is complete in wedlock and the cerebro-spinal rings up the sympathetic system, and this hands over the reins to the biophores and germ cells, which now assert their dominance over those of the soma. In the most unitary of all acts, which is the epitome and pleroma of life, we have the most intense of all affirmations of the will to live and realize that the only true God is love, and the center of life is worship. Every part of mind and body participates in a true pangenesis. This sacrament is the annunciation hour, with hosannas which the whole world reflects. Communion is fusion and beatitude. It is the supreme hedonic narcosis, a holy intoxication, the chief ecstasy, because the most intense of experiences; it is the very heart of psychology, and because it is the supreme pleasure of life it is the eternal basis and guarantee of optimism. It is this experience more than any other that opens to man the ideal world. Now the race is incarnated in the individual and remembers its lost paradise. (2: 122–23)

And so on, for another thirty-three lines. Clearly, Hall saw something of the synthetic character of sexual intercourse, its basis in psychic as well as physical life, and its important role in mental health and happiness. These ideas were almost drowned, however, in biological and religious wrappings. By the end of the passage, one sees the heavens, the earth, the species, the germ cells coupling, certainly not two people. Hall's idealization of sexual intercourse was only a more enthusiastic and positive rendering of the doctrine propounded by guardians of Victorian respectability, that physical love, to be permissible, had to be hallowed by respectable ends beyond itself. As such it was typical of many reformers of sex in America during this period.[37]

It was to be expected, then, that Hall went on to say that "nature designs this experience to be long circuited" (1:455).

The most rigid chastity of fancy, heart and body is physiologically and psychologically as well as ethically imperative until maturity is complete on into the twenties, nor is it hard if continence is inward. . . . (2: 120–21.)

To insure chastity, Hall recommended such restraints as the old regime of hard work and cold baths, as well as a more imaginative prescription of active pursuits, from dancing to religious, aesthetic, and intellectual enthusiasms (1:205, 225–27, 465–69; 2:74).

37. See Peter T. Cominos, "Late-Victorian Sexual Respectability and the Social System," *International Review of Social History* 8 (1963): 24–25; Hale, *Freud and the Americans,* pp. 29–47, 446–47.

These last, Hall thought, were most important, for the outcome of restraint was sublimation into the highest pursuits of civilization. As civilization advanced, an ever longer period of continence would be necessary (1:456; 2:119, 140–41).

Hall discussed at some length the close relation between sexuality and religion and the importance for the adolescent of sublimating his sexual feelings into higher, religious endeavor. Hall was concerned at times to explain that the tie between the two fields was only one of similarity:

Perhaps Plato is right, and love of the good, beautiful and true is only love of sex transfigured and transcendentalized; but the Gospel is better, which makes sex love at the best the type and symbol of love of God and man. (2:293, 295–300)

Both sexuality and religion in adolescence were "predominantly emotional and the contiguity of emotional states is then most liable to produce extension of excitement to other areas by contagion" (2:301). Hall often suggested a "unity" as well as a similarity between the two, however, and urged modern educators to construct a ladder up the same path Plato had climbed (2:119, 300).[38] Indeed, he delighted in showing that even the Christian religion had been "slowly sublimated and refined" out of primitive sexual consciousness and was still centrally concerned with sexual temptation: "the burden of the Bible has sprung from the very heart of Man's deepest nature and his direst need" (2:100, 123, 333).

Hall made somewhat vaguer arguments in regard to the relation between sexuality and intellectual and creative activity of all kinds. "Sex asserts its mastery in field after field," he said (1:xiv). "Knowledge at its best is a form of love." "Interest is intellectual love" (2:136–38). "Love sensitizes the soul to the influences of nature," he asserted, and hence it was a genetic factor, a potency, in the creation of art, literature, and even science (2:129). Hall's analysis had the radical effect of showing that the highest pursuits of civilization were at least partly rooted in the crude energies of sexuality. His purpose was not to debunk these pursuits, however, but to applaud their control of sexuality. What Hall wanted most for adolescents was freedom to sublimate.

38. See also "Universities and the Training of Professors," 1894, p. 303.

Hall naturally considered adolescent girls even better adapted to this goal than boys. Hall acknowledged their sexuality and assumed the existence of female masturbation as of male, but he believed sublimation was even easier and more natural for the girl (1:419–24, 432–53).

To be a true woman means to be yet more mother than wife. The madonna conception expresses man's highest comprehension of woman's real nature. Sexual relations are brief, but love and care of offspring are long. (2: 627)

Hall did not therefore feel any great need to insure or provide for female chastity during adolescence, as he did with young men. His chief concern was with their physical health, specifically the establishment of regularity in the menstrual cycle, which many physicians of the day thought would insure the later ability to bear children (1:472–512; 2:569–83).

Religious feelings and their proper culmination in conversion held almost as central a place in Hall's concept of adolescence as sexuality and its proper outcome in sublimation. If Hall appeared to ground religious enthusiasm in sexual energies, he also subordinated sexual desires to religious goals. Sexuality was the primary sphere in which the adolescent accomplished the principal task of his life, the shift from selfishness to altruism, from concern for self to that of the race.[39] It was thus, Hall said

the most critical revolution of life, to successfully accomplish which is to make catharses of our lower nature and to attain full ethical maturity without arrest or perversion; this is the very meaning of adolescence. (2: 337)

This shift was accomplished, Hall believed, through religious conversion—a circumscribed, intense, emotional experience which brought the adolescent to the brink of despair, extracted from him a surrender of self, a "full self-sacrifice," and gave him in return new love for and acquiescence in the order of existence, a new sense of participation in its powers. This experience, Hall believed, was a natural development of the religious impulse at this period. By it, nature herself insured that the child's hitherto amoral nature was brought within the ethical bounds of civilization. Hall described the

39. Comte had described altruism as the product of the adolescence of the individual and humanity. *System of Positive Polity,* 3:156–57.

"full ethical maturity" which resulted in such conventional terms as "temperance," living by "the golden mean," living "for others and not for self" (2:301–52). Under these traditional rubrics he sometimes seemed willing to subordinate his newer ideals of health and maximal individual development.

Hall's concept of adolescence, then, was founded on a basic ambivalence—on a desire for wide freedom of self-expression and development of potential coupled with the wish to control and direct that development into respectable, ethical forms. This same ambivalence shaped his view of the ultimate outcome of adolescence. Hall spoke of the maturity which should result from a normal adolescence chiefly in terms of "mental unity," of desires, beliefs, and volitions organized into a harmonous personality which would work as one, rather than be divided against itself (2:90–91). This ideal received frequent praise in Hall's writings, as did the "full ethical maturity" which would accompany it. Hall appeared to think of this mature unity as a final equilibrium of the personality, a static period and not a stage of further growth.

Hall was thus not entirely happy with maturity. It could not compete with adolescence itself, "this golden stage when life glisters and crepitates" (2:132). He called adolescence "the apical stage of human development . . . before the decline of the highest powers of the soul in maturity and age" (2:361). Ordinary maturity might be acceptable for most people, Hall implied, but for the elite who reached the heights of human development, it was not the goal.

The ordered, regular life of maturity involves necessarily more or less degeneration for simple tendencies. Indeed, the best definition of genius is intensified and prolonged adolescence, to which excessive or premature systematization is fatal. (2: 90–91)

What was true of the individual was also true of the race. The broader and higher development reached in adolescence would be progressively inherited until a higher evolutionary product, the superman of the future, was created. Adolescence, Hall asserted, "and not maturity as now defined, is the only point of departure for the super anthropoid that man is to become" (2:94). Only the superman would finally achieve an ideal unity. He would be the "cosmic" man who would "co-ordinate from every race and land every typical expression by word or deed of every tendency, element and stage" (2:359). In the meantime, maturity disappeared into an apotheosis of adolescence itself, or the decline of old age. The only other stage of life after childhood and adolescence which Hall described in any detail was senescence.[40]

Hall's concept of adolescence was probably the first systematic portrayal of that stage of life in the modern world.[41] The components of which it was formed, however, were already fairly commonplace in the nineteenth century, and Hall's synthesis of them was greeted with instant recognition. Rousseau and other European romantics had already described adolescence as a period of great storm and stress, and Rousseau's *Emile* specifically linked the onset of this troubled period to puberty and the development of the sexual passions. Rousseau also urged that sexual knowledge, both physical and imaginative, be withheld from the adolescent as long as possible —he thought twenty the outside limit—so that the youth would gain strength and vigor through the retardation of development.

A good deal of this view was implicit or explicit in the popular conception of youth as a stage of life which appeared in the cautionary literature in America addressed to young people or their parents. Youth was seen as a plastic, formative stage of vigorous and fluctuating passions, during which the youth must avoid the ever-present danger to sin. As the century progressed, the sexual component of the passions and dangers was more explicitly discussed, and by Hall's day, there was a large medical and popular quack literature on sexual hygiene for youths.[42]

Hall put these Rousseauian and popular ideas of adolescence into the framework of post-Darwinian biology. He linked the turbulence of adolescence to a wide spectrum of physiological and psychological changes determined by evolution. The retardation of sexual activity in the interests of higher individual development and civilization

40. GSH, *Senescence; the Last Half of Life*, 1922.
41. A near competitor is Antonio Marro, *La Puberta* (Torino: Fratelli Bocca Editori, 1898), 2d ed., 1900, which treats of puberty and its after-effects extending to about the age of twenty.
42. John Demos, "Adolescence in Historical Perspective," *Journal of Marriage and the Family* 31 (1969): 632–35; Hale, *The Psychoanalytic Movement in America*, pt. 1.

was grounded in a specific psycho-physiological process of inhibition and irradiation. Most important, Hall's doctrine of evolutionary progress sanctioned the claim of adolescence on the future. The popular view of youth as carrying both the dangers and promise of change in the mobile American society was linked to the dynamics of the evolutionary process. The moral superiority which the future holds in all theories of progress thus attached to adolescence itself, justifying the free expression of adolescent nature and its prolongation.

Hall drew into this new, biologically based concept still another common idea about youth in nineteenth-century America, the idea that youth was particularly susceptible to religious conversion. Hall claimed in *Adolescence* to be the first person to have proved this connection when he pointed to it in his very first pedagogical article, "Moral and Religious Training of Children"; and he collected statistics on it from various religious societies, which he briefly reported (2:292). The connection was, however, common knowledge in the clerical literature on conversion and was implicit in the traditions of the academies and colleges which specifically set aside certain periods to stimulate conversion in their adolescent students.[43] Hall himself had been exposed to this tradition at Williams College and had experienced a rather conventional conversion in his freshman year.

Although Hall maintained the basic pattern of traditional religious experience in his discussion of adolescent conversion, what he really described was the crisis of belief of the nineteenth-century intellectual whose religious commitment had been undercut by modern science, the crisis of Tennyson in his *In Memoriam* and of Hall himself in his youth and again in middle-age, when he struggled to escape from the coils of idealism and accept the benign dispensation of evolutionary nature. Although Hall often stated that adolescents needed a sectarian religious affiliation, the outcome of this conversion experience was described in strictly nonsectarian terms—as the kind of pantheistic feelings to which science had reduced religion in Hall's mind, and as the purely ethical goal of altruism, the ideal of

43. Joseph Kett, "Adolescence in the Nineteenth Century," paper delivered at the Clark Conference on Childhood and Youth in History, 20 May 1970.

Comte's religion of humanity. Religion had been the field on which Hall had enacted his early emancipation. His concepts of adolescence and of the natural education of children were worked out first in the context of religious feelings. It was natural then for Hall to maintain the religious framework to describe what was essentially a newer experience of intellectual doubt and return, a confirmation of one's place not in the religious universe but in the natural world.

Hall's synthetic transformation of these earlier ideas of youth into the modern concept of adolescence clearly owed much to the social setting of the 1890s in America. The decade was rife with fear of the new urban, industrial society and its destruction of the older rural and village ways which most Americans still knew at firsthand. It was also beginning to spawn a more optimistic desire to find new sources of vitality and new norms for the emerging society. Both conservatives and liberals looked to nature, to a nostalgic image of the rural past or a confident image of the dynamism and intelligence ever present in the nature of man and society. Both had what John Higham has so suggestively described as the desire to find in nature the "vivifying experience" which industrial and urban civilization increasingly denied its members.[44]

Characteristically, Hall responded to all these pressures. In *Adolescence*, he worried over the degeneration of modern life and recalled an idealized version of a simpler and purer youth. He also sought in adolescent nature the energy and standards appropriate for the humanity of the future, and he gloried in the passionate life of youth, which rose above the flat, workaday world of maturity and age. As he often declared,

There is really no clue by which we can thread our way through all the mazes of culture and the distractions of modern life save by knowing the true nature and needs of childhood and adolescence.

"Other oracles may grow dim," he concluded, "but this one will never fail."[45]

The popular reviewers of *Adolescence* were divided between

44. John Higham, "The Reorientation of American Culture in the 1890s," in *The Origins of Modern Consciousness* (Detroit: Wayne State University Press, 1965).

45. GSH, "Child Study and Its Relation to Education," 1900, p. 700.

those who approved Hall's firm response to the degeneration threatened by modern life and saw his view of sublimation and religious
conversion as the center of adolescence;[46] and those who approved
his sympathetic, vivid portrait of adolescence and saw the importance of sex and natural development as his central concepts.[47] With
his sympathies so well attuned to the needs of the day and so widely
scattered among them, it is understandable that *Adolescence*
achieved a remarkable popularity for such a weighty tome, reportedly selling over twenty-five thousand copies in America.[48]

Among all the reviewers of *Adolescence*, the one who most fully
grasped the central thrust of the book was Patrick Geddes, the
Scotch biologist and urban reformer. Geddes declared that the
faults of Hall's book soon disappeared from view, "leaving a work
profound and original in its thought," especially

as we divine how fully the writer must have lived, not only amid but
through much of the experience he describes—giving fuller proof than
perhaps he knows of the truth of his own general doctrine of the association of the powers and the difficulties of adolescence.

Pointing directly to the normative concept which most clearly expressed Hall's view of adolescence, Geddes declared that "the highest critical and practical idea" of the book was Hall's "interpretation of Genius, one again doubtless not wholly new, but now
developed towards fuller possibilities and applications." Buoyed by
this confirmation of his own romantic prophecy, Geddes declared
that "the Paper Age of mere book-learning has virtually ended,
and . . . a new world of education, of life and health, of growth
and action—nay of evolutionist culture of genius, of redemption of
evil, has fully begun."[49] With his combination of evolutionary biology, romantic idealism, and Carlylean earnestness and passion,

46. "The Critical Period of Life," *Outlook* 78 (1904): 238–40; Mrs. Theodore W. Birney, "Adolescence," *Delineator* 64 (1904): 272–74. See also J. M.
Greenwood, "Adolescence," *ER* 29 (1905): 342–63.
47. "Adolescence," *Reader Magazine* 4 (1904): 469; A. K. Rogers, "Adolescence," *Dial* 37 (1904): 82–85.
48. *DAB*, s.v. GSH; David Gibbs to GSH, 17 Aug 1904, CUP. A shorter, one-
volume edition, *Youth, Its Education, Regimen and Hygiene*, 1906, omitted much
of the material on sex contained in the larger work and achieved great popularity
as a normal-school text.
49. Patrick Geddes, "Adolescence," *Paidologist* 7 (Feb 1905): 33–41.

Geddes was, perhaps more than any other man of their age, close to Hall in spirit. In their different ways—Geddes moving into urban development and planning, and Hall into the expansion and revaluation of the individual life-cycle—both expressed the romantic resurgence at the turn of the century and the desire to build organic values into the increasingly specialized and mechanized urban, industrial, scientific civilization.[50]

Hall may also have responded to the social fact of adolescence itself. It has been suggested that by the end of the century adolescents constituted a distinct social group in urban settings and were causing their elders increasing difficulty.[51] The presence of visible and troublesome adolescents is clearly reflected in Hall's book and undoubtedly influenced him. The reviewers, too, commented on the practical helpfulness of the book to parents, particularly the chapters on sex, health, disease, faults and delinquency, and adolescent social institutions.[52] Middle-class urban parents by 1904 must have been aware of adolescence as a special stage of life, with special problems, requiring special nurture. This social fact may not of itself have demanded attention, however. Such adolescents may have been present earlier and were not to become the highly visible, institutionalized social group we know until some decades after Hall's formulation of the concept.[53] Hall's development of the concept appears related to a number of social factors which converged more centrally on his own life experience.

Hall was led by his social and cultural position to experience a long and troubled adolescence. The injunction against premarital sex; the necessity of securing an occupational position and financial

50. Probably as a result of Geddes's response to the book, he and Hall struck up a correspondence; at Geddes's invitation, Hall traveled to Edinburgh in 1906 to deliver a lecture at the University. *Educational News,* 5 Oct 1906. When Geddes visited the United States, he stopped in Worcester to see Hall, but their correspondence was apparently infrequent. Geddes to GSH, 1 Jan 1916, HP. Hall may have had this relationship in mind when he regretted at the end of his life not making fuller contact with like-minded intellects around the world.

51. Demos, "Adolescence in Historical Perspective," pp. 636–38.

52. Mrs. Birney, "Adolescence," pp. 272–74; *Outlook* 78 (1904): 239. Hall also called for an adolescent specialty in medicine and received some favorable attention among physicians. GSH, "Adolescence: The Need of a New Field of Medical Practice," 1905. See also *PNEA*, 1905, p. 709.

53. Kett, "Adolescence in the Nineteenth Century."

independence before marriage; the desire for an intellectual occupation outside the ministry; and the temperament and intelligence which required the integration of more traditional and newer modes of thought—all these contributed in Hall, as they did in William James, to an adolescent crisis which was not finally resolved until his thirties.[54] The storm and stress, the ambivalence, the sublimation, the prolonged effort to find a vocation which would create the broadest possible unity among his divergent impulses, all these elements of Hall's experience were related to those conditions and were echoed in his theory.

In addition, emotional difficulties had made Hall's mature equilibrium rather fragile; so as he was approaching the age of fifty, a series of personal and professional losses forced him to reopen the problems of his adolescence and revise the solutions he had earlier reached. In the midst of this second reliving of his adolescent crisis, Hall began work on his book on adolescence, and his theory reflected his experience of this second crisis as well as the first.

Beyond this, Hall's theory was a product of the frustrations of his own maturity. As in his view of childhood, Hall hoped through his concept of adolescence to stave off for a time the narrow specialization and cognitive focus decreed by his occupational role. He also used his concept of adolescence to escape the narrow limits of his sex role. The idea contained and expressed his enlarged concern with the "feminine" realm of the feelings, religious experience, and youth. It was really a means by which he could restore these aspects of human nature to masculinity. In adolescence, the normal male could indulge in the feelings Hall's own constraints and narrow view of masculinity had denied him.

54. Emotional difficulties prolonged James's adolescent crisis as they did Hall's. See Cushing Strout, "William James and the Twice-Born Sick Soul," *Daedalus* 97 (1968): 1062–82. His difficulties abated when he took his first professional position at the age of thirty, and married at thirty-six. The comparable ages for Hall were twenty-eight and thirty-five. The average age of marriage for Harvard and Yale graduates toward the end of the century was twenty-nine to thirty-one. Nathan Hale, *The Psychoanalytic Movement in America*, pt. 1. It may be that the experience of Hall and James was representative only of a particular group of young, late-Victorian intellectuals whose adolescent turmoil was exceptionally prolonged and shaped by ascertainable historical conditions. The tightening of civilized morality after 1840 described by Hale, ibid., must have been one such condition.

Hall himself was vaguely aware of what he was doing. In adolescence, he said,"those who up to that time seem like their father begin to show maternal traits."[55] Or again,

Woman at her best never outgrows adolescence as man does, but lingers in, magnifies and glorifies this culminating stage of life with its all-sided interests, its convertability of emotions, its enthusiasm, and zest for all that is good, beautiful, true and heroic. (2:624)

Adolescence, he said, included a "generalized or even feminized stage of psychic development" (2:625). When Hall was called upon to outline his program of separate education for young women, he proceeded to outline very largely the same program of "repose, leisure, art, legends, romance, idealizations, in a word, humanism," which he would suggest for the adolescent male (1:xvii). Suddenly struck by this similarity, he remarked that if this program was good for young men, it was even more so for women.[56] To Hall, adolescence was filled with those qualities of which woman was the incarnation. By means of this passionate stage of life, Hall succeeded in putting these qualities into a masculine context.

Hall's development of a concept of adolescence, therefore, was part of his solution—an extremely creative solution—to a set of personal conflicts which had been reinforced by the specialization of occupational roles and the rigidly differentiated sex roles of Victorian culture. In that light, his idealization of adolescence and his failure to work out a satisfactory concept of maturity reflected an inability to face his underlying problems. This failure was a kind of regression, which allowed the basic problems of vocation and of the proper identification of male and female to go unresolved, both within himself and for the culture at large. Nonetheless, implicitly, Hall was attempting to redefine maturity, to make it a period of continued growth, strong feeling, and personal exploration. In his own life, if he failed to achieve an adequate integration of his personality, he did continue to grow to the very end.

Hall's concept of adolescence, of course, persists to the present

55. GSH, "On Specialization," 1897.
56. GSH, "Address on Founders Day at Mount Holyoke College," 1896, pp. 64–72. See also *Adol*, 2:636–46, which adds to the joint Hallian program education in manners and domesticity but also ends confusedly by contrasting and likening education for young men and women.

day, together with its fundamentally ambivalent attitudes toward freedom or control, toward perennial youth or maturity, toward the dangers of an unprecedented society or the promise of youth to overcome them.[57] Hall would nonetheless hardly recognize the forms his ideas have taken. The ideal of broadened personal experience and exploration now often sanctions adolescent sexual activity. The prolongation of adolescence has been carried backward, as well as forward, often destroying latency as a period of drill and discipline. The sublimation required of youth has been asked in the name of an increasingly specialized, work-oriented education, rather than allowing the leisurely acquisition of humanistic culture. In formulating the modern concept of adolescence Hall achieved the prophetic role he sought, but prophecy, like all else in history, moves beyond personal intentions.

57. This despite a steady current of opposition to the theory in academic circles. Thorndike early asserted that "the emotional instability, the alternation of happiness and misery, satisfaction and remorse or self-depreciation, is of no value, and the many boys and girls who do not manifest it are to be congratulated." "Notes on Child Study," *Columbia University Contributions to Philosophy, Psychology and Education* 8, nos. 3–4 (1901), p. 141. He later found that for most teenagers personality changes were neither so sudden or large as Hall had suggested. "Magnitude and Rate of Alleged Changes at Adolescence," *ER* 54 (1917): 140–47. A recent study confirms this view: Daniel Offer, *The Psychological World of the Teen-Ager: A Study of Normal Adolescent Boys* (New York: Basic Books, 1969). As opposition to biological determinism mounted in the 1920s, Hall's theory also came under attack for its failure to recognize the cultural determination of the storm and stress of adolescence. See Margaret Mead, *Coming of Age in Samoa* (New York: W. Morrow, 1928). The psychoanalytic view of adolescence, however, has always focused centrally on the upsurge of libidinal energies and stressed the upheavals of the period and their ultimate adaptive value. Psychoanalysts have shown, however, a firm sense of the maturity to which adolescence leads. See Peter Blos, *On Adolescence* (New York: Free Press of Glencoe, 1962); Erik Erikson, *Identity and the Life Cycle*, pp. 1–171; *Identity: Youth and Crisis* (New York: W. W. Norton, 1968).

17   FAILURE IN SUCCESS

In 1898, at the height of the child study enthusiasm, and several years before Hall presented his full theories of education and adolescence, spokesmen for scientific psychology openly turned against the movement, thereby starting the wave of disillusion which helped to bring Hall's child study movement to an end by 1911. James Mark Baldwin, speaking for the community of scientific psychologists who had been involved in the movement only marginally, or not at all, declared in 1898, "I think the time has come for the emphatic expression of opinion in this matter."[1] Baldwin, William James, and particularly Hugo Münsterberg of Harvard proceeded to attack the movement in the popular press and at teachers' meetings, as bad science and bad for the teacher.[2]

Münsterberg, like all the other critics of the movement, focused his attack on the questionnaire method and its involvement of teachers in a scientific program. In a passage that echoed Hall's own criticism of psychical research when he was a young champion of science, Münsterberg declared that

progress in our science has depended upon the most laborious, patient work

1. *PR* 5 (1898): 219.
2. William James, *Talks to Teachers* (New York: Henry Holt, 1899); Hugo Münsterberg, *Psychology and Life* (Boston: Houghton Mifflin, 1899), contains criticisms of the movement he had published in 1898 in the *Atlantic Monthly* and *ER*. See also Claparède, *Experimental Pedagogy,* pp. 6–7, and Buck, *Social Sciences at Harvard,* p. 253.

of our laboratories and the most subtle and refined methods, and . . . all this seductive but rude and untrained and untechnical gathering of cheap and vulgar material means a caricature and not an improvement of psychology.[3]

Not only was fragmentary data collected by untrained observers useless, it was harmful if it led the teacher to think it could in any way replace the intuitive understanding and tact of her art, or if the teacher was misled to believe that the ideal ends of education were implicit in scientific findings.[4]

The criticism of such eminent psychological scientists undoubtedly shook the confidence of many child study workers in the authority of their leader and the value of their efforts. Hall's own criticisms of many child study doctrines the following year further alienated his supporters. Among educators, one observer remarked, Hall

suffered from . . . devotion to topics that have been looked upon with more or less suspicion. He has never failed to carry his audiences with him, but when those who heard him went home and reported what they had heard the coolness of its reception cooled their own ardor.[5]

The suspect subjects, of course, were his approval of corporal punishment, his willingness to allow children and adolescents—at least male ones—to break the customary code of civil behavior, his opposition to the coeducational high school and equal education for women, his dislike of the complete democratization of public education, and finally, his defense of latency as a period of intensive drill, partly set off from the freer methods suitable for infancy before and adolescence after. These views may well have found sympathetic chords in his audiences but not chords deep enough to withstand the prevailing progressive, moralistic, and humanitarian consensus.

Beyond these specific views, Hall's ideal system of education was uncomfortably demanding of the educational profession. As one major pedagog commented, "The first requisite is a teaching class educated far beyond the present attainments of those who now fol-

3. Münsterberg, *Psychology and Life*, p. 116.
4. Ibid., pp. 139–40, and James, *Talks*, pp. 5–14, 133–43.
5. *Journal of Education* 55 (Mar 1902): 167–68.

low that vocation."[6] Hall's ideal, he said, was thus very far distant, if attainable at all.

As the first decade of the twentieth century proceeded, Hall's disagreement with the main direction of his followers became even more pronounced. Hall not only repeated his belief in these unpopular doctrines in *Adolescence,* he asserted several times afterward that "the educational situation here is grave." Laying his blows on all sides with equal force, Hall criticized both the misdirected progressivism of the schools and their traditional imperviousness to the romantic message. "Kindergarten methods have leavened the grades," Hall complained, bringing with them too much sewing and basket-weaving and not enough work on fundamentals. Children are sometimes even allowed to choose their own topics of study in a misplaced obeisance to children's rights, thus gearing education to their whims rather than to their real needs. On the other hand, "time is wasted in training for orderliness in going, standing, sitting," and "antediluvian methods" still prevail.[7] He continued to berate the low intellectual quality of texts and teachers. "The sorest point in the whole American system is the insufficient professional training of teachers."

Hall also complained of "the alarming predominance of female teachers" and the "socialistic" paternalism of the state which lavished free education on so many who did not deserve it.[8] He spoke more frequently of the need for moral education in the schools and sometimes even urged that it include explicit religious instruction.[9] While he continued to promote his romantic message after the turn of the century, he also brought into sharper focus the intellectual and conservative principles with which he hoped to contain it.

One other suspect subject contributed to Hall's divergence from the educational mainstream during these years. In his occasional

6. George P. Brown, "The School of the Future," *School and Home Education* 21 (1901): 119.

7. GSH interview, Worcester *Telegram,* 28 Jan 1906; GSH, "Some Dangers in Our Educational System and How to Meet Them," 1907; GSH, "The German Teacher Teaches," 1907.

8. GSH in Worcester *Gazette,* 7 Jan 1908; GSH in Boston *Post,* Feb 1908; GSH, "What Is to Become of Your Baby?" 1910.

9. GSH, "What Changes Should Be Made in Public High Schools," 1906; *EP,* 1:220–344; GSH in Worcester *Post,* 24 Oct 1911.

discussion of adolescence during the 1890s, Hall had stressed the importance of the development of sexuality and urged that educators learn how to turn youthful sexual energies into acceptable and fruitful nonsexual channels.[10] Though his goal was eminently respectable, his stress of the subject was not, and his students were often more direct and heated than he. Attempts to discuss his views at educational meetings invariably ended early with an admonition from the floor, "the less our young teachers and would-be teachers had to say about this subject the better."[11] The great length and frank detail in which Hall dealt with sexuality in *Adolescence* was a serious breach of custom. Nothing could have alienated him more from the teachers and pedagogs who composed the child study movement, and *Adolescence* was quickly banned from some libraries.[12] Many of the normal school educators, it was reported, lived in dire fear of Hall's ideas actually being put into practice.[13]

Joined to the vocal opposition of eminent psychologists, Hall's open criticism of the direction of educational reform and his increasingly strenuous assertion of unpopular views helped to end the child study movement. A tenuous alliance at best of scientists and educators, Hall's inspirational enthusiasm was needed to glue the movement together. While a science of education had initially been an attractive prospect to the better educated and professionally minded teachers, it was difficult in practice to maintain their allegiance to a scientific program. Even these teachers found scientific terminology and discussion difficult; so their meetings had to be composed of "brief evangelizing addresses" rather than long scientific papers.[14] The normal school teachers who constituted the heart

10. GSH, "Child Study: The Basis of Exact Education," 1893, pp. 440–41; "Universities and the Training of Professors," 1894, pp. 301–4.

11. *PNEA*, 1895, p. 258. See also, *PNEA*, 1897, p. 851. For his more enthusiastic students, see ibid., pp. 843–51 and M. F. Libby to GSH, 24 Nov 1907, CUP.

12. Joseph Jastrow, "Adolescence," *Popular Science Monthly* 66 (Mar 1905): 465.

13. Michael V. O'Shea, "Adolescence," *PB* 2 (Apr 1905): 134.

14. Wm. L. Bryan to GSH, 31 Dec 1894, CUP. Among educators outside the child study movement, there had always been a good deal of skepticism about the scientific pretensions of the movement and its claim to override ordinary common sense. See, for example, B. A. Hinsdale, "American Education," *Dial* 28 (May 1900): 354.

of the movement also discovered that the pedagogical and scientific purposes of the work were not easily joined. Most of the data collected by normal school students was never analyzed, and when the students discovered that they were not really gathering data for science, but only for themselves, their interest declined considerably.[15] As early as 1897, the less serious and less capable teachers began to drift away. Attendance at the Clark summer school began to decline after 1900, and complaints mounted over the repetitiousness and lack of practical bearing of the summer school programs. After 1903, Hall discontinued them altogether.[16]

Thus, while the critical outbursts of psychologists and of Hall himself did much to drive teachers away from child study, the decline of the movement was ultimately due to more fundamental factors: the work of child study became increasingly scientific and specialized, and the interest of educational reformers turned toward the social aspects of education. In part, of course, these two developments reflected basic failures of child study as Hall had conceived it. Neither the questionnaire method, with its reliance on amateur assistance, nor the decree to follow biological nature were adequate to the complex realities which faced the scientists and educators who seriously attempted child study work. The momentum of research and argument within a decade carried child study and educational reform beyond Hall's conceptions.

It is equally true, however, that these new developments reflected the success of the movement in stimulating interest in educational reform and the scientific study of children. Hall's child study program created a great demand in education for scientific, psychological expertise, a demand which quickly brought psychologists into the field. Some, like James, stayed only for brief *Talks to Teachers*; others, like Thorndike, permanently tied the two fields. Moreover, the broad suggestiveness of the material Hall uncovered and the issues he raised, and the fruitful cross-contact he stimulated between different fields, were extremely important in generating the more viable forms of science and pedagogy which replaced child study, even when these successors were hostile to his program. A great deal

15. *PNEA*, 1893, pp. 784–85.
16. *ER* 14 (1897): 192–93; *Clark University Summer School*, CUP.

of Hall's vision, transformed to be sure, eventually made its way into the later efforts of science and education. For a time, Hall himself tried to follow on these new paths before entirely forsaking the movement.

The chief exemplar of the growing scientific sophistication of child study work was Edward L. Thorndike. A student of James and Cattell, Thorndike had performed at Columbia one of the first laboratory experiments on animal learning. He had gone to Western Reserve University in the late 1890s as professor of psychology and pedagogy and in 1901 to the Teachers College of Columbia University as adjunct professor of genetic psychology. Finding himself in the midst of the child study ferment, he proceeded to enter the field and soon began to sort out and codify the child study findings.

Thorndike brought to child study the methodological sophistication and statistical skill of a student of Cattell. He early recognized the weaknesses of the questionnaire method and was second to none in informed criticism of it. Thorndike responded to Münsterberg's criticism of child study, however, as a member of the movement, defending its larger purposes and hoping for reform from within. Disputing Münsterberg's categorical statement that psychology had nothing to teach the teacher, Thorndike encouraged

everyone even in normal schools and child study societies to go ahead making judgments about mental facts . . . . Very poor psychology it may be. . . . But they can do work as good for the purposes of mental science as much of the work of naturalists has been for biology. . . . Any attempt to improve the judgments of common sense about any sort of facts may prove fruitful.[17]

Thorndike's chief hope, as he demonstrated in his first book, *Notes on Child Study,* in 1901, was to give the child study workers an elementary understanding of probabilities and of the kinds of difficulties involved in coming to more reliable conclusions about child nature. "That child study has few exact statements as yet is due to the incompetence or thoughtlessness of its students, and not to the nature of the subject. Such a condition of affairs should be speedily overcome."[18] Thorndike proceeded to outline some of the more reliable child study findings, together with some of the considerations involved in disputed points.

17. E. L. Thorndike, "What Is a Psychical Fact," *PR* 5 (1898): 645–50.
18. E. L. Thorndike, "Notes on Child Study," p. 20.

Beginning with his introductory statement on the qualitative difference between the child mind and the adult, Thorndike outlined the child study work in much the same terms that Hall had conceived it, although he organized some of the material around the conventional labels of scientific psychology, as Hall did not. Thorndike pointed out to his readers, however, when a line of Hallian research was inconclusive—as in the many attempts to study children's interests at various ages. And he sharply criticized some of Hall's theoretical foundations, particularly the whole recapitulation argument. Thorndike showed that the individual seems to repeat the race "only in its most general features. The attempts at concrete parallelism break down again and again." His criticism of recapitulation echoed growing skepticism about the validity of the theory among biological scientists.[19] Throughout, Thorndike treated the mind as a congeries of "unlearned reactions" or instincts, which were developed and improved by learning, but went much further than Hall in analyzing the ways in which instinctive reactions could be strengthened, directed, or inhibited—the learning process itself.

In 1903 and periodically thereafter, Thorndike recast this material and the results of his own investigations into an educational psychology.[20] He continued to emphasize the importance of the "original nature of the race" and to comment on the issues Hall had raised, but the heart of the work was now his own experiments and quantitative studies of the psychology of learning. In 1913 he acknowledged his debt to his two teachers, James and Cattell, "and to that intrepid devotee to concrete human nature, Stanley Hall, whose doctrines I often attack, but whose genius I always admire."[21] A just estimate of his debt to Hall is implied in his review of Hall's *Adolescence:*

The great service of President Hall's studies may be to inspire others which will replace their data and refute their conclusions, but which will nonetheless be true offspring.[22]

19. See, for example, J. Arthur Thomson, *The Science of Life* (London: Blackie and Son, 1910), pp. 133–37, and Waldo Shumway, "The Recapitulation Theory," *Quarterly Review of Biology* 7 (1932): 93–99.
20. E. L. Thorndike, *Educational Psychology* (New York: Lemke and Buechner, 1903).
21. Thorndike, *Educational Psychology* (2d ed., 1913), vol. 1, preface.
22. *ER* 28 (1904): 227.

Thorndike accepted the biological framework Hall had brought to the study of child nature, and injected into it methodological sophistication and systematic concern for the learning process itself, thus transforming child study into educational psychology. Unfortunately, Hall's rich suggestiveness and his radical, reforming motive did not equally survive the change.

Hall's response to the criticism of the questionnaire method and the more sophisticated scientific program offered by Thorndike was twofold. For one, he and his disciples repeatedly attempted to defend the questionnaire method—at least the better examples of it—as no more unreliable than most methods in psychology.[23] Hall himself argued that there was a distinct and legitimate difference between what was required of untrained observers, like the missionaries or animal breeders who provided data for anthropology or biology, and the work of the scientific expert who went over their data and eliminated much error: "the gathering of raw material and the manufacture of it into forms of value [are] processes as distinct as the work of the quarryman and the sculptor."[24] Although Hall had tried to overcome the methodological sources of error in a few of his questionnaire studies, he evidently never understood the intricate relationship between the methods by which data are gathered and the results they can reliably yield. His best defense of the method was the quantity of suggestive data it produced and, he could have added, the insights it could provide a sensitive student of human nature, as many of his own questionnaire studies proved.

The problem with suggestive data and insights, however, is that they must at some point lead to more definite concepts and hypotheses, and here Hall's understanding failed. In 1902 and 1903, under the challenge of Thorndike and his other scientific critics, Hall resolved to undertake the task. Given a small grant from the new Carnegie Institute of Washington, Hall hired a full-time research assistant and proposed to organize child study workers more closely "to place the work upon a strictly scientific basis." He also wanted to open systematic contact with child study workers in other coun-

    23. GSH, "Child Study and Its Relation to Education," 1900; Theodate L. Smith, "The Questionnaire Method in Genetic Psychology," *PS* 10 (1903): 405–9; *PNEA*, 1904, pp. 762–70.
    24. GSH, "Child Study and Its Relation to Education," 1900, p. 692.

tries so as "to base conclusions on many subjects upon a comparative study of data from different countries."[25] Moreover, on each topic of child study considered at his summer school of 1903, Hall announced, the student must "bring out the logic of this work, its errors and defects," and his own lectures at Clark would henceforth deal with "the sources of error, the different methods and their evaluation."[26]

Hall's resolve, however, was greater than his powers of execution. Except for the report in his journals of more fragmentary data from foreign countries, nothing of this program was ever realized. Hall could hardly expect untrained pedagogs in his summer school or a research assistant in correspondence with child study workers to supply the methodological sophistication and conceptual analysis he himself lacked.

The one effort at conceptual clarity Hall made was extremely revealing of his weakness as a systematic thinker. In 1902 and 1903, Hall and a number of students authored a new series of questionnaire studies which explicitly attempted to prove his theory that mental development of the individual recapitulated that of the race.[27] Hitherto, Hall had merely assumed its truth and never tested it critically against his data. Hall chose for his study topics which could most easily disclose the value of the theory—children's attitudes toward clouds, light and dark, and fire and cold—all universal elements of man's experience. All the studies came to conclusions similar to those in the study of clouds: the forms children saw in clouds were clearly the products of environment, but the "picture-making impulse" itself was probably a racial inheritance. Emotional responses to clouds, like the fear of dark thunderclouds, were also found to parallel those of racial experience rather than the child's own.[28] Such studies, of course, could not prove the recapitulation

25. MS, President's Report, 31 Aug 1903, CUP; "Circular," Apr 1903, CUP.
26. GSH, "Child Study at Clark University: An Impending New Step," 1903, p. 96.
27. GSH and J. E. W. Wallin, "How Children and Youth Think and Feel About Clouds," 1902; GSH and T. L. Smith, "Reactions to Light and Darkness," 1903; GSH, "Note on Cloud Fancies," 1903; GSH and C. E. Browne, "Children's Ideas of Fire, Heat, Frost and Cold," 1903, and "The Cat and the Child," 1904. See also Alice Thayer, "A Study of Children's Interest in Flowers," *PS* 12 (1905): 107–40.
28. GSH and Wallin, "Clouds," 1902, pp. 503, 505.

theory; they did make as strong a case for the impulses they described as Hall had ever done before.

Hall's strategy, however, only displayed more poignantly the weaknesses of the theory. Recapitulation seemed most plausible for those aspects of child behavior most far removed from the central learning experiences of children. While Hall waxed eloquent about the pedagogical value of encouraging children to gaze at clouds and open fires, educators and psychologists must have been justifiably disappointed at such conclusions.[29] In 1903, Hall and his assistant published a new questionnaire study on curiosity and interest in children but again could only promise that a comprehensive chart of children's interests, showing their curves of rise and fall by years, was "impending."[30]

Hall had neither the investigative techniques nor the conceptual ability to analyze the innate components of childhood development or to relate them systematically to what and how the child learned from experience. He could only loosely hang his insightful descriptions of the pattern of development on the recapitulation theory, already in the early years of the twentieth century a weak reed upon which to hang anything. After 1903, Hall continued to predict that genetic psychology would someday fulfill its promise and produce a science of education, and he continued to contribute toward that end, but he no longer spoke of performing the critical sifting and intellectual synthesis himself.[31]

Other scientific offshoots of child study besides Thorndike's appeared after 1900 to challenge Hall's vision, and the most important of them appeared in his own circle at Clark: mental testing and clinical psychology. Although the mental testing movement is not usually considered a product of child study, it was given great impetus by the child study movement as a whole and by the open atmosphere Hall stimulated at Clark for interchange between educational, psychological, and psychopathological subjects.[32]

29. GSH, "Note on Cloud Fancies," 1903.
30. GSH and T. L. Smith, "Curiosity and Interest," 1903, p. 356.
31. Hall stated, *PNEA,* 1904, p. 787, that in his method "there lies implicit an imposing genetic logic. . . . But the time for development of this logic has not yet come."
32. The role of Clark University in catalyzing the mental testing movement

Some attention was drawn to the problem of gauging intellectual capacities in the first decade of child study. Although special classes had often been available in urban schools for some kinds of defective children, more stringent compulsory attendance laws and child studies, like those on sight and hearing defects, made increasingly visible the heterogeneous capacities of children in school and their wide variety of special needs.[33] After 1900, teachers and guardians of the mentally deficient and discussions of mental abnormalities made more frequent appearances at child study meetings.[34] Hall himself and other child study workers elsewhere were inundated with letters from parents asking for guidance in the treatment of some abnormality or for a personal examination for their child.[35] One of the functions given to the Child Study Department of the Chicago public schools, the first institutionalization of child study in a local school system, was the examination of exceptional children to determine their need for special treatment.[36]

The tools at hand for such determinations were meager. Measurements of elementary functions, like reaction times and perceptual discrimination, had been taken in the laboratory. The idea of using them to test individual capacity had been put forward by Cattell as early as 1890 and was widespread among scientific psychologists during the decade.[37] By 1901, however, it was shown that these tests were not an adequate guide to general capacity.[38] The effort which finally led to practicable tests of intelligence was that of

is mentioned by William Kessen, ed., *The Child* (New York: John Wiley, 1965), p. 208, and given considerable attention by Kimball Young, "The History of Mental Testing," *PS* 31 (1924): 1–48.

33. Mark Haller, *Eugenics; Hereditarian Attitudes in American Thought* (New Brunswick: Rutgers University Press, 1963), p. 198. See also, E. W. Scripture, "Tests on School Children," *ER* 5 (1893): 52–61; *PNEA*, 1895, pp. 895–98, 910.

34. See, e.g., *PNEA*, 1902, pp. 710–16; 1904, pp. 738–44 and ff.; 1905, p. 708.

35. GSH to Adolf Meyer, 23 Aug 1909, Meyer Papers; Carl Emil Seashore, "Autobiography," in Murchison, *History of Psychology in Autobiography*, 1:265.

36. *PNEA*, 1902, pp. 710–16.

37. Cattell, "Mental Tests and Measurements," *Mind* 15 (1890): 373–81, and "Tests of the Senses and Faculties" *ER* 5 (1893): 257–65; "Physical and Mental Tests," *PR* 5 (1898): 172–79; Samuel Fernberger, "The A.P.A., A Historical Summary, 1892–1930," *Psychological Bulletin* 29 (1932): 42–43.

38. R. S. Woodworth, "James McKeen Catell, 1860–1944," *PR* 51 (1944): 203.

Alfred Binet—himself a representative of the child study impulse in France. Binet's tests of the higher intellectual capacities, organized according to an age scale, were first translated, disseminated, and improved in America by a group of Hall's students.[39]

Beginning in the late 1890s, Hall attracted to Clark a number of very able men, often from normal school backgrounds, where they had been influenced by one of his disciples. They flourished in the Clark atmosphere, kept in touch with each other's work and sometimes stimulated each other to pioneer in the fields of testing and clinical psychology. H. H. Goddard and Edmund B. Huey took their degrees from Hall in 1899; J. E. W. Wallin did postgraduate study with Hall in 1901 and 1902; Fred Kuhlmann, Lewis M. Terman, and Arnold Gesell all worked with Hall and then took their degrees under the more methodical Sanford between 1903 and 1906.[40]

These students had the benefit of Hall's concern with psychopathology, as well as child study and education. In 1893, when he returned to teaching, Hall had begun taking his students to the Worcester State Hospital for the Insane for demonstrations. Two years later, when Adolf Meyer was appointed pathologist at the Worcester Hospital, Hall named him docent at Clark and had him conduct at the hospital an annual series of lectures and demonstrations on psychopathology for Clark students. Goddard, Huey, and Wallin studied with Meyer. After 1902, when Meyer left for New York, Dr. Edward Cowles of the MacLean Hospital in Boston conducted the lectures and demonstrations.

In 1908, H. H. Goddard, then director of the research laboratory of the Vineland Training School for the Feeble-Minded, one of the most progressive of such institutions, discovered Binet's efforts and in 1910 published in his school journal and the *Pedagogical Seminary* a translation of his test and a report of his own successful efforts to use the Binet tests and scale. In 1910, Huey, Kuhlmann, Wallin, and Terman all tried the tests and began to report success-

---

39. Kimball Young, "History of Mental Testing," pp. 11–31.
40. Terman, "Autobiography," pp. 298 ff.; J. E. W. Wallin, *The Odyssey of a Psychologist* (Lyndalia, Delaware: by the author, 1955), pp. 17–26; Arnold Gesell, "Autobiography," in Murchison, *History of Psychology in Autobiography,* 4:125–28.

ful results.[41] Huey and Kuhlmann had both gone on from their Clark studies to become, with Goddard, among the first psychologists employed at institutions for the feebleminded. Wallin had decided on the basis of his Clark experience to apply psychology to education and would open the following year at the University of Pittsburgh a clinical department of psychology. Terman had just gone to Stanford University to teach psychology and school hygiene, after putting in several years on the normal school circuit.

In 1910 and 1911 Goddard and Terman talked of this work to the annual child study department meetings of the NEA, a natural outlet for Hall students who recognized immediately its educational implications.[42] Eventually both Terman and Goddard worked with Robert Yerkes on the wartime testing program in which the movement came of age, and it was Terman who was responsible for the first standardized IQ test widely used in this country, the Stanford-Binet.[43]

Hall's influence on these Clark students worked against, as well as for, the development of tests. He tried to discourage Terman from undertaking his pioneer doctoral project on tests that would differentiate exceptionally bright from exceptionally dull students; so Terman took the project to Professor Sanford.[44] Hall voiced frequent doubts to all his students about the testing effort. He doubted the contribution such work would make to a basic, genetic psychology, and he was irritated and bored by the substantial methodological and statistical efforts the work involved.[45] On the other hand, he was reluctant to disown such a successful stepchild, and at the time of the Great War, was publicly and enthusiastically endorsing the work.[46] Ultimately, some of his skepticism returned.

Hall's greatest influence was indirect. He supplied his students

41. Kimball Young, "History of Mental Testing," pp. 35–37.

42. *PNEA*, 1910, p. 890; 1911, pp. 870–78. Terman called the first professional conference on the subject of the Binet-Simon tests in connection with the Fourth International Congress on School Hygiene in Buffalo, N.Y., 1913, which he was planning with Burnham. *PS* 20 (1913): 549–54.

43. Young, "History of Mental Tests," p. 40.

44. Terman, "Autobiography," p. 318.

45. GSH to Abraham Flexner, 5 Apr 1917, CUP.

46. GSH, "Practical Relations between Psychology and the War," 1917, p. 16; GSH, "Some Possible Effects of the War on American Psychology," 1919, pp. 48–49.

with the stimulus to put psychology to work in educational and medical settings, to join insights from a variety of different fields in novel combinations, and to attack directly the larger, functional units of behavior. In this environment, talented students could break out of the atomistic categories of traditional experimental psychology in which Cattell's testing efforts were trapped, though they could not acquire the necessary statistical competence which Cattell and others supplied for the movement. Hall's hereditarian imprint, reinforcing the work of Francis Galton and the evolution-ism of the day, remained with Goddard, Terman, and through Thorndike as well, much of the subsequent intelligence testing effort.

Out of this same group of students came a substantial stimulus to clinical psychology, a field closely bound up with the development of testing techniques.[47] According to Wallin, Clark University was in those days the mecca for would-be clinical psychologists, and even those pioneers who had already been trained elsewhere and were embarked on their careers came to study at Clark for at least a year during this period, to "get" Hall.[48] Somewhat later, a number of talented women students, including Miriam Van Waters, Florence Mateer, and Phyllis Blanchard, went on from Clark to distinguished careers in clinical psychology. Here, again, Hall's in-fluence was chiefly one of stimulation and freedom, in an atmo-sphere full of concern for education, the child, abnormality, and pathology. And, again, Hall's direct influence sometimes countered the indirect one. His opposition to the individual case-study method drove Miriam van Waters to take her degree under Chamberlain, and, when she later decided to work with delinquent girls, Hall urged her not to do so, on the grounds that such work was unbe-coming a woman.[49] Hall was also hampered by incapacity. As God-dard noted rather bitterly, when he wrote Hall for advice on how to

47. Theodate L. Smith, "The Development of Psychological Clinics in the United States," *PS* 21 (1914): 143–53.

48. Wallin, *Odyssey of a Psychologist*, p. 20.

49. Rowles, *"The Lady at Box 99,"* pp. 92–95; GSH to Mrs. John A. Gun-dry, 20 May 1912, CUP. Florence Mateer did her thesis under Burnham, a pioneer effort in the use of conditioning techniques in the experimental study of children. See Florence Mateer, *Child Behavior* (Boston: Badger, 1918).

study the mentally deficient, Hall's reply was useless.[50] When Hall wrote Adolf Meyer in 1909, asking for advice on how to set up a children's clinic at Clark University, he said that he had had last year alone nearly six hundred letters from "anxious parents, . . . with which I am able to do practically nothing. I find this the most difficult of all the departments." Hall was eager, however, to find young men who would be willing to pioneer in the field.[51]

The most direct line of influence that outlived Hall into the new era of substantial study of child development was carried by Gesell. After getting his degree from Clark, Gesell thought of going into clinical psychology and worked for a while with Terman and Goddard. Finding himself limited to the normal school positions Hallians could most easily secure, he decided to get a medical degree to increase his competence. In 1911 an opportunity appeared at Yale to teach education and Gesell went there, finished his medical studies, and devoted the rest of his career to the study of the developmental stages of childhood. Many aspects of his work followed Hall's, from his emphasis on the primary role of heredity in determining growth, to his method of collecting large masses of observations and organizing them into descriptive patterns at ascending stages of the age cycle. Through most of his career, too, he found himself with a wide popular following and much opposition from his behavioristic academic colleagues for his persistent hereditarianism.[52]

As child study was spawning more viable, specialized efforts among psychologists after 1900, the teaching profession was show-

50. Henry H. Goddard, "In the Beginning," *Training School Bulletin* 40 (1943): 154–55. Hall's letter of advice was a perfunctory list of topics with some genetic interest such as he had assigned questionnaires on, from automatisms to play. He told Goddard, "It is very easy to make such superficial suggestions . . . and you can indefinitely extend the list." GSH to H. H. Goddard, 9 Feb 1906, Archives of the History of American Psychology, University of Akron. When faced with concrete data, Hall could often sense significant meaning, but his recapitulation theory, in the abstract, gave him no real sense of where to look for meaning.

51. GSH to Adolf Meyer, 23 Aug 1909, Meyer Papers; GSH to W. H. Holmes, Jr., 9 Nov 1909, CUP.

52. Gesell, "Autobiography"; Arnold Gesell to GSH, 24 Sept 1910, CUP; Kessen, *The Child,* pp. 209–11.

ing greater concern for the social aspects of education. An informed observer of the educational scene commented in 1909 that the interest in reforming education on the basis of psychology had ended around 1900; now the profession was turning toward the relations between education and society.[53] As the programs of the NEA disclose, this change did occur among the articulate, pace-setting portion of the profession. The social aspect of education was, however, a rather vague catchall for interests and motives even more diverse than those represented in child study.

On a theoretical level, the renewed awareness of the role of society in education in part grew out of argument with Hall's naturalism. The social ends of education, moral and intellectual, had traditionally been at the center of American educational thinking. Hall's bold declaration that the substance and goal of education instead lay implicit in the child's nature challenged every educational thinker of his day. Harris's reliance on the intellectual tools of civilization, Dewey's view of the school as a form of community, and Thorndike's turn to analysis of the learning process were all sharpened by their encounter with Hall.

Much of the educators' social concern was not theoretical, however, but drew from attitudes and reform efforts typical of the progressive period. Reflecting the work of child labor reformers and settlement house workers, educators talked about making the school into a community center, for adults as well as children. Child study itself had sometimes led teachers to examine the home and community surroundings of their children and to adopt this view.[54] A still more pervasive theme was the socialization of the child. Partly this was the old concern to create an inner moral guide to direct the child through a rapidly changing society. In part, it expressed the progressives' desire to substitute social cooperation for the competitive and socially destructive individualism of the old order.[55] The writings of

53. Ellwood P. Cubberley, *Changing Conceptions of Education* (Boston: Houghton Mifflin, 1909), pp. 49–68. See also *PNEA*, 1902, pp. 703–10; *Forum* 34 (1902); 269–74.

54. *PNEA*, 1897, pp. 859–65; 1899, p. 1035; 1900, pp. 585–90; 1905, pp. 721–24.

55. A good example of this line of thinking, with its emphasis on "service," is Cubberley, *Changing Conceptions of Education*, pp. 49–68.

John Dewey most clearly articulated this theme and rose to popularity among educators partly on its strength.

Of all the ancillary participants in the child study movement, Dewey was certainly the most important. Fifteen years Hall's junior and for two years his student at Johns Hopkins University, Dewey was in the 1890s still a minor figure on the scene of educational reform.[56] Dewey's exposure to Hall's psychology had helped to lead him to redefine his Hegelian standpoint and to make naturalism the foundation of his thinking, although it was his reading of William James's *Principles* in 1890 which most definitively shaped his new viewpoint.[57] Hall's lingering interest in education at Hopkins may also have had its effect in focusing Dewey's attention.

At the time Dewey arrived at Chicago in 1894 as professor of psychology and pedagogy, he found himself in the midst of the child study ferment. Dewey's concern for the relationship between individual and society, fortified by Hegelian philosophy, assured the fact that his conception of education would from the start include and mediate between both individual nature and the social order. Hall's articulate naturalism, however, may well have led Dewey to enrich the biological basis of his conception of child nature and to try to derive from it the social means and ends of education. In Dewey's early educational essays he accepted the romantic prescription to follow nature, as well as much of the Hallian interpretation of it, including the desire to recapitulate the history of the race and to derive the curriculum from the child's inherent interests. A central motive of his early effort appeared to be to link these natural instincts to social activities and socially desirable ends.[58]

56. Maxine Greene, "Dewey and American Education, 1894–1920," *School and Society* 87 (1959): 381–86.

57. Morton G. White, *The Origins of Dewey's Instrumentalism* (New York: Columbia University Press, 1943), particularly pp. 34–48; Marshall J. Cohen, "Dewey in Process," *Perspectives in American History* 3 (1969): 497–508. A note from Dewey to E. G. Boring, n.d., Boring Papers, states that Dewey "read a great deal" in psychology under Hall at Johns Hopkins, but "after James's *Principles* came out that influence outweighed all this put together."

58. The best discussion of Dewey's relation to and use of the child study doctrine is Strickland, "The Child and the Race," pp. 269–76, 306–14, 333–34. Dewey's solution was to base the curriculum on those "instincts which find their conscious outlet and expression in occupations. . . . In a rough way, all occu-

The relationship between the two men was inevitably difficult. From the time of their Hopkins experience, no great liking existed between them. In personal contact and in their published writings, they avoided each other as much as possible.[59] Neither man was anxious to admit the large area of similarity in their views, though Hall occasionally delighted in criticizing Dewey for precisely the reliance on biological norms and on recapitulation theory for which Dewey criticized him.[60] As Hall's personal influence in education declined after 1910, Dewey's began to rise. With his easy accommodation to the moral and religious standards of the past and his real concern for the reform of society, Dewey could speak to later generations with a fluency that Hall's pious, biological rhetoric could never attain. Hall made the doctrine of education according to child nature the dominant theme of educational reform in the 1890s, but it was through the medium of Dewey's social naturalism that the romantic, child-centered educational approach would reach its largest influence.

The different direction of their views also resulted in their having a different impact on the continuing stream of progressive education. By virtue of his lack of social concern, Hall's theory lacked the emphasis on adjustment to the immediate social world which pervaded Dewey's work. Dewey liked to chide Hall for thinking that the child's imagination could only be exercised on myths and distant events, when in fact the child was most interested in his immediate environment and community.[61] Hall in turn declared that teachers' attention to things near at hand to adolescents' lives and immediate social concerns was crippling their capacity for far-ranging ideals and abstract thought.[62]

This subtle divergence of their theories also had a moral dimen-

---

pations may be classified as gathering about man's fundamental relations to the world in which he lives. . . . It is hardly unreasonable to suppose that interests which have such a history behind them must be of the worthy sort." *The School and Society* (Chicago: University of Chicago Press, 1899), pp. 135–37.

59. Frederick Eby to the author, 15 Sept 1962.

60. GSH, "Some Social Aspects of Education," 1902, p. 89; Dewey, *School and Society*, pp. 135–37.

61. Ibid., p. 146. Strickland, "The Child and the Race," pp. 301–5, has pointed out that the experience of Dewey's Laboratory School could have confirmed Hall's contention.

62. *Adol*, 2:463–65.

sion. Dewey's emphasis on the social goals of education may have
seemed to many teachers to sanction their traditional moralism in a
way that Hall's naturalism did not. For all his overt moralizing,
Hall's talk of making room for sex and savage impulses was probably more abrasive to the traditional American teacher than Dewey's
desire to create a socially cooperative adult, albeit a politically liberal
one. Traditional moralists quickly saw the possibility of using the
social group, the child's peer group, to inculcate and enforce their
moral demands.[63] Dewey's social program in the early years of the
century, moreover, did not always make as clear as some of his later
writings that he wanted the child socialized in the image of the ideal
society of the future and not the imperfect one of the present.[64]
Hall, whose educational thinking always remained rooted in his
experience around the turn of the century, later explained Dewey's
rise to popularity as based on the fact that "the average conservative
teacher who reads him thinks himself progressive, but never to a
degree that makes him feel unsafe or even much unsettled. . . . He is
best described as a mediator between child study and the old philosophical orthodoxies of Herbart, Hegel, Hamilton and other
more or less metaphysical thinkers."[65] Hall could never understand
why Dewey's theory was so popular, when to his mind it merely
reintroduced the older metaphysical view that the ends and aims of
the society ought to control education. Considering the fate of
Dewey's theory in the hands of some of his followers, Hall may well
have been correct in suggesting that the more traditional interest in
social education did, in fact, underlie some of Dewey's support.

Differences also appeared in their attitude toward reorganization
of the classroom. Hall never had Dewey's opportunity at Chicago to
actually organize a progressive school, and hence he never focused
as clearly as Dewey on the issues involved. Dewey believed that the

63. See *PNEA*, 1905, pp. 734–40.
64. See for example Dewey's talk to the NEA in 1902, "The School As a
Social Center," where he approved the purposes of this educational movement
"to keep the individual properly adjusted to a rapidly changing environment,"
to interpret to him the intellectual and social meaning of his work, to educate him
to compensate for "the decay of dogmatic and fixed methods of social discipline,"
and to bring people and beliefs together so as to "lessen friction and instability."
PNEA, 1902, p. 381. Cf. *Forum* 34 (1902): 269–70.
65. *LCP*, pp. 499–500.

traditional authoritarian classroom, in which teachers ruled over competing students, and the whole curriculum and pace of advance was set from outside, could not possibly respect the child's nature, no matter what the attitude of the teacher. He therefore reduced classes to small groups of about twelve, in which the teacher took a directing part, but in the context of organizing the group's own activities, usually projects which involved a good deal of making and building. The cooperative activities of the group thus became the source of the curriculum and the determinant of advance.[66]

Although Hall never specifically addressed himself to the organization of the classroom, his influence went in a direction different from Dewey's. Hall's magnification of the role of the teacher as purveyor of information, and his masculine protests against the decay of traditional discipline and the discouragement of fighting and competition in the schools, suggest that he was not willing to abandon the authoritarian, competitive classroom. Hall did want to change the classroom, however, and his very reliance on the teacher allowed his theory to escape some of the drawbacks of Dewey's design of the curriculum around constructive group activities.

Hall's conception of the teacher-student relationship was inspired by the Platonic ideal of master and pupil and found its embodiment in the ideal German school teacher.[67] The teacher was to remain the unquestioned authority and the chief source of the curriculum. Hall once commented in an implied criticism of Dewey's methods:

My chief scruple is whether or not the receptive powers of children get that relative predominance which the very nature of childhood requires, for active as it is, its observing, listening, afferent faculties are still greater.[68]

Except for the needed drill during latency, however, the teacher was to employ his art imaginatively and sparingly, providing the student with suggestions and inspiration, rather than masses of knowledge or ready-made answers, so that the student would be prepared and stimulated to conduct much of the learning process

66. Mayhew and Edwards, *The Dewey School.*
67. See "The German Teacher Teaches," 1907.
68. GSH, "Some Social Aspects of Education," 1902, p. 89.

himself.[69] Hall's conception of active learning, despite all his emphasis on physical training, was still one of *mental* activity, not physical.

Hall was also not willing to limit the freedom of study and pace of the individual by that of the group. Along with his outspoken opposition to the standardized, lockstep organization of the schools, Hall often suggested that the pupil should be promoted or held back separately in each subject, at any time of the year, and by merely the word of the teacher, and praised efforts to institute individualized systems.[70] He particularly supported Preston W. Search in his pioneer efforts to start a program of individualized instruction and promotion. Search was criticized from the right by Harris, who accused him of returning to the chaos of the ungraded school, and from the left by Parker, who praised the social benefits of group instruction and activity.[71] Hall alone wrote a favorable introduction to Search's account of his experiment, published in 1899, and the book was dedicated to him.[72] Something of this attitude may well have been transmitted to Frederic Burk, who took his degree with Hall in 1898 and went on to become president of the San Francisco State Normal College, which introduced the "Individual System," and thence to two of his students, Carleton Washburne and Helen Parkhurst, who originated the individualized Winnetka and Dalton plans.[73]

From its beginnings at the turn of the century, Hall was aware of the rising interest in the social aspects of education and tried, one way and another, to draw it into his own orbit. Hall not only named his ideal high school the "People's College," he also began to talk about the "social aspects of education," dutifully repeating all the catchwords of the social theorists. Hall cleverly showed how a number of his favorite doctrines could be turned to the purposes of the

69. *EP*, 1:vii–viii.

70. GSH in Worcester *Gazette*, 29 Jan 1903; "How Can We Make the Average Public School a Good School?" 1909, pp. 10–13.

71. *PNEA*, 1895, pp. 406–11.

72. Preston W. Search, *An Ideal School* (New York: D. Appleton, 1901). Hall said Search's principles were the basis of progressive education. Search called Hall "America's Greatest Educator."

73. Cremin, *Transformation of the School*, pp. 295–99, describes this line of progressive development without linking it to Hall's individualistic bias.

social theorists, as indeed later they were. His ideal of adolescent development, for example, could support the conception of the high school as

the embryo of future society which we cannot forecast, and to merely train for the present is to dwarf talent and originality. . . . Thus to feed the new centers of all-sided interest should be our end. . . . the best possible social education now is to develop the fullest possible maturity of the individual in as many directions as possible.[74]

Though Hall continued to add some of the social slogans to his talks on child study during the following years, the structure of his thought remained tied to the polarities of the individual and the race.

Hall nonetheless made one last effort to restore the child study movement, by trying to combine it with the child welfare movement. His ideas were sympathetic to many reformers in the areas of child health, recreation, and delinquency, particularly the playground movement, children's libraries, drama, music, dancing, and nature study organizations. The heart of the child welfare movement, however, lay in the child labor and juvenile protective associations which had grown during the progressive period and mounted a campaign to establish in the federal government a children's bureau to investigate and recommend improvement in the condition of children.[75] On these issues, Hall could not keep himself from publicly alternating between professions of sympathetic concern for "dependent, delinquent and defective children"[76] and reactionary condemnation of the excessive paternalism of the state and excessive restriction of child labor.

There is a considerable difference . . . between different social classes, and . . . what would really seem hardship to one may be luxury to another. . . . the children of the poor . . . thrive well under a certain degree of neglect.[77]

With such an attitude, Hall could hardly expect to gain the confidence of child welfare workers.

74. "Some Social Aspects of Education," 1902, p. 90.
75. Robert H. Bremner, *From the Depths: The Discovery of Poverty in the United States* (New York: New York University Press, 1956), pp. 212–13, 220–22.
76. In Worcester *Telegram*, 11 Nov 1910.
77. GSH, "What Is to Become of Your Baby?" 1910, p. 664.

Nonethless Hall sensed the need of cooperation among the welfare organizations themselves as their number multiplied. He sent out a circular early in 1909 proposing to organize a permanent conference on child research and welfare, to meet that summer at Clark University. Receiving a universally favorable response, Hall said, he went ahead with the plan, and in July 1909 the first national child welfare congress was held at Clark and the conference was formed, with Hall as president and his disciples and allies, chiefly, as officers.[78] The meeting attracted a broad spectrum of the welfare movement and was repeated the following year at Clark with an even more distinguished list of speakers. After 1910, however, the national conference lapsed, and a third congress on child welfare was not held until 1914, when it appeared under the auspices of the National Mother's Congress, with no tie to Clark University or child study.[79]

Hall said later that the joining of the two movements failed because the child welfare people were not really interested in scientific child study.[80] He might also have said that he was not really interested in abolishing child labor. The child welfare workers must also have sensed Hall's desire to use them to gain a new base of support for his movement, financial as well as moral. By 1909, research in child development already required sums of money unavailable in Clark's budget. With Hall's teacher-workers fallen away and the questionnaire method discredited, he needed an institutional setting and a budget adequate to secure experts and facilities for experimental and clinical work.

Hall urged from the start of his union campaign that child study be incorporated into the proposed federal children's bureau, but he recognized this was an unlikely possibility.[81] He therefore announced at the first joint conference in 1909 the formation at Clark of a children's institute, which would engage in scientific and pedagogical research, open a children's clinic and experimental school, and undertake to coordinate efforts among child welfare

78. *Proceedings of the Child Conference for Research and Welfare* 1 (1909): ix–xvi.
79. *Proceedings of the Child Conference* 2 (1910).
80. *LCP*, p. 401.
81. "The Children's Institute of Clark University," 30 Apr 1910, CUP.

workers and between them and the scientists. The Clark trustees pledged $5,000 to start the institute, but Hall would need larger sums to keep it going. Hall apparently hoped that the tie of the institute to child welfare work would bring it funds from philanthropists who had hitherto been impervious to his pleas.[82] In addition, he may well have hoped that the welfare groups would fund their national conference sufficiently to support the institute.[83] Although child welfare philanthropy would indeed fund the major child development programs of the 1920s, neither possibility materialized for Hall, and after 1910 the institute was reduced to whatever work along its lines Hall's fellows could manage, and disappeared altogether after 1914.[84] Hall's designs on them, meanwhile, may well have frightened off the child welfare organizations.

The inability of Clark University adequately to finance Hall's child study plans was part of the general decline of the influence of Clark, as an institution, in the educational profession. Before 1900, Hall's Ph.D.s and summer school students constituted a formidable, strategically placed force in the profession. After 1900 the Teachers College at Columbia University began to send a far larger number of graduates into the field, trained to respect the statistical methods of Thorndike and the theories of Dewey.[85] This shift of institutional power sealed the death of the child study movement.

In 1911 Hall published his last major educational work, his two-volume collection of essays on *Educational Problems*. A typical Hallian compilation of old and new data on his series of favorite topics, the book was noted chiefly for its treatment of sex and received several scathing reviews.[86] Thereafter, Hall's message and reputation survived intact only in more backward outposts, where

82. "Records of the Board of Trustees, 1901–1909," 17 June 1909, CUP. GSH to Starr J. Murphy, 21 Mar 1907; GSH in Worcester *Telegram*, 18 June 1909.

83. Open letter from GSH et al., 20 Sept 1909, in Jacques Loeb Papers, Library of Congress.

84. *Clark Register*, 1909–15.

85. Cremin, *Transformation of the School*, pp. 171–73.

86. "Morbid Pedagogism," *Nation* 93 (July 1911): 80–81; Paul Shorey, "An Educational Culture-Bouillon," *School Review* 20 (1912): 73–80. See also *Bookman* 34 (Sept 1911): 88–90.

his disciples still presided, and he himself still came occasionally to repeat the old stirring lectures. Except for such brief forays, Hall did, as he told a correspondent in 1912 he would, "go back to psychology, my first love, and . . . let education henceforth entirely alone."[87]

In 1911 the Child Study Department of the NEA changed its name to the Department of Child Hygiene. The change reflected the more specific interests of two groups in the department, the school health officers and the scientific students of school hygiene and mental testing.[88] The testing work soon dropped away from this department, and in 1924 the guardians of school health joined with gym teachers to form the Department of Health and Physical Education—in outward form, at least, a fitting heir of Hall's great emphasis on health and physical development.

The schools themselves showed only a partial willingness to respond to Hall's message. The educators and teachers who were actually involved in child study constantly testified to the enlightening effect it had on their understanding of childhood. But that effect did not go very deep into the teaching profession. Teachers after 1910 more often became interpreters of culture rather than mere drillmasters, but they still most often relied on formalized methods tied to inferior textbooks.[89] Child study never proved to be the perennial solvent of formalism in the schools, and indeed, no other has been found.

Nor did public school teachers always acquire the knowledge of their subjects which Hall thought would also vitalize teaching. Hall called for the increased *professional* education of the teacher, not quite seeing the difficulty of raising the commitment to knowledge in institutions designed for elementary vocational preparation. When normal schools began to demand the right to train secondary teachers as well, he reluctantly acquiesced if those normal schools were connected with a university.[90] That connection, however, proved merely formal. Understandably in his day, when only a

87. GSH to Ripley Hitchcock, 19 Jan 1912, CUP.

88. *PNEA*, 1911, pp. 870–78.

89. The distinction between drillmaster teachers and interpreters of culture is drawn by Finkelstein, "Governing the Young," pp. 23–24.

90. GSH, "Normal Schools," 1902, pp. 180–92; *Adol*, 2:501.

minority of the elementary teaching force had even some normal
school training, Hall worked to build up and strengthen the normal
schools, not realizing that this system, even while raising standards
within the profession, would perpetuate the inferiority of intellectual standards in the teaching profession vis à vis the university.

Hall's chief influence on the high schools came after 1910 when
he had abandoned education and his influence was carried chiefly by
his disciples and writings. Hall's emphasis on the distinct pedagogical needs of the adolescent period coincided precisely with the trend
of democratization in the high school and hence reinforced the
deemphasis of the traditional, college-oriented curriculum for such
other goals as health and the repackaging of the intellectual disciplines into dilute forms presumably more educational. His disciples also claimed that his ideas were extremely influential in two
reforms which he never advocated: the establishment of junior high
schools and the "democratizing" of high school teacher training, by
placing it in the newly upgraded state teacher's colleges after 1915.[91]
At the end of his life, Hall was pleased with many of the changes
that had been made, yet critical of the many ways in which the
schools still fell short of his ideals.[92]

As with any figure so closely bound up with his times, Hall's role
in child study and education was very complex. Without any viable,
systematic body of ideas to perpetuate his influence and with the
offspring of his labors scattered amidst several professions, Hall's
importance in his own day was not long remembered. His principal
educational doctrines, moreover, rode the tide of popular thinking
and were then lost in it. His offer of science and romantic naturalism
appeared at the strategic moment to gain wide popular and educational currency. Those substantial elements of his thinking that
opposed the tide were criticized or ignored in his own day and
quickly forgotten to history; and when the tide turned toward
social concerns, most of his ideas were absorbed and submerged in
the new popular viewpoint.

The imprint of Hall's own effort was most deeply felt in the brief
tie he was able to effect between the educational, psychological, and

91. "G. Stanley Hall," *Journal of Education* 98 (Mar 1923): 257–58; Frederick Eby to the author, 6 Nov 1962.
92. *LCP*, pp. 479–547.

to some extent, medical professions around the center of child study. It took Hall's voracious appetite for experience, and his enormous desire to unify the divergent elements of that experience, to bring together for a time the variety of needs and viewpoints involved. The tie was clearly doomed, and yet it was the most important and fruitful of Hall's creations. From it came central, formative impulses of progressive education, child development, educational psychology, clinical psychology, school hygiene, and mental testing. Certainly, without penetrating systematic thinkers around him, Hall's broad, suggestive viewpoints would have gone for naught. Without Hall's unorthodox synthetic urges, however, both psychology and education might have been considerably poorer.

Beginning in 1896, when Hall saw that child study could form the basis of a genetic psychology, his work in the popular pedagogical movement always had a second dimension. Not only could the best of the child investigations enter into a developmental science, but Hall's own studies constantly probed beyond the school-oriented boundaries of the movement to earlier and later stages, and to more basic considerations. The genetic psychology Hall outlined over the following years concerned aspects of the life cycle from infancy to senescence, and included the study of psychopathology and of primitive peoples as devolutionary phenomena. Finally he incorporated into its framework the psychoanalytic theories of Sigmund Freud.

Hall was genuinely impressed by the questionnaire data generated by the studies of the child's basic emotional patterns. Although unreliable on many counts, and only fragments torn from the personal and developmental contexts that could give them meaning, the data did provide revealing material for an insightful student of human nature. The data confirmed to Hall the formative influence of childhood and adolescent experience and suggested an adult amnesia covering the intimate experiences of these earlier stages. The striking gap in appropriateness between some elements of behavior and the child's or adult's present environment suggested their origin in earlier developmental stages and an earlier environment. Since only a small amount of the wide range of feelings and needs disclosed in the data actually showed on the surface of any individual, Hall was impressed by the importance of the unconscious.[1]

Hall did a questionnaire study on tickling and the comic sense in 1897 in which he suggested that sexual feelings had their genetic origin in the tickling sensations of infancy and proposed a "reversionary" theory of wit and humor perhaps not recognized before: our laughter at forbidden, obscene topics, Hall said, represented the feeling of liberty and joy at breaking through the restraints on primitive feelings established by civilization.[2]

In 1898, Hall attempted a brief, pioneer study of the development of the sense of self. Beginning with the infant's formation of a sense of his own body, Hall suggested that "man's primitive body consciousness has been largely disguised and transformed into clothes-consciousness." The core of the ego was unconscious, Hall said, and ever remained so. He placed the child's relationship to the mother at the center of development. The child early established two tendencies, one toward the mother and home, the other outward toward the social sphere. The child grew, Hall felt, by a dynamic process in which its expansive instincts overcame the fears attached to leaving mother and home, a theory which found ample confirmation in Hall's own life.[3]

In the summer of 1898, Hall set about to evoke and examine his own memories of his childhood by systematically visiting three old farmhouses in which he had lived as a boy and recording his impressions on the spot. Moved by nostalgia for his lost home, Hall doubted "if there ever has been a better school of infancy than the old New England farm in its best days." But Hall was also impressed by the way "the physical features of this old farm had such amazing power to play upon my deeper sentiments and emotions." The emotional tone of his memories was the chief finding Hall drew from this experience. He speculated that it was due either to the merger of these early memories with ancestral ones, "Weismann to the contrary notwithstanding," or that these were "baby stages of mind," formed when the senses were so closely related to

1. GSH, "A Study of Fears," 1897, p. 147, 246; *Adol*, 2:91.
2. GSH and Arthur Allin, "The Psychology of Tickling, Laughing and the Comic," 1897, p. 31.
3. GSH, "Some Aspects of the Early Sense of Self," 1898, pp. 351–95.

feelings that "the emotional tone which colored all impressions may have been the organ of experience." These baby impressions were then covered over by later, more mature strata of mind and uncovered only partially in memory.[4]

Hall's study of pity in 1900, an insightful, yet formless, discussion of everything from social compassion to self-pity, brought Hall virtually to his knees:

> I confess at times, as I do now, how poor, weak and utterly inadequate all the resources at my command are to fathom such abysmal processes of the heart. Yet psychologists now must face these and triumph or decay. . . .[5]

Using introspective insight into his own feelings and difficulties, as well as an educated sense of the nature of developmental problems, Hall was attacking in a fragmentary way some of the key items on the agenda of a genetic psychology, items which Freud, too, a few years later would grasp more profoundly in working out his own developmental psychology.

Hall brought together his genetic insights as fully as he ever would in his two-volume work on *Adolescence* in 1904. In the course of describing this prime period of life, Hall imposed some system on human development, its relation to pathology and primitive peoples, and his own philosophy of life. Although his ideas would evolve further after 1904, particularly under the influence of Freud, *Adolescence* would remain the most comprehensive statement of Hall's genetic psychology.

Beginning at the biological font Darwin's theory suggested, Hall's starting point in psychology was "the will to live," the fundamental drive of the human body and mind. This life force expressed itself in two principal forms, as hunger and love; and these two "feeling-instincts," as Hall called them, were the original sources of energy for, and the directing guides of, individual growth, development, reproduction, and behavior. Over the course of the evolution of the species, they had been molded and subdivided into numerous—indeed, innumerable—subsidiary feeling-instincts; and these acted as the "psychophores or bearers of mental heredity" of the race (2:9, 60–62, 69–70). Anger was such a

---

4. GSH, "Note on Early Memories," 1899, pp. 485–512.
5. GSH and F. H. Saunders, "Pity," 1900, p. 572.

derivative feeling-instinct, developed in the course of sexual competition and aroused when the ego was thwarted. But his list ran the gamut to the "truancy instinct," the instinct to run away from home, inherited from primitive man's nomadic ages.

Hall based his theory of mental development on the recapitulation theory and on the neo-Lamarckian view of the inheritance of acquired characteristics. Hall took account of the criticisms that had been made of the recapitulation theory. He recognized the difficulty of using a record of parallel development of the individual and the species that was so distorted and inverted in detail, and the near impossibility of distinguishing inherited instincts from acquired responses (1:viii; 2:93–94). He declared his belief, however, in the possibility of using the theory when evidence suggested it and expected that ultimately it would be vindicated by science. Hall could not abandon a theory which so powerfully conveyed his own inner vision, that

we are influenced in our deeper, more temperamental dispositions by the life-habits and codes of conduct of we know not what unnumbered hosts of ancestors, which like a cloud of witnesses are present throughout our lives. . . . our souls are echo-chambers in which their whispers reverberate.

"We have to deal," Hall concluded, "with the archaeology of mind" (2:61).

This view likened the mind of the child and the adolescent not only to earlier evolutionary forebears but to existing primitive peoples, on the theory that these peoples represented arrested forms of the childhood and adolescence of the race (2:648–748). Like E. B. Tylor and other early ethnologists, he assumed that the characteristic animism and concreteness of primitive thinking resembled those qualities of the childish mind.[6] Hall constantly found parallels between youthful forms of play, social organization, religious feeling, and the like, and those of various primitive tribes. The recapitulation theory allowed Hall to use the biological and anthropological record as a limitless store of analogies with which to thicken his text and, occasionally, sharpen his sense of developmental levels in the individual. For despite his reliance on the

6. Robert Lowie, *The History of Ethnological Theory* (New York: Farrar and Rinehart, 1937), pp. 82–85.

theory, his focus was on the process of individual development, not that of the race.

The period of most rapid growth of any instinct in the individual Hall called its "nascent" period, and the way in which the instinct was molded at this critical time determined how its energies would be used later on in life (1:53–55).[7] Hall was aware that a balance had to be struck in the adjustment between inherited impulses and the requirements of civilization. Suppression or "inhibition" of the early forms of many desires by the higher, more civilized faculties was necessary to maturity. Aspects of the theories of nervous function of Hughlings Jackson led Hall to propose that inhibition of the nerve impulse involved "irradiation or long-circuiting to higher and more complex brain areas." On this neurological model, Hall pictured repression as antecedent to the thoroughly desirable process of "irradiation" or sublimation. Sexual energies, for example, could in normal development be largely diverted into higher and more socially acceptable channels (1:107–11, 162, 455–57).[8]

On the other hand, Hall wanted to give due expression to all the latent possibilities of human nature and criticized many of the "suppressions" and "repressals" which society forced upon individuals. "Faculties and impulses which are denied legitimate expression during their nascent periods," Hall warned, "break out well on in adult life—falsetto notes mingling with manly bass as strange puerilities" (2:90, 368–69, 381–82).

7. William James, *Principles of Psychology*, vol. 2, chap. 24, noted the same phenomenon under the "law of transitoriness" of instincts and also drew educational conclusions from it similar to Hall's.

8. According to Henri Ellenberger, *The Discovery of the Unconscious: The History and Evolution of Dynamic Psychiatry* (New York: Basic Books, 1970), pp. 274, 505, the term and concept of sublimation were well known by the end of the nineteenth century and had been used by Novalis, Schopenhauer, and most extensively, by Nietzsche. Hall chose, however, to use a term borrowed from neurophysiology, where the neural impulse was often spoken of as radiating or irradiating from one point in the nervous mechanism to adjacent or connected areas. This neural image is congruent with the concept of diversion common in the nineteenth-century English and American literature on sexual hygiene, where it was assumed that energy diverted from sexual activities could be channeled into civilized pursuits. Hale, *The Psychoanalytic Movement in America*, p. 44. In the first case, the energy is specifically sexual and retains something of its sexual character in its higher transformations. In the latter case, the energy is neutral and simply diverted elsewhere. Despite his terminology, Hall most often used irradiation in the first sense, of sublimation.

Hall was thus aware that the impulses released during development were not entirely outgrown. The healthy adult in play, and
characteristically, the adolescent and the genius, retained "mobility
up and down the genetic ladder," Hall said. "This functional
reversion [is] a resource of very great economic value for achievement," for it allows one "to tap the freshness and resources of
earlier years" (2:402). On the other hand, the appearance of impulses characteristic of earlier levels of development was also a sign
of pathology. If an impulse was allowed to develop precociously,
through overuse or premature elaboration, it could be arrested in this
childish form and persist into adult life. Hereditary or environmental damage could also, as in the popular concept of degeneration, lead to the persistence into adulthood of an earlier, regressive
trait; or the weakening of later, unifying and inhibiting functions
could allow primitive traits to appear unchecked (1:163–65, 264,
293–97, 321–22).

Especially at such critical stages of rapid development as early
adolescence, something could go awry, turning a normal trait into
an extreme, pathological form and arresting or erasing normal
growth. Hall speculated that many sexual perversions originated in
early adolescence, when the emerging sexual instinct was plastic and
indeterminate and could therefore be transferred onto "almost any
act or object." The same plasticity, of course, could produce more
normal "irradiations" (1:286). He also thought that dementia
praecox was likely to prove a functional product of the emotional
stresses and imbalances of adolescence, particularly in the sexual
sphere, rather than a product of toxic physical agents, as Kraepelin
thought it to be. We will never have an adequate idea of mental
pathology in adolescence, Hall stressed, until we have a clearer
understanding of the normal pattern of development (1:303–6).

In all his speculations on psychopathology, Hall was not exclusively wedded to theories of congenital, hereditary predisposition.
He accounted for an overgrown, childish impulse, a weak ego, or a
sexual malfunction by either a congenital predisposition or by unfavorable environmental conditions which disturbed normal function, or by both.

In the normal person as well as the ill one, the result of these
processes of sporadic growth, suppression, and reversion was to produce a psyche which "seems built layer upon layer of partly isolated

yet strangely interacting strata," a psyche in which much of the dynamic structure is unconscious and ill-coordinated, yet acts powerfully on behavior. These unconscious layers, Hall said, revealed themselves in

the many-voiced comments, the sense of assent and dissent, pleasure and pain, the elation of strength or the esthetic responses, the play of intuitions, the impulses to do or not to do, automatic tensions or contractions . . . the mild or incipient insanities [which anyone] that is honest and has true self-knowledge will . . . confess to recognizing in his own soul. (2: 67–68)

Personal insight obviously led Hall to recognize the complexity of mind.

The core of Hall's theory was his attribution of this complexity to the continued effective presence in the individual of prior developmental levels of psychic organization. Darwin had suggested as much in his study of expression in man and animals, and it was Darwin, Hall claimed, who also alerted him to look for the subtle clues left by development, "automatisms, acts, behaviour, things neglected, trivial and incidental, such as Darwin says are often most vital" (1:vii).

At bottom, Hall's insight into Darwin and developmental complexity was—as his evolutionary thinking had always been—historical. It was the conditional character of history, always subject to revision by later generations, which informed his evolutionism and his desire to search below the surface record of intentions to deeper causes. In psychology, as in history, Hall said,

one must always reason from what is said to what is meant in quest of another and deeper continuum, always finding what were thought to be causes turning out to be only effects, what seemed finalities to be beginnings or means, forces deemed supreme only provocatives of others that lie deeper. (2: 448)

In Hall's genetic psychology, not only did the mind become quite literally the product of the historical experience of the species, but it became itself a miniature historical realm, its layers conditioned by, and meaningful in relation to, the changing epochs of development. Historicism, as it were, entered the psyche, bringing in its train the problem of judging among relative values and problematic directions of growth.

In line with this historical view, Hall saw the historical series of religions and philosophical schools as part expressions of the total nature of man:

All thinking men are all of these in differing proportion and are any one of them at most, as it were, only by a small majority, if they are not dwarfed or maimed. . . . Age, mood, culture-stage, perhaps sex, demand a differing succession of isms already beginning to be slowly made out. (2: 50).

Beginning with his early recognition that he had "outgrown" Hegel, to this view of the fluidity of all beliefs, Hall turned historical criticism into psychological relativism.

His judgment of the various stages and products of development was not always neutral and inclusive, however. Hall was led by the high value he placed on feelings and unconscious processes to devalue consciousness and maturity.

The conscious adult person is not a monad reflecting the universe, but a fragment broken off and detached from the great world of soul, always, maimed, defined by special limitations. . . . Not so much our birth, but every year of growth and every degree of mental illumination "is a forgetting" of preexisting states and involves a lapse of other sections and activities of soul, as it were, to lower meristic levels.

. . . [Consciousness] may be a wart raised by the sting of sin, a product of alienation or a remedial process. We have no warrant that natural selection . . . determines what rises above the highest of the series of thresholds in mind. Consciousness seems in some of its aspects more likely a fall or a process of purgation so far as it is merely adaptive, and that which is best and survives is that which sinks deepest, beyond the test of recallability, and so becomes most fundamental. (2: 66 67)

From the time of *Adolescence* onward, Hall's turn away from consciousness as the center of psychology involved him in a basic dilemma. For he did not, by the same token, abandon his high regard for science. Indeed in the same passage in which he termed consciousness a secondary, remedial process, Hall went on to praise the only agents which could bring order to "all this flux and chaos" of the layered psyche: "common sense, that knows and adjusts to facts and to the external world, and the sciences of nature" (2:69).

Hall's genetic view of the psyche brought fully home to him the problematical character of progress. A few years later, in outlining the evolutionary basis of his psychology, Hall wondered aloud if evolution were really a case of devolution. "Which way really lies up and down, progress and retrogression in the vast continuum we call the universe . . . ?" he asked.[9] Hall continued nonetheless to laud both science and the unconscious and to evade the problem of progress as long as he could. The world war forced him, as so many of his contemporaries, to face the issue again.

Even as Hall was formulating his theory of development around the turn of the century, the theory of recapitulation, and its corollary, the theory of degeneration, were being discredited in better scientific circles; after World War I, they had all but disappeared from the American intellectual scene. For those who have since gone back to examine Hall's views, these theories have often exercised the fascination of strange antiques, drawing all attention to themselves and obscuring the content of the ideas they expressed. For Hall, however, these theories were admittedly loose and imperfect systematizations of his core belief in the human psyche as a composite of the developmental experience of the race.[10] If one looks past the idiom to the ideas themselves, one finds a relatively sophisticated viewpoint, a distillate of the evolutionary wisdom in regard to human development before Freud and Piaget, on which their theories also drew.

Hall's theory was, first of all, dynamic. He defined the psyche as "a quantum and direction of vital energy" (2:69). Hall tied this dynamism to a conventional and vague concept of instinct, which could do equally well for love and truancy, but he clearly linked instinctual impulses to emotion. Hall's exploration of intellectual development bore a few similarities to ideas developed by Jean

9. GSH, "A Glance at the Phyletic Background of Genetic Psychology," 1908, p. 181.

10. For all his advocacy of the genetic *approach*, Hall considered his systematic ideas to be in the nature of guesses which would, he hoped, be confirmed by more viable efforts in the future. When one of his disciples, George E. Partridge, wrote a neat summary of his theory which emphasized its systematic core of recapitulation theory, Hall's initial reaction on reading the manuscript was surprise. "It makes me sit up and respect myself more highly and what is much more important, it makes me begin to query whether after all, down below consciousness, I may have some kind of system that, if I live a decade or two more, might be put into a sort of scheme of things called perhaps geneticism." GSH to G. E. Partridge, 1 Mar 1911, CUP. See Partridge, *Genetic Philosophy of Education* (New York: Sturgis and Walton, 1912).

Piaget, but because Hall centered his theory on feelings, it more nearly resembled the work of Freud.[11]

Hall distinguished between the conscious and the unconscious and put in this latter category traces of childhood and adolescent experience, as well as traces of the evolutionary experience of the entire species. Hall never developed any systematic idea of how these different kinds of consciousness operated, however, beyond conventional discussions of association and dissociation. Perhaps extending the idea of erotic fetishes common in the literature on sexual perversions, Hall did notice that the questionnaire data showed how a fragmentary object, like a particular facial expression or kind of dress could bring forth very strong feelings of love, anger, or fear which obviously belonged to earlier experiences in which that object figured, ontogenetic and phylogenetic. Hall likened them to fetishes, and spoke of one's ultimate love object as conforming to and synthesizing such partial traces of past love experiences (2:113–15).[12]

Hall also had a vivid sense of the importance of confession and recognized that its psychology was "deep and complex." Confession was efficacious in several ways:

By showing others how vile we seem to ourselves, and taking them behind the veil of conventionalities, restraints, and hypocrisies, which had disguised our leprosy, we find at once a certain relief proportionate to the strain these falsities had caused us, and some energy is freed for inner reconstruction.

The shame of confession, Hall said, also acted as a motive to repair the public image one had just lost. But most important,

the very act of putting our sins into words and acknowledging them to others means that the long-festering sores have suppurated into consciousness. . . . Consciousness is a remedial process, a therapeutic agent. (2: 308).

But again, Hall did not apply this insight to the division between consciousness and the unconscious except in the most general way.

Hall more systematically applied his concepts of inhibition, irra-

11. Grinder, "The Concept of Adolescence in the Genetic Psychology of GSH," pp. 365–66, and McCullers, "The Contents of Children's Minds," pp. 2–3, suggest parallels between aspects of Hall's work and that of Piaget.

12. See also "Anger," 1899, p. 28.

diation, and regression. He pictured all three processes as involved in both healthy growth and pathology. These mechanisms expressed Hall's general sense of struggle going on in the psyche, but he did not see the specific way in which opposing forces motivated them, nor did he believe sublimation had any real limit.

Hall's theory was, finally, skewed toward biological rather than cultural factors. Hall by no means ignored the importance of environmental influence; indeed, his whole emphasis on education depended on the fact that the way in which the environment treated inherited impulses was crucial to their ultimate formation. Hall's concept of the "nascent period," taken over to psychological function from its earlier use in embryology, was somewhat similar to what has now been accepted as the "critical period" in the development of certain animal and human impulses. Hall's view of adolescence, moreover, like the theories of such recent analysts as Eric Erikson, stressed the fact that the experience of these later years significantly affected personality.[13]

Hall traced the primary impulses, which gave each stage of development its particular character, to phylogenetic sources, however. Hall's general sense of the importance of man's animal inheritance has recently found support in the investigations of animal ethology. But the specific terms in which Hall traced that inheritance blinded him to some of the complementary environmental influences. As Freud himself noted in his *Three Essays on the Theory of Sexuality*, it was strange that commentators on childhood should reach into the distant and obscure past for causes of behavior which had a much more obvious source in the child's own early experience in the family.[14] The crowd of ancestors whom Hall imagined as inhabiting his psyche were obviously more welcome tenants than the ambivalent images of his parents and siblings. By the same

13. J. P. Scott, "Critical Periods in Behavioral Development," *Science* 138 (1962): 949–58. According to the recapitulation theory, "the influence of the environment in producing acquired characters transmissable by heredity is greatest on the soma during adolescence." *Adol,* 1:50. Robert E. Grinder and Charles E. Strickland, "GSH and the Social Significance of Adolescence," *Teachers College Record* 64 (1963): 390–99, point out Hall's strong environmentalism, but do not note that it stopped short of the essentially stressful character of adolescence, which was biologically determined.

14. Trans. James Strachey (London: Imago, 1949), p. 51.

token, Hall sensed only sporadically, as did Freud himself, the ways in which the culture at large shaped the behavior characteristic of the different life stages.[15]

Hall's biological, genetic approach was different from the kind of psychology his scientific colleagues generally pursued, but in some ways Hall's work was highly characteristic of the direction in which American psychology was moving. When Hall announced his intention to formulate a genetic psychology in 1896, Baldwin and Dewey, at the University of Chicago, were beginning the attack on the Titchenerian-Wundtian analysis of consciousness in the name of a more "functional" approach to psychological problems. Hall's leap into educational and genetic psychology formed another kind of functional break with the Titchenerian core of the profession and he openly declared that "we seek nothing less than to raise new problems, find different methods of approach, and bring about a transvaluation generally" (2:58). Hall helped stimulate the search for new standards which overtook the profession during the following two decades.[16]

Like the newer American psychologies which would emerge from this period of transition, Hall's psychology had abandoned the study of generalized man for a study of the wide range of psychic experience among men, indeed, among all sentient forms of life. Hall expressed his search for new norms not in statistical investigations, but in evaluations of health and disease and in the attempt to segregate natural from cultural factors in development.

Hall's psychology was also practical. In his early praise of "pure" science, he had always assumed that advances in knowledge would of necessity and easily lead to practical application. After the collapse of his hopes for a "pure" university, he was more willing to accept the responsibility of science to address itself directly to pressing practical problems. But he did not thereby abandon his central concern for the internal values of science, for he came to believe that psychology would develop most fruitfully as a science if it was based

15. Hall was chiefly aware of the way in which urban civilization threatened to pervert or arrest the natural tendencies of development. See, for example, *Adol*, 1:xv–xviii, 321–22.

16. See Cattell's comment on *Adolescence* in Poffenberger, *James McKeen Cattell*, 2:203.

on consideration of the most critical problems of modern life—the problems of education, health and disease—as his own genetic psychology was. Hall could thus place his weight solidly behind the goal of psychology applied to life, and at the same time criticize merely technological applications of psychology, applications which did not feed back into basic science or did not contribute to the most vital problems of life.[17]

Hall's psychology was also vaguely behavioristic. Hall urged that the objective observation of animals, children, and all natural forms was a far better means of understanding the psyche than introspection. He made the study of consciousness the chief villain of his psychology and constantly urged its limitations as a source of psychological knowledge.[18] Hall's predilection for dynamic considerations and muscular processes led him into passages redolent of old myths and the future behavioristic doctrine. He announced that all mental processes were "efferent in their psychophysical nature" (1:ix):

Modern psychology thus sees in muscles organs of expression for all efferent processes. Beyond all their demonstrable functions, every change of attention and of psychic states generally plays upon them unconsciously, modifying their tension in subtle ways so that they may be called organs of thought and feeling as well as of will, in which some now see the true Kantian thing-in-itself, the real substance of the world, in the anthropomorphism of force. Habits even determine the deeper strata of belief, thought is repressed action, and deeds, not words, are the language of complete men. The motor areas are closely related and largely identical with the psychic, and muscle culture develops brain-centers . . . (1: 132, 165–66; 2: 449–50)

and so on. In a series of major professional forums over the next decade, Hall focused his polemic against consciousness itself—the most superficial aspect of mind, he said, whose study had trapped psychology in the introspective mold of the old philosophical psychology.[19] As the decade went on, Hall's charges lost more and more of their earlier special animus toward James's psychology and took on more and more the aspect of the behavioristic attack against the

<hr/>

17. GSH, "Mental Science," 1904; Willard S. Small in "Clark Alumni Banquet," p. 30.
18. GSH, "Mental Science"; *Adol*, 1:v–vi.
19. GSH, "Mental Science," 1904; GSH, "The Affiliation of Psychology," 1906; GSH, "Fifty Years of Darwinism," 1909.

study of consciousness, which was to focus psychological discontent after 1914. How much influence this could have had on John B. Watson or the development of behaviorism is problematical. It does show the undergrowth of conventional ideas and the trend of motor emphasis within psychology which may have contributed to the ready response Watson received in the profession.

In the years ahead, Hall moved his conception of genetic psychology closer to both psychoanalysis and the practical concerns of his colleagues, but it is chiefly for his efforts in bringing Freud to America and stimulating the spread of psychoanalytic ideas that Hall's later work in psychology is remembered. The interests which led him most directly to Freud were his concerns with psychopathology and sex.

At Clark University, as at Johns Hopkins before, Hall was alert to the constructive influences which might flow in both directions between a scientific psychology and a progressive psychiatry. Hall exposed his psychological students to the Worcester State Hospital for the Insane and to lectures there by Adolf Meyer, and he also contributed to efforts in the state to reform psychiatry according to the canon of science. Hall's efforts and the presence of Clark University nearby had been one of the factors which first brought Meyer to Worcester.[20] The open, biological atmosphere at Clark also encouraged Meyer to formulate his own "psychobiological" approach, which stressed the relation of mental illness to the whole life history of the individual. Meyer evidently saw in Hall's mature stance against the narrow framework of the experimental psychologists a support for his own efforts to break out of the narrow somaticism and nosology of current psychiatry.[21]

During the 1890s Hall began to pay increasing attention to the

20. On Meyer's coming to Worcester, and his tenure there, see Gerald Grob, *The State and the Mentally Ill: A History of Worcester State Hospital in Massachusetts, 1830–1920* (Chapel Hill: University of North Carolina Press, 1966), pp. 268–316. On the influence of Hall's activities at Clark on reforming psychiatry, see also New York *Evening Post*, 6 Feb 1891; *New York Scientific American*, 17 Oct 1891.

21. Adolf Meyer, "A Functional Approach to Dementia Praecox," in *Lectures and Addresses Delivered before the Departments of Psychology and Pedagogy in Celebration of the Twentieth Anniversary of the Opening of Clark University, September, 1909* (Worcester: Clark University, 1910), pp. 156–57.

new ideas emerging from European psychiatry. A number of European neurologists and psychiatrists were experimenting with new techniques of psychotherapy. Charcot's treatment of hysterics by hypnosis, Bernheim's use of suggestion therapy, and Janet's "cathartic method" were inspiring similar attempts by Breuer and Freud in Vienna, August Forel in Switzerland, and others. News of this work was occasionally being reported in American journals, and a group of psychologists and physicians in the Boston area, with Dr. Morton Prince, Dr. James J. Putnam, and William James at Harvard at their lead, began to use various kinds of psychotherapy during the late nineties. The chief source of their theory was Janet, and, in 1904 and 1906, Janet delivered notable academic lectures in this country. In 1906 Prince also started the *Journal of Abnormal Psychology* to publicize the new psychotherapy.[22]

In choosing to bring August Forel to this country in 1899 to speak at the Clark Decennial celebration, Hall was probably aware of the importance of this new frontier of psychiatry. In his Clark lecture on "Hypnotism and Cerebral Activity," Forel discussed the work of Breuer and Freud, pointing out the only partial success met by therapies using hypnosis, and he described his own attempts at suggestion therapy.[23] That year Hall's *American Journal of Psychology* reviewed favorably the work of Breuer and Freud on hysteria.[24]

Hall's interest continued in the following years. According to J. E. W. Wallin, both Hall and Meyer briefly mentioned Freud in their lectures at Clark during 1901–2. Lewis M. Terman, remembered Hall lecturing about Freud between 1903 and 1905.[25] In his discussion of psychopathology in *Adolescence,* Hall referred several times very favorably to Freud's theories of the mid-1890s on hysteria and morbid anxiety, though he did not appear to know *The*

---

22. Ackerknecht, *Short History of Psychiatry*, pp. 72–83; John C. Burnham, "Psychoanalysis in American Civilization before 1918" (Ph.D. diss., Stanford University, 1958), pp. 17–21; Hale, *Freud and the Americans,* chap. 6.
23. *Clark University, Decennial Celebration,* pp. 409–32.
24. *AJP* 10 (1899): 592–94.
25. J. E. W. Wallin to the author, 27 Oct 1962; David Shakow and David Rapaport, *The Influence of Freud on American Psychology,* Psychological Issues, vol. 4, no. 13 (New York: International Universities Press, 1964), p. 71.

Interpretation of Dreams, published in 1900.[26] Freud reinforced
Hall's own ideas concerning the etiological importance of psychic
trauma in early adolescence, the harmful effects of repression, and
the necessity of emotional catharsis. Hall particularly noted in
Freud's work the importance to health of normal sexual function
and the centrality of the sexual instinct in pathological development.[27]

When Hall was asked to make a major address at the American
Psychological Association meeting in Cambridge in 1905, he made
the new direction of psychiatry the keynote of his remarks.

Psychiatry is just now coming our way. Its extreme subserviency to neurology is abating. Wernicke and the somatologists whose chief paradigm was
general paresis . . . is giving way to Ziehen, Janet and Hughlings Jackson,
whose type diseases are epilepsy, hysteria, etc., and who proceed from
function to structure and not conversely. This opens up an unprecedented
opportunity for normal psychology to influence psychiatry.

Even more important, it opened the way for psychology to "deal
effectively with the great problems of human life, health, reproduction, disease and vital experience."[28] Hall was aware of the
quickening interest in psychotherapy among the Boston group and
attended at least one of their meetings.[29]

Another line of interest which brought Hall to Freud was his
emphasis on the importance of sexuality in psychic life. Hall's interest in the subject dated at least from 1894 when his personal
crisis may have created or augmented personal sexual difficulties.
His students investigated love in childhood and adolescence; one
study by Sanford Bell produced one of the earliest acknowledg-

26. Hall knew Breuer and Freud's *Studies on Hysteria,* 1895, and Freud's
papers, "On the Grounds for Detaching a Particular Syndrome from Neurasthenia
under the Description 'Anxiety Neurosis,'" 1895, and "The Aetiology of Hysteria," 1896. See James Strachey, ed., *The Standard Edition of the Complete
Psychological Works of Sigmund Freud* (London: Hogarth Press), vol. 3.
27. *Adol,* 1:233, 178–87; 2:121–22. Interestingly, Hall ignored Freud's assertion in his 1896 paper that sexual traumas of puberty invariably can be traced
back to "occurrences of premature sexual experience" in early childhood (pp.
202–3).
28. GSH, "Affiliation of Psychology," 1906, pp. 297–301.
29. Ives Hendrick, ed., *The Birth of an Institute: Twenty-fifth Anniversary
The Boston Psychoanalytic Institute November 30, 1958* (Freeport, Me.: Bond
Wheelright, 1961), p. 7.

ments of sexual feelings in children.[30] Hall's public concern with sex reached a new level of intensity in his *Adolescence* and continued unabated thereafter. Hall was among the earliest and most influential participants in the effort by many scientists and professionals in the years before the war to remove public reticence and raise the level of knowledge and purity in sexual matters.[31]

In 1907, Hall began repeatedly to urge sex education in the schools. The program of enlightenment and sublimation he offered was the one he had already advocated in *Adolescence*. He asked "that we awake not only to the dangers but to the almost unlimited possibilities and potencies here involved." When urged to outline exactly what he would say about human reproduction to school children, however, Hall took refuge in his doctrine of instruction by hints and suggestion.[32] Hall's own efforts at talks on the subject collapsed under the weight of his reticence.[33]

Hall's public intellectual discussion of sex really advertised and disguised his inner preoccupation with the subject. As in the whole of Hall's intellectual life, so with sexuality, Hall seemed to crave self-exposure. In 1899, in his "Note on Early Memories," Hall described how on his annual summer visits to the Ashfield countryside, he would entirely undress, roll around naked in the grass, and glory in the feeling of freedom this brought him. In *Adolescence*, Hall not only confessed to his own early problems with nocturnal emissions and masturbation, but much of the other comment on sexuality seemed to emerge from his personal experience, as well, such as his descriptions of feelings of rage and then "almost feminine" passivity in the male after intercourse.[34] His frequent discussions of adolescent enthusiasm, or "erethism" as he called it, were always laced with allusions and metaphors of male sexuality.[35]

30. *AJP* 13 (1902): 330. On the work of Hall's students, see Hale, *Freud and the Americans,* pp. 137–41.

31. Hale, *The Psychoanalytic Movement in America*, pp. 323–53.

32. GSH, "How and When to Be Frank with Boys," 1907; GSH, "The Needs and Methods of Educating Young People in the Hygiene of Sex," 1908; GSH in Boston *Transcript*, 21 Oct 1909; GSH, "In Life's Drama Sex Plays the Leading Part," 1911; GSH, "The Teaching of Sex in Schools and Colleges," 1911.

33. *LCP*, p. 407; *Adol*, 2:141.

34. *Adol*, 2:117, 313.

35. E.g., "Pedagogical Methods in Sunday School Work," 1895, p. 720: "especially young men, as I have learned from my experience in teaching all these

When in 1909 and 1910 Hall took the presidency of the New
England Watch and Ward Society, and resolutely attempted to make
their work scientific and up to date, he was following an old line of
sexual preoccupation, externalized and disguised in scientific interest.[36]

It would be a mistake, however, to see only prurience in Hall's
strategy. He seemed to be seeking not merely morbid advertisement
but a way of bringing his problems to greater consciousness, and
thus, possibly, solution. He turned to science and to Freud for insight as well as cover. His desire, moreover, to dispel some of the
prudish silence and moralistic exaggerations of danger which en-
veloped the subject of sex grew from an honest reading of his own
experience and required in his day a great deal of courage.

Hall earned for his public discussion of sexuality considerable
criticism and insult. Among psychologists, the subject was not in
good taste. As early as 1900, a leading experimental psychologist
wrote Titchener, "Is there no turning Hall away from this d——d
sexual rut? I really think it a bad thing morally and intellectually
to harp so much on the sexual string, unless one is a neurologist."[37]
Hall's style of treatment, moreover, made him an easy target. In his
review of *Adolescence* in *Science,* Thorndike reported to his colleagues that

the acts and feelings, normal and morbid, resulting from sex are discussed
in a way without precedent in English science. To realize the material presented one must combine his memories of medical text-books, erotic poetry
and inspirational preaching.

He then proceeded to quote in his review the entire passage on
sexual intercourse we have noted. Privately, Thorndike wrote Cattell that Hall's book was "chock full of errors, masturbation and
Jesus. He is a mad man."[38]

---

years—need first to feel emotion. They must tingle, burn. The erectile tissues
must be brought into exercise. It is necessary that the new-forming tissue of
every part of the body should be supplied with blood, that they should glow with
excitement. If they cannot get excited about their lessons . . . then they will paint
the town red, they will have dissipations." See also *Adol*, 2:74.

36. GSH memo, "The New England Watch and Ward Society," 24 Feb 1910;
GSH to Rufus B. Tobey, 3 Mar 1910, CUP.

37. Frank Angell to Titchener, 19 Mar [1900], TP. See Pruette, *GSH*, p. 197.

38. *Science,* n.s. 20 (1904): 144; Thorndike to Cattell, 6 July 1904, CP.

If not carried too far, this hostile reaction merely strengthened Hall's determination to preach the truth. He surely expected to be punished for his sexual exposures and took some delight in shocking his colleagues. His taste for public abuse was not unlimited, however. As in the past, public criticism could awaken his own internal censors and send him back to denouncing what he had surreptitiously praised.

Beyond the outlets Freudian psychology gave him for his interest in psychopathology, sexuality, and heretical opinions, another factor quickened Hall's interest in Freud. In 1908 Hall began planning the second decennial celebration of the anniversary of the founding of Clark University for the following year. The previous celebration in 1899 had been immensely successful, and Hall undoubtedly hoped to bring to Clark intellectual leaders of as great importance as he had done before. He also planned to hold in conjunction with the academic meetings for July 1909, the conference on child research and welfare which would, he hoped, restore the child study movement.

In looking around for people to bring to Clark, Hall first consulted his faculty, and in November 1908, they proposed to the trustees to bring from abroad only the psychologists Herman Ebbinghaus and Ernst Meumann, pioneers in the experimental study of memory, learning, and intelligence.[39] The following month evidently on his own initiative, Hall also invited Sigmund Freud. In his letter of invitation Hall wrote Freud that

Janet, who has visited this country and given a similar course of public lectures, has had a profound influence in turning the attention of our leading and especially our younger students of abnormal psychology from the exclusively somatic and neurological to a more psychological basis. We believe that a concise statement of your own results and point of view would now be exceedingly opportune, and perhaps in some sense mark an epoch in the history of these studies in this country.[40]

Freud was unable to come to America for the July date, but Hall

39. "Records of the Board of Trustees, 1901–9," vol. 2, 6 Nov 1908. Ebbinghaus accepted, but died before the conference, in February 1909. *Lectures and Addresses, 1909,* p. 159. Meumann declined the invitation. "Proof: Preliminary Announcement: The Second Decennial Celebration of the Opening of Clark University," CP.
40. GSH to "Siegmund" Freud, 15 Dec 1908, CUP.

wrote him again in February 1909 that the date of the conference
had been changèd to early September, and this time Freud accepted.[41]

Hall replied that even though he had not publicized Freud's
acceptance,

news of your coming has reached a number of people in this country who
have been profoundly interested in your work and have written us expressing
their pleasure and their desire to hear whatever you may have to say to us.[42]

Hall was quite conscious of the fact, in inviting Freud, that interest
in his work was increasing, particularly among the influential group
of psychotherapists. At some point during these proceedings, Hall
also asked to Clark, Carl Gustav Jung, Freud's most important adherent, already known in psychology for his pioneer work on association tests.[43]

In sensing the rising interest in Freud and bringing to Clark the
leaders of a movement in favor among the Boston circles from
which he was still substantially excluded, Hall was exercising his
familiar and formidable ambitions. Freud's later observation of Hall
clearly held truth: "there was a touch of the 'king-maker' about him,
a pleasure in setting up authorities and in then deposing them."[44]
Freud's observation was sharpened by the fact that he later felt
"deposed" by Hall, but Hall clearly relished his role as the evangel
of new and controversial thinkers and saw the 1909 celebration as
an occasion to install himself in the lead of a promising and heretical movement.

Hall wrote Freud several times again during the spring and
summer of 1909 about travel arrangements, offering him the hospi-

41. GSH to "Siegmund" Freud, 16 Feb, 13 Apr 1909, CUP.
42. Ibid., 16 Feb 1909.
43. Jung late in his life claimed that he had been invited simultaneously with
and independently of Freud, but there is no firm evidence about when he was invited or when he accepted. Jung, *Memories, Dreams, Reflections,* p. 141. Freud
first heard that Jung had been invited in a letter from Oskar Pfister, 13 June
1909; Jones, *Freud,* 2:54, 466. As late as 28 May 1909, Sanford wrote Titchener
(TP) that "with Stern, Freud, Meyer, Boas and Jennings, we shall be pretty
heavily loaded on the side of applied psychology." Presumably, Sanford would
have included Jung's name had he accepted an invitation by that date.
44. Sigmund Freud, *An Autobiographical Study,* trans. James Strachey (London: Hogarth Press, 1935), p. 94.

tality of his own home or a hotel, as Freud preferred, and giving him complete freedom on the topic of his lectures, their number, and their delivery in English or German.[45] Freud arrived in Worcester on Sunday, 5 September, with Jung and Sandor Ferenczi, his disciple from Budapest whom he had asked to accompany him,[46] and the following day, Freud and Jung moved into Hall's home. According to Jung, Hall greeted them "with the kindest hospitality," and Mrs. Hall "promptly took over Freud and me as her 'boys' and plied us with delicious nourishment and noble wine, so that we began visibly to recover."[47] Freud delivered five lectures in German, each day from Tuesday to Saturday at 11 A.M., Hall's own cherished lecture hour.[48] Jung delivered at least three lectures during the course of the week, also in German, on the association method.

The conference which brought Freud to America was equal in intellectual distinction and even larger in scope than the previous conference of 1899. There were altogether fourteen lectures delivered on psychology, six on education, and even larger numbers delivered as part of concurrent sessions in mathematics, physics, chemistry, biology, and history. The most distinguished of the speakers in all fields received honorary degrees at formal academic ceremonies. The physicists honored with Freud were no less than Ernest Rutherford of the University of Manchester, and Albert A. Michelson of Chicago, both already Nobel prize winners, and Vito Volterra, of the University of Rome.[49]

Besides Freud, those honored in psychology were E. B. Titchener, leader of the Wundtian experimentalists in America, the Munich

45. GSH to "Siegmund" Freud, 15 Apr 1909; GSH to Freud, 9 Aug, 31 Aug 1909.
46. Jones, *Freud*, 2:54.
47. Jung to Emma Jung, 6 Sept 1909, in Jung, *Memories, Dreams, Reflections*, pp. 365–66.
48. Worcester *Telegram*, 9, 11, 12 Sept 1909.
49. *Lectures and Addresses*, pp. v–viii. See also *Chemical Addresses Delivered at the Second Decennial Celebration of Clark University in September, 1909* (Clark University and the American Chemical Society, 1911), and *Lectures Delivered at the Celebration of the Twentieth Anniversary of the Foundation of Clark University under the Auspices of the Department of Physics* (Worcester: Clark University, 1912).

psychologist, Wilhelm Stern, already known for his pioneer work in individual psychology and testing, and the anthropologist, Franz Boas, the biologist, Herbert S. Jennings, and the psychiatrist, Adolf Meyer, probably the most eminent members of their professions in America. Honorary degrees in education and hygiene went to Jung and to Leo Burgerstein of Vienna, the preeminent figure in the scientific study of school hygiene.

The other psychologists who lectured themselves or heard Freud were a distinguished group, though by no means representative of all American psychology or psychiatry. Although it is not entirely certain who was present or absent at the meetings, or for how long,[50] Hall apparently limited the conference chiefly to psychologists, and few psychiatrists were present beyond the analytic band of Ferenczi, Jones, and A. A. Brill, a New York analyst who had studied with Jung and Freud. There is evidence only of the psychiatrists Meyer, Putnam, and Isador H. Coriat of Boston attending. The psychotherapy group in Boston was represented by Putnam, and Coriat, and by the psychologists around Harvard, William James, Edwin B. Holt, Edward W. Katzenellenbogen, and Frederick L. Wells. The other psychologists represented chiefly those trained at Clark, those at Cornell under Hall's ally Titchener, and those from Harvard and Yale who were interested in educational and clinical psychology. Except for Cattell, none of the Columbia psychologists attended, nor any from the University of Chicago. Few psychologists from the Middle or Far West were present. Probably the largest single representation was of psychologists who would work in clinical, developmental, or educational psychology, around ten in all, including Bird T. Baldwin, H. H. Goddard, Carl Seashore, F. L. Wells, and Guy M. Whipple.

Freud spoke, therefore, to a highly trained and distinguished group, dotted with men of real eminence in psychology and related fields, in the course of an event of widely acknowledged intellectual distinction. Despite the marginal position of Clark University and

---

50. Except for scattered letters or notes, the only record of attendance is in the list of speakers and the large group picture, evidently taken the fifth day of the conference, Friday, 10 September. On attendance at the conference, see Burnham, "Psychoanalysis in American Civilization before 1918," pp. 43–46.

The Psychological Department at Clark University posed for a photograph on June 4, 1892, just before Boas, Donaldson, and others left for Chicago.

First row (sitting): Thaddeus Bolton, Franz Boas, H. H. Donaldson, G. Stanley Hall, Edmund C. Sanford, William H. Burnham, E. W. Scripture

Second row (standing): J. S. Lemon, Gerald M. West, W. O. Krohn, F. B. Dresslar, James E. LeRossignol, W. L. Bryan, Alexander Fraser, J. A. Bergstrom

Photo courtesy of Clark University

This famous record of the Clark Conference of 1909 was probably taken on Friday, September 10, and does not include everyone who attended.
Photo courtesy of Robert G. Hall

1. Franz Boas
2. E. B. Titchener
3. William James
4. William Stern
5. Leo Burgerstein
6. G. S. Hall
7. Sigmund Freud
8. C. G. Jung
9. Adolf Meyer
10. H. S. Jennings
11. C. E. Seashore
12. Joseph Jastrow
13. J. M. Cattell
14. E. F. Buchner
15. E. Katzenellenbogen
16. Ernest Jones
17. A. A. Brill
18. W. H. Burnham
19. A. F. Chamberlain
20. Albert Schinz
21. J. A. Magni
22. B. T. Baldwin
23. F. L. Wells
24. G. M. Forbes
25. E. A. Kirkpatrick
26. Sandor Ferenczi
27. E. C. Sanford
28. J. P. Porter
29. Sakyo Kanda
30. Kikoso Kakise
31. G. E. Dawson
32. S. P. Hayes
33. E. B. Holt
34. C. S. Berry
35. G. M. Whipple
36. Frank Drew
37. J. W. A. Young
38. L. N. Wilson
39. K. J. Karlson
40. H. H. Goddard
41. H. I. Klopp
42. S. C. Fuller

Hall singled out his psychoanalytic guests for this separate memorial of the Clark Conference of 1909.

First row (sitting): Sigmund Freud, G. Stanley Hall, C. G. Jung
Second row (standing): A. A. Brill, Ernest Jones, Sandor Ferenczi
                                        Photo courtesy of Robert G. Hall

Stanley Hall's study on the second floor of his home in Worcester. Portraits of Hall's parents are on the wall to the right of his desk.

Photo courtesy of Clark University

the sometimes dubious reputation of Hall, there was real reason for Freud to take pride in the recognition this event afforded him. As he recalled many years later,

> my short visit to the new world encouraged my self-respect in every way. In Europe I felt as though I were despised; but over there I found myself received by the foremost men as an equal. As I stepped on to the platform at Worcester to deliver my *Five Lectures upon Psycho-Analysis* it seemed like the realization of some incredible day-dream: psycho-analysis was no longer a product of delusion, it had become a valuable part of reality.[51]

This was, as Freud said on the occasion, the first recognition of his work he had anywhere received, and both he and Jung took great pleasure in it.[52]

The atmosphere surrounding the conference at Worcester and in the press was very favorable to Freud, augmenting the feeling of recognition and acceptance he drew from it. It is too much to say, as William Burnham reminisced some years later, that Freud was "the great drawing card of the celebration,"[53] but his extraordinary views were already known among American psychologists in outline, there was already a distinguished group in New England anxious to know more of him, and the local public evidently knew of and were interested in his ideas.

At the conference, Wells commented unfavorably to Hall about Freud's views,[54] and other psychologists such as Titchener were not favorably inclined; but there was no public opposition expressed. Three of the most eminent men present were actively interested in him and his work: James, Putnam, and Meyer. Jung helped substantially to create the favorable impression psychoanalysis made on this occasion. As Freud himself was acutely aware, Jung's Aryan presence was an impressive credential.[55] Moreover, his lectures on the association test and his convenient theory of "complexes" were

51. Freud, *An Autobiographical Study*, p. 95.

52. Jones, *Freud*, 2:57; Jung to Emma Jung, 8 Sept, 14 Sept 1909, in Jung, *Memories, Dreams, Reflections*, p. 366.

53. Worcester *Gazette*, 24 Mar 1938. The Burnham interview also contains some recollection of other minor incidents involving Freud and Jung.

54. Frederic L. Wells, interview with the author, 6 Mar 1962.

55. Adelbert Albrecht, "Prof. Sigmund Freud," Boston *Transcript*, 11 Sept 1909; R. G. Hall, interview with the author, 17–20 May 1961.

the most easily assimilated and congenial products of psychoanalysis for the American psychologists.[56]

The local newspaper coverage was entirely favorable and regretted that Freud did not speak in English so that more people could understand him. Echoing what must have been Hall's words, the local papers often referred to psychoanalysis as "the psychology of the future" and claimed it was rapidly gaining recognition all over the world.[57] A notice in the *Nation,* probably written by Hall, was similarly respectful and enthusiastic.[58] In a long interview with Freud published in the Boston *Transcript,* the reporter gave a faithful account of Freud's views on psychotherapy, its promise, and its difficulties and described him sympathetically:

> One sees at a glance that he is a man of great refinement, of intellect and of many-sided education. His sharp, yet kind, clear eyes suggest at once the doctor. His high forehead with the large bumps of observation and his beautiful, energetic hands are very striking. He speaks clearly, weighing his words carefully, but unfortunately never of himself. Again and again, he emphasizes the merits of his colleagues, particularly of his friend, Dr. Jung of Zurich, who is staying with him at President Hall's.[59]

Thanks to Stanley Hall, Freud appeared in this first American contact far more respectable and eminent than he did in Europe.

How influential the conference was in disseminating Freud's ideas in America has already been the subject of considerable discussion.[60] Knowledge of Freud in this country came chiefly from the speaking, writing, and translations of Jones, Brill, and those who joined them in the psychoanalytic movement. A number of lines of direct influence can be traced to the Clark conference, however, and it appeared to mark a major acceleration of interest in Freud in all public and professional spheres, as notice of his work increased

56. Hale, *Freud and the Americans,* pp. 230–57; John C. Burnham, *Psychoanalysis and American Medicine, 1894–1918,* Psychological Issues, vol. 5, no. 4 (New York: International Universities Press, 1967), pp. 18–19.
57. Worcester *Telegram,* 8, 9, 11, 12 Sept 1909.
58. GSH, "Twentieth Anniversary of Clark University," 1909.
59. Boston *Transcript,* 11 Sept 1909.
60. See particularly the estimates of Hale, *Freud and the Americans,* p. 2, and Burnham, "Psychoanalysis in American Civilization before 1918," pp. 41–46.

substantially from 1909 onward. The conference also strongly influenced two key figures in American psychiatry, James J. Putnam,
who dated his adherence to Freud from his American visit, and
Adolf Meyer.[61]

Among psychologists, the Clark conference marked the first
substantial notice of psychoanalysis, and considerable discussion of
the Freudian theories and Jung's association test occurred at psychological meetings in the following years.[62] Although unable to attend
the conference, Lewis M. Terman wrote Hall enthusiastically after
reading Freud's lectures that they had "stirred up more thoughts
than had come to my brain for many a day." If Freud and Jung were
correct, "their work is the biggest bomb that has struck the psychologists camp in recent years."[63] Yet little of the Freudian viewpoint ever showed in Terman's work. On further reflection, Freud's
ideas proved very difficult to assimilate. The influence of psychoanalysis entered into scientific psychology very slowly, stimulating
and strengthening the inclusion of dynamic and developmental
factors in psychology, though hardly ever making its way in toto or
intact.

The psychologist most affected by psychoanalysis was Hall himself. Hall never disclosed what effect his meeting with Freud had
upon him, though a personal encounter with the doctor reputed to
have uncovered man's inner secrets would naturally have had its
difficulties for Hall. Jung recalled an incident which occurred on
Thursday evening, when James arrived as a guest at Hall's home, to
stay only that evening and the following day for Freud's lecture.[64]

After dinner William James appeared and I was particularly interested in
the personal relation between Stanley Hall and William James, since I
gathered from some remarks of President Hall that William James was not
taken quite seriously on account of his interest in Mrs. Piper and extra-
sensory perceptions. Stanley Hall had prepared us that he had asked James
to discuss some of his results with Mrs. Piper and to bring some of his

61. Meyer recorded something of his immediate reaction to Freud and Jung
in a series of letters to Titchener, beginning 18 Sept 1909, TP.
62. On the impact of psychoanalysis in psychology, see Burnham, "Psychoanalysis in American Civilization before 1918," pp. 174–219, and the longer-
range estimate of Shakow and Rapaport, The Influence of Freud.
63. L. M. Terman to GSH, 27 Apr 1910, CUP.
64. Wm. James to GSH, 8 Sept 1909, GSH Memorial Volume, CUP.

material. So when James came, (there was Stanley Hall, Professor Freud, one or two other men and myself) he said to Hall: "I've brought you some papers in which you might be interested." And he put his hand to his breastpocket and drew out a parcel which to our delight proved to be a wad of Dollar bills. In consideration of Stanley Hall's great merits for the increase and welfare of Clark University and his rather critical remarks as to James' pursuits, it looked to us as a particularly happy rejoinder. James excused himself profusely. Then he produced the real papers from the other pocket.[65]

Although bested in the exchange, Hall got even with James in the reports of the conference he circulated for years afterward. He told his students that James and Freud did not get along at all and that James had told him that Freud was "a dirty fellow."[66] In view of the classical psychoanalytic interpretation of the symbolic meaning of money, this could be a gloss on the incident. It seems clear from subsequent events, in any case, that Hall was quite sensitive to the "dirty" connotations of Freud's theory.

Another incident during the conference brought home to Hall his amateur status in the field of therapy and his embarrassment at bringing sexuality into the open. Hall and two colleagues at Clark had seen during the year a young girl who had come to them claiming spiritualist powers. It had taken Hall many interviews to discover a sexual motive behind her behavior. Hall mentioned the case to Freud and Jung and they asked to see her.

In a short interview with her they at once diagnosed the true nature of it all, and to my surprise she frankly confessed that her chief motive from the first had been to win the love of her adored one. . . . The erotic motivation was obvious and the German savants saw little further to interest them in the case, and I was a trifle mortified that now the purpose so long hidden from us was so conscious and so openly confessed.[67]

Despite these embarrassments and perhaps because of the skill Freud displayed in the course of them, Hall was drawn to Freud's views.

65. Jung to Virginia Payne, in Payne, "Psychology and Psychiatry at the Clark Conference of 1909," (Medical thesis, University of Wisconsin, 1950), pp. 49–50.
66. Carroll Pratt, interview, 10 Mar 1962; Harry Elmer Barnes to the author, 12 Apr 1962. On William James's response to Freud, see Shakow and Rapaport, *The Influence of Freud*, pp. 67–68.
67. GSH, "A Medium in the Bud," 1918, p. 156; *AJP* 21 (1910): 169.

Whatever personal impression Freud made on Hall, however, counted less than the veracity and the genetic content of his theories. Psychoanalysis, like Hall's own genetic vision, gave him an insight into reality, as he knew it, which he found nowhere else. As Hall had told his colleagues in 1900, he refused to

work in the very narrow limits prescribed for psychology in the over-elaborate classifications and definitions of some of my contemporaries. Wherever life is most intense and reality seems most real, there the student of the inner life should find his theme and seek to be at home.[68]

Hall clearly felt this reality in Freud's developmental theory.

Even before the Clark conference, Hall asserted that the new psychotherapy heralded a genetic synthesis in psychology. Affective, unconscious "complexes," Hall said, "dominate psychopathic symptoms and also our normal lives." They "irresistibly suggest past evolutionary stages of mentation," that is, phylogenetic experience, and the long list of instincts and impulses whose shaping of development he had already described. [69] Freud's genetic viewpoint, interpreted as congruent with his own, more than any other factor, made Hall an advocate of psychoanalytic ideas for the remainder of his life. Hall's relative isolation in American psychology as the champion of geneticism appeared now to be at an end and some, at least, of his pioneer views to be confirmed in a most promising way.

68. GSH, "College Philosophy," 1900, p. 421.
69. GSH, "Fifty Years of Darwinism," 1909.

19   DENOUEMENT

The period from 1910 to 1920 was Hall's last decade as a professional psychologist, and he began it as a staunch advocate of Freud's theory of psychoanalysis. During the course of the decade, however, Hall's attraction to Freud weakened under the challenge of his sexual theory and Hall's adherence fell into the more familiar mold of his own genetic psychology. Calling for a new synthetic, genetic psychology, a grand union and perfection of his own and Freud's genetic theories, Hall spent the decade making partial advances in the direction of Freud's former adherents, Alfred Adler and Carl Gustav Jung, and exploring some of the implications of psychoanalytic ideas on the variety of genetic topics which concerned him.

At the start of the decade, however, just after the Clark conference, Hall was enthusiastic about Freud, and Freud himself was delighted with Hall's support. "Who could have known," Freud wrote,

that over there in America, only an hour away from Boston, there was a respectable old gentleman waiting impatiently for the next number of the *Jahrbuch,* reading and understanding it all, and who would then, as he expressed it himself, "ring the bells for us"?

At the meeting of the American Psychological Association in Cambridge in December 1909, Hall joined Putman in defending Freud against the attack of Boris Sidis.[1] In the next issue of his

1. Jones, *Freud,* 2:57–58.

American Journal of Psychology, Hall published Freud's Clark lectures under the title, "The Origin and Development of Psychoanalysis," along with Jung's lectures and a paper by Ferenczi.[2] He wrote Freud that he hoped the publication "will do good," and he described his defense at the APA in such a way as to show himself a loyal supporter, more faithtul even than Putnam.[3]

Hall also set his fellows at the new Children's Institute to work on Freud's theory and the association test. He established a division at the institute devoted to the "Psychology, Pedagogy and Hygiene of Sex," which would consider, among other problems, "the Freud-Jung theory that sex manifests itself from infancy."[4] That year Hall also became a charter member of the American Psychopathological Association and, in 1911, of the American Psychoanalytic Association, an affiliate of Freud's international society.[5]

In his two-volume work on *Educational Problems,* Hall published a long chapter on "The Pedagogy of Sex," in which he hailed Freud's theory in the highest terms. The main outline of Hall's treatment of sex was the same as his earlier discussion in *Adolescence*: shame, repression, and sublimation were still described as the natural course of development of the sexual instinct. Hall remarked that "for all our boys and girls today the old ideals of absolute purity in thought, word, and deed are impossible," but he continued to stress purity of deed: chastity before marriage, and after marriage, sexual relations for procreation only.[6] His criticism remained chiefly directed at the repression of speech and false reticence.

Hall did, however, discuss and approve Freud's theory of the development of the sexual impulse from infantile components of "passionate sucking . . . interest in all that pertains to both excrementations, various autoeroticisms which may later evolve into self-abuse," and he accepted the characterological effects of such impulses, as well. Freud's psychological view, Hall said,

has brought more unity and insight into the very nature and operations of the soul, and the mechanism of the conscience than any other in our gen-

2. *AJP* 21 (Apr 1910).
3. GSH to Freud, 30 Dec 1909, CUP.
4. "The Children's Institute of Clark University," pp. 14, 69, CUP.
5. Hale, *Freud and the Americans,* pp. 412–13.
6. *EP*, 1:477–79.

eration. It marks the end of the old and the dawn of a new era. It is the most triumphant vindication of the genetic mode of conceiving the mind. . . . This is quite true apart from its bearings upon sex, for it includes a far wider domain which cannot even be glanced at here. Into the whole domain of sex, however, it brings sudden order and harmony by showing the relations between the different morbid manifestations among themselves and between these and normal activities. . . . [it] gives sex, which had been neglected by all contemptuously and dismissed by some psychologists as of the slightest significance, its rightful and dominant place.[7]

Hall's praise could hardly have been more forthright.

After the publication of *Educational Problems* in 1911, however, there was a sudden absence of any public support on Hall's part for Freud, and he ceased to answer several cards of greeting Freud sent him.[8] Hall announced at Clark that he would lecture on "the Freud school" as part of his courses those years, and he continued to direct his doctoral students to the Freudian literature and to problems raised by Freud.[9] But there was none of the public advocacy or discussion of Freud's theories that would be expected to follow his previous initiatives.

The first real indication of a turnabout in Hall's attitude toward Freud came in his articles on Berkeley and Kant, published in April and July of 1912. Perhaps the need to seriously evaluate Freudian psychology once again drove Hall back to a reconsideration of the basic problem of his intellectual life—philosophical idealism. For the last time, at any rate, Hall attempted to summarize his understanding of these two philosophers and to pay off his "ancient grudge" by subjecting them to a "psychoanalysis."

Most expressions of psychic life are more or less symbolic, and . . . their half-concealed, half-revealed meaning will be brought out only when we can get through and back of their form in consciousness and tell what deeper tendencies they express and how historically they came to take on their present forms.[10]

By "psychoanalysis," therefore, Hall meant to trace back ideas to the

7. *EP*, 1:445, 447.
8. GSH to Freud, 26 Sept 1913, CUP.
9. *Clark Register, 1910*, p. 78; *1911*, p. 91; *1912*, p. 86; *1913*, p. 90; GSH to Miriam Van Waters, 10 Nov 1911; GSH to Mr. Bivin, 6 Feb 1912, CUP.
10. GSH, "The Genetic View of Berkeley's Religious Motivation," 1912, pp. 137–38.

historical situation of the subject—"age, race and nation"—as well as to his personality. His insight was an extension of the historical relativism he had long since made a part of his psychology-as-natural-history. As he declared in his study of Kant,

> The impending analysis of all the great systems is the inevitable result then of the new dominance of genetic psychology and owes little save terms and suggestions to the Freudian analysis of neuropaths, and yet we must do the latter ample justice and there is one very suggestive analogy and difference between them. As Freudians find sex, so our analysis finds religion at the root of all. Religion is a passion of the soul comparable in universality and intensity with sex. . . . As the root impulse of sex is to propagate another generation, so the root impulse of religion is to prolong the life of the individual by getting his soul born into another world. Both are forms of Schopenhauer's will to life, which is the *Grund-Trieb* of all life.[11]

Hall occasionally thereafter spoke of "psychoanalyzing" the major figures of psychology and philosophy as part of his genetic program, but he did not again raise the religious impulse to equal status with the sexual impulse at the core of psychic energy. Temporary though this strategy was, it was clearly aimed at the sexualism of Freud's psychology.

The following year, in March 1913, in a letter to Dr. Smith Ely Jelliffe, a young psychiatrist already practicing psychoanalysis, Hall claimed that he had just now caught up on his reading of the Freudian literature of the past two years and was "immensely impressed with the vitality of it all" but disturbed at the sexual symbolism.

> I believe certain of these newer tendencies, particularly those in the direction of the extreme of symbolism, are far-fetched and that salt, the forms of chemical formulae, synaesthesias of numbers and letters, musical notation, etc., are sexual in the sense some of these extremists imply, I cannot believe. If I were educating Freudians I would insist that they have as a propaedeutic a good course in such things as the old phallic theories . . . and second, . . . the mythological curiosities that were perpetrated by men like Cox, when everything straight was a sun ray and everything round its disk.[12]

In May 1913, delivering an invited address at the American Psychopathological Association meeting in Washington on "Sex-symbolism

11. GSH, "Why Kant Is Passing," 1912, pp. 420–21.
12. GSH to Smith Ely Jelliffe, 8 Mar 1913, CUP.

in the Psychology of Freud," Hall repeated his criticism of the Freudians for attributing sexual symbolism to all manner of objects. A few months later, in 1914, Hall retreated from his earlier advocacy of sex education. He told Worcester educators that

the tendency now is toward conservatism in the matter of sex hygiene being taught in the schools. . . . sex hygiene should not be taught to a class, but . . . the teacher should answer all questions relating thereto individually. . . . he commended the view of the Catholic Church on the matter of sex hygiene.[13]

That same month, Hall told the American Psychological Association that the Freudian child was just "a fragment of a child" and that traits discovered in the study of abnormality could not be applied so broadly to normal children and adults.[14]

What happened between 1911 and 1914 to turn Hall against the Freudian emphasis on sex is partly a matter of record and partly a problem for speculation. The first element was clearly the abusive criticism he incurred for his writing on sex. In July 1911, the *Nation* reviewed his *Educational Problems* under the head "Morbid Pedagogism." The *Nation* objected particularly to the chapters on the "Pedagogy of Sex" and "The Budding Girl":

193 pages of sexual detail which are not surpassed even by Krafft-Ebing or Mantegazza for quantity of nastiness and nudity of statement. The facts might be bolted (where they are facts) if they were served without the perfume of tender sentiment, but the combination nauseates. . . . At intervals in his recital of abnormalities, the author pauses to wipe away a tear and explain that, "It is painful to write these things." But we beg leave to doubt it. He dwells too long and lovingly upon the theme, too caressingly upon its nastiest aspects; and we are compelled to believe that "bathing in this cosmic ocean" of subconsciousness and sex is altogether to his taste.[15]

There was, of course, a good deal of truth in this reviewer's charges. Hall clearly relished the subject, even while denouncing his data as "vicious" or "immoral." He again lyricized at great length and even greater detail on sexual intercourse. His section on forms of "degeneracy" in the early adolescent girl, which the *Nation* seemed particularly to dislike, added to his old portrait of "the bud" two pages

13. Worcester *Telegram*, 17 May 1914. See also GSH, "Education and the Social Hygiene Movement," 1914.
14. GSH, "The Freudian Child," 1914, p. 68.
15. *Nation* 93 (1911): 80–81.

of moralistic comment on girls, "steeped in vice and disease, body and soul," whom "nothing but physical restraint . . . can prevent from sinking upon the first occasion into the lowest depths."[16]

Hall himself confessed some anxiety about his attraction to the subject of sexual abandon in young girls. He concluded, "But enough and too much of this. . . . perhaps even the author's ideal of completeness in treating this subject may hardly justify even these allusions."[17] It seems likely that Hall's information about young girls in "certain institutions" was acquired during his term as president of the New England Watch and Ward Society in 1909–10. He may well have felt uneasy about his own interest in such work, and apparently dropped it in 1910.

The reviewer's objection to "quantity of nastiness and nudity of statement," however, seems both overdrawn and puerile. Hall did use, along with such vague language as "vice" and "the lowest depths," such clinical terms as masturbation or homosexuality, and he discussed such problems as venereal disease at length. His attention to sexual perversion was rather brief, however, and his melodramatic treatment of vice in adolescent girls and his lyrics on sexual intercourse were exceptions to a largely straightforward approach. His passage on Freud's theory of infantile sexuality was probably the most "nude" statement of the volume. It was precisely in making such plain statements that Hall's work now seems most enlightened.

Hall was extremely shaken by this review. He had long been the recipient of criticism on the grounds of his sexual interest, but, as he wrote his old friend Hamilton Mabie, "I never had anything in the way of criticism that rankled like this . . . what touches me is that the critic says I love these subjects and treat them caressingly."[18] When Goddard wrote personally to the anonymous reviewer, Warner H. Fite, to ask for a retraction, Fite answered that "the criticism embodied in the review is a very general [i.e., widely held] one," and the *Nation* never printed Hall's rejoinder.[19] After this

16. *EP*, 2:26–27.
17. Ibid., p. 29.
18. GSH to Hamilton W. Mabie, 8 Sept 1911, CUP.
19. H. H. Goddard to Warner H. Fite, 10 Jan 1912; Warner H. Fite to H. H. Goddard, 6 Feb 1912, CW, vol. 27.

painful episode, Hall may well have been reluctant to publicly support the sexual emphasis of psychoanalysis.

Hall was not, however, entirely driven off by this incident. When
Jelliffe and William Alanson White, another young analytically oriented psychiatrist, approached Hall late in 1912 for advice on starting a journal to represent the psychoanalytical movement in its
widest genetic scope, Hall began thinking of getting his own
Journal onto the bandwagon. Hall offered White a quarter or third
of the space in his *Journal* to edit under his own name, with the
right to go off on his own any time he wished.

You see I am rather coveting a little sponsorship because for these many
years I have been rather derided by many of my psychological colleagues for
my geneticism. I have an impression that things are going to set that way,
however, very strongly indeed, though probably the tide won't be full on for
a decade.[20]

Hall claimed to understand when White and Jelliffe insisted re-
spectfully on going their own way, and they repeatedly urged him
to write up his views for their journal and to advise them on various
points relating to genetic psychology.[21]

This was, undoubtedly, another of Hall's *Journal* escapades,
which would lead to retraction of his offer as soon as the other
party showed interest. It may nonetheless have symbolized a real
desire to assume leadership in the movement, a desire frustrated by
his difficulty in handling the issue of sexuality and his lack of experience in psychotherapy.

It was after his rejection by these young analysts that Hall wrote
Jelliffe early in 1913 of his opposition to the sexual symbolism of
the Freudians, but it was evidently his experience at the Washington
meeting in May of that year, where he delivered his critical lecture
on sex symbolism, that turned him firmly against this aspect of
Freud. Hall wrote Titchener,

The Freudian point can be dropped for it is a natural misunderstanding on
your part. True, sometime ago I did think of taking on Jelliffe and White

20. GSH to Wm. A. White, 11 Dec 1912, CUP.
21. Wm. A. White to GSH, 11 Feb 1913, GSH Memorial Volume; GSH to
White, 18 Feb 1913; GSH to Smith Ely Jelliffe, 19 Jan 1916, CUP.

and printing some of their material, but as a result of several interviews and
of the Psychoanalytic Conference which I attended at Washington, I have
definitely given up having their or any other new names or special contributors. The whole Freudian situation has immensely changed since three
or four years ago, when we printed articles which were then by no means so
crude as they seem in the light of developments since. In my address at
Washington and in my class my attitude has been that while some of the
mechanisms and particularly the genetic methods appeal very strongly to my
geneticism, the symbolism is not only cheap and crude but vicious, morally
and intellectually. Some of the worst and some of the best things are in it
and they about balance. I am even more interested in Pawlow. Thus you
will see that any idea of making propaganda for Freud is probably about as
repugnant to my mind as it is to yours.[22]

This sudden moralistic attempt to castigate psychoanalysis as cheap,
crude, and vicious suggests that at the bottom of his retreat from
Freudian sexuality was an effort of self-defense.

Two things reported in the public record of the Washington conference may have bothered Hall. In countering Hall's criticism, all
the psysicians present except Morton Prince argued that the sexual
meaning of the symbols they discussed was not something they
assumed, but which their patients, in case after case, revealed themselves. Drs. Trigant Burrow and A. A. Brill were particularly frank
in their discussion of some of the symbols, dreams, and vocational
sublimations of sexual impulses confessed by their patients.[23] With
his own vivid fantasy life and his sensitivity to the way in which the
plastic sexual impulse can pervade all experience, Hall may well
have felt threatened by these disclosures.

In addition, Ernest Jones, in a paper on "The Case of Louis
Bonaparte, King of Holland," analyzed Louis's attachment to his
brother Napoleon as being homosexual in nature.[24] In the discussion
which followed, Hall asked Jones on what evidence he had decided
that Louis had homosexual impulses and indulged them. Jones
replied that he had never said that Louis indulged them, but the
evidence for his having them,

probably quite unknown to himself, is the fact of his delusions of jealousy
and of persecution, the significance of which is definitely established through

22. GSH to Titchener, 27 May 1913, TP.
23. *Journal of Abnormal Psychology* 8 (1913-14): 336-42.
24. Ibid., pp. 289-301.

psychopathological researches, his behavior toward his wife and other women, and his attitude toward men, particularly toward Napoleon.

Jones had described his attitude toward women as being one of misogyny and, toward Napoleon, as an attachment alternating between love and hate. Hall then asked, "How far may homosexuality be assumed to exist when there is never any direct manifestation of it?" Jones replied that it could exist without any expression, just as in the case of the heterosexual impulse.[25] Although Hall focused his public criticism on the issue of sexual symbolism, the issue of latent homosexuality Jones raised may have been even more disturbing to him. Consciously or unconsciously, Hall must have sensed something of himself in Jones's talk of delusions of persecution, misogyny, and passionate, ambivalent relations with men.

It is also possible that another factor entered into the situation. This may have been the period in which Hall made his aborted attempt at his own psychoanalysis. Hall reported in his autobiography that at some point he started a self-analysis, "but finding the task too hard, called in an expert to finish the work."[26] Hall wrote White early in 1913 that

We had last year a Dream Club of advanced students, which resulted in all studying their dreams, out of which I got some genetic and other conceptions. We have a Freud and Catharsis Club too which is thrashing out considerable material.[27]

Hall's high opinion of the Freudian theory in 1911, followed by the public accusation of pathology which was leveled at him, may have led him into an attempt at psychoanalysis during 1912.

The way in which Hall later described the process of psychoanalysis suggests that his attempt was rather short-lived and did not succeed. Hall claimed that the good results sometimes obtained from analysis were really the product of the patient's shame at revealing his morbidities. Shame would force him to suppress the symptoms and problems he had hitherto experienced.[28] In 1915 Hall told the American Psychoanalytic Association that the widespread "aversion" to the sexual emphasis of the Freudians was

25. Ibid., pp. 345–46.
26. *LCP*, p. 449.
27. GSH to Wm. A. White, 18 Feb 1913, CUP.
28. *LCP*, p. 12.

part of a complicated protest of normality, found in all and even in the resistance of subjects of analysis, which is really a factor basal for self-control, of the varying good sides of which Freudians tell us nothing.[29]

Hall's brief psychoanalysis may have ended with a "flight into health," which left him determined to suppress his own symptoms, and with them, the overt sexuality of the Freudian theories.

Unlike many who showed resistance to Freudian theories, however, Hall did not allow himself to be entirely carried away by hostility. For one thing, there was a realistic and rational basis for his criticism of Freud's sexual emphasis. Apart from the personal evidence Hall wanted to deny, he lacked the evidence of the importance of sexual problems and symbolism available to practicing psychoanalysts; many therapists who later converted to psychoanalysis were unconvinced on this issue until faced with the repeated evidence of their patients.[30] Hall approached Freud's theories, therefore, on a theoretical level, and from that point of view, Freud was open to criticism. He still believed at this time that apart from the ego instincts, to which he paid little attention, instinctual energy was entirely libidinal in nature. It was only later that he counted aggression a primary instinct of equal depth, and it was chiefly through his followers that the ego instincts and the role of the ego came to assume a prominent place in psychoanalytic theory.[31] Even Freud's loyal follower, James J. Putnam, agreed with Hall that Freud unduly slighted the "social motives other than sexual, and not to be classed as sexual without some forcing."[32]

Hall thus came to a balanced view of psychoanalysis in which his personal blindness and rational judgments were closely intertwined. In September 1913, writing Freud evidently for the first time in the past two years, Hall expressed high regard for him. He excused his inability to accept the "rather wild use of sex symbolism" on the grounds that "I am only a novice, and only a student of normal psychology, so that I am debarred from the vaster and richer field of

29. GSH, "The Freudian Methods Applied to Anger," 1915, p. 439.

30. Hale, *Freud and the Americans,* chap. 8.

31. On the changes in Freud's own views, see Edward Bibring, "The Development and Problems of the Theory of the Instincts," *International Journal of Psychoanalysis* 22 (1941): 102–31.

32. James J. Putnam, *Addresses on Psycho-Analysis* (London: International Psycho-Analytic Press, 1921), pp. 350, 356.

abnormal psychology." Probably it was by holding to this distinction that Hall achieved some distance from the more disturbing aspects of the Freudian literature. Hall also informed Freud of the somewhat different direction his own thinking was taking. Hall was still impressed with "the immense genetic significance of it all," including Freud's theory of infantile sexuality. He added, however,

I cannot but feel that sooner or later psychologists must break into the big open field of phylogeny and postulate many rather specific influences of the development of the race upon that of the individual, as Stekel seems to have gone far in doing in some respects.

He reported that he was trying "to apply your mechanisms to the study of children's fears and anger, which seem to me to have plenty of *Verdrängung, Verschiebung,* and most of the rest."[33] Hall was, in other words, trying to enlarge Freud's psychological framework in such a way as to lessen the centrality and importance of the sexual impulse in individual development.

Even without the sexual issue, Hall's predilection for phylogenetic experience must have led him to bring this factor into the center of psychology. Freud himself believed in the inheritance of acquired characteristics, though the phylogenetic factor remained a secondary motif in his work. In speaking of applying the Freudian "mechanisms" to fear and anger, Hall was really asserting that the development and transformations of fear and anger were equal in importance to that of the libido. This view was in keeping with the genetic framework Hall had outlined early in 1909, when he identified the unconscious with the long series of instincts inherited from phylogeny. Hall's broadened genetic framework, with its overview of evolutionary progress and bypass of the emotional conflicts rooted in the family, was one of the many liberalized and moralized versions of Freud which his early American adherents generally adopted.[34]

The least worthy of Hall's attempts to enlarge the Freudian theory was the one he alluded to first in his mention of Pavlov. Hall interpreted the experiments of Pavlov to show the importance of hunger in generating learning, and he presented the instinct for

33. GSH to Freud, 26 Sept 1913, CUP.
34. See Hale, *Freud and the Americans,* pp. 433–61.

nutrition as one of the major drives which Freudian theory underestimated. Hall had lectured on the subject of food and nutrition
since his child study work of the 1890s. Other than citation of
Pavlov's experiments, Hall had little beyond his old rhetoric to
contribute to this position, and the intermittent lyrics on the subject
"you are what you eat" which appeared throughout the remainder
of his career were among those aspects of his work which most
justifiably subjected Hall to the ridicule of his colleagues.[35]

   Hall's more sober efforts to deal with the nonsexual instincts led
him to begin in 1914 a series of restudies of some of the major
feeling-instincts in order to reach a new "synthetic genetic" view,
that is, one in which the new insights of psychoanalysis were both
incorporated and enlarged in his own genetic framework. In the
first of these studies on fear, Hall drew at several critical points on
the work of Alfred Adler, one of the early students of psychoanalysis who broke with Freud and was read out of the movement in
1911 and 1912. Hall had been impressed by a collection of Adler's
essays which appeared in 1914, *Heilen und Bilden,* and promptly
wrote him of his interest.[36] He even thought of inviting Adler to
speak at Clark, though the invitation either was never actually issued or was brought to naught by the advent of World War I.[37]

   Hall used particularly the idea of compensation, "which Alfred
Adler has best characterized and which is the most important key
not only for abnormal, as he deems it, but as we believe, for normal
genetic psychology." As Hall interpreted the idea,

man is a congeries of many organs in various stages of evolution and decline, [and] the nervous system when it comes to power establishes a set
of interrelations. . . . Leaving some to decline and powerfully stimulating
others to unfold and develop, by keeping them sufficiently but not too much
in exercise, it reinforces both atrophy and hypertrophy. . . . Where the
brain fails to establish a compensatory system we have all the hosts of
neuroses and psychoses. Very much of the total energy of all of us and still
more of that of neurotics and psychotics is spent in developing and using

   35. See Pruette, *GSH,* pp. 132–38; *LCP,* pp. 414–21. Kern, "Freud and the
Emergence of Child Psychology," pp. 74–75, shows, however, that a number of
studies by Hallians resulting from this interest in the psychology of nutrition
contained uncommon insights.
   36. GSH to Alfred Adler, 18 Apr 1914, CUP.
   37. Jones, *Freud,* 2:134.

devices of concealment of diseases and defects. Thus often the higher protective and defensive mechanisms come to do the work of the subnormal
function even better than it would do it.[38]

Hall thus understood Adler to be talking of *Minderwertigkeit,* or
inferiority, rather than *Minderwertigkeitsgefühls,* feelings of inferiority.[39] Hall's older conception of psychic impulses fighting a
kind of struggle for existence until a coherent pattern of unity was
reached, and his view of consciousness as remedial, thus absorbed
and reshaped the Adlerian idea.

Hall drew another conclusion from this "horror of mediocrity."
Man's "dearest wish is esteem, fame and to maximize himself."
Freud was wrong, therefore, in believing that anxiety was rooted in
sex:

Sex anxieties are themselves only symbols of this deeper sense of abatement
of the will to live, to be powerful, to illustrate in our personality the whole
estate of man, to glow with the humanistic totalising motive to be citizens
of all times and spectators of all events.[40]

Here, presumably, was a new center for his psychology, one which
found strength as Freud's had earlier, in Hall's own sense of himself and of evolutionary process.

In fact, Hall never systematically developed these ideas, but
remained in the more eclectic standpoint of his genetic psychology.
The following year he wrote one of his former students that he was
trying to make "anger one of the *Leitlinien* in Adler's sense, along
with libido, play, reactions to death, etc., for I am trying to block out
a dozen special lines of geneticism."[41] In his study of anger, delivered that year to the new American Psychoanalytic Association
Hall urged that anger, fear, and hunger were "just as primary,
aboriginal and independent as sex." He briefly cataloged how anger
could be considered a dynamic agent, subject to repression, sublimation, and other forms of abreaction. In short, "the movement

38. GSH, "A Synthetic Genetic Study of Fear," 1914, pp. 165–67.
39. Heinz L. Ansbacher, "Alfred Adler and G. Stanley Hall: Correspondence
and General Relationship," MS, p. 17. Hall had earlier used the term "Minderwertigkeit" after the usage of Koch and Trüper, as evidences of developmental
failures. See *Adol*, 1:239–40.
41. GSH to R. F. Richardson, 1 Feb 1915, CUP.
40. GSH, "Synthetic Study of Fear," 1914, pp. 167, 381.

inaugurated by Freud opens up a far larger field than that of sex,"
the field of the unconscious and the feelings, "and in that the chief
merit of Freudianism consists."[42]

Hall brought not only Adler into his genetic version of Freud but,
for a time, Jung as well. Hall's study of the fear of death and desire
for immortality, published in 1915 evidently led him back to his
first love, the psychology of religion.[43] He was thus ripe for the
appearance in 1917 of Jung's *Psychologie der unbewussten Pro-
zesse*. Here Jung presented his theory of the unconscious as the
reservoir of racial psychic experience and religious images. Hall's
own theory of the unconscious as the repository of the whole
species's experience of evolutionary development, the remnant in
man of the whole of "Mansoul," bore striking similarities to Jung's
concept, and it has been suggested that Hall's idea, which clearly
antedated Jung's, might also have influenced it.[44]

Hall wrote Jelliffe that Jung's book "seems to me one of the very
most important things in the psychoanalytic field for years, whatever we think of it."[45] This last qualifier represented Hall's ambivalence toward his own mystical leanings. Together with Jung's
noncommittal reply to his request to have a student translate the
book,[46] this skepticism dampened his ardor. Still he wrote a former
student in 1919 that "psychoanalysis in its larger scope, such as
Jung has seen better than Freud, marks the advent of geneticism" in
psychology. The Freud he wanted to take over psychology, he said,
was "Freudism, ridded of its excessive stress on sex and broadened
into a philosophy of life."[47] Publicly, however, Hall hardly men-

42. GSH "The Freudian Methods Applied to Anger," 1915.
43. GSH, "Thanatophobia and Immortality," 1915.
44. Emmett A. Hinkelman and Morris Aderman, "Apparent Theoretical
Parallels between GSH and Carl Jung," *JHBS* 4 (1968): 254–57. In *Adol*, 2:341–
42, for example, Hall described "the larger unconscious life, on which consciousness floats" in terms very similar to Jung's. The unconscious, Hall said, is "of
the race." The conscious individual communes with it, appeals to its "wise,
benignant and energetic powers." Again, "the motifs of the choicest human documents are due to its initiative and control. . . . What successfully appeals to it
and receives its sanction, we call sacred, divine, biblical, and its messages are
revelations."
45. GSH to Jelliffe, 30 Nov 1917, CUP.
46. GSH to Jung, 29 Oct 1917, CUP; Jung to GSH, 5 Dec 1917, GSH Memorial Volume, CUP.
47. GSH to Martin L. Reymert, 21 July 1919, CUP.

tioned Jung except to comment condescendingly on his mysticism.[48]
The following year, Hall came full circle. He was asked by Edward Bernays to write a preface to the English edition of Freud's
Introductory Lectures on Psychoanalysis. Evidently honored by the
task, he wrote a most favorable little essay, calling Freud "by far the
most original and creative psychologist of this generation" and
emphasizing the wide value of his insights, quite apart from what
many considered his undue emphasis on sex. Adler and Jung were
mentioned as disciples who were carrying Freud's work on in other
directions, and whom he hoped Freud would not too quickly disown.[49]

As psychology picked up again after the war, Adler and Hall
resumed correspondence, Hall directed the work of a number of his
students to Adler's ideas and his journal, and in 1923 he consented
to become one of his "contributing editors."[50] That same year, in
his final exchange with Freud, Hall acknowledged that he had
found much of value in Adler and Jung but that by far his greatest
debt was to Freud himself. "For me, your work has been the chief
inspiration of most that I have done for the past fifteen years. It
has given me a totally new view of psychic life, and I owe to you
more than to anyone else living or dead."[51] During the last years
of his life, the chief topic of his conversation with psychological
colleagues and former students was the importance of psychoanalysis.[52]

To Freud, determined to preserve his vision undiluted, Hall's
course over the years was a puzzling trial. Freud was hurt by the

48. *LCP*, p. 411.
49. Bernays, *Biography of an Idea: Memoirs of Public Relations Counsel Edward L. Bernays* (New York: Simon and Schuster, 1965), p. 253; Sigmund
Freud, *A General Introduction to Psycho-Analysis* (New York: Boni and Liver-
ight, 1920).
50. Ansbacher, "Alfred Adler and G. Stanley Hall," pp. 11–16.
51. GSH to Freud, 24 Sept 1923, printed in John C. Burnham, "Sigmund
Freud and G. Stanley Hall: Exchange of Letters," *Psychoanalytic Quarterly* 29
(1960): 314. The exchange of letters contains an interesting discussion of the
defection of Adler and Jung, in which Hall shrewdly remarked to Freud that
"both illustrate the revolt against the father which you have so well explained.
I do not know that psychoanalysis tells us what is the instinctive, or what ought
to be, the attitude of the father toward his revolting sons." Ibid., p. 313.
52. Cattell, "The Founding of the Association," *PR* 50 (1943): 64; GSH
to L. R. Emerson, 22 May 1919, CUP.

interest Hall showed in Adler and finally decided Hall was "whimsical, unreliable."[53] Adler, determined to mark out an independent sphere for himself and grateful for any attention, immediately enrolled Hall as an adherent to his school, evidently blinking whatever contrary evidence came to his attention.[54] In fact, Hall was neither a Freudian or an Adlerian in the sense in which those men used the terms. He was, simply, a Hallian, who put psychoanalysis into the framework of his own genetic psychology. As such, he had no need to enter into the sectarian distinctions which grew up within the psychoanalytic camp. From the beginning, however, when he approved a number of Freud's major theories, through the whole period after 1913 when he tried various ways to desexualize them, he always thought of Freud as the primary figure of the group, to whom Adler, Jung, and he himself owed most of their new insight into psychological development.

The use of psychoanalytic ideas sometimes strengthened Hall's genetic psychology but also made its inherent weaknesses more apparent. His restudies of the major instincts were most insightful where they followed Freud or Adler. His own commentary still bore the mark of his methods of data collection and run-on style and seemed in contrast to the more systematic ideas of the psychoanalysts, now hopelessly inadequate. Even his knowledge of psychoanalysis often appeared superficial, and Hall admitted to Freud that, lacking clinical experience, he had not been able to understand a good deal of what he had read on the subject.[55]

Hall never finished the series of genetic studies he had planned beyond "Thanatophobia and Immortality," nor did he ever write the final, systematic account of his synthetic, genetic psychology, the treatise on the feelings, which he had so long planned. But systematic psychology had never been Hall's forte. In these last years, Hall's value as a psychologist again lay in recognizing and popularizing the drift of new ideas and extending the professional horizon to new areas of concern.

In his teaching at Clark, Hall gave considerable currency to

53. Jones, *Freud*, 2:105, 134, 205.
54. Ansbacher, "Alfred Adler and G. Stanley Hall," pp. 4, 5, 14, 16.
55. GSH to Freud, 24 Sept 1923, in Burnham, "Sigmund Freud and GSH," p. 314.

psychoanalytic ideas. Many of his students were initiated into the psychoanalytic literature and used Freudian, Adlerian, or other psychoanalytic ideas in their own work. Although enthusiastic about Freud, their knowledge of him was somewhat superficial.[56] One of Hall's best students of these years, Phyllis Blanchard, who was to become a prominent clinical psychologist, remembered that she could not begin to use psychoanalytic techniques seriously in her own work until she had been analyzed, some years after leaving Clark.[57] Nonetheless, one historian has concluded that "American attention to Freud occurred so frequently in work done under Hall's direction and by his students that Hall himself was a major factor in the history of psychoanalytic ideas in the United States, quite apart from his role as organizer of the Clark conferences."[58]

Hall recognized quickly that Freud had profoundly deepened the understanding of child nature. Often citing the new psychoanalysts as his source, he several times during these years addressed audiences of parents and teachers on these new findings in the area of child study. Hall now urged the importance of the first three years of life. During that time the "nascent" impulses which determine the major character traits could be shaped by proper parental training. The spirit of Hall's message remained the same: "give ample vent for spontaneous expressions and . . . avoid excessive repressions," but with the aid of the Freudians, he gave it a more liberal content. Hall remarked, for example, that interest in excretory functions should be moderately gratified; that absolute obedience should not be required; that the child's sense of his own competence should be nurtured.[59]

The overall purpose remained, however, the one of encouraging sublimation.

56. Burnham, "Psychoanalysis in American Civilization before 1918," pp. 189–213; Carroll Pratt, interview, 10 Mar 1962; E. G. Boring to Titchener, 8 Apr 1920, TP.
57. Phyllis Blanchard to GSH, 21 July 1920, CUP; Phyllis Blanchard, interview with Nathan Hale, Jr., May–June 1961, MS, p. 4.
58. Burnham, "Psychoanalysis in American Civilization before 1918," p. 212.
59. See GSH, "Recent Progress in Child Study," 1914; "Child Training," 1915; "New Lights on Childhood," 1915; "A General Survey of Child Study," 1918.

The practical psychologist is like a hydraulic engineer who builds an irri-
gation system, so that waters that went to waste in floods are stored, and
rightly distributed to produce harvests and to turn the mills of industry.[60]

Occasionally, moreover, there was a new element of puritanism introduced. In his *Educational Problems* of 1911, Hall cautioned,

In general the inculcation is to avoid all erethic states, even in the nursery,
beginning with those of sucking itself, which the rubber nipple very distinctly favors. Parents must realize that the masturbatory diathesis may be
cultivated by excessive coddling, by frictions anywhere, especially pattings
and strokings that tend to crescendo or culminating sensations.[61]

In his later lectures, Hall only cautioned against pacifiers and relationships with a parent that were "too close," thus making it difficult for the child to select a spouse.[62] Such warnings were common
among the early analysts. John B. Watson, who was attracted to,
and then rejected, psychoanalysis during these years, drew on this
observation in framing a popular and extremely rigid and depriving
method of child rearing.[63]

On the subject of sex education in the schools, Hall continued to
take the conservative position he had adopted in retreat from Freud.
Emma Goldman, the anarchist agitator who had lived in Worcester,
recorded her disappointment on happening to hear Hall lecture in
1916 in Denver, where he "talked badly and endlessly on the need
of the churches' taking up sex instruction as 'a safeguard for chastity,
morality and religion.' "[64] She had stumbled unwittingly into one
of Hall's lectures designed for the provincial popular culture and
compiled from amongst the less enlightened of his views.

In his social attitudes, Hall's thinking remained after Freud very
much what they had been before. It is not too much to say that Hall's
chief social concern throughout his mature life was the health and
continued biological evolution of the human race. He saw education,
science, improvements of all kinds, as leading not only to social or

60. GSH, "New Lights on Childhood," 1915, p. 578.
61. *EP*, 1:447–48.
62. GSH, "Recent Progress in Child Study," 1914, pp. 214, 216.
63. Hale, *Freud and the Americans*, pp. 481, 535. On Watson, see Kessen,
The Child, pp. 228–44.
64. Emma Goldman, *Living My Life* (Garden City: Garden City Publishing
Co., 1936), p. 575.

cultural progress but, through that, to improvements of the racial stock and production of the superman. It was this concern which made him pay so much attention to women as childbearers of the race, and which gives his work now such a dated flavor. Hall's stance on the eugenics movement, however, was moderate. As an old-fashioned believer in the inheritance of acquired characteristics, he never believed that eugenics was the only road to racial improvement. In 1910 and 1911 when the American eugenics movement was first organized, he spoke frequently on the subject. Hall sometimes echoed his student Goddard on the danger of the feeble-minded, and he often favored sex education as a means of promoting eugenic marriage. He shrunk, however, from advocating the more extreme reforms, and he gave the subject less attention after 1912.[65]

Hall also accepted the loose definitions of race common in his day. He spoke of Negroes, Jews, southern Europeans, and Anglo-Saxons as distinct races and worried particularly that the Anglo-Saxons were committing "race suicide" through their declining birth rate.[66] All those who used these categories were not equally racist, however, in the sense that one could accord races other than the Anglo-Saxon more or less dignity.

Given Hall's view of childhood and adolescence, his belief that primitive peoples represented the childhood and adolescence of the race had a positive, as well as negative, content. Primitive peoples represented human qualities not always cultivated in the West, and could any of them begin to develop in new ways, they might eventually outstrip our own civilization in the move toward the superman. Hall believed in the right of each race to be left alone to develop its indigenous culture in its own way. Christianity had no inherent merit over primitive religions on the scale of evolutionary development if it was imposed from without. Individualism, not uniformity, was the goal of racial policy, as of educational policy.[67]

In 1898, Hall urged in a letter to the New York *Evening Post*

65. See *Adol*, 2:722; GSH, "The Co-ordination of the School with the Three Score Other Child Welfare Agencies," 1910; GSH, "Eugenics: Its Ideals and What It Is Going to Do," 1911; GSH in Boston *Post,* 29 Oct 1911.

66. *Adol*, 2:594–612; GSH, "From Generation to Generation: With Some Plain Language about Race Suicide and the Instruction of Children During Adolescence," 1908; *LCP*, p. 114.

67. See *Adol*, 1:57, 72; 2:648–748.

that we stay out of Cuba, and he repeatedly and publicly thereafter opposed American colonial policy in the Caribbean and the Pacific. He argued that our knowledge of how to deal with foreign peoples was too infirm to allow us to administer their interests properly; after we had taken on imperial duties, he urged that we allow the peoples in our charge to develop in their own way.[68] Characteristically, Hall was not entirely comfortable in the radical camp and denounced anti-imperialists who attacked the president personally for his policies.[69] He reported voting for McKinley in 1896 and 1900 "because I fear free silver more than I do imperialism."[70]

Hall's anti-imperialism was nonetheless quite consistent for many years. When stories of atrocities against the natives of the Congo began to circulate, Hall became active in efforts to restrain Leopold of Belgium. He was president in 1906 and 1907 of the Kongo Reform Association, which petitioned the American government to intervene and for a time monitored developments after Belgium took over the Congo.[71] Hall thought of putting together "another organization in the interests of primitive people generally, a kind of society of societies," but the society never got beyond his daydreams.[72]

Hall took a continuing, though not as prominent, interest in racial minorities within the country. From the 1880s onward, Hall often mentioned the problem of "mixed bloods" as one of the key

68. GSH, "The Business Point of View," in New York *Evening Post*, 28 Feb 1898; GSH, "Colonial Policy," in Greenfield, Mass., *Gazette and Courier*, 25 Aug 1900; GSH, "The Point of View toward Primitive Races," 1910; GSH, "Mission Pedagogy," 1910.

69. Sara Norton and Mark A. De Wolfe Howe, eds., *The Letters of Charles Eliot Norton* (Boston: Houghton Mifflin, 1913), 2:455; Edward Jewell to GSH, 23 Aug 1901, CUP.

70. GSH in Boston *Journal*, 15 Oct 1900.

71. Worcester *Telegram*, 21 Jan, 11 Apr 1906; GSH to Thomas S. Barbour, 5 Feb, 2 July 1907; GSH to Elihu Root, 21 Aug 1908, CUP. In 1912 Hall was still active in the Anti-Imperialism League. Worcester *Telegram*, 10 Jan 1912.

72. GSH to Thomas S. Barbour, 2 July 1907, CUP. Hall's enthusiasm probably helped to interest George S. Blakeslee, professor of history at Clark, in international relations, and Blakeslee became one of the founders of the study in America. In 1910 Hall was included as co-editor of Blakeslee's *Journal of Race Development*, which later merged with *Foreign Affairs*. Harry Elmer Barnes, "Clark University: An Adventure in American Educational History," *American Review* 3 (1925): 286; Harry Elmer Barnes to the author, 30 Nov 1962; Samuel Flagg Bemis to the author, 24 Oct, 3 Nov 1962.

Denouement

problems of American society. While pointing to the difficulties mixed racial heritage brought to growing up in America—it increased the stresses of adolescence, for example, by providing a more disparate racial inheritance to express and unify—Hall generally concluded that the resultant personality would be stronger and higher because of its wider racial foundation.[73]

Except for a few commonplace references to the southern Europeans after 1900, Hall gave specific attention to only two minorities in the country, the Jews and the Negroes. Hall was most favorable in his treatment of the Jews, perhaps because of his early pleasant contact with the Seligmans and their cultured friends in New York. Hall's essay reports from Germany had contained an extended and highly critical account of the anti-Semitism which was already pervading German popular culture and entering the universities.[74] As anti-Semitism in America rose in connection with the influx of Eastern European Jews into the country, Hall spoke often to Jewish groups, comparing Jews very favorably with Yankees, and urging that Jews in America retain their religious and cultural identity.[75]

Hall's comments on black Americans read now like the attitudes of a typically prejudiced man of the progressive era. Hall's positive valuation of emotionalism, however, the chief characteristic of the black stereotype, carried his views in a more favorable direction than appeared on the surface. Hall regarded himself as something of a liberal on the race question. He thought the program of Booker T. Washington, with its effort at self-improvement and indigenous development, was the key to black improvement, which whites ought to encourage and support.[76]

Hall's social analysis on the basis of racial categories thus produced a generally moderate stance. He did not become a virulent racial alarmist of the right nor did he see through the stereotypes of race as the more progressive social theorists were doing during these years. His thinking belonged rather to the era before 1900, when

73. See *Adol*, 2:722.
74. GSH, *Aspects*, pp. 51–57.
75. Worcester *Telegram*, 27 Oct 1913; GSH, "Yankee and Jew," 1915; GSH, "A Suggestion for a Jewish University," 1917.
76. GSH, "A Few Results of Recent Scientific Study of the Negro in America," 1905; GSH, "The Negro in Africa and America," 1905; GSH in the Worcester *Telegram*, 28 Jan 1906; Thomas P. Bailey to GSH, 30 Jan 1908, CUP.

biological determinism and racial categories could be taken for granted and yet allow a good deal of room for environmental influence and optimistic meliorism. As was his temperamental wont in any case, Hall could in this earlier vein utter the conventional conservative fears of racial decline while continuing to explore more liberal approaches to international and domestic race relations.

On the subject of woman's rights, Hall similarly remained in the nineteenth-century mold. As he wrote a former student, "in these days of suffragettes, . . . so many people who have generally been enrolled among the antis are, like myself, finding the fence a most comfortable position."[77] He continued to urge women not to become more like men and he came to approve women using their new power only in their own special sphere of public morals. He made an exception, however, for the few brilliant women he found enrolling at Clark during his last years and whose company he found himself greatly enjoying.[78]

Another of Hall's long-standing concerns, which came to fruition in these years after his initiation into psychoanalysis, showed little change from his earlier pre-Freudian attitudes. The psychology of religion had been the earliest thread of Hall's own, distinctive psychology. Two of his students had made substantial contributions to the subject in the 1890s: James H. Leuba stressed the moral content of religious experience and Edwin D. Starbuck, a student of James as well as Hall, analyzed conversion as a variation of normal processes in adolescence.[79] Hall's attention to the subject of religion began to increase in 1900, just as child study was running into difficulties among scientists and educators. Perhaps sensing a new interest in liberal ideas among the clergy, Hall forecast that "a new Universal religion" was "at Hand."[80]

In 1901, moreover, William James began his course of Gifford Lectures at the University of Edinburgh which resulted the following year in his book, *The Varieties of Religious Experience*. James

77. GSH to Luther M. Gulick, 4 Apr 1913, CUP.
78. GSH, "Points of Difference between Men and Women, Inherent and Acquired," 1919; *LCP*, p. 318.
79. See *Adol*, 2:292, and "Clark List of Religious Papers," 1911, in *CULP*, vol. 2.
80. GSH, "A New Universal Religion at Hand," 1901; GSH, "Some Fundamental Principles of Sunday School and Bible Teaching," 1901.

probably had Hall's early statements about the connection of sexuality and religion in mind when he subjected the view to a strong
critique in his *Varieties*.[81] In his extensive discussion of religion and
conversion in *Adolescence*, Hall had James's views very prominently
in mind and criticized them sharply. Hall called James's parade of
pathological religious experiences "the yellow literature of religious
psychology."[82] Widely hailed at the time of its appearance and since,
James's treatment of religious psychology must have been a challenge to Hall to publicize his own views.

The same year *Adolescence* appeared, Hall announced a new
journal, *The American Journal of Religious Psychology and Education*, which he would edit in cooperation with Leuba, Starbuck,
and others not directly his disciples. Claiming that psychology would
bring to a moribund Christianity "a new revival of a kind and degree that the Christian world has not known in recent centuries,"
and paying heed as well to the condition of workers which was then
stirring the clergy to social action, Hall thought to cultivate another
field of future promise.[83] Starbuck was worried about Hall's intentions and relieved that James had already given the subject a solid
and respectable intellectual basis. As he wrote James,

One thing I had suspected and a bit feared is about to happen . . . Hall is
about to start a Journal devoted to the psychology of religion. But it is happening too late to give the subject such a period of unenviable history to
outgrow as was the case with child study.[84]

Hall did not, however, devote much attention to the *Journal* or the
subject for the next decade, and he soon passed the editorship to
Chamberlain, who held it until his death in 1914. Claiming that he
could find no one to take over the editorship thereafter, Hall discontinued publication.[85]

Hall finally brought his religious speculation to fruition a few

81. William James, *The Varieties of Religious Experience* (New York: Longmans, Green, 1902), pp. 10–11.
82. *Adol*, 2:292–93. A more balanced critique is found in "A Statement of
My Differences with William James' Psychology of Religion," 9 May 1907, in
Clark CW.
83. GSH, "Editorial," 1904.
84. E. D. Starbuck to Wm. James, 13 Feb 1904, JP.
85. *LCP*, pp. 317–18. The Clark librarian stated in 1911 that the journal "has
not accomplished all that was hoped for." "Clark List of Religious Papers," p. 1.

years later, in 1917, when he published his *Jesus the Christ in the Light of Psychology*. He had had the book nearly finished in 1900 but decided to "hold it off for some time." Even in 1917 Hall was afraid "that I risk what future career remains to me by publishing so frank a book."[86] Hall still did battle with religious fundamentalists in his lectures in the provinces and worried that such attitudes persisted even in university circles.[87] The book was indeed criticized severely in the conservative religious press but taken in stride in other quarters.[88]

Jesus was, according to Hall, a mythic creation of humanity who "incorporates all the good tendencies in man." He was particularly a man of passion and vitality, the apotheosis of adolescence, a young man physically large, with great strength, beauty, and personal magnetism. The story of his death and resurrection embodied the fundamental rhythm of psychic life, from pain to joy; to experience and understand this rhythm in conversion was the supreme lesson of life. The message Jesus left was not to be projected "upon the clouds" or to be made into a cult for assuring immortality, but was to be realized within each individual, in this world, in service to his fellow man.

Hall's rendering of the Christian story harked back to very personal themes: Jesus as a kind of adolescent superman, the cyclic swing from despair to joy, and Hall's messianic desire to bring about a new Reformation. Hall assumed throughout that the primary religious impulse was that of love, but the link between religion and sex, which had been such a prominent aspect of his earlier treatment, was conspicuously absent. Aside from an occasional use of the psychoanalytic mechanisms in explaining the actions of Christ or his followers, Hall's picture of Jesus owed little to Freud.[89] It was, in reality, a historical study of Jesus' life and its humane meaning, rather than an analytical study of religion; the historical

86. GSH to W. T. Harris, 11 June 1900, Harris Papers, University of Southern California Library; GSH to Patrick Geddes, 7 July 1916, CUP.
87. Worcester *Gazette*, 5 May 1908; GSH to F. K. Saunders, 15 Sept 1915; GSH to J. H. Leuba, 5 Jan 1917; J. H. Leuba to GSH, 10 Jan 1917, CUP.
88. William Byron Forbush, "G. Stanley Hall," *Congregationalist and Christian World* 86 (1901): 169–70; Elwood Worcester, "Jesus in the Light of Psychology," *Churchman*, 17 Nov 1917, p. 627; GSH to E. S. Conklin, 21 June 1918, CUP.
89. GSH, *Jesus, the Christ, in the Light of Psychology*, 1917, p. xviii.

419   *Denouement*

problems of evidence and changing interpretation most intrigued
him in writing it.[90]

The last major episode of Hall's career as a psychologist, and the
last great enthusiasm to overtake him, was the First World War.
From the moment war broke out in Europe, in August 1914, Hall
spoke a great deal about it and urged that the war be taught in
school. Hall was convinced that the subject could be taught fairly to
both sides and wanted to put the great interest generated by the
event to use in lessons in geography, history, and politics.[91]

Hall maintained his own neutrality bravely, though "like so
many of my class, I have felt my soul almost torn in two between a
sense of loyalty to and admiration of civic and cultural Germany,
from whom we have yet so much to learn, and German militar-
ism."[92] Once we were in the war, however, Hall thought, we should
"let loose the vials of righteous wrath." Though he supported the
right of socialists to speak their contrary views, he could not see

how a pacifist can conscientiously and consistently advocate neutrality. This
is a war unlike other wars. It is a war to end war. . . . We are in the war to
realize the high purposes and principles which the pacifists profess.[93]

Still, Hall tried to maintain some balance. His oft-repeated lectures
on the war typically left his audiences undecided whether he
thought "the benefits of war outweigh its cruelty." Moved by the
rationale of his optimistic evolutionism Hall predicted that a new
and better world would emerge from "what now seems the greatest moral catastrophe that has ever befallen Christendom."[94]

Amidst these conventional sentiments, Hall suddenly emerged
in the forefront of psychology's response to the war. Once again,

90. Carroll Pratt, interview, 10 Mar 1962. Hall's focus on Jesus and his human
experience was characteristic of liberal Protestant thinking during Hall's formative years in the 1870s and 1880s. See Daniel Day Williams, *The Andover Liberals,* p. 22.

91. GSH in Boston *Herald,* 27 Aug, 6 Oct 1914; Worcester *Telegram,* 15
Nov 1914; GSH, "Teaching the War," 1915; GSH, "Forward, with a Discussion
of the Psychology of the Present War," 1916.

92. GSH, "Psychological Notes on the War," 1916, p. 358.

93. GSH in Worcester *Telegram,* 10 Sept 1917. Hall allowed, for example,
Dr. Harry W. Laider, secretary of the Intercollegiate Socialist Society to speak at
Clark. Worcester *Telegram,* 21 Feb 1918.

94. New York *Evening World,* 10 July 1916; GSH, "The War and Some of
Its Relations to Education," 1916, p. 120.

at the end of his career, as had happened at the beginning, Hall's own predilections and his keen sense of what his audience wanted to hear combined to make him the spokesman for the mainstream of psychology. Addressing a joint session in New York of the American Psychological Association and the American Association for the Advancement of Science in December 1916, a few months before America entered the war, Hall told the psychologists how applied psychology had made the German and French war efforts so efficient. The Freudian literature, too, could offer insight into how and why soldiers broke down under fire. This announcement of the practical value of psychology was, according to the *New York Times*, "discussed by many of the scientists yesterday as one of the most appealing of the convocation," and the *Times* itself, naming Hall, editorialized in favor of the "practical" academic expert.[95]

Hall quickly followed up this lead by launching in March 1917, with two of his younger colleagues at Clark, *The Journal of Applied Psychology*, the first journal in America devoted to applications of psychology to business problems and vocational aptitudes. A form of vocational selection would in fact be the chief contribution of organized psychology to the war. Stanley Hall was promptly made a member of the psychology committee of the National Research Council, which began to organize professional efforts. It soon was apparent, however, that he was too old and his ideas too far removed from practical application to be of any use.

Hall wanted to work up tests of morale and "second-breath," the "readiness to get into the erethic state, that draws upon . . . reserves or racial qualities after a period of being all in," or to study the hereditary or childhood aggressiveness of soldiers to determine the best fighters. The younger psychologists finally set him to work summarizing and analyzing the thousands of letters received by the army from young recruits, for their bearing on the subject of morale.[96]

The only result of Hall's war efforts, therefore, was a long article and a book written after the war, both titled *Morale*. His conception of morale was imbedded in a series of religious and Freudian meta-

95. *New York Times*, 29, 30 Dec 1916.
96. GSH to Robert M. Yerkes, [spring 1918]; GSH to R. S. Woodworth, 17 Apr 1918; GSH to J. W. Baird, 12 Sept 1918, CUP.

phors on the energy of the life force, and the subject was no more than a literary device for joining together vivid accounts of a variety of subjects affecting the conduct of the war and of American society. On most subjects, Hall could only repeat the judgments which he had made all his mature life. Even the soldier, he counseled, should maintain "chastity and self-control." On political affairs, however, Hall was moved to a new concern and a more outspoken call for reform. In his enthusiasm for the national viewpoint and vigorous government induced by the war, Hall often sounded sympathetic to socialism, as he had been in his youth. His firm belief in academic freedom also led him to advocate the right of socialists to speak and teach at universities. In the reaction of the postwar years, however, Hall stressed the dangers of communism and called for voluntary reconciliation and mutual adjustment of needs between capital and labor. To forestall the spread of Bolshevism, American capitalism should be brought to share its profits with labor, Hall asserted, but the principle of competition should be regulated and not destroyed.[97]

With the end of the war, Hall's influence in psychology was substantially at an end. In June 1920, he resigned from his professorship and the presidency of Clark University, to spend his last few years facing old age and death and looking backward over his life. To Titchener, Hall had seemed for some years already a "historical figure" whose mind was formed in the seventies of the past century.[98] Yet Hall had generated interests and issues from that Victorian matrix which were genuinely modern and which genuinely challenged his colleagues.

The influence of Hall's early career in psychology had gone in the direction of making his profession more rigorously and self-consciously scientific. The influence of his mature career went toward making scientific psychology in America a discipline very much oriented to practical application. Hall generated popular desire for psychological knowledge in education and child rearing,

97. GSH, "Morale in War and After," 1918, pp. 424–25; GSH, *Morale: The Supreme Standard of Life and Conduct,* 1920, pp. 316–41; GSH in Worcester papers, 19 July 1899, CW, vol. 7.

98. Titchener to T. A. Hunter, 22 Oct 1925; Titchener to L. N. Wilson, 24 June 1925, TP.

health and disease, work and play, and he drew in after him wide professional concern with these problems. His importance in stimulating the study of child psychology and development was fundamental. He also did much to encourage the study of dynamic processes in behavior, in part under the guidance of psychoanalytic conceptions. Hall's specific methods and doctrines aroused so much opposition, however, that the wide impact of his activities and ideas was often lost to view.

The psychologists who followed Hall's lead did not always recognize their debt to him, for Hall did not leave a systematic body of ideas behind to be accepted or modified by later psychologists. He did leave an approach and direction of concern—most perhaps of what James bequeathed to his profession—but unlike James, Hall had not captured that respect and affection of his colleagues which would lead them to identify with his larger concerns, even while rejecting his invalid or irrelevant ideas. Among most of his students Hall was held in great esteem, but as Boring has shown, most of Hall's students did not themselves sire psychological disciples of the first rank; so no continuing school of Hallians long survived him.[99] More of Hall's students went into education than psychology, and many of them went to small colleges or to the less-developed state universities in the Middle and Far West. Terman and Gesell almost alone made their way to institutions of the first rank and left their mark clearly on the structure of the profession.[100]

99. Mollie D. Boring and Edwin G. Boring, "Masters and Pupils among the American Psychologists," *AJP* 61 (1948): 527–34. The lines of continuing influence they find seem to be located at the larger and wealthier university departments which were able to attract high-caliber students over several generations.

100. A tabulation of a random sample of entries in L. N. Wilson, ed., "Clark University Directory of Alumni, Faculty and Students," *CULP* 4, no. 6 (1915), shows the occupations of former Clark students as follows: In the educational hierarchy, as school teachers, principals, or superintendents, 22 percent; in normal schools or university departments of education, 34 percent; in departments of psychology or philosophy at colleges and universities, or presidents thereof, 25 percent. This tabulation includes those who did not receive a Clark degree as well as those who did, but the same pattern apparently holds true for those who received the Ph.D. degree. Up until 1916, Clark awarded more Ph.D. degrees in psychology than any other university in the country. See Harper, "Tables of American Doctorates in Psychology," 580–81. Among members of the American Psychological Association in 1916, however, more members held degrees from Columbia, Harvard, and Chicago than from Clark, suggesting that many Clark

There is, however, one line of substantial current effort in psychology which bears Hall's stamp, and that, appropriately, at Clark University. In 1947, Heinz Werner, an Austro-German psychologist who had earlier fled Hitler's Germany, was appointed G. Stanley Hall Professor of Genetic Psychology at Clark University. Trained in Vienna and in Hamburg under Wilhelm Stern, Werner was concerned with tracing developmental processes in the full spectrum of psychobiological phenomena and was familiar with Hall's work from the respectful comments of Stern.[101] At Clark, Werner cast his genetic theory into experimental forms, thus joining the university's experimental and genetic traditions. Unique among American developmental psychologists for working on hypotheses which link developmental and disintegrative phenomena, intrapsychic processes, individual development, and cultural evolution, Werner nonetheless established his genetic approach on firm scientific bases.[102] He thus continued in more modern form at Clark the developmental tradition which earlier included Stanley Hall.

---

degree-holders did not actually become psychologists. See Cattell, "Psychology in America," in Poffenberger, *James McKeen Cattell,* 2:455. It was also a commonplace among Clark alumni that their university was better known in the West than the East. C. N. Boynton to E. C. Sanford, 22 Jan 1914, CUP.

101. Heinz Werner, interview, 10 Dec 1962; Bernard Kaplan and Seymour Wapner, eds., *Perspectives in Psychological Theory; Essays in Honor of Heinz Werner* (New York: International Universities Press, 1960), pp. 13–19.

102. See Alfred L. Baldwin, *Theories of Child Development* (New York: John Wiley & Sons, 1967), pp. 495–533.

20

END OF A CAREER

When Hall retired from Clark University in 1920, he left an enormous vacancy, for the university was, through most of his thirty-one-year presidency, very much his own domain. The pattern of relations he had early established with students and colleagues persisted throughout his term. Hall continued to offer great stimulus and opportunity for research, and his catholicity of interests and willingness to adjust standards to each individual allowed a great variety of type and quality of work to go on at Clark over the years.

Hall attracted promising students from the educational hinterlands and occasionally rebels against the more conventional and rigid standards of the larger universities. There was always a core of first-rate students, surrounded by more mediocre minds, and beyond them, a "lunatic fringe" of assorted odd characters, some of them with only a grade school education.[1] In most periods of its history, one could find a few ministers working on religious psychology or education and some pedagogs working up a favorite idea.[2] During the middle and late 1910s, the university had a decidedly radical flavor, with students avidly discussing Freud, and iconoclastic young social scientists like Frank Hankins and Harry

1. Lewis M. Terman, "Autobiography," pp. 317–18; Edwin D. Starbuck to Wm. James, 29 Jan 1896, JP; "Clark Alumni Banquet, 1907" pp. 7–9; Frank Hankins, interview, 8 Mar 1962.
2. See, for example, *Ann. Rep. Pres. Clark, 1916*, pp. 35–57.

Elmer Barnes making radical gestures under the umbrella of Hall's support.[3]

Hall gave his students broad, stimulating, often superficial, vistas in his lectures, keen competition and suggestive criticism in his seminar, and as much of his personal office time as they wished to occupy. After Sanford abandoned his chair for the presidency of Clark College and turned the laboratory over to a Titchenerian, the experimental students felt themselves somewhat separate from the "Hallians," but everyone always attended Hall's seminar.[4]

Hall carried to great lengths his belief in adjustment to the individual student. He quickly recognized the strong minds and set them high standards. He demanded much less from the others and sometimes fed them as much as they would swallow.[5] Hall's admirers believed that he was thus bending in kindness to the human and practical needs of his students.[6] His rivals at Harvard and Columbia accused him of admitting students with inadequate preparation and granting the Ph.D. for inferior work merely to augment the number of his students.[7]

Hall gave his students suggestions which sometimes amounted to a word-by-word blueprint of his own ideas on the subject and inconsistent reactions to ideas and to themselves. Some of the best of Hall's students blossomed in this atmosphere. They rose to his stimulating suggestions without being cowed by them and, often taking their thesis topics to Sanford, learned to build a solid intellectual support under their Hallian inspiration. It required great independence to do so, however. As Terman confessed, "to go into anything at Clark without the backing of Dr. Hall, makes un-

---

3. Frank Hankins, interview; Carroll Pratt, interview, 10 Mar 1962. For an overly favorable description of Clark in these years, see Barnes, "Clark University," *American Review* 3 (1925): 271–88. Fleeing the repressive atmosphere of Columbia University, Barnes was at Clark from 1918 to 1922 and claimed Hall's insipration in writing *The New History and the Social Studies* (New York: Century, 1925). See pp. xi, 76–77, 82, 91–101, 569.

4. Carroll Pratt, interview; Edwin G. Boring, interview, 5 Mar 1962.

5. The registrar's files at Clark University and CUP contain correspondence with students which illustrate Hall's extreme flexibility in setting standards. See, for example, the correspondence with Walter Libby, A. J. Uppvall, A. A. Cleveland, and Frederick M. Smith. Also GSH to Mr. Hori, 20 Feb 1915, CUP.

6. Pruette, *GSH,* p. 202; M. Evelyn Douglass to the author, 11 June 1962.

7. GSH to Norman Triplett, 9 Feb 1914, CUP; Frank Hankins, interview.

pleasant business." Understandably, the more mediocre minds tended to imitate Hall, and often they copied the worst rather than the best of him.[8]

Hall's personal impression on his students was as varied as his pedagogical impact. Some responded straightforwardly to what they felt was a pleasant and unaffected manner, genuine interest in one's work, quick humor, and real personal power. Some, however, felt the reserve at the core of Hall's personality and regarded his approaches as experimental gestures, never quite escaping self-consciousness. A number of his bright women students during his last years found him an understanding father figure, wise and uncensorious. Still others were baffled by his inconsistent anger or approval, his evidences of harshness, meanness, and selfishness. His most perceptive student sensed that he was a very accomplished actor.[9]

Hall's administrative methods continued unchanged over the years. His admirers blinked at what they called his "artistic mendacity" and the tight personal control he continued to wield over university affairs.[10] For all Hall's praise of the "Cattell movement" for greater faculty control of the university which gained strength after 1913,[11] he continued to believe Clark's small size and his own dedication to freedom in teaching and research sufficed to exempt it from the general rule. Faculty meetings were nonexistent, and attempts in 1914 and after to have the faculty represented on the board of trustees were met with killing silence.[12] Hall did agree in

8. Terman to Arnold Gesell, 19 Jan 1906, Gesell Papers, Library of Congress. For different reactions to Hall's teaching style, see Terman, "Autobiography," pp. 312–18; Rowles, *The Lady at Box 99*, pp. 80–95; Harvey A. Carr, "Autobiography," in Murchison, *History of Psychology in Autobiography*, 3: 72–73.

9. Pruette's *GSH* records the most perceptive impression of Hall's personality on a student during his later years, but it is an extremely appreciative one. For contrasting views, see Rowles, *The Lady at Box 99;* Edmund S. Conklin's review of Pruette in *AJP* 38 (1927): 135; A. E. Hamilton, "Stanley Hall: A Memory," *American Mercury* 2 (1924): 287–92; George E. Dawson, in "Clark Alumni Banquet 1907," pp. 9–11; and Phyllis Blanchard, "G. Stanley Hall: Mental Hygienist," *Understanding the Child* 1 (1931): 20. Similarly diverging impressions were also presented by Carroll Pratt and Frank Hankins in interviews with the author.

10. Barnes, "Clark University," pp. 273–74.

11. GSH, "Contemporary University Problems," 1914.

12. "Twenty-Fifth Anniversary of Clark University," p. 34; *Inauguration of*

1915 to reestablish the long defunct university senate, composed
only of full professors, and it was the debates of these elders which
Hall's later students remembered as the mark of administrative
freedom at the university.[13] There was, however, a certain irony in
the freedom to disagree that Hall allowed his faithful band of colleagues, for they knew, as he did, that their objections could create
only minor detours in the basic course which Hall himself always,
indisputably, set.

The fate of the few men who clung to Clark and Hall over those
thirty years shows much of his personal strength and weakness.
Hall could attract their loyalty to his high ideals and keep it despite
the meagerness of their salaries, and he allowed Webster in physics
and newer men in chemistry and biology to establish traditions of
excellence which long outlasted his administration. The men in
his own fields were subtly and inevitably submerged by him, however, and neither Sanford, Burnham, nor Chamberlain ever achieved
in their profession what their intellectual power seemed to
promise.[14]

Their staying at Clark and their submergence to Hall were facts,
of course, of their own making as well as Hall's; yet Hall showed
them little of the gratitude he owed for their loyalty. In countless
ways which he could easily have foregone, he upstaged them and
held them back.[15] Though he regarded them as his closest friends,
there remained always a distance and reserve.[16] Even among
this small band, Hall was self-absorbed and alone. At the end, pon-

Wallace Walter Atwood As President of Clark University (Worcester: Clark
University Library, 1921), p. 40.

13. "Record, The University Senate, The Academic Council," CUP; Barnes,
"Clark University," p. 273.

14. L. N. Wilson, ed., "Alexander Francis Chamberlain. In Memoriam,"
CULP 4 (1914); "In Memoriam. Edmund Clark Sanford," ibid. 8 (1925).

15. Titchener said that Sanford "has always been pressed down and kept
under; he was held assistant professor so long that I used annually to remonstrate
with Stanley Hall about him." Titchener to E. G. Boring, 9 Nov 1923, TP. For
many years Burnham edited the *Pedagogical Seminary*, though Hall remained as
editor on the masthead, adding after 1905, "with the Assistance of" Burnham.
See also the correspondence between Burnham and Arnold Gesell in the Gesell
Papers.

16. E. C. Sanford to Titchener, 25 Apr 1924, TP; Pruette, *GSH*, pp. 253–54;
LCP, pp. 311–12.

dering his isolation, he wondered why he had never attained congenial and friendly relations with intellectuals around the world, but he hardly saw the failure which lay closest to home.[17]

Understandably, Hall clung tenaciously to his post at Clark as he advanced in age. He had early dropped off two years from his official age and, until near the end, he maintained his spry gait and prodigious capacity for work. As his last decade at Clark proceeded, however, the difficulties that faced the small university became increasingly apparent and Hall was clearly past solving them.[18] After the war he could no longer ignore the depleted condition of his university. Chamberlain of the anthropology department was dead. Physics and mathematics struggled on with a few students. Only chemistry and psychology remained in any strength, and he and Sanford were well past their prime. Inflation meanwhile had cut their small budget almost in half. Reluctantly, Hall told the trustees in 1919 to begin looking for a replacement.[19]

Typically, Hall allowed no word of his retirement to escape and would not permit the presence or announcement of his successor at his last commencement exercises of 1920, lest his authority be diminished before it had run the last minute of its course.[20] It was only then that Hall relinquished his *American Journal of Psychology* to Titchener's student, Karl M. Dallenbach, asking in the bargain the last possible dollar, so that the feeling of even this most loyal colleague cooled toward him in his last years.[21]

The Clark board of trustees, looking for a president to unite the college and university, hoped first to find a psychologist of stature. Titchener and others refused, however, for they would gain by the presidency the critical financial problems of the small school, as well as their own department of psychology. The board finally chose Wallace W. Atwood, professor at Harvard and a noted geographer.

17. *LCP,* p. 571.
18. The predicament of the college was vividly felt in 1914, in "Twenty-Fifth Anniversary of Clark University."
19. Edmund C. Sanford, "A Sketch of the History of Clark University," *CULP* 7 (1923), pp. 8–9.
20. Wallace W. Atwood, "Administrative Report of the President, 1920–1945," *CULP* 9 (1945), p. 17.
21. Karl M. Dallenbach to Titchener, 4 Apr 1921, TP; E. G. Boring to the author, 20 Mar 1962.

It was understood that like Hall before him, Atwood would be a teaching president who would build up his new and promising department at Clark. It was clear to Hall as he acquiesced in the choice, that psychology would probably continue at Clark but that geography might well attain to the first position in size and resources.[22]

The transition to the new regime proved difficult, in part because the new president had a very limited notion of academic freedom and in part because he did not appear to have the high intellectual aims of his predecessor. As a result, a number of the strongest young faculty left, including Edwin G. Boring, whom Hall had hoped would give psychology a firm hold in the new Clark.[23] Hall might have eased the strain had he discussed the transition with his faculty beforehand, but he clothed it entirely in silence. After his successor had taken over, and Hall lived on quietly in the old President's House, his silence was a virtue. His old colleagues and students brought him news of Atwood's reactionary stance and the disquiet among the faculty, but he was determined to let the new man have his day and hopeful that somehow the university he had made would continue.[24] In fact, psychology did survive at Clark, along with the tradition of supporting valuable, but idiosyncratic, scientific ventures.[25]

The cultural turmoil following the war added to Hall's personal plight. He was struck particularly by the loss of morale and purpose which overtook the country, so that instead of the determination to solve the country's economic and social problems there was labor

22. *Inauguration of Wallace Walter Atwood As President of Clark University,* particularly, pp. 35, 39.
23. On the difficulties over academic freedom at Clark under Atwood, see E. G. Boring, "Autobiography," in Murchison, *History of Psychology in Autobiography,* 4:37–38, and the more extended version in Boring, *Psychologist at Large* (New York: Basic Books, 1961), pp. 35–39; Arthur O. Lovejoy et al., "Report of Committee of Inquiry concerning Clark University," *Bulletin of the American Association of University Professors* 10 (1924): 40–105; and for a radical account, Upton Sinclair, *The Goose-Step* (Pasadena, Calif.: by the author, 1924), pp. 287–302.
24. Pruette, *GSH,* pp. 233–37; E. G. Boring, interview.
25. E.g., the work of Robert H. Goddard in rocketry. Goddard had been partly trained by Webster and later took over his chair. See Milton Lehman, *This High Man; the Life of Robert Hutchings Goddard* (New York: Farrar, Straus, 1963).

unrest, class antagonism, a retreat from international responsibilities, and a lapse into mere money-getting.[26] In this falling apart, as in the German devotion to the Nietzschian superman,, he began to see an unbridled individualism as the principal culprit.[27] Hall composed in 1920 a utopian fantasy called *The Fall of Atlantis,* in which his ideal state of perfect health, morality, cooperation, and advancing knowledge was slowly destroyed by the strife of often valid, progressive, individualistic wants. As a utopia, Atlantis was merely an intensified and simplified form of his several reforming concerns during the course of his life rather than a compelling and unitary vision. But in his account of its progressive disintegration, Hall was quite perceptively realistic and utterly without recourse. His romance gave form to his earlier sense that the Golden Age was after all in the unconscious past and that evolution might only be regression.[28] Yet Hall could not hold this insight in steady focus, for so much of his life and thought was rooted in the ideal of individual development. The following year he again aspired to be one of the "true Supermen who, like Zarathustra, are all old, very old, with the sapience that long life alone can give."[29]

Hall promptly and publicly scolded himself for his utopian flight from reality and its depressing pessimism. The present crisis deserved all one's attention, he said, and sometimes with more confidence, at other times with less, he offered his only remedies— education, a total devotion to the advancement of knowledge, love-conversion-moral regeneration.[30]

Hall offered his solutions as the fruits of the wisdom of old age, and old age was the chief of the trials Hall now had to face. Fighting off the desolation which came over him as he finally abandoned his daily round of duties for a more formless and purposeless existence, Hall determined to look honestly at old age and death.[31] He had worked intermittently on a study of senescence since he had turned

26. GSH, *Morale,* pp. 147–51; GSH, "Salvaging Civilization," 1922, pp. 830–34.
27. GSH, "Psychological Notes on the War," 1916, p. 361.
28. Published in GSH, *Recreations,* 1920, pp. 1–127.
29. GSH, "Old Age," 1921, p. 31.
30. GSH, "The Message of the Zeitgeist," 1921; "Salvaging Civilization," 1922.
31. GSH, "Old Age," 1921.

fifty, but now he attacked it in earnest. The result, *Senescence,* published in 1922, completed Hall's examination of the life cycle. The book is disappointing in one major respect, for it fails to deal with the critical problem of Hall's own life-line—the fact that his greatest creativity and accomplishment came after he reached the age of fifty. Hall hinted in an earlier article on "The Dangerous Age" that he would deal with this problem. He concluded there that

leaving out of consideration here the initial prepubertal stage and the terminal one of the post-climacteric or old age proper, all the rest of life which lies between these is divided into two parts, adolescence and senescence, that the latter begins where the former ends [at about forty-five years of age], and that all that we have thought characteristic of middle life consists of only the phenomena which are connected with the turn of the tide.[32]

Such a conception would fit our evidence of a major psychological crisis in Hall's life between the ages of forty-five and fifty and throw some light on his own conception of the changes involved between the earlier and later period, but Hall never elaborated on this idea in his book. However, the fact that Hall subsumed his own period of greatest intellectual creativity under a category of decline can only suggest how little inner satisfaction his intellectual solution to the crisis of his middle years had brought him. In *Senescence,* Hall gives us a more conventional outline of the life stages, in which maturity follows adolescence, from twenty-five or thirty to forty or forty-five, and senescence, lumped together with old age, constitutes, as in the book's subtitle, "The Last Half of Life." The differences between senescence and old age, therefore, are blurred, and Hall tells us far more about the advanced years he was currently living than the previous, more important decades.

Facing old age was itself a courageous effort. Like most of his writings, the book consisted chiefly of data about the various aspects and problems of old age, together with vivid descriptions of the psychological state of older people. In the course of it, Hall disclosed how in his own last years he tried a variety of doctors, diets, and regimens of exercise and sleep in the hope of preserving his health and life; how he grappled with his changing moods and indulged his cravings for novels and movies; how he was constantly tempted

32. GSH, "The Dangerous Age," 1921, p. 294.

to fall into self-pity and into dependency on his attentive house-keeper. In the end, facing death and the absence of immortality stoically, he opted for living to the full whatever life was left, for making an "Indian summer," in which the gifts of the old for prophecy and clairvoyance would be realized.

Hall did, in fact, wring a good deal of enjoyment from his last years, and took a keen interest in the spirit of the postwar world. He was an appreciative student of the new cinema, as well as the new dance.[33] He even approved the "flapper" in a little essay, "Flapper Americana Novissima," published in the *Atlantic Monthly* in 1922. Several times before Hall had published articles on the young adolescent girl, but under the Victorian title "The Budding Girl" and written, for all their occasional charm, in his heavier, serial style. Somehow, in this last rendering, the old rhetoric disappeared, the facts and theories were nicely integrated into the line of argument, and a single, sympathetic, yet somewhat ironic and amused point of view prevailed throughout. Hall felt, quite obviously, a real rapport with his teenage girl subjects and their budding femininity. Whatever difficulties this subject earlier had for him were now absent. The new simplicity and frankness in manners and social conventions must have helped to free him from his own constraints.

The "flapper" Hall drew was, as he said himself, the same girl she always was, the same combination of surface sophistication and inner naiveté, of confidence and self-consciousness, of outer mystery and inner preoccupation with her real role in life, that of "loving and being loved." While thus largely repetitious of his older analysis, which idealized the conventionally feminine qualities of her role, Hall also caught much of the contemporary spirit of freedom in manners and the resulting tension between her and her mother's generation.

Without even the hint of a leer, Hall described how he followed for a few minutes one "specimen" sixteen-year-old girl as she passed the university on her way home from school, and described her dress and manner with graceful, but telling, accuracy. Hall concluded,

---

33. GSH, "What Dancing Means," 1918; GSH, "Gesture, Mimesis, Types of Temperament, and Movie Pedagogy," 1921.

Underneath the mannish ways which she sometimes affects, she really vaunts her femininity, and her exuberance gives it a new charm. The new liberties she takes with life are contagious, and make us wonder anew whether we have not all been servile to precedent and slaves to institutions that need to be refitted to human nature, and whether the flapper may not, after all, be the bud of a new and better womanhood.

For a seventy-eight-year-old man, who had all his life bowed to the Victorian image of Woman, this position was quite remarkable. The qualities he assigned to femininity were, of course, precisely the same ones convention had decreed all his life, but he was able to see into and through very different styles to his old ideal, and he responded sympathetically, as in his best moments he had in the past, to personal freedom.

Hall hoped, for a time, to contribute to psychology, as well, with a crowning systematic work. He had big books almost ready, he said, on the feelings and on food and nutrition, but they never appeared; and when a former student later went through his papers, he could find only disconnected notes.[34] Hall did write a kind of "summa" nonetheless, and an appropriate one for him, his autobiography, *Life and Confessions of a Psychologist,* which was published in 1923.

Hall's account of his life is, perhaps, the most interesting of all the documents he has left us. He dwells most lovingly on his parents and early years in Ashfield, and gives an excellent and perceptive account of his family relations, budding ambitions, early troubles over sexuality, and the life of the New England country side at mid-century. His stay at Williams College, too, is well described and he is pleased now with Williams's ability to combine modern education with the best of her old traditions.

As he proceeds Hall gives us a lively account of his growing desire to see life and the world and of his growing radicalism, but not of the conflict, hesitance, and disguise that always accompanied it. When he begins on his intellectual career, moreover, he conveniently distorts much of the truth. Harvard and James sink into obscurity. His account of the early Johns Hopkins is informative, but not of his own ambitions and conflicts there. To reveal the

34. *LCP,* p. 590; Edmund S. Conklin, in *AJP* 38 (1927): 135.

truth about Clark University was one of his chief reasons for writing
the book, Hall said, but his "truth" remains his own unrealistic view
of the situation.

Hall's discussion of his work in psychology is revealing of his
final attitudes and of the long road he took to reach them. He admits
that

there is a sense in which all my active conscious life has been made up of a
series of fads or crazes, some strong, some weak; some lasting long and
recurring over and over again at different periods of life and in different
forms, and others ephemeral. (p. 367)

He describes vividly the thread of evolution which tied the whole
together, but tells us little that is enlightening about child study, and
virtually nothing about *Adolescence*. Hall confessed that once having gathered up one of his favorite subjects in book form, he was
too acutely aware of its shortcomings ever to want to open the book
or the subject again (p. 585).

He has, however, decided opinions on contemporary psychology.
He fears that testing, as mere technology, has come too much to
dominate psychology after the war. The real job is to work on a
basic genetic science and to fit present institutions to the nature of
man, rather than vice versa. His great hope for the future of psychology is psychoanalysis, and he thinks now that a psychoanalysis
will become a central part of the education of youth. He has finally
absorbed Freud well enough to say that autoeroticism is a normal
stage through which all pass (p. 397).

His account of education is a description of changes that have
taken place in the field over his lifetime, rather than of his relation
to them, and betrays the fact that he had not been much involved in
the field for over a decade. He takes a favorable view of the improvements that have been made while still calling for more of his
old remedies. So, too, he merely incorporates the ambivalent social
analysis of his last few years, without adding to it any fresh insight.

But it is chiefly as a personal document that the book is most
revealing, both for what Hall has come to understand of himself
and for what he still obscures. Hall admitted at the outset that self-
exposure, the desire to exhibit his weaknesses, was undoubtedly one
of his motives in publishing the work. He is frank about many

things, but he did not try to tell all that he knew about himself. One chapter, the result of his psychoanalysis, he said, had been burned, and he leaves us only the tantalizing clue that "certain passages are only keys to rooms in my house of life that I cannot open to the general reader, at least during my life" (p. 575). The most obvious rooms to which we are not allowed entrance contain his two marriages and his children.

At the beginning of the book Hall tells us revealingly how much he is like his mother in his ambition and in his almost masochistic desire to avoid argument and accept the frustrations of life stoically, but this is, he says, a similarity of genetic inheritance. Reading his parents' intimate, affectionate letters, he also comes to feel that "if I have found more public ways of self-expression, I feel that I have lost something very essential that they possessed" (p. 85). At the end of the book, Hall tries a more analytic approach to these themes. He has come to feel his isolation most painfully, and he wonders why he has made so many enemies in his life and found so few congenial friends, why he has sometimes been able to show his students that he is really a "good fellow" while with his equals and superiors he has felt somehow inferior and so struck out at them critically.

Hall finds running underneath his life a pattern of alternating periods of passiveness and aggressiveness (pp. 567–89). The passive periods he mentions were those of insecurity about his competence and his future: at Williston, in New York and Antioch, and during the first years at Clark; the aggressive periods were at Williams, during the second trip to Germany, at Johns Hopkins, and again later at Clark. The main rhythm comes to an end there, but Hall recognizes another "oscillation of less amplitude" which has run clear through his life, the high points representing his periods of intense work and creativity, driven on by "a certain fervor," the low points, periods of inactivity and impotence.

The feelings and behavior Hall assigns to these two categories of passive and aggressive really range further than these two qualities. With the passive periods he associates the desire to sink into obscurity (like the "almost masochistic subjection of my mother to the will of God"), feelings of worthlessness, and desires to be punished. With the aggressive periods, there comes an exhilaration at breaking through to aggressive attack, an "I can" mood that drives him to attempt much beyond his powers, grandiose fantasies that "would very likely be the inception point of megalomania or delusions of greatness if I ever fell a victim to this; while the dread of discord would make a rich soil for delusions of persecution."

Hall is describing, apparently, a cyclic manic-depressive trend in his life which halted around the time of his crisis in the mid-1890s into a more permanent adjustment, one which allowed him to sublimate some of his "feminine" desires and hostility in creative work, though milder cycles of manic intensity and depression continued to shape the pattern of his work throughout his life. He was, at the end, just becoming aware of the gross outlines of this pattern, and perhaps of some of the paranoid tendency of his character. At the end of his autobiography, however, he was still alternating between regret over his failures and assurance that he could "see the 'upward Path' just as clearly as Jesus or Buddha did" (pp. 594–96).

Hall carried on his labors into 1924 and that year Sanford initiated a movement in the APA which resulted in Hall being elected president of the association for a second time, an honor accorded only to James before him.[35] He died on 24 April 1924, after a series of illnesses which ended in pneumonia.[36] At the small funeral in Worcester, the local minister caused a brief scandal by criticizing Hall for not having appreciated the importance of the institutional church, a scandal which Hall surely would have relished.[37] He was buried in Ashfield cemetery.

When his will was published and probated, it was discovered that Hall had left an estate valued at over $233,000, of which over $172,000 was deposited in small amounts in seventy-eight Massachusetts banks.[38] Living modestly all his mature life, he had secretly hoarded the fees from his books and his thousands of lectures. By

35. E. G. Boring to the author, 27 Mar 1962.
36. Pruette, GSH, p. 256. Hall's death certificate records the cause of death as acute nephritis. Henry H. Donaldson, "A Study of the Brains of Three Scholars: Granville Stanley Hall, Sir William Osler, Edward Sylvester Morse," The Journal of Comparative Neurology 46 (Aug 1928): 9, lists the cause of death as pneumonia, with arteriosclerosis and nephritis present.
37. Pruette, GSH, p. 198.
38. Report to the Probate Court, Worcester, Massachusetts, 13 June 1924.

his will, most of the estate—eventually a sum of over $160,000—
went to Clark University, where the income was "to be strictly and
solely devoted to research in genetic psychology."[39] By this means
the professorship in his name was established which perpetuates
genetic psychology at the university.

39. Will of G. Stanley Hall, 27 June 1922; *The First Fifty Years* (Worcester:
Clark University, 1937), p. 112.

ABBREVIATIONS

Adol   G. Stanley Hall, *Adolescence* (New York: D. Appleton, 1904), 2 vols.

AJP   *American Journal of Psychology.*

CP   James McKeen Cattell Papers, Library of Congress, Washington, D. C.

CULP   *Clark University Library Publications.*

CUP   Clark University Papers, Clark University Library; some few letters are kept in the G. Stanley Hall Memorial Volume, Department of Psychology.

CW   Collected works of G. Stanley Hall, Clark University Library.

DAB   *Dictionary of American Biography.*

EP   G. Stanley Hall, *Educational Problems* (New York: D. Appleton, 1911), 2 vols.

ER   *Educational Review.*

FPM   Franklin P. Mall Papers, The Carnegie Institution of Washington, Baltimore.

GP   Daniel Coit Gilman Papers, Lanier Room, Johns Hopkins University Library, Baltimore.

GSH   G. Stanley Hall.

HP   G. Stanley Hall Papers, formerly in possession of the author, now at Clark University.

JHBS   *Journal of the History of the Behavioral Sciences.*

JP   William James Papers, Houghton Library, Harvard University, Cambridge.

JSP   *Journal of Speculative Philosophy.*

LCP   G. Stanley Hall, *Life and Confessions of a Psychologist* (New York: D. Appleton, 1923).

MP   Hugo Münsterberg Papers, Boston Public Library, Boston.

NP   Charles Eliot Norton Papers, Houghton Library, Harvard University, Cambridge.

PNEA   *Proceedings of the National Education Association.*

PR   *Psychological Review.*

PS   *Pedagogical Seminary.*

TP   Edward Bradford Titchener Papers, John M. Olin Research Library, Cornell University, Ithaca.

WRH   William Rainey Harper Papers, University of Chicago, Chicago.

BIBLIOGRAPHY

A SELECTION OF HALL'S PUBLISHED WORKS

1866   "Bryant." *Williams Quarterly* 13 (June): 245–49.

"The Student's Sin." *Williams Quarterly* 14 (Aug): 19–26.

"A Life without a Soul." *Williams Quarterly* 14 (Aug): 36–41.

"The Inventive Mood." *Williams Quarterly* 14 (Nov): 108–17.

1867   "Editor's Table." *Williams Quarterly* 14 (Apr): 195–96.

"Philanthropy." In *An Oration by John M. Taylor and a Poem by G. Stanley Hall, Delivered on Class Day, June 27, 1867.* North Adams: James T. Robinson.

"John Stuart Mill." *Williams Quarterly* 15 (Aug): 18–29.

1872–74   "Anti-Materialism." *JSP* 6 (July 1872): 216–22.

"Outlines of Dr. J. A. Dorner's System of Theology." *Presbyterian Quarterly and Princeton Review,* n.s. 1 (Oct 1872): 720–47; 2 (Jan, Apr 1873): 60–93, 261–73.

"Hegel As the National Philosopher of Germany." *JSP* 6 (1872): 53–82, 97–129, 258–79, 340–50; 7 (Jan 1873): 17–25, (July 1873): 44–59, (Oct 1873): 57–74; 8 (Jan 1874): 1–13. Translations from Karl Rosenkranz. *Hegel als deutscher Nationalphilosoph.* Leipzig: Duncker and Humblot, 1870.

1876   "College Instruction in Philosophy." *Nation* 23 (Sept): 180.

1878   "Notes on Hegel and His Critics." *JSP* 12 (Jan): 93–103.

"Color Perception." *Proceedings of the American Academy of Arts and Sciences,* n.s. 5:402–43.

"A Leap-Year Romance." *Appleton's Journal,* n.s. 5 (Sept, Oct): 211–22, 319–30.

"The Muscular Perception of Space." *Mind* 3 (Oct): 433–50.

"The Philosophy of the Future." *Nation* 27 (Nov): 283–84.

1879   "Philosophy in the United States." *Mind* 4 (Jan): 89–105.

"Ueber die Abhängigkeit der Reactionszeiten vom Ort des Reizes." With J. von Kries. *Archiv für Anatomie und Physiologie; Physiologische Abtheilung,* supp., pp. 1–10.

"Die willkürliche Muskelaction." With Hugo Kronecker. *Archiv für Anatomie und Physiologie*; *Physiologische Abtheilung*, supp., pp. 11–47.

"Laura Bridgman." *Mind* 4 (Apr): 149–72.

1881 "Recent Researches on Hypnotism." *Mind* 6 (Jan): 98–104.

"Getting Married in Germany." *Atlantic Monthly* 47 (Jan): 36–46.

"American and German Methods of Teaching." *Harvard Register* 3 (May): 319–21.

Aspects of German Culture. Boston: James R. Osgood.

1882 "The Moral and Religious Training of Children." *Princeton Review* 10 (Jan): 26–48.

"Chairs of Pedagogy in Our Higher Institutions of Learning." *Bureau of Education Circulars of Information*, no. 2, pp. 35–44.

"The Education of the Will." *Princeton Review* 10 (Nov): 306–25.

"Optical Illusions of Motion." With H. P. Bowditch. *Journal of Physiology* 3 (Aug): 297–307.

1883 "Educational Needs." *North American Review* 136 (Mar): 284–90.

"Reaction-Time and Attention in the Hypnotic State." *Mind* 8 (Apr): 170–82.

"The Contents of Children's Minds." *Princeton Review* 11 (May): 249–72.

"The Study of Children." Privately printed, N. Somerville, Mass.

1884 "Bilateral Asymmetry of Function." With E. M. Hartwell. *Mind* 9 (Jan): 93–109.

1885 "New Departures in Education." *North American Review* 140 (Feb): 144–52.

"The New Psychology." *Andover Review* 3 (Feb, Mar): 120–35, 239–48.

"Pedagogical Inquiry." *PNEA*, pp. 506–11.

"A Study of Children's Collections." *Nation* 41 (Sept): 190.

"Overpressure in Schools." *Nation* 41 (Oct): 338–39.

"Motor Sensations on the Skin." With H. H. Donaldson. *Mind* 10 (Oct): 557–72.

1886 "Studies of Rhythm." With Joseph Jastrow. *Mind* 11 (Jan): 55–62.

1887 "Dermal Sensitiveness to Gradual Pressure Changes." With Jujiro Motora. *AJP* 1 (Nov): 72–98.

"Editorial Note." *AJP* 1 (Nov): 3–4.

"Psychological Literature." *AJP* 1 (Nov): 128–64.

1888 "The Story of a Sand Pile." *Scribner's Magazine* 3 (June): 690–96. Reprinted. New York: E. L. Kellogg, 1897.

1889 "Address Delivered at the Opening of Clark University." In *Clark University, Worcester, Massachusetts: Opening Exercises, October 2, 1889* (Printed by the University), pp. 9–32.

1890 "Children's Lies." *AJP* 3 (Jan): 59–70.

"A Sketch of the History of Reflex Action." *AJP* 3 (Jan): 71–86.

"The Training of Teachers." *Forum* 10 (Sept): 11–22.

"The Relations of Physiology to Psychology." *Christian Register* 69 (Oct): 698–99.

"The Educational State; or The Methods of Education in Europe." *Christian Register* 69 (Nov): 719.

"The Modern University." *Christian Register* 69 (Dec): 785–86.

1891 "Educational Reforms." *PS* 1 (Jan): 1–12.

"Boy Life in a Massachusetts Country Town Thirty Years Ago." *Proceedings of the American Antiquarian Society*, n.s. 7: 107–28.

"Review of William James's *Principles of Psychology*." *AJP* 3 (Feb): 578–91.

"Contemporary Psychologists, I. Professor Eduard Zeller." *AJP* 4 (Apr): 156–75.

"Phi Beta Kappa Oration." *Brunonian* (17 June), pp. 109–16.

"Notes on the Study of Infants." *PS* 1 (June): 127–38.

"University Study of Philosophy." *Regents' Bulletin* no. 8 (University of the State of New York) (July): 335–38.

1892   "Health of School Children As Affected by School Buildings." *PNEA*, pp. 682–91.

"Ecstasy and Trance." *Christian Register* 71 (Jan): 56.

1893   "The New Movement in Education, An Address Delivered before the School of Pedagogy of the University of the City of New York, December 29, 1891." Printed by the University.

"Child Study As a Basis for Psychology and Psychological Teaching." *Report of the Commissioner of Education for the Year 1892–93*, pp. 357–70.

"Child Study: The Basis of Exact Education." *Forum* 16 (Dec): 429–41.

1894   "Psychological Progress." In *The Liberal Club, Buffalo, 1893–1894*, pp. 13–47. Buffalo: Mathews-Northrup.

"On the History of American College Text-Books and Teaching in Logic, Ethics, Psychology and Allied Subjects." *Proceedings of the American Antiquarian Society* n.s. 9 (Apr): 137–74.

"American Universities and the Training of Teachers." *Forum* 17 (Apr): 148–59.

"Universities and the Training of Professors." *Forum* 17 (May): 297–309.

"Scholarships, Fellowships, and the Training of Professors." *Forum* 17 (June): 443–54.

"Research the Vital Spirit of Teaching." *Forum* 17 (July): 558–70.

"Child Study in Summer Schools." *Regents' Bulletin* no. 28 (University of the State of New York) (July): 333–36.

"Remarks on the Report of the Committee of Ten." *Regents' Bulletin*, no. 28 (July): 303–7.

"The New Psychology As a Basis of Education." *Forum* 17 (Aug): 710–20.

"Address at the Bryant Centennial, Cummington, Massachusetts, August 16, 1894." In *Bryant Centennial,* pp. 67–69. Springfield, Mass.: Clark W. Bryant Co.

"Address at the Dedication of the Haston Free Public Library Building, North Brookfield, Massachusetts, September 20, 1894." In *The Haston Free Public Library,* pp. 11–21. Brookfield, Mass.: H. J. Lawrence.

"Child Study." *PNEA* pp. 173–79.

"Remarks on Rhythm in Education." *PNEA,* pp. 84–85.

"Practical Child Study." *Journal of Education* 40 (Dec): 391–92.

1895   "Laboratory of the McLean Hospital, Somerville, Massachusetts." *American Journal of Insanity* 51 (Jan): 358–64.

"Editorial." *AJP* 7 (Oct): 3–8.

"Pedagogical Methods in Sunday School Work." *Christian Register* 74 (Nov): 719–20.

1896   "Modern Methods in the Study of the Soul." *Christian Register* 75 (Feb): 131–33.

"The Case of the Public Schools: I. The Witness of the Teacher." *Atlantic Monthly* 77 (Mar): 402–13.

"The Methods, Status, and Prospects of the Child Study of To-day." *Transactions of the Illinois Society for Child Study* 2 (May): 178–91.

"Psychological Education." *American Journal of Insanity* 53 (Oct): 228–41.

"Nature Study." *PNEA,* pp. 156–58.

"Some of the Methods and Results of Child Study Work at Clark University." *PNEA,* pp. 860–64.

"Child Study." *School Education* 15 (July-Aug): 5.

"Address on Founder's Day at Mount Holyoke College." *Mount Holyoke* 6 (Nov): 64–71.

"A Study of Dolls." With A. Caswell Ellis. *PS* 4 (Dec): 129–75.

1897   "A Study of Fears." *AJP* 8 (Jan): 147–249.

"On Specialization." In *One Hundredth Anniversary of the*

Founding of Union College, pp. 230–44. New York: Union College.

"Some Practical Results of Child Study." In *The Work and Words of the National Congress of Mothers,* pp. 165–71. New York: D. Appleton.

"The Psychology of Tickling, Laughing and the Comic." With Arthur Allin. *AJP* 9 (Oct) : 1–41.

1898   "Some Aspects of the Early Sense of Self." *AJP* 9 (Apr) : 351–95.

"The Love and Study of Nature, A Part of Education." *Report of the State Board of Agriculture of Massachusetts, 1898,* pp. 134–54.

"Heredity, Instinct and the Feelings." *Proceedings of California Teachers' Association, Santa Rosa, December 27–30, 1898,* pp. 46–48.

"Food and Nutrition." *Proceedings of California Teachers' Association, Santa Rosa, December 27–30, 1898,* pp. 59–62.

1899   "Resume of Child Study." *North Western Monthly* 9 (Mar-Apr) : 347–49.

"The Education of the Heart," "From Fundamental to Accessory in Education," "Needed Modifications in the Theory and Practice of the Kindergarten," *Kindergarten Magazine* 11 (May) : 592–95, 599–600, 604–6.

"A Study of Anger." *AJP* 10 (July) : 516–91.

"The Line of Educational Advance." *Outlook* 26 (Aug) : 768–70.

"Corporal Punishments." *New York Education* 3 (Nov) : 163–65.

"Note on Early Memories." *PS* 6 (Dec) : 485–512.

1900   "Some New Principles of Sabbath School Work." In *Minutes of Worcester Baptist Sunday School Convention, May 10, 1900,* pp. 10–12. Worcester: G. G. Davis, 1900.

"College Philosophy." *Forum* 29 (June) : 409–22.

"Pity." With F. H. Saunders. *AJP* 11 (July) : 534–91.

"Child Study and Its Relation to Education." *Forum* 29 (Aug): 688–702.

1901   "Confessions of a Psychologist." *PS* 8 (Mar): 92–143.

"The Ideal School As Based on Child Study." *Forum* 32 (Sept): 24–39; also *PNEA,* 475–88; *Review of Education* 7 (Oct): 88–94.

"How Far Is the Present High School and Early College Training Adapted to the Nature and Needs of Adolescents?" *New England Association of Colleges and Secondary Schools, Official Report of the 16th Annual Meeting,* pp. 72–104; also *School Review* 9 (Dec): 649–65.

"A New Universal Religion at Hand." *Metropolitan* 14 (Dec): 778–80.

"Some Fundamental Principles of Sunday School and Bible Teaching." *PS* 8 (Dec): 439–68.

1902   "The High School As the People's College." *PS* 9 (Mar): 63–73.

"Some Social Aspects of Education." *PS* 9 (Mar): 81–91; also *ER* 23 (May): 433–45.

"Normal Schools, Especially in Massachusetts." *PS* 9 (June): 180–92.

"Pre-Established Harmony." *PS* 9 (Sept): 379–84. Reprinted in *Recreations of a Psychologist,* 1920, pp. 175–83.

"How Children and Youth Think and Feel about Clouds." With J. E. W. Wallin. *PS* 9 (Dec): 460–506.

1903   "Reactions to Light and Darkness." With Theodate L. Smith. *AJP* 14 (Jan): 21–83.

"The Secondary School Curriculum." A syllabus of six conferences conducted by GSH for the Education Committee of the Twentieth Century Club.

"Child Study at Clark University: An Impending New Step." *AJP* 14 (Jan): 96–106.

"The Relations between Lower and Higher Races." *Proceedings of the Massachusetts Historical Society,* 2d ser. 17 (Jan): 4–13.

"Children's Ideas of Fire, Heat, Frost and Cold." With C. E. Browne. *PS* 10 (Mar): 27–85.

"Note on Cloud Fancies." *PS* 10 (Mar): 96–100.

"Showing Off and Bashfulness As Phases of Self-Consciousness." With Theodate L. Smith. *PS* 10 (June): 159–99.

"Curiosity and Interest." With Theodate L. Smith. *PS* 10 (Sept): 315–58.

"Co-Education in the High School." *PNEA*, pp. 446–60.

"Psychic Arrest in Adolescence." *PNEA*, pp. 811–13.

1904   *Adolescence: Its Psychology and Its Relations to Psysiology, Anthropology, Sociology, Sex, Crime, Religion and Education.* 2 vols. New York: D. Appleton.

"The Cat and the Child." With C. E. Browne. *PS* 11 (Mar): 3–29.

"Editorial." *American Journal of Religious Psychology and Education* 1 (May): 1–6.

"Co-Education." *PNEA*, pp. 538–42.

"The Natural Activities of Children As Determining the Industries in Early Education." *PNEA*, pp. 443–47.

"Unsolved Problems of Child Study and the Method of Their Attacks." *PNEA*, pp. 782–87.

"Mental Science." *Science*, n.s. 20 (Oct): 481–90.

1905   "A Few Results of Recent Scientific Study of the Negro in America," *Proceedings of the Massachusetts Historical Society*, 2d ser. 19:95–107.

"The Negro in Africa and America." *PS* 12 (Sept): 350–68.

"Adolescence: The Need of a New Field of Medical Practice." *Monthly Cyclopedia of Medical Practice* 8 (June): 241–43.

1906   "What Changes Should Be Made in Public High Schools to Make Them More Efficient in Moral Training?" *Proceedings of the Third Annual Convention of the Religious Education Association, Boston, February 12, 1906*, pp. 219–23.

"The Affiliation of Psychology with Philosophy and with the Natural Sciences." *Science*, n.s. 23 (Feb): 297–301.

Youth, Its Education, Regimen and Hygiene. New York: D. Appleton.

1907   "Some Dangers in Our Educational System and How to Meet Them." *New England Magazine* 41 (Feb): 667–75.

"The German Teacher Teaches." *New England Magazine* 42 (May): 282–87.

Aspects of Child Life and Education, By G. S. Hall and Some of His Pupils. Edited by Theodate L. Smith. Boston: Ginn.

"How and When to Be Frank with Boys." *Ladies' Home Journal* 24² (Sept): 26.

1908   "The Needs and Methods of Educating Young People in the Hygiene of Sex." *PS* 15 (Mar): 82–91.

"A Glance at the Phyletic Background of Genetic Psychology." *AJP* 19 (Apr): 149–212.

"Feminization in School and Home." *World's Work* 16 (May): 10237–44.

"From Generation to Generation: With Some Plain Language about Race Suicide and the Instruction of Children during Adolescence." *American Magazine* 66 (July): 248–54.

"The Awkward Age." *Appleton's Magazine* 12 (Aug): 149–56.

1909   "Education of the Heart." In *Southern California Teachers' Association, December 21–24, 1908,* pp. 31–38. Redlands Review Press.

"The Budding Girl." *Appleton's Magazine* 13 (Jan): 47–54.

"Fifty Years of Darwinism." In *Centennial Addresses in Honor of Charles Darwin before the American Association for the Advancement of Science, Baltimore, Friday, January 1, 1909.* pp. 251–67. New York: Henry Holt.

"How Can We Make the Average Public School a Good School?" *Housekeeper* 32 (Feb): 10–13.

"Twentieth Anniversary of Clark University." *Nation* 89 (Sept): 284–85.

1910   "Education in Sex Hygiene." *Eugenics Review* 1 (Jan): 242–53.

"What Is to Become of Your Baby?" *Cosmopolitan* 47 (Apr): 661–68.

"The Point of View toward Primitive Races." *Journal of Race Development* 1 (July): 5–11.

"Mission Pedagogy." *Journal of Race Development* 1 (Oct): 127–46.

"The Co-Ordination of the School with the Three Score Other Child Welfare Agencies." In *Annual Report of the 56th Annual Meeting of the New Jersey State Teachers' Association*, pp. 63–79.

1911   *Educational Problems.* 2 vols. New York: D. Appleton.

"Eugenics: Its Ideals and What It Is Going to Do." *Religious Education* 6 (June): 152–59.

"In Life's Drama Sex Plays the Leading Part." In *Sagamore Sociological Conference, June 28–30, 1911*, pp. 27–31.

"The Problem of Dependent Races." *Report of the 29th Annual Lake Mohonk Conference, Lake Mohonk, New York*, pp. 225–32.

"The Teaching of Sex in Schools and Colleges." *Social Diseases* 2, no. 4, pp. 1–19.

1912   "The Genetic View of Berkeley's Religious Motivation." *Journal of Religious Psychology* 5 (Apr): 137–62.

"Why Kant Is Passing." *AJP* 23 (July): 370–426.

Founders of Modern Psychology. New York: D. Appleton. Also *Die Begrunder der modern Psychologie (Lotze, Fechner, Helmholtz, Wundt).* Translated by Raymond Schmidt. Leipzig: Meiner, 1914.

1913   "Social Phases of Psychology." *American Journal of Sociology* 18 (Mar): 613–21.

1914   "The Freudian Child." *Psychological Bulletin* 11 (Feb): 67–68.

"Recent Progress in Child Study." *Child Welfare Magazine* 8 (Feb): 212–16.

"A Synthetic Genetic Study of Fear." *AJP* 25 (Apr, July): 149–200, 321–92.

"Education and the Social Hygiene Movement." *Social Hygiene* 1 (Dec): 29–35.

1915 "Teaching the War." *School and Society* 1 (Jan): 8–13.

"Yankee and Jew." *Menorah Journal* 1 (Apr): 87–90.

"Child Training." *Woman's World* 31 (May): 5, 31–32.

"Anger As a Primary Emotion and the Application of Freudian Mechanisms to Its Phenomena." *Journal of Abnormal Psychology* 10:81–87.

"Thanatophobia and Immortality." *AJP* 26 (Oct): 550–613.

"New Lights on Childhood." *Youth's Companion* 89 (Oct): 577–78.

1916 "Foreword, with a Discussion of the Psychology of the Present War." In *Problems and Lessons of the War*, edited by G. H. Blakeslee, pp. ix–xxiv. New York: Putnam.

"Psychological Notes on the War." *Journal of Race Development* 6 (Apr): 357–69.

"Teaching the War." *American School* 2 (July): 205–7.

"The War and Some of Its Relations to Education." *School and Society* 4 (July): 115–20.

1917 "Practical Relations between Psychology and the War." *Journal of Applied Psychology* 1 (Mar): 9–16.

"A Reminiscence." *AJP* 28 (Apr): 297–300.

Jesus the Christ in the Light of Psychology. 2 vols. New York: Doubleday, Page.

"A Suggestion for a Jewish University." *Menorah Journal* 3 (Apr): 98–101.

1918 "What Dancing Means." *Designer* (Mar).

"A Medium in the Bud." *AJP* 29 (Apr): 144–58.

"A General Survey of Child Study." *PS* 25 (Sept): 308–18.

"Morale in War and After." *Psychological Bulletin* 15 (Nov): 361–426.

1919 "Some Possible Effects of the War on American Psychology." *Psychological Bulletin* 16 (Feb): 48–49.

1920   "Points of Difference between Men and Women, Inherent and
        Acquired." *Proceedings of the International Conference of
        Women Physicians, 1919*, 4: 90–99. New York.

        Preface to *A General Introduction to Psycho-analysis* by Sig-
        mund Freud. New York: Boni and Liveright.

        Morale: The Supreme Standard of Life and Conduct. New York:
        D. Appleton.

        Recreations of a Psychologist. New York: D. Appleton.

1921   "The *American Journal of Psychology.*" *AJP* 32 (Jan): 1–3.

        "Old Age." *Atlantic Monthly* 127 (Jan): 23–31. Published
        anonymously.

        "Gesture, Mimesis, Types of Temperament and Movie Peda-
        gogy." *PS* 28 (June): 171–201.

        "The Message of the Zeitgeist." *Scientific Monthly* 13 (Aug):
        105–16.

        "The Dangerous Age." *PS* 28 (Sept): 275–94.

1922   *Senescence; the Last Half of Life.* New York: D. Appleton.

        "Flapper Americana Novissima." *Atlantic Monthly* 129 (June):
        771–80.

        "Salvaging Civilization." *Century Magazine* 104 (Oct): 830–40.

1923   *Life and Confessions of a Psychologist.* New York: D. Appleton.

BIBLIOGRAPHICAL NOTES
Autobiographical and Biographical Sources

The biographer of Stanley Hall is well served, for Hall included many
direct and indirect autobiographical references in his writings and left a
large and revealing autobiography. The *Life and Confessions* is often
unreliable as to facts and judgments, but its manner of deviating from
the truth is itself instructive. Wilson draws much of his information
directly from Hall and hence his book is often inaccurate. Pruette's
biography is an affectionate and perceptive account of Hall by a student
of his later years and contains some firsthand information not available
elsewhere. The best general account of Hall's work is Fisher's article in

AJP; it surveys his early studies at Johns Hopkins, as well as his mature work, and relates them briefly to basic themes in his life and thought.

Burnham, William H. "The Man, G. Stanley Hall." *PR* 32 (Mar 1925): 89–102.
Donaldson, Henry H. "A Study of the Brains of Three Scholars: Granville Stanley Hall, Sir William Osler, Edward Sylvester Morse." *The Journal of Comparative Neurology* 46 (Aug 1928): 1–11.
Fisher, Sara Carolyn. "The Psychological and Educational Work of G. Stanley Hall." *AJP* 36 (Jan 1925): 1–52.
Hall, G. Stanley. "Boy Life in a Massachusetts Country Town Thirty Years Ago." *Proceedings of the American Antiquarian Society,* n.s. 7 (1891): 107–28.
———. "Confessions of a Psychologist." *PS* 8 (Mar 1901): 92–143.
———. *Life and Confessions of a Psychologist.* New York: D. Appleton, 1923.
———. "Note on Early Memories." *PS* 6 (Dec 1899): 485–512.
———. *Recreations of a Psychologist.* New York: D. Appleton, 1920.
Hamilton, A. E. "Stanley Hall: A Memory." *American Mercury* 2 (July 1924): 287–92.
Hankins, Frank H. "G. Stanley Hall, 1846–1924." *Medical Journal and Record* 120 (July 1924): 22–23.
Jastrow, Joseph, "The Mind and the Man." New York *Evening Post, Literary Review,* 28 June 1924, pp. 849–50.
Meyer, Adolf. "In Memoriam, G. Stanley Hall." *American Journal of Psychiatry* 4 (July 1924): 151–53.
Odum, Howard. "G. Stanley Hall." *Journal of Social Forces* 3 (Nov 1924): 139–46.
Pruette, Lorraine. *G. Stanley Hall: Biography of a Mind.* New York: D. Appleton, 1926.
Sanford, Edmund C. "G. Stanley Hall, 1846–1924." *AJP* 35 (July 1924): 313–21.
Sheldon, Henry D. "G. Stanley Hall." *DAB.*
Starbuck, Edwin Diller. "G. Stanley Hall As a Psychologist." *PR* 32 (Mar 1925): 103–20.
Straker, Robert L. "The Apprenticeship of G. Stanley Hall, 1872–1876." *Antioch Alumni Bulletin* (May 1934), pp. 5–13.

Thorndike, E. L. "G. Stanley Hall, 1846–1924." National Academy of
Sciences, *Biographical Memoirs* 12 (1928).
Wilson, Louis N. *G. Stanley Hall: A Sketch.* New York: G. E. Stechert,
1914.
————, ed. "Granville Stanley Hall. In Memoriam." *CULP* 7 (May
1925).

Several articles deal specifically with the question of Hall's date of
birth, the most important one by Swift.

Chidester, Albert J. "In What Year Was G. Stanley Hall Born?" *School
and Society* 60 (Dec 1944) : 420–21.
Finner, Paul F. "Concerning the Centennial of G. Stanley Hall." *School
and Society* 60 (July 1944) : 30–31.
Swift, Fletcher H. "Sleuthing for the Birth Date of G. Stanley Hall."
School and Society 63 (Apr 1946) : 249–52.

The genealogy of the Hall and Beals families can be traced in a number of printed sources.

Alden, Ebenezer. *Memorial of the Descendants of the Hon. John Alden.*
Randolph, Mass.: Samuel P. Brown, 1867.
Hall, David B. *The Halls of New England.* Albany: Joel Munsell's Sons,
1883.
Howes, Joshua Crowell. *Genealogy of the Howes Family in America.*
Yarmouthport: Fred. Hallett, 1892.
Jones, Emma C. B. *The Brewster Genealogy, 1566–1907.* New York:
The Grafton Press, 1908.
May, Samuel P. *The Descendants of Richard Sares (Sears).* Albany: Joel
Munsell's Sons, 1890.

Works by G. Stanley Hall

Hall was a prolific and repetitive writer. He published eleven books,
several of them in two volumes, and several of them compilations of
previously published work. His articles and copies or reports of many
of his speeches have been collected in two unpublished sets of collected
works (CW), each running to twenty-nine volumes. One set was in
possession of the author and is now deposited at Clark University; the
other set has always been at the Clark University Library. The contents

of the two sets are not identical, some work being included in each that is not found in the other. The set permanently at Clark has a thirtieth volume containing articles about Hall published after his death.

Louis N. Wilson, ed., "Bibliography of the Published Writings of G. Stanley Hall, 1866–1924," in "Granville Stanley Hall. In Memoriam," *CULP* 7 (May 1925): 109–35, is nearly complete, except for several early items which are cited in this book. The Wilson bibliography runs to 439 items. The published works by Hall which are cited in this book, generally his most important pieces, are listed here separately.

Hall's *Adolescence*, 1904; *Aspects of Child Life and Education*, 1907; and *Educational Problems*, 1911, compile a great deal of his previously published work and provide a representative sample of his mature views in psychology, child study, and education.

Manuscript Sources

According to Henry D. Sheldon, in *DAB,* Hall left at his death a voluminous collection of letters. These came into the possession of his son, Dr. Robert G. Hall. Sheldon went through the collection and made copies of what he felt to be the most important letters, in the hope of publishing a book of Hall's selected correspondence. No publisher would take his manuscript, however; the final publisher approached rejected it as having no historical, scientific, or literary value. Dr. Robert Hall then insisted on having Sheldon's manuscript returned to him. Sheldon did this but on his own initiative also sent copies of some of Hall's most important professional correspondence to the Clark University Library. In cases where it has been possible to check the Sheldon copies against the originals, they have proved to be very largely accurate.

A large portion of the papers in the possession of Dr. Robert Hall were destroyed over the years. Those that survived are mostly Sheldon copies of letters to and from Hall and his family, and hence chiefly of value to the student of Hall's early life and development. The papers also contain some scattered professional correspondence, the most important being some original letters from William James. Dr. Robert Hall graciously lent these papers to the author and they are now deposited at the Clark University Library. Deposited along with them are letters to the author and typescripts of interviews by the author of various people, all of this material relating to Hall. The letter from Martin Schmitt of the University of Oregon Library to the author, 18 May 1960, describes the fate of Sheldon's efforts and the papers.

The Clark University Papers are the largest extant collection of Hall materials. They include considerable original correspondence of Hall, Jonas Clark, and Louis N. Wilson relating to Hall's affairs and the university, as well as the Sheldon copies of Hall's professional correspondence. Two drawers of correspondence from the University Registrar's Office between Hall and his Clark students and colleagues are particularly revealing. There is besides a bound volume of miscellaneous Hall materials in the library office and a number of letters kept in the G. Stanley Hall Memorial Volume in the G. Stanley Hall Memorial Room of the Department of Psychology at Clark. The Memorial Room still contains a substantial part of Hall's original library; few of the books are annotated, however.

Of materials in the collection relating to the history of the University, Amy Tanner, "History of Clark University through the Interpretation of the Will of the Founder," May 1908, is the most important. Despite the fact that Miss Tanner was Hall's assistant, she tried to present a balanced account and was scrupulous in documentation. Her typescript contains reports of many source materials no longer available. A number of books of newspaper clippings about Hall and the university are also useful.

On the quarrel with the faculty, the memo by the dissident members of the faculty, of events at Clark University from October 1891 to 16 February 1892, is the most important source in the Clark collection. For a balanced view, however, the Mall, Harper, Nef, and Donaldson Papers are also essential.

For Hall's intellectual development and activities during the 1870s and 1880s, the Gilman, Norton, and James Papers are particularly useful. For Hall's mature career, the Cattell, Titchener, and Clark University Papers are rich sources.

The following manuscript collections yielded items on Hall cited in the text. Of these, the Adams, Antiochiana, Davidson, Eliot, Goddard, Harris, Hosmer, Loeb, Meyer, Newcomb, Ticknor, University of Chicago, and White Papers were consulted for only a limited number of selected letters, some at long distance. The James and Norton Papers are quoted by permission of the Harvard College Library. The Mall Papers are quoted by courtesy of Carnegie Institution of Washington.

Herbert Baxter Adams Papers, Lanier Room, Johns Hopkins University Library, Baltimore.

Antiochiana Collection, Olive Kettering Library, Antioch Library, Antioch College, Yellow Springs.

Franz Boas Papers, American Philosophical Society, Philadelphia.

Henry Putnam Bowditch Papers, Harvard University Medical School Archives, Boston.

James McKeen Cattell Papers, Library of Congress, Washington, D.C.

Clark University Papers, Clark University Library, Worcester.

Thomas Davidson Papers, Yale University Library, New Haven.

Henry H. Donaldson Papers, American Philosophical Society, Philadelphia.

Charles W. Eliot Papers, Harvard University Archives, Cambridge.

Arnold Gesell Papers, Library of Congress, Washington, D.C.

Daniel Coit Gilman Papers, Lanier Room, Johns Hopkins University Library, Baltimore.

Henry H. Goddard Papers, Archives of the History of American Psychology, University of Akron Library, Akron, Ohio.

G. Stanley Hall Papers, Clark University Library, Worcester.

William Rainey Harper Papers, University of Chicago Archives, Chicago.

William Torrey Harris Papers, Hoose Library, University of Southern California, Los Angeles.

George Frisbie Hoar Papers, Massachusetts Historical Society, Boston.

James K. Hosmer Papers, Minnesota Historical Society, St. Paul.

William James Papers, Houghton Library, Harvard University, Cambridge.

Johns Hopkins University Correspondence, Alumni Records Office, Johns Hopkins University, Baltimore.

Jacques Loeb Papers, Library of Congress, Washington, D.C.

Franklin P. Mall Papers, Carnegie Institution of Washington, Baltimore.

Adolf Meyer Papers, William H. Welch Medical Library, Johns Hopkins University, Baltimore.

Hugo Münsterberg Papers, Boston Public Library, Boston.

John Ulric Nef Papers, University of Chicago Archives, Chicago.

Simon Newcomb Papers, Library of Congress, Washington, D.C.

Charles Eliot Norton Papers, Houghton Library, Harvard University, Cambridge.

Benjamin Holt Ticknor Papers, Library of Congress, Washington, D.C.

Edward Bradford Titchener Papers, John M. Olin Research Library, Cornell University, Ithaca.
University of Chicago, Frederick T. Gates, ed., "Correspondence of the Founder and His Associates," University of Chicago Archives, Chicago.
Andrew D. White Papers, John M. Olin Research Library, Cornell University, Ithaca.

Secondary Sources

In addition to the sources cited specifically in the footnotes, a number of theses, books, and articles have been useful in understanding the intellectual and cultural history of Hall's era.

Merz's study of European philosophical and scientific thought in the nineteenth century is an indispensable guide to that intricate subject. Ueberweg's *History of Philosophy* and Cassirer's *Problem of Knowledge* provide entrance into the philosophical thinking in Germany during the third quarter of the century, and Ueberweg is especially important for Trendelenburg and the Ideal-realists. On Trendelenburg, see also Rosenstock and George S. Morris. Randall's *From the German Enlightenment to the Age of Darwin* is excellent on Comte, Schleiermacher, and Schelling, and particularly illuminating on Hegel from the point of view of his later English and American influence. See also Kaufmann's *Hegel*. Randall's history is also good on liberal German theology and its important role in reconciling American opinion to natural science. On liberal Protestant theology see also McGiffert, Cross on Schleiermacher, and Pfleiderer on Dorner. Nineteenth-century definitions of materialism are discussed in Lange's history, and a modern perspective on materialism is provided by Ernest Nagel.

For American philosophy the basic source is Schneider's *History of American Philosophy*. On Mark Hopkins, see his own works, as well as Schneider. Haroutunian and Foster are useful for American Protestant thought in the mid-nineteenth century and Foster deals specifically with Henry B. Smith. On St. Louis Hegelianism, the standard sources are Pochmann, Charles Perry, Schaub, and Snider. The richest source for later nineteenth-century thinking in the area of Cambridge is still Perry's biography of William James. On James himself, Perry should be supplemented by Strout's fine study of William James's personal development.

Peirce is ably discussed in Brent's biography and Murphy's analysis of his philosophical thought. On the influence of Darwin on American thinking, see the articles by Randall and Schneider, White's study of the influence of science on religion, and Hawkin's essay on Eliot. Houghton's *Victorian Frame of Mind* is the major account of the intellectual attitudes which literate Americans of the middle and late nineteenth century often shared with Victorian Englishmen.

A useful guide to the history of American psychology is Boring's basic textbook on experimental psychology. Müller-Freienfels' history, however, provides a deeper analysis of the basic tendencies at work in psychology during Hall's lifetime. An important source for the psychological thinking of Hall's generation, and a delightful one, is James's *Principles*. Ribot's examinations of German and English psychology are also very useful. Hearnshaw briefly describes the British physiological tradition which influenced James and Hall. Brett, Murphy, Flugel, and Watson are also useful surveys of the origins and development of psychology.

The biological strain within American psychology still needs to be pieced together. On the development of the recapitulation theory and its links to a revived Lamarckianism, see Nordenskiöld's excellent *History of Biology*; Grinder's extended treatment of the intellectual sources of Hall's genetic theory; and Eiseley's *Darwin's Century*. Haller's basic study of hereditarian thinking in American social science is also very useful. See also Stocking's brief survey of American Lamarckianism. On some of the difficulties involved in applying the criteria of scientific explanation to biological and behavioral phenomena, see Nagel's *The Structure of Science*.

Ben-David and Collins, and Ross discuss the social origins of scientific psychology as a profession. Rosen surveys the influence of Ludwig on the development of physiology in America. On the early development of the psychological profession in America, and some of the tensions within it, Albrecht's thesis on the new psychology is the pioneer and indispensable work. Two suggestive articles by Bakan and Burnham's article on behaviorism are also important.

On the development of clinical psychology in America, see the articles by Sexton, Smith, and Watson, and Reisman's book. In the area of child and developmental psychology, Hall's work can best be placed by reference to Anderson's survey of American work, Kern's definitive investigation of European and American thinking on the child at the time of

Freud, and Kessen's perceptive account of the major contributors to the modern understanding of childhood, particularly Preyer, Baldwin, Watson, and Gesell. On the history of child psychology, see also the articles by Bradbury, Dennis, English, and McLean and the first chapter of Watson's *Psychology of the Child*.

On the child study movement itself, no adequate account exists. The theses by Dutton and Hendricks contain some useful information, but are generally imprecise and superficial. Belden traces a few major changes in the kinds of child study in Europe and America, but lacks a detailed historical context. The most penetrating study of some of the ideas involved in the movement is Strickland's thesis, "The Child and the Race." Kett's paper, "Science and Sentiment," treats the social roots of the movement very suggestively. For contemporary formulations of the child study program other than Hall's, see Claparède, Luckey, Tanner, and Tracy.

In the area of psychiatry, Ackerknecht's classic history and Shakow's survey of the American scene are extremely useful, as is Sicherman's study of concepts of mental health during the late nineteenth century. See also Sicherman's biographical sketch of Adolf Meyer. The American background to psychoanalysis and the Clark conference is very perceptively presented by Hale, and Burnham's thesis contains important additional material. Jones's biography of Freud is the basic source for Freud's development of psychoanalysis. Ellenberger's study is the best general account of the development of dynamic and psychoanalytic ideas in Europe, including those of Jung and Adler.

Veysey's *Emergence of the American University*, Hofstadter and Hardy's *Development and Scope of Higher Education*, and Ryan's *Studies in Early Graduate Education* set the framework for an understanding of American higher education in this period. Hawkin's *Pioneer* is an excellent account of the formulative years of The Johns Hopkins University.

On primary and secondary education, see the texts by Cubberley, Butts and Cremin, and Edwards and Richey; and the basic study of progressivism in American education, Cremin's *Transformation of the School*. Cubberley's contemporary comments on the educational scene are also useful. The most penetrating study of the ideology and motives of educators in the nineteenth century is Katz's monograph. Their essential moralism is also well described in Finkelstein's study of teacher behavior and Elson's examination of textbooks. For Hall's place in the stream of progressive education, see also Smith's religious interpretation of progressivism and Feuer's linkage of John Dewey and the "Back to the People" movement.

On the major educational theorists and their influence in nineteenth-century America, see the following. For Rousseau: his *Emile* and *Julie; or the New Eloise,* and Boyd's study of his educational theory. For Pestalozzi: his *Leonard and Gertrude* and the studies by Barnard and Monroe. For Froebel: his *Education of Man,* Barnard's study of Froebel's kindergarten, and Forest's history of preschool education. For Herbart: his *Outlines of Educational Doctrine* and the studies of Herbart and Herbartianism by Compayré, DeGarmo, and Dunkel. For Herbert Spencer: his *Education.* For all the romantics, see George Boas, *The Cult of Childhood.* For Locke and his precursors, who also made a limited application of appeal to the child's natural inclinations and development of his physical health and character, see Gay's edition of Locke's *Some Thoughts Concerning Education* and Smith's article, "Some Ideas on Education Before Locke." Ariès, *Centuries of Childhood,* explores the social and ideological background of these modern ideas.

On the major American educators of Hall's generation, see the following. For Harris: his *Psychologic Foundations of Education,* his essay in Lang's *Educational Creeds,* and the biography by Leidecker. For Parker: his collected talks, Patridge's account of the Quincy experiment, and Campbell's biography. For Dewey: his *Lectures in the Philosophy of Education,* the new edition of which contains a bibliography of his early educational work; his *School and Society* and *Child and Curriculum;* his perceptive analysis of *The Educational Situation* in 1902, and Mayhew and Edwards's detailed account of Dewey's experimental school. The most perceptive analysis of the ambiguities of Dewey's educational thinking is Hofstadter's "The Child and the World." See also Hofstadter's discussion of Dewey and Hall in his *Anti-Intellectualism.* On Thorndike and the development of educational psychology, see Woodworth's biographical memoir; Joncich's selection of his writings, which is more coherent than her full biography of Thorndike; and Watson's brief history of educational psychology.

A number of works deal specifically with Hall's educational ideas, the most important being Strickland and Burgess's selection of his writings, *Health, Growth and Heredity.* The authors argue that Hall's ideal was a "stable social order under the direction of an elite, and glorifying physical vigor and juvenile idealism over intellect and mature judgment," a social order which was "ominously parrallel to twentieth century totalitarianism" (pp. 22–26). The term "totalitarianism," however, gives far too great coherence and emphasis to the authoritarian and primitivist aspects of Hall's thinking, and ignores the contrary strains of genuine individualism, intellectualism, and libertarianism in his thought.

The "totalitarian" interpretation of Hall apparently derives from Burgess's thesis, "The Educational State in America." Burgess argues that in Hall's early praise of Germany as "the educational state," he meant chiefly to praise the ideal of a strong, centralized state to which individual values must be wholly subordinated. Since Hall was too timid to enuciate this view clearly, Burgess argues, his ultimate meaning has to be supplied by the interpreter; and so whenever Hall goes on to praise the ideals of service or physical health, Burgess adds, "in the service of the State." When Hall admires Nietzsche, Burgess sees more evidence of a desire to turn adolescents into hordes of marching, brown-shirted youth. Burgess's interpretation involves a gross distortion of the whole tenor of Hall's thinking, innumerable distortions of the contextual meaning of Hall's statements, and the ignoring of overt contradictions to his theory. For example, Hall closed his talk, "The Educational State," 1890, with the statement "I never expect to see this German system adopted as a whole in this country. Its centralization makes it forever impossible here; but the momentous lesson for us is that the one source of vitality in every true educational system is at the top [the university], and not at the bottom. To conserve knowledge is indispensable, to diffuse it is noble, but to increase it is life itself." Burgess's interpretation also vitiates Grinder and Strickland, "GSH and the Social Significance of Adolescence." Grinder's later article is a more perceptive discussion of Hall's concept of adolescence as rooted in the theory of recapitulation. The description of Hall's "subserviency to the existing social system" in Curti's *Social Ideas of American Educators* is still the best treatment of his political ideas. In Wilson's study of the ideal of community in America, Hall is miscast as a social philosopher whose aim was a return to the unconscious past.

Ackerknecht, Erwin H. *A Short History of Psychiatry*. New York: Hafner, 1959.

Albrecht, Frank M. "The New Psychology in America: 1880–1895."
Ph.D. dissertation, Johns Hopkins University, 1960.

Anderson, John E. "Child Development: An Historical Perspective."
Child Development 27 (June 1956): 181–96.

Ariès, Philippe. *Centuries of Childhood; a Social History of Family Life.*
New York: Knopf, 1962.

Bakan, David. "The Influence of Phrenology on American Psychology."
JHBS 2 (1966): 200–220.

————. "Behaviorism and American Urbanization." *JHBS* 2 (1966):
5–28.

Barnard, Henry, ed. *Papers on Froebel's Kindergarten.* Hartford: American Journal of Education, 1881.

————, ed. *Pestalozzi and Pestalozzianism.* New York: F. C. Brownell,
1862.

Belden, Ernest. "A History of the Child Study Movement in the United
States, 1870–1920." Ph.D. dissertation, University of California at
Berkeley, 1965.

Ben-David, Joseph, and Collins, Randall. "Social Factors in the Origins
of a New Science: The Case of Psychology." *American Sociological
Review* 31 (August 1966), pp. 451 ff.

Boas, George. *The Cult of Childhood.* London: The Warburg Institute,
1966.

Boring, Edwin G. *A History of Experimental Psychology.* New York:
Appleton-Century-Crofts, 1957.

Boyd, William. *The Educational Theory of Jean Jacques Rousseau.* New
York: Russell and Russell, 1963.

Bradbury, Dorothy E. "The Contribution of the Child Study Movement
to Child Psychology." *Psychological Bulletin* 34 (1937): 21–38.

Brent, Joseph L. Jr. "A Study of the Life of Charles Sanders Peirce."
Ph.D. dissertation, University of California at Los Angeles, 1960.

Brett, George S. *History of Psychology.* London: G. Allen and Co.,
1912–21.

————. *Brett's History of Psychology,* revised and edited by R. S. Peters.
London: George Allen and Unwin Ltd., 1962.

Burgess, Charles O. "The Educational State in America: Selected Views
on Learning As the Key to Utopia, 1800–1924." Ph.D. dissertation,
University of Wisconsin, 1962.

BIBLIOGRAPHY

Burnham, John C. "Psychoanalysis in American Civilization before 1918." Ph.D. dissertation, Stanford University, 1958.

————. "On the Origins of Behaviorism." *JHBS* 4 (1968): 143–51.

Butts, R. Freeman, and Cremin, Lawrence A. *A History of Education in American Culture*. New York: Henry Holt & Co., 1953.

Campbell, Jack K. *Colonel Francis W. Parker, The Children's Crusader*. New York: Teachers' College Press, 1967.

Cassirer, Ernst. *The Problem of Knowledge: Philosophy, Science and History since Hegel*. New Haven: Yale University Press, 1950.

Claparède, Eduard. *Experimental Pedagogy and the Psychology of the Child*. New York: Longmans Green, 1911.

Compayré, Gabriel. *Herbart and Education by Instruction*. New York: Thomas Y. Crowell, 1907.

Cremin, Lawrence A. *The Transformation of the School*. New York: Alfred Knopf, 1961.

Cross, George. *The Theology of Schleiermacher*. Chicago: University of Chicago Press, 1911.

Cubberley, Ellwood P. *Changing Conceptions of Education*. Boston: Houghton Mifflin, 1909.

————. *Public Education in the United States*. Boston: Houghton Mifflin, 1934.

Curti, Merle. *The Social Ideas of American Educators*. Patterson, N. J.: Littlefield, Adams & Co., 1959.

De Garmo, Charles. *Herbart and the Herbartians*. New York: Charles Scribner's Sons, 1895.

Dennis, Wayne. "Historical Beginnings of Child Psychology." *Psychological Bulletin* 46 (1949): 224–35.

Dewey, John. *Lectures in the Philosophy of Education: 1899*. Ed. Reginald Archambault. New York: Random House, 1966.

————. *The School and Society*. Chicago: University of Chicago Press, 1899.

————. *The Child and the Curriculum*. Chicago: University of Chicago Press, 1902.

————. *The Educational Situation*. Chicago: The University of Chicago Press, 1904.

Dunkel, Harold B. *Herbart and Herbartianism: An Educational Ghost Story*. Chicago: University of Chicago Press, 1970.

Dutton, Harvey. *The Child-Study Movement in America from its Origin*

*(1880) to the Organization of the Progressive Education Association
(1920).* Ph.D. dissertation, Stanford University, 1945.

Edwards, Newton, and Richey, Herman G. *The School in the American
Social Order.* Boston: Houghton Mifflin Co., 1963.

Eiseley, Loren. *Darwin's Century.* Garden City: Doubleday, 1958.

Ellenberger, Henri F. *The Discovery of the Unconscious: The History
and Evolution of Dynamic Psychiatry.* New York: Basic Books, 1970.

Elson, Ruth Miller. *Guardians of Tradition.* Lincoln: University of
Nebraska Press, 1964.

English, Horace B. *Trends in Child Psychology.* In Philip Harriman, ed.
Twentieth Century Psychology. New York: The Philosophical Library,
1946, pp. 705–10.

Feuer, Louis. "John Dewey and the Back to the People Movement in
American Thought." *Journal of the History of Ideas* 20 (1959) : 545–
68.

Finkelstein, Barbara. "Governing the Young: Teacher Behavior in
American Primary Classrooms, 1820–1880." Ph.D. dissertation,
Teachers College, Columbia University, 1970.

Flugel, J. C. *A Hundred Years of Psychology.* London: Gerald Duckworth, 1951.

Forest, Ilse. *Pre-School Education.* New York: Macmillan, 1927.

Foster, Frank H. *A Genetic History of the New England Theology.*
Chicago: University of Chicago Press, 1907.

Froebel, Friedrich. *The Education of Man.* New York: D. Appleton,
1887.

Gay, Peter, ed. *John Locke on Education.* New York: Teachers College,
1964.

Grinder, Robert E. *A History of Genetic Psychology: The First Science
of Human Development.* New York: John Wiley, 1967.

————. "The Concept of Adolescence in the Genetic Psychology of G.
Stanley Hall." *Child Development* 40 (1969) : 355–69.

Grinder, Robert E., and Strickland, Charles E. "GSH and the Social Significance of Adolescence." *The Teachers College Record* 64 (Feb
1963) : 390–99.

Hale, Nathan, Jr. *Freud and the Americans: The Beginnings of Psychoanalysis in the United States, 1876–1917.* London: Oxford University
Press, 1971.

Haller, Mark H., Jr. *Eugenics: Hereditarian Attitudes in American Thought.* New Brunswick: Rutgers University Press, 1963.

Haroutunian, Joseph. *Piety Versus Moralism. The Passing of the New England Theology.* New York: Henry Holt, 1932.

Harris, William T. *Psychologic Foundations of Education.* New York: D. Appleton, 1898.

Hawkins, Hugh. *Pioneer: A History of the Johns Hopkins University, 1874–1889.* Ithaca: Cornell University Press, 1960.

————. "Charles W. Eliot, University Reform, and Religious Faith in America, 1869–1909." *The Journal of American History* 51 (Sept 1964): 191–213.

Hearnshaw, L. S. *A Short History of British Psychology, 1840–1940.* New York: Barnes & Noble, 1964.

Hendricks, James Dale. "The Child Study Movement in American Education, 1880–1910: A Quest for Educational Reform Through a Systematic Study of the Child." Ph.D. dissertation, Indiana University, 1968.

Herbart, Johann Friedrich. *Outlines of Educational Doctrine.* New York: Macmillan, 1901.

Hofstadter, Richard. "The Child and the World." *Daedalus* 91 (1962): 501–26.

————. *Anti-Intellectualism in American Life.* New York: Knopf, 1963.

Hofstadter, Richard, and Hardy, C. DeWitt. *The Development and Scope of Higher Education in the United States.* New York: Columbia University Press, 1952.

Hopkins, Mark. *Lectures on Moral Science.* Boston: Gould and Lincoln, 1862.

————. *The Law of Love, and Love as a Law.* New York: C. Scribner, 1869.

————. *An Outline Study of Man: or The Body and Mind in One System.* New York: Scribner, Armstrong, 1873.

Houghton, Walter E. *The Victorian Frame of Mind.* New Haven: Yale University Press, 1957.

James, William. *The Principles of Psychology.* 2 vols. New York: Henry Holt, 1890.

Joncich, Geraldine, ed. *Psychology and the Science of Education.* New York: Bureau of Publications, Teachers College, Columbia University, 1962.

Katz, Michael B. *The Irony of Early School Reform: Educational Innovation in Mid-Nineteenth Century Massachusetts.* Cambridge: Harvard University Press, 1968.

Kaufmann, Walter. *Hegel: Reinterpretation, Texts, and Commentary.* Garden City: Doubleday, 1965.

Kern, Stephen. "Freud and the Emergence of Child Psychology, 1880–1910." Ph.D. dissertation, Columbia University, 1970.

Kessen, William, ed. *The Child.* New York: John Wiley, 1965.

Kett, Joseph F. "Science and Sentiment: The American Child Study Movement, 1880–1910." Paper delivered at the Organization of American Historians, April, 1970.

Lang, Ossian H., ed. *Educational Creeds of the Nineteenth Century.* New York: E. L. Kellogg, 1898.

Lange, Frederick Albert. *The History of Materialism.* 3 vols. in 1. New York: Harcourt, Brace, 1925.

Leidecker, Kurt. *Yankee Teacher: the Life of Wm. Torrey Harris.* New York: Philosophical Library, 1946.

Luckey, G. W. A. *The Essentials of Child Study.* Chicago: The University Publishing Co., 1917.

Mayhew, Katherine Camp, and Edwards, Anna Camp. *The Dewey School: the Laboratory School of the University of Chicago, 1896–1903.* New York: D. Appleton-Century, 1936.

McGiffert, Arthur C. *The Rise of Modern Religious Ideas.* New York: Macmillan, 1915.

McLean, Dorothy. "Child Development: A Generation of Research." *Child Development* 25 (1954): 3–8.

Merz, John Theodore. *A History of European Thought in the Nineteenth Century.* 4 vols. Edinburgh: William Blackwood & Sons, 1896–1914.

Monroe, Will S. *History of the Pestalozzian Movement in the United States.* Syracuse: C. W. Bardeen, 1907.

Morris, George S. "Friedrich Adolf Trendelenburg." *The New Englander* 33 (Apr 1874): 287–336.

Müller-Freienfels, Richard. *The Evolution of Modern Psychology.* New Haven: Yale University Press, 1935.

Murphy, Gardner. *An Historical Introduction to Modern Psychology.* London: Kegan Paul, Trench, Trubner & Co., 1929.

Murphy, Murray G. *The Development of Peirce's Philosophy.* Cambridge: Harvard University Press, 1961.

Nagel, Ernest. "Naturalism Reconsidered," "Are Naturalists Materialists?" In *Logic Without Metaphysics*. Glencoe: The Free Press, 1956, pp. 3–38.

———. *The Structure of Science*. New York: Harcourt, Brace and World, 1961.

Nordenskiöld, Erik. *The History of Biology*. New York: Tudor, 1928.

Parker, Francis. *Notes on Talks on Teaching*. Reported by Lelia Patridge. New York: E. L. Kellogg, 1883.

———. *Talks on Pedagogics*. New York: E. L. Kellogg, 1894.

Patridge, Lelia. *The "Quincy Methods" Illustrated*. New York: E. L. Kellogg, 1885.

Perry, Charles M., ed. *The St. Louis Movement in Philosophy*. Norman: University of Oklahoma Press, 1930.

Perry, Ralph Barton. *The Thought and Character of William James*. 2 vols. Boston: Little, Brown, 1935.

Pestalozzi, Johann Heinrich. *Leonard and Gertrude*. Boston: D. C. Heath, 1885.

Pfleiderer, Otto. *The Development of Theology in Germany Since Kant and its Progress in Great Britain Since 1825*. London: Swan Sonnenschein, 1890.

Pochmann, Henry A. *New England Transcendentalism and St. Louis Hegelianism*. Philadelphia: Carl Schurz Memorial Foundation, 1948.

Randall, John H., Jr. "The Changing Impact of Darwin on Philosophy." *Journal of the History of Ideas* 22 (Oct 1961): 435–62.

———. *The Career of Philosophy, 2: From the German Enlightenment to the Age of Darwin*. New York: Columbia University Press, 1965.

Reisman, John M. *The Development of Clinical Psychology*. New York: Appleton-Century-Crofts, 1966.

Ribot, Theodule. *English Psychology*. New York: D. Appleton, 1874.

———. *German Psychology of Today*. New York: Charles Scribner's Sons, 1886.

Rosen, George. "Carl Ludwig and His American Students." *Bulletin of the History of Medicine* 4 (Oct 1936): 609–50.

Rosenstock, Gershon George. *F. A. Trendelenburg, Forerunner to John Dewey*. Carbondale: Southern Illinois University Press, 1964.

Ross, Dorothy. "On the Origins of Psychology." *American Sociological Review* 32 (June 1967): 466–69.

Rousseau, Jean Jacques. *Emile*. London: J. M. Dent, 1911.

————. *Julie; or the New Eloise.* University Park: Pennsylvania State University Press, 1968.

Ryan, W. Carson. *Studies in Early Graduate Education: The Johns Hopkins, Clark University and the University of Chicago.* New York: The Carnegie Foundation for the Advancement of Teaching, 1939.

Schaub, Edward, ed. *William Torrey Harris, 1835–1935.* Chicago: The Open Court Publishing Co., 1936.

Schneider, Herbert W. *A History of American Philosophy.* New York: Columbia University Press, 1946.

————. "The Influence of Darwin and Spencer on American Philosophical Theology." *Journal of the History of Ideas* 6 (Jan 1945): 3–18.

Sexton, Virginia S. "Clinical Psychology: An Historical Survey." *Genetic Psychology Monographs* 72 (1965): 401–34.

Shakow, David. "One Hundred Years of American Psychiatry." *Psychological Bulletin* 42 (July 1945): 423–32.

Sicherman, Barbara. "Adolf Meyer (1866–1950): Profile of a Swiss-American Psychiatrist." *Swiss-American Historical Society Newsletter* 5 (Dec 1969): 2–24.

————. "The Quest for Mental Health in America, 1880–1917." Ph.D. dissertation, Columbia University, 1967.

Smith, Constance I. "Some Ideas on Education Before Locke." *Journal of the History of Ideas* 23 (1962): 403–6.

Smith, Theodate L. "The Development of Psychological Clinics in the United States." *PS* 21 (1914): 143–53.

Smith, Timothy L. "Progressivism in American Education." *Harvard Educational Review* 31 (1961): 168–93.

Snider, Denton J. *St. Louis Movement in Philosophy, Literature, Education, with Chapters of Autobiography.* St. Louis: Sigma Publishing Co., 1920.

Spencer, Herbert. *Education: Intellectual, Moral and Physical.* London: G. Manwaring, 1861.

Stocking, George W. "Lamarckianism in American Social Science, 1890–1915." *Journal of the History of Ideas* 23 (1962): 239–56.

Strickland, Charles E. "The Child and the Race: The Doctrines of Recapitulation and Culture Epochs in the Rise of the Child-Centered Ideal in American Educational Thought, 1875–1900." Ph.D. dissertation, University of Wisconsin, 1963.

Strickland, Charles E., and Burgess, Charles. *Health, Growth and*

Heredity: G. Stanley Hall on Natural Education. New York: Teachers College Press, 1965.

Strout, Cushing. "William James and the Twice-Born Sick Soul." *Daedalus* 97 (1968): 1062–82.

Tanner, Amy. *The Child; his thinking, feeling and doing.* New York: Rand McNally, 1904.

Tracy, Frederick. *The Psychology of Childhood.* Boston: D. C. Heath, 1893.

Ueberweg, Friedrich. *History of Philosophy from Thales to the Present Time.* Trans. George S. Morris. 2 vols. New York: Charles Scribner's Sons, 1872–74.

Veysey, Laurence Russ. *The Emergence of the American University.* Chicago: University of Chicago Press, 1965.

Watson, Robert I. "A Brief History of Clinical Psychology." *Psychological Bulletin* 50 (1953): 321–46.

———. *The Psychology of the Child.* New York: John Wiley, 1959.

———. "A Brief History of Educational Psychology." *Psychological Record* 11 (1961): 209–42 .

———. *The Great Psychologists from Aristotle to Freud.* Philadelphia: J. B. Lippincott, 1963.

White, Edward A. *Science and Religion in American Thought.* Stanford: Stanford University Press, 1952.

Wilson, R. Jackson. *In Quest of Community: Social Philosophy in the United States, 1860–1920.* New York: John Wiley, 1968.

Woodworth, Robert S. "Edward Lee Thorndike, 1874–1949." National Academy of Sciences, *Biographical Memoirs* 27 (1952).

INDEX